THEORETICAL MODELS OF COUNSELING

AND PSYCHOTHERAPY

SECOND EDITION

THEORETICAL MODELS OF COUNSELING

AND PSYCHOTHERAPY

SECOND EDITION

KEVIN A. FALL, JANICE MINER HOLDEN, ANDRE MARQUIS

Routledge
Taylor & Francis Group
New York   London

Routledge
Taylor & Francis Group
270 Madison Avenue
New York, NY 10016

Routledge
Taylor & Francis Group
27 Church Road
Hove, East Sussex BN3 2FA

© 2010 by Taylor and Francis Group, LLC
Routledge is an imprint of Taylor & Francis Group, an Informa business

---

Library of Congress Cataloging-in-Publication Data

Fall, Kevin A.
    Theoretical models of counseling and psychotherapy / Kevin A. Fall, Janice Miner Holden, and Andre Marquis. -- 2nd ed.
        p. cm.
    Includes bibliographical references and index.
    ISBN 978-0-415-99476-7 (hardcover : alk. paper)
    1. Counseling. 2. Psychotherapy. I. Holden, Janice Miner. II. Marquis, Andre, Ph. D. III. Title.

BF636.6.F35 2010
158'.3--dc22

2009033904

Visit the Taylor & Francis Web site at
http://www.taylorandfrancis.com

and the Routledge Web site at
http://www.routledgementalhealth.com

Contents

	Preface	vii
	Authors	ix
Chapter 1	Introduction	1
Chapter 2	Classical Psychoanalysis	27
Chapter 3	Self Psychology	65
Chapter 4	Adlerian Counseling–Individual Psychology	101
Chapter 5	Existential Counseling	139
Chapter 6	Person-Centered Counseling	169
Chapter 7	Gestalt Counseling	201
Chapter 8	Behavioral Counseling	229
Chapter 9	Cognitive Counseling	259
Chapter 10	Rational Emotive Behavioral Counseling	297
Chapter 11	Reality Therapy and Choice Theory	323
Chapter 12	Constructivist Approaches	347
Chapter 13	Systems Approaches	387
Chapter 14	Integral Counseling: The Prepersonal, Personal, and Transpersonal in Self, Culture, and Nature	433
Author Index		493
Subject Index		503

Preface

I (Kevin A. Fall) am writing the preface of this new version of *Theoretical Models of Counseling and Psychotherapy* in the same manner as I wrote the preface to the original: at the end of the writing process. Upon reflection, I am not sure why I choose to write the preface at the end. I even remember thinking about doing things a little different with this edition. I recall that I considered writing the preface at the beginning of the process, as a way to motivate myself and perhaps my coauthors to plow into the project ahead of us. I did not write it at that point. Change is difficult.

Change. That one word really sums up the core theme of this book. In fact, it characterizes the change in content as well as the process of revising the book. We were actually pretty satisfied with the first edition of the book. I have to admit, I was a bit reluctant to go back and revise it—as if doing so was an admission of lack of quality. Each author spent some time with the material and, in our own ways, we made peace with adapting and evolving the book. In some ways and at some times, each of us felt excited and motivated. At other times the process seemed a bit overwhelming and even boring. I cannot help but believe that this is how our clients feel at times. One of the most fascinating elements of revising the book was to observe the parallel process of change as it relates to books and counseling. What seems apparent to me, now more than ever, is that *learning about theory is the most important step in learning about change*. We hope you keep this idea in mind as you read about the various approaches covered in this edition.

Obviously, because this is a revised edition, you are expecting change. We are pleased to offer the following to you in the spirit of change:

- We updated each chapter for content, references, and resources. In come chapters, we dramatically revised and improved the material to deepen readers' understanding of the theory.
- We added a new chapter on Constructivist approaches. We thought this was an important addition to the text and a theory about which many of our students were interested in learning more. In our survey of other texts, we noticed that many covered only Solution-focused, Narrative, or a combination of the two. We have chosen to be a bit daring and cover Solution-focused, Narrative, and Mahoney's contribution to the field. We hope you enjoy this new chapter!
- An authorship team—De La Garza, Holden, Kantor, and Marquis—has developed a Teacher's Manual as an adjunct resource. This material provides a valuable supplement for theory course instructors to use in expanding student learning opportunities.

With any change process, modifications may be made but some of the original remains. Along with the updates and improvements, the core of this book is intact as is our commitment to provide you with a text that makes theory accessible and practical without sacrificing any of the depth inherent in each approach. If you are new to this text, by way of an orientation on how to use this book, the following is taken from the first edition:

> Most of you are probably using this book as a required text in a graduate course on theory. We have been there, so we know that theory texts can seem abstract and distant, which can lead to your putting the book back on your shelf to collect dust until your comprehensive or licensure exams. We hope you use this book as a resource in your personal development as a mental health professional. We purposefully did not include a comparison chapter because we want you to compare and contrast the theories on your own. Explore! Get personally involved in the theories! The book is designed for you to literally work your way through the personal theory development process by reading the chapters, flipping back and forth and comparing sections, and using your class time to discuss the deeper aspects of the theory.

Very seldom are changes facilitated in isolation. Most changes occur through effort on the part of the individual with aid and support from others. We could not have completed this project without the help of several key people. First, we want to thank Fred Coppersmith for his patience and gentle encouragement on this revision. We also send our gratitude to our reviewers. Thank you, also, to Gail Kerrigan for applying her considerable graphic art talent in designing some of the figures in the book.

As I write this paragraph, I am aware that what ends a process for me, begins a process for you. Jan, Andre, and I wish you well as you learn about the process of change and hope you take the time to challenge yourself in the same way that you will learn to challenge your clients. Best wishes in your learning!

Kevin A. Fall
Janice M. Holden
Andre Marquis

Authors

Kevin A. Fall, PhD, is an Associate Professor in the Professional Counseling program at Texas State University. He worked for 11 years as a faculty member and served as Chair of the Department of Counseling at Loyola University–New Orleans. He has co-authored several textbooks including *Group Counseling: Concepts and Procedures* with Robert Berg and Garry Landreth (Routledge, 2006), *Translating Theory into Practice* with Justin Levitov (Waveland, 2009), and *Alternatives to Domestic Violence* with Shareen Howard (Routledge, 2004). He is a frequent presenter at the state and national level on the topics of group work, ethics, counseling adolescents, and Adlerian theory. He also maintains a small private practice, focusing on adolescents and their families. He is currently working with a colleague, Justin Levitov, to research and publish material on an innovative treatment modality for high conflict couples.

Janice Miner Holden, BS, MS, PhD, earned her degree in psychology with honors from the University of Illinois–Champaign (1972), her master of science (1978), and doctoral (1988) in Counselor Education from Northern Illinois University. In 1988, she joined the Counseling Program faculty at the University of North Texas where she now is a professor and serves as Chair of the Department of Counseling and Higher Education. She is a Licensed Professional Counselor–Supervisor, Texas Licensed Marriage and Family Therapist, and National Certified Counselor. At the University of North Texas, Jan teaches courses in counseling theory, the transpersonal perspective in counseling, and dreamwork in counseling. Having focused her scholarship on near-death experiences, Jan was a past president of the International Association for Near-Death Studies, was first editor of *The Handbook of Near-Death Experiences: Thirty Years of Investigation* (Praeger, 2009), and is editor of the quarterly, peer-reviewed *Journal of Near-Death Studies*. The nature of human consciousness, particularly at death, its implications for counseling, and for meaning and purpose in life and death continue to be Jan's primary research interests.

Andre Marquis is assistant professor of counseling and human development at the University of Rochester who believes that there is much to be gained with integrative and unifying approaches to counseling that capitalize on the strengths and complementary nature of various counseling approaches. Marquis's teaching, research, and scholarly interests include counseling theories, psychotherapy integration, group therapy, relational psychodynamics, constructivist counseling, and the integral philosophy of Ken Wilber and its application as an integrative approach to counseling, teaching, and supervision. Marquis has recently published *The Integral Intake: A Guide to Comprehensive Idiographic Assessment in Integral Psychotherapy* (Routledge, 2008); this book describes integral theory, assessment via the integral intake, and how they both pertain to the practice of integral psychotherapy. Marquis is also the author of numerous articles in such publications as *Journal of Psychotherapy Integration*, *Constructivism in the Human Sciences*, *Psychoanalytic Inquiry*, *Counseling and Values*, *Journal of Humanistic Psychology*, and *Journal of Mental Health Counseling*. He is currently co-authoring *Psychopathology for the Helping Professionals: An Integral Exploration* and co-editing the *Handbook of Integral Psychotherapy*.

CHAPTER 1

Introduction

There is nothing so practical as theory.

—Kurt Lewin, social psychologist

There is no therapy without theory.

—Earl Ginter, counselor educator

COUNSELING THEORY

What Is Counseling Theory?

Imagine this: You are conducting your first individual counseling session. You have oriented your client to procedures and to ethical and legal considerations in the counseling process. You are ready to turn the focus to your client and her reason for being in counseling. You might facilitate the beginning by saying, "Well, Kim, now that we have dispensed with the paperwork, where would you like to start today?" That sounds easy enough. No problem. We do not need theory to do that, right? Now the client begins to tell her story, and the information begins to accumulate. Having begun, how do you proceed? What is your purpose, what are your goals, and how do you pursue them? How do you conceptualize your client's psychological dynamics? How do you determine what you can do to help her reach her counseling goals?

In a standard 50-minute session, you have a myriad of choices. How do you decide whether and when to follow your client and/or direct her? How do you decide whether and when to address the counseling relationship, assessment of the client, or strategies for change? With each communication, your client will provide you with additional information; how will you organize and interpret that information? With each client communication, you have a variety of responses from which to choose; how will you choose the one response you make? Your choices are crucial; they will influence the direction of the session and the experience your client has in the session. Under the pressure of limited time, how do you make these multileveled, multilayered decisions? If these choices sounds complicated, it is because the process of counseling is a complex inter- and intra-personal journey, one involving several questions for each counselor to answer—questions about how best to help one's client.

It is these very questions that counseling theory answers. Good application of theory brings some sense of order and meaning to what, otherwise, would be a meaningless jumble of data. It consists of concepts, along with corresponding terms, that are related to each other and are internally consistent with each other, that is, that do not contradict each other (Patterson, 1973). It provides a rationale for action.

In essence, a counseling theory is *a story of a person*. It is the theorist's story of each human being's life, including yours. Like any good piece of literature, a good counseling theory provides good character development. In the case of counseling theory, this means an explanation of how each person was innately endowed and developed throughout one's lifetime so far: how one became who one is today. Good theory also provides an explanation for problems people encounter in life and how they address those problems and seek further development through counseling. Within this storyline of change a new character emerges: the counselor. Good theory includes a description of a counselor's role in facilitating a main character's ongoing development.

What are the Advantages of Counseling Theory?

Almost certainly, you have had the experience of setting out on a journey to a place you have never been before. You probably appreciated any information you could get regarding what to expect and how best to go about the journey. If you ever have been—or could imagine being—a tour guide, then you know that your need to be prepared probably multiplied exponentially; You now have a contract whereby the members of your tour group pay you in exchange for your provision of a particular kind and high quality of service. How helpful it would be if someone had already done the legwork you need to provide that service and had put their collective wisdom into one resource book for you: a guidebook.

A tour guide using a guidebook can be compared to a counselor using a counseling theory. Counseling theory constitutes an organized, consistent way for you to anticipate, understand, and respond to the variety of clients and issues you will encounter as a counselor. Counseling theory is your *guidebook* about how to accompany and assist clients in the journey of change. This is the *conceptual* advantage of a guidebook.

A tour guide using a guidebook is also advantaged in other ways. The guide can feel secure in the structure the guidebook provides yet retain flexibility to respond to unique situations that will inevitably arise. That structure and flexibility can help both guide and traveler feel confident and relaxed, secure in *how* they will proceed and able to focus on the sights—*what* they will encounter along their journey together. Thus, a guidebook advantages both guide and traveler in the *process* of their journey. Similarly, a counseling theory provides both counselor and client with a secure yet flexible process for the activity of counseling.

Another advantage is that, through experience, a guide can evaluate the quality of the guidebook and continue revising it with improvements that reflect current "best practices." Similarly, counseling theory provides a basis for counselors, both in their own experiences and through larger scale research, to evaluate and improve their service to clients. This is the *quality* advantage.

And, having done so, if—heaven forbid—a disgruntled traveler should sue the tour guide, a well-organized guidebook that has been evaluated for its effectiveness and improved based on those evaluations would serve as a cornerstone of the tour guide's defense. Similarly, a key feature of a counselor's defense in the case of a malpractice suit is the ability to justify one's treatment based on theory that is supported by the traditional and/or current professional literature. This is the *legal* advantage.

Why are there so Many Counseling Theories?

Having grasped the advantages of identifying *a* theory of counseling to guide one's practice, your next logical question is likely to be *which* theory. A trip to the travel section of any bookstore can reveal that, for any travel destination, several different guidebooks exist. Compared with each other, the guidebooks have certain similarities and certain differences. Correspondingly, as the table of contents in this book shows, not just one but numerous counseling theories exist, also with certain similarities and differences. They are similar in their sharing of a few very core assumptions: that each person is born with certain innate tendencies and psychological functions; that each person's environment contributes to the kind of person one becomes; that, as a result of some interaction of innate tendencies, environment, and perhaps other factors, people develop; that some modes of functioning are preferable to others; that, once developed, people can develop further—can change in the direction of the more preferable mode of functioning; and that an interpersonal process called *counseling* can facilitate that change. Beyond these basics, each theory includes its own beliefs about *how* people are innately endowed, *how* the environment influences people, *how* people develop, *what* constitutes preferable modes of functioning, *how* people change, and *how* counseling facilitates that change— and the beliefs of each theory in some way contradict the beliefs of every other theory.

Why is there not one single theory of counseling upon which everyone agrees? The answer to this question may be illustrated by the story of the five blind men and the elephant:

> Five men from India, all blind from birth, met each day and passed the time by making up elaborate, amusing stories. One day, while visiting together, they heard a rustling. Unbeknownst to them, an elephant had wandered nearby. Sensing that the sound came from a harmless source, they each approached and reached out to the source of the rustling sound. Touching different parts, they immediately fell into disagreement in their attempts to explain what the thing was. The first man, feeling the elephant's body, interpreted it to be a mud wall and expressed confusion as to how it suddenly could have materialized in that location. The second, touching a tusk, interpreted it to be an ivory spear. The third, feeling the elephant's moving trunk, interpreted it to be a python hanging from a tree. The fourth, tugging gently on the elephant's tail, interpreted it to be a rope. The fifth, reaching around the elephant's leg, interpreted it to be a palm tree. Just then, a small boy passing by asked why they all were examining that elephant. At first, the men were uncharacteristically at a loss for words, but once the boy had passed, the first three men expressed a sense of foolishness and shame at having so boldly asserted their limited interpretations as the complete story or the whole truth. " 'Perhaps it's better to be silent,' suggested the fourth man. 'But better still,' concluded the fifth man, 'is to learn the truth from one who directly knows it.' " (Das, 1996, p. 59)

Another helpful analogy is the hologram. A regular photographic negative, if cut into pieces, shows only a part of the picture. By contrast, if a holographic negative is shattered, each piece contains *a dim reflection of the whole picture*. Each piece is accurate to the extent that it reflects the whole picture; simultaneously, each piece is inaccurate to the extent that it only dimly reflects the full richness of the whole picture.

At least until recently, the human psyche may very well have been to counseling theorists what the elephant was to the blind men and what the holographic fragment is to the complete hologram. Humanity, the human psyche, and human behavior are so diverse and complex that each person who tried to comprehend it did so to some degree accurately but incompletely. What was left, then, was that each person who tried to grasp these phenomena held a piece of the truth. Illustrated most clearly by the blind men and the elephant, the various pieces of truth appeared to contradict each other. To the extent that a particular piece of truth resonated with some people, they became adherents to that perspective, and the perspective was affirmed and reified. Yet each piece of truth, if projected to represent the whole truth, was done so only erroneously.

This analogy is particularly true of most of the theories we describe in this text. Each one represents the perspective of a *separate* school of thought that developed some time between 1900 and around 1980; their development constituted the first phase of the history of psychotherapy (Anchin & Magnavita, 2008). Culminating in the 1980s, some theorists and researchers pursued an *integrative* perspective, seeking to identify commonalities and reconcile differences between the separate schools; these pursuits constituted the second phase. Perhaps at least in part because every separate school of thought contradicts every other school in some way, and integrationists found that they could not reconcile those differences by remaining on a parallel perspective with the various schools, some theorists and researcher assumed a metaperspective and began developing *unifying* theories. In these umbrella systems of thought, the theorists honored the differences between the schools while placing each school—often along with pertinent knowledge from other fields, such as genetics and physics—into a systematic "grand scheme" of psychotherapy. They assumed the role of the small boy who, from something of a distance, could see how the various unique features of the elephant interrelated in a unified whole. In this text, we present two such metatheories: Mahoney's in Chapter 12, and Wilber's in Chapter 14.

Most beginning counselors find this plethora of theoretical perspectives rather dizzying. Before we offer some hopefully stabilizing advice, we address another question.

What are some Disadvantages of Counseling Theory?

In summary, just as a guidebook is an invaluable resource to a tour guide, a counseling theory is an invaluable resource to a counselor. Nevertheless, just as every guidebook is limited in that it reflects the author's particular take on the travel destination, every counseling theory is limited to the degree that it reflects the theorist's particular take on human experience and behavior.

To elaborate, most guidebook authors highlight some features of the territory and make little or no mention of other features. Consider the traveler whose purpose is to visit other countries' museums. On the journey itself, she sees a building in the distance, but because her guidebook does not mention it, she misinterprets an actual museum for some unimportant store, and she misses the exact kind of experience for which she undertook the journey. Or the traveler who is very focused on the features mentioned in the guidebook may not even have noticed the building–museum. In the extreme, when later encountering other tourists who claimed to have visited the museum, the traveler may doubt their veracity and disbelieve that the museum even existed, for surely it would have appeared in the guidebook if it existed and were of any importance.

Similarly, a counseling theory can become a perceptual filter through which a counselor might miss, dismiss, misinterpret, or deny important data about a client. For example, some theories have little to say about the meaning or value of dreams as an instrument of change. Others downplay the influence of biology in personality functioning. Yet others have little to say of spiritual experience or reduce it to a rationalization. A client who had a meaningful dream, who suspects a strong biological influence in one's lifelong struggles, or who had a profound spiritual experience runs the risk of being poorly served by a counselor bound to any of these respective theories.

This disadvantage is more likely to occur with a theory associated with a separate school of thought. The answer might seem to be to focus on a unifying metatheory, because it's likely to be more comprehensive. The problem is that such a theory, to a neophyte counselor-in-preparation, can seem overwhelming. Imagine being a brand new tour guide and trying—in one course, or even one entire master's degree—to know *everything* about *any* location in the world!

How can you Reconcile the Advantages and Disadvantages?

Again, to summarize, counseling theory has its advantages, but it also is quite plural and has disadvantages. Considering all this, how are you, the student of counseling, to approach counseling theory?

- If, in an attempt to be as comprehensive as possible, you seek to master a unifying metatheory in your master's degree, you probably set yourself up for overwhelm and failure.
- If you try to be at least somewhat more comprehensive by seeking to master more than one separate-school theory, you encounter contradictions and set yourself up for dilemmas and inconsistent functioning.
- If you align with one separate-school theory, you function with blinders.
- If you throw up your hands and try to counsel without a theory (which we consider impossible in any case), you lose the several vital advantages of functioning on the basis of a guiding theory.

A hint at the answer we endorse comes from metatheorists like Mahoney and Wilber. Both have described evolving in their beliefs as they grew in knowledge and experience. To varying degrees, their developmental processes reflect our own. For example, one of us (JMH) identified first as a behaviorist, then as person-centered, then as cognitive, and currently as integral. As a starting place, and as a realistic goal for a master's degree, we believe the best alternative is for a student counselor to identify one guidebook—one separate-school theoretical basis—and master the complexity and intricacy of that approach as a foundation for practice. Within the master's course of study, once a firm foundation is established, we endorse a student counselor consulting others guidebooks for enhancements (ideas and techniques) that do not contradict one's fundamental approach to counseling. The most mindful student counselor will undertake this process with the awareness of the down side (the blinders one's theory inevitably creates) and will endeavor to minimize that detriment as much as possible. The mindful student will also remain aware that one's identification of a guiding theory (one's best current answer to the question of a guiding theory) will evolve as one continues to learn both didactically and clinically–experientially and continues to assess the truth value of one's identified theory (Brabeck & Welfel, 1985).

To identify what guidebook you will use as your main resource, you must first familiarize yourself with each one. One purpose of this textbook, then, is to present an introduction to each of the guidebooks that most current counseling professionals use. As you become acquainted with each one in turn, you will probably find that you resonate with more than one. This reaction makes sense, considering that the elephant *does* have tusks, *does* have a tail, and *does* have a trunk—that each theory *is* an accurate reflection, albeit dim, of the whole truth. The fact that each theory is at least partially correct, however, raises another crucial question that we address next.

Which is the Best Counseling Theory?

The next question might very well be *which* guidebook (counseling theory) is *best* to use as your foundation. In fact, quite a bit of controversy exists in the field of counseling in this regard. We will address this issue by responding to several related questions.

Has Research Shown One Theory of Counseling to be More Effective than Another?

In a nutshell, we believe the best answer is no. As a result of the most comprehensive investigations, no one counseling approach has emerged as clearly superior to all others (Elliott, 2002; Lambert, 2004; Wampold, 2006). Again, this finding is probably due to the fact that the elephant does have a trunk, a tail, and so on. Research on the effectiveness of psychotherapy is, however, a crucial and somewhat more complex topic, one to which we will turn very shortly in a later section of this chapter. For the purpose of identifying one best theory, however, research gives little direction.

Are Proponents of One Theory Any Wiser than those of Another?   This question is somewhat more difficult to answer. As Richards and Bergin (1997) said regarding the three primary worldviews to which humans adhere (see Table 1.1), wise and thoughtful people align with each of these mutually exclusive perspectives. In other words, at the most fundamental level of how they see the world, intelligent, insightful people disagree. What Richards and Bergin said about worldviews can also be said of counseling theories: At the most fundamental level of how counseling theorists see people—people's nature, how they develop, and how they change—wise and thoughtful theorists disagree. Because the evaluation of what is "more wise" is a subjective one, you are encouraged to keep this question in mind as you sequentially explore each of the theories we describe in this book.

Assuming for the moment that popularity reflects collective wisdom, *to which theory do most current practitioners subscribe?* Research into this question yields only a somewhat clearer answer (Bechtoldt, Norcross, Wyckoff, Pokrywa, & Campbell, 2001; Glass, Victor, & Arnkoff, 1993; Jensen, Bergen, & Greaves, 1990). Of the counselors who specify one guiding theory, in some studies they indicate psychodynamic (as represented in this text by Chapter 3), whereas in others they identify cognitive-behavioral and existential theories followed by psychodynamic, person-centered, and system approaches. We encourage you not to allow yourself to be swayed too much by these findings. Throughout the history of Western psychotherapy over the past century, the answer would have been very different depending on when the question was asked. The most popular theory today may be in relative disfavor tomorrow.

Considering that a counselor does best to identify one primary theory from an informed knowledge of those that are most widely endorsed, but that no one best theory can be identified on the basis of research, relative wisdom, or collective wisdom, how do you, a counselor in training, identify your own guiding theory? It is to this question that we now turn.

How do you Identify your Guiding Theory of Counseling?

This discussion may, so far, seem to imply that theory is "out there" apart from you, a guidebook external to you that you consult as needed. This implication is partly true. It is equally true, however, and perhaps more important to know, that *you already have a counseling theory*. That is, you already have beliefs about what causes people to be as they are and what they need in order to continue in their development; in the process of living, you already have begun to develop your own fledgling guidebook. And the basic

TABLE 1.1 Three Major Worldviews Among Humans

Naturalistic (Scientific)	Subjective Idealistic (Western or Monotheistic)	Objective Idealistic (Eastern)
Metaphysical assumptions about the nature of reality:		
Naturalism	Supernaturalism	Naturalism and Supernaturalism
Everything is exclusively a phenomenon of nature.	Phenomena exist that transcend nature.	Some belief, disbelief in transcendent phenomena.
Atheism	Theism	Atheism and Polytheism
God is not real.	God is real.	No single transcendent God.
Determinism	Free will	Free will
Every event is determined by a cause.	Humans have freedom to choose though often within biological and environmental limits.	Humans have freedom to choose.
Universalism	Contextualism	Contextualism
Universal laws exist whereby phenomena are generalizable and repeatable.	Some real phenomena are unique and unrepeatable.	Some real phenomena are unique and unrepeatable.
Reductionism	Holism	Holism
Any phenomenon can be understood by reducing it to its parts.	The whole is greater than the sum of its parts.	The whole is greater than the sum of its parts.
Atomism	Holism	Holism
The foundation of reality is found in increasingly smaller parts.	Reality is increasingly lost with successively smaller parts.	Reality is increasingly lost with smaller parts.
Mechanism	Mechanism	Mechanism
The universe is like a machine.	The universe is a manifestation of some intentional intelligence.	The universe is a manifestation of intentional intelligence.
Materialism	Materialism	Materialism
The universe is essentially matter.	The universe is essentially spirit.	Some belief, some disbelief, universe is spirit.

(Continued)

TABLE 1.1 Three Major Worldviews Among Humans (Continued)

Naturalistic (Scientific)	Subjective Idealistic (Western or Monotheistic)	Objective Idealistic (Eastern)
Axiological assumptions about what is valuable, good, and right:		
Ethical hedonism	Ethical altruism	Ethical altruism
Optimal good is a maximum of pleasure and minimum of pain.	Optimal good is foregoing pleasure and bearing pain to benefit others.	Optimal universal "good" and "rights" exist.
Ethical relativism	Ethical universals and absolutes	Ethical universals and absolutes
"Good" and "right" are never universal, always relative to a context.	At least some universal "goods" and "rights" exist.	Some universal "goods" and "rights" exist.
Epistemological assumptions about what can be known:		
Positivism	Noesis	Noesis
Observable facts are our only source of positive knowing.	Some source(s) of knowing transcend what is observable.	Some knowing transcends the observable.
Classical realism	Theistic realism	Theistic idealism
The universe is separate from human consciousness, which can know it.	God is separate from human consciousness, which cannot know it.	Where theistic, consciousness is a part of God.
Empiricism	Epistemological pluralism	Epistemological pluralism
Our physical senses are the only reliable source of knowledge.	Some source(s) of knowing transcend the senses.	Some source(s) of knowing transcend the senses.

Source: Adapted from Richards, P. S. & Bergin, A. E., *A spiritual strategy for counseling and psychotherapy*, American Psychological Association, Washington, DC, 1997.

philosophy you have established probably matches one of the existing theories better than any of the others. We believe this match constitutes the best basis upon which to identify a starting place for your counseling theory foundation—to discover with which theory you initially, philosophically have the strongest allegiance and use that theory as a starting place for your practice of counseling (Luborsky et al., 1999).

The problem is that you've probably developed your guidebook informally and without conscious awareness. If you are to find the best match, you must become aware of your own basic beliefs about how people develop and change, and you must subject those beliefs to scrutiny.

Let us first address the idea that you already have a counseling theory. One way to discover you already have a theory is to realize that, if you had to conduct a counseling session right now, you could do so. You would make choices about how to begin, how to proceed, how to respond moment-to-moment. You would make at least some of those choices based on your belief that those choices would be more effective than other choices. Although you couldn't say *how* effective your choices would be, nevertheless, you likely would have some rationale for at least much of what you do.

Another way to know that you already have a theory of counseling is to answer questions that theories of counseling address, such as those in the box.

As briefly as possible, give your current answer to each of the following questions:

HUMAN NATURE

At the core, are people basically good, evil, or neutral?

How much of personality is inborn, that is, determined or influenced by biological and/or other innate factors?

What, if any, inborn drives, motives, tendencies, or other psychological or behavioral characteristics do all humans share?

How much of a person's individuality is the result of innate factors, such as heredity?

ROLE OF THE ENVIRONMENT IN PERSONALITY DEVELOPMENT

How influential is one's physical and/or social environment in the development of one's personality?

How does the environment influence personality development?

MODEL OF FUNCTIONALITY

What constitutes functionality–mental health in a person? Dysfunctionality–mental unhealth?

How do innate and environmental factors interact such that a person manifests relatively more healthy or unhealthy functioning?

PERSONALITY CHANGE

Once a personality has developed to a lesser or greater degree, how does it change?

What conditions are necessary but not sufficient for change to occur?

What conditions are both necessary and sufficient?

You almost certainly had some ideas in response to the above questions. Those ideas constitute your current theory of counseling. Now that it is clear that you have a theory of counseling (whatever its degree of development) a next question might be, how *good* is your theory? How might you evaluate the quality of your theory? One way to explore this question is to put yourself in the role of a counseling client.

THE SEVEN C's

Think back to a time when you felt the most vulnerable, the most in need of assistance in coping with some aspect of yourself or your environment. Imagine that, at the time, you went to a counselor. By placing an X on each continuum below, rate the qualities you hope you would find in your counselor.

MY IDEAL COUNSELOR WOULD HAVE A THEORY OF COUNSELING THAT IS

Very complete 0—0—0—0—0 Very incomplete

(Indicates how comprehensive your counselor's beliefs about people are, how well her beliefs prepare her to work effectively with a wide variety of people and issues.)

Very clear, straightforward 0—0—0—0—0 Very complex, obscure

(Indicates how easily you and others can understand your counselor's belief system, how straightforward it is, how free it is of an excess of complicated terms and concepts, how "elegant" it is.)

Very internally consistent 0—0—0—0—0 Very internally inconsistent

(Indicates how much your counselor's belief system contains elements that complement rather than contradict each other.)

Very concrete 0—0—0—0—0 Very abstract

(Indicates how easily the concepts in your counselor's belief system can be perceived in real life, can be measured; especially how easily your progress in counseling—and, thus, the effectiveness of the theory itself—can be assessed.)

Very current 0—0—0—0—0 Very out-of-date

(Indicates how well your counselor's beliefs match what the best contemporary research has shown to be true of people and to be effective in helping people change.)

Very creative 0—0—0—0—0 Very rigid, fixed

(Indicates how well your counselor's belief system can accommodate new information and the extent to which it provides her with the foundation to develop innovative approaches to unique people and situations.)

Very conscious 0—0—0—0—0 Very unconscious

(Indicates how aware your counselor is of her belief system, how purposefully she can access and utilize specific concepts and skills; how well she can devise a course of action based on a rationale and explain her rationale when asked to do so.)

If you are like many counseling theorists (Combs, 1989, p. 159), you value a coun-selor whose guiding theory of counseling is complete, clear, consistent, concrete, current, creative, and conscious: the seven c's. (Perhaps our next book will be titled *Counseling Theory: Your Guidebook to Sailing the Seven C's!*) In other words, most people prefer a counselor who uses a well thought out, up-to-date approach that is sensitive to individual needs and can be understood by clients and counselors alike.

Now return to your own answers to the questions about personality development and change. How confident are you that your ideas fulfill the criteria of the seven c's?

Personal Theory Development as Process

The process of identifying a guiding theory can, at first, seem a formidable task. It is not a matter of *choosing* a theory, like you might choose whether to eat strawberry or vanilla ice cream. Rather, it is a process of *identification*. We use this term in two senses. One is in the sense that you are sure to *identify with* or *resonate with* the different theories to various degrees and identify with one more than the others. The other sense is in relation to the concept of your *identity*: that your guiding theory of counseling is a reflection of your identity, of who you are. Just as identity is a phenomenon that develops over time and experience, so is guiding theory (Brabeck & Welfel, 1985). Identification of a guiding theory is not a single decision but, rather, is an ongoing process involving several steps or stages.

Watts (1993) developed a four-stage model to describe the process of identifying a guiding theory. Beginning with the exploration stage, he encouraged students to conduct an internal inventory of values and beliefs, as you began to do by answering the ques-tions posed earlier in this chapter. From this foundation of self-awareness, you are in the best position to explore the major theories of counseling. You can learn about prominent theories through classroom study, audio and video recordings, consultation with practi-tioners, and texts such as this one. The goal of the exploration stage is to begin to com-pare and contrast your beliefs and values with those represented in the various theories.

Watts, like we, recommended that you enter the second, examination stage by iden-tifying from among all the theories the one that seems closest to your views. Once you have made this tentative commitment, immerse yourself in primary resources (print and visual media produced by the original theorist or those who, themselves, identify the theory as their guiding theory). Recommended resources at the end of each chapter pro-vide you with an opportunity to explore primary sources of each theory. Also examine research on the effectiveness of the theory—both by proponents and nonproponents of the theory—to evaluate its truth value (Brabeck & Welfel, 1985). As the immersion pro-gresses, if you begin to feel that the fit between theory and yourself is awkward, then return to the exploration stage to revisit your personal values and your understanding of existing theories.

If you continue to feel a resonance with the theory, you are ready to proceed with the examination stage by beginning to apply your theory with clients under supervision in a prepracticum or practicum course. When beginning to counsel, as when beginning to develop any skill, it's natural for you to experience a certain amount of awkwardness. Remember when you were first learning to drive? You may have sincerely believed in the appropriateness of all the skills your instructor was helping you learn, but doing them all simultaneously and well was another thing altogether! You probably felt somewhat over-whelmed, whereas by now you have probably had the experience of driving from point

A to point B without even thinking consciously of what you were doing! In driving, as in counseling, it is important to persevere in practicing skills that you believe in but that might feel initially quite foreign until those skills become second nature.

Another factor to consider in this second part of the examination phase is the enormous amount of anxiety that most beginning counselors feel initially. The stress of getting out of the classroom and into the counseling room can be very disequilibrating. Consider the following metaphor for this experience: During your academic preparation you are learning to create a set of filters, of glasses, which guides your view of self, others (clients), and the world. The better you are able to integrate personal values and theory, the better your glasses will fit. You walk into the clinical experience able to see reasonably well, and consequently you feel rather confident, even proud of your glasses and your ability to use them. During your first session as the counselor, and repeatedly after that, you begin to feel pressure to be or to do something you are not; it is as if a giant hand comes down from the sky and knocks the glasses off your head. You have difficulty seeing the client through your glasses. Anxiety sets in and you feel you must desperately grasp for any technique that works. It might be helpful to know that the big hand of anxiety is normal at this stage and that your glasses cannot be completely removed (leaving you blind) because they are a part of you: They are your beliefs. In reality, the filters are only moved off their previous position, knocked sideways, and can be repositioned or altered as you gain more experience. Confidence in your abilities and your theory grow in the remaining stages. However, if you have persevered on the basis of a good understanding of the counseling theory you have identified, yet you continue to feel awkward, you have trouble putting the theory into practice, you are not seeing positive outcomes with many of your clients, and/or your ongoing critical examination of the theory leaves you doubting that it is your current best guide to the practice of counseling, you probably do not have a good fit. In this case, you probably need to cycle back to the exploration stage.

Assuming you experience an increasing sense of good fit with your guiding theory throughout the examination stage, the third and fourth stages include taking the mesh between theory and personal values to a level of integration and personalization. Integration occurs when you have assimilated the theory such that you think and act according to the theory in a way that is consistent and that feels natural and spontaneous. This aspect of the process is similar to the student of a new language who, after considerable immersion in it, awakens one morning to the realization that the new language is so deeply integrated that the person was actually *dreaming* in the new language. At this point in the theory identification process, technical eclecticism may become fitting, whereby you evaluate techniques from other theories for compatibility with the philosophy of your personal theory and adopt or adapt those you find compatible. Personalization involves a lifelong commitment to refining, expanding, and clarifying your personal beliefs, values, knowledge, and skills in continuing to develop an internally consistent and ever-richer approach to counseling.

Whereas the first two of Watts's stages are achievable within the structure of your graduate program, your achievement of the last two stages depends largely on your investment in the process as you proceed professionally after graduation. Many counselors never reach the integration stage because they fail to develop the necessary level of self-understanding. Some therapists choose the path of "I attended a workshop on hypnotism. I think I will try that with my 3:00 client," using any new technique regardless of rationale and, unethically, without sufficient preparation. Exploring self and theory takes persistence and passion. This exploration is characterized not by blind devotion but by intellectual and personal openness and curiosity. The payoff of the journey is greater self-understanding, clearer client conceptualization, greater effectiveness, and a reduced likelihood of burnout (Boy & Pine, 1983).

To return to our analogies from earlier in the chapter, in this process of coming to understand and work with the elephant that is the human psyche, each counselor is probably neither as ignorant as the blind men nor as omniscient as the small boy. Rather, each is in the process of perceiving the elephant ever more clearly and accurately—and working with it more effectively. Thus, the best any counselor-in-training can do is identify the guiding theory that best approximates her own beliefs about people, then commit to the ongoing process of refining those beliefs in light of personal experience and current, high-quality research. In the final section of this chapter, we will discuss yet more rationale in support of this approach to a difficult but important issue in your development as a professional counselor.

HOW THIS BOOK IS ORGANIZED

To help you approach each theory in the most understandable way and to help you in your comparison of the various theories, we have organized the theory chapters with a particular format. By reading the following outline overview, you will prepare yourself to make the most of the chapters that follow.

I. Background of the theory

   Historical context. What was the historical and cultural context in which this theory developed?

   Founder's biographical overview. What were the major experiences of the founder's life, and how did his life relate to his theory?

   Philosophical underpinnings. What philosophical perspectives provided the conceptual foundation of this theory?

II. Personality development. Beginning at an infant's birth and proceeding chronologically into adulthood, how does a person's personality develop, according to this theory?

   Nature of humans. What factors in personality are inborn at birth and influential across the life span?

   The function of the psyche. What inborn motives, such as drives, needs, or tendencies, consistently animate the person across the life span? What operating principles are fundamental to the psyche?

   The structure of the psyche. What psychological constructs exist at birth either actually or as potentials? Psychic structure typically is either aggregate, having parts that can operate independent of or in opposition to each other, or holistic, being a unified whole whereby any parts operate in the service of the whole.

   Role of the environment. How do factors other than innate factors influence personality development?

   Impact of the familial environment. What is the role of one's early familial environment, and how important is the influence of that environment throughout one's life?

   Extrafamilial factors. What is the role of one's environment besides one's early familial environment, and how important is the influence of that environment throughout one's life?

The healthy–adaptive versus unhealthy–maladaptive personality. What characterizes optimal and less-than-optimal human functioning? How do the influences of human nature, the environment, and any other factors interact to result in optimal and less-than-optimal functioning?

III. The personality change process. Each theory rests on the basic assumption that personality, whether partially, substantially, or fully formed, can develop beyond its current form, that is, can change. How does this theory conceptualize and promote personality change, particularly through the counseling process?

Basic principles of change. In general, how do people change, either in or out of the counseling setting? What is the "prime mover" of change: feelings, thoughts, and/or actions?

Change through counseling. In particular, what characterizes the change process in the counseling setting?

The client's role. What is the client's part in the change process?

Motivation to change. Why do clients seek counseling? If a client is mandated to counseling, what influence will that fact have on the change process?

The client's experience. From the client's perspective, what provokes a client to seek (or in the case of a mandate not seek) counseling?

The counselor's conceptualization. From the counselor's perspective, what dynamics underlying the client's experience provoke (or don't provoke) the client to seek counseling?

Capacity for change. How much is the client's personality determined, and, consequently, how free is the client to change?

Responsibility for change. How passive or active must the client be in the counseling process?

Source of resistance. To what extent does the theory embrace the idea that clients in counseling sometimes resist change? To the extent that it does, how does the theory conceptualize the psychological dynamics at work in resistance?

The counselor's role. What is the counselor's role in the client's change process?

Goals of counseling. What does the counselor conceptualize to be the aim of the counseling process?

Characteristics of an effective counselor. What attitudes and behaviors characterize the counselor who is most likely to facilitate client change?

Stages and techniques

The therapeutic relationship. What constitutes a "good" therapeutic relationship, how important is it, and how is such a relationship established and maintained throughout the counseling process?

Assessment. To what extent is formal and/or informal assessment used, when during the counseling process is it used, and what form(s) does it take?

Change strategies. What specific techniques does the counselor employ to facilitate developmental change?

Addressing client resistance. In each theory that embraces the concept of client resistance, how does the counselor recognize and respond to resistance?

IV. Contributions and limitations of the theory

　　Interface with recent developments in the mental health field. (These topics are discussed in depth in the next section of this chapter.)

　　The nature–nurture question

　　DSM–IV–TR diagnosis

　　Pharmacotherapy

　　Managed care and brief therapy

　　Technical eclecticism

　　Diversity issues, including client ethnicity, gender, sexual orientation, and spirituality

　　The effectiveness of psychotherapy

　　What limitations have proponents and nonproponents noted regarding the applicability and/or effectiveness of this theory?

　　What distinguishing addition has this theory made to counseling and psychotherapy?

V. Current status. Since its original inception, how has the theory developed to its current status?

VI. Summary

VII. Recommended resources: print, audiovisual, and Web site.

VIII. References

RECENT DEVELOPMENTS IN MENTAL HEALTH PERTINENT TO COUNSELING THEORY

In this final section of this introductory chapter, we will address in more detail one aspect of the outline that appears above. A crucial ingredient in the evaluation of a counseling theory is the extent to which the theory has incorporated, or could incorporate, information that has been discovered since the theory was created. Most of the theories we describe in this text were developed prior to 1980. However, over the past three decades, research and practice in the mental health field, along with social change, have yielded new information and perspectives. It is no fault of traditional theorists that they did not consider these developments when they were formulating their theories; they cannot be held responsible for knowledge that did not exist at that time. You, however, a counseling student of the early twenty-first century, are in a position to consider these developments as you study each counseling theory. You are responsible for knowledge that exists at this time. The following discussion addresses several of these developments and their implications for you in your process of identifying your guiding theory of counseling.

The Nature–Nurture Question

To what extent is personality a manifestation of nature (the influence of heredity), or of nurture (the influence of experience in the natural and social environment)? In 1990, the American Counseling Association's *Journal of Counseling and Development* published a special feature on the genetic origins of behavior (Baker & Clark, 1990). They cited such researchers as Thomas Bouchard (Skovholt, 1990), director of the Minnesota Center for Twin and Adoption Research, whose research team has studied dozens of identical twins separated by adoption at or shortly after birth and reunited as adults for the first time at the center's research site in Minneapolis. These research participants have provided a unique opportunity to study concordance rates, the extent to which personality traits are shared in two people who possess identical genes but who were raised in different environments. Findings from these and other studies have yielded several results that contradict or challenge prevailing beliefs up to and including the late twentieth century:

- For most personality traits, genes explain at least 30% and up to 50%, of the variance in the trait (Gatz, 1990, p. 601).
- Environmental factors—all effects except genetic—explain the remaining 50% to 70% of variance (Gatz, 1990, p. 601).
- Of the environmental factors that explain the remaining variance, shared factors, such as growing up in the same family, have little or no influence on personality traits. Rather, nonshared experiences, those unique to the individual, have the greatest effect (Gatz, 1990, p. 601). Therefore, "parenting styles and traditional family variables may be relatively unimportant in understanding problem behavior" (Baker & Clark, 1990, p. 598). Rather, in understanding the environmental contribution to the development of a particular personality trait, counselors might do well to focus on a client's *unique* experiences with caregivers or other people or situations (Baker & Clark, 1990, pp. 598–599). Unique experiences include such things as illness, accidents, specific interactions with a specific caregiver, and receiving awards. It should be noted that some critics have questioned the validity of this particular assertion.
- Caregiver behavior may be the result rather than the cause of a child's genetically predisposed behavior, a kind of "reverse causality" (Rowe, 1990, p. 609).
- "Genes may be expressed at one age and not another" or only under specific circumstances (Baker & Clark, 1990, p. 599).
- "Biology is *not* necessarily destiny" (Baker & Clark, 1990, p. 599). When a genetic influence is known to exist, environmental accommodations often can maximize or minimize the genetic influence.
- Several phenomena that are the focus of counseling or are addressed in counseling have a known or a strongly suspected genetic influence: schizophrenia, depression, manic depression, and Alzheimer's Disease (Gatz, 1990); chronic anxiety and panic disorder (Carey, 1990); reading disabilities (LaBuda, DeFries, & Pennington, 1990); antisocial behavior (Raine & Dunkin, 1990); and extreme introversion (Ellis & Robbins, 1990).
- The prevailing view in the mental health field is that distressing psychological symptoms are the result of some combination of genetic vulnerability and environmental factors. Even more specifically, in the diathesis-stress model (Elwood, Hahn, Olatunji, & Williams, 2009), two factors (hence "di"), genetic endowment and early learning, create some degree of latent vulnerability to or protection from psychopathology that later manifests when a person encounters particular type(s) and intensity(s) of stressors.

Near the end of each chapter, we will help you apply this information to the theory at hand by offering our answers to the following questions:

What do people of this particular theoretical persuasion believe about the nature–nurture question?
How do those beliefs compare with the recent developments described above?

If they differ, could the recent developments cited above be incorporated into the theory without violating the theory's basic premises?

DSM–IV–TR Diagnosis

In 1952, the American Psychiatric Association published the first edition of its *Diagnostic and Statistical Manual of Mental Disorders*. The most recent fourth edition with text revision, *DSM–IV–TR*, was published in 2000 (American Psychiatric Association, 2000, p. xxiv ff.). The purpose of these publications was to identify categories of, establish nationally acceptable nomenclature and descriptions of, and determine incidences for the various mental disorders.

A complete *DSM–IV–TR* diagnosis includes five "axes." For Axis I, the clinician indicates any clinical disorders other than personality disorders and mental retardation. Axis I includes psychotic, adjustment, anxiety, mood, sexual, eating, and sleep disorders. Axis II includes personality disorders and mental retardation. If a general medical condition seems relevant to the mental condition specified on Axis I or II, it is indicated on Axis III. Axis IV indicates psychosocial and environmental problems potentially relevant to the mental disorder. Axis V indicates the clinician's assessment of the extent to which the mental disorder impairs the client's overall functioning, from 1 (extremely severe impairment) to 100 (no impairment; American Psychiatric Association, 2000, p. 34).

The acceptability of diagnosis—and even of the concept of "mental disorder"—varies from one counseling theory to another. In the extremes, some theories eschew the diagnosis of clients, whereas others consider it essential. Although *DSM* authors claim its categorizing system is atheoretical, critics have demonstrated its empirical perspective that frequently neglects to acknowledge such important contextual factors in diagnosis as clients' subjective meanings, cultures, and systems (Douthit & Marquis, 2006). Even in those orientations in which diagnosis is considered vital, clinicians are often quite mindful of the power of labeling and, consequently, handle a diagnosis with requisite care. Community agency counselors are often required, and private practice counselors seeking third party payment from managed care providers are almost always required to render a *DSM–IV–TR* diagnosis for clients.

Near the end of each chapter, we will help you apply this information to the theory at hand by offering our answers to the following questions:

How does each theory view the act of diagnosing, and even the concept of "mental disorder"?

If you will be dealing with managed care, which almost always requires the mental health practitioner to diagnose each client, how compatible is that requirement with the theory?
How might you reconcile any discrepancy between the theory's view on diagnosis and the pragmatic necessity of rendering diagnoses?

Pharmacotherapy

Psychiatrists and other physicians can prescribe any of a number of medications that reduce or eliminate distressing psychological symptoms. Some research has indicated that psychoactive medication can be as effective as, or even more effective than, psychotherapy, at least in the short run; other research has indicated the superiority of psychotherapy over psychoactive medication; and yet other research has indicated that medication in conjunction with psychotherapy is often most effective (Holiner Psychiatric Group, 1998). An excellent source on the subject of pharmacotherapy is Preston, O'Neal, and Talaga's (2008) *Handbook of Clinical Psychopharmacology for Therapists*.

Evaluating the potential benefits and drawbacks of pharmacotherapy can be complex and value laden. For example, premature ejaculation abates with certain psychoactive medications, but the disorder recurs as soon as the medication is discontinued. Conversely, premature ejaculation is highly responsive to certain quite simple and easy sexual exercises; the symptoms abate for as many as 95% of men within just a few weeks, and the men then have a skill that will serve them for their lifetime (LoPiccolo, 1998). In cases such as this, counselor tend to value "skills over pills." However, some conditions require pills along with or in addition to skills.

Near the end of each chapter, we will help you apply this information to the theory at hand by offering our answers to the following questions:

To what extent does the theory address pharmacotherapy, providing guidelines about if and when pharmacotherapy should be considered or used?

To the extent that the theory does not address this issue, how compatible is the theory with pharmacotherapy?

To what extent could pharmacotherapeutic considerations be added to the practice of this theory without violating the theory's basic premises?

Managed Care and Brief Therapy

Prior to approximately 1980, when a mental health practitioner worked with a client who received insurance reimbursement for expenses incurred from psychotherapy, the typical arrangement was for the client to choose the psychotherapist, for the psychotherapist to determine the length of therapy and therapeutic approach, and for the client or therapist to file directly to the insurance company for reimbursement. Since about 1980, managed care has changed that process. Managed care refers to health maintenance organizations (HMOs), preferred provider organizations (PPOs), and government-funded programs such as Medicaid and Medicare (Glosoff, Garcia, Herlihy, & Remley, 1999). Organizations such as these restrict those mental health professionals they will reimburse, determine how many sessions for which they will reimburse, require substantial paperwork describing treatment protocol and client progress, and reimburse only for certain favored psychotherapeutic approaches. The favored approaches are those that are brief and that have been supported by empirical evidence, in particular, cognitive-behavioral. We have heard some counselors refer sardonically to managed care as "managed cost" or, even more pointedly, "mangled care."

Some counselors work in environments heavily dependent on managed care for reimbursement, such as the community agency or the private practice. If you anticipate possibly being such a counselor, near the end of each chapter, we will help you apply the above information to the theory at hand by offering our answers to the following questions:

Does this therapeutic approach constitute a form of brief therapy?

If not, have recent practitioners published guidelines for adapting the approach to a brief therapy format?

If not, could the approach be adapted to a brief therapy format?

How amenable is the theory to incorporating the counseling techniques favored by managed care?

Technical Eclecticism

Recent surveys reveal an increasing tendency for mental health professionals to identify their theoretical orientation as "eclectic" (Bechtoldt et al., 2001). Eclecticism means "selecting what seems best from various systems" (Morris, 1976). This practice suggests an atheoretical or polytheoretical approach to counseling. As we discussed earlier in this chapter, we disagree with either of these approaches. Following is a summary of our viewpoint.

First, we believe it is simply impossible for a counselor to be atheoretical. The counselor must make choices about how to respond to a client from moment to moment; those choices are based on some rationale, however conscious or nonconscious; and a rationale is based on beliefs about how people develop and change—theory. Whereas a counselor cannot be atheoretical, a counselor can be nonconscious of one's guiding theory.

Second, we also value consistency in thought; consequently, we eschew a polytheoretical approach to counseling. Any two counseling theories directly contradict each other in some way. For example, one cannot believe both that people's innate tendency is always to do what is self-gratifying and that it is always to do what is self-actualizing.

With these two points in mind (the impossibility of being both rationale-based and atheoretical and the impossibility of being both internally consistent and polytheoretical) the inevitable consequence is for each counseling student to identify the one theory that best reflects one's own beliefs about how people develop and change. This process is supported by research results: The evidence in favor of certain psychotherapeutic treatments is outweighed by an absence of evidence for the superiority of any one psychotherapeutic approach over another.

Having stated the case for *theoretical purity*, we also endorse the concept of *technical eclecticism*, a term first coined by Arnold Lazarus (Lazarus & Beutler, 1993). Technical eclecticism involves the adoption or adaptation of a technique that grew out of a theory other than one's own guiding theory. In other words, the technically eclectic counselor uses any technique adopted or adapted from another theory that does not violate the basic tenets of one's own guiding theory. We believe counselors who subscribe to *theoretical* eclecticism are seeking flexibility, but they achieve flexibility at the expense of self-awareness and internal consistency. Those who are theoretically pure and *technically* eclectic find flexibility while achieving self-awareness and internal consistency.

Near the end of each chapter, we will help you apply this information to the theory at hand by offering our answers to the following questions:

How amenable are proponents of this theory to technical eclecticism?

To the extent that they are amenable, what specific techniques from what other theories can a counselor adopt or adapt for use in a conceptually consistent way with the theory at hand?

Diversity Issues

The United States contains a diverse (and, regarding some domains of diversity, an increasingly diverse) population (U.S. Census Bureau, 2009). Consider the distribution in three domains of diversity: ethnicity, sexual orientation, and religious affiliation (see Figures 1.1 through 1.3). These figures indicate that you inevitably will encounter issues of diversity in your professional counseling experience. In its *Code of Ethics*, the American Counseling Association (2005) asserted that "counselors do not condone or engage in discrimination based on age, culture, disability, ethnicity, race, religion/spirituality, gender, gender identity, sexual orientation, marital status/partnership, language preference, socio-economic status, or any basis proscribed by law" (p. 10, C5). "Respecting diversity means that [counselors] are committed to acquiring the knowledge, skills, personal awareness, and sensitivity that are essential to working effectively with diverse client populations" (Herlihy & Corey, 1996, p. 295).

Contrast these facts about diversity with the fact that almost every theory described in this text was originally developed by a Western (European, European-American, or European-Australian), Caucasian, apparently heterosexual, male from a Judeo-Christian background. In addition, almost all the theories originally were formulated many years before diversity issues came to prominence in the mental health field. Existing counseling theories might reflect characteristics—values, beliefs, and practices—that are incompatible with the characteristics of certain diverse populations.

Near the end of each chapter, we will help you apply this information to the theory at hand by offering our answers to the following questions:

How, if at all, does the theory address diversity issues?
How flexibly does or could the theory accommodate specific characteristics of various diverse populations?

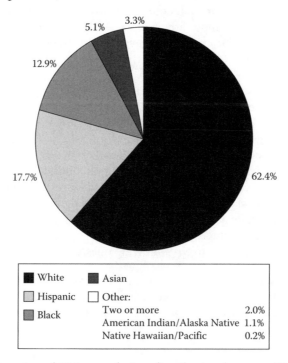

FIGURE 1.1 2015 projected U.S. population distribution by race. (U.S. Census Bureau, *The 2010 statistical abstract.* Retrieved from http://www.census.gov/compendia/statab/cats/population.html, 2010. Due to arithmetic rounding and to some overlap in categories, total exceeds 100%.)

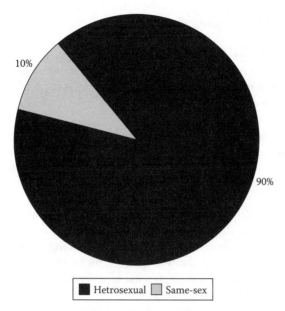

FIGURE 1.2   Sexual orientation among U.S. population. (Mean estimate of predominant same-sex orientation. Based on Gonsiorek, J. C., Sell, R. L., and Weinrich, J. D., *Suicide and life-threatening behavior*, 25, 1995. Cited in Kinsey Institute for Research in Sex, Gender, and Reproduction, Inc., Prevalence of homosexuality, 2009.)

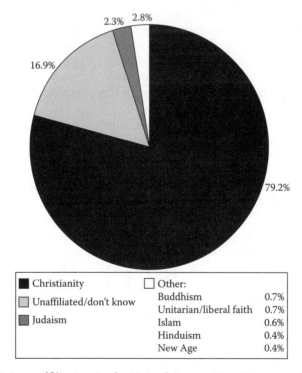

FIGURE 1.3   Religious affiliation in the United States. (Pew Forum on Religion & Public Life, *Religious affiliation*. Retrieved from http://religions.pewforum.org/reports, 2008. Due to arithmetic rounding, total exceeds 100%.)

The Effectiveness of Psychotherapy

How effective is psychotherapy, what factors play a role in its effectiveness, and, in particular, what role does counseling theory play? In their thorough review of the quantitative research on the effectiveness of psychotherapy, Asay and Lambert (1999) summarized several conclusions.

- Psychotherapy works. Most clients report a positive outcome (observed and reported improvement in feelings and functioning) following counseling. At least half of clients will achieve a beneficial outcome in 5 to 10 counseling sessions, whereas one fifth to one third will need more than 25 sessions. Counselors need to quickly identify and address client characteristics that contraindicate brief therapy or even predict a lower likelihood of success in longer term therapy: poor motivation, hostility, a history of poor relationships, and passivity in the counseling process. Most clients who achieve a beneficial outcome will maintain their gains, especially when counselors help them adopt an active role in their progress, help them expect the likelihood of temporary setbacks, and help them rehearse how to handle such setbacks.
- At least 40% of positive outcome in psychotherapy can be attributed to extratherapeutic factors, that is, factors essentially outside the counseling setting and out of the counselor's hands. These include client factors such as the severity and chronicity of the client's problem; the client's level of motivation to change; the client's capacity to relate to other people; the client's ego strength, that is, such characteristics as the ability to tolerate and manage emotional pain and the ability to create and follow through on plans; the client's psychological mindedness, that is, an understanding of psychological dynamics and insight into motivation and cause–effect aspects of behavior; and the client's ability to identify a focal problem. Extratherapeutic factors also include the quality of the client's social support system and the client's ability and willingness to access and use self-help and community resources.
- About 15% of positive outcome be attributed to the client's expectation of improvement, a factor for which both the client and the therapist share responsibility. The client brings a history of relative optimism or pessimism, in general, as well as prejudices about the probable effectiveness of psychotherapy, in particular. The therapist can instill hope while avoiding the ethical breach of guaranteeing any particular outcome.
- At least 30% of beneficial outcome can be attributed to the therapeutic relationship, on which the counselor exerts the most influence. It is the counselor's responsibility to establish and maintain, and consistently communicate, acceptance of, warmth toward, and empathy for the client. In this regard, certain counselors may feel challenged when working with certain clients, such as a previously emotionally abused counselor working with a client who reports having emotionally abused a child. Still other clients represent a challenge to virtually any counselor, such as clients who meet the criteria for certain personality disorders. In either case, it is the counselor's responsibility to establish and sustain accepting, warm, and empathic interaction with the client. If a counselor finds oneself behaving toward a client in a "critical, attacking, rejecting, blaming, or neglectful" way (Asay & Lambert, 1999, p. 44), the counselor has the responsibility to take action to remediate oneself or refer the client to another

therapist. Counselors also need to integrate these qualities of a good therapeutic relationship with appropriate limit setting when therapeutically and ethically indicated. In addition to the counselor undergoing high-quality training to learn how to facilitate a good therapeutic relationship, a counselor should undertake self-care to avoid burnout, continually collaborate with the client to maintain a sense of joint cooperation in the therapeutic process, and assess client progress at the beginning of each session.

- Finally, 15% of beneficial outcome in psychotherapy can be attributed specifically to the techniques the therapist uses. In 1993, the Clinical Psychology Division of the American Psychological Association created a task force to identify psychotherapeutic approaches validated by research to be effective or probably effective (Crits-Christoph, 1998). Members of the task force established criteria, including a minimum number of studies with acceptable research design that had involved the use of standardized treatment manuals and had yielded statistically significant results. Then they surveyed the vast psychotherapy research literature and generated a list of empirically supported techniques. Counselors need to be aware that critics have argued against both the empirically validated treatments in particular (Marquis & Douthit, 2006) and the use of treatment manuals in psychotherapy and in the training of psychotherapists in general. Nevertheless, "keeping an open mind, but a balanced perspective, in considering the use of treatment manuals and empirically validated treatments [later changed to "empirically supported treatment" and currently called "evidence-based treatments"] will give clinicians more options" (Asay & Lambert, 1999, p. 45; bracketed material added).

Near the end of each chapter, we will help you apply this information to the theory at hand by offering our answers to the following questions:

To what extent does the theory, at least, address or, at best, incorporate these factors?

To the extent that it does not, to what extent could the theory be modified to incorporate these factors without violating the theory's basic premises?

CONCLUSION

Your task as a developing counselor is to identify the theory that will serve as your guidebook in the practice of counseling. The purpose of this textbook is to help prepare you to do so. Each theory consists of a unique system of beliefs about how people develop and change. By coming to a good understanding of each theory, and by assessing how well the beliefs of a particular theory coincide with your own beliefs, you will provide yourself with the means to identify the theory that is a best fit for you. Because that theory offers a more conscious elaboration of ideas similar to your own along with a set of conceptually consistent techniques, it can serve you as you launch into your development as a counselor.

In addition, throughout your counseling career, your guiding theory can be a resource to which you turn when feeling challenged in your work with a particular client. As you develop, and to the extent that your theory embraces it, you may expand your repertoire of counseling techniques by—in a way that is conceptually consistent with your guiding theory—adapting or adopting techniques that grew originally out of other theories. By using your own experience of success and failure along with an ongoing awareness of current research, you can refine your approach, ultimately creating a theory—an internally consistent system of beliefs and techniques—that is both increasingly accurate and uniquely your own. In doing so, you become progressively less like the blind men and more like the small boy in your discovery of how to work with the elephant that is the human psyche; you incorporate ever greater clarity and depth in your understanding of, and workings with, the hologram of human existence.

REFERENCES

American Counseling Association. (2005). *Code of ethics*. Alexandria, VA: Author.

American Psychiatric Association. (2000). *Diagnostic and statistical manual of mental disorders* (4th ed., text rev.). Washington, DC: Author.

Anchin, J. C., & Magnavita, J. J. (2008). Toward the unification of psychotherapy: An introduction to the journal symposium. *Journal of Psychotherapy Integration, 18,* 259–263.

Asay, T. P., & Lambert, M. J. (1999). The empirical case for the common factors in therapy: Quantitative findings. In M. A. Hubble, B. L. Duncan, & S. D. Miller (Eds.), *The heart and soul of change* (pp. 23–55). Washington, DC: American Psychological Association.

Baker, L. A., & Clark, R. (1990). Introduction to special feature. Genetic origins of behavior: Implications for counselors. *Journal of Counseling and Development, 68,* 597–605.

Bechtoldt, H., Norcross, J. C., Wyckoff, L. A., Pokrywa, M. L., & Campbell, L. F. (2001). Theoretical orientations and employment settings of clinical and counseling psychologists: A comparative study. *The Clinical Psychologist, 54,* 3–6.

Boy, A. V., & Pine, G. J. (1983). Counseling: Fundamentals of theoretical renewal. *Counseling and Values, 27,* 248–255.

Brabeck, M. M., & Welfel, E. R. (1985). Counseling theory: Understanding the trend toward eclecticism from a developmental perspective. *Journal of Counseling and Development, 63,* 343–348.

Carey, G. (1990). Genes, fears, phobias, and phobic disorders. *Journal of Counseling and Development, 68,* 628–632.

Combs, A. W. (1989). *A theory of therapy: Guidelines for counseling practice*. Newbury Park, CA: Sage.

Crits-Christoph, P. (1998). Training in empirically validated treatments: The Division 12 APA task force recommendations. In K. S. Dobson & K. D. Craig (Eds.), *Empirically supported therapies: Best practice in professional psychology* (pp. 3–25). Thousand Oaks, CA: Sage.

Das, A. S. (1996). *Vedic stories from ancient India*. Borehamwood, Hertfordshire, Ahimsa.

Douthit, K. Z., & Marquis, A. (2006). Empiricism in psychiatry's post-psychoanalytic era: Contemplating DSM's "atheoretical" nosology. *Constructivism in the Human Sciences, 11,* 32–59.

Elliott, R. (2002). The effectiveness of humanistic therapies: A meta-analysis. In D. J. Cain & J. Seeman (Eds.), *Humanistic psychotherapies: Handbook of research and practice* (pp. 57–81). Washington, DC: American Psychological Association.

Ellis, M. V., & Robbins, E. S. (1990). In celebration of nature: A dialogue with Jerome Kagan. *Journal of Counseling and Development, 68,* 623–627.

Elwood, L. S., Hahn, K. S., Olatunji, B. O., & Williams, N. L. (2009). Cognitive vulnerability to the development of PTSD: A review of four vulnerabilities and the proposal of an integrative vulnerability model. *Clinical Psychology Review, 29,* 87–100.

Gatz, M. (1990). Interpreting behavioral genetic results: Suggestions for counselors and clients. *Journal of Counseling and Development, 68,* 601–605.

Glass, C. R., Victor, B. J., & Arnkoff, D. B. (1993). Empirical research on integrative and eclectic psychotherapies. In G. Stricker & J. R. Gold (Eds.), *Comprehensive handbook of psychotherapy integration* (pp. 9–25). New York, NY: Plenum.

Glosoff, H. L., Garcia, J., Herlihy, B., & Remley, T. P., Jr. (1999). Managed care: Ethical considerations for counselors. *Counseling and Values, 44,* 8–16.

Gonsiorek, J. C., Sell, R. L., & Weinrich, J. D. (1995). Definition and measurement of sexual orientation. *Suicide and Life-Threatening Behavior, 25*(Suppl.), 40–51.

Herlihy, B., & Corey, G. (1996). *ACA ethical standards casebook* (5th ed.). Alexandria, VA: American Counseling Association.

Holiner Psychiatric Group. (1998, October). *What's new in psychopharmacology for the 21st century.* Paper presented in Dallas, TX.

Jensen, J. P., Bergen, A. E., & Greaves, D. W. (1990). The meaning of eclecticism: New survey and analysis of components. *Professional Psychology: Research and Practice, 21,* 124–130.

Kinsey Institute for Research in Sex, Gender, and Reproduction, Inc. (2009). *Prevalence of homosexuality.* Retrieved from http://www.iub.edu/~kinsey/resources/bib-homoprev.html

LaBuda, M. C., DeFries, J. C., & Pennington, B. F. (1990). Reading disability: A model for the genetic analysis of complex behavioral disorders. *Journal of Counseling and Development, 68,* 645–651.

Lambert, M. J. (Ed.). (2004). *Bergin and Garfield's handbook of psychotherapy and behavior change* (5th ed.). New York, NY: Wiley.

Lazarus, A. A., & Beutler, L. E. (1993). On technical eclecticism. *Journal of Counseling and Development, 71,* 381–385.

LoPiccolo, J. (1998, October). *Postmodern sex therapy.* Paper presented at the meeting of the American Association of Marriage and Family Therapists, Dallas, TX.

Luborsky, L., Diguer, L., Seligman, D., Rosenthal, R., Karuse, E., Johnson, S., . . . Schweizer, E. (1999). The researcher's own therapy allegiances: A "wild card" in comparison of treatment efficacy. *Clinical Psychology: Science and Practice, 6*(1), 95–106.

Marquis, A., & Douthit, K. (2006). The hegemony of "empirically supported treatment": Validating or violating? *Constructivism in the Human Sciences, 11,* 108–141.

Morris, W. (Ed.). (1976). *The American heritage dictionary of the English language.* Boston, MA: Houghton Mifflin.

Patterson, C. H. (1973). *Theories of counseling and psychotherapy.* New York, NY: Harper & Row.

Pew Forum on Religion & Public Life. (2008). *Religious affiliation.* Retrieved from http://religions.pewforum.org/reports

Preston, J. D., O'Neal, J. H., & Talaga, M. C. (2008). *Handbook of clinical psychopharmacology for therapists* (5th ed.). Oakland, CA: New Harbinger.

Raine, A., & Dunkin, J. J. (1990). The genetic and psychophysiological basis of antisocial behavior: Implications for counseling and therapy. *Journal of Counseling and Development, 68,* 637–644.

Richards, P. S., & Bergin, A. E. (1997). *A spiritual strategy for counseling and psycho-therapy*. Washington, DC: American Psychological Association.

Rowe, D. C. (1990). As the twig is bent? The myth of child-rearing influences on personality development. *Journal of Counseling and Development, 68,* 606–611.

Skovholt, T. M. (1990). Counseling implications of genetic research: A dialogue with Thomas Bouchard. *Journal of Counseling and Development, 68,* 633–636.

U.S. Census Bureau. (2009). *The 2009 statistical abstract*. Table 11. Resident Population by Race, Hispanic-Origin Status, and Age—Projections: 2010 and 2015. Retrieved from http://www.census.gov/compendia/statab/cats/population.html

Wampold, B. E. (2006). Not a scintilla of evidence to support empirically supported treatments as more effective than other treatments. In J. C. Norcross, L. E. Beutler, & R. F. Levant (Eds.), *Evidence-based practices in mental health: Debate and dialogue on the fundamental questions* (pp. 299–307). Washington, DC: American Psychological Association.

Watts, R. E. (1993). Developing a personal theory of counseling. *Texas Counseling Association Journal, 21,* 103–104.

CHAPTER 2

Classical Psychoanalysis

BACKGROUND OF THE THEORY

Historical Context

Sigmund Freud's life spanned the late nineteenth and early twentieth centuries almost entirely in Vienna, Austria. When Freud was born, Europe was in the Age of Reason—also termed the Age of Enlightenment or Modernity. The premodern worldview was that religious or supernatural forces could explain everything. By contrast, modernist thinkers emphasized "unbiased rationality" and sensory experience; they were in awe of the mechanistically ordered universe that Newton had revealed; and many of them questioned, and in some cases denounced, the existence of God. Their prevailing belief was that "the advance of science and the general extension of education assured the progressive perfection of society" (Huizinga, 1936, cited in Kreis, 2000a, p. 1). It was through science, which integrates empirical observation with rational theories, that Freud himself, along with other social and intellectual forces, helped to advance the Age of Modernism (Kreis, 2000a).

With the conclusion of World War I came widespread disillusionment and an Age of Anxiety about the potential for human peace and the meaning of life. Europeans saw an increase in fascism, the belief in government by power and authority by "a special breed of man ... a Philosopher/King" (Kreis, 2000b p. 1). This philosophy contributed to the development of World War II, at the beginning of which Freud died.

Economically, Freud's era was a time of industrial expansion, of general prosperity punctuated by periods of relative impoverishment, which Freud experienced both as a child and in the aftermath of World War I. One social force, until the death of Queen Victoria in 1901, was the Victorian value of sexual restraint.

Another social force with which Freud contended throughout his life was anti-Semitism. Partly in response to it, his family of origin moved before he was five years old, and solely because of it, his family of creation moved when Freud was 81, less than two years before his death, to escape Hitler's persecution. In between, anti-Semitism played a significant role in Freud's choice of vocation and his ability to exercise and advance in it.

Founder's Biographical Overview

> I am not a man of science at all, not an observer, not an experimenter, not a thinker. I am nothing but a conquistador by temperament, an adventurer ... with all the inquisitiveness, daring, and tenacity of such a man. (Sigmund Freud, cited in Gay, 1988, p. xvi)

Freud expressed a distinct distaste for the "lies ... concealment ... hypocrisies ... and embellishments" (cited in Gay, 1988, p. xv) of the biographical enterprise. As early as age 29, Freud reported with glee that he had undertaken to frustrate his future biographers by destroying "diaries ... letters, scientific notes and ... [publication] manuscripts ... [sparing] only family letters" (cited in Jones, 1953, Vol. 1, pp. xii–xiii). However, over the ensuing years, Freud actually provided biographers with much more revealing—and potentially damning—material: his own extensive self-analysis, which he conducted and published in the service of his passion for the development of his theories.

His memories from his first few years included feeling jealous when his newborn brother deprived Sigmund of sole access to his mother's breasts, then guilt when, only months later, Julius died; seeing his mother naked, which aroused sexual feelings toward her; entering his parents' bedroom out of sexual curiosity only to be banished by his angry father; and displacing his resentment toward his father as rival for his mother's affection to his brother, Phillip. Having revealed his early childhood memories, as well as his dreams and innermost wishes, he later witnessed these intimate disclosures misused and abused by his detractors. In response, Freud and his family wholeheartedly endorsed one person, Ernest Jones, to present the most truthful account possible of Freud's life. Jones's (1953) three-volume work is the official biography of Sigmund Freud, authorized by "Professor" (as Freud was known among his friends) himself (Roazen, 1992).

Peter Gay (1988), whom many experts consider the most reputable of Freud's contemporary biographers, offered the perspective on Freud's commentators that "every worshipper who has hailed him ... has been matched by a detractor who has derided him" (p. xvi). Gay continued:

> Unlike other great figures in the history of Western culture, Freud seems to stand under the obligation to be perfect. No one acquainted with the psychopathology of Luther or Gandhi, Newton or Darwin, Beethoven or Schumann, Keats or Kafka, would venture to suggest that their neuroses damaged their creations or compromised their stature. In sharp contrast, Freud's failings, real or imagined, have been proffered as conclusive evidence for the bankruptcy of his creation. It has become a common tactic to strike at psychoanalysis by striking at its founder. (p. xix)

Although "no statute of limitations pertains to unearthing flaws in Freud's character, there must be some point in the development of a discipline when questions about its founder no longer bring the whole structure into doubt" (Moore, 1999, p. 37). With these considerations in mind, we embark on a biographical sketch of Sigmund Freud.

Since Freud considered early parental influence to be formative of a child's—and, later, that child's adult—personality, we begin with his parents. At age 40 and already a grandfather, Jakob Freud, a merchant who primarily sold wool, entered his second marriage, to Amalie Nathansohn. Amalie maintained her vibrant personality throughout her life. Six weeks prior to her death at age 95, a local newspaper featured her photograph, upon which she commented, "A bad reproduction; it makes me look a hundred" (cited in Jones, 1953, Vol. 1, p. 3).

Amalie's and Jakob's first child, Sigmund, was born on May 6, 1856, at 117 Schlossergasse, in the small, quiet, Moravian town of Freiberg, about 150 miles northeast of Vienna, Austria. Schlossergasse was renamed Freudova in his honor and is currently Příbor in the Czech Republic.

Although Freud's middle class Jewish parents subsequently bore five daughters and two more sons, Sigmund's mother's intense love for and pride in him left an indelible impression: "A man who has been the indisputable favorite of his mother keeps for life the feeling of a conqueror, that confidence of success that often induces real success" (Freud, cited in Jones, 1953, Vol. 1, p. 5). Freud (1949a) came also to believe that, as a child's primary caretaker, the mother is "the first and strongest love-object ... the prototype of all later love relations" (p. 70). Perhaps the doting he experienced from his mother influenced his later choice of a wife—Martha Bernays. Early on, Martha recognized and deeply appreciated her husband's greatness and she enjoyed his fame. She went beyond the call of duty, even for those days, in assuring that Freud and his work were undisturbed—from keeping their home quiet and orderly to applying toothpaste to his toothbrush! A pupil of Freud's once joked, "If I had had such a wife, I too could have written all those books" (cited in Roazen, 1992, p. 57).

Freud also believed that a child "identifies with" caretaking and authority figures, taking on their characteristics as the child's own, which forms a template for later identifications. Jakob would have played such a role for Sigmund. Despite popular opinion, evidence does not indicate that Jakob was any more stern that the average father but, instead, suggests he was gentle, kind, tolerant, and affectionate, as well as just and "objective." Perhaps Sigmund's identification with him facilitated Freud's later identification with men established in their professions who served to influence and even mentor Freud. There was Ernst Brucke, the physiologist under whom Freud studied in medical school and in whose research laboratory Freud worked immediately after receiving his MD. There was another of Brucke's students, Joseph Breuer, whom Freud credited with the creation of psychoanalysis and with whom Freud published *Studies on Hysteria* in which Breuer's patient, Anna O., became the founding patient of psychoanalysis. There was Jean-Martin Charcot, the celebrated French neurologist whose use of hypnosis contributed to Freud's shift away from purely physiological explanations of psychopathology to more psychological ones involving mental processes, and whose valuing of empirical observation over theory contributed to Freud's lifelong willingness to revise his theories based on new observations. And there was Wilhelm Fliess, an MD ear, nose, and throat specialist and Freud's longtime and intimate friend, with whom Freud engaged for years in "an immensely revealing and scientific correspondence" (Gay, 1989b, p. xxxiii).

Freud's heroes also reveal his identifications. As a boy, Sigmund marked the backs of his toy soldiers with the names of Napoleon's marshals. Napoleon and Hannibal fulfilled Sigmund's martial ideals, and Freud's fondness for military language and imagery pervaded his later system of thought: conflict, struggle, enemies, resistance, and defenses (Roazen, 1992). Also later in life, he enjoyed quoting the saying of Heine: "One must ... forgive one's enemies—but not before they have been hanged" (cited in Roazen, 1992, p. 181). Freud also admired Shakespeare for his understanding of human nature and his power of expression and Nietzsche whom Freud believed had achieved an unmatchable degree of introspection (Roazen, 1992, p. 192).

Freud believed that human personality resulted from the interplay of innate disposition with environmental circumstances. No better example exists than the matter of Freud's intellect. Jones (1953) referred to innate disposition when he said that, unlike characteristics that could be traced to the influence of identification, "[Freud's] intellect was his own" (Vol. 1, p. 4). Nevertheless, Freud's parents influenced its development by valuing intellectual achievement. Twice before the time Freud was five years old, his parents moved the family, finally to Vienna, in part to find better educational opportunities for their children. Both of Sigmund's parents encouraged him to cultivate high ambitions and catered to him, which, he would probably say, provided him with a psychological ideal involving achievement. Year after year, he was first in his class. At age nine, Sigmund entered high school—a year earlier than normal for the time. He graduated summa cum laude at age 17.

One month later, Freud enrolled in the University of Vienna to study law. However, driven by his "greed for knowledge" (Freud, cited in Gay, 1989a, p. x), coupled with his recent reading of Darwin's *The Origin of Species* and hearing a lecture concerning Goethe's essay on nature, Freud's interest in science was sparked, and he shifted his focus to the only other profession available to Jews: medicine (Hergenhahn, 1992). Originally, Freud planned to pursue a career in research, so he might come to understand some of the great riddles that had puzzled him since childhood (Gay, 1988). His studies were so stimulating and vast that he did not graduate with his MD until 1881, after which he worked briefly in Brucke's laboratory.

In April 1882, Freud fell in love with Martha. To make the kind of money he needed to establish what they both considered a respectable bourgeois household, Freud reluctantly left the laboratory to become a physician. He first worked at the Vienna General Hospital, where he became a recognized expert in the diagnosis of brain damage and honed his skills as a neuroanatomist.

In the spring of 1884, Freud began "experimenting" with cocaine. He found that the "magical substance" (Hergenhahn, 1992, p. 458) relieved his depression, helped him work, cured his indigestion, and seemed not to have negative side effects. As a result of his patients' apparent improvements from cocaine, he published six articles in the following two years advocating the drug for its benefits. Gradually, reports of cocaine addiction from around the world proved Freud's advocacy unfounded. He was severely criticized, a development that both harmed his reputation as a physician and, later, contributed to the suspicion and skepticism with which the medical community responded to his radical ideas (Hergenhahn, 1992).

Although Freud was never addicted to cocaine, the same could not be said of nicotine. He smoked, on average, 20 cigars a day for most of his adulthood. Aware of the health risks of smoking, he tried several times to quit but failed. Even when he developed cancer of the jaw and palate and experienced almost continual pain and extreme difficulty with speaking, he would not cease smoking. He himself might attribute this situation to a rational mind insufficiently strong to hold rein over irrational impulses.

Freud once said that, "second only in intensity to his nicotine addiction" was his "addiction … for the prehistoric" (cited in Gay, 1988, p. 170). Over his lifetime, Freud collected in excess of 2000 objects of antiquity (p. 171). His consulting room and study overflowed with sculptures and statuettes. One of Freud's patients remarked that "there was always a feeling of sacred peace and quiet" (p. 170) with an atmosphere more like that of an archeologist's study than a doctor's office. Such a passion on Freud's part invited interpretations, and Freud himself told a patient that "the psychoanalyst, like the archeologist in his excavations, must uncover layer after layer of the patient's psyche, before coming to the deepest most valuable treasures" (p. 171).

In 1886, five months after opening his own practice in Vienna, Sigmund and Martha married. The Freuds had six children together. The youngest, Anna, would become her father's confidante, secretary, disciple, and representative. Eventually, she achieved the stature of a leading figure in her own right in the field of ego psychology, a development within psychoanalysis (Gay, 1988). One of the mysteries of Freud's life was his decision, as part of Anna's training, to psychoanalyze her himself, despite his own writings admonishing analysts not to take on analysands with whom they shared a close bond.

Freud remained in Vienna for most of the remainder of his life. Perhaps the best way to understand that expanse of years is conceptually. Greenberg and Mitchell (1983, pp. 24–25) characterized Freud's development of psychoanalysis in three phases. The first, from the late 1880s to 1905, began when Freud adopted Breuer's cathartic method to treat hysteria, a condition in which physical symptoms, such as numbness or blindness, arise with no identifiable medical cause. Breuer had found that, by hypnotizing the patient, having her trace a symptom back to its original circumstances, usually a trauma, and facilitating catharsis, which is the release of emotion surrounding the traumatic experience, the symptom would usually disappear. Anna O. called the process "the talking cure," and Freud believed during this time that the original trauma inevitably involved sexual abuse: "childhood seduction." During this time he also found that hypnosis was not necessary; that the same outcome resulted from the conscious but unfettered reporting of everything that came to mind: free association. In 1900, Freud published *The Interpretation of Dreams* (1900/1965), and during this phase he achieved appointment as associate professor at the University of Vienna.

The second phase, 1905–1910, began when Freud published *Three Essays on the Theory of Sexuality* (1905/1949b) in which he abandoned the seduction theory and asserted instead that *fantasies* of seduction were the source of neurotic symptoms. Controversy still rages around this development: Did Freud make this fundamental change in his theory more in response to empirical observation or to social pressure? During this five-year period, "he developed and articulated many of the concepts which define the drive/structure model" (Greenberg & Mitchell, 1983, p. 25) that we will describe later in this chapter. In 1906, the Wednesday Psychological Society first met. This group went on to become the Vienna Psychoanalytical Society, eventually including Freud's medical colleague, Alfred Adler.

During the remaining years between 1911 and Freud's death in 1939 at age 83, he developed his ideas about how relationships with others relate to innate biological drives. He made many of his theoretical revisions and expansions "in response to dissents, particularly those of Adler and Jung" (Greenberg & Mitchell, 1983, p. 25). These years also encompassed World War I and the beginning of World War II, which most likely contributed to Freud's application of psychoanalytic principles to societal phenomena. One of his more widely read volumes is the 1929 *Civilization and Its Discontents*. In response to the establishment of the League of Nations, Freud and Albert Einstein corresponded about "the possible prevention of war" (Gay, 1989b, p. xlv) and their correspondence was published in 1933.

Although both of Sigmund's grandfathers were rabbis, his only religious exposure was from the Catholic Mass he attended with his nanny who helped raise him in his early years. By the time he entered medical school, he was an avowed atheist, and he remained so throughout his life. In 1927, he published *The Future of an Illusion*, his "most sustained psychoanalytic assault on religion" (Gay, 1989b, p. xliv). Despite his disaffiliation from the Jewish religion, he could not disaffiliate himself from his Jewish heritage, and he experienced anti-Semitism throughout his life, culminating in 1938 when, shortly after Hitler entered Vienna, the Freuds fled to London. Less than a year later, Freud's cancer returned and was inoperable. Nine months later, Freud's condition had so deteriorated and he was in such agony that his physician complied with Freud's request for euthanasia by morphine overdose. Though Freud did not believe in personal or spiritual immortality, he nevertheless continues to live on through the pervasive influence of psychoanalysis on the field of psychotherapy and on Western culture in general.

Philosophical Underpinnings

Freudian psychology is based on a Newtonian view of the world, including concepts such as the conservation of energy, forces, and deterministic cause and effect. From his mentors, he became opposed to metaphysical explanations for phenomena, those based purely on speculation and abstraction. Instead, he became committed to positivism, focusing only on what could be positively confirmed and reconfirmed by direct observation through the senses, and to the scientific method of developing and revising theories on the basis of observation.

In time, as Freud developed psychoanalysis, he would be criticized for putting forth an understanding of human nature that reduced it to biological forces. What you would do well to realize, however, is that "Freud's mechanistic metaphors and his technical vocabulary ... were the language of his world.... His attempt to establish psychology as a natural science on the solid basis of neurology fits the aspirations of the positivists with whom Freud had studied" (Gay, 1988, p. 79).

PERSONALITY DEVELOPMENT

Nature of Humans

Function of the Psyche

Psychoanalysis begins with the concept of energy. *Roget's II Thesaurus* (1995) defined energy as the "capacity or power for work: animation, force...." Energy is the animating force of the universe and of the human being. Energy is characterized by several principles. It takes a variety of forms such as "mechanical, thermal, electrical, and chemical" (Hall, 1999, p. 36). It can transform from one form into another. It can be displaced from one object to another. It can be free, or it can be bound, that is, trapped—and it can shift between the free and bound conditions.

From a psychoanalytic perspective, even prior to birth, an infant's source of energy is the nourishment it receives through the placenta, and after birth, the source is food nutrients. Throughout life, a human's expenditure of energy is through physical functioning, such as metabolism, growth, sensing, and movement, and psychological functioning, such as perceiving, remembering, imagining, and thinking, while both awake and asleep. Freud referred to the totality of mental life as the *psyche*, and the energy potentiating mental life as *psychic* or *psychological energy*. He assumed that physical and psychological energy is always present in a fixed amount in the closed system of a human and that it continuously transforms back and forth between the physical and psychological forms through some unspecified process.

According to Freud (1949a), "the true purpose of the individual organism's life [is] the satisfaction of its innate [biological] needs" (p. 17). When a need arises, the body releases stored energy that activates the need-related *drive** (Arlow, 2000, p. 28). The

---

* Arlow (2000) made the excellent point that "these impulses have been loosely and inaccurately referred to as *instincts*. The correct term in psychoanalytic theory, translated from the German *Treib*, is *drive*" (p. 28). However, he went on to say that because of widespread use of the term *instinct*, he would use the two terms interchangeably. For three reasons, we will use the term *drive*. One is that it is the accurate translation. A second involves modern psychology's distinction between instincts and drives. Instincts are innate, unlearned, complex behaviors that are stimulated by a sign stimulus, are carried out stereotypically by every member of a given species, and are impervious to modification. An example is the specific migration pattern of the peregrine falcon in response to seasonal changes. Biological drives also are innate and unlearned, but, unlike instincts, they are inferred, not directly observable, states shared by numerous species and carried out uniquely by each species and even within each species. An example is the hunger drive, which a fish might satisfy by eating fish food or its own offspring, a Kalahari bushman by eating live grubs or native roots, and an American by eating a hamburger, salad, or any of a myriad of possibilities. When Freud referred to hunger, sex, elimination, and so on, he was referring to them as drives, in the way we have just defined them.

drive is experienced as a disturbing, unpleasant *tension*. More specifically, a drive has a *source*: the need; an *aim*: the discharge of tension through imagination or action, which results in regaining a relaxed state of quiescence; an *object*: some image of a thing, person, and/or activity that will achieve the aim; and an *impetus*: an urge to achieve the aim (Hall, 1999, p. 37). For example, in the hunger drive, the source is the need for nutrition; the aim is the discharge of hunger–tension through imagination or action that results in quiescence; the object could be, for example, the mental image of food or the actual eating of food; and the impetus is the urge to produce the object—the image or action. (How anorexia and obesity develop is the more advanced stuff of psychoanalysis that we will address below.)

Though Freud (1949a, p. 17) hypothesized a myriad of drives, he concluded that they all could be reduced to two fundamental ones: a *life drive* and a *death drive*. Freud called the energy of the life drive *libido*. He believed that, during childhood and adolescence, libido invests itself in a particular sequence of areas of the body, called *erogenous zones*. This process gives rise to particularly intense needs at particular times of development, which, in turn, makes an important contribution to personality development. Libido could be *mobile*, moving from investment in one object to another as needs dictated, or could become *fixated*, that is, bound to a particular object of desire. Although Freud saw evidence of the death drive in aggression, destructiveness, and the ultimate fate of every person, he did not name an energy of the death drive or specify developmental stages for it (Arlow, 2000, p. 28).

To the drive-related process, an individual brings the two types of functioning that characterize all of human mental life. *Primary process* is the nonlogical thinking that comprises the mental functioning of a newborn and dominates the functioning of a young infant. Freud believed that infants are born with some fundamental images inherited from frequently repeated experiences of their ancestors, such as the image of food in response to hunger, and that they also can learn rudimentary associations based on their own experiences, such as generating the image of the mother's breast or a bottle in response to hunger. In primary process, images are fleeting and are not distinguished from reality; thus, the images themselves can momentarily satisfy the need. Through *predicate thinking*, a kind of association process, two similar objects are experienced the same, despite their differences (Hall, 1999, p. 40). Thus, energy can be *displaced* from one object to another: If a breast or bottle is unavailable, an infant might suck a thumb; later in life, if a repair person does not show up for a third time, the frustrated customer might lose his temper with his child.

In the case of any drive, the underlying and most basic motive is that of the *pleasure principle*: to minimize the pain of tension related to an unmet need and maximize the pleasure of relaxed quiescence when a need is satisfied. As already indicated, primary process continues throughout life. Additional examples are the person who experiences momentary relief from stress by imagining oneself on a tropical beach, or someone sleeping who, needing to urinate, repeatedly dreams of doing so and feels momentary relief each time. Indeed, primary process can be most readily observed during the psychical function of *dreams*, a topic to which we will return.

Obviously, primary process has its advantages and its limitations. Thus, from the moment of birth, as one continually interacts with the "real" outside world, one develops one's ability for *secondary process*: to distinguish between inner experience and outer reality and to use thinking and problem solving to plan and enact a way to produce desired objects *in reality* (Hall, 1999). Secondary process also involves a phenomenon crucial to personality development, *identification*: the ability to incorporate "the qualities of an external object, usually those of another person, into one's personality" (Hall, 1999, p. 74).

So far, we have mainly used a simple example of the hunger drive that illustrates both the essential force of *cathexis*, the investment of psychological energy—desire—and physical energy—acquisition—in objects of gratification, and the smooth process of drive gratification. However, due to a variety of additional factors, psychological dynamics are rarely so smooth. For example, among the numerous drives, two or more can, and often do, conflict—as with the exhausted, famished person who is torn between sleep and food. In addition, conditions in the outside world, such as the unavailability of a cathected (desired and/or acquirable) object, often result in what is termed *external frustration* (Hall, 1999). Innate in the infant's psyche is the potential, beginning a few months after birth, to develop *anticathexis*, the withdrawal of energy from an object of gratification. Anticathexis results in *internal frustration*. We will explain below why a person develops anticathexis, but for now, it is most important to realize that primary process involves only cathexis, whereas secondary process involves both cathexis and anticathexis. Thus, for a variety of reasons, the dynamic interaction of forces at work in the psyche, or *psychodynamics*, range from relative harmony to profound conflict. Profound conflict from within oneself can be as threatening as actual danger from outside oneself, resulting in the unpleasant emotion of *anxiety*. As you will see, anxiety is an important factor in psychopathology.

Anxiety is always perceived consciously, meaning that it is in a person's awareness (Hall, 1999). However, the cause of anxiety is not always conscious. *Unconscious* function involves psychological material that was never in one's awareness—or that *was* in awareness but, because of its painfulness, was relegated to unawareness—a process called *repression*.

Unconsciousness, repression, and other dynamics come into play with the innate function of sleep. Regarding the origin of sleep, Freud (1949a) explained that "there arises at birth an instinct to return to the intra-uterine life that has been abandoned—an instinct to sleep. Sleep is a return ... to the womb" (pp. 39–40). Freud believed that the innate function of dreaming enabled a person to remain for a prolonged period of time in the state of sleep. Since a complete understanding of the functions of sleep and dreams relies on an understanding of certain psychological structures, we will return to this topic in the next section.

Finally, it is an axiom in psychoanalysis that the function of the psyche is lawful and explainable. Through the principle of *determinism*, Freud asserted that every manifestation of a person's psyche is determined, that is, caused by conditions and events from both the recent and distant past. The source of any aspect of a person's current mental life can be traced back to its roots: the interaction of one's *innate disposition*, or inborn resiliency or susceptibility to the effects of experience, with one's experiences, particularly the *experiences of infancy and/or early childhood*—hence the psychoanalytic term *infantile determinism*.

Structure of the Psyche

Over the years that Freud developed psychoanalysis, he formulated two models pertaining to psychical structure: the topographical and the structural models. In the following discussion, we explain both models and how they relate to each other.

The Topographical Model According to the *American Heritage Dictionary* (2000), one definition of topography is a "graphic representation of the surface features of a place or region on a map, indicating their relative positions and elevations." In the psyche, the "elevation" is the availability of mental contents (sensations, perceptions, thoughts, memories) to awareness.

At the surface level is the *conscious* domain of the psyche, containing material not only available to, but actually in, awareness. "We can be conscious of only one thing at a time" (Hall, 1999, p. 57). Thus, although consciousness itself—the process of being aware—is usually continuous, the contents of consciousness are quite fleeting. You can experience this fact by setting a timer for three minutes and tracking the contents of your consciousness by noting repeatedly to yourself, "Now I am aware...."

Where do the contents of consciousness come from and where do they go? The unconscious? Yes, although Freud distinguished between two domains of unconsciousness that actually represent a continuum of availability to consciousness. He called the domain of mental material that is easily accessible to awareness the *preconscious*. You can experience your preconscious right now: by turning your attention to your right foot. Just a moment ago, the sensation of your right foot was *available* to consciousness but was not *in* it, until you turned your attention to it. And once you resumed reading, that is, turned your attention back to this text and made it the object of your attention, awareness of the sensation of your right foot probably returned to your preconscious mind. Here's another experience of your preconscious: Think about your last meal. Again that memory was probably easily available to consciousness, awaiting, so to speak, your bringing it "up" from the domain "just below" awareness. The vastness of the repository of the preconscious was brought home to one of us (JMH) recently when I attended a reunion: Lyrics to songs I had not sung in 40 years popped back into my conscious mind—in some cases, entire songs consisting of several verses. Material can lie latent in the preconscious mind for a lifetime. You've experienced the deepest level of the preconscious when you've had something on the tip of your tongue. And if you think *that is* maddening, wait until you find out about the potential of the unconscious itself to madden!

An understanding of the unconscious can be clarified by understanding the two criteria for mental material to reside in the preconscious. First, the mind must be able to represent the material in language, that is, it must be describable in words (Hall, 1999). Thus, every infant's and young child's experience that developed prior to the child's having language to describe the experience exists in the unconscious. These memories are not forgotten; they exert their influence on the older person, but outside the person's awareness.

The second criterion involves the pleasure principle: The mental material must not be too painful. Experiences that are overwhelmingly painful are repressed—relegated to the unconscious mind where they do not represent an immediate, conscious threat—but, again, where their influence continues to be exerted on the psyche. Repression is like preventing a helium balloon from rising by holding one's hand over it: The task is a continuous one of opposing forces. And unlike real life, where the helium in a balloon disperses over the course of a few days, the energy of a repressed memory does not disperse but remains intact and bound—a force within the psyche that requires continuous opposition.

Freud believed that, as vast as the preconscious is, the *unconscious* (phenomena such as nonverbal images, emotions, and desires, as well as preverbal memories) is exceedingly more vast. This belief implies that, inherently and unavoidably, humans for the most part do not know who they really are.

The topographical model is depicted in Figure 2.1. Notice the relative sizes of the domains. Notice also the border between topographical structures. The conscious–preconscious border is relatively open, indicating the great ease with which psychic material (verbal thoughts of phenomena like desires, images, memories, and plans) can move

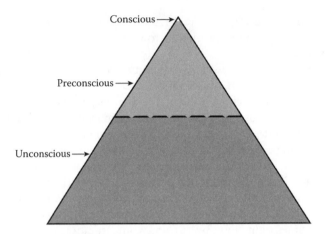

FIGURE 2.1   The topography of the psyche.

between the conscious and preconscious. By contrast, the preconscious–unconscious border is much more dense and of a unique structure, indicating the ability of deeply preconscious material to sometimes "funnel" into the unconscious but the difficulty with which unconscious material moves into preconsciousness.

The Structural Model   The psychical structure that Freud theorized somewhat later in his career, and the one that became the foundation of personality theory in psychoanalysis, brings together all the functions and structures described so far in this section on Personality Development. It is a three-part model of a phenomenon that does not correspond directly to the brain yet does, Freud (1949a) believed, have "the characteristics of being extended in space" (p. 13).

The foundation of the personality is the *id*. *Id* is Latin for "it," implying a primitiveness so extreme as to be unnamable. The id *is* the entire personality of the infant at birth. It is biological in orientation, being made up of the drives, as well as drive-related phenomena such as inherited, rudimentary object images. The id's contact with the real world is extremely limited, consisting only of the sensing of external stimuli and the acquisition of rudimentary object images through its cortex, or outermost "surface." The id is capable of only two means of discharging drive-based tension: imagining objects, that is, need/ drive-satisfying things, people, and actions; and reflex action, such as sucking, swallowing, urinating, defecating, squinting at bright light, pulling away from extreme pain, and numerous other simple, innate behaviors.

Operating entirely by primary process, the id has several characteristics. It knows only cathexis, the force of urging desire, and nothing of anticathexis, the force of inhibition. It is atemporal, living entirely in the "now," having no sense of past or future. It is irrational: In it, opposing drives exist side by side with no means to be reconciled; thus, a person can, at once, feel an urgent desire for two opposite and mutually exclusive things. Another aspect of id's irrationality is its predicate thinking, treating similar objects as if they were identical.

Without a sense of time or the ability to reason, and with numerous urgent, often conflicting desires and only minimal contact with reality, the id has no awareness of itself as a separate entity, yet it is totally self-centered—often referred to in psychoanalysis as *narcissistic*. It is insistent in its demands while, simultaneously, having no ability to execute voluntary action and thus no way to produce needed objects in reality (an apt description of a young infant). Also as a result of its limitations, it is amoral, with no sense of right or wrong. Since the infant as yet has no language, the id is totally unconscious—as evidenced by the universal phenomenon of infantile amnesia: Who can remember the first two (or more) years of life? Yet this id is the source of all energy of the personality. It is the beginning of the story of personality development, but clearly, considering the range and complexity of adult personality, it is not the end.

Innate in the id lies the potential for the development of another, qualitatively different part of the personality: the *ego*. *Ego* is Latin for "I." Beginning at birth and continuing throughout childhood, as the id, at its cortex (outermost surface), is in contact with outer reality, some of its energy is "given over" to the formation of the ego. As a result of experience in the "real" outer world, the infant gradually comes to differentiate its inner experience from outer reality. Inner experience comes to comprise one's sense of a separate self. This sense of self begins to emerge as the child acquires language comprehension, even prior to when the child is actually able to speak. Thus the sense of self is capable of being preconscious and thus conscious. In fact, the ego contains all three topographical dimensions.

As the sense of self consolidates, so does the motive to preserve the self, a motive of which the atemporal, irrational id is incapable. Also, as the self consolidates, so do a variety of psychological abilities. The child discovers increasingly that "If I do *this, that* will happen." Thus, the ego is able to employ secondary process to reason, plan, and execute voluntary action. The ego is the mentally oriented part of the personality that operates by the reality principle: Do whatever actually produces objects of gratification with a maximum of pleasure and minimum of pain. The ego learns through processes such as trial-and-error and identification.

Originally, the ego arises to serve the id. However, with development the ego realizes that, at times, to truly maximize pleasure and minimize pain, gratification must be delayed, displaced, sometimes even denied. To accomplish these feats, the ego creates anticathexes, the inhibitory forces that oppose urging desires. Through this opposition and the ego's other qualitatively different ways of functioning, it becomes increasingly—but never completely—differentiated from the id. As it does, it progresses in its ability to act in opposition to the id. It might be said that the ego begins as slave to the id but usually becomes, to one degree or another, but never completely, master of it.

Within the ego lies the potential for the third and final personality dimension: the *superego*. *Superego* is Latin for "above-I," suggesting images of both a judge in an elevated position above the courtroom and an ideal perched high on a pedestal. Superego develops because the pleasure principle is not served entirely by the id and ego alone. An ego strategy for drive satisfaction can be perfectly gratifying and perfectly reasonable, but not perfectly acceptable, such as one of our (JMH's) favorite examples: eating strawberry shortcake for breakfast. How different is the strawberry shortcake from a Belgian waffle covered with strawberry and whipped cream? Yet eating strawberry shortcake for breakfast *just is not done*. Yet other ego strategies that are gratifying and reasonable, such as stealing something I want that belongs to someone else, carry potentially painful social consequences. To avoid the pain of punishment, a child begins to learn very early in life to restrict behavior within certain acceptable limits—limits that do not necessarily make sense to the reasoning, pragmatic ego.

Whereas the ego cathects objects that are most practical and expedient and anticathects those that are not—as in the process of continuing to desire something–someone attainable and "letting go" of desire for something/someone realistically unattainable;

the superego, being socially oriented, cathects objects that are socially and morally appropriate and anticathects those that are not—as in the process of continuing to desire something/someone socially/morally acceptable and "letting go" of desire for something/someone socially/morally unacceptable. The superego develops based on the punishments and rewards from anyone who has authority over the child: first, one's primary caretakers, usually the parents, then other authority figures such as teachers. The child identifies with these people, internalizing their principles of right and wrong and the ideals they represent, to form the superego. Eventually, the child also identifies with other powerful and idealized figures, like movie stars and politicians.

The superego has two aspects. One is the *conscience*, acquired through experiences of punishment, comprising what is "wrong" to do, and capable of self-punishment through guilt. The other is the *ego-ideal*, acquired through experiences of reward, comprising what is "right" to do, and capable of self-reward through pride. Since the processes of punishment, reward, and identification typically begin prior to language comprehension and continue well into childhood, the superego, like the ego, contains all three dimensions of mental topography: unconscious, preconscious, and conscious.

Just as, in the service of the pleasure principle, the ego arises out of the id, becomes differentiated from it, and develops the capacity to act in opposition to it, the superego follows a similar developmental course with respect to the ego. It operates on what might be called the "perfection principle," cathecting only objects that conform to its sense of acceptability and its high ideals and anticathecting those that do not. Though the superego may seem totally opposed to the id, their objects often coincide: Consider the high school student who gets a date with the most attractive, intelligent, popular person in class.

Yet even when their objects conflict, id and superego share at least one important characteristic: both are irrational. It is just as unreasonable to expect always and immediately to get exactly what is wanted, as it is to expect always to get and do what is perfect. In addition, Freud (1949a) noted that "the super-ego often displays a severity for which no model has been provided by the real parents, and moreover … it calls the ego to account not only for its deeds but equally for its thoughts and unexecuted intentions" (p. 95). You may begin to realize the difficult spot in which the ego often finds itself: trying to satisfy, and survive in the face of, the often powerful conflicting demands of the id, the superego, and the outside world.

An illustration of Freud's structural model appears in Figure 2.2, and the relationship between Freud's topographical and structural models is shown in Figure 2.3. With an understanding of these structures, you are now prepared to understand Freud's views on sleep and dreams.

Dreams   Sleep, you may recall, results from the drive to regress—to go back in developmental history—to the pleasurable state of prebirth existence in the womb. To whatever extent the ego and superego have developed, when sleep is desired, they relax, nearly ceasing functioning to allow the regression, which gives the id more play in the psyche. Both the more powerful of the unconscious wishes in the id and the unconscious roots of unsatisfied conscious wishes from the ego energize drives. That increased energy threatens to arouse the person from sleep. To safeguard sleep, the relaxed-but-not-completely-inactive ego fantasizes a fulfillment of the wish. Then it makes the whole process even less anxiety producing by distorting and transforming the entire "story" into symbols that disguise the original cause of the dream. Thus, an unattainable and/or unacceptable, id-related wish is transformed into a sense of attainment through a scenario that is mysterious but not objectionable.

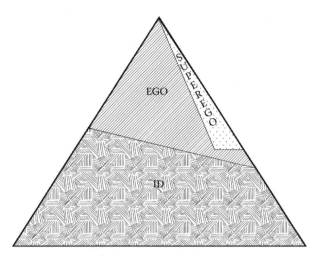

FIGURE 2.2   The structure of the psyche.

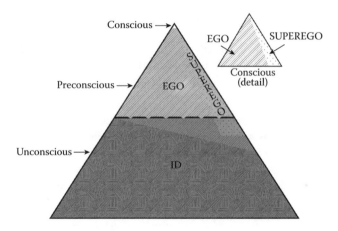

FIGURE 2.3   The relationship between the topography and structure of the psyche.

This process makes sense in the case of the sleeper with a full bladder who dreams of urinating, the sleeper who dreams in the morning that she has awakened and gotten ready for school, or the sleeper who dreams of having sex with an anonymous partner. But what of nightmares? How can they reflect wish fulfillment? Freud explained that nightmares are the ego's *failure* to produce an adequate fantasy. In other words, a sleeper awakens from a nightmare of being chased by a bear, not because the bear is chasing him but because his ego was unable to generate a fantasized escape. The *wish* to escape from pain, to "master" situations involving the threat of severe pain, was still the cause of the dream.

Few chase dreams involve chasers (bears, criminals, aliens) that the dreamer has actually experienced. They clearly represent something or someone else that has made the person feel chased or threatened. Yet, upon awakening, it is the symbols that one remembers, not what they represent. These symbols (what one remembers of a dream) Freud called the dream's *manifest content*. What they represent (the hidden meaning of the dream) the original wishes that the symbols are disguising, he called the *latent content*.

Freud (1949a) found in dreams the single best source of his understanding of the workings of the unconscious mind and its primary process.

- Dreams "may be confused, unintelligible, or positively nonsensical ... may contradict all that [our egos] know of reality ... [yet] so long as we are dreaming," dreams feel absolutely real; indeed, they *are* our reality (pp. 38–39).
- Dreams bring up long-forgotten memories and can even bring up memories we had not remembered—had repressed—but, upon awakening, recognize to be accurate.
- They sometimes include words that do not make sense to the dreamer (at least initially) or are not even "real" words.
- Dreams can include "material which cannot have originated either from the dreamer's adult life or from his forgotten childhood" and, thus, appear sometimes to arise from "the archaic heritage which a child brings with him into the world, before any experience of his own, influenced by the experiences of his ancestors ..." (p. 40).
- Dreams employ a process of condensation,

    an inclination to form fresh unities out of elements which in our waking thought we should certainly have kept separate. As a consequence ... a single element of the manifest dream often stands for a whole number of latent dream-thoughts ... a combined allusion to all of them ... and [can even] have the meaning of its opposite. (pp. 42–43)

- Dreams employ a process of displacement, in which psychical energy is moved from one dream element to another. The result is that a highly charged latent element may appear as an unimportant manifest element, and a highly charged manifest element may actually represent an unimportant latent element.

The undoing of dream formation—the decoding of symbolic manifest content to reveal its hidden, wish-fulfillment meaning—is called *dream-work*. Below, we will describe how an analyst enacts this process.

Defense Mechanisms   The ego faces multiple pressures, often contradictory and unrelenting: id frustration, superego guilt, and the demands of reality. To survive these pressures, the ego employs defensive mechanisms. These defense mechanisms constitute the final topic of this section.

All *defense mechanisms* share two characteristics. First, they in some way *distort or deny inner or outer reality*—the actual demands of the id, the superego, and/or the real world. Second, they *operate unconsciously*: The ego can only "fool itself" into the experience that the pressures are less than they really are as long as it remains unaware of the true nature of those pressures. Nevertheless, you might recognize occasional *conscious* use of some of these mechanisms.

We have already described *repression*, in which the ego avoids pain by relegating extremely painful mental material to unconsciousness, such as the person who genuinely forgets a dental appointment to have a root canal. In *fantasy*, one avoids frustration by conjuring up in imagination what is unavailable in reality, as with the person who fantasizes a romantic liaison with a favorite movie star. Involving secondary process, fantasy is more complex than, but draws upon, the id's primary process of mere momentary object imagining. In *rationalization*, one avoids guilt by generating a reasonable explanation for something that actually arose from an unacceptable motive, such as the parent who abuses a child "for the child's own good." In *identification*, one avoids frustration or guilt by taking on the characteristics of another person, as in the case of a victim of abuse who may take on the abuser's view that the victim deserves the abuse or, conversely, escapes the victim role by taking on the abuser's abusive behavior. In *projection*, one attributes the source of inner anxiety to the outside world, as with the miserly person who perceives everyone *else* as trying to cheat *her*. In *reaction formation*, one escapes guilt by strongly enacting behavior opposite of an unacceptable urge, such as the performer with a selfish desire for public attention and recognition who develops a performance phobia.

Two defense mechanisms relate specifically to development. In *fixation*, one avoids the frustration and/or guilt of inadequacy by not progressing to the next developmental level of functioning, as in the case of the student who feels unprepared to commence life after high school and, despite his seemingly best efforts, fails a course in the last semester, disqualifying himself from graduation. In *regression*, one reverts to an earlier mode of functioning to escape current pressures, such as the jilted lover who withdraws into her room for days to cry.

Three additional defense mechanisms involve the concept of substitution. In *displacement*, one avoids frustration by substituting a less desirable but available object for the desired but unavailable one, as in the popular song, "If you can't be with the one you love, love the one you're with" (Stills, 1970). In *compensation*, someone incapable of a desired activity avoids feelings of inadequacy by substituting a lesser activity, such as the person who didn't make the team becoming the team's equipment manager. *Sublimation* involves a socially lauded substitution, such as the channeling of socially unacceptable sexual and aggressive wishes and impulses into "intellectual, humanitarian, cultural, and artistic pursuits" (Hall, 1999, p. 82). For Freud, such pursuits are always an expression of sublimation: the redirection of more base desires into more elevated outlets. A specific example that comes immediately to mind is the writing of a theory textbook that, Freud would say, is energized by the unconscious diversion of the authors' sexual and/or aggressive inclinations. Freud attributed the intellectual and technological advancements of culture to sublimation.

Defense mechanisms always leave a residual of anxiety. As already stated, repression involves a continuous anxiety analogous to persistently holding down a helium balloon. Mental manipulations, such as rationalization and reaction formation, hide original motives but do not alleviate them. Developmentally related defenses leave the person unprepared to deal with reality, prone to further frustration, guilt, and/ or actual pain. Substitutive defenses allow for the partial, but never complete, gratification of a desire; the pressure of residual desire persists in the personality. We will return to the topic of defense mechanisms in the section on healthy and unhealthy personalities.

Summary The human psyche consists of material at various levels of availability to awareness. Conscious material is what is momentarily in awareness. Preconscious material is available to consciousness. Unconscious material is relatively, and usually deeply, unavailable to consciousness. At birth, the psyche consists of the completely unconscious, irrationally self-centered, demanding id. With practical experience, some id energy is given over to the development of the functionally different, rational ego, which retains some unconscious aspects but also involves preconsciousness and consciousness. With moral instruction, some ego energy is given over to the development of the yet again functionally different, irrationally perfectionistic and idealistic superego that also contains unconscious, preconscious, and conscious aspects. As the ego becomes differentiated from the id, it can act in opposition to it; similarly as the superego becomes differentiated from the ego it can act in opposition to the ego. The entire dynamics of personality arise from the ego seeking to meet and manage the urgent, sometimes conflicting demands of the id, the often oppositional and equally irrational pressures of the superego, and the necessities of the outside, real world. In the process of coping, the ego employs a variety of mechanisms to defend against frustration and guilt.

Role of the Environment

"The child," Freud (1949a) said, "is psychologically father to the adult ... [T]he events of his first years are of paramount importance for his whole later life" (p. 68). Though Freud's writings predominantly addressed the internal dynamics of the personality, he attributed to the environment, especially the social environment, a powerful role in personality development. Human children are, at first, totally dependent on their caretakers and they continue to be dependent for years.

The fledgling ego is extremely vulnerable to damaging assaults from the environment to which the ego can respond only with defensive strategies. Psychological assaults come in three forms. In *privation*, a desired object is simply unavailable in the environment. In *deprivation*, it is available but withheld or withdrawn by other(s). In *trauma*, internal drive demands from the id and/or external drive excitations from the environment produce more energy than the ego can manage. For example, in sexual abuse of a child, the child is likely to feel entrapment, physical pain, sexual arousal, death anxiety, and/or guilt in amounts too great for the fledgling ego to manage. Environmental assaults, whether small or large, are ubiquitous. They represent psychological obstacles, and "the ways in which a person meets and attempts to overcome or adjust to these obstacles shape [one's] personality" (Hall, 1999, p. 75).

Hall (1999) asserted that "the ability to displace energy from one object to another is the most powerful [instrument] for the development of personality.... The same energy source can perform many different kinds of work" (p. 84). Other people, especially authority figures, powerfully influence the objects of substitution in displacement, compensation, and sublimation "by sanctioning certain object-choices and prohibiting others" (p. 80). For example, presumably Freud would have said of himself that he chose cigars, rather than his thumb or lollipops, as a means of *oral gratification* because cigars were an object that external authorities considered age-appropriate and socially appropriate. Note that values change in this regard, as evidenced by the current general disfavor in which cigars and cigarettes are held by society at large due to their now widely known, serious health risks.

Similarly, Freud might have considered his prolific writing to be an object—in this case, an activity—that compensated for feelings of inadequacy in other areas of his psyche and/or that sublimated frustrated sexual energy. The fact that he wrote prolifically rather than won recognition for productivity on a factory line or for skill at jai alai could be attributed to his having been urged by significant others to "cultivate high ambitions" and to being unable to pursue jai alai due to its absence from his culture. Again, the influence on particular personality manifestations by outer circumstances is extensive and carries profound effects.

Regarding *familial* influence, the influence of primary caretakers (usually parents and especially the mother) on a child's personality is paramount. In Freud's (1949a) words,

> A child's first erotic object is the mother's breast … later completed into the [entire] person of the child's mother. [She also becomes important to the child] by her care of the child's body…. In these two relations [feeding and body care] lies the root of a mother's importance, unique, without parallel, established unalterably for a whole lifetime as the first and strongest love-object and as the prototype of all later love relations—for both sexes. (p. 70)

The child's ego and superego are formed through training and education by, and identification with, significant others: the mother, then the father, then other family members. In summary, family members constitute significant others who are the source of environmental gratification or deprivation and with whom the child identifies.

Regarding *extrafamilial* influence, around the time a child reaches school age, other people exert influence on the child's developing personality. The child is disciplined by, and identifies with, personally acquainted authority figures such as teachers and religious leaders. Not long afterward, the child extends identification to impersonally known public figures.

Interaction of Human Nature and Environment

If a person could freely fulfill all drives, one would be anxiety-free, though perpetually primitive. However, for at least three reasons, this hypothetical situation will never happen. One is internal: The id often presses for opposite and mutually exclusive aims, which means that, at times, at least one drive must go unsatisfied. Another is environmental: Everyone experiences in the external nonsocial and social worlds the privations, deprivations, and traumas that make drive satisfaction impossible in the short-term and/or the long-term; "stuff happens," as the saying goes (natural and socioeconomic disasters) and in the social arena, people are inevitably both unintentionally and intentionally cruel. A third condition is also environmental: the universality with which authority figures exert their influence through moral training intended to curtail or redirect drive gratification.

Although Freud acknowledged all of these sources of frustration, he believed that the most influential sources of personality development—and, particularly, personality psychopathology—are conflicts that arise when one experiences urgent drives along with authority figures who use moral training to control those drives. The two drives he believed authorities particularly target in this way are the aggressive drive, one of the death drives, and the sexual drive, one of the life drives. Furthermore, the aggressive drive could rather readily find outlet in a variety of displacements, such as watching or playing competitive games and sports. The sexual drive, however, being more suppressed in Western society and undergoing certain universal and inevitable family dynamics, as shall be discussed below, represents the single most conflictual experience for a young child that, consequently, exerted the most influence over personality.

In reading the term *sexual drive*, you may have immediately thought of the drive that culminates in sexual intercourse. Although this was, in part, Freud's meaning as well, he also meant something broader: the drive whereby pleasure is derived from the manipulation of, and the discharge of tension from, any bodily zone, apart from any value to the survival of the individual or the species. The zones to which he particularly referred included the genitals, which provide pleasure not only in the act of reproduction, which is usually, but not always, beneficial to a species, but also in a myriad of nonreproductive activities. The zones also included the mouth and anus. For example, sucking and biting appear to be pleasurable in their own right, apart from the intake of nutrition, as evidenced by smoking, chewing gum, and overeating. The expulsion of feces—defecation—is pleasurable even when it exacerbates dehydration; and the retention of feces, which arguably has no survival value whatsoever, can be pleasurable. For Freud, the term *sexual* referred to any of these three bodily areas made especially sensitive to excitation by the concentration there of libido or life energy. These, then, are the erogenous zones.

Psychosexual Development

The interaction between the sexual drive and related environmental factors plays out in the process of *psychosexual development*. Though psychosexual development tends to occur in a series of five stages, the stages sometimes overlap or even proceed concurrently.

Freud believed that at birth, and usually for approximately the first year of life, libido is invested primarily in the mouth. In the *oral stage*, pleasure is derived first from sucking and then, with the emergence of teeth, from biting. The caretaking activity critical to oral gratification is feeding. How the mother (or other primary caretaker) manages feeding can have a lasting effect on the infant's, and later that infant's adult, personality. More specifically, sucking is associated with the infant's most basic experience of dependency on the mother. If the mother employs a feeding pattern that somehow does not satisfy the child, the child is likely to develop oral dependency, which can manifest not only as straightforward general dependency but also in a variety of transformations: reaction formation into defiant independence, or projection into seeing not oneself but others in need and providing assistance through becoming a counselor. Oral dependency can take two forms: a preoccupation with taking in, as with the person who becomes obese through overeating or who would rather observe than participate in social situations, or with holding in/holding on, as with the person whose hobby is collecting bottles. (I, JMH, just had an interesting experience: While trying to type the word "hobby," I at first kept typing and deleting "bo," "bo," as if through some unconscious pressure to type the word "bobby" or "booby." In the example, bottles represent the mother's breast. Thus, Freud would undoubtedly interpret this variation on a slip of the tongue as some repressed oral dependency in me.)

"Oral aggressiveness by biting is the prototype for many kinds of direct, displaced, and disguised aggressions" (Hall, 1999, p. 106). A child's desire to discharge tension by biting is almost universally met with a caretaker's admonition "Do not bite!" Later in life, one might displace the urge by making a "biting remark," or might try to control such an urge by "biting one's tongue." One might aggressively undertake an activity by really "biting into it." Oral aggression has its sublimation in careers such as the law or politics that draw heavily on argument and debate.

Other gratifying oral activities include spitting out and closing up against what is distasteful. "The spitting-out type of personality is characterized by disdainfulness and contempt, the closing up type by a shut-in, guarded quality" (Hall, 1999, p. 106). Anorexia, or self-starvation to control body weight, is understood orally as a "closing up" oral fixation. Conversely, if a child is punished for these oral activities, he might employ reaction formation, becoming gullible, prone to "swallow anything."

Around the first year of life, and lasting less than two years, is the *anal stage*. To the extent that libido has been satisfied in the oral stage, it moves to the anus. Tension develops as fecal matter collects in the rectum, and pleasure is experienced as the tension is released with the expulsion of the feces. "Expulsive elimination is the prototype for emotional outbursts, temper tantrums, rages, and other primitive discharge reactions" (Hall, 1999, p. 107). The crucial caretaking activity is toilet training, which usually represents the first time the child is required by external authority to bring a reflex under voluntary control. "A person naturally resists having a pleasurable activity interfered with and regulated" (Hall, 1999, p. 108). Therefore, if the mother (or other caretaker) is rigid and harsh in her demands, the child may fixate and become rebellious or, conversely, compulsive about cleanliness and orderliness. If she pleads with the child and praises her successes at bowel control, the child may become productive, even philanthropic. If she overemphasizes the importance of bowel control, the child may fixate, developing personality traits such as thriftiness. These traits are manifestations of the anal-expulsive theme.

As previously stated, retention of feces also is pleasurable. A fixation on retention can result in personality traits such as possessiveness and compulsive collecting. A reaction formation to the retentive urge can result in compulsive expulsion, such as overgenerosity and compulsive spending and gambling.

Beginning before age three and lasting until age five is the *phallic stage* in which libido, for the first time, becomes invested most intensely in the genitals. The crucial caretaking activity is the mother's (or other caretaker's) reaction to the child's genital preoccupation. Though phallus means penis, this stage is experienced by both boys and girls. But because boys' and girls' genitals differ, their courses through this stage also differ.

As a boy's genital urges increase, he learns to manipulate his genitals for the pleasurable sensation. Simultaneously, through accompanying fantasies, his mother (already his firmly established love object) naturally becomes his primary sexual object. In Freud's (1949a) own words, "he becomes his mother's lover. He wishes to possess her physically in such ways as he has divined from his observations and intuitions about sexual life" (p. 71). He begins to see his father as a rival who stands in the way of his exclusive relationship with his mother; his rivalrous feelings reach murderous proportions. Freud called this state of affairs the *Oedipus complex* after the Greek legend of Oedipus who unknowingly killed his father and married his mother.

"Under the conditions of our civilization," Freud (1949a) wrote, the Oedipus complex "is invariably doomed to a frightening end. The boy's mother has understood quite well that his sexual excitation relates to herself. Sooner or later she reflects that it is not right to allow it to continue" (p. 71). She first forbids him to touch his genitals; failing that, she threatens the boy with castration by his father. At this point the boy, either remembering or seeing female genitals that lack a penis, develops *castration anxiety*. To reduce this anxiety, he may renounce (repress) his attraction to his mother and identify with the aggressor, his father.

As with the other psychosexual stages, a variety of psychodynamics result in a variety of possible outcomes. The boy may remain to some degree fixated on his mother, resulting in a kind of excessive dependence and "bondage to women" (Freud, 1949a, p. 73). He also may retain resentment of his father, resulting in a compulsively competitive attitude toward other men throughout life. Or, out of fear of the consequences of sexual attraction to his mother and, through predicate thinking, other women, as well as fear of the consequences of hostility toward his father, he may completely repress women as a sexual object and, instead, feel sexually attracted to men. This latter dynamic was Freud's explanation of homosexuality. He believed everyone is born bisexual and that most people, through the Oedipal resolution of maternal renunciation and paternal identification, develop a "normal [hetero]sexual aim" (p. 26). He saw homosexuality as a fixation, a "developmental inhibition" (p. 26) involving the inversion (Arlow, 2000, p. 31) of that aim.

A girl's course through the phallic stage is different. Acutely aware that she is lacking a penis, she feels inferior, blames her mother for the lack, "[wishes] to have [her father's] penis at her disposal" (Freud, 1949a, p. 77), feels rivalrous toward her mother as a block to the fulfillment of that wish, and displaces her wish for a penis into "another wish—to have a baby from [her father] as a gift" (p. 77). Though she represses this wish, it need not be transformed through any other defense: Through predicate thinking, "she will … choose her husband for his paternal characteristics and be ready to recognize his authority" (p. 77), and through compensation for her basic sense of inferiority, she will want to bear children.

Freud (1949a) concluded that "the whole occurrence [of the phallic stage] … may probably be regarded as the central experience of the years of childhood, the greatest problem of early life and the strongest source of later inadequacy" (p. 74). In both sexes, memories of the phallic stage are powerfully repressed such that all sexual urges become unconscious—and libido withdraws from investment in any bodily area—until puberty. Thus, between the ages of five or six and about 11, the child is in the *latent* stage, during which the child focuses on education and socialization outside the home. Thus, Freud saw sexual development in humans not as one continuous, monophasic process, but as *diphasic*, consisting of the pregenital phases and the later genital phase, interrupted by the latent phase.

Puberty provokes the onset of the *genital* phase that lasts for the remainder of one's life (Hall, 1999) and in which libido is reinvested in the genitals. The first three pregenital phases were narcissistic—focused on self-gratification—and involved isolated drives that were, so to speak, disorganized in relation to reproductive sexuality. In the genital stage, the dynamics of those pregenital stages become organized into a pattern of not only other-focused, reproduction-oriented sexuality but of personality in general. Recall that every imaginable personality trait and pattern can be understood as having roots in those first three stages of life, the result of the interaction of the person's innate drives and constitution with the person's experiences in the natural and, especially, social world. We now turn to the subject of how well, and how poorly, that interaction can go, culminating, respectively, in healthy and unhealthy functioning.

Model of Mental Health

Healthy Functioning

Healthy functioning begins with innate disposition. Although Freud did not elaborate on the qualities of such a disposition, we might presume that the person is endowed with at least normal cognitive abilities and with an absence of propensity for excessive anxiety. Hall (1999) succinctly described the environmental conditions that maximize healthy functioning, one in which:

> the child [is offered] a succession of experiences that are synchronized with his capacities for adjustment. At no time should the dangers and hardships be so strong as to be incapacitating to the child or so weak as to be unstimulating. In infancy the hazards of existence should be small ones, in early childhood the threats should be a little stronger, and so on throughout the years of growth. In such a graded series of environments the ego would have an opportunity to shed its defense mechanisms … and replace them by more realistic and more efficient mechanisms. (p. 97)

Thus, the ego develops through both moderate gratification and moderate frustration: Enough gratification to experience that one can discharge unpleasant tension and achieve pleasant quiescence, and enough frustration to encourage the development of strategies to obtain objects in reality and in accord with social, moral guidelines.

Hall (1999) distinguished between the stabilized personality and the mature and/or well-adjusted personality. He asserted that it is possible to have the former without the latter. The primary feature of the stabilized personality is that the ego meets its goal of survival with a minimum of anxiety. The ego is in executive control, so to speak, finding realistic ways to manage the demands of the id, the superego, and the external world. This strong ego needs to rely on defense mechanisms only minimally or, at most, moderately. In addition, for Freud (1949a, pp. 26–27), the "normal" person was heterosexual, having learned to cathect a whole object—a person—and, in particular, a person of the other sex for the ultimate purpose of survival of the species through procreation.

In the bulk of his writing, Freud addressed the sources of distress in people and how to alleviate that distress. Consequently, he wrote very little about his view of the well-functioning personality. One exception is a passage from *Civilization and Its Discontents* (Freud, 1929/1989), which Freud wrote at the beginning of the last decade of his life. In it he asserted that functioning well and being happy are not synonymous: "The programme of becoming happy, which the pleasure principle imposes on us, cannot be fulfilled; yet we must not—indeed, we cannot—give up our efforts to bring it nearer to fulfillment by some means or other" (p. 733). He further mused that "work ... perhaps ... [comes] nearer to this goal [of a positive fulfilment (*sic*) of happiness] than any other method." He continued, "I am, of course, speaking of the way of life which makes love the centre of everything, which looks for all satisfaction in loving and being loved" (p. 733). Hence it has been said that Freud's view of mental health, of genuine maturity, is the capacity to strive relatively successfully for happiness through work and love.

Unhealthy Functioning

In the parlance of Freud's day, psychopathology was generally divided into two categories: neurosis and psychosis. *Neurosis* was characterized by impaired functioning and/or chronic subjective distress with an underlying presence of anxiety and an observable presence of self-defeating behavior. Neuroses included what are now called phobias—irrational fears of specific objects or situations; conversion disorders—loss of sensory or motor function, such as blindness or paralysis that follow a conflict or trauma and that have no apparent organic cause; and dissociative amnesia—"an inability to recall important personal information, usually of a traumatic or stressful nature, that is too extensive to be explained by normal forgetfulness" (American Psychiatric Association, 2000, p. 520). *Psychosis* involved more severe loss of contact with outer reality, as in what are now called schizophrenia, delusional disorder, and bipolar disorder. Though Freud's writings mentioned psychosis, he focused almost exclusively on neurosis. It appears that he viewed the normal state, neurotic disorder, and psychotic disorders on a continuum rather than as discrete phenomena. For example, he said that "the neuroses ... shade off by easy transitions into ... the normal, and, on the other hand ... scarcely any state recognized as normal [does not contain] indications of neurotic traits" (Freud, 1949a, p. 63).

Freud (1949a) conceptualized the neurotic as having a "weakened ego" (p. 60). That is, the ego is not up to the task of managing the demands of the id, the superego, and external reality. This condition is the result of some combination of innate disposition—presumably, cognitive deficits and/or affective tendencies toward excessive anxiety—and certain kinds of experiences. Those experiences can involve excessive indulgence, in which the ego is not induced to fend for itself, so to speak, and/or in which a lack of discipline fails to provide for superego development. At the other extreme, those experiences can involve excessive trauma—extreme privation, deprivation, and/or abuse that overwhelms the ego and forces it to rely excessively on defensive strategies just to keep itself afloat, to avoid disintegrating back into the id from which it strives to remain differentiated.

In either case of environmental excess, the ego does not develop, and/or has impaired access to, memory and action capabilities. The consequence is unmanaged anxiety. Thus, the ego employs coping strategies that manage anxiety in the short run but, in the long run, defeat the ego in its own goal of self-preservation. Consider, for example, the soldier who, upon seeing the horror of combat and experiencing acute death anxiety, goes psychogenically blind; he protects himself in the short-term from the immediate source of anxiety, but he renders himself disabled and, therefore, actually more vulnerable to death. (Note that this conversion disorder involves regression to an infantile state in which sensory processes occurred without conscious awareness.)

Freud (1949a) asserted that:

> neurotics have approximately the same innate dispositions as other people ... the same experiences ... the same tasks to perform. The "weak points" in a normal organization [arise from] one instinctual demand ... one period of life which comes in question exclusively or predominantly in connection with the generation of neurosis. (pp. 64–65)

That demand is the sex drive and that period is the phallic stage. Neuroses could appear in childhood as general anxiety, nightmares, tics, compulsions, or behavior disorders (Arlow, 2000). Commonly, however, though the roots of neurosis lie in childhood, the manifestation is latent until later in life. At any time in the genital stage, a marginally developed ego can "decompensate" (lose its ability to cope) if the demands of normal, daily life become too challenging, if one encounters profound traumas, or if a later situation resembles, and thus reactivates, an earlier unresolved conflict (Arlow, 2000, p. 34).

THE PERSONALITY CHANGE PROCESS

Personality change occurs with *insight*: when one becomes conscious of the conflicts underlying one's distressing feelings and self-defeating behavior, when one understands the true nature of those conflicts, and when one is able, rarely, to resolve them, or, much more commonly, to learn to deal with them more maturely and rationally (Arlow, 2000). However, much of psychological life never emerges naturally from unconsciousness. Furthermore, the ego, the part of the personality that has the capacity for consciousness, maturity, and reason, strives actively to spare itself anxiety by keeping conflictual dynamics *out* of consciousness. For these reasons, insight is highly unlikely to occur in the normal course of life; it is likely to occur only in the special circumstance of the psychoanalytic situation.

Before we address the therapeutic process, we want to say a word about terminology. The profession of counseling did not exist in Freud's time. If we assume that counseling primarily addresses normal developmental challenges, psychoanalysis might better be referred to as belonging in the broader domain of psychotherapy rather than the more specific subdomain of counseling. Nevertheless, this distinction becomes foggy in the professional literature. For example, because Freud and most psychoanalysts have been medical doctors, they have made reference to their analysands as *patients*. The term *client* was introduced by Carl Rogers after Freud's death. Nevertheless, current psychotherapists who rely heavily on psychoanalytic principles make reference to their "clients" (Kahn, 2002). We also will use the term *client* and will make reference to counseling, trusting that you now are aware of the ambiguity around this matter of terminology.

Client's Role

Clients' motives to seek counseling arise directly from their basic motive: to maximize pleasure and minimize pain. They are in pain, experiencing moderate to extreme emotional distress and/or engaging in self-defeating behavior that produces the anxiety of frustration and/or guilt. They are inherently motivated to alleviate their pain; on this point, client and psychoanalyst overtly agree.

However, although clients may say they are motivated to change as a means of alleviating their pain, the process of gaining insight puts clients directly in touch with the sources of anxiety and, thus, with painful anxiety itself. In other words, change is an inherently painful process. For this reason, from the psychoanalyst's perspective, the client is consciously motivated to change and unconsciously resistant to that very same change.

The client's experience in psychoanalysis reflects this dynamic. The potentially successful psychoanalytic client is in significant—not minor—psychological pain that is due to subjective dynamics rather than objective circumstances. As Arlow (2000) so poignantly put it, regarding objective circumstances such as severe congenital deformity or crippling disease, "No psychological insight can compensate for the injustices of life" (p. 39).

> The potentially successful psychoanalytic client also is strongly motivated to overcome their difficulties through honest self-scrutiny … in a position to commit the time necessary to carry the analysis through to successful termination…. [willing to] accept the discipline of the conditions proposed by the psychoanalytic contract…. [and] able to accept … frustration and to express thoughts and feelings in words rather than action. (Arlow, 2000, p. 38)

The successful client also has the financial resources necessary for the process, which usually involves two or three sessions a week over the course of at least 12 months and more typically, 2 or more years.

The client's primary role in psychoanalysis is to free associate. In *free association*, one reports one's stream of consciousness without interruption and without censorship. The client brings to the psychoanalytic session concerns and/or dreams, describes them, and then proceeds to free associate anything that comes to mind pertaining to the concern or dream—and any other topic where the process might take them. In the proper therapeutic environment, free association enables the client to relax defenses and reveal unconscious material. The client also must be open to the analyst's interpretation of what the client reveals; even if the interpretation does not ring true, the client must consider the possibility, or even probability, that one's lack of resonance with the interpretation is due to the client's repression rather than any error on the analyst's part.

As the preceding material indicates, the client bears a great deal of responsibility for one's own change through psychoanalysis. However, even the client best equipped to benefit from psychoanalysis is, according to Freud, limited in the capacity to change. Conflict, being inherent in the human condition, can never entirely be overcome, and the unconscious, with its vast reserves of irrationality, can never be understood or harnessed entirely.

The concept of psychotherapeutic resistance has its origin in psychoanalysis. *Resistance* refers to anything on the client's part that interferes with the achievement of insight. Resistance can take many forms. In all forms, the client's ego is seeking to protect itself from the threat of painful frustration or guilt that would occur if unacceptable impulses and their associated conflicts became conscious. Freud (1949a) said that "the maintenance of certain internal resistances is a *sine qua non* of normality" (p. 33). Thus he considered resistance in psychoanalysis to be normal and expectable—indeed, inevitable.

In one category of resistance, the client may *avoid free association* by arriving late to a session or forgetting it altogether, or by failing to pay on schedule, thus forcing the analyst to spend session time on financial matters. Another category of resistance occurs *during free association*: The client may fail to bring in any focal issues or dreams, may skip superficially from one subject to another, or may fall asleep.

In yet another category of resistance, the ego *disbelieves interpretations* offered by the analyst. Freud (1949a) explained that:

> When we attempt to [make another person's unconscious conscious], we should not forget that the conscious filling-in of the gaps in his perceptions—the construction we are presenting him with—does not mean as yet that we have made the unconscious material in question conscious to him. All that is true so far is that the material is present in him in two records, once in the conscious reconstruction he has been given, and besides this in its original unconscious state. Our continued efforts usually succeed eventually in making this unconscious material conscious to him himself, as a result of which the two records are brought to coincide. The amount of effort we have to use, by which we estimate the resistance against the material becoming conscious, varies in magnitude in individual cases. (pp. 32–33)

Regarding this latter category, Freud (1949a) noted particularly his clients' resistance to interpretations regarding the phallic stage of psychosexual development. The "reconstruction [of the castration complex] during the work of analysis is met in adults by the most decided disbelief" (p. 74). And, again, "if we ask an analyst what his experience has shown to be the mental structures least accessible to influence in his patients, the answer will be: in a woman her wish for a penis, in a man" the acceptance of feminine tendencies in himself, which he associates with castration and its accompanying anxiety (pp. 77–78).

Counselor's Role

Since the terms *analyst* and *psychoanalyst* are not legally protected, anyone can use them, even a person completely untrained in psychoanalysis (American Psychoanalytic Association, 2003). The ethical, appropriately trained psychoanalyst begins with a thorough understanding of psychoanalytic principles derived from both the intellectual study of psychoanalysis and the experience of one's own analysis. Beyond this, Arlow (2000) identified three critical analyst characteristics. The first is *empathy*, the ability to identify temporarily with both the cognitive and emotional aspects of a client's experience while simultaneously retaining a sense of separateness from the client. The second is *intuition*, whereby "the myriad data communicated by the patient are organized in the analyst's mind into meaningful configurations outside the scope of consciousness" (p. 44). The third is *introspection*, in which the analyst, in her own private process of free association, consciously apprehends the meaningful configuration, which constitutes the basis of an interpretation. For example, with a client who is in analysis for a pattern of leaving romantic relationships just as they verge on commitment, an analyst might empathize with the client's traumatic memory of her dear father's sudden death when she was young, might intuit that the woman avoids commitment out of fear of another traumatic abandonment, and might introspect to bring that intuition into consciousness and offer it to the client as an interpretation.

The analyst understands that, at this point in the process of understanding the client's psychodynamics, a given interpretation may have more or less merit—and may even be downright wrong. Once the configuration first becomes conscious, the analyst elaborates it, that is, cognitively develops the idea, and seeks to confirm or deny it by examining how it fits with the analyst's repeated observations of the client and her overall understanding of the client. If the analyst has employed the crucial skill of *timing* the delivery of the interpretation when the client is most likely to be receptive, such as while the client is exploring a case-in-point on the very same theme as that of the interpretation, client denial is less likely to be the result of resistance and more likely to be an indication that the interpretation is somehow off target. If client response includes surprised recognition of the validity of the interpretation, further association of related material congruent with the interpretation, and/or the spontaneous emergence of forgotten memories congruent with the interpretation, the analyst considers that interpretation confirmed.

Throughout this process, the analyst strives to remain as detached and objective as possible. That stance can be threatened by *countertransference*, in which the analyst has reactions to the client based not on material the client has presented but on the analyst's own unresolved psychological dynamics. For example, if the client reminds the analyst of his own mother and ways he felt traumatized by her, he may have difficulty remaining objective about the client. A vital task for analysts is to monitor their reactions to clients and, if they find countertransference, address it in their own analysis. It is because of countertransference that training to become a psychoanalyst includes undergoing one's own analysis—in great part to identify aspects of one's own psyche that are unresolved, resolve those aspects as much as possible, and remain vigilant about their potential reactivation in the process of conducting analysis of future clients.

Stages and Techniques

Stages

Opening Phase   In the first three to six months, the therapist works to establish a constructive therapeutic relationship and undertakes an assessment of the client. In the first part of this phase, the client and analyst meet for a few sessions of face-to-face talk in which the analyst purposely gives the client the lead in deciding when and how much to say. In this way, the analyst pieces together the client's history, identifies the client's concerns, and begins to develop a superficial understanding of the client's personality dynamics.

One of the analyst's early tasks is to assess whether the nature of the client's distress is appropriate for treatment with psychoanalysis. Freud (1949a) asserted that "the neuroses ... alone seem accessible to the psychological methods of our intervention" (p. 63). Consequently, the psychoanalyst would discontinue work with clients who are, at one extreme, "impulsive, willfull, ... highly narcissistic ... basically dishonest, psychopathic, or pathological liars [or psychotic]" (Arlow, 2000, pp. 38–39). The analyst also would discontinue work with clients who are, at the other extreme, experiencing only minor difficulties, because she would consider them insufficiently motivated to endure the challenges of psychoanalysis. In addition to this assessment, the analyst also would continue only with clients who demonstrated the qualities described in the "Client's Role" section above.

Having established the client's appropriateness for psychoanalysis, the analyst explains how psychoanalysis works. According to Arlow (2000), "the understanding of the analytical situation must be clearly defined at the outset and the respective responsibilities of both parties explicitly stated" (p. 36).

If the client agrees to the verbal psychoanalytic contract, he proceeds to the second part of the opening phase by reclining on the couch in the analyst's office, angled such that the client cannot see the analyst's face. Both lying down (a position associated with vulnerability, regression, and relaxation) and not seeing any analyst responses are conditions the analyst intends will maximize the client's revelation of unimpeded and uncensored psychological material, which is most likely to contain heretofore unconscious material. During these sessions, the analyst continues to learn about the client's psychological dynamics and offers occasional interpretations that mostly address the client's conscious conflicts and that, therefore, the client is most likely to recognize and accept.

Transference Typically, somewhere between three to six months after the client has assumed the couch, a distinctive dynamic in the client–analyst relationship develops. According to Arlow (2000), as "the patient is just about ready to relate his or her current difficulties to unconscious conflicts from childhood, concerning wishes over some important person or persons in his life" (p. 37), the client begins to have feelings for and expectations of the analyst that are excessive, unwarranted, and inappropriate in light of the psychoanalytic contract and the analyst's unfailing fulfillment of it. The client has somehow come to distort the relationship with the analyst, and rather than focusing exclusively on his own dynamics and their roots in the past, the client's attention, reactions, and needs becomes focused on the analyst. For example, the client may feel desperately dependent on the analyst, may feel "in love" with her, and/or may feel profoundly betrayed by something she has said or done.

As untoward as this client shift may seem, the analyst is not surprised. She *anticipates* the development of transference, in which, through predicate thinking, the client unconsciously transfers onto the analyst his unresolved conflicts with significant others from his past, usually his parents. The word *anticipates* is used here purposefully for both of its meanings: The analyst both *expects* transference to develop and, professionally speaking, *looks forward* to it, believing that it alone offers the client the opportunity for the lasting, healing insight into his most basic conflicts that are most fundamentally responsible for his current distress.

Working Through Since unresolved conflicts usually developed and became entrenched through myriad childhood experiences over time, and because of the power and pervasiveness of amnesia for those childhood experiences, insight into those conflicts and their manifestation in transference and the resolution and/or development of more realistic management of those conflicts does not occur with just one interpretation. In other words, the analyst cannot realistically expect an unresolved conflict that was years in the making to be resolved in one analytic session. Rather, the client needs to repeatedly revisit the theme in all its pervasive manifestations. To facilitate this, the analyst takes every opportunity to elaborate and amplify the theme. In this process, the ongoing recall of additional memories and the understanding of the themes playing out in transference reciprocally facilitate each other.

> It would be a mistake to believe that … the actual emergence of a repressed … traumatic memory of childhood regularly takes place…. [More commonly,] many strands of

evidence ... coalesce into an inescapable conclusion that a certain event did actually occur and had specific psychological consequences that have persisted throughout the patient's life. (Arlow, 2000, p. 38)

Consider, for example, the client who felt traumatized by her mother's constant and inappropriate invasiveness throughout her childhood and adolescence: walking in while the client was bathing, reading the client's diary without the client's permission, listening in on the client's phone calls, and so on. Such a client might display a related pattern of responses. Although it is the analyst's job to offer interpretations of the client's dreams, the client might become suddenly and extremely angry at some "presumptuous" interpretation the analyst offers. Although it is the analyst's job occasionally to inquire benignly into the client's life, the client might express resentment at the "nosiness" of the analyst. And when the analyst makes a suggestion pertaining to the client's relationship with her husband, the client might protest that the analyst is "usurping my power" and threaten to discontinue analysis. In each case, the analyst would use empathy, intuition, and free association to hit upon an interpretation involving the theme of perceived invasion and disempowerment that had more to do with the client's mother than with the analyst, and she would use timing to offer this interpretation when the client seemed most receptive.

Resolution   In this final phase of analysis, when analyst and client agree that they have achieved the client's therapeutic goals and the client has resolved any transference, they agree upon a date to terminate. At this point, to avoid separation from the analyst, the client is likely to experience a resurgence of symptoms. Also at this time, the client is likely to express disappointment that he has not achieved the fantasy of a conflict-free existence. The analyst anticipates both of these seeming setbacks as issues necessary to address for the client to avoid relapse, and he responds to them with the same approach as he has responded to all previous material: using free association and interpretation. When the client has made relative peace with the process of separation and the fact of the ongoing struggle inherent in life, the analysis is complete, and analyst and client part.

Techniques

The primary techniques of psychoanalysis are free association and interpretation. The analyst employs these techniques to address both the concerns and the dreams that the client brings to analysis. We will illustrate their use with regard to one of Freud's psychotherapeutic innovations: dreamwork.

Dreamwork   You will recall that people engage in dream *formation* to *encode primitive wishes into symbols*, thereby creating the *manifest* content—the obvious, remembered account of the dream—that *hides the dream's true meaning*. Analyst and client engage in *dreamwork* to *decode symbols* into their underlying *primitive wishes*, thereby discovering the *latent* content that *reveals the dream's true meaning*. In the dreamwork process, the client tells the dream and takes time to free associate on each element of the dream, whether seemingly important or unimportant. The analyst and, hopefully, the client offer interpretations regarding the latent content and its relationship to the client's unresolved childhood conflicts.

An example is the adult female client who reported the following dream:

This dream was very simple. It began with a baked potato with a lengthwise cut and the white part of the potato "plumped" up through the opening. A single green pea came and landed in the potato. The potato was dry, and the pea was supposed to moisten it, but the pea was completely inadequate to the job.

The client was completely mystified by the dream but remembered it so vividly that she was sure it carried a hidden meaning that she was eager to discover. Some of her associations to the dream were:

- The plumped out potato: A vegetable she liked; an outside that was somewhat rough that protected a smoother, "purer" inside; fullness; abundance; readiness, and eagerness to be consumed; warm and inviting; open; innermost contents revealed and available to be taken; the word "pot"—a receptacle, in this case, for moistening agents like butter and sour cream.
- The green pea: A vegetable she felt neutral about, her husband's favorite vegetable, small, powerless by itself, sweet but dry.

As she said the word "pea" a few times, she said "pee-wee," then "pee-pee," then "penis." She noted that, in the dream, the potato was passive, and the pea was active.

A psychoanalyst might interpret that the potato represented female genitals, and the pea represented male genitals. The analyst might further interpret that the dream harkened back to the client's childhood-based feelings of inferiority, of envy for the penis she did not have. She might suggest that the dream arose from the client's id-wish to have the powerful instrument of connection that males have, and from the unresolved ego-conflict between that wish and the reality of her anatomy and its related powerlessness. She might inquire into any experiences the client had had the day before the dream—experiences carrying the theme of inadequacy or powerlessness, experiences that may have reawakened the old, unresolved conflict from the client's earliest years of life. The dream may have indicated that the client had unresolved feelings pertaining to this complex and might not have developed adequate strategies to compensate for her feelings of inferiority. By understanding the nature of this long-standing conflict, and possibly developing relatively realistic compensations, she might reduce the force of the conflict and free her mind to attend to other matters. (For an alternate understanding of the dream, see Chapter 10 on cognitive counseling.)

Due to predicate thinking, in which one experiences as identical something similar but not identical, symbols often reveal their underlying meaning by virtue of their physical characteristics or their word associations. Hence, a penis might be represented by a banana or an umbrella as well as by the word pea. Thus, the analyst, again, uses her own intuition as well as the client's free associations to uncover the wish behind the symbol.

Addressing Resistance   The analyst's response to resistance depends on the type of resistance. He responds to avoidance by acknowledging it to the client and analyzing it, making it the focus of free association and interpretation. He responds to disbelief by temporarily discontinuing interpretation and watching for opportunities to restate an interpretation when the client seems receptive.

CONTRIBUTIONS AND LIMITATIONS

Interface With Recent Developments in the Mental Health Field

The Nature–Nurture Question

Beginning with his own early adherents, Alfred Adler and the Swiss psychiatrist, Carl Jung, and extending through the behaviorists and humanists of the second half of the twentieth century, Freud was criticized for attributing too much to biological forces within the person. These critics attributed more influence on personality development to various factors: environmental, especially social, influences; innate strivings to actualize all of one's potential; one's own creativity; even spiritual factors.

With recent research on the influence of genetics on personality development, the pendulum has swung back toward Freud's (1949a) original conception. His attribution of psychopathology to " 'traumas,' particularly if they are met halfway by certain innate dispositions" (p. 65), sounds amazingly similar to current views of genetic vulnerability in which unique experiences interact with an individual's genetic susceptibility to psychopathology (Gatz, 1990). Though Freud might have offered a higher proportion, even the new view in genetics that approximately 40% of variation in personality traits can be attributed to heredity seems not far afield from Freud's perspective.

On a related point, results from genetics research are prompting revision of a legacy of psychoanalysis: the tendency to point a blaming finger at parents for having "nurtured" their children's maladjustment. As this thinking goes, if a person is not functioning well, it must be due to parental deprivation, overindulgence, or induction of trauma. The greater attribution of children's behavior to the child's own hereditary tendencies tends to reduce the blame of parents (and, for that matter, of children) and tends to place all parties in a collaborative stance with the counselor to identify and respond constructively to a child's innate tendencies that may be contributing to an identified problem. This development is a far cry from the psychoanalytic perspective.

DSM–IV–TR *Diagnosis*

Clearly, Freud did not hesitate to conceptualize in terms of psychopathology and to use diagnostic terms such as phobia and psychosis. Presumably, he would have had no problem with rendering *DSM* (American Psychiatric Association, 2000) diagnoses if the *DSM* had existed in his time.

Pharmacotherapy

Pharmacotherapy came into being after Freud's death. However, one can hardly fail to be impressed by the sagacity of his musings on this topic as well as on the future regard in which psychoanalysis might be held overall:

> We are concerned with therapy only in so far as it works by psychological means.... The future may teach us to exercise a direct influence, by means of particular chemical substances, on the amounts of energy and their distribution in the mental apparatus. It may be that there are other still undreamt-of possibilities of therapy. But for the moment we have nothing better at our disposal than the technique of psycho-analysis, and for that reason, in spite of its limitations, it should not be despised. (Freud, 1949a, p. 62)

Managed Care and Brief Therapy

Psychoanalysis might be considered the polar opposite of brief therapy. Rather than aiming at expedient relief from discrete symptoms, psychoanalysts aim to deeply restructure personality, a process that is costly in both time and money. Combined with its failure to be identified among empirically supported approaches to psychotherapy (Crits-Christoph, 1998) and the limited number of disorders Freud considered it appropriate to treat, psychoanalysis is antithetical to brief care and is not covered by managed care. As previously stated, psychoanalytic principles have been incorporated into briefer forms of therapy (Broderson, 1994; Kahn, 2002), and many of the brief forms of therapy are outgrowths of psychoanalysis.

Technical Eclecticism

In classical psychoanalysis, analysands lie on a couch and free associate. Psychoanalysts employ these techniques for the specific purpose of facilitating analysands' unconscious material to come into consciousness. This purpose and its associated techniques are unique among approaches to psychotherapy. In virtually every other approach, the counselor encounters the client face to face and employs an approach and techniques with different goals than those of psychoanalysts. Thus, techniques from other approaches by and large do not align with the goals of psychoanalysis, so analysts do not employ technical eclecticism.

Diversity Issues

Regarding ethnicity, Freud was an upper middle-class Caucasian Westerner who developed a theory from working with others of his own sociocultural background. Although he was fascinated with the archeology of more diverse groups, and he believed the principles he developed applied at least to all Western cultures if not to others, he undertook neither to study diverse cultures nor to take members of those cultures as patients. Thus, psychoanalysis is frequently criticized for being extremely culture-bound.

Regarding gender, feminists have denounced psychoanalysis for reflecting and promoting the male chauvinism of Freud's time. Concepts like the phallic stage, named for male genitals; penis envy, with its lifelong implication of not only feelings of inferiority but actual inferiority of women; and the readiness of a well-adjusted wife to submit to her husband's authority, reflect an inherently superior view of men and inferior view of women. However, not all of Freud's ideas were sexist, for example, his basic drive theory and his psychoanalytic techniques and processes.

Regarding sexual orientation, most health professionals now consider Freud to have been heterosexist by virtue of his belief that heterosexuality was normal and his reference to homosexuality as a developmental inhibition and a perversion. Research findings have not substantiated Freud's views about the origin of homosexuality—nor heterosexuality, for that matter (Bell & Weinberg, 1978). The fundamental assumption that homosexuality is inherently psychopathological, at one time reflected in its listing in the *DSM* as a mental disorder, does not reflect the current prevailing view in the field of psychology, as evidenced by its absence as a diagnostic category from the *DSM* for the past four decades and the growing view that homosexuality is a normal minority variation in sexual orientation comparable to left-handedness in hand dominance. It is interesting to me (JMH) that even before homosexuality was depathologized, people looked with profound skepticism at Freud's Oedipal explanation for the development of heterosexual orientation but continued to hold fast to that same theory as an explanation for homosexual orientation.

Regarding spirituality, Freud addressed only religion, not spirituality, in his writings and reduced religion to psychological origins. He considered religion to result from the universal wish to regress to submission to idealized authority: a deity. In particular regarding monotheism, he believed not that God created humans, but that men created God, so to speak, to assuage their unconscious guilt over their unconscious wishes to kill their fathers (Brunner, 1998). The possibility of a spiritual domain inherent in human nature was alien to Freud's thinking.

Research on Personality Development and Function

Since psychoanalysis is the oldest of psychotherapeutic theories, it is most prone to disproval by subsequent discoveries. Interestingly, time also has favored some Freudian concepts with an accumulation of confirmatory evidence. Though a complete review is beyond the scope of this chapter, we will address a few of these topics.

Researchers have disconfirmed some of Freud's beliefs. For example, Harry Harlow's research on infant rhesus monkeys exposed only to "surrogate mothers" made of wire or cloth demonstrated that the infant's bond to the mother is not based on the oral stimulation of feeding but on the stimulation of physical embraces that Harlow called "contact comfort" (WGBH, 1998). In addition, "some aspects of Freud's thoughts on dreaming (such as the idea that the dream is the guardian of sleep) have not withstood the test of science" (Luborsky, O'Reilly-Landry, & Arlow, 2008, p. 34).

Regarding aggression, Freud (1949a, p. 20) proposed that hostility and aggression are inevitably bound up in the personality as a by-product of socialization and that death is hastened when such feelings are not released through expression. However, current researchers have established that expressing anger promotes, rather than reduces, the subsequent experience and expression of anger, and that people who are high in the chronic experience and expression of anger are more prone to stress-related diseases, including coronary disease, that actually shortens their lives (Australian Broadcasting Corporation, 2003; Radio National, 1998). Consequently, current approaches to aggression deemphasize cathartic expression of anger and emphasize the reduction of aggressive feelings and actions through anger management (see Chapter 10).

Researchers also have confirmed others of Freud's ideas. Freud's contention of childhood sexuality has been confirmed by sonograms showing male infants *in utero* with the sexual reflex: penile erection. It also has been confirmed through research on child sexual behavior, such as how masturbation, even among preschoolers, is normal and, especially if parents respond in appropriate ways, is likely to be healthy (Steele, 2002). In addition, every human is sexually aroused during dreaming, which dominates a newborn's sleep and constitutes about 2.5 hours each night in an adult, no matter how sexual, or seemingly nonsexual, the content of the dream. These latter facts could be construed as support not only of Freud's theory of infantile sexuality but also of the sexual basis and latent sexual meaning of dreams.

Other areas of confirmation include the concept from attachment theory of "inner working models" of self and others in relationships that people develop in childhood and that tend to remain stable throughout life (Main, Kaplan, & Cassidy, 1985) and, on a related note, the existence of transference and the value of addressing it in psychotherapy (Luborsky & Crits-Christoph, 1998; Luborsky & Luborsky, 2006). Finally, regarding the concept of the unconscious mind, foremost brain researcher Antonio Damasio (1999) asserted that, "Throughout the [20th] century, and through work unrelated to the original proposals of Freud and Jung, the evidence for unconscious processing has not ceased to accumulate" (p. 297).

The Effectiveness of Psychotherapy

Psychoanalysis is not listed among the American Psychological Association's empirically supported approaches to psychotherapy (Crits-Christoph, 1998). Lacking a treatment manual, it didn't even get into the running in that sweeping analysis of psychotherapeutic approaches.

Even among analysts themselves, appraisal of the effectiveness of psychoanalysis is contradictory, at best. For example, Arlow (2000) confirmed that "unfortunately, no adequate study exists evaluating the results of psychoanalytic therapy" (p. 40) and offered that "the claims of psychoanalysis must be modest at best" (p. 40) because, at most, it enables a client to achieve a stable equilibrium that continues to be vulnerable to distressing external circumstances in the client's life. However, he went on to conclude that "the fact remains that when properly applied to the appropriate condition, psychoanalysis remains one of the most effective modes of therapy yet devised" (p. 40). In the absence of adequate study of psychoanalysis, that conclusion should remain in the realm of opinion rather than fact. Luborsky et al. (2008) claimed effectiveness of psychoanalysis on the basis of general studies of psychotherapy rather than studies of analysis itself (pp. 50–51).

A controversy continues to rage over whether psychoanalysis proper is an effective treatment. Kahn (2002) offered a perspective that probably represents most psychotherapists' views: that psychoanalysis includes some concepts that are not therapeutically helpful and others that powerfully inform the therapeutic process. Those latter concepts can often be very usefully incorporated or adapted into a therapeutic structure that differs fundamentally from classical psychoanalysis.

Limitations

We have already implied several weaknesses of psychoanalysis. Among them are its questionable effectiveness, its unavailability to the masses in need of psychological help, its culture-boundedness, its aspects that have been invalidated by subsequent research, and its failure to consider and/or account for a genuine spiritual domain in humans, in general, and profoundly meaningful and constructive spiritual experiences, in particular.

Another potential weakness is inherent in the theory itself. Any specific content in the psyche can be simply itself; can, through predicate thinking, stand not for itself but for something similar; or can, through reaction formation, stand not for itself or for something similar but for precisely its opposite. This openness of interpretation, combined with the authoritative stance of the analyst, in which any failure of the client to agree with the analyst's interpretation can be attributed to client repression, has the potential to disempower the client as an authority on his own reality. This state of affairs has led more than one exasperated client to abandon psychoanalysis.

Contributions

Most counseling theorists since Freud have adopted or adapted free association and/or interpretation in the approaches they developed. Adlerians, for example, conceptualize psychological processes differently than Freudians, yet they propose to clients their interpretations of client's nonconscious mental workings, albeit in a less authoritative and more tentative way: "Could it be that you...." Every approach to dreamwork (Adlerian, Rogerian, Gestalt, cognitive, and others not mentioned in this book) relies fundamentally on clients associating to the remembered dream and on the counselor and/or client interpreting those associations: intuiting connections, themes, and patterns that elucidate clients' inner workings and that potentiate constructive change.

Perhaps Freud's most distinguishing contribution to counseling and psychotherapy is that he is credited as its founder. Prior to psychoanalysis, no well-organized, psychologically based system of Western thought existed to understand the human psyche. Virtually every subsequent approach arose either as an extension of psychoanalysis or in opposition to it. As you proceed to read subsequent chapters in this book, you undoubtedly will recognize many concepts similar to those you read about in this chapter.

Another contribution is the extent to which psychoanalysis "psychologized" Western culture at large through the pervasion (some might say perversion!) of psychoanalytic terms and concepts into popular thinking. We all, knowingly or not, speak Freud's language. Freud's concept of infantile determinism—that early experiences have a lasting effect on personality—has, for many Westerners since Freud's time, achieved the status of an a priori assumption. It also is commonplace to refer to someone as "defensive" or "neurotic," or to speak of repression, rationalization, projection, sublimation, narcissism, sibling rivalry.... The list goes on and on. A layperson uses such words and another nods in glib agreement, unconscious that they are affirming aspects of Freudian thinking that resonate intuitively.

CURRENT STATUS

Psychoanalysis persists as a force in the field of psychology, though a decreasingly powerful one. However, Kahn (2002) noted that the number of psychoanalytic training institutes in his area have increased rather than decreased. Such institutes exist around the world, and scholars and practitioners continue to publish psychoanalytically oriented journals and books about the theory, practice, and social impact of psychoanalysis.

Luborsky et al. (2008) listed numerous fields from which current psychoanalysts have incorporated ideas, including empirical findings about sexual trauma and neuroscience and concepts from feminist theory (p. 28). An example of recent research is Vaillant's (1977, 2002) longitudinal studies of Harvard students showing that "the use of more mature defenses, such as sublimation ... and humor, as opposed to those that are less mature and [more] pathological, such as projection, is highly predictive of both physical and mental health later in life" (Luborsky et al., 2008, p. 30). A recent trend is for psychoanalysts to consider that some countertransference reactions may not be reflections of the analyst's own unresolved psychological material but useful clues about how others in the client's life experience the client (Luborsky et al., 2008, p. 20).

Arlow (2000) identified what he considered "the most significant and powerful trend concerning modern-day psychoanalytic technique" (p. 45): The movement among some analysts from a position of objectivity in relation to the client, to one of *intersubjectivity*. From this latter perspective, the analyst is not an all-knowing entity who can stand apart from the client and presume with certainty to know the client even better than the client knows himself. Rather, the analyst, like all humans, is limited in her knowledge and experiences client material in an unavoidably subjective way, based on her own wishes and defenses. Rather than fight these realities, the analyst accepts them. In the process, she becomes more collaborative with the client and self-disclosing of her experience of the client, believing that, through a more mutual search for the dynamics underlying the client's distress, they are most likely to find the best approximation of truth.

SUMMARY

Sigmund Freud wrote that, "My life has been aimed at one goal only; to infer or guess how the mental apparatus is constructed and what forces interplay and counteract in it" (cited in Hall, 1999, p. 15). It appears that, to the best of his ability, within the limits of his personal potential and the philosophical, social, and technological systems within which he worked, he met that goal. Many ideas that originated with Freud are pervasive in current Western culture. Some of his ideas have lost credibility in light of subsequent research on behavior, genetic influences on personality, and the use of psychoactive medication to treat psychopathology; others have been confirmed through empirical research on sexuality, sleep, dreams, and consciousness. Clinicians continue to practice psychoanalysis as a form of psychotherapy, both in its original form and as an adapted form in brief therapy. It has been extremely fruitful to the field of psychotherapy by spawning most other approaches that are either an outgrowth of it or a reaction against it.

RECOMMENDED RESOURCES

Books

Arlow, J. A. (2000). Psychoanalysis. In R. J. Corsini & D. Wedding (Eds.), *Current psychotherapies* (7th ed., pp. 15–51). Belmont, CA: Brooks/Cole-Thomson. Short on personality theory, this chapter provides a systematic explanation of the process of psychoanalysis as psychotherapy.

Freud, S. (1949a). *An outline of psychoanalysis.* (J. Strachey, Trans.). New York, NY: Norton. Freud did not complete this, his last work. However, because it was his last, it reflects in a fairly concise form his ultimate formulation of psychoanalysis as a theory of personality and an approach to psychotherapy. Though I (JMH) found his writing obscure at times, I also found it startling to read in his own eloquent words (albeit translated) some of his most outrageous-by-current-standards ideas as well as some ideas with which I agreed immediately and which resonated deeply with me.

Gay, P. (1989). Sigmund Freud: A chronology. In P. Gay (Ed.), *The Freud reader* (pp. xxxi–xlvii). New York, NY: Norton. This listing condenses into 17 pages the most critical facts pertaining to Freud's life. The ambitious student who wants to read excerpts of Freud's work throughout his lifetime may proceed to read this entire volume; those who want to read Freud's biography in depth are referred to Gay's 1988/1998 *Freud: A life for our time.*

Hall, C. S. (1999). A *primer of Freudian psychology.* New York, NY: Meridian. Although a close reading begins to reveal holes and discrepancies in psychoanalytic theory, this clear and dense volume still represents the best introductory overview of the personality theory of psychoanalysis. It does not address the psychoanalytic psychotherapy process.

Audiovisuals

A&E Television Network. (1995). *Sigmund Freud: Analysis of a mind* [Television broadcast]. An excellent 50-minute biography. Available for about $25 at http://www.amazon.com

Learning Corporation of America (Producer). (1970). *Sigmund Freud: The hidden nature of man* [Motion picture]. New York, NY: Learning Corporation of America. An excellent overview of Freud's life and ideas. Although it is an older production, its content and production values have held up over time. Available for about $60 at http://www.amazon.com

Probably because psychoanalysis is difficult to depict in one short video, we know of none that attempt to demonstrate it. However, videos are available that demonstrate psychodynamic approaches derived from psychoanalysis:

Broderson, G. (Producer/Director). (1994). *Short term dynamic therapy* [Motion picture]. Washington, DC: American Psychological Association. (Available from the American Psychological Association, 750 First Street, NE, Washington, DC 20002-4242 or at http://www.apa.org/videos/4310330.html) A mock therapy session with "Dorothy" conducted by Donald Freedheim is the focus of this 36-minute video. The video is available for about $100.

Strupp, H. (1986). Psychodynamic psychotherapy. *Three approaches to psychotherapy III*, Part 1 [Motion picture]. Corona Del Mar, CA: Psychological & Educational Films. (Available from Psychological & Educational Films, 3334 East Coast Highway, #252, Corona Del Mar, CA 92625 or http://www.psychedfilms.com/id1.html). In this 46-minute video, Hans Strupp briefly introduces psychodynamic psychotherapy, conducts a 30-minute session with "Richard," and briefly debriefs the session. The video is available for about $400.

Web Sites

A listing of psychoanalytic journals and publishers can be found at http://www.dspp.com/links/psapubs.htm

Rich with information about psychoanalysis in the United States, the American Psychoanalytic Association's Web site is http://www.apsa.org/

Rich with photos and information about Freud, the Freud Museum in London's Web site is http://www.freud.org.uk/

REFERENCES

American heritage dictionary of the English language (4th ed.). (2000). New York, NY: Houghton Mifflin.

American Psychiatric Association. (2000). *Diagnostic and statistical manual of mental disorders* (4th ed., text rev.). Washington, DC: Author.

American Psychoanalytic Association. (2003). *About psychoanalysis.* Retrieved from http://www.apsa.org/

Arlow, J. A. (2000). Psychoanalysis. In R. J. Corsini & D. Wedding (Eds.), *Current psychotherapies* (7th ed., pp. 15–51). Belmont, CA: Brooks/Cole-Thomson.

Australian Broadcasting Corporation. (2003). Hostility and cholesterol. *News in Science* (1998, October). Retrieved from http://www.abc.net.au/science/news/stories/s13934.htm

Bell, A. P., & Weinberg, M. S. (1978). *Homosexualities: A study of diversity among men and women.* New York, NY: Simon & Schuster.

Broderson, G. (Producer/Director). (1994). *Short term dynamic therapy* [Motion picture]. Washington, DC: American Psychological Association. (Available from the American Psychological Association, 750 First Street, NE, Washington, DC 20002-4242 or at http://www.apa.org/videos/4310330.html)

Brunner, J. (1998). Oedipus politicus: Freud's paradigm of social relations. In M. S. Roth (Ed.), *Freud: Conflict and culture: Essays on his life, work, and legacy* (pp. 48–61). New York, NY: Alfred A. Knopf.

Crits-Christoph, P. (1998). Training in empirically validated treatments: The Division 12 APA task force recommendations. In K. S. Dobson & K. D. Craig (Eds.), *Empirically supported therapies: Best practice in professional psychology* (pp. 3–25). Thousand Oaks, CA: Sage.

Damasio, A. (1999). *The feeling of what happens: Body and emotion in the making of consciousness*. New York, NY: Harcourt.

Freud, S. (1949a). *An outline of psycho-analysis*. (J. Strachey, Trans.). New York: Norton.

Freud, S. (1949b). *Three essays on the theory of sexuality*. (J. Strachey, Trans.). Oxford, UK: Imago. (Original work published 1905)

Freud, S. (1965). *Interpretation of dreams*. (J. Strachey, Trans.). New York, NY: Avon. (Original work published 1900)

Freud, S. (1989). Civilization and its discontents. In P. Gay (Ed.), *The Freud reader* (pp. 722–772). New York, NY: Norton. (Original work published 1929)

Gatz. M. (1990). Interpreting behavioral genetic results: Suggestions for counselors and clients. *Journal of Counseling and Development, 68*, 601–605.

Gay, P. (1988). *Freud: A life for our times*. New York, NY: Norton.

Gay, P. (1989a). Sigmund Freud: A brief life. In S. Freud, *An outline of psycho-analysis* (J. Strachey, Trans.; pp. vii–xx). New York, NY: Norton.

Gay, P. (1989b). Sigmund Freud: A chronology. In P. Gay (Ed.), *The Freud reader* (pp. xxxi–xlvi). New York, NY: Norton.

Greenberg, J. R., & Mitchell, S. A. (1983). *Object relations in psychoanalytic theory* (Part 1: Origins, pp. 9–78). Cambridge, MA: Harvard University.

Hall, C. S. (1999). *A primer of Freudian psychology*. New York, NY: Meridian.

Hergenhahn, B. R. (1992). *Introduction to the history of psychology* (2nd ed.). Monterey, CA: Brooks/Cole.

Jones, E. (1953). *The life and work of Sigmund Freud* (Vols. 1–3). New York, NY: Basic.

Kahn, M. (2002). *Basic Freud: Psychoanalytic thought for the 21st century*. New York, NY: Basic.

Kreis, S. (2000a). *The history guide: Lectures on twentieth century Europe: Lecture 1: Random thoughts on the intellectual history of 20th century Europe*. Retrieved from http://www.historyguide.org/europe/lecture1.html

Kreis, S. (2000b). *The history guide: Lectures on twentieth century Europe: Lecture 9: The Age of Anxiety: Europe in the 1920s (2)*. Retrieved from http://www.historyguide.org/europe/lecture9.html

Luborsky, L., & Crits-Christoph, P. (1998). *Understanding transference: The CCRT method* (2nd ed.). Washington, DC: American Psychological Association.

Luborsky, L., & Luborsky, K. (2006). *Research and psychotherapy: The vital link*. Lanham, MD: Jason Aronson.

Luborsky, E. B., O'Reilly-Landry, M., & Arlow, J. (2008). Psychoanalysis. In R. J. Corsini & D. Wedding (Eds.), *Current psychotherapies* (8th ed., pp. 15–62). Belmont, CA: Thomson.

Main, M., Kaplan, N., & Cassidy, J. (1985). Security in infancy, childhood and adulthood: A move to the level of representation. *Monographs of the Society for Research in Child Development, 50*(1–2), 66–104.

Moore, R. (1999). *The creation of reality in psychoanalysis: A view of the contributions of Donald Spence, Roy Schafer, Robert Stolorow, Irwin Z. Hoffman, and beyond*. Hillsdale, NJ: Analytic Press.

Radio National. (1998). *The health report: Anger kills*. Retrieved from http://www.abc.net.au/rn/talks/8.30/helthrpt/stories/s10309.htm

Roazen, P. (1992). *Freud and his followers*. New York, NY: Da Capo.

Roget's II: The new thesaurus (3rd ed.). (1995). New York, NY: Houghton Mifflin.

Steele, R. (2002). *Masturbation: Is this normal for preschoolers?* Retrieved from http://parenting.ivillage.com/tp/tpdevelopment/0,,3q9m,00.html

Stills, S. (1970). Love the one you're with. On *Stephen Stills* (record). New York, NY: Atlantic.

Vaillant, G. E. (1977). *Adaptation to life.* Cambridge, MA: Harvard University Press.

Vaillant, G. E. (2002). *Aging well.* Boston, MA: Little, Brown.

WGBH. (1998). *People and discoveries: Harry Harlow.* Retrieved from http://www.pbs.org/wgbh/aso/databank/entries/bhharl.html

CHAPTER **3**

Self Psychology

BACKGROUND OF THE THEORY

Historical Context

Self psychology is the most recent of the four main schools of psychodynamic thought that emerged from Freud's pioneering psychoanalysis, the other three being *drive theory, ego psychology,* and *object relations.* Since the early 1970s, most psychodynamic theorists have worked primarily in analytic institutes. Consequently, most therapist–educators in academia today, even those who regularly teach the theories of Freud and Erik Erikson, know relatively little about significant developments in psychodynamics (McWilliams, 1994). Nevertheless, in at least one major study, mental health professionals most often named psychodynamic theories as their exclusive or primary guiding theories (Jensen, Bergin, & Greaves, 1990). For this reason and others that we will discuss in this chapter, it is fitting that counselors be knowledgeable about psychodynamic theories. In this chapter, we present a very brief overview of the first three schools and a more in-depth introduction to Heinz Kohut's self psychology. Since the historical foundation of self psychology is relatively richer than that of other theories, this section will be somewhat longer than comparable sections in other chapters of this text.

In the primary literature of psychoanalysis and psychodynamics, authors often use the terms *psychoanalytic* and *psychodynamic* interchangeably. "Psychoanalytic" usually refers to traditional psychoanalysis; however, after Kohut's radical departure from traditional psychoanalysis, he continued to use the classical terms "psychoanalysis," "analyst," and "analysand–patient." In this chapter, we will use "therapy–counseling," "therapist–counselor," and "client," respectively, whereas we will retain Kohut's original terminology in our quotations from him.

Each of the psychodynamic theories retains significant similarities to psychoanalysis. Each adheres to the central concept that a person's feelings, thoughts, and behaviors are profoundly influenced by psychological processes and mental representations that are, to some degree, *unconscious.* Each affirms the *formative impact of early caretaker–child interactions* on one's present experience, the *development of personality through invariant stages,* and the presence and importance of *defenses, transference, and the interpretation of the client's psychic material in the therapeutic process* (Perry, Cooper, & Michels, 1986).

Students studying psychodynamic theories for the first time can probably best understand them in relation to Freud's theory of psychoanalysis that evolved through three primary phases, each characterized by a model. His first phase involved the *topographical model.* This model accounted for the relative degree of access a person has to one's psychic material: from completely unconscious, to preconscious, to fully conscious. It included the concept of *drives* along with *defenses* a person uses to repress intolerable emotions to some level of unconsciousness. Freud's second phase emphasized drives in the context of a *structural model* whereby the *ego* mediates the primitive desires of the *id* and the moralistic demands of the *superego*. In his final *relational model* phase, Freud highlighted how *early experiences with significant others* interact with a child's innate topography and structure to determine adult personality (Greenberg & Mitchell, 1983).

The current school of psychodynamics that remains closest to psychoanalytic theory is *drive theory,* which emerged quite early in the history of psychoanalysis. As drive theory is nearly indistinguishable from psychoanalysis, no particular proponent of this school exists apart from Freud himself. The emphasis in drive theory is on people's libidinal and aggressive drives that energize psychological processes. Libidinal drives are not merely sexual but refer more broadly to impulses toward bodily pleasure, excitement, anticipation, love, or happiness (Greenberg & Mitchell, 1983).

For almost 50 years, only classic psychoanalytic theory and its very close relative, drive theory, existed. By the 1940s, however, a few individuals began to create alternative psychoanalytic perspectives: Harry Stack Sullivan, Melanie Klein, Karen Horney, Erich Fromm, Clara Thompson, and Frieda Fromm-Reichman. However, none of these theorists developed their theories sufficiently and/or attracted a sufficient number of proponents to warrant calling their respective approaches one of the four primary analytic schools of thought (Greenberg & Mitchell, 1983).

The second actual school to emerge was that of *ego psychology*, primarily associated with Anna Freud and Heinz Hartmann. They named their perspective ego psychology because they emphasized not drives themselves but the ego's capacity to regulate, control, and channel drives. Anna Freud's foremost contribution to this school was a much more detailed elaboration of the mechanisms of ego defense. Hartmann's foremost contribution was the concept that, in the interest of adaptation, the ego could actually alter drives, that is, change what one experiences as pleasurable; and the conceptual separation of the self—which is largely a locus of the felt-sense of "I" and of all personal experience—from the ego—which refers more specifically to the psychological defenses and other functions that serve to maintain and consolidate one's sense of self. If you are interested in a succinct overview of clinical applications of ego psychology, we refer you to Chapter 5 of Bellak, Hurvich, and Gediman (1973).

In the 1940s and 1950s, while ego psychologists were refining their model of personality, various theorists in Europe, such as W. R. D. Fairbairn, D. W. Winnicott, and Margaret Mahler, established the school of *object relations;* their work independently paralleled that of Edith Jacobson and Otto Kernberg in the United States. In this theory, the term *object* can be understood to mean object of desire that satisfies a drive, and usually refers to a person, most importantly one's primary caregiver(s) in early childhood, as well as significant others throughout the rest of one's life.

The object relations pioneers worked with clients who would now be diagnosed as psychotic or borderline—children and adults without a well-developed ego. They found existing psychoanalytic and psychodynamic theories inadequate to understand such clients because those theories proceeded on the assumption that a client already had a developed ego. To more thoroughly explain how the ego developed, object relations theorists focused on the quality of the primary objects (people) in a person's infancy and very early childhood, how the person had experienced and internalized those objects, and how the internal representations of significant objects persisted in the person's unconscious mind throughout life, greatly influencing the quality of the person's experience (McWilliams,

1994). All of these dynamics profoundly impact the development of one's sense of self. Object relations theorists acknowledged the often very real actions of the object but *considered the client's perception of the object even more important than the actual object,* because the client's preegoic, prerational perception was likely to have involved misinterpretations. For example, a 1-year-old girl whose mother had to be hospitalized for a year felt abandoned; that is, she misinterpreted that her mother had abandoned her. In later relationships with other objects, she was hypersensitive to possible abandonment and misperceived it where it actually had not occurred (McWilliams, 1994). Clinically, the fact that her mother had not intentionally abandoned her was unimportant; her perception that she had been abandoned and her feeling of having been abandoned were key in her later relationship difficulties.

Object relations theory is complex; even a competent introduction is beyond the scope of this chapter. Suffice it to say that the theory has made several unique contributions to psychotherapy. One was the elaboration of theory regarding stages of psychological development in very early childhood (Klein, 1948; Mahler, Pine, & Bergman, 1975). Another was the understanding and treatment of severely disturbed clients, many formerly considered untreatable, such as those with borderline personality disorder (Kernberg, 1975). A third was a new appreciation of and perspective on countertransference in the psychotherapeutic process: In contrast to Freud's perspective of viewing strong emotional reactions to the client as an analyst's failure to maintain psychological neutrality, distance, and objectivity, the perspective of object relations theorists such as Harold Searles and D. W. Winnicott was that such reactions provided them their best tools for understanding and treating their highly distressed clients (McWilliams, 1994). When some therapists talk about "use of self," they mean what Searles and Winnicott suggested: a therapist using one's own reactions to a client to assess and to navigate interventions with that client. A fourth contribution was the shift away from the impersonal therapeutic relationship of psychoanalysis toward a therapeutic alliance characterized by the therapist's personal involvement, engagement, and even self-disclosure (McWilliams, 1994). A fifth was Hartmann's initial conceptualization of a self that is more than the ego.

Self psychology, the fourth school of psychodynamics, was born with Heinz Kohut's 1971 publication of *The Analysis of the Self.* However, in this book, Kohut actually continued with ideas he had been developing over the previous 12 years. Prior to 1971, not only had Kohut been deeply committed to the teachings of classical psychoanalysis and its technical prescriptions, but he had also been a prominent member and leader of the psychoanalytic community. It was, therefore, only with great difficulty that he gradually revealed to himself and the analytic community what ultimately became a radical reformulation of psychoanalytic theory. Reflecting on his career, Kohut (1984) wrote that "in 1971, I was simply trying to pour new wine into old bottles, attempting to make new ideas appear less radically new and more acceptable not only to my fellow analysts, but above all to myself" (p. 193). However, by 1977, with the publication of *The Restoration of the Self,* Kohut presented his work as superordinate to mainstream psychoanalysis. Today, most mental health professionals view self psychology not merely as an elaboration of psychoanalysis but as a genuinely new school of psychotherapy (Kohut, 1979; Masek, 1989).

Like the object relations theorists, Kohut never considered classical psychoanalysis and the first two psychodynamic schools invalid or unimportant. He did, however, view them as limited, particularly in that they inadequately prepared therapists to understand and treat people with more severe psychological disturbances. Kohut termed the more severe disturbances *disorders of the self* that include narcissistic, borderline, and

TABLE 3.1   Psychodynamic Listening

Drive theory	What does this client want?
	Are the client's wishes and fantasies developmentally appropriate?
Ego psychology	What defenses does this client primarily employ?
	How does this client go about getting what she wants?
Object relations	How does this client recall the significant people from the various stages of development in her life?
	Whom does this client behave, think, and feel like?
Self psychology	To what extent does this client like, value, and admire herself?
	How does this client respond to events that insult her self-esteem?

Source: Adapted from Ursano, R., Sonnenberg, S., & Lazar, S., *Psychodynamic psychotherapy: Principles and techniques in the era of managed care,* American Psychiatric Press, Washington, DC, p. 35, 1998.

psychotic conditions (Kohut, 1979; Masek, 1989), all of which we will explain and discuss in a later section of this chapter. In particular, Kohut described narcissism far more completely and broadly than it was—and is—described in the *Diagnostic and Statistical Manual of Mental Disorders* (*DSM–IV–TR*; American Psychiatric Association [APA], 2000). Consequently, he considered narcissism to be far more pervasive than did most other mental health professionals.

Before proceeding with a more in-depth description of self psychology, we want to make one last overview point. Of the four theories we just described, most psychodynamically oriented therapists resonate more with one theory than the others but, clinically, call upon all four (or at least the latter three) to conceptualize their clients (Perry et al., 1986; Ursano, Sonnenberg, & Lazar, 1998). In so doing, the therapist explores with the client the primary concerns addressed in each school of thought. This "psychodynamic listening" (Ursano et al., 1998, p. 35) is summarized in Table 3.1.

In summary, psychodynamic theories, having evolved from Freud's psychoanalytic theory, have emerged primarily through four schools of thought. Proponents of the first school, drive theory, emphasized the role of drives in psychological life. Those of the second, ego psychology, emphasized the ego's ability to manage drives. Those of the third, object relations, emphasized how the person develops through early experience with objects. Those of the fourth, self psychology, emphasized the development and treatment of the self, a larger, broader structure/function than the mere ego. Following is a biographical overview of Heinz Kohut, who developed self psychology.

Founder's Biographical Overview

Born in Vienna on May 3, 1913, Heinz Kohut was an only child. His parents treated him as especially talented. World War I took his highly cultured father, Felix, away for Heinz's first five years, during which time Heinz lived with his mother, Else, and her parents. Although his father returned from the war physically, he apparently remained absent psychologically (Strozier, 1985).

In her relationship with Heinz, Else seemed to alternate between oppressive closeness and distance. Since his parents maintained busy social lives, Kohut reported a sad and intensely lonely childhood. Nonetheless, "there was something deep and abiding between Heinz and his mother, whatever the residues of ambivalence" (Strozier, 1985, pp. 4–5).

Even by the Viennese elite's high standards, Heinz's education was remarkable. Beginning with two years of private tutoring, he proceeded to the Doblinger Gymnasium where he studied Latin for eight years and Greek for eight, in addition to French, history, athletics, and more. At the age of 19, he attended the University of Vienna, where he completed his medical degree in 1938.

Kohut enjoyed telling the story of his only encounter with Freud. It was June 4, 1938, and Freud and his entourage were departing from Vienna for England to flee Nazi persecution. As the train was leaving, Kohut could see Freud looking out the window. Kohut tipped his hat to Freud, who returned the gesture as the train departed. This contact with Freud left an indelible impression on the young Kohut, who sensed a certain mission he was to serve in the history of psychoanalysis (Strozier, 1985).

In 1940, Kohut also emigrated from Austria. Arriving in Chicago, Illinois with only 25 cents to his name, Kohut secured an internship at a small hospital and, later, a coveted residency in neurology at the University of Chicago. In 1947, he began to focus exclusively on psychiatry. It appears that he was consciously modeling himself after Freud: "There was, in other words, an early sense of purpose in Kohut, an inner fire and lofty ambition to be Freud's successor, long before those thoughts had any basis in actuality" (Strozier, 1985, p. 7).

Kohut spent the majority of his life in Chicago, enthusiastically teaching and training analysts and maintaining a full clinical practice until he died in 1981 (Goldberg, 1989). Throughout the 1960s, he proudly bore the title "Mr. Psychoanalysis" and was the most eminent spokesperson for traditional psychoanalysis (Strozier, 1985), serving as president of the American Psychoanalytic Association (1964–1965), vice president of the International Psychoanalytic Association (1965–1973), and vice president of the Sigmund Freud Archives (1971–1981).

However, after the 1971 publication of *The Analysis of the Self,* he tended to elicit extreme reactions from the psychoanalytic community—from abject devotion to contemptuous disregard (Strozier, 1985). Whereas many colleagues simply withdrew from him, some viciously attacked his bold new ideas. These reactions genuinely hurt Kohut, who never completely reconciled himself to them. The orthodoxy of classical psychoanalysis was a gargantuan opponent, and Kohut's fortitude was emotionally costly. However, despite his difficult struggles, Kohut always persevered with humor and playfulness (Strozier, 1985).

In formulating self psychology, Kohut created a new theory of how the self develops, how that development can go awry, and how therapists can treat the resulting disturbances. Although he authored only three books, many mental health experts consider them to be among the most important contributions anyone has made to the professional psychodynamic literature (Strauss, Yager, & Strauss, 1984). Even John Gedo, Kohut's first apostate, wrote that "Kohut's personal contribution to psychoanalysis was so important that in the past two decades all pioneering work in the field deserves to be called 'post-Kohutian'" (Gedo, 1989, p. 415). Prior to his death at the age of 68, Kohut also wrote on the application of psychoanalytic formulations to the understanding of a variety of phenomena: music, literature, creativity, humor, group psychology, charisma, and wisdom (Akhtar, 1989).

Kohut became increasingly humanistic at a time when humanism was on the rise in U.S. culture. However, he actually worked in relative isolation and disclaimed most influence from other theorists or from the Zeitgeist of the time. Like Carl Rogers, with whom Kohut was not affiliated but whose theory shows striking similarity to Kohut's, Kohut maintained consistently that he developed his ideas out of his own professional experience with his clients.

Philosophical Underpinnings

"Kohut has been a theorist in perpetual transition," according to Greenberg and Mitchell (1983, p. 357). They divided his work into three phases that corresponded to his philosophical evolution. In his classical phase, prior to 1971, his ideas aligned with those of psychoanalysis, including philosophical concepts of determinism: people are at the mercy of their biological drives and childhood experiences that, together, determine adult personality; and objectivity: the best way for one person to understand another is as a distant, uninvolved observer.

In Kohut's second, transitional phase, from 1971 to 1977, he began to conceptualize the self. With that conceptualization, he began to shift philosophically.

That shift culminated in his third, radical phase, in which he departed from psychoanalysis and aligned philosophically with humanism. In this philosophical transition, he criticized psychoanalysts' mechanistic focus, which he believed caused them to miss the vital aspects of their own and their clients' human experience. He supplanted a belief in determinism with a belief in a fundamental human tendency to proactively overcome developmental arrests and mature into one's potential, while he continued to affirm the tendency for a person to be powerfully influenced, but not determined, by one's biology and environment. He also supplanted a belief in objectivity in favor of subjectivity: that the best way for someone to understand a phenomenon is to enter it; that knowing a phenomenon inescapably involves subjective, personally unique perception; that, indeed, objectivity is impossible because the very act of observing a phenomenon changes the phenomenon; that both the clinical and theoretical domains of psychoanalysis are defined and demarcated by that which is accessible to empathy and introspection, neither of which are objective. He expressed this shift in his realization in the 1950s that *reality per se, whether extrospective or introspective, is unknowable; we can only describe what we see within the framework of what we have done to see it*" (Kohut, 1982, p. 400). He reflected these shifts in his psychotherapeutic system by emphasizing not biological but social urges in humans, not clients' pathology but their developmental potentials, not a negative view of clients' lifelong irrational drives but a positive view of their lifelong legitimate psychological needs, not a therapeutic stance of distant objectivity about clients but one of experience-near subjectivity with clients, and not insight about clients but empathy for and with them as curative of their psychological disorders.

A feel for the shift Kohut underwent is reflected in his criticism that psychoanalysts' mechanistic view of the psyche missed the vital aspects of human experience. He contended that analysts should focus not on a client's drives themselves but on a client's *experience* of drives. He advocated a profoundly phenomenological approach, what he called "experience near," in which the therapist should be close to the client's subjective experience—in fact, enter into it—to avoid "experience distant" *empiricide,* that is, killing that which is most human through the objectification of human experience (cited in Masek, 1989, p. 184). In his last paper, he likened the experience-distant approach of drive theorists, with their focus on a client's drives at the expense of understanding how the client's self experiences drives, to an attempt to understand a painting by merely analyzing its pigments. Kohut maintained that the *meanings* of drives and conflicts *emerge only from the perspective of the self* (Greenberg & Mitchell, 1983). Although Kohut still viewed interpretation of transference as essential to therapy, he believed that effective interpretation required not the neutral, experiential abstinence of the objective, distant scientist-observer but, rather, an experientially rich introspective and empathic inquiry—a process of being experience-near.

PERSONALITY DEVELOPMENT

Nature of Humans

Structure of the Psyche

In discussing psychic structure, Kohut (1984) admonished his readers to remember that theorized structures are not actual things but conceptual tools that help people understand and communicate ideas. To increase the likelihood that readers would maintain this awareness, Stolorow, Brandchaft, and Atwood (1987) presented Kohut's theorized "structures," such as the self, as *functions* or *dimensions of experience*. To help you keep this disclaimer in mind as you read the following material, we use the term *structure/function*.

According to self psychology, at birth, the infant's psyche consists of a continuous onslaught of immediate experiences—disorganized, unmanaged, unregulated, and lacking cohesion. The infant is born with the potential to develop a psychological structure/ function that Kohut (1977) called the self: "the center of the individual's psychological universe" (p. 311), a recipient of impressions and a center of initiative that provides a person cohesion, organization, and continuity in space and time (Kohut, 1984). The self is the consistent sense of identity, the "I" that brings a sense of organization to perception and action. Although each person has the potential for a fully developed self, different people realize that potential to varying degrees, for reasons that we will explain below.

Beyond the basic ability to organize experience in a manner characterized by a cohesive and continuous sense of identity, Kohut's concept of self also included three poles. One's *nuclear ambition* is comprised of one's general desire and level of initiative to achieve goals. One's *talents and skills* consist of the resources one brings to the achievement of goals. One's *guiding ideals* consist of the final goals one aspires to achieve. For example, Jane is a young adult who has a cohesive, consistent sense of "I" that enables her to organize, regulate, and manage her experiences. She has a high level of nuclear ambition, desire, and initiative; her talents include extremely good interpersonal skills, psychological mindedness, and understanding of counseling theory; and, among several guiding ideals, one is to be of substantial service to others by becoming a highly effective counselor.

Kohut differentiated the self from the personality. The personality consists of relatively persistent feelings and actions. For example, if I feel anxious much of the time, anxiety is one of my personality characteristics. If I usually behave outspokenly, or quietly, that typical behavior characterizes my personality. But chronic feelings and habitual actions are not as central to one's experience as one's sense of reality, of initiative, of identity. These latter features—the "I" that *experiences* feeling anxious and behaving in a particular way—constitute the self that underlies the personality characteristics of relatively persistent feelings and actions.

Another way to understand the concept of the self is by contrast to Freud's concept of the ego. In psychoanalysis, the ego is an essentially reactive juggler constantly challenged to manage three balls with minds of their own: the id with its irrational demands for gratification, the superego with its irrational demands for perfection, and the environment with its demands of reality. Whereas Freud's ego was reactive, seeking merely to keep the balls under control, Kohut's self was proactively and creatively imagining and seeking to achieve goals, to do more than a basic juggling act. Another point of comparison is that whereas the idealistic superego was fundamentally different than and separate from the ego, Kohut's self included guiding ideals. Overall, whereas Freud's concept of psychic structure consisted of aggregates in conflict, Kohut's consisted of a single, more unified, purposeful structure/function, though not without its own internal tensions.

Function of the Psyche

From the perspective of self psychology, the primary function of each human being is to relate with other human beings. Kohut affirmed the existence of biological and psychological drives. However, like object relations theorists, he saw drives not as primary to psychological life but rather as secondary, serving to establish and ensure continuation of what is primary to each person: *relationship*. Thus, self psychology is essentially a social psychology. It is based on the contention that humans do not relate with others as one means to reduce the pressure of drives; rather, humans have drives to ensure that they will continually relate with others.

Self and Selfobjects   Relating with others is not only the purpose of psychological life; it is the means for achieving the fundamental lifelong human need: to develop and maintain a self. For Kohut, the self actually is several interrelated *intrapsychic functions* that include organizing experience and restoring psychological cohesion that has been jeopardized; validating subjective experience; maintaining homeostasis through tension regulation, the soothing of physical and emotional distress; and esteeming one's abilities and felt-sense of "I" (Bacal, 1990; Kohut, 1971). The infant, overwhelmed with a cacophonous onslaught of experience, is not innately endowed with these functions. He is, however, born with the ability to form bonds with selfobjects and, through those bonds, develop those functions. *Selfobjects* are external objects (usually people) that an individual subjectively experiences as providing one or more intrapsychic functions. Beginning in infancy and throughout life, one naturally feels an emotional connection and a desire for continued interaction with selfobjects, what Kohut called the self–selfobject bond/relationship.

Transmuting Internalization   Beginning at birth, as the infant experiences selfobjects providing its intrapsychic functions, the infant has the potential to develop the ability to provide those functions for oneself via a process called *transmuting internalization*. In this process, the infant and, later, child slowly, gradually, bit by bit, transform the external selfobjects' capacities to provide one's intrapsychic functions into one's own internal capacities. These capacities comprise the structure/function of the self (Kohut, 1977).

Kohut described transmuting internalization as a type of psychological metabolism, analogous to physical metabolism, in which the physical system breaks food down and absorbs and integrates aspects of it, usually fulfilling physical needs. Analogously, in psychological metabolism, the psychological system absorbs and integrates selfobject experiences such that they become one's own internal capabilities. Kohut contrasted this process with the psychoanalytic concept of identification in which one internalizes an entire person.

Kohut elaborated on some specific selfobject experiences that constitute the "food" of psychological metabolism. In the following material, we will discuss each type along with an example. It is important to keep in mind that just as an infant initially takes in physical food and digests and metabolizes it nonconsciously, an infant also metabolizes psychological food—selfobject experiences—initially in a nonconscious, nonrational, organismic way. Then, throughout life, although a person usually becomes more conscious of intake, one continues to digest and absorb nutrients nonconsciously. This explanation does not mean that a person cannot or should not understand the digestion process; on the contrary, one can come to understand physical digestion and, as a result, choose foods more purposely and healthfully. Nevertheless, one continues to be mostly unaware of the digestion process as it occurs. Analogously, one can come to understand the metabolism of psychological nutrients and, as a result, choose potential selfobjects more purposely and healthfully. Nevertheless, people are often unaware of transmuting internalization as it occurs.

As we said, Kohut conceptualized the self as consisting of three poles—like the three points of a triangle. As primary caretakers meet each of three of a child's innate selfobject needs—as well as a fourth that pervades all three poles—the corresponding poles of the child's self develop.

1. Empathic Attunement and Empathic Mirroring The first innate human selfobject need, which emerges at birth and lasts throughout life, is for empathic attunement and empathic mirroring. Empathy is "intrinsically [comprehending] the experience of others from their own unique perspective, which is often very different from 'what I would feel if I were actually in their place'" (Baker & Baker, 1987, p. 2). In empathic attunement and mirroring, the infant's caretaker accurately perceives the infant's emotional states and emerging abilities and responds with acceptance, validation, admiration, and caring action. An example is a father who always enjoyed the taste of bananas but finds that when he introduces his infant daughter to mashed bananas, she grimaces. Despite the fact that he himself has never disliked bananas, when he sees her grimace, he empathizes by looking at her; by grimacing as if his face were a mirror reflecting her facial expression; by saying "Oooh! You don't like that!" in a way that expresses understanding, affirmation, even pride in her knowing and expressing herself; and by discontinuing to feed her the bananas. Through transmuting internationalization in repeated similar experiences, the infant comes to differentiate certain aspects of experience that a more mature self might label as "not liking things," "avoiding not-liked things," and "the taste of bananas" and to organize these aspects of experience into a broader category of commodities and activities that are and are not liked.

Another aspect of empathic mirroring occurs when the child perceives that her primary caretakers (usually her parents) respond to her developing abilities, such as the ability to crawl, with delight and pride, which they convey verbally and/or nonverbally. "The gleam in the mother's eye" (Baker & Baker, 1987, p. 3) is a nonverbal example of a parental response that communicates a sense of value and self-worth to the child. It is natural that, at first, the child will respond to such mirroring with grandiosity, a sense of unbounded esteem and omnipotence. It is as if the child thinks, "I am wonderful! I can do anything!" However, with ongoing empathic attunement and mirroring experiences, the child will develop a more moderate and realistic matrix of responses that comprises one aspect of self, specifically, *the self pole of nuclear ambition*: the child's core sense of motivation and initiative to achieve goals. However, when parents respond with chronic indifference, hostility, or excessive criticism, the reflection of self the child receives lacks a sense of worth, and the child is likely to show a decreased sense of self-esteem and decreased self-assertive ambitions.

2. Idealization A second innate selfobject need is idealization. Beginning in somewhat older infancy, the child needs to perceive in at least one other person an image of greatness, all-powerfulness, and all-knowingness with which the child can connect and merge. Kohut called this image the "idealized parental imago." Kohut believed that children, being less competent to function in the world, tend naturally to perceive primary caretakers as omniscient and omnipotent. When they are not disabused of this perception, they have their need for idealization met, and the groundwork is laid for the child's development of *the self pole of guiding ideals*: the child creates an internal image of, and strives to become, more than she currently is, an image of an ideal.

3. Twinship A third innate selfobject need is for the experience of twinship. Also called alter ego needs, twinship needs refer to an individual's "need to experience the presence of essential alikeness" (Kohut, 1984, p. 194). Research suggests that this need emerges developmentally last, at approximately 18 months of age (Kriegman & Solomon, 1985, p. 245). When the child perceives opportunities to perform tasks and carry out responsibilities like her idealized parental imago, she feels her twinship need met. Fulfillment of this need may take a form as simple as a parent allowing one's child to join in raking leaves or dusting furniture. Fulfillment of this need contributes to the development of the child's *self pole of talents and skills.*

Kohut (1984) underscored the strength of a child's need to develop a self by asserting that the child who does not receive mirroring responses from primary caretakers will intensify the search for idealizing or twinship experiences. Kohut likened this tendency to a tree's ability to grow around obstacles that prevent its exposure to the sun's life-sustaining rays. In addition, to the extent that a child is unable to meet any of these needs, one will proceed to seek to meet them relatively more intently throughout adulthood. If the person seeks therapy, one's relatively intent pursuit of fulfillment of a particular need will emerge as a particular type of transference.

In a way, fulfillment of the three selfobject needs provides the sane foundation for a well-developed sense of self. Without the three pillars of empathic attunement and mirroring, idealization, and twinship, a stable sense of self cannot develop. No sane, no gain (of a self).

4. Optimal Empathic Failures Kohut believed humans must meet one additional need in order to complete the process of transmuting internalization and, thus, form a self. He termed this need *optimal empathic failures.* In a way that at first might seem paradoxical, these "beneficial" failures occur in the context of a well-established self–selfobject relationship, when a young child experiences the selfobject failing to empathize in some mild, nontraumatic way. In the temporary absence of a selfobject fulfilling a child's particular need, the child gradually acquires the ability to fulfill it oneself. For example, a little boy is routinely terrified when he sees a monster in a certain TV commercial. His mother usually notices his fear and comforts, consoles, and reassures him that the monster cannot hurt him and that he is safe. Then one day, just as this commercial is broadcasting, the mother must turn her complete attention to an urgent phone call. The young boy, in the absence of his mother's optimal empathic mirroring, has only himself to provide him comfort, which he is capable of doing to some extent.

Optimal empathic failures can also include idealization and twinship failures. Occasional mild disillusionment in the all-powerfulness of selfobjects fosters one to create and rely on an internal ideal. Occasional failures in twinship provide an opportunity for one to develop one's talents and skills on one's own—perhaps in creative ways that even surpass those of the selfobject.

The more "optimal opportunities" a child has (occasionally rather than chronically and mild rather than intense) the more fully he will be able to perform tasks intrapsychically himself that he formerly relied on his selfobjects to perform for him. Adults express an understanding of this process when they comment ruefully that they've learned and matured the most as a result of their most challenging life experiences: No pain, no gain (of a self).

Selfobject Needs Throughout Life   In summary, through the selfobject's empathic responsiveness to the child's needs, and the child's participation in the selfobject's organized experience, the self gradually develops (St. Clair, 2000). People never outgrow their selfobject needs. Recall that selfobjects refer to any aspect of any thing or person that fulfills self functions. Thus, it is natural that, throughout life, external selfobjects evolve, typically from caretakers in one's infancy, to teachers during primary school years, to peers during later childhood and adolescence, and to spouse, boss, colleagues, even one's culture, in adulthood.

In addition to the innate tendency for selfobjects to evolve through various forms, the nature of the needs themselves—their form and intensity—also evolve. All very young children are absolute, archaic, and global in their insistence for unceasing selfobject fulfillment. As transmuting internalization occurs, one becomes increasingly capable of doing for oneself what others used to do, including the ability to organize, understand, and validate one's own experience; to respond nurturingly to one's own feelings—to celebrate when elated, to soothe oneself when distressed; and to esteem oneself. As the self thus develops, one becomes less demanding on external selfobjects to provide fulfillment, that is, one requires less frequent, intense, and blatant external response, although the seeking for selfobjects never completely disappears—nor should it.

In this section, we have addressed the inborn functions—the drives, needs, tendencies, and processes—that play a role in a person's psychological development throughout life. For some infants, specific innate conditions, such as temperament and physical or mental handicap, complicate the likelihood that the infant will be able to fulfill its selfobject needs. We will address these conditions in more detail below.

Role of the Environment

Familial

By now, it is probably clear to you that, from a self psychology perspective, a child's family usually plays the most central role in development of the child's self. The child is most likely to perceive selfobjects among her primary caretakers—those who interact most frequently with her and actually fulfill her intrapsychic needs. The child can perceive empathic attunement/mirroring only in people who actually express it, can perceive idealization only in people who actually offer themselves as ideals, and can perceive twinship only in people who actually provide opportunities for the child to perform tasks and carry out responsibilities similar to themselves. The extent to which caretakers provide empathy, idealization, and twinship are crucial factors in the child's self development.

In addition, empathic failures are inevitable occurrences in a child's environment. However, the extent to which such failures are optimal (mild, occasional, and occurring in the context of an established self–selfobject relationship, thereby facilitating the child's self development) or suboptimal (severe, chronic, and occurring outside the context of a well-established self-selfobject relationship, thereby hindering the child's self from developing) clearly plays a formative role.

Kohut observed and theorized in a cultural environment very different from that of Freud. Since the Victorian era, family structures had loosened and family interactions had reduced. These changes created the conditions for a higher incidence of what Kohut termed disorders of the self: narcissistic, borderline, and psychotic disorders. Perhaps Freud had not theorized about such individuals with these disorders because fewer such individuals existed. Conversely, as Kohut encountered more such clients, he experienced the need to develop an understanding of them (St. Clair, 2000).

Extrafamilial

Any aspect of a thing or person that or who fulfills one or more of a child's self functions, whether within or outside of the family, is a selfobject. As previously stated, selfobjects tend to change as a person develops, moving from caretakers in the original family to include such people as peers and teachers in the wider social environment and then to include a spouse or partner in the created family. For many people, less personal aspects of culture can serve as selfobjects. Information from newspapers can help one make sense of events, and both fictional characters and public figures can provide idealization and even twinship for the ongoing structure/function of one's self.

Model of Mental Health

Healthy Functioning

> Self psychology holds that self-selfobject relationships form the essence of psychological life from birth to death, that a move from dependence (symbiosis) to independence (autonomy) in the psychological sphere is no more possible, let alone desirable, than a corresponding move from a life dependent on oxygen to a life independent of it in the biological sphere. The developments that characterize normal psychological life must, in our view, be seen in *the changing nature* of the relationship between the self and its selfobjects [italics added]. (Kohut, 1984, p. 47)

When an infant or young child's innate needs for selfobject relationships that provide empathic attunement and mirroring, idealization, twinship, and optimal empathic failure are met with an environment that meets those needs, then, through transmuting internalization, the young child will develop the structure/function of a self. Thus, she can increasingly meet her own needs, becoming less intensely needful, though never independent, of external selfobjects. This process is summarized in Figure 3.1.

Under ideal conditions, the child's mirrored grandiosity becomes more realistic, and the child channels it into plausible ambitions; the self is characterized by vitality for life and life undertakings. Similarly, the child introjects the idealized parental imago, which emerges as one's values and ideals (St. Clair, 2000). Following suit, the child's experiences of twinship transform into her talents and skills, which she enlists in the pursuit of her ambitions and ideals.

Kohut (1984) insisted that no one ever completely outgrows the need for selfobjects. To support this contention, he cited how the artist Picasso, the philosopher Nietzsche, and Kohut's own conceptual mentor, Freud, relied on selfobjects, particularly during episodes of intense creativity and intense self-questioning and self-doubt. With this contention, Kohut defied Western culture's tendency to equate mental health with physical and emotional autonomy. Rather, Kohut asserted that in healthy development, the *quality* of one's selfobject needs change from absolute demands to more moderate, mature, resilient, and realistic desires. A healthy self is one that, except in the midst of extreme circumstances, is relatively cohesive and that the individual experiences as balanced, whole, continuous, organized, strong, and harmoniously vigorous. In addition, a person with a well-developed self knows how to select, establish, and utilize relationships to fulfill one's selfobject needs (Baker, 1991). Since the healthy individual can, to a great extent, fulfill

| Establishment of selfobject bond | → | Fulfillment of four selfobject needs | → | Transmuting internalization | → | Formation of self-structure/function |

FIGURE 3.1   Sequence in development of healthy self.

selfobject needs internally, and because, consequently, one's dependence on external others to fulfill those needs is reduced, one does not need others to be continuously empathically attuned to him; he can, so to speak, psychologically afford to see others as separate and different from himself. Thus is born one's own ability to empathize: "to intrinsically comprehend the experience of others *from their own unique perspective*" [italics added] (Baker & Baker, 1987, p. 2).

Anticipating a "so what" response from people learning about his theory, Kohut (1984) remarked,

> What an anticlimax! The reader may well think. Indeed, what a seemingly insipid, everyday occurrence compared to the drama of the primal scene, of the child's sexual excitement and death wishes, that Freud wrested from the unconscious. Perhaps so, but I would point out that dramatic excitement and truth value do not necessarily go hand in hand. The self sustenance that a little girl might get from silently working in the kitchen next to her grandmother, that a little boy might get from shaving next to his daddy or from working next to his daddy with daddy's tools in the basement; these are indeed undramatic everyday events. The drama ensues or, more correctly, the tragedy ensues when a child is chronically deprived of such experiences. (p. 197)

Hopefully, you can forgive Kohut for the sexist flavor of his remark and hear his belief in the critical nature of selfobject need fulfillment for the formation of the self.

Unhealthy Functioning

It follows, then, that when an infant's or young child's caretakers are neglectful and/or abusive, exhibiting physical and/or emotional indifference and/or hostility, the child's self-development proceeds quite differently. In neglect and abuse, the child experiences chronic and traumatic empathic failures and thus perceives little or no empathy, nothing or no one to idealize, and little or no opportunity for twinship. Thus, the child does not bond with caretakers and, consequently, does not form—or forms tenuous—selfobject relationships in which the child experiences no or little fulfillment of selfobject needs. Since optimal empathic failures occur, by definition, in the context of well-established selfobject relationships, the child with neglectful and/or abusive caretakers experiences such failures infrequently or not at all. In turn, the child's self remains undeveloped and/or its fledgling development is arrested or reversed.

Baker and Baker (1987) likened the psychological development of the self to the physical development of muscles. Optimal empathic failures comprise a kind of resistance, and some resistance adds bulk, whereas chronic, severe empathic failures are like extreme physical strain in the absence of conditioning and strength, a kind of "excess [that] exhausts, or can even tear, the muscle" (p. 4).

Kohut believed that when primary caregivers chronically fail to meet the child's selfobject needs, the child will develop a less-than-optimal self and will exhibit psychopathology. It is important to note that severe self disorders result only if all three selfobject functions are chronically absent. Yet Kohut believed that the single greatest contributor to people's psychopathology was their primary caretakers' failures to empathize with them. Stolorow et al. (1987) focused even more specifically on what they called "reliable affect attunement" (p. 87): Even a person's most fundamental ability to experience and acknowledge her feelings, rather than dissociate from or disavow them, depends on her having experienced, as an infant and young child, primary caretakers who provided a steady, attuned responsiveness to her ever-changing emotions. Thus it is that, later in life, people are emotionally crippled *not* by "the unconscious fear of forbidden erotic love that generates anxiety," wrote M. Basch in reference to psychoanalytic theory, but by "the anticipation of reexperiencing the devastating, potentially disintegrating disappointment of early empathic failures if they dare once again reach for emotional fulfillment" (cited in Baker & Baker, 1987, p. 7).

Kohut posited that the earlier and more extensively the child experienced empathic failures, the more severe the psychopathology. Thus, a person develops psychosis as a result of experiencing the earliest and most extensive empathic failures on the part of caretakers, develops borderline conditions as a result of somewhat later and/or less extensive failures, develops narcissism as a result of yet later and/or less extensive failures, and develops neuroses as a result of even later and/or even less extensive failures. These mental disorders reflect degrees of self-development.

The person suffering from a psychosis has not yet developed a self. The person's contact with consensus reality, the reality shared by most people, is impaired by their delusions, "false belief[s] based on incorrect inference about external reality that [are] firmly sustained despite what almost everyone else believes and despite what constitutes incontrovertible and obvious proof or evidence to the contrary" (APA, 2000, p. 765), and/or hallucinations, "sensory perceptions[s] that [have] the compelling sense of reality of a true perception but that [occur] without external stimulation of the relevant sensory organ[s]" (p. 767). From a self psychology perspective, delusions and hallucinations are among the self-defenses a person generated in response to frequent, severe empathic failures.

The person suffering from a borderline personality disorder has only the most tenuous and remote sense of a self. Such a person exhibits "a pervasive pattern of instability of interpersonal relationships, self-image, and affects, and marked impulsivity that begins by early adulthood and is present in a variety of contexts" (p. 650). One symptom people with borderline disorders generate in response to the frequent, severe empathic failures they perceive is splitting the perception of another person as either all good or all bad.

People who suffer from narcissistic disorders have a vague and unstable outline of a self. Kohut's description of narcissistic clients is quite different from that in the *DSM–IV–TR* (APA, 2000). He agreed that such clients may exhibit grandiosity, may lack empathy, and may desire admiration. However, he noted a more common fragile manifestation in which the person feels emptiness and boredom (lacks feelings of worth, zest, humor, and meaning) none of which the authors of *DSM–IV–TR* mentioned in the section on narcissism. Thus, Kohut (1971) included in his conceptualization "circumscribed defects in self-esteem or self-esteem regulations, or broad disturbances in the patient's systems of ideals" (p. 22). Narcissistic individuals are unable to esteem themselves and thus live ever archaically, vigilant for cues from others to use in evaluating their own self-worth. What appears to an outsider as an inconsequential, minor insult, an individual with narcissism is likely to experience as an overwhelmingly negative evaluation of one's very being, resulting in either depression or *disintegration anxiety,* which Kohut (1984) argued was "the deepest anxiety man [*sic*] can experience" (p. 16). In this circumstance, this vulnerable person will employ any behavior that wards off the impending sense of annihilation—most commonly some form of withdrawal or rage—even if that behavior is ultimately self-destructive.

Finally, with regard to a person with some form of neurosis, such a person has developed a sense of self, but it is characterized by rather pervasive internal conflict. As we noted previously, traditional psychoanalysts focused on treating these types of disorders.

In each of these disorders, the person somehow strives for fulfillment in relatively archaic, immature ways (St. Clair, 2000). Self-psychologists view most symptomatic behavior as the person's best attempt to avoid intolerable emotions and to regain some sense of self-cohesion, self-comforting, and self-worth (Baker, 1991). For example, the (grandiose) narcissist who repeatedly demands admiration and praise for his professed greatness does so because, deep down, he feels empty and incompetent; by receiving positive "strokes" from others—who are functioning as selfobjects for him—he temporarily is able to avoid the painful emotions that often plague him.

Although Kohut blamed psychopathology predominantly on early chronic and/ or severe empathic failures, he did not intend to blame primary caretakers for their empathic failures. He believed caretakers enacted such failures for a variety of reasons that self-psychologists could understand by, again, employing their empathy. For example, even relatively able caretakers will likely be challenged to maintain consistent empathic attunement if the child in their care is extraordinarily needy, having severe physical or mental disabilities; if the caretakers' and child's temperaments are extremely discrepant; or if caretakers are functioning under harsh environmental circumstances such as the chronic stressors of war or poverty. In addition, caretakers themselves may be severely limited in their ability to empathize due to their own psychopathology (Baker & Baker, 1987; Kohut, 1984). Kohut implied that primary caretakers frequently feel challenged to access adequate self-resources, and although they are responsible for the role they play in the psychopathology of the children for whom they care, they are struggling under some burden of their own and, thus, do not deserve indiscriminant blame or criticism. In summary, Kohut's purpose in theorizing about caretakers' roles in the psychopathology of their children was less to focus blame on parents than to help counselors understand how their clients developed psychopathology and understand the challenges counselors face in providing clients what they missed in their processes of self-development.

THE PERSONALITY CHANGE PROCESS

Kohut disagreed with Freud's view of the essence of change, to make the client's unconscious conscious, or "where id was, there shall ego be" (cited in Kohut, 1984, p. 103). Rather, from a self psychology perspective, change throughout life involves a person developing one's self, and it occurs through the same process that occurs in an ideal childhood (Kohut, 1971). Therapeutic life experiences involve self–selfobject relationships in which one continues to experience empathic attunement and empathic mirroring, idealization, twinship, and optimal empathic failures and, through transmuting internalization, comes increasingly, but never exclusively, to meet one's own self-needs.

The difficulty is that the individual most in need of this experience is least able to manifest it for oneself. For person A, with a poorly developed self, to establish and sustain a healthy relationship with person B, person B must have unusual insight, patience, and persistence—the characteristics of an unusually well-developed self—with which to meet person A's relatively demanding selfobject needs and her tendency to notice even the slightest empathic failure and perceive it as catastrophic. Occasional empathic failure may be inevitable in even the healthiest relationship, but in the relationship between persons A and B, person A is highly likely to experience it as a reenactment of the traumatic empathic failures of childhood—and respond with the archaic emotions of a child. In addition, because person A is powerfully invested in her own selfobject needs, she is less able to perceive and respond to even the moderate and realistic selfobject needs of person B. The more severe the disorder of person A's self, the more well-developed person B's self must be for the relationship to endure. In addition, a manifestation of person B's healthy self is that she exercises discrimination in close personal relationships, involving herself only in those relationships in which she experiences appropriate—that is, moderate, reciprocal—selfobject need fulfillment. Thus, she is less likely to establish or maintain the relatively more one-way relationship with person A. For these reasons, the more severe is person A's immaturity of self, the less likely she will be to find and secure therapeutic life experiences for herself and the more her hope for self-development rests in professional psychotherapy.

For Kohut, the organizing principle of the psychotherapeutic process can be thought of as reparenting, whereby the therapist provides selfobject functions for the client that the client's primary caretakers did not provide. In this process, the therapist communicates consistent empathic attunement and mirroring. In response, the client initially perceives the therapist as a consistent selfobject, forms a self–selfobject relationship with the therapist, and allows the establishment of selfobject transference(s): seeking—in fact, demanding—that the therapist meet not only the reasonable, moderate selfobject needs of a developmentally mature adult but also the client's unmet archaic selfobject needs. In the basic therapeutic process (a) the client experiences a reactivation of previously unmet needs and both looks to and finds fulfillment by the therapist (selfobject transference), (b) the counselor then occasionally does not fulfill some client needs (optimal frustration/empathic failure), and (c) the counselor (selfobject) and client (self) reestablish the empathic bond. This sequence must occur many, many times throughout the course of therapy until the client not only acquires a stable perception of the counselor as a selfobject who is reasonably consistent in meeting the clients needs but, even more importantly, the client very gradually develops an increasing ability to meet his own needs.

An important component in the therapeutic process is the therapist's interpretations: communications to the client about the therapist's understanding of the client's psychological dynamics. Unintentionally, but inevitably, the therapist will make an inaccurate interpretation that does not match the client's experience. These misinterpretations constitute empathic failures, which the transference-laden client experiences as reenactments of traumatic empathic failures from early life, and thus to which she reacts with emotional intensity: the sum of the current pain plus all the associated pain of the past. If the ensuing process is to be therapeutic, the therapist must respond to this emotional intensity by remaining empathically attuned. As a result, the client experiences reestablishment of the self–selfobject relationship. In addition, feeling understood, attended to, and nurtured even in response to extreme emotional reactions, the client will likely take a step in understanding and nurturing oneself the next time one perceives another person failing to empathize. In this way, the client enacts transmuting internalization: fulfilling self-functions for oneself that one previously had demanded the therapist and other selfobjects fulfill.

With numerous repetitions of the last step in the therapeutic process, the client gradually develops an increasingly coherent and cohesive self. As one's self develops, one's behavior in relationships changes, marked by a decrease in demanding insistence and in disproportionate emotional reactivity and an increase in the capacity for selfobject reciprocity. This reciprocity occurs first in a client's relationship with the therapist, and then with other selfobjects in the client's life.

To separate the client's and therapist's roles in this process is difficult because, from a self psychotherapeutic perspective, effective elements of the therapy are intersubjective and involve the interplay of both the client's and the therapist's subjective perceptions. Nevertheless, in the following two sections, we attempt to tease apart the two respective roles.

Client's Role

Most clients seek counseling for relief from suffering that, from the self-psychologist's point of view, is a manifestation of one or more disorders of the self. The client's suffering may take any number of forms: feelings of emptiness—their lives seem to lack zest, joy, humor, meaning, and purpose; feelings of anxiety, depression, or fragmented instability; feeling satisfied or worthwhile only when others respond to them in certain ways; an inability to maintain intimate relationships; hypersensitivity to perceived slights; difficulties in concentration; consequences of addictive behaviors such as gambling, drugs, or sex clients use to ward off distressing feelings; or hypochondria, insomnia, irritability, phobias, or obsessive-compulsive disorders (Bacal, 1990). However, from the self-psychologist's point of view, underlying all these symptoms is the client's central motive: the search for a selfobject with whom to have experiences that contribute to the development of the client's self.

Transference

Regarding clients' potential for change, Kohut was generally optimistic. He believed that, provided that their selfobjects are affectively attuned and empathically responsive, people with disorders of the self are capable of resuming their arrested development. Kohut (1971) referred to the establishment of selfobject transference as the client's primary responsibility in therapy. For a transferential relationship to develop, a client must be willing to allow the therapist to become psychologically important to him, as well as to persevere through the process of empathic failure and repair, which, in turn, enables the client to reactivate, and experience fulfillment of, needs that went unmet during his development.

Kohut viewed selfobject transference as the soil from which therapeutic progress could grow. Stolorow et al. (1987) described transference as "the tidal wave of the past that washes over the present, leaving its unmistakable residues" (p. 28). They also wrote that it refers to:

> all the ways in which the patient's experience of the analytic relationship is shaped by his own psychological structures—by the distinctive, archaically rooted configurations of self and object that unconsciously organize his subjective universe ... an expression of the universal psychological striving to organize experience and create meanings. (Stolorow et al., 1987, pp. 36, 46)

As such, the client, to use Piaget's (1970) term and concept, *assimilates* the therapist into his existing conceptual structure, shaving off the therapist's uniqueness and perceiving her as fitting the mold of previous selfobjects, rather than *accommodating* his conceptual structure, that is, modifying it to include the uniqueness of the therapist as a separate individual on whom the client can rely to be reasonably selfobject need-fulfilling, the latter process being a function of a healthy self.

Selfobject transference involves the reactivation in therapy of those client needs that the client's selfobjects in early life did not meet (Kohut & Wolf, 1978). Stolorow et al. (1987) believed selfobject transference is not a type of transference but, rather, a dimension of all transferences.

In self psychotherapy, clients enact transference in one or more of three primary ways. In *mirroring*, the client tries to elicit approval and affirmation (mirroring of his worth) from the therapist. For example, a client may try to maximize his therapist's affirmations and validations by denying the importance of ongoing problems. In *idealizing*, the client idealizes and seeks to merge with the therapist. An example is a client who consistently conceives of her therapist as perfect and no longer having to struggle with "problems of living"; consequently her goals in therapy are unrealistic: to be free from any difficulties whatsoever. In *twinship,* the client primarily needs to experience the therapist as someone essentially similar (Kohut, 1984). For example, a client might rejoice when he discovers that his therapist enjoys a hobby, a favorite author, or cuisine similar to what he enjoys and may want to spend inordinate amounts of therapeutic time discussing these similarities. In any of these cases, the therapist might fail to provide what the client seeks for any number of reasons, including empathic failure or the ethical–legal imperative to maintain appropriate boundaries in the therapeutic relationship. Whatever the form of transference or reason for the therapist's nonfulfillment of the client's need, when the therapist fails to provide what the client seeks, the client often responds intensely.

Resistance

Regarding client resistance, Kohut reframed the concept in a very humanistic fashion, as "the principle of the primacy of self preservation" (1984, p. 143):

> The so-called defense-resistances are neither defenses nor resistances. Rather, they constitute valuable moves to safeguard the self, however weak and defensive [the self] may be, against destruction and invasion. It is only when we recognize that the patient has no healthier attitude at his disposal than the one he is in fact taking that we can evaluate the significance of defenses and resistances appropriately. (p. 141)

Thus, self-psychologists view resistance as the client's best attempt to protect a fragile self so that this self may grow in the future. They also consider that such resistant behaviors may have been the client's greatest assets in early life, because they protected the client's self from potentially devastating insults to its fragile structural integrity. For this reason, self-psychologists view resistance as "a welcome indicator that the striving to complete the development of the self had never been totally given up" (Kohut, 1984, p. 209).

Counselor's Role

The primary responsibility of the self-counselor is sustained empathic inquiry into the meaning of the client's experience of the therapeutic (self–selfobject) relationship, which fosters the overarching goal of self psychotherapy: the establishment, strengthening, and/or maintenance of the client's self such that his self–selfobject relationships are relatively mature, realistic, reciprocal, and resilient. The therapist's role in this process is to reparent the client, that is, to permit the client to dwell in and consolidate the transferential relationship, while the therapist consistently experiences and communicates empathy to the client. She can communicate her empathy, her caring and understanding, by offering interpretations that mirror the client's point of view as well as offer him insight into the processes at work in his psyche. The therapist's consistent efforts to empathically understand the client offer him hope that his present and future need-related experiences will not be repetitions of the past and that "the sustaining echo of empathic resonance is indeed available in this world" (Kohut, 1984, p. 78). To provide this kind of reparative relationship, the therapist must, oneself, have a very well-developed self.

Ironically, to be maximally therapeutic, the therapist must, at times, offer misinterpretations. Such misinterpretations are inevitable, for "there is no analyst whose responses are so 'optimal' as to preclude the patient's recurrently experiencing frustrating and hurtful discrepancies between what he is after and what he gets" (Bacal, 1990, p. 258). Although the therapist can expect to misinterpret without intending to do so, when the client reacts to misinterpretations, her intentional response to the client's reaction constitutes the very essence of self psychotherapy. When an earlier selfobject failed to repair a rift in the selfobject relationship, the client's self-development arrested, and the client experienced the rift as a kind of open wound that the current failure touches—hence the client's strong reaction. If the therapist succeeds in repairing the current empathic rift, the client's self-development will proceed once again. An important aspect of the counselor's responsibility is to acknowledge her very real role in the rift and resume an accurately empathic stance.

Therapists typically find it much easier to remain empathically attuned to a client when that client's disappointment is directed at someone other than the therapist. In the wake of empathic failures by the therapist, the client is likely to either withdraw from or attack the therapist. Such reactions may be clear and overt, such as concrete expressions of blame, criticism, anger, rage, or inordinate appeals for apology or reassurance, or they may be subtle and covert, as when the client briefly breaks eye contact with the therapist, crosses his arms, makes a sarcastic remark or joke, falls silent, or changes the subject. The therapist's responsibility is to remain empathic: to detect that an empathic failure has occurred; to nondefensively acknowledge to the client what she has detected; to acknowledge her error in whatever form, usually a misinterpretation (her very real role in the failure); to understand that any disproportionate intensity in the client's response reflects traumatic residue from past similar situations; and, if and when these steps seem to have repaired and reestablished the selfobject bond, to offer the latter understanding to the client in the form of an interpretation, making sure to emphasize that only some of the client's response is rooted in the past, while some of it appropriately emerged in response to the therapist's actual failure.

To own her fallibility and to detect and respond constructively to client reactions requires that the therapist have a very strong sense of self. She may feel challenged in this regard because, in allowing the client to be important to her, in allowing herself to care about the client, she has opened herself to her own selfobject transference reactions. Therapists may react with countertransference: feeling her self threatened and responding with some self-defense, such as not noticing or bypassing the client's response; noticing it but failing to take responsibility for her error, perhaps by justifying and insisting on the reasonableness and correctness of her own point of view; and/or withdrawing emotionally from the client, becoming emotionally distant or indifferent, or counterattacking the client with blame or with a subtly critical interpretation. In any of these cases, the therapist has abandoned an empathic disposition, and the potential for client self-development from the experience is lost.

The more disordered the client's self, the stronger the therapist's self must be for her to be able to sustain the level of empathy required for the client's self-development. In other words, the therapist must be able to acknowledge her imperfection without loss of self-integrity or self-esteem. In the face of client withdrawal, the therapist must not feel abandoned or must be able to quickly and effectively self-soothe any such feelings. Likewise, in the face of client attacks, the therapist must not feel overwhelmingly threatened by annihilation or loss of self-esteem. Sustained by a strong self, in the wake of an empathic failure, the effective self psychotherapist attends empathically to the client's subjective experience and accepts her role in the failure. She abandons the misinterpretation that led to the failure, admits her mistake, and seeks to understand the client's reaction. Through her ability to rally her empathic resources, the rift in the self–selfobject relationship becomes the very foundation for an even deeper, stronger relationship bond and a strengthening of the client's self. Such occurrences, if the therapist handles them constructively, are blessings in disguise, the essential struggles that result in client self-development, the goal of therapy.

One interesting form of countertransference deserves particular attention: a therapist's rigid beliefs about psychological dynamics. Kohut (1971) urged therapists to resist the

> temptation to squeeze his understanding of the patient into the rigid mold of whatever theoretical preconceptions he may hold, be they Kleinian, Adlerian or, yes, self psychological.... [A]n observer needs theories to [help him] observe ... [but] these theories must be the helpmates of the observer, not his masters. (p. 67)

In Kohut's theory, the most fundamental curative factor is the therapist's empathic attunement to the client; conjecture about the client's psychological dynamics is secondary. Putting herself in the position of experiencing what the disordered client experiences is much like placing one's hand very near a flame. The therapist who cannot take the heat may resort to the use of psychological dynamic constructs to create emotional distance and, thus, defend her own self against the threat of burning up and annihilation; this process may result in the therapist labeling the client "untreatable." Presumably, the effective self psychotherapist would be aware of the many ways she might manifest countertransference; if she perceived herself engaging in it, she presumably would work through it or, if unable to do so, would seek whatever supervision or even personal psychotherapy she needed to strengthen her own self such that she could resume and maintain an empathic stance with the client.

In summary, the counselor's role in self psychotherapy is to provide the client with a reparenting experience characterized most essentially by the therapist's sustained empathic attunement. In relationship with a highly self-disordered client, a therapist's ability to maintain and communicate consistent empathy is no easy task (Bacal, 1990). Yet the capacity to empathize with others is an ability one can develop with sustained practice (Nissim-Sabat, 1989). Effective self psychotherapists undertake this practice to develop what they consider to be their single most important therapeutic skill.

Stages and Techniques

The self–selfobject relationship that forms between the client and the self counselor is truly the medium, the "holding environment," in which the client's self emerges. Although Kohut never explicitly described the physical conditions of the self psychotherapy situation, it appears that, unlike the psychoanalytic situation, Kohut and his client faced each other, seated. The topics the self psychotherapy client and therapist address appear to generally follow a sequence from immediate symptoms and related concerns in the client's life; to the client's history, with particular attention on selfobject relationships; to the nature of the immediate relationship between client and therapist; to the manifestations and resolutions of the client's selfobject transference that is at work in the rift–repair cycle of the client–therapist self–selfobject relationship.

Transference does not occur immediately.

> After an initial period during which his analysand has responded with outside behavioral improvement as well as with a degree of gratitude toward the analyst and his interventions within the psychoanalytic situation, [the analyst] is suddenly confronted with a seemingly ominous worsening of the analysand's condition. Such deterioration is characteristically accompanied by a barrage of reproaches from the side of the analysand that the analysis is ruining him, that the analyst's inept, misguided, bull-in-a-china shop interventions are destroying him. Why is there this period of calm before the storm? Why can the patient at first tolerate the analyst's unavoidable mistakes and errors in empathy only to become suddenly intolerant of them? The answer is simple to the point of triteness: What happens

is nothing else but the transference clicking into place. Thus, during the calm before the storm, the analyst and the patient have jointly explored the patient's traumatic past, allied in the shared pursuit of a goal; once the storm breaks loose, however, the analytic situation has *become* the traumatic past and the analyst has *become* the traumatizing selfobject of early life. (Kohut, 1984, pp. 177–178)

In pursuing the sequence of topics from the client's present life to past life to the immediate therapeutic relationship, self psychotherapists repeatedly employ two phases that Kohut explicitly identified: the *understanding* phase and the *explanatory* phase. The understanding phase involves the counselor's efforts to empathically understand the client's experience and communicate to the client that, to some degree, the therapist has actually experienced the client's inner condition. Some clients do not require a great deal of this. In such cases, the therapist:

> can employ the total understanding-explaining sequence from the start. Furthermore, in many instances, either ab initio or later, there is no clear operational separation between the two steps. Even though the division between them remains valid in principle, the actual activity of the analyst combines them or oscillates between them so rapidly that the operational distinction becomes blurred even with respect to a single intervention. But during particular phases of many analyses, especially analyses of certain severely traumatized patients, the understanding phase of treatment must remain the only phase for a long time. (Kohut, 1984, p. 177)

The explanatory phase is actually an expansion and deepening of the understanding phase. Although still necessitating therapist empathy, this phase enlists the therapist's theoretical understanding of psychodynamic processes, especially her comprehension of selfobjects and how they relate to the client's experiences, both in childhood and in the transference. Still residing in a state of empathy, she formulates these understandings into interpretations and offers them to the client. "It bears stressing that the analyst's essential activities in each of [these phases], not only the first one are based on empathy" (Kohut, 1984, p. 176). In addition, the greater the therapist's theoretical understandings regarding psychological dynamics, the more likely it is that her interpretations will be deeply accurate, which provides more proof to the client that the counselor understands. Again, however, more important than the objective correctness of interpretations is the manner in which the therapist communicates them: They should be expressions of the therapist's optimal responsiveness that the client experiences as restoring the cohesion and resilience of his sense of self.

In fact, Kohut believed that even if the therapist's inference about the client's psychological dynamics is incorrect, as long as the therapist also communicates accurate empathy of the client's subjective experience of the (mis)interpretation, the process of interpretation would have a healing effect. So, for example, imagine that therapist and client are walking into a session, and the therapist small-talks the comment, "I see you're wearing bright blue again this week." The client immediately feels defensive and says, "Do you think I should vary my wardrobe more?" The therapist detects that her remark has triggered a transferential reaction. As they sit down, the therapist might respond with genuine empathy, "It seems that you felt criticized by what I said about your clothes. Perhaps you think I made that observation because I found fault with what you were wearing." After processing this occurrence to the point that the client feels understood, the therapist might offer an interpretation: "Perhaps my comment reminded you of your father whom, for as long as you can remember, you experienced as so critical." The part about the father could be wrong; it may, in fact, have been the client's mother who was vigilant and critical regarding the client's wardrobe, a fact of which the counselor had been unaware but that yielded yet another empathic failure. But Kohut believed that the accuracy of the therapist's empathy for the client's feeling criticized, perceiving the therapist as critical, and experiencing some residual reaction to perceived criticism from the past, would override the erroneous inference about the father. The client could correct the therapist regarding that specific point, to which the effective therapist would respond with something like, "I see. It was your mother by whom you felt so criticized. I was mistaken in attributing your reaction to your relationship with your father. Now I see it was your mother."

Then, client and therapist could explore the emotional residue from the client's relationship with his mother and how the therapist's original remark activated it. When the therapist perceived the client to be feeling quite understood and the empathic bond reestablished, the therapist could reaffirm that her intention was actually to observe and affirm a client preference rather than find fault with a client choice. Assuming the client's ability, unobstructed by further transference, to truly grasp and believe the counselor's self-described motive, the client would take a step in accommodating into his self a previously unaccommodated experience: "When people who are important to me make observations about me, they sometimes are empathizing and affirming rather than criticizing."

From a self psychotherapy viewpoint, this piece of therapeutic progress occurred despite the therapist's erroneous interpretation. Rather, the progress occurred because of all the aforementioned steps the therapist took in responding to the client's experience of the (mis)interpretation. Kohut believed that each time the client receives an interpretation or other communication that does not feel right, he experiences anxiety regarding whether or not the therapist, unlike previous selfobjects, will recognize the empathic failure and process it with the client. By recognizing and processing it, the therapist transforms a potential retraumatization into a "development-enhancing structure-building optimal frustration" (Kohut, 1984, p. 207). Kohut wrote that such failures occur hundreds of times in good therapy, with each attended-to failure resulting in enhanced resiliency and the firming of client self-structure and self-esteem:

> Whether this pivotal transference is a mirror transference, an alter ego transference, or an idealizing transference, it is the repetition of the two-step interventions of the analyst, the experience, over and over again, of understanding followed by explaining, that leads to structure building via transmuting internalizations. (Kohut, 1984, p. 206)

It might be said that this process, which is central to self psychotherapy, is not merely a corrective emotional experience, but a corrective selfobject experience.

Kohut (1984) described his own experience of this process in an example of a client with whom Kohut cancelled several appointments in a short space of time due to several trips. When they finally had a session, the client expressed strong emotional distress, to which Kohut responded prematurely, before he had succeeded in fully empathizing with the client, with several interpretations. Kohut continued,

> The patient, as I finally grasped, insisted, and had a right to insist, that I learn to see things exclusively in *his* way and not at all in *my* way.... [T]he content of *all* my various interpretations had been cognitively correct but incomplete in a decisive direction. The patient had indeed reacted to my having been away.... What I had not seen, however, was that the patient had felt additionally traumatized by the feeling that all these explanations on my part came only from the outside; that I did not fully feel what he felt, that I gave him words but not real understanding, and that I thereby repeated the essential trauma of his early life. To hammer away at the analysand's transference distortions brings no results; it only confirms the analysand's conviction that the analyst is as dogmatic, as

utterly sure of himself, as walled off in the self-righteousness of a distorted view as the pathogenic parents (or other selfobject) had been. Only the analyst's continuing sincere acceptance of the patient's reproaches as (psychologically) realistic, followed by a prolonged (and ultimately successful) attempt to look into himself and remove the inner barriers that stand in the way of his empathic grasp of the patient, ultimately have a chance to turn the tide. (p. 182)

For Kohut, this counselor process was central to psychotherapy and he added that

If some of my colleagues will say at this juncture that this is not analysis—so be it. My inclination is to respond with the old adage that they should get out of the kitchen if they cannot stand the heat. (p. 183)

Self counselors will offer interpretations about a client's resistance, although they also acknowledge their own role in the matter. Like transference, resistance involves the client's organization of experience, the fears and expectations that the therapist will respond to one's needs and emotions in the same traumatic way one's early selfobjects responded (Bacal, 1990; Kohut, 1984; Stolorow et al., 1987). Following this conceptualization, self therapists conceptualize client resistance as the result of the client's *not* experiencing the therapist as a selfobject. Therefore, resistance is not merely an intrapsychic function of the client but, rather, a product of the intersubjective field between client and counselor, with the counselor's actions always playing a role (Stolorow et al., 1987). Unless the therapist is able to empathically identify the client's sense of impending fear or danger, which results in the client's felt need to enlist resistance, analysis of resistance will be therapeutically useless. Conversely, the client's feeling understood in a moment of great fear reestablishes the self–selfobject bond and creates the image of an object (the therapist) that is *not* a repetition of the client's past traumatic parental images. Stolorow et al. (1987) summarized:

Among the most noxious of early pathogenic situations are those in which a child's attempts to communicate an experience of being psychologically injured or undermined by a caregiver result in a prolonged disruption of the vitally needed tie. When the child consistently is unable to communicate such experiences without perceiving that he is damaging or unwelcome to the caregiver, a watershed in the relationship occurs whereby a painful inner conflict becomes structuralized. It is this pathogenic process that is repeated in [analysis when the analyst tells the patient he is resistant].... Such ideas generally occur to an analyst when his own feeling of well-being is threatened by the patient's expressions, and interpretations of resistance under these circumstance serve primarily to reconstitute the analyst's own sense of self. (pp. 51–52)

In conclusion, the essence of the self psychotherapeutic process occurs in two phases: understanding and explanation. The therapist's repeated ability, in the wake of empathic failure, to take responsibility for her errors and to offer accurate empathic understanding and interpretation of the client's psychological dynamics, creates the conditions for the client's self-development through transmuting internalization.

CONTRIBUTIONS AND LIMITATIONS

Interface With Recent Developments in the Mental Health Field

The Nature–Nurture Question

Kohut (1984; Kohut & Wolf, 1978) posited that the self emerges from the interaction between the child's innate or genetic potentials and the empathic attunement of the child's selfobject environment, though he emphasized the influence of the familial environment over genetics. However, the reader should note that Kohut was referring to influences on the *self*—a *core* construct pertaining to a person's experience of relatively enduring identity, coherence, resilience, and feelings of worth—*not* to temperament or personality traits such as shyness, activity level, intelligence quotient (IQ), dominance, fretfulness, impulsivity, and so forth (Efran, Greene, & Gordon, 1998; Rowe, 1990).

Nonetheless, Kohut acknowledged that constitutionally inherited factors significantly affect a child's potential to develop selfobject relationships and, thus, a healthy self. Usually, infants' brains are innately structured for crying, looking for faces, and so forth; with subsequent neurological development, the baby will smile and coo, all of which function to encourage and enhance selfobject relations (Horowitz, 1988). If an infant's brain is somehow structured in ways that do not potentiate these behaviors, its caretakers may fail to respond as selfobjects. Moreover, a child's temperament, which is genetically influenced, most likely affects his ability to establish selfobject relationships; to evoke, maintain, and tolerate different types and intensities of emotional arousal; and to negotiate selfobject failures. Both of these cases exemplify a conclusion genetic researchers have offered: that caregiver behavior may partly be the result, rather than the cause, of a child's genetically predisposed behavior, a kind of "reverse causality" (Rowe, 1990, p. 609). Finally, Kohut (1971) stated that parents' own inherited psychological propensities have a profound impact on their ability to serve effectively as selfobjects. Thus, Kohut (1984) did, both directly and indirectly, acknowledge a role of genetics in the unfolding development of the self, and he also acknowledged its influence to be far more complex than he was able to understand entirely.

However, the self psychology conceptualization of psychosis as a response to the earliest and most severe neglect and/or abuse is at odds with the results of current genetics research indicating that a child's genetic predisposition plays at least a mildly, if not profoundly, facilitative role in the likelihood the child will manifest psychosis at some time in life. From a genetic perspective, a child born with a propensity for psychosis might manifest it in the face of stressors—such as caretakers' empathic failures—that would hardly faze a child with a different genetic endowment. Although we believe self-psychologists could assimilate a diathesis-stress (genetic vulnerability–environmental stressor) model of psychosis into their approach, we are unaware of literature in which self psychology authors have done so.

DSM–IV–TR *Diagnosis*

Kohut (1971) responded to the question of how to differentiate narcissistic disorders from borderline and psychotic conditions by writing that "my approach in this area does not conform with the traditional medical aim of achieving a clinical diagnosis in which a disease entity is identified by clusters of recurring manifestations" (pp. 15–16). Although he did not favor diagnostic labels, he did attend to diagnostic *levels* of structural development. For instance, individuals with psychoses and borderline conditions have not yet established a nuclear self.

However, Kohut (1984) also wrote that, "to my mind, the terms 'psychosis' and 'borderline state' simply refer to the fact that we are dealing with states of prepsychological chaos which the empathic instrument of the observer is unable to comprehend" (p. 9). In other words, when a client's deficit of self is so severe that a therapist cannot empathically grasp it, the therapist's tendency may be to label the client "psychotic" or "borderline" and thus untreatable. Clearly, this label expresses and/or interferes with the therapist's willingness to take the heat of empathizing with profound intrapsychic chaos and thus aborts any potential therapy. Presumably, Kohut would not have objected to therapists using *DSM–IV–TR* diagnosis for the purposes of third-party payment as long as the diagnosis did not undermine the therapist's willingness to sustain empathy for the client's ongoing experience.

Pharmacotherapy

The only mention Kohut made in this regard was to a case of a client with agoraphobia. He noted how tricyclic medication functioned as the precursor to psychological structure by providing the calming and anxiety-curbing required for the client's self to emerge (Kohut, 1984). However, Baker (1991), one of the most outspoken current self-psychologists, stated more broadly that "careful assessment of possible biological factors is essential. Combined psychopharmacological and psychotherapeutic interventions may be ideal" (p. 297).

Managed Care and Brief Therapy

Kohut's psychotherapeutic approach tended to be long enough for transference to develop and for empathic failures and reparations to recur many, many times. However, Crits-Christoph, Barber, and Kurcias (1991) presented nine brief psychodynamic shorter term self-psychological approaches to therapy that illustrated the primary difference between brief and long-term therapy. Whereas in long-term therapy the therapist focuses predominantly on the client's selfobject interactions both within and outside of session, in brief therapy, the therapist gives equal attention to the management of specific client concerns as to the client's self–selfobject interactions. Thus, although Kohut's form of therapy was largely incompatible with current demands of managed care, other self-psychologists, such as Baker & Baker (1987), and therapists who incorporate self psychology, such as Levenson (1995), have adapted Kohut's form to develop approaches that meet those demands.

Technical Eclecticism

Therapists can find self psychology amenable to technical eclecticism. We hope you have noticed the humanistic commonality of Kohut's therapeutic approach and Rogers's, particularly the paramount importance they assigned the act of empathy. Since Kohut's death, self-psychologists have become increasingly cognitive and constructivist, especially in their views of resistance and transference as pervasive ways people construct and organize their experience. We believe self-psychologists could incorporate from cognitive counseling Socratic questioning techniques and collaborative investigation to facilitate their empathic understanding of clients, as long as the therapist maintains primary focus on whether the client appears to be experiencing empathic attunement and responsiveness from the therapist. Similarly, regarding constructivism, therapists could incorporate techniques such as personal journaling, life review exercises, narrative reconstruction, stream of consciousness, and mirror time (Mahoney, 2002). Presumably, self-psychologists would not draw techniques from approaches that can lack warmth and can involve pressing a client to adopt a different perspective than one's own, such as rational emotive behavior therapy (REBT). Similarly, they would need to be careful in adapting techniques that arose from approaches that objectify people's behaviors, such as behaviorism. Finally, self-psychologists interface extremely elegantly with integral and transpersonal approaches to counseling, both in their concern for what may be the most core of all psychological constructs, the self, and also in their devotion to understanding how a person's early developmental difficulties affect subsequent self-development.

Diversity Issues

With regard to diversity issues, Kohut made significant strides beyond psychoanalysis in honoring each client's unique experience. As self-psychologists adhere to the constructivist and relativist notions that all meaning requires interpretation and all interpretation requires an understanding of the cultural context in which one seeks meaning, they avoid many of the cultural biases inherent in some other therapies. Rather than trying to fit the client into the preexisting conceptual structures, the self psychotherapist engages in the *experience near* approach of striving constantly to understand and experience what it is like to be a particular client. Through this effort, they free themselves substantially from cultural preconceptions.

Altman (1996) proposed that psychoanalysts, who supposedly employ objectivity in analyzing the analysand's subjective experience, are limited in their capacity to accommodate racial, cultural, or socioeconomic differences. He suggested that only in the context of two- or three-person relationship in which all participants acknowledge and engage their subjectivity can therapists understand diversity-based differences among their clients. Kohut's self psychology and Atwood and Stolorow's (1984) intersubjective approach, an expansion of self psychology, are examples of therapeutic approaches in which therapists employ the latter relational context.

Roland (1996) explored the question of how universal and variable is the construct of the self across cultures. He noted the Pakistani we-self, an experiential aspect of a Pakistani's sense of self that includes inner representations of one's extended family and community. He also highlighted the psychoanalytic work of Takeo Doi who acknowledged various aspects of dependency relationships (amae), public self (omote), and private self (ura) in Japanese culture that psychoanalytic theorists had not recognized. Roland (1996) concluded that psychoanalytic theorists and practitioners need a new paradigm, and he posited the following constructs as universal:

> Developmental stages, selfobject relationships, self and object representations, self-identity, internal object world, affects and drives, transference, resistance, and dream-analysis, among others. One must then decontextualize them of their current Northern European/North American content and forms—the particular variability they are accorded by psychoanalytic theory—and then proceed to recontextualize them using the clinical data of persons from significantly or radically different cultures. (p. 86)

Kohut's reformulations also have relevance for gender issues. Westerners have tended to devalue women's emphasis on relationship and communion in favor of men's emphasis on autonomy and agency (Chodorow, 1978; Gilligan, 1982; Jordan, Kaplan, Miller, Stiver, & Surrey, 1991). Kohut's redefinition of the psychologically healthy person as someone with a mature dependence on selfobject relationships reduces the stigma associated with interdependence. Whereas traditional analytic theory is rooted in the Western value of individualism and the "secularized Protestant values of independence and self-reliance" (Roland 1996, p. 80), the primacy of relationship in object relations theory and self psychology "lessens the press for the independent, internally structured adult" (Jordan et al., 1991, p. 2). Roland went so far as to assert that, from a self psychology point of view, the values of extreme American individualism and mobility are not ideals for which people should strive but are actually pathogenic, contributing to problematic selfobject relationships and instability of the self.

Regarding sexual orientation, although Kohut never directly pathologized homosexuality as a disorder demanding treatment, he did counsel individuals who sought counseling because they were disturbed by their homosexuality. Moreover, he clearly viewed clients' homosexuality not as a primary disorder but as a secondary manifestation of a narcissistic/self disorder and of far less concern than tendencies toward depression, sensitivity to criticism, lacking zest, and so forth (Kohut, 1971). In fact, in his final book, Kohut (1984) wrote that homosexuality, as well as sibling rivalry, voyeurism, mother attachment, and so forth, should be viewed as a healthy psychic activity because it functions to safeguard the self's future growth.

Regarding spirituality, Kohut (1971) wrote that "the relationship between the true believer and his God ... corresponds to the ancient omnipotent self-object, the idealized parent imago" (p. 106). His statement might best be understood in the context of Wilber's (1999, Vol. 3) distinction between a person merely believing in God, a form of *legitimate religion*, and having a contemplative and direct experience of God, an aspect of *authentic religion*. Considering this context, Kohut appears to have reduced all spirituality to a form of legitimate religion—in which the self creates a projection of an ideal selfobject—and to have not perceived in people a potential to have authentic religious experiences.

In light of this observation, you might be surprised to learn that psychodynamic theories, such as object relations and self psychology, play a major role in approaches of the vast majority of transpersonal and integral theorists, those who theorize a domain of human spiritual experiences that transcends the ego or self—that characterize authentic religion. In fact, Boorstein (1997) described at length how self psychology interfaces with both Buddhist meditation and Christian-based contemplative practices. Kohut's work is infused throughout Boorstein's transpersonal approach to psychotherapy. So although self-psychologists do not appear to have accommodated a broader view of humans that includes a transpersonal domain of authentic religion, transpersonal psychologists have assimilated self psychology into their broader conceptualization of the human psyche.

Affirming both Kohutian and transpersonal contentions regarding spirituality, research suggests that a person's level of object relations development correlates positively with one's image of God and that both correlate positively with spiritual maturity (Hall & Brokaw, 1995; Magaletta, 1996; McDargh, 1986). Self-psychologists and object relations theorists posit that one's relationships with other people constitute the foundation of one's experience. According to proponents of the perennial philosophy—the distillation of commonalities among the world's major spiritual traditions, people can comprehend the highest realms of human experience and development only in the context of the self's relation to others and, ultimately, of the self's identity as spirit (Wilber, 2000). Contemporary spiritual teachers also express this psychological perspective, for example: "The ego that is to be transcended exists only in the context of relations.... [T]he most fundamental [spiritual] disciplines, are those in the domain of relations" (Avabhasa, 1993, p. 12).

The Effectiveness of Psychotherapy

Psychodynamic researchers have focused more on people's developmental issues than on psychotherapy outcomes. From Mahler et al.'s pioneering research (1975) on children's separation–individuation process to a host of analytic researchers (Basch, 1985; Demos, 1987; Stern, 1985) who studied patterns of early infant–parent interactions, it seems clear that *the intense emotions that infants experience in relationship with their caregivers are primary and pervasive organizers of self-experience* (Stolorow et al., 1987). In fact, experimental research with many different species has revealed that "even mild forms of trauma may cause significant biochemical and behavioral changes" in the traumatized individual, confirming "the psychoanalytic insight that disturbances in early development can produce delayed psychopathological changes" (Gabbard, 1999, p. 4). Kohut's reformulations of transference and resistance as activities of self-organization also interface well with developmental research in cognitive psychology and constructivism (Mahoney, 2002; Piaget, 1970).

Psychoanalytic researchers have mostly published outcome research in the form of case studies, a practice that can be traced to Freud's methods (Bornstein & Masling,

1994). Case studies yield individual participants' anecdotal, but not large scale experimental and statistical, outcome data. Researchers may not have pursued experimental studies because they faced several challenges: the relative newness of self psychology, the absence of a manual defining its method, and its originally long-term nature.

However, research corroborating the importance of a good therapeutic alliance in positive client outcomes is indeed relevant to Kohut's concept of the self–selfobject relationship between client and counselor. Moreover, findings from the Vanderbilt I and II process/outcome studies (Strupp & Hadley, 1979) offered "evidence that regardless of how much 'warmth', 'friendliness', and 'support' may be present, if expressions of hostility (direct or indirect) are not effectively handled, there will be repercussions on the development of a positive therapeutic alliance and on outcome" (p. 1129). This is exactly the issue Kohut (1971, 1977, 1984) addressed in his admonishment to therapists that they attend to and repair disturbances in the self–selfobject bond when clients react with hostility or even rage to the therapist's empathic failures.

Other findings also have substantiated various aspects of self psychology. Reports that clients tend to do better in therapy with therapists they perceive to be similar to them has corroborated Kohut's view of the importance of twinship. Moreover, Kegan (1982), whose seminal developmental research many mental health professionals have held in awe, wrote that the "special kind of empathy [à la Rogers and Kohut] is crucial at every phase in the lifespan because it is actually intrinsic to the process by which we develop" (p. viii).

Kohut probably would concur with Asay and Lambert (1999) regarding the factors in positive psychotherapeutic outcome. Self-psychologists agree that the quality of the therapeutic relationship, specific interventions, extratherapeutic factors, and the client's expectations about therapy all play a role in positive outcome. However, Kohut probably would have viewed somewhat differently the relative proportions of these factors, believing that an exquisitely empathic therapeutic relationship, in which the therapist succeeds in maintaining empathy even in the face of extratherapeutic factors such as severe and chronic pathology, can overcome the potentially therapeutically detrimental effects of those latter factors.

Limitations

One weakness of self psychology is that, in formulating it, Kohut failed to acknowledge predecessors on whose ideas he may have based his theory. These contributors include Fairbairn, who posited that drives are not primary but are manifestations of relational disturbances; Winnicot, whose concepts of the "good enough mother" and a "holding environment" (one optimal for healthy development) point to the profound influence of the familial environment on a person's development and pathology; and Mahler, whose work on separation and individuation underscored the importance of primary caretaker relationships in a child's development. Critics have repeatedly found fault with Kohut for these and other omissions. He both quasiapologized for and justified his method:

> Let me emphasize initially that my continuing lack of integration of their contributions with mine is not due to any lack of respect ... but to the nature of the task that I have set for myself ... an attempt to struggle toward greater clarity.... [M]y focus is not on scholarly completeness; it is directed to the direct observation of clinical phenomena and the construction of new formulations that would accommodate my observations. (Kohut, 1977, pp. xx–xxi)

A second weakness of his theory involves Kohut's use of the term and concept of *restoration*. Kohut posited that humans are born whole, hence the notion of the restoration of the self through psychotherapy. It is one thing to view newborns as full of potential, which Kohut did, and quite another to posit that they are born whole and complete. The latter scenario would suggest that the structure of the self is already established at birth, which Kohut surely would not have argued. Moreover, nowhere else in nature does one encounter a developmental sequence that begins with wholeness and is followed by a condition requiring restoration. The concept of restoration of the self, therefore, appears to be internally inconsistent with the bulk of Kohut's theory. Perhaps a more accurate, though less elegant, phrasing would be "resumption of the self's development."

A third weakness, one we consider arguable, is some mental health professionals' view that Kohut focused his attention too narrowly on narcissistic issues. In so doing, they say, he neglected the full spectrum of development (Gedo, 1989).

Finally, Stolorow et al. (1987) cited a weakness in the form of confusion regarding the concept of the self as both a person and a psychic structure. They gave an example of a typical self psychology sentence: "The fragmented self strives to restore its cohesion" (p. 18). They pointed out that the "self" in this sentence refers to both a psychic structure that has fragmented (after all, the person has not fragmented), and an active agent, the person, striving to organize its experience. They recommend restricting the use of "self" to psychic structure and function as the organization of experience and using "person" for the agent initiating actions. They would reword the sentence thus: "The person whose self-experience is becoming fragmented strives to restore his sense of self-cohesion" (Stolorow et al., 1987, p. 19).

Contributions

Kohut (1984) wrote that his work "has supplied analysis with new theories which broaden and deepen the field of empathic perception" (p. 175). His primary distinguishing contributions to the field of psychology and psychotherapy were his *reformulations of narcissism;* his description of the formation of psychic structure via *transmuting internalization;* the concept of *selfobjects* and the three *selfobject transferences;* and recognizing the profound importance of *empathy* and the *centrality of the client's self-experience.* With these four primary contributions, Kohut provided mental health professionals for the first time with conceptual and clinical tools to treat people suffering from severe developmental arrests.

Kohut (1971) radically *redefined narcissism* not by the object or target of the drive as Freud had defined it but, rather, *by the nature or quality of the relationship to the (self) object.* Thus, narcissism is a developmental line that a person never outgrows, much like cognitive or moral lines of development. Within this line, one's narcissism develops from the form of archaic, absolute, desperate demands on selfobjects to the form of more mature, differentiated, flexible, and resilient relationships with selfobjects. Kohut's radical reformulation not only emphasized the developmental potential in a person exhibiting narcissistic (selfobject) transferences, but also provided mental health professionals with a rationale to reevaluate Western culture's emphasis on absolute autonomy as an ideal of psychological health.

The concepts of selfobjects and selfobject transferences enabled counselors to understand and treat clients whom they had previously considered untreatable. The simple realization that a client may experience a counselor's mere presence as a calming and esteeming component of the client's self-organization can forever alter a counselor's view of therapy (Stolorow et al., 1987). Kohut and subsequent self-psychologists revisioned many psychotherapeutic phenomena in a kind of positive reframe. Therapists no longer saw transference as an obstruction to therapeutic work but as the foundation for it. They saw clients' intense emotional reactions not merely as symptoms of psychopathology but as prime therapeutic material and opportunities for client self-development.

For Kohut, consistent empathic inquiry replaced insight as the primary goal of analysis. The relinquishment of preexisting beliefs that makes a therapist capable of such inquiry includes relinquishment of cultural preconceptions. This same process of inquiry characterized Kohut's process of theory development, rendering his theoretical framework:

> Exquisitely self-reflexive and potentially self-corrective.... [T]he consistent application of the empathic-introspective mode not only to the psychological phenomena being studied but also to the theoretical ideas that guide our observations provides us with an ongoing basis for critically evaluating, refining, expanding, and, when necessary, discarding these theoretical constructs. (Stolorow et al., 1987, p. 17)

In other words, self psychology includes itself in the domain under investigation, thus preventing its adherents from idealizing it as a final, all-encompassing theory. "Kohut's ultimate legacy to his followers is therefore likely to be this warning from the grave not to congeal his writings into self-psychological dogma" (Gedo, 1989, p. 419).

CURRENT STATUS

Stolorow, Atwood, and Orange (1999) portrayed Kohut as "a pivotal transitional figure in the development of a post-Cartesian, fully contextual psychoanalytic psychology" (p. 381). Toward the end of his life, Kohut acknowledged that although his investigations and reformulations were significant, they "should be considered to be a progress report about the present state of a step in the evolution of psychoanalysis that is itself only in its very beginning" (Kohut & Wolf, 1978, p. 413). Moreover, Kohut (1984) wrote that

> Much remains to be done; we need investigations of the special needs of adolescents and the elderly, for example ... [and of] those shifts to a new cultural milieu that deprive a person of his "cultural selfobjects," during his mature years or when he has to deal with debilitating illness, or the confrontation with death. (p. 194)

Self psychology is a relatively young approach with many adherents carrying forward its flame. An excellent review of recent developments in self psychology is Buirski and Kottler (2007). Since 1985, editors of *The Progress in Self Psychology* series have published a volume each year. In these books, authors discuss the cutting edge of self psychology, which they continue to expand, refine, and articulate. These contributors have tightened Kohut's theoretical loose ends, of which there were few. Individuals and teams like Goldberg; Stolorow and Atwood; Baker; Bacal; and Detrick have broken new ground, for example, by investigating objects other than selfobjects (Goldberg, 1989). Stolorow et al.'s (1987) intersubjective approach is an expansion of Kohut's self psychology and demonstrates how theorists' and therapists' own subjective worlds profoundly influence their experiences and understandings of others. The popularity of this approach in Europe is evidenced by a journal devoted solely to it: *Self Psychology: European Journal for Psychoanalytic Therapy and Research*. In recent years, practitioners have expanded the self psychology literature by addressing a variety of formerly under- or unaddressed topics: addictions counseling (Ulman & Paul, 2006), couples counseling (Leone, 2008), family therapy (Leone, 2007);

group counseling (Levine & Mishna, 2007; Livingston, 2006); multicultural counseling (Berzoff, Flanagan, & Hertz, 2008); play therapy (Kindler, 2007); and time-limited self psychologically based psychotherapy (Havneskold, 2006). Moreover, authors have integrated self psychology with cognitive-behavior therapy (Meckes, 2005; Silverstein, 2007), Buddhism (Kinst, 2003; Kulka, 2006; Noe, 2005), Christianity (Preston, 2005), and end of life pastoral counseling (Koppel, 2004).

As we stated at the beginning of this chapter, a 1990 survey revealed that mental health professionals most frequently named psychodynamic theories as their exclusive or primary guiding theories of psychotherapy (Jensen et al., 1990). It is likely that self psychology, in particular, provides a therapeutic framework for this majority of psychotherapists. It is not hard to see why this would be the case, given that self psychology addresses issues so close to what it means to be human, as well as so vast an array of clinical practice.

SUMMARY

For Kohut, the reason people should not equate human finiteness and death with meaninglessness and despair is that we can empathize with each other's subjective experience (Nissim-Sabat, 1989). Kohut did far more than merely rejuvenate and expand psychoanalytic theory. With his emphasis on the centrality of empathy, he brought the counselor's humanity into the therapy room.

"If one will only listen," wrote Goldberg (1989), "what Kohut and self psychology have to say is very hard to ignore" (p. xviii). Regardless of whether one chooses a self-psychological orientation or not, counselors will better serve their clients if they are at least aware of Kohut's key contributions, especially how counselors serve as selfobjects for their clients. Kohut formulated a theory that both underscores the need for empathy and enhances therapists' capacity to empathically access their clients' subjective experiences in more of their rich diversity. He also knew that his work had uncovered more questions than it answered. He therefore created an integrating framework capable of accounting for both clinical phenomena and self psychology itself (Stolorow et al., 1999). His approach is an important contribution to the continuing human search for self-understanding and the realization of human potential.

RECOMMENDED RESOURCES

Print

Kohut, H. (1971). *The analysis of the self.* New York, NY: International Universities Press; and Kohut, H. (1977). *The restoration of the self.* New York, NY: International Universities Press. Good primary source readings provide a comprehensive foundation to the theory. Somewhat of a dense read, but worth the theoretical information.

St. Clair, M. (2000). *Object relations and self psychology: An introduction* (3rd ed.). Pacific Grove, CA: Brooks/Cole. Excellent for the beginning counselor who is new to the theory. Good explanation of concepts and good case illustrations.

Stolorow, R. D., Brandchaft, B., & Atwood, G. E. (1987). *Psychoanalytic treatment: An intersubjective approach.* Hillsdale, NJ: Analytic Press. Good discussion of the similarities and differences in the various psychoanalytic/psychodynamic approaches.

Audiovisuals

To our knowledge, there are no published videos demonstrating the self psychology approach.

Web Sites

http://www.selfpsychology.com/ and http://www.psychologyoftheself.com/ These pages provide useful information including definitions of relevant concepts and a fairly comprehensive bibliography separated by special topics. Information about conferences is also available.

REFERENCES

Akhtar, S. (1989). Kohut and Kernberg: A critical comparison. In D. W. Detrick & S. P. Detrick (Eds.), *Self psychology: Comparisons and contrasts* (pp. 329–362). Hillsdale, NJ: The Analytic Press.

Altman, N. (1996). The accommodation of diversity in psychoanalysis. In R. M. P. Foster, M. Moskowitz, & R. A. Javier (Eds.), *Reaching across boundaries of culture and class: Widening the scope of psychotherapy* (pp. 195–209). Northvale, NJ: Jason Aronson.

American Psychiatric Association. (2000). *Diagnostic and statistical manual of mental disorders* (4th ed., text rev.). Washington, DC: Author.

Asay, T., & Lambert, M. J. (1999). The empirical case for the common factors in therapy: Quantitative findings. In M. A. Hubble, B. L. Duncan, & S. D. Miller (Eds.), *The heart and soul of change* (pp. 23–55). Washington, DC: American Psychological Association.

Atwood, G. E., & Stolorow, R. D. (1984). *Structures of subjectivity: Explorations in psychoanalytic phenomenology*. Hillsdale, NJ: The Analytic Press.

Avabhasa, D. (1993). *The incarnation of love*. Clearlake, CA: Dawn Horse Press.

Bacal, H. (1990). Heinz Kohut. In H. A. Bacal & K. M. Newman (Eds.), *Theories of object relations: Bridges to self psychology* (pp. 240–252). New York, NY: Columbia University Press.

Baker, H. S. (1991). Shorter-term psychotherapy: A self psychological approach. In P. Crits-Christoph & J. P. Barber (Eds.), *Handbook of short-term dynamic psychotherapy* (pp. 287–323). New York, NY: Basic Books.

Baker, H., & Baker, M. (1987). Heinz Kohut's self psychology: An overview. *The American Journal of Psychiatry, 144*(1), 1–9.

Basch, M. (1985). Interpretation: Toward a developmental model. In A. Goldberg (Ed.), *Progress in self psychology* (Vol. 1, pp. 33–42). New York, NY: Guilford Press.

Bellak, L., Hurvich, M., & Gediman, H. K. (1973). *Ego functions in schizophrenics, neurotics, and normals: A systematic study of conceptual, diagnostic, and therapeutic aspects*. New York, NY: Wiley.

Berzoff, J., Flanagan, L. M., & Hertz, P. (Eds.). (2008). *Inside out and outside in: Psychodynamic clinical theory and psychopathology in contemporary multicultural contexts*. Lanham, MD: Jason Aronson.

Boorstein, S. (1997). *Clinical studies in transpersonal psychotherapy*. Albany, NY: State University of New York Press.

Bornstein, R. F., & Masling, J. M. (1994). Introduction: From the consulting room to the laboratory: Clinical evidence, empirical evidence, and the heuristic value of object relations theory. In J. M. Masling & R. F. Bornstein (Eds.), *Empirical studies of psychoanalytic theories: Volume 5. Empirical perspectives on object relations theory.* Washington, DC: American Psychological Association.

Buirski, P., & Kottler, A. (2007). *New developments in self psychology practice.* Lanham, MD: Jason Aronson.

Chodorow, N. (1978). *The reproduction of mothering.* Berkeley, CA: University of California Press.

Crits-Christoph, P., Barber, J. P., & Kurcias, J. S. (1991). Comparison of the brief dynamic therapies. In P. Crits-Christoph & J. P. Barber (Eds.), *Handbook of short-term dynamic psychotherapy.* New York, NY: Basic Books.

Demos, E. V. (1987). Affect and the development of the self. In A. Goldberg (Ed.), *Frontiers in self psychology* (pp. 27–53). Hillsdale, NY: Yale University Press.

Efran, J., Greene, M., & Gordon, D. (1998). Lessons of the new genetics: Finding the right fit for our clients. *Networker, 22,* 26–41.

Gabbard, G. O. (1999, January). Psychodynamic therapy in an age of neuroscience. *The Harvard Mental Health Newsletter, 15*(7), 4–5.

Gedo, J. E. (1989). Self psychology: A post-Kohutian view. In D. W. Detrick & S. P. Detrick (Eds.), *Self psychology: Comparisons and contrasts* (pp. 415–428). Hillsdale, NJ: The Analytic Press.

Gilligan, C. (1982). *In a different voice: Psychological theory and women's development.* Cambridge, MA: Harvard University Press.

Goldberg, A. (1989). Foreword. In D. W. Detrick & S. P. Detrick (Eds.), *Self psychology: Comparisons and contrasts* (pp. xvii–xxi). Hillsdale, NJ: Analytic Press.

Greenberg, J. R., & Mitchell, S. A. (1983). *Object relations in psychoanalytic theory.* Cambridge, MA: Harvard University Press.

Hall, T. W., & Brokaw, B. F. (1995). The relationship of spiritual maturity to level of object relations development and God image. *Pastoral Psychology, 43*(6), 373–391.

Havneskold, L. (2006). Focused (time-limited) self-psychologically based psychotherapy. *Self Psychology: European Journal for Psychoanalytic Therapy and Research, 7*(25–26), 300–311.

Horowitz, M. J. (1988). Short-term dynamic therapy of stress response syndromes. *Introduction to psychodynamics: A new synthesis* (pp. 116–198). New York, NY: Basic Books.

Jensen, J. P., Bergin, A. E., & Greaves, D. W. (1990). The meaning of eclecticism: New survey and analysis of components. *Professional Psychology: Research and Practice, 21*(2), 124–130.

Jordan, J. V., Kaplan, A. G., Miller, J. B., Stiver, I. P., & Surrey, J. L. (1991). *Women's growth in connection: Writings from the Stone center.* New York, NY: Guilford Press.

Kegan, R. (1982). *The evolving self: Problem and process in human development.* Cambridge, MA: Harvard University Press.

Kernberg, O. (1975). *Borderline conditions and pathological narcissism.* New York, NY: Jason Aronson.

Kindler, R. C. (2007). A peek into the playroom: A contemporary self psychological approach to work with children. In P. Buirski & A. Kottler (Eds.), *New developments in self psychology practice* (pp. 69–84). Lanham, MD: Jason Aronson.

Kinst, J. M. (2003). Trust, emptiness, and the self in the practice of Soto Zen Buddhism: An exploration including the insights of self psychology, Erik Erikson, and D. W. Winnicott. *Dissertation Abstracts International: Section A: Humanities and Social Sciences, 64*(6-A), 2122.

Klein, M. (1948). *Contributions to psycho-analysis 1921–1945.* London, UK: Hogarth Press.

Kohut, H. (1971). *The analysis of the self.* New York, NY: International Universities Press.

Kohut, H. (1977). *The restoration of the self.* New York, NY: International Universities Press.

Kohut, H. (1979). The two analyses of Mr. Z. *International Journal of Psychoanalysis, 60,* 3–27.

Kohut, H. (1982). Introspection, empathy, and the semi-circle of mental health. *International Journal of Psychoanalysis, 63,* 394–407.

Kohut, H. (1984). *How does psychoanalysis cure?* Chicago, IL: University of Chicago Press.

Kohut, H., & Wolf, E. (1978). The disorders of the self and their treatment: An outline. *International Journal of Psychoanalysis, 59,* 413–425.

Koppel, M. S. (2004). Self psychology and end of life pastoral care. *Pastoral Psychology, 53*(2), 139–152.

Kriegman, D., & Solomon, L. (1985). Cult groups and the narcissistic personality: The offer to heal defects in the self. *International Journal of Group Psychotherapy, 35,* 239–261.

Kulka, R. (2006). The human condition between emergence and dissolving: Self psychology as a harmonious bridge between psychoanalysis and Buddhism. *Self Psychology: European Journal for Psychoanalytic Therapy and Research, 7*(25–26), 312–321.

Leone, C. (2007). Toward a more optimal selfobject milieu: An intersubjective, self psychological approach to family treatment. In P. Buirski & A. Kottler (Eds.), *New developments in self psychology practice* (pp. 103–126). Lanham, MD: Jason Aronson.

Leone, C. (2008). Couple therapy from the perspective of self psychology and intersubjectivity theory. *Psychoanalytic Psychology, 25*(1), 79–98.

Levenson, H. (1995). *Time-limited dynamic psychotherapy.* New York, NY: Basic Books.

Levine, D., & Mishna, F. (2007). A self-psychological and relational approach to group therapy for university students with bulimia. *International Journal of Group Psychotherapy, 57*(2), 167–185.

Livingston, M. S. (2006). New applications of self psychology to group psychotherapy: Introduction. *International Journal of Group Psychotherapy, 56*(1), 1–4.

Magaletta, P. R. (1996). An object relations paradigm for spiritual development with highlights from Mertons's spiritual journey. *Pastoral Psychology, 45*(1), 21–28.

Mahler, M. S., Pine, F., & Bergman, A. (1975). *The psychological birth of the human infant: Symbiosis and individuation.* New York, NY: Basic Books.

Mahoney, M. (2002). Constructivism and positive psychology. In S. J. Lopez (Ed.), *Handbook of positive psychology* (pp. 745–750). London, UK: Oxford University Press.

Masek, R. J. (1989). On Maurice Merleau-Ponty and the psychology of the self. In D. W. Detrick & S. P. Detrick (Eds.), *Self psychology: Comparisons and contrasts* (pp. 175–192). Hillsdale, NJ: The Analytic Press.

McDargh, J. (1986). God, mother and me: An object relational perspective on religious material. *Pastoral Psychology, 34,* 251–263.

McWilliams, N. (1994). *Psychoanalytic diagnosis: Understanding personality structure in the clinical process.* New York, NY: Guilford.

Meckes, J. (2005). Building a conceptual bridge between behavioral, cognitive-behavioral, and self-psychology models of oppositional defiant disorder. *Dissertation Abstracts International: Section B: The Sciences and Engineering, 66*(5-B), 2832.

Nissim-Sabat, M. (1989). Kohut and Husserl: The empathic bond. In D. W. Detrick & S. P. Detrick (Eds.), *Self psychology: Comparisons and contrasts* (pp. 151–174). Hillsdale, NJ: Analytic Press.

Noe, A. (2005). Self-psychology, Buddhism, and mindfulness meditation: An integrated conceptualization and treatment approach for women experiencing post-abortion stress. *Dissertation Abstracts International: Section B: The Sciences and Engineering, 65*(10-B), 5416.

Perry, S., Cooper, A., & Michels, R. (1986). The psychodynamic formulation: Its purpose, structure, and clinical application. *The American Journal of Psychiatry, 144*(5), 543–550.

Piaget, J. (1970). *The child's conception of movement and speed* (G. T. Holloway & M. J. MacKenzie, Trans.). New York, NY: Basic Books.

Preston, L. (2005). A Christian self psychological perspective. In M. B. Weiner, P. C. Cooper, & C. Barbre (Eds.), *Psychotherapy and religion: Many paths, one journey* (pp. 207–232). Lanham, MD: Jason Aronson.

Roland, A. (1996). How universal is the psychoanalytic self? In R. M. P. Foster, M. Moskowitz, & R. A. Javier (Eds.), *Reaching across boundaries of culture and class: Widening the scope of psychotherapy.* Northvale, NJ: Jason Aronson.

Rowe, D. (1990). As the twig is bent? The myth of child-rearing influences on personality development. *Journal of Counseling and Development, 68*(3), 606–611.

Silverstein, S. M. (2007). Integrating Jungian and self-psychological perspectives within cognitive-behavior therapy for a young man with a fixed religious delusion. *Clinical Case Studies, 6*(3), 263–276.

St. Clair, M. (2000). *Object relations and self psychology: An introduction* (3rd ed.). Pacific Grove, CA: Brooks/Cole.

Stern, D. (1985). *The interpersonal world of the infant.* New York, NY: Basic Books.

Stolorow, R. D., Atwood, G. E., & Orange, D. M. (1999). Kohut and contextualism: Toward a post-Cartesian psychoanalytic theory. *Psychoanalytic Psychology, 16*(3), 380–388.

Stolorow, R. D., Brandchaft, B., & Atwood, G. E. (1987). *Psychoanalytic treatment: An intersubjective approach.* Hillsdale, NJ: Analytic Press.

Strauss, G. D., Yager, J., & Strauss, G. E. (1984). The cutting edge in psychiatry. *The American Journal of Psychiatry, 141*(1), 38–43.

Strozier, C. (1985). Glimpses of a life: Heinz Kohut. In A. Goldberg (Ed.), *Progress in self psychology* (Vol. 1, pp. 3–12). New York, NY: Guilford.

Strupp, H. H., & Hadley, S. W. (1979). Specific versus nonspecific factors in psychotherapy: A controlled study of outcome. *Archives of General Psychiatry, 36,* 1125–1136.

Ulman, R. B., & Paul, H. (2006). *The self psychology of addiction and its treatment: Narcissus in wonderland.* New York, NY: Routledge.

Ursano, R., Sonnenberg, S., & Lazar, S. (1998). *Psychodynamic psychotherapy: Principles and techniques in the era of managed care.* Washington, DC: American Psychiatric Press.

Wilber, K. (1999). *The collected works of Ken Wilber* (Vols. 1–4). Boston, MA: Shambhala.

Wilber, K. (2000). *The collected works of Ken Wilber* (Vols. 5–8). Boston, MA: Shambhala.

Adlerian Counseling–
Individual Psychology

BACKGROUND OF THE THEORY

Historical Context and Founder's Biographical Overview

Due to Alfred Adler's stature in the field of psychology, several authors have written biographies of him. Among these are Bottome (1957), Hoffman (1994), and Rattner (1983). Following is a compilation of key points from these sources. If you are interested in more detail, we encourage you to refer to the original works.

Born in Vienna, Austria on February 7, 1870, Alfred Adler was the second of six children born to Jewish parents. Adler's childhood was filled with episodes of serious health issues and interactions with death. At age three, his younger brother died of pneumonia while young Adler was in the room. At age five, Adler almost succumbed to pneumonia and later recollected hearing the physician remark on his slim chance for survival. Although he did survive, Adler was plagued with numerous health problems and was even run over in the street on more than one occasion. Despite these challenges, Adler persevered and channeled his life experiences into later ideas of compensation, organ inferiority, and courage. He also may have used these medical problems to develop a striving to overcome death, one manifestation of which may have been his pursuit and eventual completion of his medical degree in 1895.

Adler's first practice, as a general practitioner, was in an office near a Viennese amusement park. His patients consisted primarily of the park's artists and performers, and Adler was impressed with their individual areas of competence despite their social status and histories of childhood physical and emotional obstacles. Perhaps Adler recognized in them the importance of compensation that he had experienced while growing up.

In 1902, after Adler publicly defended some of Freud's ideas, Freud invited him to join a group that met weekly to discuss new ideas in psychology. Adler attended and became an active and vocal member of the group, mainly using the forum to develop and debate his emerging ideas of the human condition. Five years later, in 1907, Adler published *Organ Inferiority and Its Psychical Compensation*, outlining the process of compensation and overcompensation based on Darwin's evolutionary principles. In the years to follow, even though he became president of the International Psycho-Analytic Society, Adler openly disagreed with Freud's views of the importance of the Oedipus complex and the essential meaning of dreams, and the view that humans were driven creatures at the whim of vague energy constructs. In 1911, Adler gave several lectures openly criticizing Freud's emphasis on sexuality as the basis of personality development. Soon after, along with a group of colleagues including Carl Furtmuller, Adler left Freud's circle and formed his own school, the Society for Free Psychoanalytic Research. After this split, although Freud and Adler traded verbal barbs in various publications, the two never met again.

Adler renamed his theory "Individual Psychology," a term referring to his belief in the indivisibility of the personality into component parts. In 1912, Adler published his book, *The Neurotic Constitution*, in which he described the core tenets of his approach, thereby demonstrating that he had conceived of an original, comprehensive view of healthy and unhealthy behavior. In 1914, along with Furtmuller, Adler founded the *Journal for Individual Psychology*, which is still in circulation today.

During World War I, Adler served as a medic on the Russian front. As Adler placed such emphasis on the importance of social interaction, social embeddedness, and coopera- tion, war was especially difficult for him. Confronted with the devastating impact of war on soldiers, and later seeing its disastrous effect on children, Adler focused on integrating social interest, a feeling of community, into his theoretical framework. To further this idea, in 1918, Adler founded several child guidance clinics in Vienna and began attracting and training other professionals to develop similar programs across the world.

In 1926 Adler made his first visit to the United States. He accepted a visiting professor- ship at Columbia University, and in 1932 he assumed the first chair of Visiting Professor of Medical Psychology at Long Island College of Medicine. He lectured enthusiastically across the United States and in other countries. His family joined him in 1935 to escape the Fascists who had taken control in central Europe. Despite the fact that his followers were scattered geographically as a result of fleeing Fascism, Adler continued a tireless pur- suit of teaching others about Individual Psychology. During this time, Adler enjoyed popu- larity, and the crowds seemed to relish his presentation format that included both lecture and live demonstration. On May 28, 1937, at the age of 67, while in Aberdeen, Scotland to deliver a series of lectures, Adler collapsed while walking and died from heart failure.

Numerous followers have continued and advanced Adler's ideas and work, and several are well-established authors and educators in their own right. These Adlerians include Heinz and Rowena Ansbacher, Jon Carlson, Raymond Corsini, Don Dinkmeyer, Rudolf Dreikurs, Harold Mosak, Len Sperry, Tom Sweeney, and Richard Watts. In this chapter, you will see citations from the works of many of these leading Adlerians' works as well as Adler himself.

Philosophical Underpinnings

Unlike Freud, who attempted to develop a theory that matched the medical model of his day, Adler developed a theory based on philosophy. The following section details the main philosophical underpinnings of individual psychology.

Responsibility and Creativity

One of the most basic tenets of Adlerian psychology is the notion that people are respon- sible for their behavior, thoughts, and feelings. People choose behaviors that they believe will secure them a sense of belonging and significance in the social order. One can choose to behave usefully, that is, with social interest, or ineffectively, that is, selfishly, avoiding the tasks of life. The turning away from responsibilities is an active choice to act inferior, to give up, and this choice has its own natural consequences.

It is important to note here that the intent of the Adlerian view of responsibility is not to blame but rather to reeducate and encourage change. As Mosak and Maniacci (1999) pointed out, "choosing does not always mean wanting. Freedom to choose is not the same as freedom of choice" (p. 18). These points have important implications for the Adlerian counselor. First, a client may choose to come to a mandated group, even though he does not want to, if not going means he has to go to jail. The second statement indicates that life does present limitations that people cannot choose, such as hair color, parents, and the occurrence of traumatic events. However, people's perceptions and interpretations of those limits are always within their control. People can choose the response when they cannot control the stimulus.

As people are responsible for aspects of self, Adler believed what truly defines the human condition is not what happens to a person but, rather, how the person perceives and then uses what happens. Each individual uses one's creativity to perceive and mold experiences to fit a personal way of being. Adlerians use this conceptualization to explain why two or more people can experience the same event and respond in different ways. If it is the individual who perceives and makes meaning of events, then it is the individual who must be responsible for one's perceptions and any feelings, thoughts, or behaviors one generates.

Teleology

Teleology, derived from the Greek *teleos*, meaning "goal," connotes Adler's belief that all behavior is purposeful. To understand a person, one must understand the person's movement and the goal toward which the individual is moving.

Adlerians believe that every individual's ultimate or final goal is a striving for superiority. Superiority, in the Adlerian sense of the word, does not mean being better than someone else. It refers to an individual's sense of mastery (Adler, 1912) or competence(White, 1957) to achieve a sense of significance and belonging in the social order. In pursuit of this goal, each person creates a system of strategies that Adlerians refer to as the *style of life*. All the behavior in a person's life will be evidence of moving toward the individual's chosen means to achieve superiority. As the goal and strategies are self-created, Adlerians refer to them as fictions. Adler borrowed this idea from Hans Vaihinger (1965) who believed that a person's interpretation of truth was fictional and that all fictions serve a person's final purpose or goal.

A useful personal application of teleology for students studying counseling is to answer the question, "Why am I pursuing a graduate degree in mental health services?" There are many unique answers to this question. Some might say, "To help people," "Because my mom wanted me to," or "Because I am a good listener." Each answer provides insight into the individual purpose of getting an education to become a mental health professional. According to Adlerians that answer also enables the person (or counselor) to consider other, deeper goals. For instance, the person who answers, "To help people," could have the underlying purpose of helping people in order to feel powerful, needed, or meaningful. The underlying purpose or goal is the focus of individual psychology.

Phenomenology

Phenomenology, a term that has its roots with philosophers Husserl, Heidegger, and Jaspers, refers to the idea that each person perceives experiences in a unique and personal manner. Whereas Freud postulated an objective view of behavior, Adler relied on the individual's perceptions of events rather than on the objective events themselves, believing that it is on the basis of perceptions and interpretations that people choose thoughts, behaviors, and feelings.

Let us consider John, a 16-year-old with a history of aggressive behavior, as he details his most recent fight. John maintains he did everything he could to avoid the bully, but when the bully pushed him, John hit him back. In an attempt to connect with John, the counselor reflects, "You feel justified in striking him back. It was self-defense." John replies, "I feel horrible, I didn't want to hit … I gave in … I let him win. I'm disappointed."

The different views of the event demonstrate the importance of the subjective nature of interpretation. To fully understand clients, psychotherapists must see the world from each client's uniquely personal perspective. Zukov (1994) illustrated the concept of phenomenology:

> Reality is what we take to be true. What we take to be true is what we believe. What we believe is based upon our perceptions. What we perceive depends upon what we look for. What we look for depends on what we think. What we think depends on what we perceive. What we perceive depends on what we believe. What we believe determines what we take to be true. What we take to be true is our reality. (p. 313)

Holism

Unlike Freud, who compartmentalized the psyche, Adler believed each person to be greater than the sum of innumerable parts. Adler concurred with his contemporary, Jan Smuts, who coined the term *holism*. This view of a unified personality emphasizes that a person can be understood only by observing interconnected patterns in thinking, behaving, and feeling. Dreikurs (1989) confirmed that "the doctrine of the unity of the personality gave Individual Psychology its name … derived from the Latin word *individuum*, which literally means 'undivided', 'indivisible'" (p. 56).

The concept of holism reflects a philosophical belief that mind and body are one intertwined process that is lost when those aspects are separated. Without the mind, the body is but a shell; without the body, the mind becomes an impotent idea factory without a means to make real its abstract thoughts and dreams. Traditional holism honors the whole person and the integrated expression of the parts working as a whole. Ignoring the whole ignores the essence of humanity and blurs the clearest and most complete understanding of the person. Traditionally, the partitioned aspects of personality included physical, biological, and psychological dimensions (Dreikurs, 1997). Adler took the idea of holism one step further and believed that a person's social context and interactions must be considered as well in a complete understanding of the person, because it is in the social arena that one's mind and body finds expression.

Social Embeddedness

One of the most important aspects of Adlerian theory is its focus on the social importance of humanity. Derived from his own experiences, from reactions to the objective sciences of his day, and from the writings of Darwin, Adler viewed the role of humans' social nature to be of vital importance to the development of normal and abnormal behavior. Adler saw that, in essence, humans are social beings. From the works of Darwin, Adler concluded that species, including humans, who formed tight groups were more successful than those that preferred isolation. Thus, a sense of community has survival value. At birth, most people join their first society, their family, and then branch out into the larger world in which they strive for significance and belonging within new groups. For Adler, the social aspect of human existence became the testing ground for understanding all intra and interpersonal phenomena.

For Adler, a person's relationship to society served as a check and measure of one's mental health. Stone (2008) related the similarity between philosopher Immanuel Kant's view of private sense and common sense and Adler's view. Whereas private sense—a person's unique perspectives—come from the individual's internal world, common sense consists of perspectives the person shares with the external world—others in one's society. An extreme alignment with either world, internal or external, can be unhealthy. For example, individuals who follow only their own private sense are disconnected from society, whereas those who abide only by external frames of reference have a limited sense of self. Adler and Kant agreed that, in the healthiest people, the two perspectives are interconnected and inform one another in an ongoing process of psychosocial growth.

PERSONALITY DEVELOPMENT

Nature of Humans

Function of the Psyche

From the Adlerian perspective, human functioning can be understood in terms of two innate motives. The first is the innate *striving for superiority* that underlies all human activity "from womb to tomb." The second is *social interest*, which exists at birth as only a potential that must be developed. In the following material, these two motives are discussed.

Striving for Superiority Adlerians believe that humans are born inferior: small, naked, visually impaired, and helpless, not yet having a place of belonging and significance in their social surroundings. The most fundamental motive is to move from a sense of inferiority to one of superiority, which includes competence, belonging, and significance. Adler (1956) asserted the ubiquity of the "creative power of life, which expresses itself in the desire to develop, to strive, to achieve, and even to compensate for defeats in one direction by striving for success in another" (p. 92).

The first manifestation of this innate striving for superiority is that infants seek to survive by learning ways to elicit care from individuals in the environment. At first limited in their repertoire of skills, infants make use of what they have, such as crying, cooing, and fidgeting, and repeat whatever strategies produce the sought-after care, such as being fed, held, and rocked. Dinkmeyer and Sperry (2000) discussed how infants with deaf parents quickly realize that crying is not functional. They subsequently cry less but increase visual communications, such as making faces, turning red, and moving arms and legs in an exaggerated manner to attract parental attention and care.

According to Adlerian theory, as infants and young children face each new situation in life, they continue creatively to develop and modify strategies in the striving for superiority. In this process, children subjectively perceive and interpret their environments and draw conclusions about how best to find significance and belonging. Since children's cognitive development is limited, the conclusions they draw become convictions that often conform more to private logic than to the common sense that characterizes the consensus reality of more cognitively developed adults. By the age of five or six years, each child has created a prototypical style of life that outlines general strategies for achieving a sense of superiority, that is, for moving from an inferior "felt minus" position to a superior "felt plus" position. All future behavior will reflect this style of life, that is, the system of strategies the person developed to achieve superiority.

Social Interest Whereas social embeddedness is a fact of life—each person is born into a social context that the person must navigate in striving for superiority—social interest is the motivation to strive for superiority in a way that contributes constructively to others and to society. In other words, each person strives for superiority through strategies that can be characterized on a continuum between self-interest—concern for oneself in which one disregards others' well-being or views others as unimportant or as adversaries, and social interest—concern equally for others' well-being and one's own. Adler believed that each person is born with the innate potential to develop social interest but that significant people in the person's life must foster it through training: first parents or other primary caretakers and siblings and later other associates such as teachers and peers.

Ansbacher (1992) asserted that although Adler's term *gemeinschaftsgefuhl* has often been translated as social interest, actually the term *community feeling* is much closer to Adler's intent. Ansbacher (1992) considered community *feeling* to be the felt sense that one is part of a larger community, and he considered social interest to be the *action* of participating in that larger community in cooperative ways. Watts (2007) advocated for the use of both concepts, social interest and community feeling, as the holistic conceptualization of *gemeinschaftsgefuhl*. In Watts's description, social interest represents the behavioral and cognitive aspects of the dynamic, and community feeling makes up the emotional and motivational aspects.

By contrast, Kaplan (1991) defined social interest through the components of behaviors, feelings, and cognitions. Behaviors associated with social interest include helping, sharing, participating, cooperating, and compromising. Feelings associated with social interest include belonging, faith in others, optimism, communality, and the courage to be imperfect (p. 84). Some cognitions consistent with social interest include, "My personal goals can be attained in ways consistent with the welfare of the community," and "I believe in trying to respond to others as I would like them to respond to me" (p. 84).

An important point about social interest is that its presence is assessed in intention rather than action. For example, Martha donates to charity and volunteers at a local homeless shelter. Does she have social interest? It all depends—on her motive. If she has the financial and temporal resources to give in these ways while maintaining her own well-being, and her motive is to promote the well-being of others, she is motivated by social interest. However, if her giving in these ways takes a toll on her own well-being, such as being unable to pay her own monthly bills, or she undertakes them with an ulterior motive, such as to cite them as evidence of her civic mindedness when she runs for office next year, she is not motivated by social interest.

To summarize, Adlerians believe that all people are motivated throughout life to move from inferiority to superiority. Although all people are born with the potential to pursue superiority with social interest, that potential is relatively more or less developed among various people. Therefore, each person's striving for superiority is characterized by a relatively lesser or greater degree of social interest.

Structure of the Psyche

The structure of the psyche is the style of life. The style of life consists of convictions (basic beliefs about self, others, and the world) that the individual expresses through thoughts, feelings, and actions about how best to strive for superiority. Each person has the potential to rather easily be conscious of one's style of life. However, because each person forms one's style of life prior to formal operational cognitive development, one tends to be nonconscious of it until later in life when one might seek to become more conscious of it.

As previously stated, the style of life is based on private logic. One person's private logic may match fairly closely to the common sense, whereas another's may not match very well, containing mistaken beliefs and basic mistakes about how to strive for superiority—convictions lacking social interest. Whether relatively commonsensical or mistaken, according to Mosak and Maniacci (1999), private logic has three main components: life style goals, hidden reasons, and immediate goals.

Levels of Goals   At the core of the style of life is the lifestyle goal: a long-term goal of which a person is usually nonconscious. Although Adler stopped using the term *fictional goal*, in the Adlerian literature this goal is referred to in this way and represents the child's perception of the ultimate condition that, when achieved, will finally secure the child's superiority. The goal is a fiction because the individual person created it and because it consists of a condition that can never be attained completely or permanently, yet the person continues to strive for it. An example of a fictional goal is "To please others." To play on the saying of the nineteenth century American president, Abraham Lincoln, "You can please some of the people all of the time, and all of the people some of the time, but you can't please all of the people all of the time." Yet, if a person concluded early in life that the best way to achieve superiority is to please others, that person will have built a lifestyle around striving for this ultimately impossible goal—a goal of which the person is most likely nonconscious.

Hidden reasons are more specific principles that derive from the lifestyle goal. People tend to be somewhat more conscious of the hidden reasons for what they do. Examples include pleasing others and avoiding their rejection by being sensitive and responsive to their needs, by anticipating their preferences, by being eager to agree to their requests, and by agreeing—or at least not disagreeing—with their ideas.

Immediate goals operationalize hidden reasons; they are daily answers to long-term striving for significance. People tend to be quite conscious of their immediate goals. Examples of immediate goals are to drop everything when a friend asks for help, to give the other person the choice of where the two go together for dinner, and to say nothing when someone says something with which one disagrees.

In the examples of the three levels of the style of life, notice how each component contributes to a holistically consistent way of thinking, feeling, and acting. The actions, feelings, and thoughts that are a manifestation of immediate goals can be traced back to hidden reasons and, ultimately, to the fundamental lifestyle goal.

Personality Priorities   In the above example, pleasing was the central theme of the style of life. In fact, Adlerians believe that style of life tends to be structured around one of five themes or lifestyle typologies, termed *personality priorities,* of which pleasing is one. Adler (1956) first described four main lifestyle typologies: useful, ruling, avoiding, and getting. Dreikurs (1972) adapted the typologies to apply to children: attention, power, defeat, and revenge. Kefir and Corsini (1974) modified Adler's original categories into personality priorities: pleasing, superiority, comfort, and control (of self or of others). Table 4.1 outlines the distinguishing characteristics of each personality priority.

Nield (1979) discussed four points related to personality priorities:

Everyone has a number one priority (p. 26). People can use each of these priorities in adaptive or maladaptive ways. Discovering an individual's number one priority sheds light on the purpose of behavior.

Everyone has access to the other priorities (p. 26). Although the number one priority is the most informative, some people use other priorities in the service of the number one priority. For example, Mary may appear to please people, but her

TABLE 4.1   Adlerian Personality Priorities

Priority	Method of Belonging/ Significance	Benefit	Cost	To be Avoided	Body Movement	Counselor's Gut Response
Superiority	Being competent, right, useful, martyred	Purposeful, competent, strives to be the best	Overinvolvement, over responsibility, fatigue, stress, uncertainty about one's relationships with other	Meaning-lessness	Listening, attentive, alert, intense eye contact, constant movement	Feel inadequate or inferior
Control	Being in charge of others, authority, rule maker, boundary enforcer	Take charge, reliable	Emotional distance; others withdraw or attack	Vulnerability	None or minimal, challenging eye contact	Feel challenged (power struggle)
	Being "a rock in the storm," composed, reserved	Composed	Emotional distance, diminished spontaneity and creativity	Vulnerability	None or minimal, rigidity, impassive facial expression	Feel distanced
Comfort	Being adaptable, calm, not "rocking the boat"	Relaxed, easy going	Diminished productivity, reduced positive social interaction	Stress	Slouch, easy and fluid walk, shrug or shaking head	Feel irritated, annoyed, and/or impatient
Pleasing	Being able to fulfill the needs of others first, altruistic, caring, unselfish	Cooperative, eager to please	Stunted growth, alienation, retribution; extended relationship outcomes include rejection, disgust, frustration, despair, exasperation	Rejection	Constant eye contact, half smile, immediate forward movement when called, hands in prayer/supplication	Feel pleased

Source: Adapted from Brown, J. F., *Practical applications of the personality priorities: A guide for counselors* (2nd ed.), B & F Associates, Clinton, MD, 1976.

pleasing may be designed to control. The controlling priority surfaces when the secondary priority, pleasing, does not result in her having a sense of control.

Under stress the number one priority becomes most apparent (p. 27). By observing oneself or someone else under stress, then that person's number one priority is likely to be most clearly revealed.

No one priority is inherently better than any other priority. All priorities have their advantages and disadvantages; the disadvantages tend to be associated with an extreme rather than moderate expression of the priority. Though the priorities may differ in their proneness to include social interest, any priority can be enacted with—or without—social interest.

Life Tasks Another perspective on style of life is how a person meets the challenge of the five central life tasks that all people must confront: love, work, friendship, self, and spirituality. Adler (1956) first discussed the tasks of love, work, and friendship, and later Adlerian theorists added the tasks of self (Shulman, 1965) and spirituality (Dreikurs, 1967; Mosak & Dreikurs, 1967). Each is outlined below.

The task of *love* involves one's relative ability to establish and maintain mutually satisfying intimate relationships. According to Adler (1978), from the beginning of life the child is immersed in various examples of this task, primarily modeled by parents. Based on how the child perceives love relationships, he or she will develop basic convictions from which he or she will generate thoughts, feelings, and actions with future intimate partners. As the individual grows, personal experiences with the task begin to occur, typically in adolescence in the form of flirting and dating. Adler believed that love is commonly attached to feelings of inferiority in the forms of embarrassment and vulnerability. The following case example illustrates one client's attempt to confront the task of love:

> Bob, a 32-year-old attorney, was upset with his inability to form a lasting relationship. He reported, "I moved from town to town with my mother. She was married three different times. Although I liked my stepfathers, I remember her saying, "Don't you trust nobody, Bobby. They will rip your heart out and leave you for dead." I never dated much in high school, but I had several sex partners. I would never call them back. I figured I better dump them before they dumped me. I guess I do that now, too. I can't seem to open up. Every time I feel myself getting close to someone, I get scared and run away. 1 guess to them it looks like I'm the bad one, but it's because I'm so scared that they are going to hurt me first.

The task of *work* involves how well a person uses one's abilities to make contributions to society. Children confront the work task first through play and later through how they function in school. What occupation the person chooses indicates ultimately how the chosen style of life addresses the task of work. Equally important is what the person does within that occupation. For example, consider someone who chooses the occupation of a judge. In this position, the person could be fair and compassionate or vengeful and corrupt—reflecting, respectively, the presence or absence of social interest.

The task of *friendship* reflects Adler's belief in the social embeddedness of human beings. Here, the fundamental question is to what extent the person is connected to those in the community. This task is of vital importance to children and adolescents. As the child moves from family to the larger society, it is with friends that the lifestyle strategies, including any mistaken beliefs, become apparent. The quality of such relationships is more telling than the quantity. For example, a person may have hundreds of acquaintances but have no one in whom to confide meaningful aspects of self. It is possible for someone to meet this task with social interest by having one deep friendship, whereas someone else may be struggling even though she has 50 relationships with acquaintances that are characterized by conflict and/or a lack of genuine intimacy.

Although Adler never fully discussed the task of *self*, its importance is implied in his writings. Later Adlerians have fleshed out the task: It involves how well the person has achieved a clear sense of identity that leaves one feeling at peace with oneself and in harmony with society. Mosak and Maniacci (1999) included issues of survival (biological, psychological, and social), body image, self-opinion (how I feel about myself), and self-evaluation (perceived good and bad traits or aspects) in the task of self.

The following case vignette from an adolescent female group demonstrates various ways people struggle with the task of self. Notice how the members discuss views of self, and note the ambivalent feelings that several group members express regarding this task.

Andrea: I don't know. It seems like the boys just want one thing: pretty girls with big breasts. I don't have them, so I feel ugly.

Gina: Who cares what boys think. It's what you think that matters. I feel fine about myself. I have braces and don't feel that pretty on the outside, but I feel good most of the time. You're lucky Andrea; you are pretty and popular.

Andrea: I don't feel that way. I don't like me. I hate to look in the mirror.

Melissa: I know what you mean. I judge myself so much harder than anyone else. I know I am smart, athletic, and fun to be around. I like that about me. I don't know sometimes, I guess I forget and start to beat myself up about little things, but at the time they seem like a big deal.

Gina: I'm not saying I block everyone's opinion out. That's impossible, but no one is going to like you unless you can like yourself, you know? I know that sounds dumb, but I think it's true.

For Adler (1979), *spirituality* was a concretization and interpretation of the human recognition of greatness and perfection (p. 276), a manifestation of an ideal. The task of spirituality involves the extent to which one uses a sense of "something greater" than oneself to support and enhance one's striving for a personally defined perfection. Mosak and Maniacci (1999) delineated five subtasks that involve one's views: (1) one's definition of and relationship to a higher spirit or being, (2) the role and purpose of religion or spirituality, (3) one's relationship to the universe, (4) one's view of life and death, and (5) the fundamental meaning of life. The following statements demonstrate two ways of confronting the spirituality task. Based on your knowledge of Adlerian theory, which client is using spirituality in a healthy way? An unhealthy way?

Tom: I know my life is a wreck, but I can hang on. I really believe that whatever happens to me happens for a reason. It's all a part of a master plan. If I pray long enough, things will work out. I can't change until my higher power feels it's time for me to change. Until then, I am just riding the waves of life, living by faith.

Carolyn: There are times in my life when I feel so depressed, like the world is against me. In those times, I go to church and ask for some insight and patience to help deal with my issues. I feel a sense of inner peace. After those moments of quiet reflection, I often am able to tend to my duties. I can learn a lot from my religion's teachings, and the one thing I always try to remember is that I was given free will. I can choose to be good or evil. With help and support from my church community, I am trying to be a good person.

Final Point and Summary

A final topic pertaining to the structure of the psyche is the role of genetics in a person's style of life. Adlerians acknowledge that genetics provide some practical limitations on individuals. For example, odds are that a person who is three feet tall will never pursue the life task of work as a professional basketball player. However, Adlerians focus on how, despite apparent limitations, a person perceives and creatively uses genetically influenced propensities and characteristics. Adler asserted, "Our objections to the teachings of the hereditarians ... is that the important thing is not what one is born with, but what one makes of the equipment" (1996, p. 353). Dreikurs (1989) noted that humanity's ability to rise above genetic limitations differentiates us from other species. A child who is born with a club foot may perceive this condition as a barrier to living and may become discouraged, operating from a mistaken belief that, "Because of my deformity I can't belong. I must have others take care of me. I am helpless." Conversely, the child may perceive the disability as a challenge and compensate for the problem, channeling energy into ways of belonging that do not necessitate two fully functioning feet, such as pursuing the life task of work through a career in accounting, computers, or counseling. Adlerians emphasize that people born with similar genetic traits will perceive and use them in a wide variety of ways. Consequently, Adlerians encourage people to strive beyond their genetics and use the tools with which they were endowed to connect with other people and contribute to society instead of isolating themselves or excusing themselves not to live life to its fullest.

From the Adlerian perspective, the structure of the psyche is the style of life. The style of life consists of one's convictions about how best to achieve superiority. It is expressed in feelings, thoughts, and actions organized around a central goal. It also is expressed in one's degree of accomplishment of the life tasks. The style of life is determined not by one's heredity but by one's use of what abilities one is given.

Role of the Environment

Familial Environment

When Adlerians discuss the influence of environment on personality development, they emphasize the social environment of the family. The child is born into a society, and that society is the family—the laboratory for the development of the individual's style of life. Although Adlerians traditionally have referred to the nuclear family, in the following discussion, "parents" represent any primary caretakers and "siblings" any other people in the care of those primary caretakers.

Very early in development, children begin to question, "How can I fit into this family? How can I belong and be significant?" As they proceed to answer those questions for themselves, children are sensitive to the responses they perceive coming from parental figures and the roles they perceive siblings occupying.

Parents establish a psychological atmosphere that the child is likely to perceive and to which the child is likely to respond. This atmosphere includes values that the parents express in activities and in ways of relating to each other, to other family members, and to people outside the family. A three-year-old who remarks, "Look at me. I'm working on the computer just like daddy. I'm a hard worker, right?" perceives such work to be important in the family. By emulating the parent, the child strives to achieve belonging and significance within the family. In understanding the psychological dynamics of this situation, the Adlerian emphasis on social belonging and cooperation is very different from the Freudian emphasis on sexuality and competition.

The most important value that parents themselves can enact and can encourage in their children is social interest. As will be discussed below, Adler believed that parental nurturing of the child's innate potential for social interest is central to the child's healthy functioning.

Regarding siblings, Adlerians believe that one influence on personality development is a child's psychological birth order. Contrary to popular opinion, Adler (1958) believed that ordinal birth order, which refers to chronological birth position, is less important than psychological birth order, one's perception regarding one's birth position. The following discussion, adapted from Dewey (1991) and Sicher (1991), presents common themes often associated with psychological birth order.

Every oldest child was once an only child and, therefore, likely reaped the bounty of the family's attention. When the second child is born, the oldest usually is suddenly forced to share, and a dethronement occurs. If the child feels secure in the family, the oldest will often strive even harder to be the best, to be the star: responsible, achievement-oriented, and the bearer of the family values and ideals. If the place is less secure, the child may be increasingly hostile or take on infantile characteristics of the new baby (a form of "acting as if" one is helpless) to get care and regain a sense of significance.

The youngest child is born into a world in which, to his disadvantage, other siblings have already claimed many roles of significance within the family. However, the youngest also has a unique advantage: He never can be dethroned. Usually occupying a role opposite of the oldest, the youngest is most known for using the over responsibility of the oldest to her gain. The youngest child is usually considered the baby of the family and is, therefore, pampered. With all the older people around, it is typical for a youngest child to feel that he or she is entitled to constant care. In one case, a parent brought her four-year-old to counseling because the child rarely talked or walked. When the counselor asked the child about his day, the mother answered, "Oh, he went to the mall with me and then to the store with his brother." The counselor asked the child again, "So tell me about your brother," and the brother answered, "I'm 13 and I play...." The counselor suggested, "Perhaps your son doesn't speak or do for himself because he doesn't have to. You all get so much out of doing it for him." This case, though extreme, demonstrates a characteristic-position of the youngest child.

Like the other positions, being an only child (a small person in a world of big people) can have its advantages and disadvantages. An only child is likely to be the center of the family and can learn to feel very competent without the distractions of competing with other children. The child can use this advantage to form a responsible and helpful style of life. However, when only children attend school, they often have a difficult time socializing with peers. It is almost as if they feel threatened that, with other kids around, their significance has been lost. Often they withdraw or seem like adults trapped in children's bodies.

Shulman and Mosak (1988) described another sibling phenomenon that contributes to the uniqueness of each child: the teeter-totter effect. The sibling who finds one role space occupied will often find another, usually an opposite, role to fill. For example, if one child is athletic, the other child may choose to pursue drama or academics. Occasionally, when one sibling is quite successful, the other sibling believes herself incapable of competing and becomes discouraged that she can find a constructive role through which to achieve a sense of superiority. Out of discouragement, she may choose delinquent behavior to balance out the success of the sibling. This latter example illustrates how "belonging" is best conceptualized not as being accepted but as *finding a place* in the family. Being the black sheep of the family provides a child with a clear position and significance, even if the position and significance are achieved through opposition and conflict—a lack of social interest.

To summarize, several aspects of Adlerian theory help explain how brothers and sisters who grew up in the same family may have created styles of life that are similar in some ways and different in others. Genetic influences may be similar and family atmosphere may remain fairly stable over time, accounting for at least some similarity among siblings. Yet because of psychological birth order and the teeter-totter effect, along with each child's subjective perception and creativity, children who grow up in the same family interpret the family atmosphere in unique ways, accounting for at least some differences among siblings. In the end, Adlerians emphasize that a child creates a style of life based less on the influence of the family environment itself and more on how the child perceives that environment.

Extrafamilial Factors

To Adlerians, the first 5–6 years of life are formative, because it is during these years that a child creates a style of life. The child encounters extrafamilial factors during those first years almost exclusively through the family. For example, in the case of a child raised during a war, it is not war itself, and not even the family's response to war, but the child's perception of the family's response to war that influences the style of life that the child creates. By age 5 or 6, the child has mostly developed a style of life that she uses as a template with which to perceive and respond to extrafamilial environmental events. Although an individual can modify one's style of life in response to powerful events such as trauma or psychotherapy, typically the individual brings one's style of life to one's life circumstances and events and interprets and responds to those circumstances and events accordingly. Thus, once a child has formed a style of life, it tends to be self-perpetuating and, therefore, stable throughout life.

Model of Mental Health

Healthy Functioning

Social interest is the hallmark Adlerian concept in that it is a characteristic that Adler alone specifically honored. Social interest is tied to the Adlerian concept of healthy functioning. Indeed, Adler saw social interest as the gauge for mental health and maladjustment. In his view, a mentally healthy person will courageously meet the tasks of life with adaptable problem-solving strategies that always take into account the welfare of others. In an individual with a strong feeling of community, the striving to overcome inferiority feelings is a lifelong, adaptive movement toward optimal development. It is important to note that this striving is a fluid process, not a static goal. One does not achieve health; one continuously strives toward health.

To maximize health, children need to perceive and develop a sense of significance through contributing to others, working through inferiority feelings with courage, and feeling that they are a part of the social whole. Parents play a key role in providing an environment that maximizes the child's opportunity to perceive and develop along these lines, culminating in the child becoming a cooperative and adaptive adult. Healthy individuals recognize and respect their connectedness with the community and continuously use courage to meet the tasks of life, connect with others, and learn from personal mistakes, using the normal feelings of inferiority as a catalyst for future change. Healthy adults strive for superiority over problems in life by including and cooperating with others instead of competing with them.

Unhealthy Functioning

Adlerians believe clients are not mentally ill but, rather, are discouraged. Adler described maladjustment as pursuing a goal on the useless side of life, that is, striving for superiority with a decreased sense of social interest. This striving can be in the form of creating symptoms to escape the tasks of life or achieving superiority at the expense of others.

Inferiority Complex   A child who experiences pampering, neglect, abuse, or an inconsistent combination of any of these is likely to perceive the world mistakenly, develop convictions that reflect discouragement and provoke anxiety, and create an inflexible style of life. As the person matures, he is likely to continue to use private logic characterized by rigid, mistaken beliefs to cope with life tasks. These beliefs cannot cope with adult demands and will likely lead to increased discouragement and rigidity and a decreased likelihood of breaking out of the maladaptive feedback loop that Adler termed the inferiority complex.

To clarify, Adler believed in three forms of inferiority: *Basic inferiority* is an objective fact. It characterizes every individual at birth and to varying degrees throughout life, most clearly in physical immaturity or disability such as small stature or blindness. This concept was at the foundation of Adler's organ inferiority and compensation ideas. *Inferiority feelings* refer to a subjective evaluation of self. To feel inferior is a choice at any given moment, and in response to inevitable basic inferiority, everyone chooses to feel inferior from time to time. By contrast, an *inferiority complex* is a behavioral demonstration of inferiority based on a conviction that one is inferior. Whereas feeling inferior is not abnormal, believing and acting as if one is inferior is problematic. The inferiority complex includes symptoms to avoid the tasks of life and escape responsibility for meeting them while safeguarding one's self-esteem.

Safeguarding   Safeguarding mechanisms are the Adlerian equivalent to Freudian ego defense mechanisms, with a few important differences. Whereas Freud's defenses were intrapersonal, Adler's were primarily interpersonal. For example, whereas Freud believed the ego employed defenses to protect itself from the id and superego, Adler believed individuals use safeguards to protect themselves from physical, social, or self-esteem threats (Mosak & Maniacci, 1999). Clark (1999) outlined four patterns of safeguarding: distancing, hesitating, detouring, and narrowing the path.

People who use *distancing* withdraw from perceived threats and challenges in life. Doubting, indecision, withdrawal, and isolation are all ways to use the distancing safeguard. These purposeful strategies help the person feel a sense of superiority in acting aloof while seemingly absolving her from responsibility for solving the problem at hand. An example of distancing is a faculty member who removes himself every time a conflict arises in the department. The professor may present a holier-than-thou attitude, preferring not to bother with such immature matters. However, the professor may find himself out of the decision-making loop, even when matters concern him. In fact, he might use the safeguard to protect himself from conflict or the stress associated with making important decisions.

People who use the safeguard of *hesitating* will eagerly confront the tasks of life but will then identify reasons why they cannot complete the task. They will create symptoms to avoid the tasks of life. Examples of this approach to life include, "If only I weren't so angry, I would have good relationships with my family," or "If only I weren't so sick, I would be a good father."

A person who uses *detouring* protects oneself from failure by focusing on other matters. Typically, these matters consist of lesser tasks that take an enormous amount of time so the person has little to no time to address the larger concern. As the person cannot attend to the more significant matter, the risk of failing is minimized, at least for the short-term. For example, a man who agrees to do chores around the house but has limited aptitude for the tasks might feel anxious when his wife asks him to put up a ceiling fan on Sunday. Instead of facing embarrassment when he admits he does not know how, or experiencing failure if he tries, he sleeps late, encourages his family to go to church, takes them out to eat for lunch, goes by the park on the way home, and then feigns exhaustion when he gets home.

In the *narrowed path* form of safeguard, a person accepts only tasks that are easy to accomplish, thereby avoiding failure but also underachieving in the bargain. The client with the MBA who chooses to work in a bookstore as a clerk is one example. When he examines this choice, he discovers it is not that he likes the bookstore as much as that he is afraid he cannot succeed as a businessman. Another expression of this safeguard is the person who accepts larger tasks but chooses to finish only pieces, never quite completing the whole task. By this strategy the person can claim the larger task is a work in progress and can avoid final critique of the work.

Adler discriminated between the neurotic and the psychotic in the degree to which each one denies personal responsibility and social interest (Adler, 1956). A neurotic has a "yes, but" attitude, acknowledging social responsibilities but using symptoms as an excuse not to meet them. A psychotic has no social interest, completely cutting all ties with society, but does not experience failure because she does not even conceptualize the phenomenon of social interest. Additionally, a psychotic may create delusions, hallucinations, and other symptoms to meet life tasks (Mosak & Maniacci, 1999).

Mistaken Beliefs   Just as a lack of social interest is reflected in safeguarding strategies, it also is reflected in mistaken beliefs. Mosak (1995a) outlined the following common patterns of basic mistakes.

In *overgeneralization*, people often use one experience to contaminate future experiences. Examples include, "You can't trust women. They all just want you for your money," or "The world is a scary place. It is never safe to take risks." The underlying message in overgeneralizations is, "It's not my fault I am not succeeding in [fill in the blank]."

In *false or impossible goals of security*, individuals function under an "only if" absurdity: "Only if I can be perfect will I truly find happiness," or "Only if I can control my children will I be a good parent." People making this basic mistake set ridiculously high expectations of self and others. Often they want recognition for having such lofty goals, or they can feel justified in succumbing to hopelessness and discouragement.

Minimization or denial of one's worth is often a clear example of acting as if one is inferior. Examples include, "I'm just the vice president. I don't really make any important decisions. I'm not as smart as everyone else." The message here is a purposeful attempt to avoid responsibility.

The basic mistake of *faulty values* demonstrates a decreased sense or absence of social interest. For example, "You have to get people before they get you," or "The man has to make all the decisions in the family. There is no discussion." These beliefs circumvent any perceived need for social interest and often alienate the person from others that, in turn, leads to greater feelings of inferiority and discouragement.

Summary   People are most likely to develop maladaptive styles of life when their environments do not nurture their innate capacity for social interest. The lack of social interest is reflected in the presence of safeguarding strategies and mistaken beliefs. Although Adler believed humans were capable of health through cooperation, the negative effects of failing to develop social interest include inter- and intrapersonal difficulties at the microlevel and possible species extinction at the macrolevel.

THE PERSONALITY CHANGE PROCESS

In general, people change when they come to understand the style of life they have created, especially its mistaken aspects, and choose to modify their style of life, including thoughts, feelings, and actions. According to Adler, the typical course of life sometimes can facilitate this process, but more often the person needs the atypical process of counseling or psychotherapy to facilitate change.

Client's Role

Clients come to therapy because they are upset that life is not working out the way they expected. They themselves may report that they feel depressed, anxious, or guilty. Underneath these subjective client experiences, the Adlerian counselor sees discouragement: The strategies that formerly helped clients achieve a sense of belonging and significance are currently failing them.

Although clients' motivation to seek counseling is yet another expression of the fundamental striving for superiority, some clients (usually nonconsciously) seek it to perpetuate an unhealthy style of life. That is, they want the counselor to confirm that they are sick and stuck or that they cannot figure out new solutions to the dilemmas they face. In either case, Adlerian counselors believe clients have a great capacity to change, and they place the ultimate responsibility for change squarely on clients. Adlerians believe that pampering, as evidenced by a counselor who views clients as unwilling parties to the formation of symptoms, is disrespectful of individuals' inherent creativity and power. Although, as you will read later, Adlerian therapists see counseling as a collaborative process, they also see clients as the ones ultimately responsible for either maintaining or changing their chosen strategies for achieving significance.

Client resistance results from a misalignment of counselor and client goals. A client who is not open to being challenged by the counselor or to taking responsibility for personal thoughts, feelings, and actions will resist the counselor's encouragement to do so. A client must also be willing to explore past family-of-origin experiences and relate them to present functioning. As the counselor confronts the client's private logic, the client will often use safeguarding mechanisms to protect the style of life from change. This safeguarding is grist for the therapy mill, because it itself is a mechanism the client employed as a child and continued to use consistently throughout life to avoid the tasks of life (Dreikurs, 1989). Therefore, client resistance is not viewed as maladaptive but as information about the client's goals and methods of achieving them.

Counselor's Role

The Adlerian therapist's view of the goals of therapy differs depending on whether the client is seeking counseling or psychotherapy. Although we use the terms counseling and psychotherapy interchangeably throughout this text, Adlerians make a distinction between the two terms. Dreikurs (1967) viewed *counseling* as dealing primarily with immediate concerns, usually impacting only one task of life. He considered *psychotherapy* a longer process concerned with a more dramatic reorientation of the client's style of life. Thus, the therapist assesses what the client seeks and then chooses the specific goals, method, and depth of exploration that aligns with the client's overall therapeutic goals.

Although each client's experience in therapy is different, Adlerian therapists pursue some common goals in both counseling and psychotherapy. Mosak (1995a) outlined the following goals:

- Fostering the client's social interest
- Facilitating in the client a decrease in inferiority feelings, an overcoming of discouragement, and the recognition of one's resources
- Facilitating change in mistaken aspects of the client's lifestyle, that is, mistaken convictions, perceptions, and goals
- Facilitating change to the client's faulty motivation
- Encouraging the client to recognize equality among all people
- Helping the client become a contributing human being (p. 67).

Another way to conceptualize the Adlerian counselor's goal is that the counselor seeks to uncover the cognitive aspects of the client, particularly the basic mistakes in the private logic that constitutes the foundation of the client's style of life, so that the client can bring basic beliefs more in line with common sense and act on those revised beliefs with social interest.

The effective Adlerian counselor is an educator, collaborator, and encourager. The counselor assumes the role of educator to teach the client about social interest and the purpose of behavior. The role of teacher blends with the role of collaborator in that the counselor avoids assuming total control or responsibility for change. The discouraged client will readily act inferior to get the counselor to assume responsibility; however, the counselor must always ensure that the client is working as hard as the counselor at any given time. "The therapist must induce [the client] to face the problems [he came to treatment to resolve] while leaving him to make decisions for himself" (Dreikurs, 1989, p. 88). Additionally, the therapist encourages the client to courageously face the tasks of life with a new or renewed sense of social interest. The counselor uses oneself, including one's empathy, competence, and imperfection as a therapeutic tool to model healthy interest in others. As Manaster and Corsini (1982) noted, "An ideal Adlerian therapist acts as a whole person, encouraging confidently with sensitivity and with social purpose" (p. 168).

Adler (1983) believed that within these three roles, therapists must attempt to: (a) see things from the client's viewpoint; (b) understand why a client does the things he or she does, that is, the purpose of behavior; and (c) illuminate the style of life for the client. Adler claimed that if the therapist followed these steps, she would never experience confusion about what to do next. The simple act of being interested in the client's world, understanding personal motives, and being willing to point out patterns while encouraging the client to re-approach life, often produces change (Adler, 1930).

Stages and Techniques

The Adlerian perspective on treatment emphasizes a comprehensive understanding of the individual seeking counseling. Toward this end, the counselor enacts four phases of the therapeutic process: (a) developing the therapeutic relationship, (b) investigating and understanding the style of life, (c) understanding, and (d) reorientation (Dreikurs, 1967).

The four phases can be compared to a team putting together a jigsaw puzzle that reveals clues to hidden treasure. First, the venture is most likely to be successful if the two members of the team come together with a collaborative, cooperative working attitude. This process is analogous to the first, relationship phase of Adlerian counseling.

In the initial phase of puzzling, the puzzle solvers lay the groundwork for putting the puzzle together by emptying the pieces onto the table or other surface, turning them all face up, and beginning to organize them into groups based on how they might generally be connected. The initial phase is analogous to the second, investigative phase of Adlerian counseling. The counselor and client participate in a variety of activities to collect information and begin to identify the themes and patterns that characterize the client's unique style of life.

In the ultimate phase of puzzling, the solvers put the pieces together to form a meaningful whole—greater than each of the individual pieces—that reveals the clue to previously unrealized treasure. The ultimate phase is like the second, understanding phase of Adlerian counseling, in which counselor and client together reach a mutual, holistic understanding of the client's lifestyle—one that reveals ways the client might realize the treasure of more effective living.

In the quest phase of the venture, the team uses the completed puzzle to seek, and hopefully find, previously undiscovered treasure. The quest phase is like the fourth, reorientation phase of Adlerian counseling, in which the counselor and client use the now-revealed style of life to take action to create a more "golden" style of life.

As any puzzle solver knows, the phases are rarely distinct. In the initial process, certain pieces just come together, revealing important aspects of the whole picture. Indeed, at some points in the ultimate phase, enough of the puzzle might be revealed that the puzzle solvers leave off the puzzle solving process temporarily and venture briefly into actual treasure hunting before returning to complete the puzzle and make sure they've realized all the clues. Similarly, the investigation, understanding, and reorientation phases can overlap as exploration unintentionally yields powerful "Aha!" moments, and the power of those "Aha's!" motivates the client to take immediate action even before investigation and/or understanding are complete. And throughout the entire venture, the working relationship must be sustained, including, if it becomes stressed, stopping the puzzle process temporarily and repairing it so the two can continue together in collaborative cooperation.

Following is more detail of each phase of counseling, including the techniques the Adlerian counselor uses in each one.

Phase 1: Developing a Therapeutic Relationship

In the first phase of Adlerian counseling, developing the relationship, the counselor lays the foundation for an egalitarian working relationship. Adler disagreed with the psychoanalytic notion of the anonymous, omnipotent analyst. Adler believed that if a therapist constructed a cooperative environment, a client would more openly and actively challenge faulty assumptions and would experience the benefits of collaborating instead of competing. In essence, the therapeutic relationship serves as the retraining ground for the client's development of social interest.

The development of the relationship begins with the first contact between counselor and client. The Adlerian counselor is encouraging and supportive while emphasizing the importance of the client's active participation in the counseling process, including regular goal-setting, discussing key issues, and following through on recommendations or plans. Watts (1998) noted the congruence between Rogers's core conditions of empathy, unconditional positive regard, and genuineness and the Adlerian use of social interest within the therapeutic relationship. The following case excerpt is an example of how an Adlerian counselor encourages cooperation and client responsibility from the first phone contact.

Client: Hi, I was referred to you for counseling. So I was wondering about appointment times.

Counselor: I'm glad you called. What is it that you would like to work on in counseling?

Client: Well, I don't think I really need to come. My wife suggested it.

Counselor: Well, I certainly respect your decision to follow through on your wife's request, but I have found that counseling works best if you have some idea of what you would like to work on before you invest the time and money to come. Does that make sense?

Client: Yeah, it does.

Counselor: There must be something that you're considering; otherwise you could have declined your wife's suggestion.

Client: You're right. I have been feeling down lately. I just feel like I should be able to handle it on my own, you know …

Counselor: You're feeling embarrassed about seeking help and support, so it must have taken a lot of courage for you to make this call. Perhaps discussing feelings would be a good place to start. What do you think?

Client: That would be great.

The effectiveness of counseling depends on the maintenance of a caring relationship characterized by work between two equals: the counselor and the client. This first phase provides the foundation upon which later change is built and is the underlying structure for the counseling process.

Phase 2: Investigating Style of Life

According to Mosak (1995a) the second phase, investigating the lifestyle, is comprised of two important parts: exploration of the style of life and how the client's chosen style of life impacts the ability to meet the tasks of life. In this phase, the counselor has access to numerous techniques that can reveal fascinating information about the client. It is important for counselors in this phase to keep their eyes on the goal of all these techniques: identification of the basic convictions on which the client has founded his style of life; of the extent to which the client's private logic in formulating those convictions aligns with the common sense; and, thus, the extent to which the thoughts, feelings, and actions that arise from those convictions help—or hurt—the client in striving for belonging and significance and meeting the life tasks with social interest.

Like the development of the cooperative relationship, inquiry into a client's style of life begins with the first contact. What is the client's demeanor toward counseling? Toward the counselor? How does the client explain the presenting problem? To whom or what does the client attribute responsibility for the problem? What is the client's posture? Voice tone? Each of these bits of information is an aspect of the client's consistent way of being and helps the counselor piece together the client's style of life.

Style of life assessment can be informal or formal. Although discussions in this text are primarily general and informal overviews, Adlerians have published formal style of life inventories (Shulman & Mosak, 1988; Wheeler, Kern, & Curlette, 1993). During this phase, Adlerian counselors use a wide variety of tools and techniques to illuminate the client's patterned way of being. As the counselor gets a clearer understanding of the client's style of life, the counselor can begin to interpret and, thus, move to the next phase. The following represents a discussion of some of the more common tools counselors use for this purpose.

Family Constellation   The family is the first society people experience. It is here, in interaction with family members during the first five years of life that the child begins to crystallize a style of life. Adlerians believe that how a child perceives significance in the family becomes the blueprint for later beliefs about self and others. Therefore, exploration of the client's perception of her original family and her place within it can produce key information about the client's present functioning. Two areas of common assessment include psychological birth order and perceptions of parental figures.

The main strategy for examining the family constellation entails assessing psychological birth order. Psychological rather than merely ordinal position honors the client's perspective on, and unique interpretation of, one's place and role in the family relative to siblings. Attending to psychological positioning enables counselors to explain why some clients do not fit into the traditional birth order profiles that researchers have found to be probabilities for the various birth positions. Psychological birth order profiles can provide the counselor with information for tentative hypotheses regarding patterns in the client's style of life.

The method for exploring birth order can be varied in its formality. The client can give brief descriptions of siblings and any characteristics that stand out for each, any information regarding relationships between the siblings, and commentary on how the client feels about each sibling. Asking the client, "What made your brother, Bob, special in the family? What was his unique role?" can elicit places of significance among siblings and the client. From this information, the counselor can begin to see themes that pertain to the family group and can formulate some ideas about the client's perceived method for belonging and basic convictions about self, others, and the world that are the foundation of the style of life. These formulations are important to the present therapy. As Manaster and Corsini (1982) noted, "Clients often describe themselves as children in a way almost identical to how one would describe them as adults" (p. 181).

Personality Priorities   Typologies are constructs that allow counselors to make tentative hypotheses about a client's style of life and that help a client gain insight into personality dynamics. Although it might seem to an outside observer that typologies lump clients into catch-all categories, the Adlerian counselor is most interested in how each client is uniquely using the characteristics of the typology in the personal striving for superiority. In essence, the typology is the beginning, not the end of the assessment.

Exploring personality priorities can help the client answer the question, "What is the primary strategy I use in my striving for belonging and significance?" Brown (1976) organized a systematic method for using personality priorities with individual clients. Holden (1991, 2000) updated her method and applied it to couple counseling. As early as the first session, the counselor may begin to form a hypothesis about the client's number one priority. Sometimes the first clue is the "counselor's gut response" (see farthest right column of Table 4.1). Once the counselor has an idea of the client's number one priority, she can then explain to the client the rationale for exploring personality priorities, outline the different priorities, and collaborate with the client on identifying one that best matches the client's way of being. The counselor can reduce the likelihood of client defensiveness by assuring the client that no one priority is best. In the next counseling phase, understanding, counselor and client deepen awareness of the fundamental role of the number one priority in the client's style of life by discussing examples that illustrate how the client uses this priority and how it has both helped and hurt the client in achieving a sense of belonging and significance and meeting the tasks of life, with particular emphasis on the role it plays in the challenge(s) the client came to counseling to address. The goal of the reorientation phase is not to change the priority but to make the expression of the priority more healthy and adaptive. For example, a client with a pleasing priority can learn to say "No" before he reaches the point of feeling overwhelmed and withdraws from others. Pleasers can learn to catch themselves (see the Reorientation section below) and use self-statements such as, "I don't have to do everything that others ask of me. I can set and maintain limits and still belong and be significant."

Early Recollections   Adler believed there are no accidental memories. Recollections from one's past represent capsule summaries of one's present life philosophy. At any given time, an individual recalls certain events out of the countless experiences of one's lifetime. Adlerians believe people remember events that confirm their current ways of viewing themselves, others, and their environment. Therefore, a client's early recollection can be a useful tool to uncover the client's style of life. Additionally, research indicates that as the person modifies the view of self, others, and the world, the themes of memories recalled also change (Eckstein, 1976; Savill & Eckstein, 1987; Taylor, 1975).

A collection of 6–10 early recollections is usually sufficient for a counselor to begin to detect themes and patterns. Counselors can use their own personal styles to solicit recollections from clients. For example, "I would like you to tell me your earliest memories. Let's start with your earliest, single specific memory before age 6." It is important to start before age 6 because, as we noted earlier, Adlerians believe each child forms a style of life by this age. Additionally, the phrase "single specific memory" addresses the need to differentiate between a recollection and a report. A report is a general memory, such as, "My mother often scolded me for things I did," and is not specific enough to illicit any useful information. A recollection is a snapshot of a point in time: "One time I was sitting in my high chair with a bowl of cream of mushroom soup, which I didn't like, in front of me. While my mother was talking on the telephone, I put lots of salt and pepper into it so I wouldn't have to eat it. When she got off the phone, I showed her that it was inedible. I remember her tasting it, then looking at me for a long moment—then saying I could get down when I finished my soup. I remember sitting there for hours eating one awful spoonful at a time. I remember feeling relieved when she let me down after I was almost—but not completely—finished." Recollections have more specific information and, more importantly, allow the client clearer access to emotions surrounding the recollection.

Counselors can interpret early recollections in a number of ways. Once again, they do well to keep in mind that the purpose of early recollections is to illuminate the client's style of life and basic mistakes therein. The focus is not on what clients did in the past but, rather, on what they concluded about themselves, others, and the world from the recollected experience and how they continue to enact those convictions, for good or ill, in their current lives. To process the early recollections, write down the recollections verbatim. Focus on content and affect. Interpretation, like all aspects of Adlerian counseling, is designed to be a collaborative process in which both counselor and client are active. The interpretation process involves the counselor reviewing the collected memories and searching for consistent themes or patterns. The counselor presents the interpretations to the client and solicits client feedback on the interpretations. One method for reporting themes is the use of the syllogism (Allen, 1971): "I am ... Others are ... The world is ... Therefore...." The counselor and client work together to fill in the blanks and, at the end of the process, the style of life is clearer.

The following case examples demonstrate a collaborative interpretation of a collection of early recollections (ER). As you read them, look for patterns and try to discern the client's presenting problem.

> ER 1, age 5: 1 am at a friend's party. His name is Riley. All the other kids are gathered around the present table. Everyone gets a plastic dinosaur, but by the time they get to me, all the toys are gone. I burst into tears and run all the way home. I felt so sad and alone.
>
> ER 2, age 5: I wake up on Sunday morning to the sound of laughter. I walk into the kitchen and my whole family is sitting around the table laughing and eating bacon and eggs. They were having fun and didn't bother to include me. I felt left out and sad.
>
> ER 3, age 6: My mom and dad went on some kind of trip. They said they were going to a meeting for several days. I had to stay with Aunt Lois. I remember them driving away and watching them leave. I cried and felt like they were never coming back. I felt scared.

Even with only three recollections, the pattern is fairly clear. The client was a 12-year-old boy who was complaining of feeling isolated and weird, like no one liked him. He did not like being sad, so whenever he felt sad, he would get into a fight. His syllogism worked out like this: "I am unlikable (his word) and left out. Others are mean. The world is cold. Therefore I must fight to not be alone and sad." The early recollection process provides understanding and a place from which to establish goals for change. Readers interested in more information on utilizing early recollections should consult Clark's (2002) excellent book, *Early Recollections: Theory and Practice in Counseling and Psychotherapy.*

Dream Analysis   Unlike Freud, Adler did not believe that dreams are the domain of a raging unconscious, that they are symbolic, or that they represent struggles with past issues. Instead, Adler considered dreams to be problem-solving activities people use to prepare to deal with future challenges. The purpose of a dream is to create a mood that motivates the client into action upon awakening. For example, a client is facing the decision of proposing marriage to his girlfriend. If he does not want to propose, his dream will contain frightening material and, thus, he awakens with a lack of resolve. If he is sure about his choice of a partner, he will dream pleasant, happy dreams. The dream itself is an extension of the style-of-life patterns the dreamer has chosen and helps shed light on a client's true purpose.

The Question   "The question" (Adler, 1956) is a technique designed to uncover the purpose of the client's symptoms. "The question" follows the general format of, "If [the symptom] weren't present, how would your life be different?" By asking "the question," counselors are able to assess what the client is avoiding by using symptoms. The following vignette demonstrates this process.

Melissa: I don't know. I just feel so down all the time. I can't eat. I can't sleep. I must be sleeping only about 3 hours a night. It wears me out. All I can do is keep thinking, "Something is wrong with me. You are defective." It drives me nuts.

Counselor: If you weren't so down and anxious all the time and you could sleep, what would be different?

Melissa: Well, I would feel much better.

Counselor: I bet you would. If you could feel better, what would be different in your life? What would you be able to do that you feel you can't do now?

Melissa: Well I could go to work. When I feel so bad, I call in sick.

With this information, the counselor and client have some clue as to how the client uses depression to avoid the task of work. Further understanding and reorientation can proceed once the purpose is revealed.

Identifying Basic Mistakes   This aspect of the second phase is not so much a technique as a result of the themes emerging from each of the techniques described above. The summary provides the counselor and client with information about consistent strategies within the client's style of life that are incongruent with social interest. These self-defeating ways of being are known as basic mistakes, which typically take the form of overgeneralization, false or impossible goals of security, minimization or denial of one's worth, and/or faulty values.

Summarizing the Material   The above strategies are designed to illuminate the client's style of life. The counselor uses as many strategies as necessary to gather the information needed to help the counselor and client begin to see the client's consistent way of being, with particular focus on maladaptive patterns within the style of life that relate to the client's counseling goals. According to Dinkmeyer and Sperry (2000), the exploration of the client's lifestyle has another vital role: It helps the client feel understood:

> This type of understanding transcends establishment of rapport.... [I]t creates faith in the counselor and stimulates hope that things can change. This kind of understanding goes beyond empathy and confronts you with the fact that you are deciding to display a particular emotion [or behavior] and therefore, you can respond differently. (p. 114)

The information gathered, combined with the client's faith in the process and the counselor's understanding of the client's consistent way of being, provides the necessary foundation to move forward into the next phase.

Phase 3: Understanding

In the understanding phase, counselor and client collaborate in putting together the themes and patterns that emerged from the phase two lifestyle investigation into a mutually agreed-on conceptualization of the client's style of life. The team members come to understand the conclusions the client drew as a child about self, others, and the world in the client's process of striving for superiority. They also come to understand the extent to which the private logic involved in those conclusions do and don't reflect the common sense and social interest. By focusing on the style of life information, the client can come to understand how strategies that, at one time, were seemingly adaptive are now causing problems when applied rigidly to present and future concerns.

The primary technique in this phase is the counselor offering tentative hypotheses about client convictions and purpose, then engaging in discussion with the client until, hopefully, the two reach consensus. If a good working relationship has been established and if the counselor offers hypotheses in the spirit of collaboration, the client is most likely to receive the counselor's interpretations. To meet these criteria, it is best if the counselor presents the hypotheses tentatively and both solicits and welcomes client feedback. For example, hypotheses that begin with, "Could it be ...," "Is it possible that ...," or "I'm wondering if this fits for you ...," all demonstrate understanding in a way that also invites client response. The tentative construction allows the client to agree or disagree and thus decreases the likelihood of defensive safeguarding reactions. If the client disagrees with the counselor's guess, then the counselor can glean the benefit of collaborating with the client on a better conceptualization. Additionally, by handling the client's challenge in a cooperative and understanding manner, the counselor can model social interest and the ability to be accepting of one's own mistakes.

Although the general goal of this phase is understanding of both the adaptive and maladaptive aspects of the client's style of life, the ultimate goals for this phase are twofold: The client begins to see basic mistakes in the style of life and then begins to demonstrate this understanding by noticing thoughts, feelings, and behaviors that typify the maladaptive patterns. Dinkmeyer and Sperry (2000) suggested that the counselor can facilitate the client's active participation at times by asking, "From what you understand about your lifestyle, how would you explain the current experience you have just been describing to me?" (p. 117). As the client begins to demonstrate an understanding of the purpose of behavior, client and counselor can begin to explore how the client might reorient one's style of life.

Phase 4: Reorientation

Reorientation is the phase in which clients demonstrate *insight*. Adlerians define insight in a unique way: It is not merely the understanding of one's style of life, including its mistaken aspects, but the translating of that understanding into action in which the style of life reflects a greater degree of success in meeting the tasks of life with social interest. Adler believed that understanding was good but that it was meaningless if people did nothing with their new perspectives. Out of the clarity of understanding their purpose of behavior and means of accomplishing that purpose, clients are challenged to choose different strategies to attain significance; to shed old maladaptive ways of being, characterized by a demonstration of inferiority, an avoidance of life's tasks, and a lack of social interest; and to develop new, more adaptive ways. This challenge is often scary for clients because, to complete it, they must step out of the familiar into the unknown. Therefore, although counselors encourage clients in this phase, the decision to reorient rests with clients.

To help with the reorientation, Adlerian therapists have created and utilized a wide variety of innovative techniques including giving advice, task setting with homework, guided imagery, confrontation, and encouragement (for more on encouragement, see Table 4.2). Often, Adlerians challenge clients to act as if they were different. For example, a shy man may act as if he is assertive and then solicit feedback on how others perceive him. Counselor and client then use the client's perception of the feedback to challenge old beliefs and patterns and develop new ones. Adlerian counselors sometimes make cautious and judicious use of paradoxical intention, or antisuggestion, in which they recommend that a client actually do *more* of a certain undesirable feeling, thought, or action under controlled circumstances that do not hold the potential for long-term damage; in this way, the client is

TABLE 4.2 Praise, Encouragement, and Discouragement

Praise	Encouragement	Discouragement
1. You cleaned up your room just like I told you to!	You really worked hard at cleaning up your room!	You left a sock out. I hope you do better next time.
2. You got an "A." That's my girl!	I can tell you are very proud of your grade!	You may have made an "A" in science, but what about math?
3. You make Daddy happy when you tell the truth.	You were brave to tell the truth even though you knew you would be grounded.	I can't believe you disobeyed me! I don't want to hear another word!
4. You don't need my help. You're the smartest one in the class!	I am confident that you will do your best.	Here, just let me do it for you.
5. I like you a lot better when you are wearing your smile!	You look very happy today. Would you tell me about your day?	It's nice that one of us had an easy day! [Sarcastically]
6. You're doing great! Growing up just like your old man!	You are looking forward to going to high school and trying out all the cool new opportunities.	All teenagers are the same. They think they know everything. I was your age too. I didn't know crap and neither do you.

Source: Reprinted from Fall, K. A., & Howard, S., *Alternatives to domestic violence*, Brunner-Routledge, New York, 2004. With permission.

likely to experience more intensely than ever before the ineffectiveness of the strategy and the extent to which the strategy is under the client's control to increase or decrease. Along the same line, the push button technique can demonstrate that each person can create different emotions and beliefs at will. An angry client may be encouraged to get angry in session, then asked to choose to remove the anger and feel frustrated, then calm, then angry again. Through this process, the client learns the power of choice and control over one's self.

CONTRIBUTIONS AND LIMITATIONS

Contributions

Adlerian theory has had a lasting impact on the field of psychotherapy. Initially proposed as a socially oriented cognitive therapy, the approach provided a more human alternative to Freud's mechanistic model. Adler's most unique contribution, social interest, associates healthy functioning with contribution to a greater good and is optimistic in its thrust. In addition, by pointing out the role of courage in human existence, and the potential for people to encourage each other toward more effective living, Adler served to frame people in terms of their positive potential rather than emphasizing only their pathological vulnerabilities; for a better understanding of the critical difference between encouragement and praise see Table 4.2. Furthermore, Adler was a forerunner in advocating equality among the sexes in particular and humanity at large. Additionally, Adler's work with families and child guidance continue in many facets of society.

The most notable contribution of Adler's work is that his ideas have been blended and incorporated into almost every school of therapy included in this text, mostly without acknowledgment. It seemed as though Adler could see this eventuality coming when he stated, "There might come a time when one will not remember my name; one might even have forgotten our school ever existed. But this does not matter because everybody will act as if he had studied with us" (Manaster, Painter, Deutsch, & Overholt, 1977, p. 33). Ferguson (2000) remarked that "contemporary psychology increasingly reflects important concepts of Adler and Dreikurs" (p. 14). Watts (2000b) made a case for Adlerian influence and compatibility with a wide range of modern therapies: constructivist, cognitive, systemic, brief approaches, solution-focused, and narrative. Mosak and Maniacci (1999) showed similarities of Adler's formulations with those of family therapy, existentialism, object relations, and integration theories.

Having concepts borrowed without recognition is ironically Adlerian, in that the importance lies with the contribution, not the recognition or glory. Watts (2000b) asserted that Adlerian psychology, because of its inherent depth and applicability, was ahead of its time. He contended that its contribution and staying power rests on its flexibility: Adlerian practitioners enjoy a particular freedom in their practice because they can be both theoretically consistent and technically eclectic (p. 26). As the mental health profession moves toward integration of theoretical approaches, Adlerian theory seems well placed for future shifts.

Limitations

A review of this chapter reveals some apparent limitations of the Adlerian approach. With a theory of wide depth and scope, practitioners, especially those learning about the field, may become overwhelmed with the amount of concepts and strategies contained in the theory. Nebulous dynamics such as striving for superiority, inferiority, fictional goal, and style of life are difficult to define operationally. Even the capstone concept, social interest, is still causing confusion regarding its definition and meaning. Adlerians need to address this limitation by continuing to define and research key concepts.

Although Adler had ideas about how humans grow, he did not formulate a sound theory of development or learning (Mosak & Maniacci, 1999). For example, although Adlerians discuss how to parent, they do not have a consistently solid developmental model from which to draw conclusions and differentiate developmentally appropriate behavior. Perhaps Adler resisted formulating a developmental sequence in reaction to Freud's model. Whatever the reason for originally ignoring the issue, Adlerians have ample modern models available to integrate into Adlerian constructs.

The most debilitating limitation of any theory is stagnation. Manaster and Corsini (1982) noted that while doing research for their book, *Individual Psychology*, they noticed that almost nothing had been added in the literature that in any way contradicted what Adler said; everything new appeared to be additions to, supplements to, or further explications of his basic ideas. Carlson (2000) admonished Adlerians to expand and integrate, to become more inclusive than exclusive. He remarked that,

> If Adler were alive today, he would not be sitting around rehashing the same concepts developed 80 years ago. Instead, he would be out in the community and the world, trying to make a difference … He would look at larger systems and how to influence them. (p. 9)

The literature is full of examples outlining the attempt to integrate other theories with Adlerian concepts. For example, *The Journal of Cognitive Therapy* (1997) dedicated a special issue to exploring the integration of Adlerian, cognitive, and constructivist approaches. The *Journal of Individual Psychology* (1998) devoted a special issue to the integration of narrative and Adlerian theories, and Watts and Carlson's (1999) text, *Interventions and Strategies in Counseling and Psychotherapy*, contains chapters on the integrative application of Adlerian theory with an array of theories and a variety of special populations and clinical issues.

To this end, Adlerians must continue to strive to reinvent the theory in the light of modern times by using the very principles of community involvement and curiosity to contribute, as Adler and Dreikurs first outlined. If individual psychology is to thrive, Adlerians must bring it out of the shadows by actively educating professionals and society about their ideas. They can achieve this aim through workshops, practice demonstrations, involvement in political causes, and cooperation with other theoretical approaches and disciplines, much like Adler did in his time.

Interface With Recent Developments in the Mental Health Field

The Nature–Nurture Question

Research results have supported some aspects and failed to support other aspects of the Adlerian view of the relative roles of heredity and environment on personality/style of life. Adlerians might be considered "soft determinists," in that they acknowledge individuals' choices within the limits and probabilities of genetic and environmental influences. However, as we discussed in Chapter 1, the finding that genetics explain 30–50% of variance in most personality traits (Gatz, 1990) indicates that choice may not be as extreme as Adlerian theorists have advocated and that discouragement may be a less-than-complete explanation for disorders that researcher know or strongly suspect are genetically influenced, such as schizophrenia, depression, and manic-depression (Gatz, 1990). The finding that antisocial behavior is genetically influenced (Raine & Dunkin, 1990) brings into question whether social interest is innate as a potential in everyone and whether its absence in adulthood is necessarily the result of inadequate training during the developmental years. Nevertheless, Adlerians presumably would heartily concur with researchers who concluded that "Biology is *not* necessarily destiny" (Baker & Clark, 1990, p. 599) and would point not only to how environmental accommodations can maximize or minimize genetic effects but also how people—at least those unimpaired by choice-limiting disorders such as Alzheimer's Disease—can serve as agents of choice in their own development, including the choice of the extent of exposure to certain environments.

A related question is the extent to which a child's theoretically innate creativity and initial tendency to perceive in unique ways might actually be genetically influenced rather than the seeming wild cards with which everyone is equally endowed and that can override the influences the environment and other aspects of heredity. Ironically, until researchers definitively identify genetic influences in these regards, belief in various degrees of determinism is still largely a matter of philosophical choice.

Interestingly, longitudinal research on attachment theory has revealed that adults' descriptions of their parents' parenting, rather than being a subjective perception reflecting those adults' current functioning, quite objectively corresponds to how external observers described that parenting at the time the parents were providing it. Similarly, research indicates that "parenting styles and traditional family variable may be relatively unimportant in understanding problem behavior" (Baker & Clark, 1990, p. 598), which contradicts the Adlerian view of the role of "family atmosphere" in development of a child's style of life. However, research confirms the important role in personality/style of life development of nonshared, unique experiences, such as illness, accidents, specific interactions with a specific caregiver, and receiving awards (Baker & Clark, 1990)—the stuff of which early recollections are made.

DSM–IV–TR Diagnosis

Unlike many psychological theories that emphasize pathology, individual psychology focuses on a person's unique use and meaning of symptoms, not the symptoms themselves. Some Adlerian sources indicate that, because labeling fails to tell the true story and movement of the client, Adlerians use diagnostic labels only for nontherapeutic purposes, such as completing insurance forms (Mosak, 1995a; Sperry & Carlson, 1996). Adler (1930) commented on the pitfalls of diagnostic labeling:

> If he stops at this point and believes that when he hears the word ... "anxiety neurosis" or "schizophrenia," he has gained some understanding of the individual case, he not only deprives himself of the possibility of individual research, [he] will never be free from misunderstandings that will arise between him and the person he is treating. (p. 127)

Within the Adlerian framework, the primary axes of the *Diagnostic and Statistical Manual of Mental Disorders* (*DSM–IV–TR*; American Psychiatric Association, 2000) can be conceptualized in the following manner.

Axis I: These disorders are classified as the "Yes, but I'm sick" neurotics (Mosak & Maniacci, 1999). Instead of confronting a life task, they create symptoms to safeguard and excuse themselves from meeting the given task. For example, an anxious man states, "Yes, I would love to meet a nice woman, but I am too nervous," or a depressed woman states, "Yes, I would like to work, but I am too sad and tired."

Axis II: These personality disorders are characterized by, "Yes, but I'll do it my way." Sperry and Mosak (1996) illustrated that these clients respond to the tasks of life in idiosyncratic and inappropriate ways, usually failing to fulfill the task. Examples include: "Yes, I want to work, but I'm on a different wavelength than others, so I must use caution" (schizotypal), and "Yes, I want friends, but others hate me, so I must demand reassurance or I will withdraw" (avoidant).

Overall, diagnosis as classification is theoretically useless to the Adlerian. It tells the counselor how the client thinks they are sick, but Adlerians are more interested in what the client is doing with the symptoms and how the client is using symptoms in the striving toward superiority.

Pharmacotherapy

As we discussed in Chapter 1, the use of medication is an increasing reality in the realm of psychotherapy. In Adler's time, researchers had not yet developed psychotropic medications, but his daughter, Alexandra, had this to say about her father's probable view of medication: "I would have loved my father to have seen the effects of drugs on psychosis. I am sure he would have accepted it. He was always open to progress" (Manaster et al., 1977, p. 57). Adlerians have debated this issue, with many believing that the use of medication is an ethical adjunct to therapy. In many cases, pharmacotherapy can help clients achieve a mental state in which they can benefit from counseling (Sperry, 1990). However, honoring the perspective that psychosis as purposeful, some Adlerians have demonstrated the usefulness of therapy alone with psychotic patients (Mosak, 1995b).

Managed Care and Brief Therapy

Carlson, Watts, and Maniacci (2006) noted that Adlerian counseling has been a brief form of counseling since its inception. For Adlerian therapists, the application of brief therapy is similar to the process of long-term therapy. Adler believed the important aspects of understanding the client and the purposes or goals of behavior were the key elements of the therapeutic process that a client and counselor could achieve in a relatively short time. Adlerians adopt a therapy method that could be brief in time but emphasize the need to take time to understand the subjective experience of the client. Bitter and Nicoll (2000) outlined an Adlerian approach in which a counselor can employ functional solutions to the client's problem without sacrificing the tenets of Adlerian theory (see Figure 4.1).

The emphasis of the brief model is on using the tools and techniques, in any order, to understand the lifestyle of the individual and encourage change. For example, in Bitter and Nicoll's (2000) approach, "the data base," "meeting the person," "the subjective interview," and "the question" are all ways to form a collaborative alliance with the client and assess the presenting problem. The objective interview and family constellation/ tasks of life/early recollections phases represent a lifestyle assessment. Based on the combination of these two steps, the counselor makes tentative hypotheses about the purpose of the symptoms of the presenting problem. The client who understands and agrees will likely proceed to change, whereas the one who disagrees or resists will return with the counselor back to more lifestyle assessment.

Technical Eclecticism

Adlerian theory provides a solid foundation for counselors to be integrative in their approach. In a professional climate in which being eclectic is a common and popular answer to one's theoretical orientation, recent Alderian literature has focused on how multifaceted the theory can be with a wide range of populations (Carlson, Watts, & Maniacci, 2006; Oberst & Stewart, 2003). Whereas many practitioners are critical of tying oneself to a single theory, Adlerian therapy is philosophically positioned to be very broad in its application.

In the beginning stages of counseling, Adlerians focus on forming a relationship built on trust, cooperation, and respect. Any techniques from other theories that promote such a relationship may be incorporated into an Adlerian approach. Examples include the necessary conditions for change that Rogers espoused: empathy, unconditional positive regard, and genuineness that a counselor can operationalize primary through reflective responses (see Chapter 6). The main difference between the theories would be that Adlerians would use these attitudes and skills to deepen the counseling and move it forward but not consider them sufficient to facilitate client change, whereas Rogerians would see these elements as both necessary and sufficient for change.

In the middle phase of the counseling process, when counselors are looking to identify patterns and basic mistakes, using any technique that serves this goal is appropriate. Systems techniques such as genograms can help illuminate family of origin connections, and cognitive techniques found in REBT or cognitive theory can be useful for identifying clients' basic mistakes and private logic. In a recent dialog between an Adlerian, Jon Carlson, and the founder of Reality Therapy, William Glasser, they used a case comparison to highlight areas of convergence and divergence (Carlson & Glasser, 2004). They concluded that the theories were quite similar in their applications, with the largest

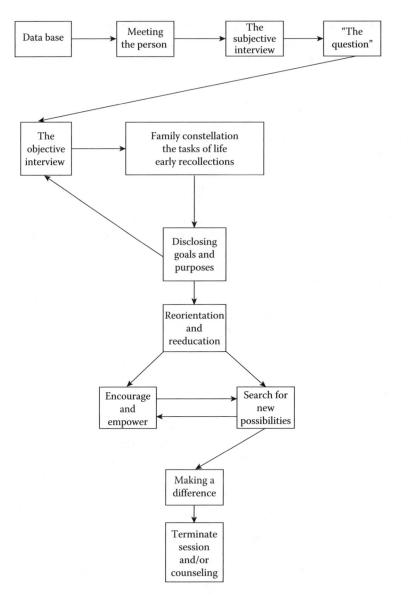

FIGURE 4.1   Adlerian brief therapy. (Adapted from Bitter, J. R., & Nicoll, W. C., *Journal of Individual Psychology, 56,* 35, 2000.)

overlap occurring in such aspects as a here-and-now orientation, focusing on the creativity and strengths of the client, and helping the client make better choices.

   In the later stages of counseling, as a client begins to experiment with reorientation, any techniques that help the client practice the chosen modifications to the style of life would be appropriate. Homework assignments found in cognitive theory literature, such as mood logs or cognitive cycles, or in behavioral theory literature, such as behavioral contracts, may be useful. The counselor can flesh out the "acting as if" technique by recording and spelling out the details in a contract. Any of these activities would involve a collaborative process between counselor and client, with the client taking on more responsibility as counseling progresses.

Diversity Issues

Gender, ethnicity, sexual orientation, and spirituality are four important diversity issues that Adlerian theorists have addressed. By contemporary standards, Adler was a true feminist, not afraid to comment on how women should be accorded the freedom of equality. As early as 1927, Adler (1978) seemed to be commenting on late twentieth century concerns by stating "that human culture is characterized by the overtowering significance of man" (p. 5) and that "the low esteem of women is expressed in far lower pay for women ... even when their work is equal in value to men" (p. 7). Adler was sensitive to the impact of inequality on both men and women and saw the resulting conflict as possibly devastating.

Dreikurs (1999) noted that the generally accepted war of the sexes was a self-fulfilling prophecy of socially useless behavior on both sides: men striving for superiority over women and women acting as if they are inferior or rebelling against men. Adler refused to accept or use the term *opposite sex*, choosing to say always *the other* sex. He wouldn't concede that the two genders must, by nature, be in opposition. Instead he preached the doctrine of social equality for all people, regardless of obvious differences. Adlerians observe the striving of each individual through the life task of love, described earlier. He advocated that for healthy love relationships to occur, the common conceptualization of the relationship between men and women as a war must be reoriented as a relationship based on cooperation, equality, and respect.

A long-time focus of Adlerian theory has been respect for diverse cultural identities through an appreciation of the subjective view of every client. Sherman and Dinkmeyer (1987) asserted that Adler's sociocultural concepts and practical, commonsense approach make individual psychology a natural fit for various ethnic groups. Arciniega and Newlon (1999) proposed that, of all the counseling theories, individual psychology best suits the needs of minority groups by focusing on the importance of community, family, cooperation, and social interest, or contributing to a larger group. Mozdzierz (1998) noted that social interest is a unifying concept among cultures that encourages various groups to consider and respect the growth and striving of other groups. A review of recent Adlerian literature demonstrated a continuing effort to further explore the efficacy of the Adlerian approach with diverse cultures and multicultural applications (Brack, Hill, Edwards, Grootbroom, & Lassiter, 2003; Carlson & Carlson, 2000; Duffey, Carnes, Carnes, & Garcia, 1998).

One area of multicultural impact has been in the area of parent training. Adler and his followers have historically had a strong interest in creating democratic-based families in which parents are the teachers of discipline and responsibility and relationships are based on cooperation and social interest. As one may expect, different cultures have differing values of the role of the parent, and Adlerians have been proactive in testing and applying their approach to various cultures. Research seems to indicate that training in Adlerian principles and practices is not only effective at improving parent–child interaction but can also extend into schools, improving student–teacher relationships (Gfroerer, Kern, & Curlette, 2004; Prinz, Arkin, & Gelkopf, 2008).

The issue of sexual orientation is a good example of how a theory must adapt to changing societal views. Adler viewed homosexuality as a dysfunctional style of life and rejected a biological basis for sexual orientation (Maucieri & Stone, 2008). Today, the majority of mental health professions and professionals consider homosexuality to be a normal variation and a nonpathological orientation possibly resulting from genetic or other biological phenomena. Several professional associations, including the American Psychiatric Association, American Psychological Association, and American Counseling Association, have amended their ethical codes and standards of practice statements to encourage fair and equitable treatment of people with any sexual orientation.

Like many theories and professions in which the founding theorist originally conceptualized homosexuality as categorically unhealthy, Adlerians have taken steps to create a dialog to reconsider and reconceptualize the theory's position on sexual orientation. In general, it is safe to say that Adlerians have moved away from the blanket assumptions that homosexuality is universally deviant and that no biological basis exists for sexual orientation. However, the discussion is far from over. Although Adlerian counselors may be well positioned to connect with clients based on the philosophical underpinnings of phenomenology, holism, and social interest, a given counselor's belief system may conflict with the style of life of the client. The most difficult issue for many Adlerians rests with the issue of choice versus biological determinism. This struggle is actually similar to dialogs regarding choice and behavioral–emotional–cognitive manifestations of schizophrenia or diabetes. In short, the answer is as it has always been: "It's not what you have; it's what you do with what you have." Conceptualized in this manner, the issue is not so much homosexual orientation itself but the degree to which homosexually oriented individuals meet the life tasks with social interest.

When most other mental health theories ignored or denigrated spirituality, Adlerians elevated it to the stature of one of the five tasks of life. Croake and Rusk (1980) and Leak, Gardner, and Pounds (1992) explored the integration of Adlerian, Eastern, and Buddhist concepts. O'Connell (1997) wrote about the importance of spirituality in Adlerian counseling and its possible impact on personal growth. Watts (2000a) applied Adlerian principles to Christian tenets. More recently, Johansen (2005) explored the overlap of Adlerian concepts with those found in the Islamic faith. In this regard, Adlerians again appeared to be ahead of their times.

Although Adlerians have made strides in the incorporation of spirituality into counseling, more work is needed. In each of the articles cited above, the authors found a great degree of overlap between the philosophy of individual psychology and various forms of spirituality. However, they also indicated points of possible divergence. It is important for Adlerian counselors to honor each client's phenomenology and respectfully explore the definition and role of spirituality in each client's life. The Adlerian litmus test of social interest—whether particular beliefs and practices contribute constructively to the social order—can apply equally to spiritual beliefs and practices. Pursuing the topic in this manner, proponents of individual psychology are well placed philosophically to respect a wide range of spiritual beliefs and practices.

The Effectiveness of Psychotherapy

As with many of the theories we covered in this book, little empirical evidence specifically substantiates the effectiveness of Adlerian theory. It is no surprise that, considering the highly specific and operational criteria the American Psychological Association task force used in their quest to identify validated approaches to psychotherapy (Crits-Christoph, 1998), they did not cite individual psychology as a validated approach. With regard to Asay and Lambert's 1999 study on the factors that make counseling effective, Adlerian theory fits well with the focus on the therapeutic relationship, the importance of the client's own motivation, and even the vital nature of external factors. As mentioned in the stages of therapy section, Adlerian theory places a heavy emphasis on the development of an egalitarian working relationship between client and counselor. Due to the philosophical foundation of personal responsibility, Adlerians would agree that the client's expectations for improvement and motivation for change are key to the success of counseling.

Although inferiority issues may influence the client's sense of personal responsibility, these issues become the centerpiece of the therapy. Adlerians also honor the impact of extratherapeutic factors noted in the study, although, perhaps in a different manner than the study intended. The study described these factors as largely outside the counselor's influence, but Adlerians are less concerned about how they can influence the issues of culture, social support, and intrapsychic dynamics and more focused on how the client uses these factors. From an Adlerian perspective, these factors are not important from an objective sense, but are vital from a phenomenological one.

Mosak and Maniacci (2008) maintained that the lack of quantitative research on individual psychology does not mean it is not effective but that the assessment was not appreciative of the more qualitative approaches Adlerians have used to study the theory's effectiveness. As the fields of psychology, counseling, social work, and psychiatry gain a greater understanding and appreciation of qualitative research, we believe researchers will increasingly find support for the effectiveness of Adlerian and other theories.

CURRENT STATUS

Adlerian theory currently enjoys popularity throughout the world. The North American Society of Adlerian Psychology (NASAP) publishes the quarterly journal, *The Journal of Individual Psychology,* which includes scholarly and clinical articles relevant to the Adlerian approach. The NASAP also holds an annual international conference and sponsors training institutes across the United States and Canada. The Adler School of Professional Psychology grants graduate degrees and certificate training with an emphasis in Adlerian counseling. The International Committee of Adlerian Summer Schools and Institutes (ICASSI) is an organization that provides Adlerian educational seminars throughout the world and coordinates the annual Rudolf Dreikurs Summer Institute.

SUMMARY

Alfred Adler created a form of therapy that emphasized the social nature of humankind. Opposed to Freud's negative and deterministic views, Adler focused on how every individual strives from inferiority toward a personal sense of superiority. The family plays an important role in development because it represents the societal training ground for the growing child. Interacting with the environment, each child forms a life plan that the individual uses throughout life as a guide for ways to be significant in the world. Although Adler viewed all behavior as purposeful, he distinguished healthy and unhealthy behavior based on whether or not the individual's underlying purpose in any action was social interest (the intention to contribute to society) or was purely selfish interest. The concept of discouragement as maladjustment is consistent with Adler's positive view of humanity: He described how maladjusted people have either never gained or lost the courage to face life's tasks in socially useful and responsible ways. Thus, the theory of change emphasizes counselors working collaboratively with clients to assess and then challenge clients' basic mistakes, faulty logic, and safeguarding strategies and then to encourage clients to find new ways of fulfilling their goals of superiority through socially interested methods.

RECOMMENDED RESOURCES

Books

Adler, A. (1956). *The individual psychology of Alfred Adler* (H. L. Ansbacher & R. R. Ansbacher, Eds.). New York: Basic Books. Excellent collected works of Adler. Difficult to read straight through, but a wonderfully comprehensive reference work.

Carlson, J., Watts, R. E., & Maniacci, M. (2006). *Adlerian therapy: Theory and practice.* Washington, DC: American Psychological Association. This is probably the best new book about the theory. The authors do an excellent job presenting the depth of the theory while highlighting its contemporary use and clinical utility.

Dinkmeyer, D. C., & Sperry, L. (2000). *Counseling and psychotherapy: An integrated, individual psychology approach* (3rd ed.). New York: Merrill. Easy to read and very practitioner oriented. The book also covers various treatment modalities such as group, couples, adolescent, and elderly applications.

Dreikurs, R. (1999). *The challenge of marriage.* Philadelphia, PA: Accelerated Development. This newly reprinted work is a must for applying the Adlerian concepts to couples. It covers a wide range of topics such as jealousy, sex, living together, and parenthood.

Manaster, G., & Corsini, R. (1982). *Individual psychology.* Chicago, IL: Adler School. This is an older book but it covers just about everything. Nice case examples.

Mosak, H., & Maniacci, M. (1999). *A primer of Adlerian psychology.* Philadelphia, PA: Brunner/Mazel. This book mainly addresses theory and is fairly light on the practice element.

Sicher, L. (1991). *The collected works of Lydia Sicher: An Adlerian perspective* (A. K. Davidson, Ed). Fort Bragg, CA: QED Press. This book has an informal feel and tackles concepts such as guilt, philosophical issue, early recollections, and generous case studies. There are even two question-and-answer chapters.

Sweeney, T. J. (2009). *Adlerian counseling: A practitioner's approach* (5th ed.). New York: Routledge. Easy to read and very practical. There is good coverage of spirituality.

Watts, R. E., & Carlson, J. (1999). *Interventions and strategies in counseling and psychotherapy.* Philadelphia, PA: Accelerated Development. Great overview of Adlerian theory with chapters on special populations and applications.

Audiovisuals

Carlson, J. (1999). *Psychotherapy with the experts: Adlerian counseling.* Needham Heights, MA: Allyn and Bacon. In an attempt to demonstrate, within a limited time, all four phases of the Adlerian counseling process, Dr. Carlson presses through with his client. Although the product is a somewhat more directive process than typifies this counseling approach, Dr. Carlson succeeded in demonstrating how the four phases relate to each other in work with the style of life of one client.

Web Sites

These Web sites supply good historical information, chat rooms, and book resources: Alfred Adler Graduate School, Minnesota: http://www.alfredadler.edu

Adler School of Professional Psychology, Chicago: http://www.adler.edu
North American Society for Adlerian Psychology: http://www.alfredadler.org

REFERENCES

Adler, A. (1907). *Study of organ inferiority and its psychical compensation* (S. E. Jeliffe, Trans.). New York, NY: Moffat-Yard.

Adler, A. (1912). *The neurotic constitution.* New York, NY: Dodd & Mead.

Adler, A. (1930). *Problems of neurosis.* New York, NY: J. J. Little & Ives.

Adler, A. (1956). *The individual psychology of Alfred Adler* (H. L. Ansbacher & R. R. Ansbacher, Eds.). New York, NY: Basic Books.

Adler, A. (1958). *What life should mean to you.* New York, NY: Capricorn.

Adler, A. (1978). *Cooperation between the sexes* (H. L. Ansbacher & R. R. Ansbacher, Eds.). New York, NY: Norton.

Adler, A. (1979). *Superiority and social interest* (H. L. Ansbacher & R. R. Ansbacher, Eds.). New York, NY: Norton.

Adler, A. (1983). *The practice and theory of individual psychology* (P. Radin, Trans.). Totowa, NJ: Littlefield, Adams.

Adler, A. (1996). The structure of neurosis. *Journal of Individual Psychology, 52,* 351–362.

Allen, T. W. (1971). Adlerian interview strategies for behavior change. *The Counseling Psychologist, 3,* 40–48.

American Psychiatric Association. (2000). *Diagnostic and statistical manual of mental disorders* (4th ed., text rev.). Washington, DC: Author.

Ansbacher, H. L. (1992). Alfred Adler's concepts of community feeling and of social interest and the relevance of community feeling for old age. *Journal of Individual Psychology, 48,* 402–412.

Arciniega, G. M., & Newlon, B. J. (1999). Counseling and psychotherapy: Multicultural considerations. In D. Capuzzi & D. Gross (Eds.), *Counseling and psychotherapy* (22nd ed., pp. 435–458). Columbus, OH: Merrill/Prentice Hall.

Asay, T. P., & Lambert, M. J. (1999). The empirical case for the common factors in therapy: Quantitative findings. In M. A. Hubble, B. L. Duncan, & S. D. Miller (Eds.), *The heart and soul of change* (pp. 23–55). Washington, DC: American Psychological Association.

Baker, L. A., & Clark, R. (1990). Introduction to special feature. Genetic origins of behavior: Implications for counselors. *Journal of Counseling and Development, 68,* 597–600.

Bitter, J. R., & Nicoll, W. C. (2000). Adlerian brief therapy with individuals: Process and practice. *Journal of Individual Psychology, 56,* 31–44.

Bottome, P. (1957). *Alfred Adler.* New York, NY: Vanguard.

Brack, G., Hill, M. B., Edwards, D., Grootboom, N., & Lassiter, P. S. (2003). Adler and Ubuntu: Using Adlerian principles in the new South Africa. *Journal of Individual Psychology, 59,* 316–326.

Brown, J. F. (1976). *Practical applications of the personality priorities* (2nd ed.). Clinton, MD: B & F Associates.

Carlson, J. (2000). Individual psychology in the year 2000 and beyond: Astronaut or dinosaur? Headline or footnote? *Journal of Individual Psychology, 56,* 3–13.

Carlson, J. M., & Carlson, J. D. (2000). The application of Adlerian psychotherapy with Asian-American clients. *Journal of Individual Psychology, 56,* 214–226.

Carlson, J., & Glasser, W. (2004). Adler and Glasser: Demonstration and dialogue. *Journal of Individual Psychology, 60,* 308–324.

Carlson, J., Watts, R. E., & Maniacci, M. (2006). *Adlerian therapy: Theory and practice.* Washington, DC: American Psychological Association.

Clark, A. J. (1999). Safeguarding tendencies: A clarifying perspective. *Journal of Individual Psychology, 55,* 72–81.

Clark, A. J. (2002). *Early recollections: Theory and practice in counseling and psychotherapy.* New York, NY: Routledge.

Crits-Christoph, P. (1998). Training in empirically validated treatments: The division 12 APA task force recommendations. In K. S. Dobson & K. D. Craig (Eds.), *Empirically supported therapies: Best practice in professional psychology* (pp. 3–25). Thousand Oaks, CA: Sage.

Croake, J. W., & Rusk, R. (1980). The theories of Adler and Zen. *Journal of Individual Psychology, 36,* 53–64.

Dewey, E. A. (1991). *Basic applications of Adlerian psychology.* Coral Springs, FL: CMTI.

Dinkmeyer, D. C., & Sperry, L. (2000). *Counseling and psychotherapy: An integrated, individual psychology approach* (3rd ed.). New York, NY: Merrill.

Dreikurs, R. (1967). *Psychodynamics, psychotherapy, and counseling: Collected papers.* Chicago, IL: Alfred Adler Institute.

Dreikurs, R. (1972). *Coping with children's misbehavior.* New York. NY: Hawthorn.

Dreikurs, R. (1989). *Fundamentals of Adlerian psychology.* Chicago, IL: Alfred Adler Institute.

Dreikurs, R. (1997). Holistic medicine. *Journal of Individual Psychology, 53,* 127–205.

Dreikurs, R. (1999). *The challenge of marriage.* Philadelphia, PA: Accelerated Development.

Duffey, T. H., Carnes, M. R., Carnes, A. W., & Garcia, J. L. (1998). The lifestyle of the middle-class Mexican American female. *Journal of Individual Psychology, 54,* 399–406.

Eckstein, D. G. (1976). Early recollection changes after counseling: A case study. *Journal of Individual Psychology, 32,* 212–223.

Fall, K. A., & Howard, S. (2004). *Alternatives to domestic violence* (rev. ed.). New York, NY: Brunner-Routledge.

Ferguson, E. D. (2000). Individual psychology is ahead of its time. *Journal of Individual Psychology, 56,* 14–20.

Gatz, M. (1990). Interpreting behavioral genetic results: Suggestions for counselors and clients. *Journal of Counseling and Development, 68,* 601–605.

Gfroerer, K. P., Kern, R. M., & Curlette, W. L. (2004). Research support for individual psychology's parenting model. *Journal of Individual Psychology, 60,* 379–388.

Hoffman, E. (1994). *The drive for self: Alfred Adler and the founding of individual psychology.* Reading, MA: Addison-Wesley.

Holden, J. M. (1991). Most frequent personality priority pairings in marriage and marriage counseling. *Individual Psychology, 47*(3), 392–397.

Holden, J. M. (2000). Personality priorities in marriage counseling. In R. Watts (Ed.), *Techniques in marriage and family therapy* (Vol. 1). Alexandria, VA: American Counseling Association.

Johansen, T. M. (2005). Applying individual psychology to work with clients of the Islamic faith. *Journal of Individual Psychology, 61,* 174–184.

Kaplan, H. B. (1991). A guide for explaining social interest to lay persons. *Journal of Individual Psychology, 47,* 81–85.

Kefir, N., & Corsini, R. (1974). Dispositional sets: A contribution to typology. *Journal of Individual Psychology, 30,* 163–178.

Leak, G. K., Gardner, L. E., & Pounds, B. (1992). A comparison of Eastern religion, Christianity, and social interest. *Individual Psychology: Journal of Adlerian Theory, Research, and Practice, 53,* 33–41.

Manaster, G., & Corsini, R. (1982). *Individual psychology.* Chicago, IL: Adler School.

Manaster, G., Painter, G., Deutsch, D., & Overholt, B. J. (Eds.). (1977). *Alfred Adler: As we remember him.* Chicago, IL: NASAP.

Maucieri, L., & Stone, M. (2008). Adler's interpretation of same-gender orientation from neurobiological perspective. *Journal of Individual Psychology, 64,* 213–223.

Mosak, H. (1995a). Adlerian psychotherapy. In R. J. Corsini & D. Wedding (Eds.), *Current psychotherapies* (5th ed.). Itasca, IL: F.E. Peacock.

Mosak, H. (1995b). Drugless psychotherapy of schizophrenia. *Journal of Individual Psychology, 51,* 61–66.

Mosak, H., & Dreikurs, R. (1967). The life tasks III. The fifth life task. *Journal of Individual Psychology, 5,* 16–22.

Mosak, H., & Maniacci, M. (1999). *A primer of Adlerian psychology.* Philadelphia, PA: Brunner/Mazel.

Mosak, H., & Maniacci, M. (2008). Adlerian psychotherapy. In R. J. Corsini & D. Wedding (Eds.), *Current psychotherapies* (8th ed., pp. 63–106). Belmont, CA: Brooks/Cole.

Mozdzierz, G. J. (1998). Culture, tradition, transition, and the future. *Journal of Individual Psychology, 54,* 275–277.

Nield, J. (1979). Clarifying concepts of the number one priority. *The Individual Psychologist, 16,* 25–30.

Oberst, U. E., & Stewart, A. E. (2003). *Adlerian psychotherapy: An advanced approach to individual psychology.* New York, NY: Brunner Routledge.

O'Connell, W. E. (1997). The radical metaphors of Adlerian psychospirituality. *Individual Psychology: Journal of Adlerian Theory, Research, and Practice, 53,* 33–41.

Prinz, J., Arkin, S., & Gelkopf, M. (2008). Hadarim: A description and evaluation of a school-based Adlerian parenting program in Israel. *Journal of Individual Psychology, 64,* 37–54.

Raine, A., & Dunkin, J. J. (1990). The genetic and psychophysiological basis of antisocial behavior: Implications for counseling and therapy. *Journal of Counseling and Development, 68,* 637–644.

Rattner, J. (1983). *Alfred Adler.* New York, NY: Ungar.

Savill, G. E., & Eckstein, D. G. (1987). Changes in early recollections as a function of mental status. *Individual Psychology, 43,* 3–17.

Sherman, R., & Dinkmeyer, D. (1987). *Systems of family therapy: An Adlerian integration.* New York, NY: Brunner/Mazel.

Shulman, B. H. (1965). A comparison of Allport's and the Adlerian concepts of life style: Contributions to a psychology of the self. *Individual Psychologist, 3,* 14–21.

Shulman, B. H., & Mosak, H. (1988). *Manual for life style assessment.* Philadelphia, PA: Accelerated Development.

Sicher, L. (1991). *The collected works of Lydia Sicher: An Adlerian perspective* (A. K. Davidson, Ed.). Fort Bragg, CA: QED Press.

Sperry, L. (1990). Personality disorders: Biopsychosocial descriptions and dynamics. *Journal of Individual Psychology, 46,* 193–202.

Sperry, L., & Carlson, J. (1996). *Psychopathology and psychotherapy from diagnosis to treatment* (2nd ed.). Philadelphia, PA: Accelerated Development.

Sperry, L., & Mosak, H. H. (1996). Personality disorders. In L. Sperry & J. Carlson (Eds.), *Psychopathology and psychotherapy: From DSM-IV diagnosis to treatment.* Washington, DC: Accelerated Development/Taylor & Francis.

Stone, M. (2008). Immanuel Kant's influence on Adler. *Journal of Individual Psychology, 64,* 21–36.

Taylor, J. A. (1975). Early recollections as a projective technique: A review of some recent validation studies. *Journal of Individual Psychology, 31,* 213–218.

Vaihinger, H. (1965). *The philosophy of "as if"* (C. K. Ogden, Trans.). London, UK: Routledge & Kegan Paul.

Watts, R. E. (1998). The remarkable similarity between Rogers' core conditions and Adler's social interest. *Journal of Individual Psychology, 54,* 4–9.

Watts, R. E. (2000a). Biblically based Christian spirituality and Adlerian psychotherapy. *Journal of Individual Psychology, 56,* 316–328.

Watts, R. E. (2000b). Is individual psychology still relevant? *Journal of Individual Psychology, 56,* 21–30.

Watts, R. E. (2007). Counseling conservative Christian couples: A spiritually sensitive perspective. In O. J. Morgan (Ed.), *Counseling and spirituality: Views from the profession.* Boston, MA: Lahaska/Houghton Mifflin.

Watts, R. E., & Carlson, J. (Eds.). (1999). *Interventions and strategies in counseling and psychotherapy.* Philadelphia, PA: Accelerated Development.

Wheeler, M. S., Kern, R. M., & Curlette, W. L. (1993). *BASIS-A inventory.* Highlands, NC: TRT Associates.

White, R. W. (1957). Review of the individual psychology of Alfred Adler. *Contemporary Psychology, 2,* 1–4.

Zukov, G. (1994). *The dancing wu-li masters.* New York, NY: Bantam.

CHAPTER **5**

Existential Counseling

BACKGROUND OF THE THEORY

Historical Context

In reaction to the dehumanizing forces prominent in the scientific, industrial, psychiatric, and political arenas of the nineteenth century, a series of nineteenth and twentieth century philosophers and writers developed existentialism. Most sources place the genesis of the existential movement at the end of World Wars I and II. However, Allers (1961) indicated that existentialism arose out of a prewar society that emphasized compartmentalization—family separated from work, religion as a lofty ideal far above the drudgery of daily existence, gender roles rigidly stratified, and industrial work involving humans as tools of production. Many people believed that such compartmentalization led individuals to surrender self-awareness, to be estranged from self, and to what the German philosopher Friedrich Nietzsche termed *herd mentality*. The seeds of discontent that several thinkers sowed before the war blossomed in the postwar environment of Europe. The prominent psychological theory of the time, Freud's psychoanalysis, represented a deterministic, humans-as-driven-automatons perspective, as did the theory that displaced it in the postwar decades: behaviorism. Both served as springboards of reaction for the growing existential movement.

The ancestry of existentialism is deep and well documented. From the seminal writings of French philosopher Gabriel Marcel, to the foundational work of Danish philosopher Søren Kierkegaard, to the work of German philosophers Nietzsche and Martin Heidegger and French philosopher Jean-Paul Sartre, existentialists developed a philosophy that, in turn, theorists and practitioners have applied to counseling and psychotherapy. Unlike other psychotherapeutic approaches in which theory and treatment are of utmost importance and philosophy is considered a necessary but often ignored aspect, existential psychotherapists place the philosophy as the guiding force in both theory and treatment. Space limitations do not allow for a complete discussion of the proponents of existential philosophy, but Table 5.1 highlights the primary thinkers and their contributions.

Founder's Biographical Overview

We chose to present a biographical sketch of Rollo May, not because he is the only "founder" of existential therapy, but because his story is one that resonates with existential themes. As with other biographies in this text, we encourage you to note how the founder's life reflected the principles of the theory long before he put the theory to paper.

TABLE 5.1   Major Contributors to Existential Thought

Philosopher	Contribution
Søren Kierkegaard	Mid-nineteenth century Danish theologian whom existential historians consider the first existential philosopher. Kierkegaard reacted against Hegel and stressed the ambiguity and absurdity of the human situation. He asserted an individual's response to this seemingly meaningless condition must be to live a "committed life," as each individual defined it. Proponent of an individualized Christian way of life that, although the element of faith seemed impractical and irrational, could be one way of leading a committed life.
Fyodor Dostoevsky	Mid-nineteenth century Russian writer who focused on individual will, freedom, and suffering. His fictional characters portrayed the intrapsychic struggle with the meaning of life.
Friedrich Nietzsche	Late nineteenth century German writer whose ideas influenced Heidegger and Sartre. Developed concepts of will-to-power and overman (*Ubermensch*). Unlike Kierkegaard, who proposed individualism while staying connected to Christianity, Nietzsche rejected religion in favor of the individual will that defies the moral conformity of the majority.
Franz Kafka	Early twentieth century novelist from now-Czechoslovakia whose themes included the human conditions of anxiety, guilt, and isolation. Explored meaninglessness by presenting life as an "absurdity."
Martin Heidegger	Mid-twentieth century German whose writings on death, *Dasein*, and authenticity influenced existential psychological thought.
Jean-Paul Sartre	Twentieth century French literary figure who noted that although human beings strive for rational explanations for existence, they will never find one. Viewed human life as a "futile passion;" his emphasis on human freedom, choice, and responsibility is well known in existential theory. He openly criticized Freudian determinism and wrote about existential psychology (see *Existential Psychoanalysis*, 1953).
Simone de Beauvoir	Twentieth century French writer who explored and applied gender issues to existential concepts. Could be considered the first feminist existentialist.
Maurice Merleau-Ponty	Mid-twentieth century Frenchman who bridged phenomenology with existentialism. Whereas phenomenology emphasizes the unique essence of the individual, existentialism is concerned with how the essence relates to existence.
Albert Camus	Mid-twentieth century French journalist and essayist who explored the concept of meaninglessness through the view that life is absurd. Contended that recognizing and resisting the absurdity becomes the balance of life.
Karl Jaspers	Mid-twentieth century German psychiatrist who coined the term *Existenzphilosophie* for his perspective on existentialism. Theistic approach that emphasized courage to face challenges of the human condition.

Rollo May was born April 21, 1909, in Ohio. May's early life was filled with family conflict. May's father worked at a job that required the family to make several geographic moves. May had five brothers as well as one older sister who spent some time in a mental hospital (Rabinowitz, Good, & Cozad, 1989). At an early age, May sought refuge from the chaos of his family life by retreating to the banks of the St. Clair River, where he would sit, play, and watch the ships. One could conclude that the precursors to many of May's ideas about anxiety and ways to cope, both healthy and unhealthy, can be found in his early struggles within the anxiety-provoking environment of his home.

After an adolescence and college career marked by sparks of defiance, anger, and a love for the humanities, he graduated from Oberlin college and soon took a job at a Greek school to teach English to adolescent boys. Early on, May thrived in his new job. He found a connection with his students and enjoyed painting in the pastoral environment of Europe. But soon he became lonely. In fact, in the spring of his second year, May reported experiencing the beginnings of a "nervous breakdown" (May, 1985, p. 8). Out of feelings of loneliness and intense fatigue, May succumbed to two weeks of bed rest where he gathered energy for a change in his life. May (1985) reported, after talking with some friends, that he began to walk. He walked approximately 10 miles to Mt. Horiati, where he then began to ascend the mountain. Six hours later, as rain soaked his body, he reached a plateau, where he stopped to think. As mountain wolves howled and approached his position, May took little notice, as he was thoroughly engrossed in his internal process. At dawn, May traveled to a small village in the mountains where he began to write, "What is life?" and other thoughts on old slips of paper. May was confronting existential issues that followers would come to recognize as the core of existential theory: meaninglessness, isolation, freedom, and death (nonbeing). Although May did not find answers on that mountain, the experience served to catalyze May's thoughts and his sense of being.

Shortly after his mountain experience, May expressed his self through art and further developed his interest in psychology. In the following spring, he chanced to see a flyer on a bulletin board about a seminar in Vienna that Alfred Adler would be conducting. May decided to spend the summer learning from Adler, a decision that became professionally and personally important to May's development. May commented, "I've often wondered to myself what would have happened had I never seen that little flyer" (May in Rabinowitz et al., 1989, p. 437).

May continued his interest in psychology by exploring doctoral programs in the United States. Much to his disappointment, he found many programs were too focused on behaviorism and neglected to focus on other approaches such as those of Adler or Jung. Fortunately, May discovered the program at the Union Theological Seminary aligned well with his interests, and he soon enrolled and met his greatest influence, Paul Tillich. Tillich's (1952) knowledge and ideas on religion, philosophy, and art provided May with a resource and friend who resonated with his own ideas. May's contact with Adler provided a rich foundation in counseling, whereas Tillich contributed the philosophical backdrop for May's search for a personal approach to dealing with life.

Due to family issues, May was unable to finish at the Union Theological Seminary and, instead, moved back home, took a college counseling job, and began lecturing and writing about counseling. In 1939, he published *The Art of Counseling*, which reads like a primer of Adlerian psychology. The next few years proved hectic yet productive for May. He pursued a doctorate in clinical psychology from Teachers College of Columbia University. While finishing his dissertation on anxiety, he taught night courses, underwent psychoanalysis, and worked to support his mother. During this time, May contracted tuberculosis and spent the next two years in a sanitarium. May spent his time thinking about anxiety and not only completed his dissertation but also wrote the book *The Meaning of Anxiety,* which was published in 1950.

Since the 1950s May continued to expand and refine the art of applying existential thought to an approach to counseling. As an author and clinician, he worked with Erich Fromm, Henry Stack Sullivan, Abraham Maslow, and Carl Rogers. For many psychotherapy theorists and practitioners, he holds the position of father of existential therapy in the United States. In his later career, as he became a prominent force in establishing existentialism as a theory of mental health, May produced several important books. After a lifetime of dealing creatively with the anxiety inherent in life and its givens, May died in 1994.

Philosophical Underpinnings

As we mentioned earlier, unlike most other theories that include only a passing, obligatory reference to philosophy, existentialism's philosophy *is* the approach to counseling. This entire chapter reverberates with the philosophy of existentialism, but we begin with a few of the overarching philosophical principles of the existential movement, the common assumptions to which all existential philosophers and psychotherapists subscribe.

Ontology

Departing radically from the mechanistic approaches of Freud and the behaviorists, existentialists developed a school of thought focused on the study of being, or ontology. Ontological issues address the spectrum of existence and the dynamic balance between being and nonbeing. Existentialists do not use "being" as a noun representing an objective fact, such as, "I am a human being." Rather, they use it as a verb, such as "how I am being in this moment," connoting movement and process. This focus on being points to a deeper understanding of each individual's approach to existence. In particular, it addresses the question of the extent to which someone is fully being, is authentic, is realizing one's deepest nature through how one lives from moment to moment—or the extent to which someone is not fully being, is inauthentic, is untrue to one's deepest nature.

Phenomenology

Existentialists hold that the only way one person can understand another is to appreciate the other's unique, subjective perspective on the world and self. Each human has the power to be aware or not to be aware, that is, to focus on or to ignore aspects of one's internal and external experience, and to integrate experiences into a meaning that is distinctly one's own. The philosophical roots of phenomenology rest with Husserl (1965), but his approach was too scientific and objective for existentialists, who modified his ideas to focus more on the ontological nature of the philosophy.

Responsibility

An approach that emphasizes the subjective study of being and how experience is interpreted by each individual naturally also places the onus of responsibility for being on that same individual. Themes of freedom, choice, and accountability are threads that run throughout all aspects of existential philosophy. Once again, existentialists assumed the focus was largely in reaction to Freud's view that unconscious forces drive humans to do what they do. Existentialists yearned to put the thinking, feeling human in the driver's seat of existence. They believed that, in addition to being responsible for one's own choices, one has a duty to one's fellow human beings with whom one is inextricably connected. As Sartre (1965) noted, "When we say that a man [*sic*] is responsible for himself, we do not only mean that he is responsible for his own individuality, but that he is responsible for all men" (p. 39). This social responsibility is best demonstrated by exercising one's freedom to choose alternatives that do not harm others or infringe on their own ability to choose and be free.

PERSONALITY DEVELOPMENT

Nature of Humans

The existential view of human nature springs from the ontological and phenomenological perspectives whereby one best understands human experience by viewing it through the eyes of the individual. As we discussed earlier, ontology is the study of being, and existentialists believe that each individual begins to understand another person and oneself by understanding the individual's subjective experience of being-in-the-world (Binswanger, 1963).

Structure of the Psyche

Existentialists rejected the elemental psychologies of their contemporaries, the psychoanalysts and behaviorists. Freud reduced the human psyche to the interaction of the id, ego, and superego, and behaviorists to the elements of stimulus and response. By contrast, existentialists asserted a perspective in which each human is understood to have a unique inner world that cannot be reduced to separate components and cannot be explained completely by natural sciences such as biology, chemistry, or physics. An analogy would be to describe a cookie as consisting of the elements of flour, sugar, eggs, and salt, formed into a shape and heated. But these elements do not capture the wholeness of a cookie. The same could be said of a piece of furniture or a nuclear power plant: the whole is greater than the sum of the parts.

Each person also is greater than the sum of one's parts. Consequently, an individual must be understood in terms of one's potential for, and movement involved in, being-in-the-world. In other words, from an existential perspective, the psyche of the individual is the whole of one's approach to existence, which existentialists term *Dasein* (Heidegger, 1927/1962). As *Dasein* includes structure, the whole of the person, and function, one's approach to existence, it is mentioned both here and in the section on the Function of the Psyche.

In the context of the caveat of holistic nonreductionism, existentialists, like psychoanalysts, conceive of the human psyche as a spectrum ranging from complete unconsciousness or unawareness to complete consciousness or awareness. Relatively unconscious psychic material either never emerged into greater consciousness or it emerged and the individual repressed it.

One outgrowth of consciousness is the development of a self. "Each individual in the dawn of consciousness create[s] a primary self (*transcendental ego*) by permitting consciousness to curl back upon itself and to differentiate a self from the remainder of the world" (May & Yalom, 2000, p. 285). The levels of consciousness and self constitute the only psychic structures to which existentialists refer.

Function of the Psyche

Each person is born with the potential, to some greater or lesser degree of consciousness, to have the core experience of the human psyche: the "I-Am" experience. This experience is the realization of one's being, one's existence. The presumably uniquely human I-Am experience is the awareness that, prior to any attribution of meaning to existence (any interpretations, evaluations, or labels) one simply exists. This concept is what Sartre meant when he asserted that "existence precedes essence." Any "essence" (any feeling, thought, or action; any perception, desire, or value) is secondary to something that is absolutely primary: the simple, factual experience that one exists.

> Human existence, however, is never static. The existing person is dynamic, at every moment becoming. Existing involves a continual emerging, a transcending of one's past and present in order to reach the future. Thus *transcendere*, literally "to climb over and beyond," describes what every human being is engaged in doing every moment when not seriously ill or temporarily blocked by despair or anxiety. Nietzsche has his old Zarathustra proclaim, "And this secret spake Life herself to me. 'Behold' said she, 'I am that which must ever surpass itself.' " (May & Yalom, 2000, pp. 277–278)

This view of human nature implies that each person is innately endowed with a unique potential that the person will inevitably realize to some greater or lesser degree. Thus, the master motive throughout life is to preserve and assert one's existence, the process of "unfolding" one's potential.

The Givens of Life   The master motive to preserve and assert one's existence is expressed in some more specific needs and wishes. Each of these needs or wishes, it turns out, is in direct conflict with the "givens" of life: conditions that are present in every moment of existence and that threaten existence. Each human is, thus, innately endowed with the potential to *perceive threats* to existence and, where they do, to *generate anxiety*. Although many existential writers have developed various lists of such givens, we have chosen to use Yalom's (1980) conceptualization because of its clarity and applicability to the therapeutic process. Yalom defined the four givens—the four fundamental threats to existence—as death, freedom, isolation, and meaninglessness. As one becomes aware of the givens of life, one inevitably feels anxiety. As you read the remainder of this section, you are encouraged to monitor your own sense of anxiety.

Death

In conflict with the master motive itself, the need to preserve and assert one's existence, stands *death*. Consequently, existentialists consider death awareness and anxiety to play a primary role in human motivation. Death is the ultimate threat to existence, the ultimate threat of nonbeing. The potential for physical death begins the moment one is born. Awareness of physical death begins early in life and reminds one that one's own physical existence is finite. Thus, a person innately perceives as threatening any insults or potential insults to the physical body. With the early development of the self comes also the potential for psychological death: A person perceives insults or potential insults to the sense of self as threatening to the very sense of being. An example of such a threat is when one person makes disparaging remarks about another's self; the other is likely to experience the remarks as attacking, threatening the self's existence. Another example is simply hearing feedback that contradicts one's sense of oneself: The individual feels threatened to realize that the self one equates with one's very existence might, in fact, not be. Another example is entering an exam unprepared: To the extent one fails to live up to one's potential, in a sense that potential has died rather than been realized. Speaking of both physical and psychological death, Yalom (1980) noted how ubiquitous death is in life: "Life and death are interdependent; they exist simultaneously, not consecutively; death whirs continuously beneath the membrane of life and exerts vast influence upon experience and conduct" (p. 29).

I (KAF) was dubious of the existential assertion that death awareness and anxiety begin early in life. Then, while riding in the car with me one day, my four-year-old son asked, out of the blue, "Daddy, will I die soon?" I was perplexed and a little nervous about this question, uncertain about how to answer. To reassure us both, I said, "No, you have a long time before you die." I hoped that would quell any more questions, but he thought about my answer and asked, "Why? What's a long time? Do you mean 10 minutes?" I was really nervous now, so I began to list all the things he had to accomplish before he died: play, go to school, teach his baby brother all sorts of things, go to high school, learn to drive, go to college, pick a career, date, get married, have kids, teach them stuff and play with them, and so on. I thought it was a good list, and even I felt relieved. He quietly thought about my list and asked, "How about learning to eat tacos?" I replied, "Yes, I guess that would be on the list." He summed up the conversation with, "Good. Now I know I will never die, because I don't think I'll ever like tacos!" As my son taught me, awareness of and concern about the finiteness of being starts very early, and each person responds to that concern in a unique way. If you feel any sense of increased tension as you contemplate the inescapability of your own death, you are experiencing the death anxiety that existentialists consider fundamental to human experience.

Freedom

One specific expression of the master motive is the "deep need and wish for ground and structure" (May & Yalom, 2000, p. 284). Groundlessness and lack of structure feel innately threatening to existence because one cannot get one's bearings to preserve one's existence; some degree of ground and structure feels safer because it provides a stable foundation for an individual to make choices that can preserve existence.

Standing in conflict with this need or wish is *freedom*. In fact, within the limits of uncontrollable circumstances, each human is completely free to do whatever one chooses. Furthermore, choice is not only a human capacity; it is a human inevitability. One cannot escape from this freedom, for even *not* to choose is a choice. For example, someone who chooses not to take action to right an injustice chooses to allow the injustice to continue unchallenged. Even when overt choices seem extremely limited—what May (1981) called "freedom of doing"—an individual always has alternatives, if not in action, then in attitude, which May termed *freedom of being*. Each choice either fosters or threatens one's existence, that is, the extent to which one realizes one's innate potential, hence the burdensome anxiety of freedom. The person who says, "I had no choice," really means, "I chose this alternative rather than another that I was unwilling to choose." For example, "I chose to turn my work in late rather than sacrifice sleep and put my health at risk," "I chose to comply with my boss's orders to repackage spoiled meat to be sold rather than lose my job," or "I chose to continue to be tortured rather than to cooperate with the enemy." Since one ultimately has the capacity to choose the attitude with which one meets even uncontrollable life circumstances, existentialists believe that each human ultimately is responsible and is the sole creator of one's own life.

Isolation

Another specific expression of the master motive is "the wish to be protected, to merge and to be part of a larger whole" (May & Yalom, 2000, p. 285). In this merging, one feels safer by virtue of access to resources greater than merely one's own in facing the potentially powerful threats to existence.

In conflict with this wish is the given of *isolation*: Despite the constant presence of others, each person is ultimately alone. Since each person's uniqueness, no one can be completely understood by someone else, can have exactly the same experience as someone else, or can ultimately be rescued by someone else. Even with the advice or influence of others, a decision maker alone is ultimately responsible for the choice one makes. In suffering, even the extensive support of others cannot entirely or indefinitely alleviate pain that the sufferer ultimately endures alone. And in dying, even if surrounded by devoted loved ones, one ultimately proceeds alone. If you are feeling in any way distressed as you read this paragraph, you are experiencing the anxiety that accompanies the awareness of isolation.

Meaninglessness

Closely related to the need for ground and structure, the master motive expresses itself also in the need for meaning. This need is evidenced in the innate human tendency to organize random stimuli into some meaningful pattern (May & Yalom, 2000, p. 286). A meaningful pattern provides a context in which an individual can pursue a valued course of action. This condition feels safer because one has guiding values for how to live and pursue the unfolding of one's potential.

In conflict with the need for meaning is the given of *meaninglessness*, the fact that objects of our perception do not have inherent meaning but only the meaning that, through an individual's own perceptual organization, one imposes on them—a meaning that, ultimately, the individual alone constructs. Meaninglessness as a given stems from the first three givens. Namely, if one's death is inevitable, if one is responsible for how one chooses to create one's life, and if one is ultimately alone, then what ultimate meaning does life hold? Meaning involves a sense of order or coherence in life along with a sense of values—a way to prioritize experiences in terms of importance. The diversity of worldviews that exist on planet Earth exemplifies the existential contention that life has no inherent meaning, or that if such inherent meaning exists, it has eluded humanity so far. Rather, meaning in life, what one values, considers important or unimportant, considers to be worthy or unworthy of one's pursuit and one's efforts is something humans create, both collectively and individually. May and Yalom (2000) posed the following question, which can serve as an assessment tool for understanding someone: "How does a being, oneself, another person, a client who *requires* meaning *find* meaning in a universe that *has* no meaning?" (p. 286; italics added). As you read this question, you may be feeling anxiety and/or responding with ideas of your own regarding the meaning of life. The psychological functions of anxiety and response to meaninglessness and the other three givens are the foci of the next few sections.

The Essential Aspects of Being   May (1961), in describing six aspects of being, elaborated and expanded on the functions discussed above. First, the concept of *phenomenological centeredness* reiterates that human experience is best understood from the perspective of the individual: that all beliefs, feelings, and behaviors flow from the center point of the individual. On a related note, May (1961) asserted the second aspect: that each person has the *potential to exist with other beings without losing centeredness,* that is, to interact with others without losing one's sense of being and identity.

May (1961) differentiated two aspects of awareness. In the third aspect of being, *awareness as self-consciousness*, the ability to sense and integrate information about oneself itself has two dimensions: subjective and objective. For example, as you read this text at this moment, awareness of your inner experience of sensations, emotions, and thoughts is your subjective self-awareness. By contrast, awareness of what you are doing and how you appear (in this case that you are reading) as if seeing yourself from the outside is objective self-awareness. The fourth aspect, *awareness as vigilance*, refers to the ability to sense and integrate information from one's surroundings, in particular to perceive threat and safety. May (1961) considered this aspect of psychological functioning to be a type of alarm that informs individuals of the presence or absence of threats to being. Of course, from an existential perspective, an individual understands all data through one's subjective view of the world, so what one person considers a threat another might not. For example, when driving in a car on a high and narrow bridge, one passenger's vigilance might register alarm, whereas another's might register delight.

May (1961) described a fifth aspect of being: *anxiety as the struggle against non-being*. When one encounters the givens of life, one naturally generates anxiety, that is, energy to fend off death, isolation, and meaninglessness, as well as energy to deal with freedom of choice. In this process, May (1961) believed, each person has the potential to generate the sixth aspect of being: the *courage to self-affirm*, that is, to take courage and to affirm oneself in the process of addressing life's givens.

Dasein   *Dasein* (Heidegger, 1927/1962), loosely translated as "being there," refers to the fact that, at each moment in the process of existence, each person has a way of being. *Dasein* is "deep" in the sense that it reflects the cross-section fullness of a person in a given moment of the process of being. (Note that authors always capitalize this German word.)

A person's *Dasein* reflects several psychological functions, some of which we have already described. The first is *awareness*, particularly a person's awareness of the inescapable givens of life and the extent to which one *perceives threat*. In response to the perception of threats to one's existence, physical or psychological, one inevitably generates *anxiety*. Thus, anxiety, the response to threats of nonbeing, is an inevitable product of living. Out of anxiety, a person naturally generates some *response*. How one responds, that is, how one manages anxiety and behaves (feels, thinks, and acts) in response to it, is characterized by some use of *defense mechanisms*. Though psychoanalysts and existentialists differ in their views of the source of anxiety, they agree that people can feel overwhelmed by anxiety and, consequently, that each person employs unconscious strategies to deny or distort reality to protect oneself from excessive anxiety. In addition to the psychoanalytic defenses, existentialists add *specialness*, belief in one's immunity from the givens of existence, and *belief in the existence of an ultimate rescuer*, some other being whom one can appease in exchange for total ultimate protection against nonbeing. A person who uses defenses in moderation assists oneself in moderating anxiety and, thus, in more successfully fulfilling the master motive to preserve and assert one's existence. Conversely, someone who uses defenses excessively becomes self-defeating in that one either largely denies or greatly amplifies anxiety, blocking oneself from effective fulfillment of the master motive. The more the person enacts the latter scenario, the more one will experience *existential guilt*. Existential guilt is a warning sign of inauthenticity: living life in a manner that ignores one's "true" potential for existence. Guilt should not be confused with shame; rather, it is an opportunity to explore one's life and move in a more authentic direction (Jacobsen, 2007).

Role of the Environment

Several existentialists have written about the role of the environment in human development. The common theme in these writings is that each individual encounters limitations
that restrict, but do not determine, one's choices. Different existentialists have expressed
this theme through different models. In this section, we summarize Binswanger's (1963)
and Deurzen-Smith's (1988) model, as well as May's (1981).

The Welts

The model that Binswanger (1963) and Deurzen-Smith (1988) offered consists of four
interacting dimensions of environment: the *Umwelt,* or physical world; the *Mitwelt,* or
interpersonal world; the *Eigenwelt,* or personal world (Binswanger); and the *Uberwelt,*
or spiritual world (Deurzen-Smith). These authors asserted that the environment provides
limits and is, therefore, an important factor in *Dasein,* one's being at any given moment.
More important in existentialists' view, however, is that the environment is an influential
rather than a causal force, affecting rather than determining an individual's being. One is
not shaped by one's environments but rather subjectively perceives and creatively uses the
environments in the struggle of existence. In the following material, we describe the four
dimensions of environment in more detail.

   Umwelt (Binswanger, 1963), the "world around," is comprised of the natural world
of physics, chemistry, biology, and ecology. It includes each person's biologically based
needs, instincts, genetics, and neurochemistry. Each human is conceived in the physical
realm through the act of sexual intercourse or in vitro fertilization followed by the complicated biology of gestation and birth. The *Umwelt* continues to be important throughout life as one comes to realize that existence in the physical world is bound by the limits
of birth, death, and a variety of physical laws throughout life.

   Mitwelt (Binswanger, 1963), the "with world," is the world of social interaction
with other people. At birth, an infant begins to experience the *Mitwelt* as one relies on
others to provide care and nourishment. Growing older, one typically forms friendships,
intimate relationships, and work relationships, usually while maintaining ties with family and ancestors. These relationships are not defined by external variables or objective
measures but, instead, are defined by each person's own subjective view. *Mitwelt* includes
the important influence of culture on how one ascribes meaning to experience and on the
moral code that one internalizes.

   Eigenwelt (Binswanger, 1963), the "own-world," refers to one's inner world or one's
relationship with oneself; it could also be understood as a sense of "me-ness" or identity.
It includes how each individual views self as well as how one perceives one's relationship
to the external world. In the inevitable striving to overcome meaninglessness, one attributes meaning to experiences, thus developing unique likes and dislikes, opinions, and
values. All of these attributions constitute the "me" environment: my sense of who I am,
of what is meaningful and important to me—my sense of myself.

   Until the 1980s, existentialism mainly emphasized the three dimensions that
Binswanger (1963) had outlined. Then Deurzen-Smith (1988) introduced the concept of
the *Uberwelt* to acknowledge the spiritual aspect of being. Literally translated as "over
world," the concept of *Uberwelt* underscores that the universe is larger than humanity.
Uberwelt also encompasses the individual's personal view of the ideal. "On this dimension of our existence we really come into the true complexity of being human, as we
organize our overall views on the world, physical, social, and personal, and generate
or are inserted into an overall philosophy of life" (Deurzen-Smith, 1997, p. 123). One's

Uberwelt is influenced by religion as one's family practices it and may be limited by what is acceptable in one's society. However, the Uberwelt can transcend social or cultural structures such as religion and, like the other dimensions, is dynamic in that it can be open and flexible to new information and ways of being, if the individual so chooses.

Destiny

May's (1981) model of the role of environment in human development included three types of environmental limits imposed on an individual. The word *imposed* signifies that the environmental factors are beyond the individual's control; thus, May called these limits "destiny." *Cosmic destiny* refers to the limits imposed by the laws of nature, such as the climate into which one is born as well as one's heredity and biological processes. *Cultural destiny* refers to the limits imposed by preexisting social patterns, such as the language, economic system, technology, social practices, and values of one's culture. *Circumstantial destiny* refers to the limits imposed by sudden situations that include cosmic and/or cultural aspects, such as a hurricane, an accident, or a poor economy that leads to a cut in pay or unemployment.

Like his philosophical colleagues, May (1981) emphasized that even if a person cannot control the three aspects of destiny, each person is responsible for how one responds to them by virtue of the ability to recognize and exercise one's available options, actions, and attitudes. For example, Robert lost his job due to poor financial judgment on the part of his boss. Although Robert did not contribute to the failing of the company or the loss of his job, his life continued along with a new series of choices. He could choose to sit at home and collect unemployment, or he could choose to search for a new job. If he opted not to search for another job, then that was his choice and not the fault of his boss. How one responds to destiny characterizes one's *Dasein*—one's unique way of being.

Familial and Extrafamilial Environments

Clearly, both the familial and the extrafamilial environments involve all aspects of both May (1981) and Binswanger (1963) and Deurzen-Smith's (1988) models. Both aspects of environment include phenomena with which each person must contend throughout existence.

In particular, one's family of origin is a crucial aspect of Binswanger's (1963) *Mitwelt*. However, existentialists have actually written very little about how the family specifically influences the individual. Maddi (1967) proposed that children are more likely to develop authenticity, the existential term for mental health, when parents create an atmosphere of respect and admiration for the uniqueness of the child and encourage the child to explore the givens of existence, both through the child's direct experiencing and through parental modeling. May and Yalom (2000) contended that people:

> who lack sufficient experiences of closeness and true relatedness in their lives are particularly incapable of tolerating isolation. . . . [A]dolescents from loving supportive families are able to grow away from their families with relative ease and to tolerate the separation and loneliness of young adulthood [whereas] those [from] tormented, highly conflicted families find it extremely difficult. . . . The more disturbed the family, the harder it is for children to leave—[they] cling to the family for shelter against [the anxiety of] isolation. (p. 293)

In summary, each individual encounters environmental limits throughout the struggle of existence. Whereas one cannot control these phenomena, one can control one's behavioral and attitudinal choices in response to them. How one responds reflects the quality of one's *Dasein*, one's being-in-the-world. Although you might have the impression that existentialists blame the victim or are unsympathetic in their approach, this conclusion would be inaccurate. Existentialism is a theory of hope in which theorists acknowledge limitations but also consider each person capable of transcending limitations by being aware of one's options and accessing the courage to explore and, when one chooses, exercise those options.

Interaction of Human Nature and Environment

Developmental Stages

Most existential sources do not delineate stages of human development. However, Keen (1970) proposed four developmental stages congruent with existential theory.

In the first stage of *fusion*, the infant has little awareness of self as separate from other people. Experiencing existence primarily through *Umwelt* and through an extremely limited sense of *Mitwelt*, the infant responds to anxiety by clinging to parents and other caregivers. As early as the first year, the child enters the second stage of *separation*, beginning to recognize differences between self and others. In this fledgling *Eigenwelt* experience of uniqueness, a child can feel exhilarated but also is likely to feel the anxiety associated with the given of isolation. In the third *satellization* stage, the child responds to anxiety and creates a sense of security by acquiescing to adults in the *Mitwelt*. Parenting styles become very influential on the child's development at this stage. The extremes of overcontrol or indulgence foster a restricted *Eigenwelt*: Too much punishment can restrict the child's *Dasein*, whereas an absence of discipline or limit setting will fail to prepare the child to confront limits and take responsibility for one's actions. According to the existential perspective, parents who encourage the child to make choices and who create and allow appropriate consequences for the child's choices foster a more authentic and courageous child. At about seven years of age, out of recognition of the balance between responsibility and choice, the child enters the final stage of *similarity*. In this stage, the child develops a sense of *Uberwelt* in which one is able to discern self from others and also to recognize similarity, a human kinship, with others in the *Mitwelt*.

To avoid contradicting the existential emphasis on a phenomenological view of being, Keen (1970) did not hypothesize the developmental stages as a rigidly sequential model. Rather, his stage model offers a view of the possible interrelationship between self and others and the possible role of the four dimensions of the environment in one's developmental experience. Again, according to existential theory, the environmental dimensions in general and the family in particular, influence rather than determine one's development. These influences may constrict or enhance one's *Dasein*.

To summarize, existentialists, in their focus on the present *Dasein* of an individual, have not addressed in detail what environmental factors contribute to the way a person at any given moment participates in life. They have hinted that a person in a *Mitwelt* characterized by unhealthy functioning is likely to be poorly prepared to participate constructively in life. However, they are much less concerned with how someone *came to be* as they are with the fact that the person is how they are and with the question of how a person can *become* more effective in preserving and asserting one's existence.

Model of Mental Health

Healthy Functioning

Existentialists conceptualize mental health as *authenticity*. Authenticity involves a particular quality of awareness, of anxiety, and of response to anxiety. A person living authentically is aware of, that is, acknowledges, accepts, even embraces, the givens of life (death, isolation, freedom, and meaninglessness) as they play out in the four interrelated spheres of being: *Umwelt, Mitwelt, Eigenwelt,* and *Uberwelt.* Authenticity involves neither avoiding nor being preoccupied with any given or sphere. Authentic awareness facilitates normal, rather than neurotic, anxiety as one confronts choices each moment of one's life (May, 1977; May & Yalom, 2000). *Normal anxiety* is proportionate to the perceived situation, which, in turn, facilitates an authentic response. In responding authentically, one employs a minimum of defense mechanisms as one courageously addresses rather than avoids anxiety and courageously uses anxiety to make each choice. Authentic choices are those that express one's deepest nature and that involve the realization of one's innate potential. Some qualities that characterize authenticity are being fully present in the moment, being fully aware, and experiencing a kind of appreciation of being.

A ubiquitous example is an impending final exam. From an existential perspective, authenticity involves a realistic awareness of the situation. That awareness would involve a reasonable appraisal of the consequences of relative success or failure for one's future opportunities that, in turn, play some role in how one makes a living, all of which impinge on one's physical and psychological existence. Someone experiencing anxiety proportionate to a final exam situation may think recurrent thoughts of the exam along with concern, but not panic, about the possible outcome. An authentic response would involve planning a study schedule rather than procrastinating, adopting study methods that accommodate one's study strengths and weaknesses, and arranging to be on time to the exam. If an emergency arises, an authentic response would be to attend to the immediate demands of the emergency and, as soon as possible, contact the professor to explore alternatives for making up the exam.

Bugental (1965) noted that authenticity exists not as an achievement or objectively measured goal but, rather as an ongoing striving, as one repeatedly confronts decisions over the span of one's existence. It also is not an all-or-nothing matter but a continuum, with authenticity at one extreme and inauthenticity at the other. Finally, authenticity and inauthenticity are not labels that one person can hang on another like an evaluation or diagnosis. Although others may believe they perceive degrees of authenticity in someone else, it is that someone alone who knows one's own level of authenticity. The degree of existential guilt that one experiences is the single best indicator of the authenticity of one's existence.

Thus, the existential model of mental health includes anxiety that one uses constructively. In a sense, the existential model also includes latitude for inevitable inauthenticity. Existentialists assume that, on the continuum of authenticity, each person strays from the ideal at least occasionally. In that instance, when one fails to live up to one's potential, one naturally feels guilty. Like anxiety, existential guilt is a normal part of being that an individual neither can nor should avoid. One may ignore or feel alienated from the *Umwelt,* let others down in the *Mitwelt,* violate one's sense of integrity in one's *Eigenwelt,* and fail to live up to the ideals comprising one's *Uberwelt.* However, one can use even existential guilt authentically by regarding it as an early warning that can lead to humility and to future constructive choices. The mentally healthy individual uses anxiety, as well as the guilt that results from inauthenticity, authentically!

Deurzen-Smith (1997) asserted that authenticity involves accepting, and even welcoming, the fluid, changing nature of life circumstances. She added that someone living authentically is characterized by a sense of caring interest and psychological investment in one's physical, interpersonal, inner, and spiritual worlds.

Bugental (1965) elaborated on how an individual can create authentic responses when one experiences the anxiety arising from the givens of existence. For example, in response to death anxiety, one can choose to have faith in one's existence and affirm that "I am." An authentic response to freedom is commitment, a willingness to make choices and be responsible for the outcome of the choices. Authentically responding to isolation involves engaging in relationship with others and accepting the fact that such connections are temporary. The authentic relationship is epitomized in the "I-Thou" relationship (Buber, 1970), in which both the connection between two people and the inherent separateness, uniqueness, and isolation of each is honored and prized. In a truly caring relationship, each person wants, in Buber's terms, to "unfold" the other, that is, one "care[s] about the other's growth and [wants] to bring something to life in the other" (May & Yalom, 2000, p. 298). Lastly, one can respond authentically to meaninglessness by engaging in meaningful activities, with meaningfulness involving social responsibility and further defined internally by oneself rather than externally by others. In the case of vocation, an activity through which many people derive meaning, a person who collects trash, another who spends a lifetime researching the mating habits of the red squirrel, and yet another who counsels people, all may find authentic meaning in their work. Existentialists do not believe in fate or a great design or plan for one's life. The answer to the search for meaning lies in an individual's acceptance of the fact that the only meaning anything has is the meaning the individual assigns to it, and that some meanings coincide with an inner sense of fulfilling one's potential more than other meanings do.

Maddi (1976) poignantly summarized the authentic approach to life: "Only when you have clearly seen the abyss and jumped into it with no assurance of survival can you call yourself a human being. Then, if you survive, shall you be called hero, for you will have created your own life" (p. 136).

Unhealthy Functioning

Just as authenticity is the existential gauge of mental health, inauthenticity characterizes unhealthy functioning. Inauthenticity involves the excessive use of defense mechanisms: on the one hand, denial or avoidance of awareness of the givens of life, or, on the other, preoccupation with the givens. Correspondingly, anxiety is disproportionate to the situation: It is either too low or too high to facilitate an authentic response. Consequently, the inauthentic response is characterized by a lack of courage and by patterns such as avoidance, excuses, blame, and overreaction. Some qualities that characterize inauthenticity are being preoccupied with the past or the future, limited awareness, and a certain lack of ability to appreciate the fact of existence. Yalom (1980) remarked that "psychopathology is a graceless, inefficient mode of coping with anxiety" (p. 110).

Inauthenticity is characterized by retreating from the natural anxiety of being or transforming that anxiety into dread rather than using it as a catalyst for courageous choice. An individual blocked from authentic existence by excessive defensiveness doubts one's own potential for creation. In this condition of self-doubt, one is prone to relinquish one's inner authority and acquiesce to external authority. As Bauman and Waldo (1988) put it, "One takes on the values, ideas and beliefs of others and loses one's individuality ... and falls away from the potential to express one's unique existence" (p. 20).

Because existentialists believe each person's most fundamental innate tendency is to preserve and assert one's existence in order to continually become who one has the innate potential to be, they consider a person experiencing inauthenticity—someone who has, in a particular moment, withdrawn from that process—to presumably be somehow blocked.

How the person became blocked is much less important than how the person *is* blocking the natural inclination to participate fully and effectively in the creation of one's life.

Returning to the example of a student faced with an impending final exam, inauthenticity might take one of several forms. One student may avoid thinking about the exam as a way to ward off anxiety about potentially failing, then procrastinate studying, then fail the exam, thus fulfilling the prophecy of the original anxiety. Another student may be preoccupied in awareness of the exam and generate so much anxiety about potentially failing that he wastes his energy in worry and dread, then, unprepared, fails to show up for the exam or drops out of the program. Another student may respond to anxiety by arranging for another, seemingly more capable, student to take the exam in her place. Yet another may reduce anxiety about his own sense of responsibility for less-than-desirable performance by blaming others, such as the teacher. And yet another may be so overcome with guilt for less-than-ideal performance that she becomes discouraged, morose, even depressed. From an existential perspective, each of these examples involves a lack of authenticity: a failure to meet the challenges and choices of life with courage and fulfillment of one's potential.

Inauthenticity often is characterized by a disproportionate involvement in one *welt* at the expense of another. An example is the client who responds to the anxiety of isolation by neglecting her *Eigenwelt* and becoming immersed in an intimate relationship in her *Mitwelt*. This is how the client describes her situation:

> I am just so unhappy, but it hasn't always been like this. I used to have a job and friends and a life. When I met him, things changed gradually, yet dramatically. I felt so alive when I was around him. Sure, I played dumb and probably had sex with him sooner than I should have, but he said he loved me. When he asked me to move in with him, I jumped at the chance. Who wouldn't? I mean, I was living alone and I hated that, but I sure miss my apartment. I moved in with him, sold some of my stuff in a garage sale, and put the rest in storage. He said it was his place and he didn't want to make it a "chick house." A few months later, I quit my job, and I just basically sit at home and wait for him. My life is now his life. He doesn't let me hang out with my friends because they are single and he calls them "whores." Maybe he's right. I don't know anymore. It's like I don't trust my instincts, you know? I am happy I am in a relationship. The singles scene is a nightmare. Maybe if we get married it will be better.

Inauthenticity can be seen in a number of symptoms for which people seek counseling. In the face of death anxiety, one person might manifest agoraphobia (develop panic symptoms and avoid leaving the house for fear of dying) whereas another might manifest driving while intoxicated and otherwise engage in highly risky behavior that denies the potential to die. In the face of isolation anxiety, one person might withdraw from relationships for fear of experiencing rejection and loneliness, whereas another might manifest sexual addiction, seeking out numerous sexual partners to ward off isolation. In the face of the anxiety that arises from meaninglessness, one person might attempt suicide to escape a life that seems devoid of current or future meaning, whereas another might develop a compulsive disorder, engaging in repetitive, necessary behavior that distracts the person from questions of meaning. In the face of the anxiety that arises from freedom, one person might take a passive, defeated, "victim" approach to life by avoiding decisions, such as the man who, rather than proactively ending a stagnant marriage, instead complains of being trapped and manifests symptoms of depression, hoping the spouse will decide to file for divorce or have an affair to precipitate a divorce. In the face of the anxiety of freedom, another person might take an active, blaming, "persecutor" approach by finding fault with outside circumstances and other people outside of one's own life situation. From an existential point of view, each of these seemingly diverse symptoms can be traced back to one underlying phenomenon: inauthenticity, a lack of courage to face the givens, experience the resulting anxiety, and proactively make realistic and creative choices as befits one's existential potential.

THE PERSONALITY CHANGE PROCESS

From an existential perspective, change consists of increased authenticity. Increased authenticity occurs when one decreasingly makes use of defense mechanisms, that is, when one experiences enhanced awareness of the givens of existence as they manifest in each of the *welts*, when one generates anxiety proportionate to the threats in each of those domains, and when one creates courageous responses to that anxiety—responses free of either inactivity or overactivity, of either despair or blame.

A person is most likely to experience constructive change in the context of an authentic relationship. The crucial dynamic in such a relationship is that the other in the relationship supports the person in becoming aware all aspects of living, both comfortable and painful. The goal is neither for the person to exaggerate nor to eliminate anxiety but to acknowledge and experience it. In so doing, one drops defenses, affirms the fullness of living, and becomes unblocked to creatively use anxiety to achieve one's deepest potential.

Though rare, an authentic relationship can occur in everyday life. The reason for its rarity is that true caring, Buber's "unfoldment" that we previously described, can occur only when the other person is relatively authentic, not needing the person to be a certain way to assuage the other's own anxiety. For example, most friends and family members, when they see someone in pain, find that their own existential anxiety is provoked; seeking to escape from that anxiety, they rescue the person from pain through comforting and distraction rather than supporting the person in experiencing their pain to facilitate a more authentic existence. In addition, many people use others to assuage their own existential anxiety; in demanding that others be a certain way, one does not facilitate one's process of becoming oneself.

In light of the rarity with which authentic relationship occurs in everyday life, the individual seeking existential growth is most likely to find the necessary conditions for such growth in the special circumstances of the existential counseling situation. Groth (2008) summarized the authentic therapeutic encounter in the following way:

> Its uniqueness among the human partnerships lies in the fact that the situation or world of one member of the pair is highlighted while the other remains more or less in the background, but it [is] still visible. Here there is no place for anonymity (as in psychoanalysis) or invisible, unapproachable authority (as in behavior modification). In existential analysis, both participants retain their autonomy. Its primary goal is illuminating the client's way of existence or being-in-the-world with a view to the affirmation of her authenticity. (p. 88)

Counselor's Role

An existential counselor's goal is to facilitate a client to gain awareness and take responsibility for courageously confronting the givens of existence. The counselor encourages the client to fully explore the givens of life and to discover ways one could lead a more authentic existence. As Deurzen-Smith (1997) summarized, the goal of existential therapy is for clients:

> to learn to open up to what is there in our lives, no matter how hard the truths of our troubles, and see our own position and orientation towards all of this in order to reclaim our central role in our own lives. (p. 188)

The role of the counselor is to more systematically and purposefully provide a client with a change-facilitating relationship, that is, a more authentic relationship, than the client is likely to experience in everyday life. According to Moustakas (1994), this genuine relationship "is the essential condition that underlies all phases of therapy, the power that permeates all methods for facilitating meaning and growth" (p. 45).

The counselor's role can be summarized as an authentic "being there," a *Dasein* encounter (Boiling, 1995), an open experiencing of both the client and the counselor's self from moment to moment throughout the therapeutic process. The counselor attends both to what the client presents and to how the counselor experiences the client within the therapeutic situation. This "being there" is based on the counselor's genuine desire to understand the client's subjective perspective and approach to existence, especially the extent to which the client does and/or does not acknowledge the givens of existence, generate appropriate anxiety around those givens, and respond to that anxiety courageously, both outside of the therapeutic setting and within it. Upon sensing inauthenticity, the counselor sensitively points it out to the client, thus offering the client the opportunity for enhanced authenticity: increased awareness, anxiety proportionate to any actual threat, and courageous response to that anxiety. The counselor's role is not to provide clients with answers but to be there with clients as they struggle toward increased authenticity.

Two psychological processes assist the counselor in maintaining authenticity. One is a continuous searching attitude. The counselor seeks consistently to discover the client's unique humanity, his or her unique approach to existence. A continuous searching attitude prevents the counselor from thinking, "I know what this person is all about. I have seen this dynamic thousands of times in other depressed clients." Existential therapists understand that this client is different from all past and future clients. The counselor's consistent honoring of the individuality of the client is one hallmark of an authentic relationship.

Another process that assists the existential counselor in maintaining authenticity is resonance. Resonance begins with the counselor's well-developed awareness of one's own struggle to be human: to be aware of, to generate proportionate anxiety about, and to respond courageously in the face of the givens of existence. On the basis of this awareness, the counselor then can resonate to the client's struggles. Resonance involves a kind of identification with the client's struggles, a feeling touched by one's commonality with the client, and a sense of connectedness based on that commonality (Deurzen-Smith, 1997). To resonate with clients, a counselor must authentically address not only the therapeutic encounter but also life outside the therapy session. According to Deurzen-Smith, "the existential therapist, rather than living some kind of holy, abstinent and devout life, needs to be immersed in the complexities of life as actively as possible" (p. 200).

The authentic therapeutic relationship is one of unfoldment: the counselor truly cares for the client, that is, the counselor cares about the client's growth and wants to bring something to life in the client from which the client is currently blocked. As the client's defensive blocks fall away, the client will naturally proceed in a constructive direction.

As stated earlier, the existential model of mental health allows for the reality that complete and constant authenticity is an ideal, a human impossibility. Therefore, the existential counselor burdens neither oneself nor the client with the expectation of perfect authenticity at all times. Rather, the counselor strives to maximize one's own authenticity and encourage it in the client as well.

Client's Role

Since the client's role involves certain requirements, existential counseling is appropriate for only some people. A client must be willing to explore the givens of existence, be ready to face the anxiety that stems from them, and be prepared to experiment with new, more courageous responses to that anxiety. If the client is looking for instant relief or is otherwise not prepared to engage in the process of exploring one's personal world, of tolerating anxiety, and of taking greater responsibility in and for one's life, then the client is not ready for existential therapy (Deurzen-Smith, 1997).

Stages and Techniques

Existentialists emphasize the relationship as the primary impetus for change, and therefore the stages of therapy and its techniques focus on the formation and development of the relationship. Although some mental health professionals may think that existentialism has no technique, they would be wrong in the sense that the technique is the relationship and the therapeutic dialogue (Mendelowitz & Schneider, 2008; Russell, 2008). As Deurzen-Smith (1997) pointed out,

> Existential therapists talk with their clients: they enter into dialogue, even into philosophical discussion and argument. They venture into the exploration of the other's world experience as if they were going into unknown territory.... This coming together is known as co-presence. (p. 218)

This dialogue is designed to create a space in which clients can explore life issues. Deurzen-Smith (1997) noted several elements of this dialog creation that resemble elements of techniques counselors enacting other theories use, but with a unique existential spin.

1. **Use of silence.** In existential counseling, informed consent about the therapeutic process provides for a dialog regarding the expectations of client and counselor within the therapeutic session. Once the two agree on ground rules, the existential therapist allows for periods of silence, inviting the client to take the step to share and work. "Welcoming silence will be one of the most significant interventions that the existential psychotherapist will use" (Deurzen-Smith, 1997, p. 227). From an existential perspective, overreliance on complex interpretation and questioning often directs the client in irrelevant directions. The existential therapist provides space for the client to explore.

2. **Constructive questions.** Existential therapists ask questions to illuminate the underlying themes of the client's story and rarely use this device as a means for information gathering. Deurzen-Smith (1997) explained the operating principle existential counselors use in asking questions: "We ask the questions that are implied in the client's words, the ones already embedded in what they have said" (p. 228). In a sense, these questions are observations of the client's patterns (quite similar to reflective responses in other theoretical approaches) with a question mark at the end to denote the tentative nature of the observations. For example, instead of asking, "How did that make you feel?" a counselor might note, "So, you felt humiliated when your dad showed up to your game drunk?" The constructive use of questions requires that the counselor listen between the lines of the client dialogue and formulate questions to make this content more explicit. For example, instead of asking a client, "How are you and your father alike?" a counselor can take the information that prompted that question and illuminate the subtext, "What you seem to be saying is that you and your father have similar ways of escaping when you get anxious."

3. **Interpretation.** Existential therapists frequently make interpretations. Interpretation is the tool for connecting various pieces of client dialog in a way that promotes growth. The existential counselor's task is to interpret elements of client dialog in ways that the client is likely to find meaningful. To avoid imposing one's worldview onto the client, the counselor doesn't use theoretical jargon. Granted, the counselor may find theoretical conceptualization helpful ("This client is struggling with an *Eigenwelt* issue"), but is rarely useful to the client if expressed to the client that way. The most effective existential counselors honor the client's perspective and language when providing constructive interpretations.

The techniques described above briefly illustrate some existential methods counselors use to interact with clients. In addition, May and Yalom (2000) described the *boundary situation*, in which a person is urgently propelled into an acute encounter with one or more of the givens of life. Most people who seek counseling are involved in boundary situations: death, usually taking the form of some type of loss; a critical decision; a disturbed relationship; or a sense of meaninglessness in life. Yalom (1980) detailed the process of exploring the givens of existence as they manifest in the therapeutic relationship and in the client's life. Through the following discussion of this process, you hopefully can get a sense of the flow and focus of existential therapy.

Addressing the Given of Death

Counselor and client can explore the given of death and nonbeing both as it impacts the counseling relationship and as a personal struggle of the client. Through the discussion of both, the two will get a sense of how the anxiety associated with death is impact the client's functioning with regard to the *Mitwelt, Umwelt, Eigenwelt*, and *Uberwelt*.

We will first examine how death affects the counseling encounter. Death is an automatic equalizer between counselor and client. Vontress (1983) noted that even if the client is vastly different from the counselor in ethnic background, gender, or beliefs, the common bond they share is that both of them will, one day, cease to be. In addition to the shared experience of death, every counseling situation has its own built-in death: termination. Clients will handle the anxiety that stems from termination in their own ways. Some will no-show several weeks in advance of the termination session, others will return to old symptomatic complaints in hopes of cheating the death and prolonging the life of the relationship, and yet others may confront the end in a courageous manner, reflecting on the changes they have made and the work they still need to address. Counselors can explore this death anxiety by preparing the client for termination, beginning with the first session, and openly processing termination concerns.

As a personal issue, death anxiety is primary and exists throughout one's life span (May & Yalom, 2000). In therapy, evidence of client anxiety over nonbeing may be more subtle than anxiety connected to the other givens, but it can most readily be accessed with clients who are grieving over life changes that involve loss, such as one's own terminal illness and impending death, the death or other loss of a loved one, or a change in careers or retirement. Existential counselors do not work to eliminate anxiety but to facilitate the client's use of anxiety as a stimulus to live life to its fullest, as defined by the client within the limits of social responsibility.

Addressing the Given of Isolation

In the therapeutic setting, the counselor encourages client awareness of the anxiety involved in the unbridgeable gap between two people. Through the authentic therapeutic relationship itself, a client is likely to gain valuable lessons on how to connect with, yet honor the separateness of, individuals one encounters in the *Mitwelt*. The authentic counseling relationship is psychologically intimate and intense by design. When clients begin to experience the warmth and acceptance of the authentic relationship, it is common for some clients to want to intensify the intimacy of the relationship, either through increased professional contact, such as additional telephone calls or sessions, or increased personal contact, such as taking the relationship to a social or sexual level. The counselor conceptualizes these actions as the client's attempt to merge with the counselor, to deal inauthentically with the anxiety of being separate or, even worse, alone. Existential counselors recognize the potency of the authentic relationship and use it to help the client understand and accept appropriate limits and deal constructively with the resulting anxiety.

Isolation as a personal issue calls for the client to become more at ease spending time on the *Eigenwelt*. A client who presents for counseling with overdependence in one's relationships needs to experience time alone. By encouraging the client to engage in activities on one's own, the counselor can help the client confront the anxiety of being by oneself in order to develop one's sense of self. The following case excerpt illuminates how an exploration of isolation issues can help a client move from paralysis to creative fulfillment:

> When Karen and I got married, I thought that we had to spend every moment together. Up until a few months ago I would get so angry if she didn't want to watch TV with me or if she didn't want me to go with her to work out. I used to think, "If she loved me she would want to be with me all the time." I used to sit at home and get so angry and depressed that she was ignoring me so much. I began to believe that she must be having an affair or planning to leave me. A few weeks ago, I gradually started to spend that time by myself writing in a journal and working on household projects. I also started to jog everyday. I became aware that it was my fear of being alone that was leading to all my misery. As I began to enjoy my time alone, I stopped noticing that she wasn't there. I mean, I stopped thinking she didn't love me because she was doing something else. I actually enjoy spending time with myself now and, to be honest, I also enjoy the time I spend with Karen a lot more, too. It feels less desperate.

Addressing the Given of Freedom

Freedom as a counseling concern is the counseling concern. The existential counselor's goal is to facilitate client awareness and to help the client gain courage to embrace the responsibility inherent in the freedom to choose. Existential counselors consistently explore and challenge their clients to access the courage needed to choose. Every situation in the client's life involves choice, so there is plenty of grist for the mill. Due to the pervasiveness of a client's unique *Dasein,* a client will enact the same patterns of decision making outside the counseling relationship as inside of it. The client who avoids choices outside of counseling will follow the therapist's lead and ask for direction during counseling. The client who resorts to the defense of the ultimate rescuer will relate to the counselor as an all-knowing expert on the client's world, a situation incompatible with an authentic relationship. These phenomena are especially precarious if the therapist lacks awareness of the dynamics at work. The lack of awareness and resulting inauthentic relationship can cement the client's avoidance of freedom and can be characterized as the counselor's exploitation of the client, however inadvertent.

A person unaware of one's choices is likely to feel trapped and restricted. The following case example demonstrates the subtle yet powerful impact the increased awareness in freedom of choice can have on someone.

Client: I don't want to be here. The court says I have to come, but I think it's crazy. I didn't do anything wrong.

Counselor: It seems you feel like you're being ordered here, like you have no choice.

Client: Yeah! I'm being pushed around, you know?

Counselor: Well, I can certainly understand why you wouldn't like being ordered around. I wonder if you actually do have some choices here, but are failing to see them.

Client: I don't get what you are saying. I don't have a choice to be here.

Counselor: I see three choices: You can choose to be here, you can choose to openly refuse the judge's order to her face and be sent to jail, or you can choose simply not to attend without letting the judge know and then take your chances with her finding out and sending you to jail. That's three choices as I count them.

Client: But jail is not a choice.

Counselor: I think it is. It might not be one you prefer, but it's one you have. You are choosing to come here because you do not want to choose to go to jail. Now, once you choose to come to counseling, your choices really expand. You can choose to discuss anything you wish or nothing at all; you can choose how you interact to me. Your way of being in counseling is up to you.

Client: I never thought about it like that. I mean, I still don't think coming here is the greatest thing, but I do see that I have some power in setting the agenda, you know, get my money's worth.

Counselor: It seems you're feeling freer in the process as you recognize that even in less than desirable circumstances, you have a few options open to you.

Addressing the Given of Meaninglessness

Counseling is a meaning-making journey. Clients are choosing to engage in a process that takes emotional endurance, time, and money. Clients will ask the question, "Is what we are doing making a difference in my life? Does this matter?" All of the existential counselor's responses to this question resonate with one theme: "To the extent that we connect, to the extent that you gain awareness of yourself and choose to face the anxiety that is a normal part of your existence, and to the extent that you develop courage to face the balance of life and death, our work together will matter." Existential counselors help the client experience meaning through the development and collaborative maintenance of the authentic relationship.

The counselor explores meaninglessness at the client's personal level by discovering how the client is creating meaning in life and then encouraging the client to create more. In this exploration, the counselor can focus on the client's personal meanings and identity, the *Eigenwelt*; interpersonal relationships, the *Mitwelt*; or how one finds meaning in one's physical–biological and natural world, the *Umwelt*; and throughout this process, the most effective existential counselor maintains attention to the ideal, the client's wishes and dreams, the *Uberwelt*. Existentialists believe that the cultivation of personal meaning is far from a selfish undertaking. The individual who makes meaning in an authentic manner inevitably contributes to others' well-being.

In summary, the method of existential therapy takes the form not of techniques but of process. The process begins and ends with the relationship. Throughout that process, the counselor focuses on gaining an accurate understanding of the client's way of being— *Dasein*—in the four spheres of the world and on encouraging the client to confront the givens of existence in a creative rather than an avoiding manner.

How do counselor and client know when existential therapy is over? The short answer is that when the client evidences the desired growth outside of the counseling hour, counseling has been successful. The real answer is that counseling is a tutorial, a laboratory experiment in being. Medina (2008) reflected,

> A key aspect of this approach is the joining with our clients as they embark upon a search for meaning … and make changes that reflect their world view and take account of the fundamental givens of their lives and of the world in which they live. (p. 130)

In that sense, the process continues to expand and contract until termination.

CONTRIBUTIONS AND LIMITATIONS

Interface With Recent Developments in the Mental Health Field

The Nature–Nurture Question

Regarding the nature–nurture question, existentialists embrace the notion that everyone has biological and genetic limitations as experienced through one's *Umwelt*. If one is born with a disease such as leukemia, one cannot merely choose it away. The disease becomes a part of one's being. However, existentialists maintain that even with genetic or biological limitations, each individual will uniquely perceive and address the limitation. For example, one person may accept the fact that the disease exists but will continue to live a life that maximizes a sense of happiness. Another person may choose to conceptualize being diagnosed with a disease as already being dead and thus will live life as if it were over. From an existential perspective, genetics provide a boundary but do not determine the whole of a person's being; what determines that whole is the action and attitude choices the person makes in light of the boundary.

Similarly, as we discussed in the development section, interactions that occur with others (*Mitwelt*) are meaningful only to the extent that one grants them importance or influence. One's *Mitwelt* can provide experiences, such as neglect, abuse, and poverty that hinder the person's ability to develop authenticity, but even in these extreme situations, a child has the ability to transcend these influences and choose a path through and beyond these circumstances. From an existential perspective, both nature and nurture foster both growth and decay (facilitate both authenticity and inauthenticity) but these biological and environmental factors are not as important as the individual's subjective interpretation of, and choices regarding them. Existential psychotherapist Viktor Frankl (1988), himself a survivor of a World War II holocaust concentration camp, succinctly summarized this perspective: "Man's [sic] freedom is not freedom from conditions but rather a freedom to take a stand on whatever conditions might confront him" (p. 16).

DSM–IV–TR *Diagnosis*

Regarding diagnosis, existentialists hold that focusing on symptoms and classifying individuals into a labeling system is destructive to the holistic view of the person. Existentialist practitioners would argue that a category such as "major depressive disorder" tells a counselor very little about the person and that person's unique way of being. Existentialism is a theory focused on the uniqueness and wellness of the client, a focus that is markedly different from the pathological focus on diagnostic symptoms. Bauman and Waldo (1988) pointed out that, "in fact … a focus on symptoms alone perpetuates the restricted being which probably brought clients into counseling" (p. 22). Although existentialists can and do use diagnostic systems as a means of communication with other health professionals and for insurance purposes, they may include an existential diagnosis that documents how the client is currently functioning in the four dimensions of the world and is addressing the givens of existence (Epp, 1988).

Pharmacotherapy

Regarding pharmacotherapy, existentialists take the position that people too often use medication as a means to escape a courageous confrontation of the normal anxieties of life. When one avoids the anxiety, instead of facing it and using it creatively, the client loses an opportunity to realize one's potential and, in effect, is living inauthentically. The painful symptoms are reminders to the client that one must face the givens of existence and experience the fullness of being. Nevertheless, existentialists acknowledge cases in which a client's symptoms are so paralyzing, so limiting that the person needs medication to reduce symptoms enough to be able to engage in existential exploration. Frankl (1988) noted that he routinely used a combination of medication and existential therapy for cases of severe phobias, depression, and psychosis. Vontress remarked, "I do not think existentialists are against the prudent use of antidepressants as much as they are against the narcotizing of our existence" (Epp, 1988, p. 10). Within this approach, a counselor may recommend that a client in an extreme situation use medication, but it is important for the client to view and use this strategy as a stepping stone to existential confrontation rather than as an escape from it. Medication may provide a person with a handhold out of the abyss, but existentialists would maintain that true health and authenticity requires a client to develop courage to face one's anxieties—one's individualized abyss—and fully experience one's being, free of medication or any other numbing agents. So do existentialists deny the concept that some people have psychophysical conditions that might require lifelong medication to maximize their freedom to live authentically? Perhaps the litmus test is not a rigid edict that no one should use medication throughout their life but whether medication—however long the individual uses it—enhances rather than limits one's ability to manage anxiety in that moderate realm in which the person has the greatest freedom to live the most authentically—to one's greatest potential.

Managed Care and Brief Therapy

Few existential authors have addressed the relationship between existentialism, brief therapy, and managed care. Existential therapy rests on the authenticity of the client–counselor relationship and on the choices the client makes regarding change. Theoretically, the authenticity of the relationship is not connected to the length of the therapy. May and Yalom (2000) asserted that counselors can pursue many existential elements such as responsibility, identity exploration, and the creative use of anxiety in a brief therapy approach. Although existential counselors may perceive compatibility, many elements of managed care are contrary to the philosophical underpinnings of the theory. Requirements of managed care companies, such as diagnostic labeling, contracts, a medical model philosophy based on pathology, empirically supported change strategies that are predominantly cognitive and behavioral in nature, and outcome assessment couched in behavioral terms (Davis & Meier, 2001), are incongruent with the existential approach.

Technical Eclecticism

Existentialists believe that their philosophy of existence represents a unique and comprehensive approach to the human condition. Practitioners of existentialism hold that a firm grounding in this philosophy is fundamental to the development of an authentic approach to life and to the counseling situation. They have frowned on theoretical eclecticism. Indeed, Bauman and Waldo (1988) proposed that the comprehensive nature of existentialism is a practical alternative to the chaos of a theoretically eclectic practice. Existential psychotherapists strongly discourage theoretical eclecticism and in most cases would conceptualize a counselor engaging in it as attempting to avoid the authentic relationship with the client by a desperate grabbing at incompatible ideas.

However, technical eclecticism may be appropriate to the degree that the techniques the counselor uses are consistent with existential philosophy (May & Yalom, 2000). May and Yalom noted, "The therapist's belief system provides a certain consistency. It permits the therapist to know what to explore so that the patient does not become confused" (p. 293). In determining the appropriateness of a particular technique, an existential counselor would presumably assess whether using it helps maintain an authentic therapeutic relationship and helps the client to face, manage, and respond creatively to anxiety such that the client lives more authentically and more fully realizes one's potential.

Diversity Issues

Despite existentialism's roots in Europe, the givens of existence are applicable to all people across all cultures, regardless of race, gender, socioeconomic status, or sexual orientation. As Vontress stated, "Existentialism is not the provincial philosophy of a European elite, it is a universal philosophy of humankind" (Epp, 1988, p. 7). Within the philosophy of existentialism, each individual perceives the world in a unique way, dealing with the anxiety that arises from the givens and striving for authenticity. Due to differences in geography and cultural expectations, the specific circumstances that provoke existential anxiety may differ among various groups, but, at the most essential level of being, each person must confront death, freedom, isolation, and meaninglessness. This shared struggle cements the bond of humanity that transcends cultural, gender, or other differences.

Diversity issues can be explored from an existential perspective by considering not only the universal givens of existence but also the four interactive dimensions of experience: *Umwelt, Mitwelt, Eigenwelt,* and *Uberwelt.* As discussed earlier, the *Umwelt* is the natural world of the individual and includes not only one's biology but also the geographic areas of one's world. A counselor understanding a client's perception of the natural world is crucial to an authentic therapeutic relationship. Vontress (1983) remarked that failure to consider this element would lead the counselor to a distorted understanding of the client and would negatively impact counseling outcome. *Mitwelt* is the interpersonal sphere of experience. Since all individuals have their own perspectives regardless of background, existential counselors expect and are open to interpersonal differences. Vontress (1983) contended that existential counselors should focus the *Mitwelt* exploration on the client's uniqueness that "transcends their developmental socialization" (p. 7). The *Eigenwelt* is the client's world of self. Existentialists believe that authentic counseling is a process of honoring the individual that, therefore, must avoid stereotyping and prejudging. Each client's view of self is much more important than objective facts that the counselor may know about a cultural, gender, or sexual orientation group. For example, Vontress (1983) noted, "in counseling Blacks, anti-Black sentiments in society are not as important as each client's attitude toward them" (pp. 8–9). Simply put, health professionals may agree that hate crimes and discriminatory actions are prevalent against a certain minority group, but to assume the level of importance these factors may play in any client's life robs the client of one's unique experience and perception. Intertwined with the other dimensions, one's *Uberwelt* makes up the spiritual world or world of the ideal as the client perceives it. For a counselor to appreciate that people have different definitions of "ideal" is crucial to understanding a client's *Uberwelt*. To further assess and apply a phenomenological cross-cultural approach to an exploration of the dimensions of experience, Ibrahim and Kahn (1987) developed the Scale to Assess World Views.

From the existential perspective, humans are vastly unique yet share a common bond of humanness that is displayed in the shared struggles with the givens of existence within the four dimensions of the world. Against this common backdrop of being runs the undercurrent of anxiety that issues from these concerns. In existentialism, diversity is a given, and understanding one's own individuality and seeing individuality in others is one dimension of an authentic way of being. In all of these spheres, considering the universality of the givens, the existential counselor is guided by one principle: to understand the client's unique way of being-in-the-world.

Sexual orientation is also conceptualized as a phenomenological dynamic to which the individual gives meaning. Over the past 10 years, existentialists have dialoged and debated about issues surrounding sexual orientation. Some authors have argued that trying to find a cause, for example a biological answer, limits the individual in awareness and exploration of the aspect of self (Cohn, 1997; Spinelli, 1997). However, others maintain that if the client is wishing to seek some answers, then that journey is a valuable part of that particular client's meaning-making process. So, the issue for existentialists is figuring out how sexual orientation is expressed in the life of the client. Medina (2008) noted that existential therapists should help the individual discern the personal meaning and definition regarding sexual orientation and view that definition "as a fundamental experience of Dasein" (p. 132).

The concept of spirituality and its place in existentialism has taken an interesting historical ride. Existentialism's early beginnings were in Kierkegaard's Christian-based writings (1843/1954, 1844/1980). He used biblical stories to illustrate the existential condition and focused on sin, suffering, and encouragement to have faith in and loyalty to God. Since that time, existential writers have largely avoided the integration of religion or spirituality into the counseling or philosophical endeavor. However, existentialists avoid complete acceptance or rejection of spirituality due to the philosophical focus on understanding the individual, which may or may not include a spiritual life. Therefore, both strands of opinion are offered here with the understanding that the subjective experience of the individual is the primary factor in considering the spiritual realm, healthy or unhealthy.

As noted, openness to religion and spirituality as a part of being has played a part in the historical development of existentialism. In recent existential writings, Frankl has provided an extensive commentary on the role of spirituality in existence. Frankl

(1988) noted that the *logos* in his logotherapy is translated as *spirit*, but that it should emphasize the human spirit, that is, the creative power and freedom inherent in humanity. Additionally, Frankl (1967) also remarked that religion and spirituality are of value to a person's health because they may provide an anchor to existence that facilitates courage to face the givens of existence.

Deurzen-Smith (1997) has made the most ambitious contribution to the integration of spiritual concerns to existential thought with her inclusion of the spiritual dimension (*Uberwelt*) as an addition to the other three dimensions of experience. The *Uberwelt* is the ideal world of the individual and inspires ultimate meaning when individuals surrender to an awareness that forces larger than self are at work in the universe. Far more than religion, the *Uberwelt* can include a multitude of belief systems. The crux of the *Uberwelt* is not the creation of a powerful superbeing to order human lives. Instead, it is to the realization that there is much that humans do not understand. Humans are neither the center of the universe nor helpless pawns of an omnipresent force but are ultimately beings searching for meaning. The *Uberwelt* inspires humans to know their limits, accept their responsibilities, and understand that they will never know everything about the ways and means of the universe. This dynamic of responsibility and meaning or lack of meaning propels people to continually create a way of life that addresses everyday concerns and encourages consistent and authentic connection to self and the world.

Just as existentialists conceptualize a positive and holistic conceptualization of spirituality, they also have comments on the inauthentic application of spiritual and religious concepts. Their criticisms largely coalesce around the tendency for people to use spirituality as a means to avoid the anxiety of life. This avoidance is considered inauthentic and robs the individual of the opportunity to fully experience existence. In many cases, this avoidance manifests itself in the belief in an ultimate rescuer (Yalom, 1980) or in the absolution of responsibility for making poor choices or for attempting to make no choices at all. The following case example provides an illustration of how individuals can use spirituality to avoid the responsibility of daily life and its inherent anxiety:

> I know my world is crashing down around me but I just have to trust that the world has something better planned for me. I don't really believe in any religion, but I do believe that there is a guiding power in the universe. It is in the trees and air and out in space. It is all around us right now. I feel "It" watching over me and pushing me in certain directions. I believe that when the world wants something to happen, it will make it happen. If I am supposed to get a job, a job will come to me. Even though I am not a Christian, I pray on things. I believe that if I pray long enough, good things will start to happen. When I left my husband, I knew I hurt him, but I prayed on it and realized it must have been part of a bigger plan. I'm a pawn in this: just a speck in the universe, waiting for my next break.

In this case, it is not one's spiritual beliefs that are inauthentic; it is how the person interprets and uses the belief system. If a person uses beliefs to abdicate responsibility and hide from the anxiety that is a part of the human condition, then the beliefs are contributing to an inauthentic way of being. If the beliefs help facilitate courage to address the anxiety of everyday existence and add a sense of meaning and humility to a person's life, the person is using them in a way that promotes authenticity. In summary, existentialism allows for spirituality as an essence of being but not as the essence of one's entire being.

The Effectiveness of Psychotherapy

Our systematic review of literature produced no specific research that addressed the efficacy of existential therapy. Many sources have reported anecdotes or case studies that included therapeutic outcomes (see Deurzen-Smith, 1988; Vontress, Johnson, & Epp, 1999; Yalom, 1989), but no publications appear to exist in which researchers reported on controlled studies. The lack of outcome studies is philosophically consistent with existentialism's emphasis on the subjective view of the client and the focus on being instead of specific necessary and sufficient elements of change. Existentialists maintain that the striving for authentic being cannot be broken down and measured, and that research invariably diminishes the power of the process and vital dimensions of each participant's own journey. However, an absence of research leaves existential psychotherapy vulnerable to criticism that it may be no more effective, if as effective as, the placebo effect—the standard of comparison in the predominantly empirical world of Western civilization.

Limitations

As illuminated in the discussion of research, either researchers have not been inclined to study, or journals have not reported the outcome of study, of what does and does not constitute the effective practice of existential psychotherapy. Nevertheless, practitioners and students need to have some way to discern good practice from malpractice. Clients also deserve to know that the method of treatment has some merit. With their lack of therapeutic structure and distaste for objective measures, existential therapists have placed their approach behind a veil of mystery and vagueness. If existentialism is to survive in the world of empirically supported approaches and patients' rights, the proponents of the theory might need to soften their resolve and use their anxiety about the meaninglessness of objectivity in a creative manner.

Another criticism that springs from the subjective nature of the theory lies in its ability to be transferred to new practitioners. In my (KAF) experience, instructors and students approach existentialism from two very different tangents. On the one hand, instructors tend to teach existentialism as the theory of the intellectual, wealthy elite, steeped in deep philosophical jargon. The unspoken implication is, "This theory is too lofty and complicated, so let's move on to something more practical." This approach discourages many students from further exploration of the theory. On the other hand, some students embrace existential counseling on the assumption that listening and being with the client afford the student freedom of action and freedom from evaluation. They translate this "being" as, "No one will know if I'm doing it right or not. It's all about sharing time and space with the client. I am beyond evaluation!" In this sense, the student is using a simplified version of the theory to avoid the anxiety of being an accountable counselor. One pattern makes existentialism too complicated; the other makes it too superficial. In either case, it is both counselors and clients who lose.

Contributions

Existentialism has provided a bedrock philosophy upon which many of the leading counseling theorists of the twentieth century have based their approaches. Theories that have existential roots include Adlerian, Gestalt, reality, person-centered, and rational emotive behavioral therapy (REBT). Out of this philosophical movement, mental health practitioners can include in their practices a greater understanding and emphasis on the humanity and uniqueness of each individual. Existential theorists and therapists also can be credited with expanding the role of the counselor from blank screen to a feeling human being striving for authenticity within life and the therapeutic endeavor, much like the clients the counselor encounters. Just as existentialists broadened the role of the therapist, they also affirmed and attributed more responsibility and freedom to the client. This focus on choice and responsibility gave a new flavor to the therapeutic relationship that was vastly different from the prevailing psychoanalytic and behavioral approaches of the time.

RECOMMENDED RESOURCES

Books

Deurzen-Smith, E. van (1997). *Everyday mysteries: Existential dimensions in psychotherapy.* New York, NY: Routledge. Emmy van Deurzen-Smith is the founder of the Society for Existential Analysis, and this book provides a very readable account of existential theory. She provides the reader with a comprehensive discussion of fundamental existential philosophy as well as a thorough overview of the existential approach to counseling, complete with detailed case studies.

Frankl, V. E. (1988). *The will to meaning.* New York, NY: Meridian. Excellent discussion of Frankl's logotherapy and applicable concepts. He has also provided nice coverage of the variety of thoughts regarding spirituality and religion as it applies to existential theory.

Yalom, I. D. (1980). *Existential psychotherapy.* New York, NY: Basic Books, and (1989), *Love's executioner: And other tales of psychotherapy.* New York, NY: Harper. The first book is Yalom's most comprehensive discourse on his proposed givens of existence and how they apply to maladjustment and therapy. The second book is a series of case studies treated from an existential perspective. The case studies are well written and provide insight into the inner thoughts of the therapist as he negotiated the counseling journey.

Audiovisuals

Yalom, I. D., & Douglas, M. (1995). *Existential-humanistic psychotherapy in action: A demonstration.* San Francisco, CA: Jaylen Productions.

Web Sites

http://www.existentialanalysis.co.uk/ This is the official Web site for the Society for Existential Analysis based in London. It contains helpful information about the application and theory of the existential approach and contains the links for additional materials and opportunities for training in existential therapy.

REFERENCES

Allers, R. (1961). *Existentialism and psychiatry.* Springfield, IL: Thomas.

Bauman, S., & Waldo, M. (1988). Existential theory and mental health counseling: If it were a snake it would have bitten! *Journal of Mental Health Counseling, 20,* 13–26.

Binswanger, L. (1963). *Being-in-the-world: Selected papers.* New York, NY: Basic.

Boiling, M. Y. (1995). Acceptance and Dasein. *Humanistic Psychologist, 23,* 213–226.

Buber, M. (1970). *I and thou* (W. Kaufman, Trans.). New York, NY: Scribner.

Bugental, J. F. T. (1965). *The search for authenticity.* New York, NY: Holt, Rinehart & Winston.

Cohn, H. (1997). *Being in the world sexually: Existential thought and therapeutic practice.* London, UK: Sage.

Davis, S. R., & Meier, S. T. (2001). *Elements of managed care: A guide for helping professionals.* Belmont, CA: Wadsworth/Thompson Learning.

Deurzen-Smith, E. van (1988). *Existential counselling in practice.* London, UK: Sage.

Deurzen-Smith, E. van (1997). *Everyday mysteries: Existential dimensions in psychotherapy.* New York, NY: Routledge.

Epp, L. R. (1988). The courage to be an existential counselor: An interview with Clemmont E. Vontress. *Journal of Mental Health Counseling, 20,* 1–12.

Frankl, V. E. (1967). *The doctor and the soul: From psychotherapy to logotherapy.* New York, NY: Bantam.

Frankl, V. E. (1988). *The will to meaning.* New York, NY: Meridian.

Groth, M. (2008). Authenticity in existential analysis. *Existential Analysis, 19,* 81–101.

Heidegger, M. (1962). *Being and time* (J. Macquarrie & E. S. Robinson, Trans.). New York, NY: Harper & Row. (Original work published 1927)

Husserl, E. (1965). Philosophy as a rigorous science. In Q. Lauer (Ed.), *Phenomenology and the crisis of philosophy* (pp. 71–147). New York, NY: Harper & Row.

Ibrahim, F. A., & Kahn, H. (1987). Assessment of world views. *Psychological Reports, 60,* 163–176.

Jacobsen, B. (2007). Authenticity and our basic existential dilemmas. *Existential Analysis, 18,* 288–296.

Keen, E. (1970). *Three faces of being: Toward an existential clinical psychology.* New York, NY: Appleton/Century/Crofts.

Kierkegaard, S. (1954). *Fear and trembling.* Princeton, NJ: Princeton University. (Original work published 1843)

Kierkegaard, S. (1980). *The concept of anxiety* (R. Thomte, Trans.). Princeton, NJ: Princeton University. (Original work published 1844)

Maddi, S. R. (1967). The existential neurosis. *Journal of Abnormal Psychology, 72,* 311–325.

Maddi, S. R. (1976). *Personality theories: A comparative analysis* (3rd ed.). Homewood, IL: Dorsey.

May, R. (1939). *The art of counseling.* New York, NY: Gardner.

May, R. (1950). *The meaning of anxiety.* New York, NY: Norton.

May, R. (1961). *Existential psychology.* New York, NY: Random House.

May, R. (1977). *The meaning of anxiety.* New York, NY: Norton.

May, R. (1981). *Freedom and destiny.* New York, NY: Norton.

May, R. (1985). *My quest for beauty.* Dallas, TX: Saybrook.

May, R., & Yalom, I. D. (2000). Existential psychotherapy. In R. J. Corsini & D. Wedding (Eds.), *Current psychotherapies* (6th ed., pp. 273–302). Itasca, IL: F. E. Peacock.

Medina, M. (2008). Can I be homosexual please? *Existential Analysis, 19,* 129–142.

Mendelowitz, E., & Schneider, K. (2008). Existential psychotherapy. In R. Corsini and D. Wedding (Eds.), *Current psychotherapies* (8th ed., pp. 295–327). Belmont, CA: Brooks/Cole.

Moustakas, C. (1994). *Existential psychotherapy and the interpretation of dreams.* Northvale, NJ: Jason Aronson.

Rabinowitz, F. E., Good, G., & Cozad, L. (1989). Rollo May: A man of meaning and myth. *Journal of Counseling and Development, 67,* 436–441.

Russell, J. M. (2008). Existential psychotherapy. In A. B. Rochlen (Ed.), *Applying counseling theories: An on-line case-based approach* (pp. 107–125). Upper Saddle River, NJ: Pearson.

Sartre, J. P. (1965). Existentialism is a humanism. *Essays in existentialism* (H. E. Barnes, Trans.). Secaucus, NJ: Citadel.

Spinelli, E. (1997). Some hurried notes expressing outline ideas that someone might one day utilize as signposts towards a sketch of an existential-phenomenological theory of sexuality. *Journal for the Society for Existential Analysis, 8,* 2–20.

Tillich, P. (1952). *The courage to be.* New Haven, CT: Yale University Press.

Vontress, C. E. (1983). An existential approach to cross-cultural counseling. *Counseling and Values, 28,* 2–12.

Vontress, C. E., Johnson, J. A., & Epp, L. R. (1999). *Cross cultural counseling: A casebook.* Alexandria, VA: American Counseling Association.

Yalom, I. D. (1980). *Existential psychotherapy.* New York, NY: Basic.

Yalom, I. D. (1989). *Love's executioner: And other tales of psychotherapy.* New York, NY: Harper.

CHAPTER 6

Person-Centered Counseling

Finally it may be stressed that [client-centered therapy] is based on a philosophy which is fully consistent with the highest development of democratic feeling ... a viewpoint built upon the assumption that the individual has worth and dignity, and has the capacity to choose to live a spontaneous, independent, and self-directed life.

—Carl Rogers, 1945

BACKGROUND OF THE THEORY

Biographical and Historical Overview

Carl Rogers developed person-centered counseling and psychotherapy in the United States roughly between 1940 and 1990. He fostered this approach in an era when science pervaded Western thinking, when psychoanalysis dominated clinical psychology, and when progressivism challenged traditional education. His ideas matured concurrently with the emergence of behaviorism as a systematic approach to psychotherapy, with which his ideas differed fundamentally. "Arguably the leading voice in the humanistic psychotherapy movement" (Kirschenbaum, 2007, p. 257), Rogers expressed his humanistic views in his own summary statement of history:

> I am well aware that ... one can place ... a primary value upon society, and only a secondary value upon the individual. But only in the individual does awareness exist. Only in the individual can alternative courses of action be most deeply and consciously tested as to their enriching or destructive consequences. The whole history of mankind [*sic*], it seems to me, shows a gradually increasing emphasis upon the significance and worth of each individual. I not only observe this trend, I concur in it. (Rogers, 1989, p. 266)

Rogers lived through World War I, the Great Depression, World War II, the Vietnam war, and most of the Cold War. He continued to refine his ideas throughout the turbulent social changes of the 1960s and 1970s, including the civil rights and women's rights movements. In these fertile times of social experimentation, Rogers and others who shared his views applied his principles to a variety of domains of human existence.

The last decades of Rogers's life occurred in a time of globalization that involved both enhanced awareness of areas of intense conflict around the world and relatively greater ease of contact between people of various cultures. Increasing globalization provided Rogers an opportunity to apply tentatively his psychotherapeutic principles internationally to the arena of cross-cultural communication and conflict resolution. Also during his last decades, information and research increased regarding experiences of altered states of consciousness, including the intuitive, paranormal, and mystical domains both in life and surrounding death. Rogers used this information and, of course most importantly, his own experiences, to speculate on the ultimate nature of reality.

Founder's Biographical Overview

In 2007, thirty years after his first biography of Carl Rogers, Howard Kirschenbaum published a second: the 600-page *The Life and Work of Carl Rogers*. In it, he drew on sources ranging from the most public to the most private—including the daily journal Rogers kept throughout his life and interviews Kirschenbaum conducted with Rogers's intimates and associates after Rogers's death (2007, p. ii). The following summary unavoidably brushes the surface of Rogers's fascinating life. If you are inclined to understand Rogers and his counseling approach in greater depth, we encourage you to read Kirschenbaum's tour-de-force biography.

Carl Rogers was born in 1902 in Oak Park, Illinois, a middle- to upper-middle-class suburb that borders the west edge of Chicago. He was the fourth of six children in a family he described as close and caring and, at the same time, strictly religious, ethical, and hard working. His family enjoyed their own company, neither socializing with others nor engaging in diversions such as card playing or dancing. Rogers accepted his parents' view that his family was different from other people. He described himself as a solitary, shy boy whose primary avocation was reading.

When Rogers was 12 years old, his family moved to a farm in a far west Chicago suburb, where he reportedly developed an appreciation for the scientific process. He began college in Wisconsin, majoring first in agriculture, then changing to history as preparation for the ministry. His attendance at an international Student Christian Federation Conference in China during his junior year prompted his development of his own religious beliefs independent from those of his parents.

During college he fell in love with fellow student Helen Elliott whom he had known since second grade. Upon college graduation, he married Helen despite his parents' wishes that they delay until he finished his education. Over the years, Rogers occasionally wrote in his characteristically personal and candid style about his marriage with Helen. They had two children: David, who became a successful physician, and Natalie, who developed an expressive arts approach to therapy based on therapeutic principles she shared with her father. Carl and Helen were still married when Helen died in 1979.

Beginning in 1924, Rogers spent two years studying at the doctrinally liberal Union Theological Seminary. During his second year, he and a small group of other students petitioned successfully to hold an instructor-less seminar in which they could explore their own questions about religion and life. Through this seminar he progressed substantially toward the development of his own unique philosophy and became aware that he was not suited to the ministry's requirement of allegiance to a specific religious doctrine.

Having enjoyed his exposure to psychology and psychiatry, he pursued these interests at Teacher's College of Columbia University, including a fellowship/internship at the Institute for Child Guidance. After graduation, he moved to Rochester, New York, to take a position as a psychologist in a child guidance center. During his 12 years there, he wrote his first book, *The Clinical Treatment of the Problem Child*. Soon after its publication in 1939, Ohio State University (OSU) offered him a full professorship in psychology.

Shortly after taking the position at OSU, he delivered a paper entitled "Some Newer Concepts in Psychotherapy," marking the birth of client-centered therapy and Rogers's discovery that people could be very threatened by his ideas. Despite controversy, he expanded and published his views in the 1942 book, *Counseling and Psychotherapy.*

Rogers held academic appointments for five years at OSU, 12 years at the University of Chicago, and four years at the University of Wisconsin. During these two decades, he expanded and clarified his theory of psychotherapy, personality, and interpersonal relationships. In 1964, Rogers left academia and moved to La Jolla, California, first taking a position at the Western Behavioral Sciences Institute and then, in 1968, helping create the Center for Studies of the Person. During the next 20 years, he expanded the application of his theory to education, marriage, administration, and politics. He was invited around the world to disseminate his views and to South Africa, Eastern Europe, the Soviet Union, northern Ireland, and Central America to engage in cross-cultural communication and conflict resolution.

Rogers's theory can be understood as having developed in three major phases. The first, *nondirective* phase focused on how the nondirective counselor's conduct differed from that of more "directive" psychotherapists, such as psychoanalysts and behavior therapists. Rogers's 1951 publication of *Client-Centered Therapy* marked the beginning of the second *client-centered* phase in which he shifted focus away from the counselor and firmly onto the client as a responsible agent whose nature provided the rationale for the counselor's therapeutic conduct. The expanded application of Rogers's psychotherapeutic principles beyond the confines of traditional psychology marked the third, *person-centered* phase of his theory.

Rogers received numerous honors during his lifetime. Among his most valued was his receipt in 1956, with two other psychologists, of the American Psychological Association's first-ever Distinguished Scientific Contribution Award. It is interesting, also, to note Rogers's reception at the first Evolution of Psychotherapy Conference in Phoenix, Arizona, held in 1985. The conference organizers had invited virtually every leading figure in the field of psychotherapy to make presentations; over 7000 mental health professionals attended, representing every imaginable specialization within the field. One of the authors of this textbook (JMH) was privileged to be among those professionals and to attend numerous presentations by a variety of speakers. Only one speaker received a standing ovation, and he received one each of the three times he presented: That speaker was Carl Rogers. The accolades his audience and presenters bestowed on him reflected the ultimate esteem in which many people held Rogers. It is no wonder, then, shortly before his death, Rogers was nominated for the Nobel Peace Prize.

A believer in the uniqueness and complexity of people, Rogers himself displayed a wide, and sometimes paradoxical, array of characteristics throughout his life. Sickly as a young child, with duodenal ulcer problems into his early adulthood, he was remarkably healthy and physically vital for most of the remainder of his life. Shy throughout his life, his early experience in parliamentary procedure and debate prepared him to accept leadership positions and speaking engagements from local to global levels. Profoundly accepting, nonjudgmental, and noncontrolling in his roles as mental health professional, educator, and peacemaker, he was competitive and ambitious, and he could be sarcastic and biting in both personal and professional relationships. Along with an externally quiet and gentle demeanor was an inner principled toughness with which he actively challenged what he saw as institutional injustice and with which he never shied away from controversy. Capable of deep intimacy with people, he preferred professional confrontation by memo rather than in person. An apparently sexually faithful husband and committed secular for over 50 years, he experienced a blossoming of his sensuality, sexuality, and spirituality (but never religion) in the last decade of his life. A prolific writer, researcher, educator, psychotherapist, and workshop provider, he also enjoyed private hobbies of making mobiles, gardening, and photography. Alongside his amazing productivity, and unbeknownst even to Kirschenbaum (2007) until after Rogers's death, he consumed large amounts of alcohol throughout his adulthood—sometimes as much as a bottle of vodka a day—such that, in the last decade of his life, he was "a high-functioning, closet drinker, self-medicating with liquor to reduce anxiety, stress and intermittent depression" and difficulty sleeping (p. 474). A staunch advocate of the innate worth of each person, at age 80 he wrote in his journal, "I believe I am lovable, but do I love myself? That is the unanswered question" (p. 475).

Rogers had arranged that upon his death, his personal papers would be left to the Library of Congress. In allowing the most private aspects of his life to be known publicly, he not only revealed a multidimensional human in a lifelong process of becoming, but he also fulfilled one of his deepest commitments—to be genuine—and one of his most valued goals—to be known not only as an iconic revolutionary but as a human: achieving, fallible, ever in the process of realizing his potential.

At the close of Rogers's (1989) essay "Growing Old: Or Older and Growing," the 75-year-old Rogers reported that having been a sickly child, he was predicted to die young, a prediction with which he had come to agree, albeit in a different sense than originally meant. That prediction and agreement proved equally accurate a decade later: At age 85, continuing, to the end, to add to his list of numerous authored books, hundreds of authored journal articles and presentations, several demonstration videotapes, and several international conflict resolution processes, Carl Rogers did, indeed, die young.

To conclude this sketch, we invite you to partake of quotations from Carl Rogers regarding what he considered to be some of his most important learnings in life.

Rogers (1961), age 59 (from Rogers, 1989):

> The more I am simply willing to be myself ... and the more I am willing to understand and accept the realities in myself and in the other person, the more change seems to be stirred up.... It is a very paradoxical thing. (p. 22)
>
> I can trust my experience.... [M]y total organismic sensing of a situation is more trustworthy than my intellect.... [E]valuation by others is not a guide for me.... Experience is, for me, the highest authority. (pp. 22–23)
>
> I enjoy the discovery of order in experience.... I find it very satisfying to pursue.... [T]he reason I devote myself to research, and to the building of theory, is to satisfy a need for perceiving order and meaning. (pp. 24–25)
>
> The facts are friendly ... so while I still hate to readjust my thinking ... these painful reorganizations are what is known as learning [that] always lead to a more satisfying, because somewhat more accurate, way of seeing life. (p. 25)
>
> What is most personal is most general.... [T]he very feeling which has seemed to me most private, most personal, and hence most incomprehensible by others, has turned out to be an expression for which there is resonance in many other people. (p. 26)
>
> Life, at its best, is a flowing, changing process in which nothing is fixed. (p. 27)

Rogers in 1972, age 70 (from Rogers, 1989):

> The things in one's private life which cannot *possibly* be talked about *can* be talked about, easily and freely. (p. 31)
>
> I have come to value highly the privilege of getting away, of being alone. (p. 45)

Rogers in 1977, age 75 (from Rogers, 1989):

I have found myself opening up to much greater intimacy in relationships ... physically ... psychologically.... I recognize how much I need to care deeply for another and to receive that kind of caring in return.... I can say openly what I have always recognized dimly: that my deep involvement in psychotherapy was a cautious way of meeting this need for intimacy without risking too much of my person.... Now I am more willing ... to risk giving more of myself. (pp. 83–84)

We are indeed wiser than our intellects ... the nonrational, creative "metaphoric mind." ... I am open to even more mysterious phenomena—precognition, thought transference, clairvoyance, human auras, Kirlian photography, even out-of-the-body experiences. These phenomena may not fit with known scientific laws, but perhaps we are on the verge of discovering new types of lawful order. (p. 83)

Ten or fifteen years ago, I felt quite certain that death was the total end of the person. I still regard that as the most likely prospect.... My belief that death is the end has, however, been modified by some of my learnings of the past decade ... near-death [experiences] ... reincarnation ... that individual consciousness is but a fragment of a cosmic consciousness.... [D]eath will be what it will be, and I trust I can accept it as either an end to, or a continuation of, life. (pp. 87–88)

Rogers in 1979, age 77 (from Rogers, 1989):

In the eighteen months prior to my wife's death in March, 1979 ... a series of experiences ... decidedly changed my thoughts and feelings about dying and the continuation of the human spirit.... [My wife, Helen] and I visited a thoroughly honest medium.... The messages were extraordinarily convincing ... involving facts that the medium could not possibly have known.... Helen also had visions and dreams of her family members, which made her increasingly certain that she would be welcomed on the other side.... [S]he "saw" evil figures and the devil by her hospital bed [whom] she dismissed [and they] never reappeared ... visions of an inspiring white light which came close, lifted her from the bed, and then deposited her back on the bed.... All these experiences ... have made me much more open to the possibility of the continuation of the individual human spirit.... I now consider it possible that each of us is a continuing spiritual essence lasting over time, and occasionally incarnated in a human body. (pp. 51–53)

Philosophical Underpinnings

Rogers (1957) noted that Walker (1956) had identified Rogers as "the successor to Rousseau [who observed] that every man comes from the hand of his Maker a perfect being. This pristine splendor is corrupted, said Rousseau, by an imperfect society" (p. 89). Denying Walker's interpretation, Rogers cited evidence that his exposure to Rousseau had been extremely limited. Rather, he was adamant that his views were the product of his direct experience working with clients in psychotherapy.

However, Rogers (Raskin, Rogers, & Witty, 2008, p. 148) did acknowledge the influence of Otto Rank and his followers, whose basic assumptions about people and psychotherapy were quite similar to his own. In particular, Rank believed in the creative power in each person, the importance of self-acceptance and reliance, the centrality of the client in the therapeutic process, the value in the counselor avoiding the role of educator, and the importance of the client experiencing the present moment in the therapeutic process. Rogers also noted similarities between his views and those of Søren Kierkegaard (p. 150), who emphasized the importance of subjective experience, who believed that ultimate truth is never reached and that knowledge is always in a state of evolution, and who concerned himself with aspects of human experience such as alienation, anxiety, inauthenticity, and choice. Rogers also affirmed a similarity between his own views and those of Abraham Maslow (p. 150), who postulated a self-actualizing tendency in humans—an innate tendency of humans to heal, grow, and fulfill their potential.

PERSONALITY DEVELOPMENT

In the 70-page book chapter "A Theory of Therapy, Personality, and Interpersonal Relationships, as Developed in the Client-Centered Framework," Rogers (1959) set forth his hypotheses about how people develop and change. He "believed this was his most scholarly, complete, and well-developed theoretical formulation, was very proud of it, and was always puzzled that hardly anyone ever seemed to know or care about its existence" (Kirschenbaum & Henderson, 1989b, p. 203). This section on personality development is based primarily on that chapter, of which an excerpted form is available in Kirschenbaum and Henderson's *The Carl Rogers Reader* (Rogers, 1989).

Nature of Humans

Function of the Psyche

Rogers's view of human nature was an expression of his view of the nature of the universe. Although he acknowledged a universal tendency toward deterioration and chaos, he tended to believe in a stronger creative force involving formation and evolution toward greater complexity and order (Rogers, 1980). He saw evidence of this *formative tendency,* this "transcendent organizing influence" (Rogers, 1979, cited in Kirschenbaum, 2007, p. 489), in everything from atoms to galaxies, including humans.

Thus, Rogers did not see the core of human motivation as negative, that is, hostile, antisocial, destructive, or evil; nor as neutral, capable of being shaped into any form; nor as perfect in itself and corrupted only by an evil society. Rather, he saw humans at their deepest level to be essentially positive, having the fundamental, innate motive of all living organisms: the *actualizing tendency* to grow, to heal when injured, and to develop one's full potential. This actualizing motive renders people essentially forward-moving, constructive, and realistic. Rogers believed that, at the core, humans tend toward development, individuality, and cooperative relationships; toward movement from dependence to independence; toward a harmonized, complex, and fluid pattern of self-regulation; and toward the preservation, enhancement, and further evolution of self, the human species, and the universe. Rogers considered humans, at their most essential level, to be trustworthy.

Note Rogers's choice of the word *tendency* rather than *drive*. Whereas a drive involves the more intent pursuit of a particular goal, a tendency involves a direction and a generally defined but less specified goal; it is more like a disposition or inclination—less forceful and more vulnerable to alteration. Indeed, Rogers believed that everyone, to one degree or another, becomes alienated from the actualizing tendency. However, although the tendency can be thwarted, the only way to destroy it is to destroy the organism. People experience the actualizing tendency as needs for phenomena that maintain or enhance the organism, such as affection, affiliation, aggression, and sex. Some needs are inborn; also inborn is the potential to acquire additional, learned needs.

To pursue the actualizing tendency, the infant is equipped with the capacity to perceive and to symbolize accurately in awareness moment-to-moment sensory experience of phenomena in the environment and visceral experience of phenomena within oneself. The infant is born also with the potential to deny experience by suppressing, selectively perceiving, or distorting how experience is represented in awareness. Experience that a person has denied to accurate conscious representation does not just go away; it presses subtly to be acknowledged in awareness, a pressure the person *subceives*—*sub*consciously per*ceives*—as vaguely threatening. The newborn infant, however, having no reason to deny or distort experience from conscious awareness, engages exclusively in accurate symbolization of experience.

The infant's actualizing tendency interacts with perception in the *organismic valuing process,* whereby one immediately experiences each object of perception in terms of the degree to which it is actualizing. Thus, one experiences each object of perception either positively as something that contributes to one's actualization, neutrally as something unrelated to one's actualization, or negatively as something that detracts from one's actualization. In other words, through the organismic valuing process, a person perceives each object of perception either as fulfilling a need, as being unrelated to fulfillment of a need, or as thwarting fulfillment of a need.

The organismic valuing process is characterized by an *internal locus of evaluation,* in which the infant's preferences reflect the input of inner visceral and sensory perception and the assignment of value based on one's own innate actualizing tendency. This process involves flexibility rather than rigidity, because one might perceive a specific object as actualizing at one moment and as contrary to actualization at another. For example, a nipple in the infant's mouth: Rather than rigidly valuing it as always positive or always negative, the infant is likely to value it positively when hungry (feeling a need for food), but negatively when quite full or satiated (feeling a need for no additional food).

Also innate in infants is the capacity for behavior: holistic action aimed at the goal of satisfying needs. A person organizes activity to approach those experiences one organismically values positively and avoid those experiences one organismically values negatively. On the basis of feedback regarding how well a past behavior actually satisfied a need, a person will adjust future behavior to more nearly approximate the maximum possible need fulfillment.

The mechanism of feedback calls upon three innate conceptual capabilities of the self-actualizing tendency: memory of past experience, consideration of alternative behaviors, and prediction of possible future outcomes. Feedback also relies on the innate conceptual tendency to organize perceptions, including differentiating dissimilarities among experiences, identifying patterns of commonality among experiences, and seeking order and consistency among perceptions.

Perhaps the most important application of these conceptual capabilities is in the formation of the self-concept. The process begins when the infant comes to differentiate some aspects of her total being and functioning as self-experience. In this process a crucial shift occurs: Rather than just simply and directly experiencing a need, the infant conceptualizes herself as experiencing the need; rather than just simply and directly valuing objects of her perception, she conceptualizes herself as valuing the objects; rather than just simply and directly behaving in response to her values, she conceptualizes herself as behaving. In this way, what was formerly direct, organismic functioning now itself becomes an object of perception (actually a constellation of self-experiences) that she organizes into her self-concept: who she thinks she is. Thus, the self-concept is the domain of self-awareness.

As objects of perception, the self-concept as a whole and each of its contents become subject to evaluation. Whereas formerly she might simply cry when sad, now she observes herself crying; with that observation is born the potential to evaluate her crying as good, neutral, or bad, apart from her organismic valuation. How the child makes that secondary evaluation will be described in the next section. Once the evaluation is made, it becomes part of the self-concept. Due to the human tendency to seek order and consistency, as a person forms a self-concept, one then sets about *defending* it psychologically against inconsistent information and experience. We will describe this process more thoroughly below.

Structure of the Psyche

Rogers hypothesized two primary structures in the human psyche. He conceptualized the newborn infant's psyche as an undifferentiated, nonconscious whole consisting of all the infant's sensory and visceral experience. Every moment throughout life, this totality of what a person is actually experiencing comprises a kind of fluid psychic structure that Rogers called *experience*.

Gradually the infant comes to identify her experience as "belonging to me" and thus develops a *self-concept*: a personal psychological representation of self. Initially, the self-concept and experience are identical or *congruent*. This condition can be illustrated by a Venn diagram in which the circle representing self-concept and the circle representing experience completely overlap (see Figure 6.1, in which we have separated the circles slightly just so you can differentiate them).

For reasons that will be explained in the next section, the infant's state of congruence changes. She creates and incorporates into her self-concept *conditions of worth*, believing she is who she believes she must be to be worthwhile, even though those qualities contradict her experience. The more conditions of worth she creates, the more of her

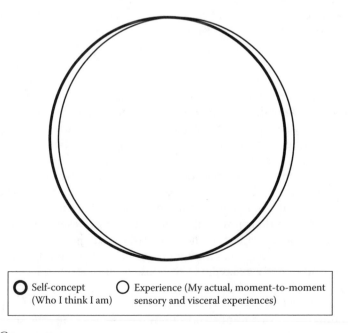

| ● Self-concept (Who I think I am) | ○ Experience (My actual, moment-to-moment sensory and visceral experiences) |

FIGURE 6.1   Congruence.

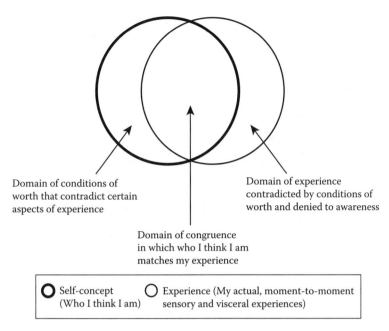

Domain of conditions of
worth that contradict certain
aspects of experience

Domain of experience
contradicted by conditions of
worth and denied to awareness

Domain of congruence
in which who I think I am
matches my experience

⬤ Self-concept   ○ Experience (My actual, moment-to-moment
(Who I think I am)   sensory and visceral experiences)

FIGURE 6.2   Moderate incongruence.

actual experience she denies, a condition Rogers called *incongruence* (see Figures 6.2 and 6.3). The degree of incongruence varies among individuals, and significant others in one's social environment play an important role in a person's development of conditions of worth and the resulting incongruence.

Role of Environment

From Rogers's perspective, a person's self-concept is profoundly influenced by relationships with significant others in the social environment—especially primary caretakers but also others in caretaking or authoritative roles. Rogers believed that as a child's self-concept begins to form, the child develops a *need for positive regard* from significant others. He wasn't sure whether this need was innate or learned, but he considered that question less important than his observation that the need is universal among humans.

Each significant other can theoretically be represented on a continuum: at one end, the significant other feels and communicates to the child a totally *unconditional positive regard,* a complete empathic understanding, acceptance, and prizing of the child's being and inner experience; at the other end, the significant other feels and communicates to the child a totally *conditional positive regard,* empathically understanding, accepting, and prizing the child only when her being and inner experience matches some condition determined by the significant other (see Figure 6.4). In reality, everyone's behavior probably exemplifies different points on the continuum at different times. It is also important to note that unconditional positive regard does not involve total acceptance and prizing of all of the child's behaviors; rather, a caretaker can accept and value the child's inner experience while setting limits on certain behaviors.

FIGURE 6.3   Extreme incongruence.

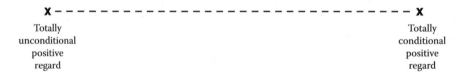

FIGURE 6.4   The positive regard continuum.

A significant other's regard for a child is reflected in all aspects of the relationship, but most notably in the forms of discipline one employs. To say, "You're a bad girl for crying like that in the restaurant" is to reject the child's total being on the conditional positive regard that "I accept and value you as a person only if you feel and act a certain way." To say, "You shouldn't get so upset when you can't have the exact drink you want" is to reject the child's inner experience on the conditional positive regard that "I accept and value your feelings only when they conform to what I think you should feel." To take the crying child to the car and to say patiently and caringly, "I know you're upset they didn't have the exact drink you wanted, and I'm sorry for that. You're so disappointed that you're crying very loudly. Since restaurants are not places for loud crying, I'll wait here in the car (or the foyer) with you until you're finished crying. Then we'll go back inside." sets limits on the child's behavior without devaluing the inner experience that gave rise to the behavior or devaluing the child as a whole.

Caretakers inevitably express to children some degree of conditional positive regard. Subsequently, the child independently associates aspects of the self with gain or loss of positive regard; this process is termed *self-regard*. The more the child's significant others genuinely empathize with whatever the child is experiencing, and they feel and congruently communicate unconditional positive regard to the child, the more likely the child will manifest *unconditional self-regard*: a sense of one's self as worthwhile no matter what one's experience. This sense of worth does not preclude at times wanting to be different and better in some ways; rather, it means that the person feels essentially worthwhile even with one's imperfection and fallibility. It is important to note that others' conditional positive regard contributes to, but is not the ultimate source or cause of, the child forming conditions of worth; the ultimate source is the child's own need for positive regard. Due to that need, the child is vigilant (on the lookout) for significant others' conditional positive regard; often perceives it in a distortedly magnified way—or even perceives it when the other was not even intending to convey it; then forms it in one's psyche in that often-exaggerated form.

Rogers also believed that the need for positive regard is so strong, so compelling, it becomes more important to a person than one's own organismic valuing process. In a sense, to receive positive regard from others, the person "sells out" her real experience and its associated organismic valuing process. Feeling the need for positive self-regard, and then perceiving others' conditional positive regard, she creates internal conditions of worth and then redefines her self-concept to match those conditions. This process constitutes an intrapsychic trade-off: the person gains positive self-regard but loses contact with actual experience—reality—and the guidance of the organismic valuing process—one's own inner wisdom.

An example of the process described above is a college student who is pursuing a premed curriculum despite the fact that she is not enjoying most of it and is getting only mediocre grades. She is very interested in law, but she perseveres in the study of medicine. The intrapsychic dynamics behind this situation are that, earlier in life, she perceived her father as communicating conditional positive regard: "I will be proud of you only if you are a physician." She created the condition of worth that, "I am worthwhile only if I am a physician." She adjusted her self-concept to align with that condition: "I am capable of succeeding and feeling happy as a physician." Although her actual experience includes disliking and performing poorly in the study of medicine, she denies this experience to her awareness or, when it manages to break through, she distorts it to fit her self-concept: "Everyone struggles at times; I'm still in the process of adjusting to doing what I'm really meant to do: become a physician." A person's degree of congruence/incongruence is the central concept in Rogers's model of mental health.

Model of Mental Health

Healthy Functioning

The relatively greater an individual's degree of congruence, the more one is aware of one's actual experiences and has access to the organismic valuing process that provides the only truly reliable means through which one can actualize one's positive potential, the healthier and more adaptive the individual will be. Rogers called the person with a high degree of congruence *a fully functioning person*.

To be a congruent, fully functioning person is not to be a conformist, nor always happy, nor in a fixed state of adjustment, homeostasis, fulfillment, or actualization. Rather, it is to be in an ongoing creative process of becoming more and more the person one has the potential to be. Being congruent, the person has no need for the defense of denial; one is open to and accurately symbolizes all experience. Existence is rich and varied as the person experiences deeply both fear and courage, both pain and ecstasy, both anger and love. Since one accepts all experiences, one does not experience subception—the vague inner sense of threat when experience that one has relegated out of awareness presses for acknowledgment. Feeling unthreatened by experience, the person does not need to control it or impose structure on it; thus, rigidity decreases. Self-structure in the fully functioning person is a fluid, integrated whole, changing as one sequentially assimilates each new experience. In each moment the person fully experiences the societal demands of the situation, one's own possibly conflicting needs, and associated relevant memories, and then openly trusts the inner wisdom of the total organism to respond holistically to all the available data with the most beneficial course of action.

Due to incomplete data from the environment, people will sometimes make choices that prove less than optimal, yet with that very feedback, they can adjust future choices to be more optimal. Thus a congruent person is engaged in an ongoing, homeostatic process, using all physiological and psychological experience to find the greatest degree of intrapersonal and interpersonal harmony. In this way the person is exquisitely capable of adapting to novel information and to changing environmental conditions with both personally and socially constructive behavior.

Again, Rogers believed that humans move toward this evolutionary potential not by incorporating influences from the environment but by being in contact with their own deepest nature. In one of his eloquent passages, Rogers (1961) asserted that:

> We do not need to ask who will socialize [a person], for one of his own deepest needs is for affiliation and communication with others.... We do not need to ask who will control his aggressive impulses, for ... his need to be liked by others and his tendency to give affection will be as strong as his impulses to strike out or to seize for himself. [As he becomes more fully functioning] he will be aggressive in situations in which aggression is realistically appropriate, but there will be no runaway need for aggression. (p. 194)

The fully functioning person's relationships with others reflect overall harmony. Rogers (1961) concluded that to be fully functioning, what he termed *the good life*, is "enriching, exciting, rewarding, challenging, meaningful.... [T]he good life is not ... for the faint-hearted" (p. 196).

Characteristics of the fully functioning person could be applied to the example of the premed student. If congruent, she would be open to her interest in the law and in becoming an attorney as well as to her disinterest and mediocre achievements in medicine and she would act accordingly. Even if she perceived her father's approval of her to be conditional on her being a physician, she would not turn that perceived conditional positive regard into an internal condition of worth. Rather, out of the organismic experience of her genuine interests, desires, successes, and failures, she would develop a self-concept ("I enjoy law and the process of becoming an attorney") that would reflect unconditional self-regard: "I am worthwhile no matter what useful profession I pursue." She would be internally congruent and flowing unobstructedly in the process of becoming the person she has the innate potential to be.

Unhealthy Functioning

Conversely, the more incongruent a person is, the less well adjusted is the person. People in a state of incongruence "are feeling some anxiety or conflict because their ... self-concepts are being threatened by … feeling or facts [that] are not consistent with their view[s] of themselves" (Kirschenbaum, 2007, p. 231).

Rogers believed that no one exemplifies the extreme of full functioning and that everyone, to some degree or another, is incongruent. With incongruence, a person encounters situations using two psychological processes. On one hand, the person includes information that does not belong to the situation, such as rigid, usually unexamined values in the form of internal conditions of worth. On the other hand, the person excludes information that does belong to the situation, that is, actual experience that, because it contradicts one's conditions of worth, one defends against by denying the experience to awareness or allowing it into awareness only in a distorted form that is less threatening.

A person's behavior is usually an expression of one's self-concept: One typically acts based on who one thinks one is, who one is aware of being. However, the more incongruent one is, the more likely one will manifest several reactions. First, the person subceives the denied experience, feels anxious, and at times, is unable to maintain the defense of denial. With the weakening of the ability to suppress, selectively perceive, or distort experience, then that experience breaks into awareness and, because it contradicts the conditions of worth in the self-concept, disrupts the self-concept. With the self-concept thus disorganized, experience has the opportunity, so to speak, to express itself in the person's behavior. The person may be mystified, or even appalled: "I don't know where that came from!" "I wasn't myself." "It wasn't me; it was the stress [or some other external factor]." Sooner or later, the self-concept may regain organization, but the more incongruent one is, the more one is likely to experience anxiety and confusion and will vacillate between behavior consistent with the self-concept and behavior consistent with experience. In general, the greater the degree of incongruence, the greater one's emotional distress and behavioral dysfunction.

To return to our premed student, as her academic term begins, she may find she feels restless and distracted; she experiences a subtle, nagging irritation, provoked by the faint yet persistent subception of her actual organismic disinterest—even dislike—of her course material. As the semester progresses, she may find she inexplicably bursts into tears and/or irresponsibly blows off important study time, pursuing instead any number of other more enjoyable activities—as her organismic experience of cumulative dislike for the material breaks through her defense that, in premed, she's "exactly where she should be and doing just fine." Thus, incongruence renders a person vulnerable to the feeling of anxiety and to behavior that is disorganized, inconsistent, and/or, to some degree, destructive. To preserve her self-esteem, her internal conditions of worth, she has psychologically waged war on herself, on her own inherent worth, and her own innate, perfectly constructive tendencies.

By now you may have gathered that incongruence creates a kind of internal tension: The more experience one denies or distorts, the more that experience "presses" to be acknowledged and reowned accurately in awareness, in the self-concept. Yet the more conditions of worth one's self-concept includes, the more one denies and distorts experience that contradicts it. Thus the individual is caught in an internal tug of war, resulting in feelings of inner conflict that people often seek counseling to resolve.

Rogers referred to incongruence in a variety of ways throughout his writings. He called it a kind of divorce *of* oneself *from* oneself, whereby one no longer knows who one really is. Rogers considered this condition the fundamental estrangement of humans from ourselves. It is no wonder, then, that the internal disconnection from experience and the reconnection with it are central concepts in Rogers's approach to counseling and psychotherapy.

THE PERSONALITY CHANGE PROCESS

Rogers hypothesized that incongruence develops in the context of a particular type of social environment, one characterized by conditional positive regard, in which a person perceived a kind of evaluative threat. Likewise, he hypothesized that congruence can be regained only in the context of a particular type of social environment, one characterized most importantly by *unconditional positive regard* along with *genuineness* and *empathy*, an environment genuinely free of evaluative threat. Rogers acknowledged that these latter three *core conditions of change* sometimes temporarily characterize everyday relationships, such as between friends, coworkers, parents and children, teachers and students, and bosses and employees. However, the consistent, persistent communication of these conditions over time is likely to occur reliably only in a special situation: psychotherapy.

In incongruence, the more one's conditions of worth *pull* one away from actual experience, the more experience *presses* to be acknowledged in awareness—to be owned in the self-concept. Thus, the boundary between experience and self-concept represents the "growing edge" of a person's potential to become more congruent (see Figure 6.5). In this situation of inner turmoil, as the person occasionally and usually very gradually allows actual experience into awareness and perceives that someone else is genuinely understanding and valuing her and her experience, she is likely to come to value and reclaim aspects of her experience that she had previously denied. In other words, when one feels no threat of external negative judgment regarding one's actual inner experience, one feels free to reconnect with and appreciate that inner experience and to trust it as a guide to making choices.

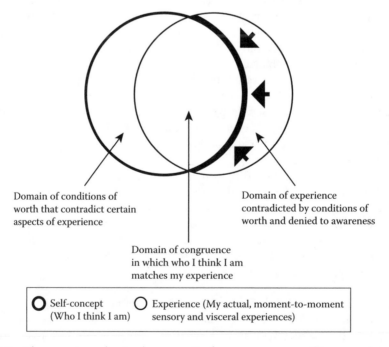

FIGURE 6.5   The growing edge in the process of movement toward increased congruence.

As a person comes to acknowledge, accept, and value one's previously denied experience, one integrates it into one's self-concept. As the self-concept aligns increasingly with experience, the person *let's go* of conditions of worth she developed in response to external conditional positive regard she had perceived, and she becomes increasingly congruent. She comes to believe that "who she actually is" is "who she should be." Thus, the person moves from the restricted and anxiety-ridden functioning of incongruence toward the full functioning of congruence; the fundamental intrapersonal alienation is repaired. With this inner reunification toward the condition represented in Figure 6.1, the person is restored to greater internal harmony, manifests harmony in relationship with others, and moves in the direction of personal and evolutionary advancement.

For example, consider again the young premed student. To the extent that she has come to equate her positive self-regard with being a physician, she is likely to deny or distort her actual experience of dislike for premed academic material. Thus she does not allow that experience into awareness and, consequently, does not integrate it into her self-concept. To the extent that she perceives unconditional positive regard—parents, teachers, friends, and/or a counselor who convey acceptance of her pursuing whatever vocation seems most fulfilling to her—she is likely to allow her experience (her actual dislike of premed coursework) into her self-concept, "I really don't enjoy studying this material! This material does not interest me! I almost certainly would not feel fulfilled in a job that required me to use this kind of material on a daily basis!" in a way that she retains positive self-regard, "And I am worthwhile even with these feelings of dislike for medicine." At the same time, she would allow into awareness her actual attraction to the study of law: "I am interested in the law. I would probably be fulfilled in a job that required me to use law-related material on a daily basis." in a way that she retains positive self-regard, "And I am worthwhile with these feelings of interest in the law." She most likely then would question, doubt, and then modify the condition of worth, "To be worthwhile, I must become a physician," into something like, "I will feel most worthwhile by pursuing a career that I find interesting and that makes a constructive contribution to society. Right now, the law seems to be my best bet for that kind of career." Based on her internal shift toward greater congruence, her actions also would reflect that congruence: She would change her major from premed to prelaw, would feel clear and decisive in doing so, and would feel enthusiastic about her new educational pursuit.

It is important to note that the reclaiming of congruence does not involve a mere return to the valuing process of infancy. Rogers pointed out that adult and infant experience are similar in fluidity, flexibility, immediacy in the moment, capacity for differentiating the uniqueness of each situation, and internal locus of evaluation. He also highlighted crucial differences: that adult experience involves greater complexity and scope, including relevant past memories, knowledge of a broader range of possible courses of action, more sophisticated hypothesizing about possible consequences of those courses of action, and more knowledge of, and ability to consider, external information. Rogers summarized that both the past and the future are included in each present moment of the ongoing adult valuing process.

Applying these principles to counseling, from early in Rogers's career up to the time of his death, he held to the hypothesis that six conditions are necessary and sufficient for a client to move in the direction of constructive personality change. The first condition, *two people in psychological contact,* is dichotomous, either present or absent, and involves both counselor and client. The remaining five conditions are continuous, existing to a relatively greater or lesser degree; the greater the strength of these conditions, the greater will be the constructive personality change in the client. The second condition pertains exclusively to the client: a *state of incongruence* is present that a client typically experiences as vulnerability, anxiety, or other presenting symptoms. The third, fourth, and fifth conditions are the aforementioned core conditions of *genuineness, unconditional positive regard, and empathy* that the counselor must feel and communicate when in contact with the client. It is not enough for the counselor to believe that he has succeeded in feeling and conveying the core conditions; the last condition requires that *the client perceive and experience the genuineness, unconditional positive regard, and empathy coming from the counselor.* These six necessary and sufficient conditions are fleshed out in the following section.

Client's Role

Motivation to Change

Client motivation is best understood by the second necessary and sufficient condition for constructive personality change. Incongruence causes the client significant distress manifesting in any number of presenting symptoms. In other words, the client must at least subceive, if not actually perceive, some degree of tension, confusion, or feeling of being unsettled in some way. From the counselor's perspective, any inner sense of anxiety or vulnerability on the part of the client is the result of incongruence between the client's self-concept and experience. Due to the innate human actualizing tendency to move toward inner consistency and harmony, the client feels a need to resolve the unsettling feelings.

Typically, the client has acted on that need by voluntarily seeking counseling. However, involuntary counseling also can result in constructive change if the client feels some inner sense of anxiety or vulnerability. Conversely, the client who has voluntarily sought counseling exclusively to achieve some ulterior agenda, such as to convince a court of his qualifications to get child custody, cannot be expected to change. In other words, whether the client is voluntary or involuntary, perception and/or subception of inner turmoil is the motivating precondition for the client to change.

Capacity and Responsibility for Change

Ultimately only the client has the capacity to change, but the responsibility for change and the extent of change rest with the six conditions, only three of which involve the client directly. The first condition, as previously discussed, requires the client to perceive or subceive at least minimal psychological tension or vulnerability. Another condition, the one Rogers listed first, is that the client be in psychological contact with a counselor who manifests certain characteristics. This statement underscores Rogers's belief that a client changes only in the context of a meaningful and nurturing relationship. In essence, the counselor is, at least to some minimal degree, a "significant other" to the client. Rogers did not clarify what factors might limit the client's perception of the counselor as psychologically important. Whatever the case, if no such person is available, or if a counselor who meets the other conditions is available but is not perceived by the client as important or significant, client change cannot be expected. A final condition is that the client must perceive and experience the counselor's communication of the three core conditions of genuineness, unconditional positive regard, and empathy. Again, Rogers was less clear about what factors might influence this client ability, but he offered some hints about how his views evolved over the course of his career.

In 1942, Rogers excluded from those who could benefit from "nondirective" psychotherapy the small minority of clients who are psychotic, cognitively defective, or unable to solve their own difficulties, even with assistance, as well as individuals faced with impossible demands from their environment. By 1957, he asserted, albeit tentatively, that the necessary and sufficient conditions for change applied to all clients, no matter what those clients' presenting problems might be. At that time, he acknowledged a contradiction to this assertion: the research finding that clients who externalize their problems, thus blaming others or outside circumstances and taking little self-responsibility, benefit from psychotherapy much less; he expressed openness to the possibility that such clients may need something more than the core conditions. Then, in 1977, he described Diabasis, an apparently successful residential treatment facility serving no more than six psychotic patients at a time and operating according to principles consistent with Rogers's core conditions. In this discussion, Rogers seemed to imply that the more severe the client's incongruence, the more pervasive, consistent, and persistent the core conditions must be. By 1986, he was hypothesizing, without qualification as to a person's degree of incongruence, that a person "has within himself or herself vast resources for self-understanding" and for changing one's own self-concept, attitudes, and behaviors (p. 135). Thus it might be inferred that someone experiencing a lesser incongruence—for example, a phobia—could benefit from a once-a-week experience of the core conditions, whereas someone experiencing a greater incongruence—for example, schizophrenia—would require the more prolonged and consistent experience of the core conditions available only in a residential environment.

Throughout his writing, Rogers did affirm the appropriateness of counselors defining the counseling situation to clients as an opportunity for client self-growth rather than for clients to receive answers from the counselor. This affirmation corresponds to his assertion that, in person-centered counseling, the locus of decision making and the responsibility for the consequences of decisions are centered unequivocally in the client.

Source of Resistance

Though Rogers (1942) referred to "the usual slight amount of difficulty in getting the client to take the lead ... and to talk freely and without restriction" (p. 273), he did not refer to this difficulty as "client resistance." Nevertheless, the person-centered counselor can, at times, experience the client resisting to take initiative in counseling. This resistance may be due to the client's lack of clarity about personal responsibility for self-growth in the counseling process, or it may be due to the client's wish, expectation, or even demand that the counselor provide answers.

Rogers (1989) did describe two types of resistance. One type is created by the client's wish to avoid "the pain of revealing, to oneself and another, the feelings that have hitherto been denied to awareness" (p. 133). The other is resistance the counselor creates, usually by rendering judgment on the client or her disclosures, but also by imposing direction on the counseling process that the client considers threatening or otherwise antithetical to the client's immediate needs. It is not as if person-centered counseling is without direction but, rather, that the direction in person-centered counseling is provided by the client's own actualizing tendency, and it is that direction alone, pursued in the client's own way and time, that the client ultimately will not resist.

Counselor's Role

> For here is demanded of you what no other person can do or point out—and that is to rigorously scrutinize yourself and your attitudes toward others. Do you believe that all people truly have a creative potential in them? That each person is a unique individual and that he alone can work out his own individuality? Or do you really believe that some persons are of "negative value" and others are weak and must be led and taught by "wiser," or "stronger" people? ... to grow oneself is the most demanding of all. (Walter Yoder, student of Carl Rogers, quoted in Rogers, 1946, p. 420).

Goals of Counseling

A person-centered counselor has one overarching goal: to create a psychological environment in which the client's actualizing tendency is free to resume its natural flow. The counselor moves toward achievement of this goal by cultivating certain attitudes toward, and attempting to communicate those attitudes to, the client.

The person-centered counselor believes that upon succeeding in conveying the core conditions, the client's psychological movement will be guided increasingly by the client's innately constructive actualizing tendency. Client movement will be toward increased congruence and thus full functioning.

Characteristics of an Effective Counselor

Five of Rogers's six necessary and sufficient conditions for constructive personality change speak to the characteristics of an effective person-centered counselor. The first condition, that the counselor and client be in psychological contact, implies not only sensory contact of some kind but also a sense that the relationship is vital to both client and counselor.

Rogers's third condition is that the counselor be genuine, real, congruent—not necessarily in every aspect of one's life, but at least in the context of the relationship with the client. That is, the counselor accurately perceives anything experienced in relationship to the client and expresses any *persistent* experiences to the client. Genuineness reflects the counselor's attempt to be completely aware of one's experience with the client and, upon experiencing something repeatedly that seems pertinent to the client's progress, to give feedback to the client in an open and honest manner. Rogers explained his own guidelines for providing such feedback. One guideline was that he would not give such feedback toward the beginning of a counseling relationship, because persistent feelings would not yet have had a chance to develop. Another was that he would own his own feelings, that is, speak in terms of his own emotions or preferences. Another was that he would usually, but not necessarily always, be specific about the client's behavior. For example, if a counselor often feels bored as a client gives a lot of information without seeming emotionally involved, the counselor might say, "Bob, I am feeling distracted as you tell your story. I want to listen, and I also find I have trouble remaining attentive when you provide a lot of details that aren't central to how you feel. I wonder if you'd be willing to express just the main point that has the most meaning for you." Or, nonspecifically, "In anticipating our session today, I felt impatient with you"—though he would probably follow such an opener with more specific feedback. Not expressing pervasive feelings might represent incongruence on the part of the therapist. As a result of the incongruence, the counselor would likely become more distracted, and the client would eventually pick up on the distraction or impatience and may even confront the counselor for "not listening to me."

Rogers's fourth condition is that the counselor experience unconditional positive regard for the client. In other words, the counselor feels a warm acceptance of all aspects of the client's experience, free of any evaluation that "I like and/or approve of you only if you are a certain way, only if your experiences meet certain conditions." The counselor values both negative and positive expressions by the client equally. According to Mearns and Thorne (1997), consistency of unconditional positive regard is the most distinctive characteristic of this person-centered attitude toward clients. Unconditional positive regard is more than acceptance; it is an unwavering respect for the humanity of the client that is not affected by the feelings, attitudes, and motives the client expresses. Since mental disturbances are an outgrowth of conditions of worth, unconditional positive regard acts as a counterconditioning process (Lietaer, 1984) whereby, in an environment conducive to self-prizing and growth, the client's conditions of worth are deconstructed and replaced, so to speak, by unconditional self-regard.

Rogers's fifth condition is that the counselor experiences a moment-to-moment, accurate empathic understanding of the client's internal perspective. The counselor senses the client's inner world as if it were the counselor's own world, yet, at the same time, the counselor consistently maintains a separate sense of self. This experience of being understood is often extremely liberating to clients. As one adolescent male client remarked, "For the first time in my life, I feel like someone is in the game with me. Not calling the shots, just trying to figure out what it means to be me. It's weird but it's like I can see me more clearly through your eyes. It's weird."

The sixth and final condition is that the counselor succeeds in communicating the previous three experiences: congruence, unconditional positive regard, and empathy to the client. In other words, the effective counselor, through nonverbal and verbal behavior, endeavors to convey the experience of the three preceding conditions to the client, realizing that success in that conveyance also rests to some degree on the client, as discussed above. To the extent that the counselor succeeds, the client will perceive the counselor as consistent, dependable, trustworthy, sincere, accepting, and understanding, and the client will feel safe disclosing inner experiences and using inner resources for self-evaluation and self-guidance. As one of our former colleagues offered, the process is like the physics principle that no two people can occupy the same space at the same time: If a counselor succeeds in conveying that he genuinely values a client and empathically occupies the exact psychological space the client is in, the client will move, and because of the counselor's absolute faith in the actualizing tendency, he can trust unequivocally that the client's movement will be in a constructive direction (G. Holden, personal communication, 1975).

For a counselor to consistently experience and convey the attitudes of genuineness, unconditional positive regard, and empathy can be extremely challenging at times. It is important to recall that probably no one succeeds perfectly in this goal. However, certain beliefs are crucial to a counselor's relative success. The person-centered counselor has an unshakable belief that each client is, at core, constructive and therefore trustworthy. The counselor believes that any destructiveness on the part of the client is the result of the client overriding the organismic valuing process of the actualizing tendency with conditions of worth based on values originally external to the client. The counselor, therefore, renounces the imposition of any evaluation, either positive or negative, onto the client, because such evaluation would constitute yet one more external value that has the potential to perpetuate the client's own intrapersonal alienation. The counselor strives to relinquish all control of the direction of counseling and to provide the client with absolute freedom to move in any direction, trusting firmly that the client will move in a positive direction. The effective person-centered counselor, when experiencing any lasting impediment to the achievement of these aims, would seek to resolve them by talking them over with the client, a colleague, a supervisor, or even one's own counselor, as appropriate.

The person-centered counselor is best conceptualized as a fellow traveler on the client's journey of self-discovery. The counselor is a midwife of change rather than its originator. In his later years, Rogers (1986) alluded to a fleeting psychological state he sometimes observed in counselors and sometimes experienced himself that he associated with profound client healing and growth along with an enhanced sense of energy. He believed it occurs when one is close to one's inner, intuitive self, "in touch with the unknown [within] ... perhaps ... in a slightly altered state of consciousness ... then simply [one's] *presence* is releasing and helpful" (p. 199). He suggested that this psychological state cannot be forced but can be facilitated by relaxing and being close to the "transcendental core" of oneself (p. 199). In this state, the counselor may behave in "strange and impulsive ways in the relationship" (p. 199), ways that cannot be justified rationally and that "have nothing to do with … thought processes" (p. 199), but that "turn out to be *right*" (p. 199). For himself, he concluded that "at those moments it seems that my inner spirit has reached out and touched the inner spirit of the other. Our relationship transcends itself and becomes a part of something larger" (p. 199).

Throughout his writings, Rogers made reference to counselors maintaining ethical standards. Presumably, his view of an effective counselor would include the counselor functioning within the limits of professional ethics.

Regarding the need for professional training, Rogers (1957) stated that the counselor's ability to experience and communicate the core conditions requires no specific intellectual knowledge but rather can be acquired through experiential training that may be, but unfortunately often is not, part of the professional training of mental health providers. Rogers was adamant that a counselor's views and values inevitably have consequences for one's clients. He therefore believed that an effective counselor has clarified one's views of human nature and one's own value orientation and can explicitly state them. The clarification process could rightly be a part of professional training.

Stages and Techniques

Rogers (1942) delineated 12 steps in the person-centered counseling process. He emphasized that these steps are not actually separate, sequential events but, rather, represent a general trend consisting of an interwoven unfolding. By reviewing these steps, you can get an overall sense of the person-centered counseling process.

1. The individual comes for help.
2. The helping situation is usually defined [as] an opportunity for self-growth, not answers.
3. The counselor encourages free expression of feelings in regard to the problem [that the client presents].
4. The counselor accepts, recognizes, and clarifies these negative feelings.
5. When the individual's negative feelings have been quite fully expressed, they are followed by the faint and tentative expressions of the positive impulses that make for growth.
6. The counselor accepts and recognizes the positive feelings which are expressed in the same manner in which he has accepted and recognized the negative feelings … which gives the individual an opportunity for the first time in his life to understand himself as he is … insight and self-understanding come bubbling through spontaneously.
7. This insight, this understanding of the self and acceptance of the self … provides the basis on which the individual can go ahead to new levels of integration.
8. Intermingled with this process of insight … is a process of clarification of possible decisions, possible courses of action.
9. Then comes … the initiation of minute, but highly significant, positive actions.
10. There is further insight.
11. There is increasingly integrated positive action on the part of the client … less fear … and more confidence in self-directed action.
12. There is a feeling of decreasing need for help, and a recognition on the part of the client that the relationship must end. (pp. 30–45)

The Therapeutic Relationship

In person-centered counseling, the client–counselor relationship that is characterized by the necessary and sufficient conditions for change is, itself, the instrument of change. Basic to this relationship is the strong valuing of psychological independence and integrity and the devaluing of conformity and the practice of having those who are seemingly more capable directing those who are seemingly less capable. In this relationship, a client discusses problems, but the focus is on the client rather than the problems because of the belief that clients psychologically equipped with congruence are able to handle reasonably well the problems that come their way. The counselor structures the therapeutic relationship by overtly or covertly reminding the client of the client's responsibility for the process. The counselor also sets and maintains ethical limits on the relationship.

In this relationship, a client will have feelings and emotions directed toward the counselor. Rogers noted two categories of such feelings. One consists of understandable reactions to the counselor's words and actions, such as positive feelings in response to a counselor's warmth, understanding, and concern, and negative feelings in response to a counselor's air of superiority, inaccurate or premature interpretation, or imposition of an agenda on the client and/or the process. A second category consists of projections transferred from another origin onto the counselor; whether or not triggered somehow by the therapist, they are identifiable by their disproportionate intensity. Rogers (1989) asserted that, from a person-centered perspective, distinguishing feelings as belonging to one of the two categories was unnecessary. "All," he said, "are best dealt with in the same way. If the therapist is sensitively understanding and genuinely acceptant and non-judgmental, therapy will move *through* these feelings" (p. 130). He believed that the therapeutic strategy of paying particular attention to transference feelings served only to create the new problems of fostering client dependency and prolonging therapy.

Assessment

Rogers's (1957) view of most psychological assessment in counseling was negative. He believed that practices such as diagnosis, analysis, and even taking a case history are not only unnecessary but also impede rather than facilitate the therapeutic process because they objectify the person of the client.

Rogers (1957) conceded only one case in which assessment, particularly diagnosis and case history, might be facilitative: when a counselor might feel more secure and therefore more accepting and understanding of the client if she has foreknowledge and/or diagnostic knowledge of the client. It would seem congruent with Rogers's thinking to believe that a counselor would be most therapeutically facilitative who, with no foreknowledge, felt secure meeting the client as an individual; however, Rogers did not state this explicitly.

Change Strategies

As early as 1942, Rogers made clear his belief that the only "strategy" in his form of counseling was the attitude of acceptance. However, he conducted a comparison of directive and nondirective counseling sessions by analyzing the actual frequency of various types of verbal responses. The results are summarized in Table 6.1.

Some of the strategies listed in Table 6.1 are self-explanatory; others may require explanation. Reflections of feelings involve the counselor paraphrasing client emotions, as in responses that begin, "You're pleased that…," "You're surprised to discover… ," or "You feel deeply sad when you consider.…" The counselor may reflect feelings in response to feelings the client expressed directly through a verbal statement, such as

TABLE 6.1   The Seven Most Frequent Types of Verbal Responses in Directive and Nondirective Therapy, Beginning With Most Frequent

Directive	Nondirective
Closed-ended questions	Reflection of feelings directly expressed
Explanation and information giving	Reflection of feelings indirectly expressed
Open-ended questions	Open-ended questioning
Proposing an activity	Reflection of content
Reflection of content	Closed-ended questioning
Persuasion	Explanation and information giving
Identification of problem in need of correction	Defining the therapeutic situation in terms of client responsibility

"I'm so mad!" or indirectly through nonverbal communication, such as body posture, facial expression, or tone of voice. Closed-ended questions can be answered by "yes" or "no," whereas open-ended questions cannot, thus requiring the client to elaborate. Both types of questions can redirect a client, but open-ended questions are less likely to do so. Reflections of content paraphrase the nonemotional content of a client communication.

Referring to questions that redirect the client, Rogers (1989) labeled them "unnecessary" and "clumsy" (p. 94), "much less profitable" (p. 101), and a "blunder" (pp. 101, 106). He labeled giving a homework assignment "unwise" (p. 106). He labeled open-ended questions "productive" (p. 93). He labeled accurate reflections "helpful" (p. 89), "productive" (p. 95), "a better response" than a "direct question" (p. 97), and as promoting "clear progress in exploration at more than a superficial level" (p. 99). He labeled the avoidance of agreeing or disagreeing with the client "wise" (p. 100). He labeled avoidance of intellectual discussion and continued focus on client feelings "to [the counselor's] credit" (p. 94). He considered defining the client's responsibility for the direction of the counseling interviews to be "helpful" (p. 106) and "defining ... what counseling can mean ... in terms of the client's symbols ... using metaphors the client has offered—to be always a sound device" (p. 99). He made the point that if a counselor misses an aspect of experience important to the client, the client will express it again. In other words, the counselor need not feel pressured to reflect everything the first time; if the client perceives the core conditions, she will persist in expressing anything important to her (p. 127).

At the same time, Rogers (1989) vehemently objected to reflection of feelings being taught as a counseling technique. Although he acknowledged that many of his transcription responses could be so categorized, he stated adamantly that during counseling sessions, "I am definitely *not* trying to 'reflect feelings' " (p. 127). Rather, he asserted, "I am trying to determine whether my understanding of the client's inner world is correct," (pp. 127–128) and suggested that these responses be relabeled "testing understandings" or "checking perceptions." Nevertheless, he affirmed that, when accurate, such responses served as a mirror, a reflection, from which the client is likely to gain clarity and insight and to move toward greater congruence.

Addressing Client Resistance

The person-centered counselor perceives resistance as yet another dimension of client experience for the counselor to address as she addresses any aspect of client experience. To again quote Rogers (1989), "If the therapist is sensitively understanding and genuinely acceptant and non-judgmental, therapy will move through these feelings" (p. 130).

CONTRIBUTIONS AND LIMITATIONS

Interface with Recent Developments in the Mental Health Field

The Nature–Nurture Question

Rogers appears to have believed that personality is influenced powerfully both by the innate actualizing tendency and by the kind of environmental positive regard one experiences. In his early writing, Rogers (1942) made rare reference to innate factors that might limit one's capacity to benefit from psychotherapy, such as being cognitively "defective" (p. 128). However, in later writings he indicated that even the person with schizophrenia could come to function well in a psychosocial environment characterized by the core conditions.

Rogers died before the research on genetic origins of behavior became widely known. Due to his respect for scientific research, we assume that he would have been open to integrating genetic research findings into his views. On a related note, in a recently reported case, a 40-year-old schoolteacher rather suddenly developed pedophilia involving, among other actions, sexual advances to his prepubescent stepdaughter. "The patient went to great lengths to conceal his activities because he felt that they were unacceptable. However, he continued to act on his sexual impulses, stating that 'the pleasure principle overrode' his urge restraint" (Burns & Swerdlow, 2003, p. 437). Legal and mental health professionals failed to detect a possible organic basis that, upon the eve of jail sentencing when he went to a hospital emergency room complaining of a headache, physicians did discover: a brain tumor. Once surgeons excised the tumor, his sexually inappropriate behavior stopped.

This patient's guilt indicated he was in a state of incongruence, and nothing in the clinical report indicated a problem with his ability to perceive the Rogerian core conditions when others conveyed them. It is difficult to imagine that the six necessary and sufficient conditions would have been sufficient in this case, but nowhere in Rogers's writings did we find reference to this type of exception. The contemporary person-centered counselor is faced with the task of reconciling findings regarding genetic and other organic factors in behavior with the tenets Rogers presented.

DSM–IV–TR Diagnosis

Rogers (1942) considered diagnostic labels to be "largely irrelevant" (p. 393) in the counseling process. As stated previously, in the case of the counselor whose empathy and genuineness would be enhanced by diagnosing a client, Rogers seemed to endorse diagnosis, albeit grudgingly. Extrapolating from that position, he might not have objected to rendering a diagnosis if it were required by managed care, although he probably would have suggested that the counselor, in her own mind, avoid objectifying the client and also that she be cautious in whether or how she communicated diagnostic information to the client.

Pharmacotherapy

Rogers's references to pharmacotherapy were sparse. Presumably, he believed that it was rarely necessary, and he would have considered current practice in mental health to involve overmedication of clients. This presumption is substantiated by a reference he made to the success of the director of Diabasis, the in-patient facility for people with schizophrenia. He exclaimed, "Dr. Perry thinks he has given [only] two tranquilizers in the past ten months!" (1989, p. 393). In other words, he believed that the necessary and sufficient conditions alone could facilitate healthy functioning in most cases. Contemporary person-centered therapists are faced with reconciling the growing role of pharmacotherapy in the standard of care in mental health counseling with person-centered tenets.

Managed Care and Brief Therapy

Person-centered therapy can be as brief as one session. However, the managed care emphasis on brief therapy seems antithetical to the person-centered philosophy that the client determine the length of counseling. The focus of managed care is on resolution of the client's immediate problem and on returning the client to her previous level of functioning as expeditiously as possible, hence the managed care emphasis on evidence-based approaches to psychotherapy. In a sense, setting a time limit on change is, in itself, a condition of worth. Rogers, on the other hand, never wavered from the position he established in 1940: that the individual, rather than the problem, is the focus of person-centered counseling. He elaborated that:

> the aim is not to solve one particular problem but to assist the individual to grow, so that he can cope with the present problem and with later problems in a better integrated fashion. If he can gain enough integration to handle one problem in more independent, more responsible, less confused, better organized ways, then he will also handle new problems in that manner.... Therapy is not a matter of doing something to the individual, or of inducing him to do something about himself. It is instead a matter of freeing him for normal growth and development, of removing obstacles so that he can again move forward. (1942, p. 379)

As a review of the 12 steps typically experienced in counseling reveals (Rogers, 1942), the process of client integration is more likely to be gradual than rapid. The contemporary person-centered counselor is faced with reconciling the philosophical perspective of the approach with practical considerations. For example, in private practice, a counselor must decide whether to seek third-party payment through managed care or offer services only to clients who can pay out-of-pocket, or, regarding work in an agency setting, whether and how to work in a setting that values or requires a brief, problem-focused approach to counseling.

Technical Eclecticism

Each theory contains perspectives that distinguish it from every other theory. In the case of person-centered counseling, the unshakable belief in the unerring trustworthiness of the actualizing tendency and a counselor's absolute avoidance of imposing any external evaluation or direction on the client represent its most salient distinguishing characteristics.

Rogers asserted repeatedly throughout his life that not only do the six conditions represent what is necessary for constructive personality change and what is sufficient for such change, but any technique or strategy in addition to those conditions is likely to represent external direction—the phenomenon that perpetuates, rather than alleviates, the fundamental problem: the client's alienation from her own deepest experience. Thus person-centered counselors have not tended to engage in technical eclecticism.

However, some practitioners have developed offshoots of person-centered counseling in which they claim philosophical consonance with Rogers's approach but use idiosyncratic techniques; these include Gendlin (1998), Elliott, Watson, Goldman, and Greenberg (2003), and Natalie Rogers (2000). In addition, a few authors (Tausch, 2007; Tursi & Cochran, 2006) have recently made the case that, under certain circumstances and conditions, incorporating techniques from other theories would not contradict person-centered tenets. In fact, Tausch (2007) reported that

> in 1986 I sent Carl Rogers an article outlining the possibility of incorporating some additional interventions. In a letter and in spoken comment, he remarked: "... you are taking realistic, modest steps toward integrating various viewpoints in therapy—a task which is much needed." (p. 5)

Thus, characteristically, Rogers expressed openness to technical eclecticism—at least in the way Tausch framed it.

Diversity Issues

Rogers (1989) believed that the same value directions, those that advance the individual, the people with whom the individual interacts, and the evolution of the entire species, are universal among humans regardless of culture, gender, or socioeconomic status. He believed that these universal values could be discovered only from inside each person rather than imposed from the outside. He believed these values would provide any person with "an organized, adaptive, and social approach to the perplexing value issues which face all of us" (p. 184).

However, Rogers did not address the fact that his beliefs represented a values position in and of themselves, a position with which some clients might fundamentally disagree at the outset, making person-centered counseling a poor fit for them. These include cultures in which people respect the wisdom of those in positions of authority, such as counselors, and look to authorities for guidance and answers. Also included are subcultures in which a person's "inner authority" is believed to be vulnerable to influence by evil forces in the universe. In such subcultures, inner authority is highly suspect, and the only trusted source of guidance is external authority represented by the collective wisdom of the culture or by some other trusted external source.

Rogers occasionally addressed the issue of the counselor defining client responsibility in the counseling process. In light of the recognition that his approach itself represents a values position, a person-centered counselor would probably do well to seek informed consent from a client at the outset of counseling. The counselor could achieve this goal by using a Professional Disclosure Statement and discussion to explain the counselor's expectations regarding the process of counseling and the client's and counselor's respective roles in that process. A client informed of these expectations could decide whether or not the person-centered approach is consonant with her own values, goals, and expectations regarding counseling. This recommendation is one of several Kirschenbaum (2007) provided in an excellent, comprehensive discussion of issues of multiculturalism and person-centered counseling (pp. 505–516). We strongly recommend this resource to anyone seeking a thorough understanding of these issues.

Regarding sexual orientation, at one point Rogers (1957) made reference to homosexuals as one category of clients seeking change; typical of the times, he implied pathology by mentioning them along with "neurotics ... psychotics ... compulsives ... etc." (1989, p. 230). However, his point in the passage was that the necessary and sufficient conditions for constructive personality change applied to all clients, regardless of characteristics, including sexual orientation. Indeed, a colleague of many years and developer of an affiliated therapeutic approach, Eugene Gendlin (2002), asserted that by virtue of the client-centered approach, Rogers was:

> ahead of the country.... In 1945, blacks, women, gay people and others found help at the [University of Chicago] Counseling Center because these therapists knew that *every* client had to teach them a new world.... These therapists never forced a policy on a client.... To therapists trained by Rogers, it was obvious that *every* person is at the directing center of a life and that one can help people only be means of their own intricacy and their own steps. (pp. xiii–xiv)

Regarding spirituality, throughout his writings Rogers made many interesting references to spirituality. He alluded, for example, to evidence indicating that, "a vast and mysterious universe, perhaps an inner reality, or perhaps a spirit world of which we are all unknowingly a part seems to exist" (Rogers, 1989, p. 424). Yet he never appears to have deviated from a radical assertion he made in 1961 that "no other person's ideas, and none of my own ideas, are as authoritative as my experience.... Neither the Bible nor the prophets ... neither the revelations of God nor man can take precedence over my own direct experience" (p. 24).

Rogers (1989) asserted that the only reality a person could possibly know is the world as that person perceives and experiences it in the present moment. Consequently, each person's reality is inevitably different. He acknowledged a consensus reality held by a group of people, and he pointed out both its benefit, providing continuity for the continuation of culture, and its detriment, the persecution of those who deviated from it. Believing the detriments to outweigh the benefits, he called consensus reality "a myth we dare not maintain" (pp. 425–426). He continued:

> It appears to me that the way of the future must be to base our lives and our education on the assumption that there are as many realities as there are persons, and that our highest priority is to accept that hypothesis and proceed ... to explore open-mindedly the many, many perceptions of reality that exist.... Might not such a society be a completely individualistic anarchy? That is not my opinion.... The natural human tendency to care for another would ... be ... "I prize and treasure you because you are different from me." ... Idealistic? ... It surely is. (pp. 426–427)

Yet, he believed, this process of mutual acceptance of unique subjective realities may be going on at an unconscious, collective level that could result, ultimately, in a shift in collective, and therefore each person's, consciousness. He concluded:

> If we accept as a basic fact of all human life that we live in separate realities; if we can see those differing realities as the most promising resource for learning in all the history of the world; if we can live together in order to learn from one another without fear; if we can do all this, then a new age could be dawning. And perhaps, just perhaps, humankind's deep organic sensings are paving the way for just such a change. (p. 428)

Rogers's statements on reality seem to indicate that he considered a spiritual domain separate from everyday reality to be a possibility; that he respected and valued each person's spiritual reality and beliefs, including the belief that no spiritual reality exists; and that he did not subscribe to any one view regarding the nature of spiritual reality. Rogers's quotes at the beginning of this chapter indicate that he was continually revising his own spiritual beliefs on the basis of new experience.

Clearly, the belief that everyone should accept one particular spiritual reality is not consonant with the person-centered philosophy nor, for that matter, with ethical and professional counseling standards. Rather, in the person-centered approach, the explicit respect for each individual's spirituality is consonant with ethical standards of the American Counseling Association and with the approach endorsed in the counselor competencies on spirituality created by a spiritually diverse group of counselor educators (Holden & Ivey, 1997).

Person-centered counseling also shares certain qualities with Buddhist mindfulness meditation. This meditation emphasizes openness to and awareness of all experiences "without wishing they were different or trying to change them" (Walsh, 1999, p. 194); paradoxically, it can result in powerful change, including powerful healing. One might think of person-centered counseling as a kind of interactive mindfulness meditation in which the counselor serves as an outside resource for enhancing client awareness.

The Effectiveness of Psychotherapy

It might appear on the surface that Rogers attributed virtually 100% of positive outcome in psychotherapy to the quality of the therapeutic relationship. However, he also alluded to client variables (extratherapeutic factors) in his first conditions that addressed the client's being in psychological contact with the counselor and sixth condition that the client perceive the counselor's communication of the core conditions; so, for example, circumstances such as a severe and chronic psychological problem might reduce the client's ability to perceive the counselor as important (Condition 1) or perceive the counselor's communication of the core conditions (Condition 6). Nevertheless, Asay and Lambert's (1999) conclusion that only 40% of positive outcome can be attributed to the quality of the therapeutic relationship, and that 55% rests with variables that are predominantly or totally out of the counselor's realm of influence, represents a clearly different emphasis than Rogers's view. If the person-centered counselor is to achieve Rogers's own criteria of effectiveness, that is, taking in new information from the environment and integrating it into an internally consistent approach to counseling, the research results on positive outcome must be reconciled with the traditional person-centered perspective.

Regarding research findings on what were originally termed empirically validated approaches to psychotherapy (Crits-Christoph, 1998), then termed empirically supported and now evidence-based, Rogers would probably have acknowledged those approaches as helpful to some people in some limited ways but not in the most important way: helping people to reconnect with their own inner wisdom. Conversely:

> accurate empathy, positive regard, nonpossessive warmth, and congruence or genuineness. Virtually all schools of therapy accept the notion that these or related therapist relationship variables are important for significant progress in psychotherapy and, in fact, fundamental in the formation of a working alliance. (Lambert, 1992, p. 104)

In the past decade, the notion of the vital role of the therapeutic relationship in positive psychotherapeutic outcome was again endorsed by the findings of an American Psychological Association task force (Norcross, 2001, 2002). Where person-centered therapists differ from other schools of thought is in believing that the six conditions are necessarily *sufficient* for positive counseling outcome.

Limitations

Some weaknesses of person-centered theory have been addressed above, such as the possible incompatibility of cultures that value collective wisdom with a psychotherapy that strongly values inner wisdom. In addition, from various other theoretical perspectives, person-centered counseling is seen as limited. According to Kirschenbaum (2007), as a result of research over the past two decades, even some strong proponents of client-centered therapy have "conceded or concluded" that the six necessary and sufficient conditions for positive therapeutic outcome "may be neither necessary nor sufficient" (p. 592). Kirschenbaum himself agreed, with the addendum that the conditions "are helpful to extremely helpful with virtually all clients" (p. 592).

Though not a limitation of the person-centered counseling approach per se, we found one aspect of the person-centered literature confusing. "Rogers, in the late [1940s], began to avoid the term 'nondirective' and began to use the 'client-centered' label almost exclusively" (Kirschenbaum, 2007, p. 163). Among his reasons was his realization that:

> nondirective was a "term of rebellion ... saying what we were against" and did not capture the essence of the approach, which was adopting the client's frame of reference. It was to [Rogers's] chagrin that, for decades, many individuals in psychology and psychotherapy continued to talk of the "nondirective method." (p. 163)

Nevertheless, the authors of important primary sources (for example, Raskin et al., 2008) have persisted in referring extensively to "the nondirective attitude." It is unfortunate that Rogers apparently never devised a term to replace nondirective. We believe the word *trusting* or some variation on it, such as *deeply trusting*, are viable contenders, and that client-centered or person-centered adherents might do well to use such a term instead of nondirective. Thus, client- or person-centered counselors approach the psychotherapy enterprise with an attitude of deep trust in the ultimate constructiveness of each client's innate actualizing tendency to provide positive direction in the client's change process.

Contributions

In tribute, Kirschenbaum and Henderson (1989b) reviewed Carl Rogers's most salient contributions to the field of counseling and psychotherapy. In addition to the pioneering of nondirective/client-centered/person-centered counseling, they cited that Rogers:

> Was the first person in history to record and publish completed cases of psychotherapy,
>   Carried out and encouraged more scientific research on counseling and psychotherapy than had ever been undertaken anywhere,
>   Spread ... professional counseling and psychotherapy ... to all the helping professions: psychology, social work, education, ministry, lay therapy, and others,
>   Was a leader in the development and dissemination of the intensive therapeutic group experience, sometimes called the "encounter group,"
>   Was a leader in the humanistic psychology movement,
>   Was a pioneer in applying the principles of effective interpersonal communication to resolving intergroup and international conflict, and
>   Was one of the helping professions' most prolific writers. (pp. 3–4)

In addition, Rogers was the first to record and transcribe counseling sessions for use in teaching and supervision. He popularized the term *client* to refer to the person utilizing psychotherapy as a responsible individual rather than as a sick *patient*. And he, more than any mental health theorist before him, brought into focus the crucial role the therapeutic relationship plays in positive psychotherapeutic outcome, a perspective that empirical researchers have substantially supported.

CURRENT STATUS AND SUMMARY

Two decades after Rogers's death, Kirschenbaum (2007) examined four trends to assess the current status of the client- or person-centered approach to counseling. First, he found that "not counting [Rogers's] own writings, more books, chapters and articles were written on Carl Rogers and the client-centered/person-centered approach in the [17] years *after* his death than were written in the [40] years before," most of which publications "encompassed new research, new theory, and new applications" (pp. 582–583). Second, as of 2004, "approximately 200 organizations and training centers located around the world [were] dedicated to researching and applying the principles developed by Rogers" (p. 584), a level of activity far greater than was the case while Rogers was alive (p. 587). Third, over the past 20 years, research on the core conditions of counseling has proliferated and has established the central role of those conditions in positive psychotherapy outcome. Fourth, "major offshoots of client-centered therapy [have] continued to develop and expand" (p. 599), characterized by "tension between the branches" (p. 601). Kirschenbaum (personal communication, June 8, 2009) estimated that at least half of practitioners who purport a person-centered philosophy practice offshoots of Rogers's orthodoxy such as focusing-oriented psychotherapy (Gendlin, 1998), emotion-focused therapy (Elliott et al., 2003), expressive therapy (N. Rogers, 2000), and other variations. From these four indicators, Kirschenbaum concluded that the person-centered approach "clearly ... has survived its founder" (p. 607) and "is alive and well" (p. 602).

In summary, Carl Rogers's person-centered approach to counseling and psychotherapy emerged during the mid-twentieth century as a major force in the humanistic psychotherapy movement. Through the humanistic perspective, person-centered counselors see humans as innately constructive at their deepest levels and also, as a result of the interaction of inner tendencies and factors in the social environment, psychologically alienated from that inner source of wisdom. The most helpful psychotherapy is the one in which the client experiences a particular psychological climate in which she can reconnect with her actualizing core. The person thus reconnected is able to use inner wisdom to live in personal and social harmony.

RECOMMENDED RESOURCES

Books

Kirschenbaum, H. (2007). *The life and works of Carl Rogers*. Ross-on-Wye, United Kingdom: PCCS Books. The most up-to-date, comprehensive review of Rogers's personal and professional lives; highly readable.

Kirschenbaum, H., & Henderson, V. (Eds.). (1989a). *Carl Rogers: Dialogues*. Boston. MA: Houghton Mifflin. Much like the other suggested readings, the dialogues provide information about the theory and illustrate Rogers's congruence with the theory.

Kirschenbaum, H., & Henderson, V. (Eds.). (1989b). *The Carl Rogers reader*. Boston, MA: Houghton Mifflin. A collection of diverse readings representing Rogers's most important ideas in his own impactful words. Coverage of several different topics makes the book attractive.

Rogers, C. R. (1961). *On becoming a person*. Boston, MA: Houghton Mifflin. In our opinion, any seminal work by Rogers would be a good read for students interested in the theory. *On Becoming a Person* provides a comprehensive discussion of the philosophical stance behind the therapeutic method.

Audiovisuals

Kirschenbaum, H. (2003). *Carl Rogers and the person-centered approach* [video recording]. Rochester, NY: Rose Films. (Available from Psychological and Educational Films, *PMB #252, 3334 East Coast Highway, Corona Del Mar, CA 92625; http://www. psychedfilms.com/id1.html). An outstanding summary of Rogers's life and work narrated by Rogers's recognized biographer and including original footage of Rogers throughout his life. In our opinion, every student of person-centered counseling will have the fullest understanding and appreciation of this approach by seeing both this video and the one we describe next.

Shostrom, E. T. (Executive Producer), Shostrom, S. K. (Producer), & Ratner, H. (Director). (1977). *Three approaches to psychotherapy II. Part 1. Carl Rogers. Client-centered therapy* [video recording]. (Available from Psychological and Educational Films, *PMB #252, 3334 East Coast Highway, Corona Del Mar, CA 92625; http://www.psychedfilms.com/id1.html). Although much has been written about Rogers's earlier *Three Approaches I* demonstration with Gloria, we find this demonstration with Kathy to be much more representative of the person-centered approach and more interesting with the inclusion of the person-centered approach to dreamwork.

Web Sites

http://www.centerfortheperson.org/ We recommend beginning with this Center for Studies of the Person Web site where visitors can find links to other person-centered resource Web sites.

REFERENCES

Asay, T. P., & Lambert, M. J. (1999). The empirical case for the common factors in therapy: Quantitative findings. In M. A. Hubble, B. L. Duncan, & S. D. Miller (Eds.), *The heart and soul of change: What works in therapy* (pp. 33–55). Washington, DC: American Psychological Association.

Burns, J. M., & Swerdlow, R. H. (2003). Right orbitofrontal tumor with pedophilia symptom and constructional apraxia sign. *Archives of Neurology, 60,* 437–440.

Crits-Christoph, P. (1998). Training in empirically validated treatments: The Division 12 APA task force recommendations. In K. S. Dobson & K. D. Craig (Eds.), *Empirically supported therapies: Best practice in professional psychology* (pp. 3–25). Thousand Oaks, CA: Sage.

Elliott, R., Watson, J. C., Goldman, R. N., & Greenberg, L. S. (2003). *Learning emotion-focused therapy: The process-experiential approach to change.* Washington, DC: American Psychological Association.

Gendlin, E. (1998). *Focusing-oriented psychotherapy: A manual of the experiential method.* New York, NY: Guilford Press.

Gendlin, E. (2002). Foreword. In C. R. Rogers & D. Russell, *Carl Rogers: The quiet revolutionary: An oral history* (pp. xi–xxi). Roseville, CA: Penmarin Books.

Holden, J., & Ivey, A. (1997, Spring). Summit on spirituality phase I, phase II, counselor competencies. *ACES Spectrum Newsletter,* 14–16.

Kirschenbaum, H. (2007). *The life and works of Carl Rogers.* Ross-on-Wye, United Kingdom: PCCS Books. (Paperback edition, 2008, Alexandria, VA: American Counseling Association)

Kirschenbaum H., & Henderson, V. (Eds.). (1989a). *Carl Rogers: Dialogues.* Boston, MA: Houghton Mifflin.

Kirschenbaum, H., & Henderson, V. L. (Eds.). (1989b). *The Carl Rogers reader.* Boston, MA: Houghton Mifflin.

Lambert, M. J. (1992). Psychotherapy outcome research: Implications for integrative and eclectic therapists. In J. C. Norcross & M. R. Goldfried (Eds.), *Handbook of psychotherapy integration* (pp. 92–129). New York, NY: Basic Books.

Lietaer, G. (1984). Unconditional positive regard: A controversial basic attitude in client-centered therapy. In R. Levant and J. Schlien (Eds.), *Client-centered therapy and the person centered approach* (pp. 41–58). New York, NY: Praeger.

Mearns, D., & Thorne, B. (1997). *Person-centered counselling in action.* Thousand Oaks, CA: Sage.

Norcross, J. C. (2001). Purposes, processes and products of the task force on empirically supported therapy relationships. *Psychotherapy, 39,* 345–356.

Norcross, J. C. (2002). *Psychotherapy relationships that work: Therapist contributions and responsiveness to patients.* New York, NY: Oxford University Press.

Raskin, N., Rogers, C., & Witty, M. C. (2008). Client-centered therapy. In R. J. Corsini & D. Wedding (Eds.), *Current psychotherapies* (8th ed., pp. 141–186). Belmont, CA: Thomson Brooks/Cole.

Rogers, C. R. (1939). *The clinical treatment of the problem child.* Boston, MA: Houghton Mifflin.

Rogers, C. R. (1942). *Counseling and psychotherapy.* Boston, MA: Houghton Mifflin.

Roger, C. R. (1946). Significant aspects of client-centered therapy. *American Psychologist, 1,* 415–422.

Rogers, C. R. (1951). *Client-centered therapy.* Boston, MA: Houghton Mifflin.

Rogers, C. R. (1957). The necessary and sufficient conditions for therapeutic personality change. *Journal of Counseling Psychology, 21,* 95–103.

Rogers, C. R. (1959). A theory of therapy, personality, and interpersonal relationships, as developed in the client-centered framework. In S. Koch (Ed.), *Psychology: A study of a science, Vol. III: Formulations of the person and the social context* (pp. 184–256). New York, NY: McGraw-Hill.

Rogers, C. R. (1961). *On becoming a person: A therapist's view of psychotherapy.* Boston, NY: Houghton Mifflin.

Rogers, C. (1980). *A way of being.* Boston, NY: Houghton Mifflin.

Rogers, C. R. (1986). A client-centered/person-centered approach to therapy. In I. Kutash & A. Wolf (Eds.), *Psychotherapist's casebook* (pp. 197–208). San Francisco, CA: Jossey-Bass.

Rogers, C. R. (1989). *The Carl Rogers reader* (H. Kirschenbaum & V. L. Henderson, Eds.). Boston, MA: Houghton Mifflin.

Rogers, N. (2000). *The creative connection: Expressive arts as healing.* Ross-on-Wye, United Kingdom: PCCS Books.

Tausch, R. (2007). Promoting health: Challenges for person-centered communication in psychotherapy, counseling and human relationships in daily life. *Person-Centered and Experiential Psychotherapy, 6,* 1–13.

Tursi, M. M., & Cochran, J. L. (2006). Cognitive-behavioral tasks accomplished in a person-centered relational framework. *Journal of Counseling and Development, 84,* 387–396.

Walker, D. E. (1956). Carl Rogers and the nature of man. *Journal of Counseling Psychology, 3,* 89–92.

Walsh, R. (1999). *Essential spirituality: The seven central practices to awaken heart and mind.* New York, NY: Wiley.

CHAPTER 7

Gestalt Counseling

BACKGROUND OF THE THEORY

Historical Context

Like many of the theories discussed in this text, Gestalt therapy grew from a reaction to classical psychoanalysis that permeated the psychological community of the early twentieth century. A psychoanalyst, cast as an anonymous blank screen, focused on interpreting a client's unconscious drives. Consciousness was a small and insignificant portion of a client's psyche, whereas the unconscious was presumably the vast entity largely responsible for a client's psychological functioning. Adherents to psychoanalytic theory believed that because a client could only rarely access one's own unconscious a client needed an analyst to unlock the mysteries of the unconscious and, through interpretation and analysis of transference, free a client from intrapsychic turmoil.

New York in the late 1940s provided the birthplace of what was to become Gestalt therapy. Yontef (1995) noted that the genesis of Gestalt thinking was in direct opposition to psychoanalytic thought and to anything regarded as "authoritarian, mechanistic, or inflexible" (p. 262). Early Gestalt thinkers disagreed with the psychoanalytic emphasis on the analyst as the expert and did not believe that clients were helpless and incapable of change. They believed that the authoritarian position of the analyst not only afforded the analyst too much power but also set up an inefficient and rigid method of psychotherapy.

> They [early Gestaltists] wanted to construct a system oriented to fostering growth more than to remediating pathology, to actual experience more than to interpretations of an unexperienced reality, and to the most authentic contact possible more than replaying of experience in the transference neurosis. (Yontef, 1995, p. 262)

Thus, Gestaltists perceived a need for an active dialog between therapist and client and honored clients as agents of their own change.

Founders' Biographical Overview

> I have often been called the founder of Gestalt Therapy.
>   That's crap.
>
> —Fritz Perls, 1969

Frederick "Fritz" Perls, born in Berlin to a lower class Jewish family in 1893, was a child and adolescent full of energy and curiosity. His early life was filled with struggle, especially with his father. "His father humiliated him continually. Therefore he always had to prove that he wasn't as his father made him look" (Perls in Bernard, 1986, p. 370). After several years of less than stellar academic achievements (he failed the seventh grade—twice), he focused his energy on earning a degree in medicine, becoming a talented neurologist and psychoanalyst. For a more detailed account of Perls's early life, consult his autobiography, *In and Out of the Garbage Pail* (Perls, 1969b).

Perls's early career path included serving as a medic in World War I and working with Kurt Goldstein at the Goldstein Institute for Brain-Damaged Soldiers. From his experiences in both of these venues, he came to appreciate the role of perception in psychological and physical problems.

It was also during this time that Perls's professional career merged with his personal life in a very meaningful way. He met Lore (Laura) Posner, an assistant to Goldstein. Although 12 years his junior, Laura had developed an interest in psychology and was working on preliminary research for her dissertation. She had studied with eminent Judeo-Christian philosophers Paul Tillich and Martin Buber and soon began psychoanalytic training supervised by leading psychoanalyst Otto Fenichel. Laura and Fritz were both drawn to psychoanalysis, Fritz working with Wilheim Reich and Laura continuing her studies. They married in 1930, but only three years later, as a result of their activism in politics and the rise of Nazi Germany, they fled to South Africa.

In South Africa, the couple established a private practice and began the seminal writings that would become Gestalt therapy. While both worked on pieces for what would become *Ego, Hunger and Aggression*, they also led somewhat independent and busy lives, a trend that would continue throughout the life of the marriage. Sensing the impending political turmoil in South Africa, the couple decided to move once again, this time to the United States.

The move to the United States proved bountiful for Fritz and Laura Perls. Their book *Ego, Hunger and Aggression* was published in 1947. The fact that Fritz was credited as the sole author, although Laura helped with the book by writing two chapters, marked a pattern that would also endure throughout their marriage: Fritz was the public face of Gestalt while Laura chose the background. In 1951, Fritz, along with Ralph Hefferline and Paul Goodman, published *Gestalt Therapy: Excitement and Growth in the Human Personality*. This work represented, and still represents, a comprehensive description of the theory and practice of Gestalt work.

Due to these two publications, the Perls's private practice activity, and Fritz's lectures, Gestalt therapy began to attract a following. While in New York, Fritz explored the founding of the Institute for Gestalt Therapy. Laura was not enthusiastic about the formation of the Institute but became more involved when the primary interest in the group came from her own group therapy patients. The group that included such Gestalt therapists as Paul Weiss and Paul Goodman helped form the Institute in 1952 as a training center designed to apprentice those interested in Gestalt therapy (Humphrey, 1986).

The New York scene bustled, and soon Fritz moved about the country, discussing and demonstrating Gestalt work. In the 1960s he settled in California where he mainly held workshops at the Esalen Institute. The Institute's laidback atmosphere seemed to be reflected in Fritz's more informal and playful tone of later works such as *Gestalt Therapy Verbatim* (1969a) and the posthumously published *The Gestalt Approach and Eye Witness to Therapy* (1973).

After Fritz died in 1970, Gestalt therapy lost its dramatic public face. Laura Perls stepped more into the spotlight at that point, but many people still see Fritz as the originator of Gestalt therapy. Laura Perls, in an interview by Janine Bernard (1986), noted that Fritz's lack of recognition of Laura's contributions had been a source of conflict between the two, but in true Gestalt form, Laura commented that she and Fritz had worked out any unfinished business between them before his death and that although they often lived and worked apart, they were on good terms in the end.

Philosophical Underpinnings

Out of a reaction to their psychoanalytic training, Fritz and Laura Perls developed a theory of counseling that incorporated elements of psychoanalysis into an existential-humanistic therapy. The primary philosophical underpinning of Gestalt is the emphasis on a comprehensive phenomenological perspective of experience. Like many existential theories that philosophers Edmund Husserl (1965) and Jean Paul Sartre (1956) had inspired, Gestalt is grounded on the assumption that meaning is best derived and understood by considering the individual's interpretation of immediate experience. Perls emphasized "immediate" experience because this is the experience that is present and, therefore, that a person can attune to and impact. "To me nothing exists but the now. Now = experience = awareness = reality" (Perls, 1970, p. 14). Therefore, the key reality is phenomenological experience that exists in the here and now and emphasizes all aspects of the individual's current perception. As Clarkson (1989) noted,

> The phenomenological method which pays total attention to the phenomenon (person, experience or object) as it presents itself, becomes the method of choice in this counseling approach. Description is more important than interpretation. Clients are able to find their own meaning through this process. (pp. 13–14)

In psychoanalysis, the analyst's interpretation of the client's unconscious processes is necessary for client change. By contrast, in Gestalt, the counselor's respect for and understanding of each client's unique perception of self, other, and environment is the basis for client change.

Influenced by interactions with philosopher Jan Smuts in South Africa, Fritz Perls grounded Gestalt theory in a holistic view of the human psyche. He believed that the psychoanalytic compartmentalization of the psyche into id, ego, and superego promoted a fragmented view of people. He considered the psyche an integrated whole in which a person's physical, emotional, and spiritual elements are intertwined and inseparable to make the whole being. The classic example of the whole being greater than the sum of its parts is that of the cookie. What makes a cookie? A typical recipe for chocolate chip cookies calls for flour, eggs, brown sugar, salt, chocolate chips, and heat. According to the concept of holism, the nature of the collection of these individual ingredients is different from the nature of the final cookie. Separating the ingredients and examining them one by one and perhaps viewing one ingredient as the "essence of the cookie" would not give someone as accurate and complete an insight into the true nature of the cookie as one would get from looking at the finished cookie as a whole. As with cookies, counselors seek to consider, and clients are encouraged to accept, all aspects of a client's self: pretty–ugly, smart–stupid, good–bad, productive–lazy. Gestaltists consider the exclusion of any aspect of self from awareness, which they consider a splitting of the whole, to be unhealthy.

In developing Gestalt therapy, Fritz and Laura Perls drew philosophically from phenomenology and holism, from modified scientific models such as Kurt Lewin's (1951) field theory, and from elements of Gestalt psychology. Lewin's field theory is also a phenomenological-holistic theory in which the field exists in the here and now and represents the interaction between an organism and its environment. In this formulation, the field is made up of the *ground*, all the information available for an organism to perceive phenomenologically, and the *figure*, the part of the ground that emerges into the organism's immediate awareness, usually because it is related to one of the organism's immediate needs. When a figure arises from the perceptual field (ground), the organism then mobilizes energy to fulfill the need. If the need is fulfilled, the figure recedes into the ground and a new figure can arise. If the need is not fulfilled, the figure does not recede and becomes a distraction to the organism. This need-fulfillment process is the basis for the Gestalt perspective on the developing human being (Perls et al., 1951).

PERSONALITY DEVELOPMENT

Nature of Humans

Function of the Psyche

The basic function of the psyche is to participate continuously in a self-regulation process of need fulfillment aimed at maintaining organismic balance (Perls et al., 1951). When *organismic self-regulation* is functioning smoothly, needs emerge, one at a time, as a figure from the ground; the organism recognizes the need and mobilizes energy and takes appropriate action to satisfy it; and the figure recedes. Thus, the individual continually experiences a sense of *closure* and approaches a state of *homeostatic balance* before the next need or figure inevitably emerges.

Perls and colleagues (1951) asserted that all human beings strive for balance through self-regulation. The self-regulation potential emphasizes the ability of the organism to participate internally and spontaneously in need fulfillment in a natural, free flowing manner. The important aspect of this potentiality is not that the organism remains balanced at all times—a condition that would be stagnant if it were even possible—but that the organism is engaged in a continuous dynamic process—one characterized by ongoing movement. That is, as a new need emerges, the organism is by definition unbalanced. The natural tendency is to be aware of the need and then fulfill it, thus achieving balance once again until a new figure (need) arises. This process exemplified each person's innate tendency toward health and growth—the fulfillment of one's positive potential.

The functioning of the psyche is such that one can experience only that which is in one's present awareness. A person can remember the past and fantasize the future but cannot directly experience either. One can experience oneself and the environment only in the present—in the now. The need that dominates the present moment also influences perception. To a hungry person, food looks attractive; to a satiated person, it can look uninteresting, even repugnant. Perception, therefore, reflects phenomenology. Objective reality cannot be known because one always perceives through the personal bias of one's current need.

Structure of the Psyche

One aspect of the structure of the psyche is the background, or simply *ground*, of awareness, and the *foreground* into which the current need (figure) emerges and becomes the focus of one's attention. As the individual meets a need, or if the original need remains unmet but another more pressing need emerges, the new need takes the foreground and the original need recedes into the ground, ready to become figure again at the earliest opportunity. Personality structure is based on this ongoing interface between individual and environment and patterns that a person forms around the need-fulfillment cycle. Korb, Gorrell, and Van De Riet (2002) explained:

> Out of the flow of experiencing, basic personality structures have coalesced in the ground of experience. These structures may be seen as a relatively constant set of constructs, attitudes, and beliefs about the individual and the environment which exists as part of the person's ground. (pp. 21–22)

Gestaltists define learning as the process of retaining in the ground images of those phenomena that have fulfilled needs. For example, if you need to start your car, you can be aware of past methods that satisfied this need, such as using your car key, and utilize the recalled method with relative ease instead of experiencing the need-fulfillment cycle of "starting the car" from scratch each time you get in your car. The patterns a person retains in one's ground represent repetitive characterological strategies for attending to life's needs: one's personality. As you will read below, they are an important focus of the therapeutic process.

Also structurally speaking, the psyche of the infant at birth is a unified whole that consists of a synergetic interaction between aspects such as feelings, thoughts, and actions; the psyche cannot be reduced to any one of these. Each person's psyche also contains the potential for every human quality such as both humor and seriousness, both selfishness and generosity, and both adventurousness and cautiousness. These qualities have the potential to become polarized, with one extreme of the polarity being disowned, that is, chronically reconciled to the ground of awareness, thereby limiting one's human potential to respond with all one's resources to an emergent need. In Gestalt therapy, client and counselor often refer to aspects of personality as "parts" while continually acknowledging that the whole of the person is greater than the sum of one's parts.

At birth, the infant experiences oneself as undifferentiated from the environment. With experience, the infant comes to differentiate what is me from what is not-me. The border between the me and the not-me, the point at which those entities make contact, is the *contact boundary*. A sense of what is not-me is never to be confused with being separate or isolated from one's environment. More accurately, an organism's boundary belongs to both the person and the environment. On the one side, the contact boundary is in some degree of contact with oneself, involving awareness of one's needs. On the other side, the contact boundary is in some degree of contact with the environment, involving awareness of phenomena with the potential to satisfy or thwart need fulfillment.

Role of the Environment

From a Gestalt perspective, the individual and one's environment are inextricably linked. Yontef (1995) explained:

> There is no meaningful way to consider a person psychologically apart from the organism-environment field, just as there is no way to perceive the environment except through someone's observational perspective. Even the need to be alone is defined in relation to others. (p. 263)

Individuals are acted upon by the environment and act upon the environment, a process that both fulfills needs and facilitates self-definition. "In Gestalt therapy theory, the sense of self is relational. There is no 'I', no person, no sense of self, isolated from interhuman environment" (Yontef, 1998, p. 89).

Every moment, every person experiences aspects of the environment on a continuum between *supportive* and *toxic*. In the process of self-regulation, each person continuously modifies the permeability of the contact boundary between self and environment, ideally making it more permeable in the presence of support and less in the presence of toxicity. In addition, when one perceives it necessary, one modifies self and/or environment, ideally to maximize exchanges between self and environment that meet one's needs and minimize those that do not.

Consider the experience of watching a movie at a theater. Throughout the movie, as always, you are in continuous contact with the environment (the film being projected on the screen, the seat in which you are sitting, the crowd around you, etc.). You probably attend to some parts of your environment more intently than others—the film dialog, for example. Attending to the crowd around you would likely be distracting, so you make contact between self and crowd less permeable and make contact between self and the film dialog more permeable. If, despite your best efforts, you could not filter out need-frustrating aspects of the environment, such as talkative audience members nearby, you might take action to modify the environment, such as asking them politely to be more quiet or moving yourself to a different seat. Focusing on the film, you are also aware that this is a movie, not real life that involves you, so although you could say you are involved in the movie, even experiencing emotion, you are aware of the boundary between self and the fictional aspect of the movie.

From a developmental perspective, the environment that comprises the infant's natural and social surroundings can be characterized as falling somewhere on a continuum between supportive at one extreme and toxic at the other, with neglectful in between. In the supportive environment, when the infant and young child attempt to meet a need, the environment provides whatever is needed. In the neglectful environment, the youngster's needs go unmet. In the toxic environment, the environment responds to the needing child with commodities antithetical to the child's well-being. For example, consider the child who needs food, experiences hunger, and is thus energized to meet that need through communication, such as crying or asking for food, and/or some other activity, such as finding commodities to put into one's mouth. The supportive environment consists of commodities, such as nutritious food and people willing to provide those commodities. In the neglectful environment, such commodities and/or people are absent. In the toxic environment, the only available commodities are unhealthful, or people respond by punishing the child expressing the need, by providing the needing child unhealthy commodities to eat, or by coercing the child to eat when the child does not need to eat.

A poignant example of the child's vulnerability to assimilate toxicity under conditions of a nonsupportive environment is a scene from the movie *King of the hill* (Soderbergh, 1993), based on the memoirs of A. E. Hotchner. It is St. Louis in the Depression of the 1930s. Twelve-year-old Aaron is living alone in his family's apartment. In desperation, his father has taken a traveling sales job. His mother is in the hospital with tuberculosis. His parents have sent his sister away to live with a relative but have left him to fend for himself, believing him capable of self-support. Despite careful attempts to conserve, he runs out of food and money. He dares not leave the apartment because the unpaid landlord will take the first opportunity to lock him out, leaving him not only foodless but also homeless. After days without food, in desperation he creates a meal for himself by placing cut out magazine pictures of food onto a plate. Then, with fantasized savor, he eats the meal, which actually ends up making him violently ill. Ultimately, he recovers and is saved from this situation, but his story illustrates how vulnerable people, and especially children, can be to assimilating what is toxic when the environment is neglectful or offers only toxicity in response to one's attempts to meet one's needs.

One form of people's toxic responses to a child's needs is "shoulds" that the vulnerable child may assimilate. By punishing a child for expressing a need, people convey the message that "You should not feel hungry." By providing unhealthy commodities, they convey, "You should eat food that is not what your body actually wants." And by coercing the child to eat when not hungry, they convey, "You should eat in response to external prompts, not internal ones." Through such internalized shoulds, children lose contact with their own needs and what actually fulfills them. Thus, such shoulds are a major source of maladjustment.

As people develop, they usually become more capable of modifying the environment to meet their needs. Nevertheless, throughout life, people continue to contend with environments that range from supportive to neutral to neglectful to toxic. Examples of the latter include adults contending with domestic violence or genocide.

You hopefully are getting a sense that, from a Gestalt perspective, the role of the environment in personality development involves a two-way street with continuous traffic. Just as people must adjust to the field, experienced as familial or cultural conditions and expectations, laws, or rules, people also shape their environment to fulfill needs. For this reason, Gestaltists attend to and promote both environmental support and self-support. A good example is eating: Each person needs food to survive, but the existence or presence of food in the environment is not enough to satisfy the need. One must actively be aware of the presence of food and take steps to ingest an appropriate amount of the necessary nutrients to survive and maximize wellness. From a Gestalt perspective, this interactive process between environment and self is true for every need throughout the life span.

Interaction of Human Nature and Environment

Healthy Functioning

Healthy individuals approach life with vigor, experiencing and fulfilling one's needs as they arise in the here and now. One consistently completes the need-fulfillment cycle with little disruption. To facilitate healthy functioning, Gestalt therapists believe individuals utilize awareness of self and environment, responsibility for self, a commitment to maturation, and a dedication to appropriate contact with the environment. To help flesh out these concepts, we use Naranjo's (1970, p. 50) general principles formulated from his "injunctions for living the good life."

1. *Valuation of actuality*: "Actuality" refers to what is actually occurring in the immediate moment. According to this principle, healthy individuals strive to live in the present rather than the past or the future. Anxiety about what has already transpired or what might occur limits one's ability to focus on the needs at hand. Attending to the here and now enables the individual to experience each moment in its fullness and increases the probability of need fulfillment. As an added bonus, as one effectively fulfills current needs, one has less to worry about regarding the past ("What did I miss?") or the future

("I am afraid of the unknown"), because one's attention is on what one can most effectively control: the present. The injunctions that arise from this principle include: "Live here. Live now. Stop imagining and experience the real" (Naranjo, 1970, p. 49).

2. *Valuation of awareness and acceptance of experience*: Healthy individuals embrace awareness of self and how self relates to and interacts with the environment. As needs arise, one must first be aware of the need; without awareness, one will not make contact with the environment and will not fulfill the need. Only with awareness of self and environment can one fully accept experience and live in the here and now. The price for not being aware of needs as they arise from the ground includes discomfort, distraction, confusion, or other more serious symptoms depending on the denied need. For example, as I (KF) am writing this paragraph, I am aware that I am thirsty. I know this because I sense dryness in my mouth, and I am repeatedly engaging in behaviors such as licking my lips and swallowing. Although I have been aware of this need to drink, I have denied the need by trying to focus on finishing this section of the book. The result: The thirst and need to drink has become a distraction interfering with my ability to work. To fulfill this need, I must both be aware of it and take steps to fulfill it, such as getting up and getting a drink of water. Having done so and quenched my thirst, I am now prepared to focus on the next emergent need, in this case, my need to finish this section.

   Healthy individuals understand and accept all aspects of self. The realizations that one can be both good and evil, healthy and unhealthy, right and wrong, at any given moment are essential to living a healthy existence. When one does not value all aspects of self, one denies self, limits one's full awareness, and thus reduces one's potential to live fully. Denial of awareness often results from the formation of polarities, a phenomenon we will discuss in more detail in the Unhealthy Functioning section below. Specific injunctions that correspond to the principle of awareness and acceptance of experience include, "Stop unnecessary thinking. Rather, taste and see. Express rather than manipulate, explain, justify, or judge. Give in to unpleasantness and pain just as to pleasure. Do not restrict your awareness" (Naranjo, 1970, p. 50).

3. *Valuation of wholeness, or responsibility*: Healthy people understand that life is a process, one that is developmental in nature. As people mature, they shed old ways of being and become more self-observing, self-understanding, and self-sufficient. The valuation of wholeness requires a commitment to the maturation process and the struggles the process brings. Consider the challenges of your development from an infant to an adult. From a Gestalt perspective, the maturation process involves you differentiating from other things and people in the environment and forming an ever-increasing sense of personality identity. I (KF) remember observing this process when my youngest child learned to walk. One day, after months of crawling and walking with the aid of my finger, he let go and toddled out into space on his own. He fell, but he tried again and again until he could walk competently. The look on his face, part terror, part astonishment, part wonder, is what Gestalt theorists envision as the experience all people encounter in the process of trusting self and actively engaging in maturation. Healthy individuals are open to this process, embracing the possibilities of letting go of unnecessary dependence on others and developing greater self-sufficiency.

Responsibility is a key to maturation. A healthy individual recognizes that one's ability to think and feel on one's own, to trust self, rests on one's willingness to take responsibility for one's own feelings, thoughts, and actions. A healthy person not only takes responsibility for self but also refrains from taking responsibility for other people's feelings, thoughts, and actions. The mantra "I am responsible only for myself. I am not responsible for others" fits the Gestalt principle of responsibility. The person who refuses to accept responsibility for self and/or who takes responsibility for others blurs the boundary between I and Thou, and this blurring interferes with one's awareness and, ultimately, need fulfillment.

Even though we have broken down the aspects of healthy living into general principles to aid in understanding, hopefully you can appreciate the interconnectedness, the holism, of the principles. Without awareness one cannot be responsible for one's feelings, thoughts, and actions. Without a here-and-now focus, one loses a sense of awareness and limits one's ability to be actively responsible. Without a valuation of the wholeness of the life process and a commitment to maturation, awareness and responsibility become moot points, and a here-and-now existence is impossible. Without responsibility, the locus of control lies outside of self and one loses the ability to be response-able, that is, aware of and able to respond in fulfilling each need as it arises in the here and now. The three general principles intertwine to create a core of healthy living in which an individual continuously maximizes need fulfillment and, therefore, balance.

Unhealthy Functioning

Each person continually and innately strives toward balance by developing methods to fulfill one's needs. Even with the innate striving toward balance, no one grows up in a completely supportive environment. Therefore, everyone's needs sometimes go unmet, and unmet needs constitute *unfinished business* with its accompanying discomforting feeling of *anxiety*. Everyone has the capacity to tolerate the anxiety of the inevitable occasional unfinished business. So, if one's environment has been primarily supportive of need fulfillment, one is likely to maintain the innate condition of an appropriately permeable contact boundary, with the ability to process through the need fulfillment cycle on a regular basis, usually restoring homeostasis.

Maladjustment occurs when, in the face of an environment chronically unsupportive of need fulfillment, one responds to anxiety by restricting awareness. In that process, one develops patterns of feeling, thought, and/or action that fail to fulfill one's needs, that end up creating more needs rather than fulfilling existing ones, or that are downright destructive to oneself or others. These patterns take the form of *disturbance at the contact boundary*. This disturbance involves some form of *disowning awareness*.

A disturbed contact boundary is overly permeable, overly impermeable, or vacillates between the two. Such disturbance takes one or more forms, and the more one manifests them, the more one impairs one's ability to contact oneself and the environment to meet one's needs.

A way to conceptualize the contact boundary is as a kind of psychological "skin" where self meets the environment. The "health" of the contact boundary is assessed by the size and shape of the "pores" of that skin. When the pores are moderately spaced and straight, the skin is, appropriately, both permeable and impermeable: Ingressly, one can assimilate self-enhancing material and block out self-destructive material (toxins) from the environment; egressly, one can put out into the environment the amount and kind of self-material that also helps one maximally meet one's needs. In this condition, one is fully aware, and one's sense of self has integrity with an appropriate amount of openness and guardedness. Figure 7.1 illustrates a healthy contact boundary.

Contact boundary disturbances can be understood as the pores having deviated in some way: size or shape. In each case, one's sense of self is disturbed and the appropriate balance of exchange between self and environment is upset. Each of the five contact boundary disturbances Yontef and Jacobs (2008) identified can be understood in this way.

Introjection   In *introjection*, pores have become so open to the environment that the individual takes in both nutritious and toxic material. With pores too ingressly open and the contact boundary too inwardly permeable, one's sense of self is not well enough defined and is vulnerable to being defined by input from the environment, which is especially problematic if the input is toxic. See Figure 7.2 for this illustrated process.

One form of introjection is taking in rules that one then holds rigidly. Consider the man who learned as a child to stop and look both ways before crossing the street. One night at 3:00 a.m., the neighbor across the street calls asking the man for help with an urgent medical emergency. Approaching the curb, he neither sees nor hears any traffic on his quiet residential street, yet he stops at the curb and looks both ways before proceeding. His response-ability to his neighbor's emergency has been impaired by his unexamined, inflexible introjection. Another form of introjection is taking in unexamined, uncensored concepts about one's self, such as the child who assimilates repeated messages from his father that he is stupid despite the child's own experience that he performs adequately in school work.

Projection   In *projection*, pores have become shaped such that one perceives personal qualities in the people and things of the environment. With one's pores too egressly open,

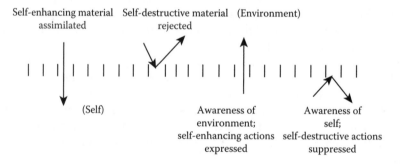

FIGURE 7.1   A healthy contact boundary.

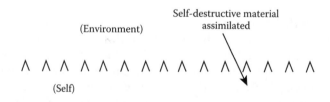

FIGURE 7.2   Introjection.

one's sense of self is not adequately contained but is projected out into the environment. See Figure 7.3 for this illustrated process.

An example of projection is the penny-pinching woman who always tries to get herself the very best deal, moneywise. In a business transaction, she is trying to manipulate the deal so that she gets more than her fair share. When others resist her strategies and persist in trying to get a fair shake, she angrily perceives them as trying to cheat her—without awareness that she began the conflict by trying to cheat them.

Confluence   In *confluence,* pores have become so open that one does not distinguish between self and the environment, especially other people. Correspondingly, one's sense of self is quite diffuse. See Figure 7.4 for this illustrated process.

An example of confluence is the person who overidentifies with others' successes, failures, or problems. I (JMH) realized I was experiencing confluence when I became upset on my husband's behalf: He felt hurt by something his stepdaughter had done. What she had done did not involve me, but was entirely between him and her; I had lost my distinction between him and myself; I had become overly identified with him. With this awareness I transcended confluence by affirming that he is he and I am I; I "gave" him the problem, which was really his problem to begin with! Another example is the person who is so much what others expect that he has little sense of himself, such as someone who is excessively pleasing or excessively rebellious in response to others' expectations; such a person tends to be out of touch with his own needs and preferences.

Isolation and Retroflection   In two additional contact boundary disturbances, the pores of the contact boundary are too closed. In *isolation,* the pores are so closed that a person rejects wholesale any material from the environment. Thus, one result is that the person rejects even nutritious material from the environment, leaving one quite isolated and

FIGURE 7.3   Projection.

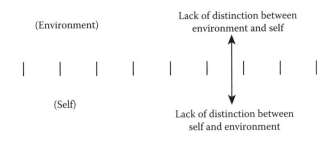

FIGURE 7.4   Confluence.

many of one's needs unmet. In *retroflection,* a person does to oneself what one would really like to do to the environment; one turns self-enhancing impulses back on oneself. These processes are illustrated in Figure 7.5.

An example of isolation is a person in distress who cannot receive support or assistance from other people. Another is a person who is impervious to others' appropriate and constructive feedback about some aspect of the person's behavior.

An example of retroflection is the person who feels angry but does not allow herself to express it, even appropriately, and instead turns it back on herself and develops a stomach ulcer. In fact, from a Gestalt perspective, psychosomatic symptoms are often the result of retroflection. Examples include the person who, rather than take action to alleviate a source of stress, develops a tension headache; or the combat soldier who, unable to take action to stop or to express fully his feelings about the horror he sees, develops temporary blindness.

Disturbances in contact produce a stagnation or paralysis in the growth process, inhibiting the person from full awareness and maturation. For example, in response to numerous unmet needs, the child may disown awareness of them. Or, if the people on whom the child depends communicate that the child should feel, think, or act differently than he or she is guided to by organismic self-regulation, the child may relegate the unacceptable aspect of self to the ground and disown it from awareness by not allowing it to emerge as figure; by allowing only the polar opposite of this aspect into awareness, the child fragments oneself and limits access to the full resources of one's self. People can avoid contact by developing one or more of the boundary disturbances described above, and their symptoms will parallel the disturbance strategy they have employed. These, then, are the symptoms of psychopathology.

Perls (1970) postulated five layers of psychopathology (see Figure 7.6), suggesting that a person or client working through these layers was much like peeling an onion. Each layer peeled not only helps the client strip away a false self but also enables the client to be more aware of the true self—and tears are a common accompaniment to peeling each layer. In the next section, we describe the specifics of how to work through these layers.

THE PERSONALITY CHANGE PROCESS

From a Gestalt perspective, change occurs with enhanced awareness. In particular, when one becomes aware of unmet needs, because of one's innate tendency to seek balance and promote health and growth, one will naturally experiment with ways to better fulfill those needs.

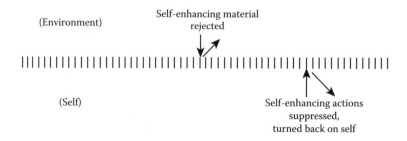

FIGURE 7.5   Isolation and retroflection.

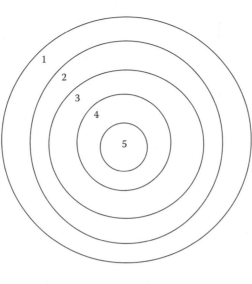

1. *The phony:* Pretend to be something we are not. Social masks; real selves are hidden so we feel liked, feared, loved, etc. Much of the disowning of certain aspects of self (polarities) occurs here.

2. *The phobic:* If we manage to try to face all that we are, this level forces us to face the fear associated with being our whole self. Catastrophes such as, "My parents will not love me if. . ." or "my wife will think I am less of a man if. . ." arise to scare us back into the phony layer.

3. *Impasse:* The impasse is a point of paralysis where we face the dual terror of moving away from external support and of relying on self. Many people freeze at this layer or retreat because it is too difficult or the pain of avoiding contact or living a life of limited awareness is preferable to the pain and fear of change.

4. *Implosive:* We step into the abyss of the unknown as we begin to explore the blind spots in our selves. The exploration often is awkward and scary, as we let go of our old ways of being and explore new ways.

5. *Explosive:* Once we let go and embrace the responsibility of self in every here-and-now moment, we will feel truly alive. Perls likened this "a-ha" as an explosion of energy; spontaneous expressions of intense anger, joy, grief, sadness are common.

FIGURE 7.6   Layers of Neurosis.

Gestalt theorists have a paradoxical view of change. They believe a person can change only when one is truly oneself; the more someone tries to be who one is not, the more stuck the person will become (Beisser, 1970). A person inhibits self-regulation by denying aspects of self, thus creating polarities and developing contact boundary disturbances. As Perls (1969a) noted,

> the aim in therapy, the growth aim, is to lose more and more of your "mind" and come more to your *senses*. To be more and more in touch with yourself and in touch with the world, instead of only in touch with the fantasies, prejudices and apprehensions. (p. 50)

The goal is not to buy into the curse of the ideal, in which one seeks to be better, but instead to be more fully aware of one's true self (Korb et al., 2002). As we discussed previously, if good health is characterized by an organism that self-regulates the fulfillment of needs as they arise, and if maladjustment consists of interruptions in that need fulfillment cycle, then the person who becomes increasingly aware of one's needs and how one interrupts the need-fulfillment process—will spontaneously return to self-regulation and balance.

According to Yontef (1995) awareness contains two vital elements: *microawareness*, which is awareness of particular content, and *awareness of the awareness process*. Microawareness is fairly easy for most counselors to grasp. For example, I am aware that I am writing about Gestalt therapy. You might be aware that you are reading about Gestalt therapy and learning about basic principles of change. A client may be aware of discussing marital problems, listening to one's child talk about the pain of the impending divorce, or hearing feedback from one's counselor. These are the contents of awareness.

Awareness of the awareness process, on the other hand, involves a person focusing on how they allow or block awareness of content. For example, someone might chronically respond to criticism from one's spouse by withdrawing, making a joke, changing the subject, or countercriticizing rather than by hearing the pain behind the spouse's criticism, considering the extent to which the criticism might be valid, and exploring possible ways of changing. According to Yontef (1995), "Awareness of awareness strengthens the ability to choose to bring automatic habits into awareness as needed and use focused awareness and phenomenological experimentation for clarification, centering, and trying out new behaviors" (p. 275). Simply put, whereas microawareness is awareness of *what* one is experiencing in the moment, awareness of the awareness process is awareness of *how* one is participating in or blocking microawareness.

The second aspect of change involves what happens after someone accesses awareness. Upon becoming aware of an interruption in the need-fulfillment cycle, a person will experiment with and experience new ways of fulfilling the need and completing the gestalt of need fulfillment. As Korb et al. (2002) pointed out, merely talking about the issue will not fulfill the need; one must experience in the here and now a way of satisfying the need.

As awareness increases, people experience a "comfort with self" and begin to take steps to move from reliance on external opinions and support to more reliance on internal support and trust in themselves. This transition, called maturity, is a hallmark of the Gestalt change process whereby people can access awareness and facilitate healthy contact on their own. Applying this principle to counseling, Perls and colleagues (1951) stated that a Gestalt therapist aims to help clients a point where "they can proceed without help ... *natura sanat non medicus*, it is only oneself (in the environment) that can cure oneself" (p. 292). In the next two sections, we will illustrate methods for facilitating these two important aspects of change: awareness and experimentation.

Client's Role

Since Gestalt therapists are active and focused on the here and now, the client plays a very important role in the therapeutic process. Greenwald (1976) outlined "ground rules for Gestalt therapy" that help conceptualize the role of the client (see Table 7.1). The author did not mean for the list of "rules" to be read as a list of commands and demands on the clients but, instead, as an assortment of elements that "create an atmosphere and attitude toward working in therapy that lead to greater awareness of the reality of oneself and how one interacts with others and how one functions in the here-and-now" (p. 269).

Counselor's Role

Akin to other existential-humanistic approaches such as client-centered and existential therapy, Gestalt therapists are considered tools of change. The therapist is both supportive and confrontational, continuously working to encourage here-and-now awareness in the client through the direct experiencing of the I-Thou relationship—the highly aware contact between two individuals. Gestalt therapists use feedback and immediacy to share

TABLE 7.1   Ground Rules in Gestalt Therapy

1. **Attune oneself to the continuum of awareness:** Clients are encouraged to pay attention to the various modes of sensory awareness over the course of the session. Sensory awareness may include thoughts, feelings, emotions, bodily sensations—anything that a client has the ability to notice internally or externally.

2. **Commit to the here and now:** Because the focus of the therapy is the here and now, clients are expected to speak in the present tense. Even when one is discussing past material, dreams, or future expectations, the client will be encouraged to bring these into the now and discuss how one experiences the impact of the issue in the present moment.

3. **Own everything:** In order to become more aware of self, clients must own all their thoughts, actions, feelings, and sensations. Just as clients are expected to speak in the present tense, they also use "I" language as an expression of self-responsibility. For example, instead of saying "You make me angry," clients may say "I feel angry when I see you."

4. **Commit to meaningful dialog:** By operating according to the preceding rules, the client is able to engage in meaningful dialog. The ability to communicate to another person in a clear and responsible manner is just one aspect of such a dialog. In addition to communicating, one must be willing to listen to the other person's (the counselor's) perception of what one just shared. A client's openness to and assessment of environmental feedback is a vital aspect of the maintenance of healthy contact that enables the need-fulfillment cycle to occur.

5. **Avoid questions:** For the most part, Gestalt therapists view client questions, whether directed to the counselor or to oneself, as ways to avoid real contact. Questions elicit explanations or justifications and rarely get to the core issues. Gathering evidence to support a position removes the counselor–client dyad from the here and now. So, for example, if a client asks, "If I start relating to my mother differently, how do you think she will react?" the counselor might encourage the client to make a statement instead, perhaps "I am afraid my mother will react negatively."

6. **Take risks:** In Gestalt therapy, one must face one's fears and risk being rejected or humiliated in order to gain awareness into one's true self. Risks involve experimenting with all aspects of one's personality, especially the parts that the client seems to be ignoring or disowning. Clients who are not willing to explore those parts of self would not benefit from Gestalt therapy.

7. **Embrace personal responsibility:** Gestalt therapists believe that clients have the power to change and have the responsibility to decide when and how that change will occur. Therefore, there exists no "I can't" in Gestalt therapy, only "I'm not willing to" or "I choose not to."

Source: Adapted from Greenwald, J. A., *The handbook of Gestalt therapy*, Aronson, New York, NY, 1976.

their impressions of and reactions to the client. This use of self by the therapist fosters contact and acts as the catalyst for here-and-now experiencing and awareness. As the client avoids contact with the therapist, the therapist challenges and brings the contact disturbances to the client's attention. Gestalt counselors often suggest exercises, which they call experiments, both during and between sessions in an effort to help client enhance awareness.

The role of the therapist is to ask "How?" and avoid the "Why?" with regard to client issues. Observing the client in the session, how she makes or avoids contact with the therapist will provide important information about the client's perspective and functioning. How the client functions in the now is the most valid representation of the client's phenomenology available to the counselor. Exploring the why only provides an explanation, a justification for experience, but does not engage in experiencing. In fact, whys are distance makers and contact breakers, whereas hows facilitate dialog and contact.

Stages and Techniques

Perhaps the most unfortunate aspect of Gestalt theory is that many practitioners have reduced it to a collection of elaborate techniques. Ask people about Gestalt therapy, and many are likely to respond, "Oh, yes, the empty-chair therapy" or something similar. It is because of this association that we are reluctant to outline various techniques. However, experimentation is an important method Gestalt therapists use to facilitate awareness, and the techniques that they have created can be wonderful tools when a counselor uses them for the purpose of establishing a continuum of awareness. Therefore, a description of some Gestalt experiments follows, and to emphasize the warning not to consider Gestalt therapy a technique-only approach, we provide a message on this point from Fritz Perls:

> One of the objections I have against anyone calling himself a Gestalt Therapist is that he uses techniques. A technique is a gimmick. A gimmick should be used only in the extreme case. We've got enough people running around collecting gimmicks, more gimmicks, and abusing them. These techniques, these tools, are quite useful in some seminar on sensory awareness or joy, just to give you an idea that you are still alive ... but the sad fact is that this jazzing-up more often becomes a dangerous substitute activity, another phony therapy that prevents growth. (Perls, 1969a, p. 1)

Although Gestalt therapy is an active, fluid process that emphasizes the here-and-now interaction between client and counselor, the traditional stages of therapy (rapport, defining the problem, exploring the problem, experimenting with change, and termination) seem to apply. The first stage of therapy involves orienting the client to the Gestalt process of experiencing here-and-now material instead of there-and-then material. Within this orientation framework, the therapist is encouraged to get a sense of the reason the client has initiated counseling and to assess the client's understanding of awareness and any fear or resistance to change. A dialog of the here and now develops at this stage, as illustrated below. Notice how the counselor uses reflection and encouragement to experience the here and now.

Client: I really don't know why I am here. I mean, I feel bad all the time, but I am used to solving my own problems. My wife says I worry too much and should be able to handle life.

Counselor: You are feeling ambivalent about being here and are considering how other people feel about your current situation. Let's focus on you right now. Focus on what you are feeling right now. Tell me the first feeling that comes to your awareness.

Client: Well, nervous, I guess.

Counselor: You are not sure? Perhaps that is your feeling, unsure. What went through your mind as I said that?

Client: That I ...

Counselor: You are editing, censoring yourself. Let it go and say it.

Client: Okay, I do feel uncertain. I feel like that all the time and I feel like that now. I also feel like I should know, and I feel like an idiot when I don't. I feel like an idiot for being here.

Counselor: That's a great place to start.

The first stage focuses on initiating contact between counselor and client and provides an introduction to the experience of working with awareness within the therapeutic dyad. This process, in Gestalt therapy as well as other approaches, is known as developing rapport or establishing a working relationship. Whereas the first stage builds the foundation, the second stage focuses on in-depth exploration of the contact disturbances and denied awareness the client experienced and/or exhibited in the first stage. To help client and counselor experience here-and-now contact, Gestalt practitioners created experiments. Each experiment is designed to help a client access and experience awareness freely within the session and promote healthy contact and meaningful dialog between client and counselor. Following are descriptions of a few Gestalt experiments.

Reversal

True awareness means experiencing and owning all aspects of self. All elements of personality exist on a continuum, but many people act as if they possess only the good side of a trait and possess none of the bad or vice versa. In the reversal experiment a client tries out expressing the polar opposite of any feeling, thought, or action and noting what awareness arises. The client might discover aspects of self that one has kept out of awareness. In becoming aware of them, the client has the opportunity to integrate them into a more whole experience of self. Consider the example below of a client who struggles with anxiety.

Client: I am anxious all the time. I cannot shake it.
Counselor: That is powerful language. Say the opposite and notice how you feel.
Client: I can't.
Counselor: I am aware of the hopelessness inherent in the phrase, "I can't." I invite you to start with "I can." Say that and tell me what you are aware of.
Client: I can. Hmm, that does feel different. I am aware of my body straightening out as I say it.
Counselor: Okay, now try the reverse of your earlier statement.
Client: I am not anxious all the time ...
Counselor: What else are you?
Client: I am calm some of the time, peaceful.
Counselor: Your body and your voice resonate with that peace. It is inside of you after all. As witnessed here, you possess the capacity for both anxiety and calm.

Dialog

This experiment, commonly referred to as the "empty-chair technique," is designed to provide enhanced awareness of parts of self that the client has not explored or has kept out of awareness. The aim is to provide the client with a means to integrate denied aspects of self. Using two chairs that face each other, the client plays the "part" in each chair, moving back and forth between chairs in an ongoing dialog. The "parts" might be such things as two aspects of self; self and another person, living or deceased; self and an object; or self and an image, such as a dream image. A common example of the experiment is the client dialog between the internal "top dog" and "underdog." Many people struggle between listening to or obeying their moralistic, judgmental, demanding side (top dog) and giving in to their side that claims helplessness, weakness, and powerlessness (underdog). Extreme manifestations of this polarity lead to clients exhibiting an overmanifestation of top dog as evidenced by a righteously rigid personality, or underdog as evidenced by helpless and victim-oriented personality traits. In the following dialog, note the shift from there-and-then material to here-and-now material and the gradual integration of the elements of this client's personality.

Client:	I am just so pissed that she won't get off her butt and do something with her life. I mean, she just wastes time!
Counselor:	Perhaps this is not so much about her as about you and your own fear of being seen as lazy or unproductive. Would you be willing to examine this possibility?
Client:	Okay, I mean, I hate being seen as lazy. I am a hard worker.
Counselor:	I wonder if you're willing to experiment with playing both sides, the lazy part and the hard worker part, and to act out a dialog between these two entities. We will work with these two chairs. Talk as if these two parts of yourself are speaking to each other. In each chair, when you feel finished with expressing what you want to, then switch chairs and respond. How would you like to begin?
Client:	I'll start with my hardworking side.
Hardworking:	I don't see why you are so damn lazy! I mean, I work hard all day. I'm doing things, and you just sit around and relax. You are useless.
Lazy:	Well, I have to relax sometime or I'll be angry all the time like you. Relaxing is good too, you know! You are always so stressed out. Wouldn't you like to take some time off?
Hardworking:	No … yes! Yes, I would, but someone has to work around here. If I don't work nothing would get done.
Lazy:	I think you could actually get more done if you took some time to rest.

Directed Awareness

Gestalt therapists believe that clients exhibit blocks to awareness and contact in a wide range of ways: behaviorally, emotionally, cognitively, spiritually, and physically. Directed awareness provides a here-and-now way for the client to focus on these blocks.

Counselor:	You seem tense, like you are anticipating something but are having a difficult time vocalizing it.
Client:	Yeah, I have a lot going on right now; too many distractions.
Counselor:	I suggest you practice some directed awareness. Find a comfortable position in your chair, and close your eyes if you like. Okay, as we have done before, as things come into awareness, verbalize with "Now I am aware of …"
Client:	(settling in) I am aware of tension in my back. Now I am aware of moving my neck to pop it. I am aware of the thought, "I am overwhelmed." I am aware of the feeling of fear. (Sighs) I am aware that I just exhaled very deeply. I am aware that it felt good, so I want to do it again. (Sighs) I am aware of the thought, "This is helping me to feel more relaxed." I am aware of my feet wiggling on the floor. I am aware of the thought, "I am not alone." I am aware that I am beginning to tear up. I am aware that the tension in my back has lessened. I am aware of the desire to open my eyes and talk about my feelings of not being alone.

As the client gains awareness, clarity, and integration of self through contact with the counselor and experimentation, the counselor invites the client to experiment with new insight outside of the session—the third stage of therapy. For example, the person who had trouble relaxing could play with (not work on) being aware of the top dog/underdog struggle during the week and practice recognizing both parts of self. The client's ability to integrate self through recognition and elimination of blocks to contact and awareness both in and outside the therapy session can be an indication of completion of the therapy.

The fourth stage is termination in which the counselor supports changes the client has made and continues to challenge the client in the here and now. Since these stages are not necessarily linear, one could view the fourth stage as an ongoing process. In fact, in keeping with the Gestalt idea of holism, the events and awareness that occur in any given stage could lead to movement into an earlier stage or to a later stage depending on the level of awareness. There is also no set time frame for stage progression. Change (awareness) can happen in an hour, or it can take many years, depending on the exact nature of the wide ranging client and counselor variables in any given session and course of therapy. The key is for the counselor and the client to be open to the moment and to be aware of issues as they surface in the here and now.

CONTRIBUTIONS AND LIMITATIONS

Interface With Recent Developments in the Mental Health Field

The Nature–Nurture Question

Gestalt theorists firmly believe in the dynamic interplay between self, biology, and environment. They acknowledge that both heredity and environment influence people's behavior. Yet, philosophically rooted in holism and self-responsibility, they do not believe that those factors cause people's behavior. Rather, people make choices that are influenced by those factors, that can transcend those factors, and that can affect them. For example, a person in a toxic environment often can choose to take steps to modify it or can leave it. From a Gestalt perspective, an individual's behavior at any moment is best understood as one's choice based on one's perception in the moment, which perception is influenced, but not caused, by nature and nurture.

DSM–IV–TR *Diagnosis*

Similar to many other holistic, phenomenological approaches to counseling, Gestalt therapists have traditionally avoided using diagnosis. They view diagnosis as an invalid compartmentalization of a being that actually is fluid and greater than the sum of its parts. Identifying a cluster of symptoms and labeling a person based on these limited aspects of self violates the basic philosophical underpinnings of the Gestalt approach.

Having noted the traditional protests regarding diagnosis, Gestalt theorists do appreciate the identification of repetitive maladaptive patterns of behavior in the form of dysfunctional methods of need fulfillment, poor boundary maintenance, or not owning all aspects of self. In fact, Gestalt authors have described the conceptualization of common diagnoses from a Gestalt perspective (Clemmons, 1997; Yontef, 1988). The key to the Gestalt perspective of diagnosis is that a diagnostic label and the symptoms that comprise the label are not static but, instead, represent the person's present pattern of contact. This perspective emphasizes a client's potential to change.

Pharmacotherapy

Regarding psychopharmacology, although modern Gestalt therapists recognize the latest research findings on the efficacy of medication in the alleviation of some symptoms, they would also argue that the client's problems do not end with the erasure of problematic symptoms. In fact, historically Gestalt therapists have criticized the medical model for focusing too much on what both client and counselor would rather not see instead of working with what both are currently experiencing (Fagan & Shepherd, 1970). Clients who take medication as a quick fix would be seen as hiding in the phony layer of existence, unwilling to take the longer road to self-awareness. From a Gestalt approach, people who merely take medication run the risk of splitting self into the "Sick me" and "Not sick me" polarity.

Conversely, Gestalt therapists would consider it appropriate for a client to take medication as a means to correct a chemical imbalance and then proceed to address personal issues that were once difficult to address. For example, a client suffering from intense hallucinations and delusions would appropriately take medication to quell these symptoms but also would seek therapy to address underlying issues of self. For an excellent account of a schizophrenic client's struggle for self within the client–counselor dialog, see Van Dusen (1975).

Managed Care and Brief Therapy

Regarding brief counseling and managed care, due to the holistic focus and here-and-now approach to the therapeutic encounter, Gestalt therapy has no definite length. However, Houston (2003) outlined a six- to eight-session model complete with in-session and homework activities. And even in standard practice, the here-and-now focus of Gestalt therapy avoids lengthy excursions into the past, and the theory favors experiencing over the lengthier process of analysis. Gestalt therapists designed the intense nature of Gestalt experiments and the immediacy of the counselor and client dialog to facilitate awareness in a short amount of time (Harman, 1995). Upon achieving awareness, clients can readily resolve conflicts, and if clients show resistance to contact, Gestalt therapists address it quickly, as well. As Yontef (1995) noted, "Frequently, open-ended Gestalt therapy spontaneously concludes in a few sessions" (p. 273).

Technical Eclecticism

Gestalt therapists encourage technical eclecticism, pulling techniques from a wide array of schools of thought in order to facilitate the awareness-enhancing dialog between client and counselor. Zinker (1977) explained that the Gestalt emphasis on creating here-and-now contact between counselor and client provides an opportunity for therapists to be creative in their approaches. However, Gestalt theorists would consider it counterproductive for Gestalt therapists to use techniques that deviate from the goals of the theory. In general, techniques that focus on the client's subjective experience, the counselor's experience of the client, facilitating awareness, and the dialog between counselor and client would fit the Gestalt framework. As psychotherapists explore avenues of theoretical integration, authors in the professional literature have begun to explore the merging of Gestalt approaches with other schools of thought (Ginger, 2008; Pack, 2008; Woldt & Toman, 2005).

Diversity Issues

Regarding issues of culture, gender, and spirituality, various aspects of the theory indicate Gestalt therapists' ability to accommodate a wide variety of client perspectives. From a philosophical standpoint, the Gestalt emphasis on phenomenology indicates that therapists understand clients' subjective perspectives on the world as seen through the lenses of culture, gender, and spiritual beliefs. Gestalt therapists consider every person unique, so clients are diverse by definition, and therapists' respect for that individuality is crucial to the Gestalt experience. In fact, as noted previously, helping the client experience and become aware of all facets of one's self is the primary goal of Gestalt therapy.

Culture constantly influences the self of the person. Gestalt therapists are not necessarily interested in the concrete specifics of a client's culture, as in "You are an African

American," but instead are more interested in what meaning a client ascribes to one's culture, as in, "What does it mean for you to be African American?" The literature contains examples of practitioners using Gestalt therapy in Latin American countries such as Argentina (Slemenson, 1998), Mexico (Munoz-Polit, 1998), and Brazil (Ciornai, 1998), and O'Hara (1998) commented that humanistic approaches such as Gestalt therapy represent credible examples of cross-cultural therapies that help people adapt to modern and postmodern crises.

On a more critical note, Saner (1989) proposed that Gestalt therapy, as practiced in the United States, has diverged from the true phenomenological base and has adopted an overemphasis on the Western value of individualism. "It is my assumption that most members of the American Gestalt therapy movement have over stressed 'I' ness because they are unaware of their cultural predisposition toward individualism with its corollary aversion or avoidance of lasting intimacy or committed 'we' ness" (p. 59). Saner contended that the emphasis on individualism profoundly distorts the therapy, as evidenced by the tendency to focus only on the client's awareness and not on how the client and counselor are making contact in the here and now. In an effort to promote client autonomy, American Gestalt therapists have shifted their focus away from the immediate therapeutic encounter and toward treating the client as an object by creating techniques and experiments to "help the client." Counselors who stress individualism may neglect the dialogic relationship or fail to recognize its importance in the Gestalt process. American counselors who do not recognize this emphasis on individualism as a personal cultural issue run the risk of damaging the process in two important ways. First, the client may not share the perspective that individualism is the only or best way to operate. Individuals from Asian and Hispanic communities, for example, may value a greater emphasis on external support and subjugating individual priorities to familial and societal ones. Second, by focusing only on client change, the counselor robs the client of the most powerful element of the change process: the coinfluencing nature and experience of the client–counselor contact.

Phenomenology provides a framework for Gestalt therapists to understand and honor gender differences among clients. How a client perceives gender roles can be rich ground for one to explore and become aware of disowned aspects of self. For many men, learning that the continuum of possible emotions extends beyond mad, sad, and glad can be a frightening yet liberating experience. Many men we have worked with firmly believe, "Vulnerable emotions are not safe. If I show fear or sadness, people will think I am less of a man. They will try to take advantage of me. I'll be seen as weak." For some women, being assertive in decision making does not fit with their concept of femininity (Enns, 1987). Their desire to get their needs met on their own terms conflicts with their view of how women are supposed to act and feel. As one client commented, "I feel that if I stand up for myself, I will be labeled a bitch." From a Gestalt perspective, how one perceives gender roles can create polarities in oneself that provide obstacles to awareness and growth. Through therapy, these clients, regardless of gender, can access their innate endowment of the full range of emotions and ways of responding to needs and can claim and integrate them into everyday life. As Polster (1976) noted, "The basic human dimension of personhood is at stake in therapy–moving beyond stereotypes of man or woman into the full articulation and integration of everything any individual can be when all aspects of one's experience are available" (p. 562).

On a more critical note, Amendt-Lyon (2008) wrote a comprehensive overview of the relationship between Gestalt theory and gender. In her critique, she noted the lack of attention authors in the Gestalt professional literature have given to gender issues and encouraged the Gestalt community to participate on a larger scale in addressing issues of gender. She also explored the effect and appropriateness of same and different gender counselor–client dyads and stressed the importance of distinguishing sexuality from gender. She made numerous other equally informative comments on the original works she reviewed (see Keppner, 2008; Olsson, 2008).

The role of spirituality in Gestalt therapy reflects the evolving and phenomenological approach of the theory. Perls (1969b) remarked that he grew disillusioned with religion early on in his family life and declared himself an atheist. Still confused and frustrated by trying to find a sense of his self in what he perceived as a chaotic universe, Perls delved into various religious perspectives, including Zen Buddhism, Tillich's perspective on Protestantism, and Gabriel Marcel's Catholicism. As a result of these experiences, Perls came to accept that one's faith could be a vital piece of one's identity, that ignoring or denying this aspect of self inhibits awareness and maturation, and, therefore, that counselors need to understand this aspect of clients. Eynde (1999) explored the similarities between Gestalt and Buddhist philosophies, and many early Gestalt works, for example Stevens (1970), integrated various spiritual paths such as Buddhism, Krishnamurti, and Native American views into the Gestalt approach.

The Effectiveness of Psychotherapy

Gestalt therapists would concur to some degree with Asay and Lambert's (1999) research findings on factors in positive outcomes in psychotherapy. Whereas Gestalt therapists seem to attribute the totality of therapeutic success to the therapeutic relationship and experiment techniques, Asay and Lambert found these factors accounted for only 30 and 15%, respectively, of positive outcome. Authors on the Gestalt approach have not tended to address the 40% effect of extratherapeutic factors or the 15% effect of client expectation of improvement. Gestalt theorists, with their phenomenological perspective, would probably say that clients' subjective experiences of these factors would be more important than the objective nature of them, yet Asay and Lambert found the objective nature of these factors to play a clear role in positive therapeutic outcome.

Regarding research on its effectiveness, Gestalt therapy suffers from the same problems it shares with other humanistic approaches discussed in this text. Many of the concepts do not mesh well with quantitative methodologies, and the phenomenological process of the client–counselor dialog makes systematic descriptions and controlled studies nearly impossible. Responding to the 1995 American Psychological Association (APA) report on empirically supported approaches to psychotherapy, Yontef and Jacobs (2008) noted, "Random Clinical Trial is not a suitable approach for Gestalt therapy, which is a complex system based on the centrality of the dialog between therapist and patient" (p. 354). They believed that should the APA include more qualitative methods, then results would demonstrate the effectiveness of Gestalt approaches.

Other research on the effectiveness of Gestalt therapy has shown mixed results. Three research teams across more than two decades (Elliot, Greenberg, & Lietaer, 2004; Greenberg, Elliott, & Lietaer, 1994; Smith, Glass, & Miller, 1980) reported that outcome studies showed Gestalt therapy to be more effective than no treatment. However Greenberg and colleagues (1994) also noted that when compared to other forms of treatment, Gestalt often demonstrated less favorable results. In perhaps the largest and most recent review, Strumpfel (2004) found Gestalt therapy demonstrated a wide range of effectiveness with various diagnoses, populations, and therapy modalities such as individual, couple, and group counseling. Another important recent review of research on Gestalt therapy is that of Brownell (2008).

Limitations

Gestalt theory emphasizes doing as a way of reaching the preferred state of awareness. Awareness is not a cognitive process as much as an experiencing process. From a Gestalt standpoint, too much thinking often gets in the way of true awareness and maturity. In the present climate of mental health practice, in which managed care companies favor cognitive-based therapies, the lack of emphasis on the cognitive aspect of existence seems to be a practical limitation of the Gestalt approach.

In my (KAF) experience with Gestalt, I have found it to be a beginning counselor's worst nightmare. Many practitioners are attracted to the theory's active and dramatic experiments. In viewing tapes on Gestalt, viewers are in awe of Fritz Perls's charisma. As students get caught up in the excitement, they often fail to recognize the philosophical and therapeutic rationale for the techniques and, instead, use the experiments as "bail out techniques"—strategies to use when they feel stuck. During a live supervision session, I observed a student counseling an adolescent boy. The student had seen the boy three times and, working from a person-centered perspective, had done a nice job establishing rapport. But apparently the therapy was not progressing fast enough for the counselor, and she blurted out, "I think you have some issues with your father. Let's pretend he is sitting in the chair next to you. Tell him how you feel." The client looked perplexed and asked, "Why?" The counselor looked at the client blankly and changed the subject.

After the session I processed the issue with the student. She stated that she felt the client needed some pushing. I asked, "Where did the empty-chair idea come from?" She responded, "I saw it on a television show last night. It was a documentary on therapy." The technique failed not because the technique lacked efficacy but because the counselor applied it improperly. The counselor had no rationale for implementing the technique, so when the client requested one, she saw no alternative but to drop the technique—and awkwardly. Due to the active nature of Gestalt and its creative use of experiments, beginning counselors, and even seasoned practitioners, are likely to grasp at them without understanding their theoretical basis or providing clients with adequate rationale and preparation. This is more a weakness of the practitioner than of the theory, but counseling students and practitioners are wise to note this dynamic and make certain that they have adequate knowledge of any Gestalt technique before attempting to integrate it into a system of counseling.

Contributions

The Gestalt approach added to psychotherapy a unique kind of activity in the interaction between client and counselor, a dynamic that was refreshingly different from the analyst-as-a-blank-screen role. Counselors who feel attracted to this theory appreciate the creativity and here-and-now aspect of the approach. The Gestalt emphasis on emotional expression gave rise to many less comprehensive styles of therapy centered around the curative nature of emotional catharsis. As one practitioner related in a personal communication,

> More than any other theory, the aspect of contact truly brings a sense of aliveness to the counseling encounter for both counselor and client. The energy that is generated through the awareness of the moment is very powerful. I know that if I can be present and engage my client in the now, then therapy is fast moving and electric.

CURRENT STATUS

Gestalt therapy remains a vital theory of practice in the United States and abroad. Gestalt institutes continue to provide training and supervision in major cities such as New York; Cleveland, Ohio; and Los Angeles, California. In Mexico, many of the larger cities have training centers, and the University of Puebla offers a postgraduate specialty program in Gestalt therapy. Gestalt therapy has also sustained a following in Europe, South America, and Australia. Four journals, *The International Gestalt Journal,* the *Gestalt Review,* the *British Gestalt Journal,* and the *Gestalt Journal of Australia and New Zealand* provide interested parties with articles devoted exclusively to theoretical, practical, and research issues pertaining to Gestalt theory.

SUMMARY

Gestalt theory, although often credited to Fritz Perls, owes its existence and development to a number of individuals. Without Fritz and Laura Perls, Paul Goodman, Ralph Hefferline, Erving and Miriam Polster, and many others, the full figure of Gestalt would be fragmented and not whole. Gestalt theory is a humanistic-experiential therapy in which clients move toward greater awareness and maturity through authentic contact with oneself and one's environment. The therapeutic relationship provides an important form of that contact. Through Gestalt therapy, clients experience, in the here and now, aspects of their true selves of which they were previously unaware, and they learn how to continue enhancing awareness of self and ever-arising needs, how to experience closure through completion of the need-fulfillment cycle, and how to move toward the wholeness of who they are and have the potential to be.

RECOMMENDED RESOURCES

Books

Brownell, P. (Ed.). (2008). *Handbook for theory, research, and practice in Gestalt therapy.* Newcastle, United Kingdom: Cambridge Scholars Publishing. This volume, with chapters authored and coauthored by many current practitioners of Gestalt and researchers in psychotherapy, focuses primarily on, and provides an up-to-date synthesis of, research on Gestalt therapy.

Korb, M. P., Gorrell, J., & Van De Riet, V. (2002). *Gestalt therapy: Practice and theory* (2nd ed.). New York, NY: Pergamon. This text provides good theoretical information paired with practical examples and applications. Students find this text a good introduction to Gestalt work.

Perls, F., Hefferline, R. F., & Goodman, P. (1951). *Gestalt therapy: Excitement and growth in the human personality.* New York, NY: Crown. This is the seminal and, many commentators say, definitive work on Gestalt therapy. It reads like many primary source materials, very dense, yet packed with good theoretical material.

Woldt, A. S., & Toman, S. M. (Eds.). (2005). *Gestalt therapy: History, theory and practice.* Newbury, CA: Sage. This is a newer book and brings Gestalt theory up-to-date while retaining the important historical information.

Audiovisuals

Gestalt Experiential Training is dated by copyright standards (1984) but timeless in its excellent presentation of the approach. In the first part, John Swanson conducts a Gestalt therapy session. In the second, he illustrates various Gestalt therapeutic concepts via excerpts from the session. Highly recommended. Downloadable excerpt, video, and manuals available at http://www.gestalt.org/GET/index.htm

Gestalt Therapy (2004). In this more recent production, Gordon Wheeler provides a discussion and a demonstration and demo debrief of the Gestalt approach. Available at http://www.apa.org/videos/4310703.html

Gestalt Therapy With Violet Oaklander: Child Therapy With the Experts Video (2002) is a quality video that demonstrates Gestalt therapy with a child client. The series also includes pre- and postsession discussion with the counselor. Contact the publisher, Allyn & Bacon and reference ISBN # 0-205-33699-X.

What's Behind the Empty Chair: Gestalt Therapy Theory and Methodology (2000) provides a unique overview of the Gestalt therapy process. It is conceptual, and students may be disappointed in its lack of practical demonstrations. Available at amazon.com.

Web Sites

http://www.aagt.org/ is the site for the Association for the Advancement of Gestalt Therapy. Not as much information as the next site listed, but appears to be a good resource for networking on an international level.

http://www.gestalt.org/ Gestalt Therapy Page: Excellent site covering historical, theoretical, and practical information and offering original transcripts of lectures by Fritz Perls and hard-to-find print resources.

REFERENCES

Amendt-Lyon, N. (2008). Gender differences in Gestalt therapy. *Gestalt review, 12,* 106–121.

Asay, T. P., & Lambert, M. J. (1999). The empirical case for the common factors in therapy: Quantitative findings. In M. A. Hubble, B. L. Duncan, & S. D. Miller (Eds.), *The heart and soul of change* (pp. 23–55). Washington, DC: American Psychological Association.

Beisser, A. (1970). The paradoxical theory of change. In J. Pagan & I. L. Shepherd (Eds.), *Gestalt therapy now* (pp. 47–69). New York, NY: Harper.

Bernard, J. M. (1986). Laura Perls: From ground to figure. *Journal of Counseling and Development, 64,* 367–373.

Brownell, P. (Ed.). (2008). *Handbook for theory, research, and practice in Gestalt therapy.* Newcastle, UK: Cambridge Scholars.

Ciornai, S. (1998). Gestalt therapy in Brazil. *Gestalt Review, 2,* 109–118.

Clarkson, P. (1989). *Gestalt counselling in action.* Thousand Oaks, CA: Sage.

Clemmons, M. C. (1997). *Getting beyond sobriety: Clinical approaches to long-term treatment.* San Francisco, CA: Jossey-Bass.

Elliot, R., Greenberg, L. S., & Lietaer, G. (2004). Research on experiential psychotherapies. In M. Lambert (Ed.), *Handbook of psychotherapy and behavior change* (5th ed.). New York, NY: Wiley.

Enns, C. (1987). Gestalt therapy and feminist therapy: A proposed integration. *Journal of Counseling and Development, 66,* 93–95.

Eynde, R. (1999). Buddhism and Gestalt. *The Gestalt Journal, 22,* 89–100.

Fagan, J., & Shepherd, I. L. (1970). *Gestalt therapy now.* New York, NY: Harper.

Ginger, S. (2008). Enriching Gestalt therapy through EMDR. *International Journal of Psychotherapy, 12,* 13–20.

Greenberg, L. S., Elliott, R., & Lietaer, G. (1994). Research on experiential psychotherapy. In A. E. Bergin & S. L. Garfield (Eds.), *Handbook of psychotherapy and behavior change* (4th ed., pp. 509–539). New York, NY: Wiley.

Greenwald, J. A. (1976). The ground rules in Gestalt therapy. In C. Hatcher & P. Himelstein (Eds.), *The handbook of Gestalt therapy* (pp. 268–280). New York, NY: Aronson.

Harman, R. (1995). Gestalt therapy as brief therapy. *Gestalt Journal, 18,* 77–85.

Houston, G. (2003). *Brief Gestalt therapy.* London, UK: Sage.

Humphrey, L. (1986). Laura Perls: A biographical sketch. *The Gestalt Journal, 9,* 5–11.

Husserl, E. (1965). *Phenomenology and the crisis of philosophy.* New York, NY: Harper and Row.

Keppner, J. (2008). Commentary II: Gender differences in Gestalt therapy. *Gestalt Review, 12,* 124–129.

Korb, M. P., Gorrell, J., & Van De Riet, V. (2002). *Gestalt therapy: Practice and theory* (2nd ed.). New York, NY: Pergamon.

Lewin, K. (1951). *Field theory in social science.* New York, NY: Harper & Row.

Munoz-Polit, M. (1998). Gestalt therapy in Mexico. *Gestalt Review, 2,* 119–122.

Naranjo, C. (1970). Present centeredness: Technique, prescription and ideal. In J. Fagan & I. L. Shepherd (Eds.), *Gestalt therapy now* (pp. 47–69). New York, NY: Harper.

O'Hara, M. (1998). Gestalt therapy as an emancipatory psychology for a transmodern world. *Gestalt Review, 2,* 154–168.

Olsson, J. (2008). Commentary III: Gender differences in Gestalt therapy. *Gestalt Review, 12,* 130–133.

Pack, M. (2008). 'Back from the edge of the world': Re-authoring a story of practice with stress and trauma using Gestalt and narrative approaches. *Journal of Systemic Therapies, 27,* 30–44.

Perls, F. (1947). *Ego, hunger and aggression.* Winchester, MA: Allen & Unwin.

Perls, F. S. (1969a). *Gestalt therapy verbatim.* Moab, UT: Real People.

Perls, F. S. (1969b). *In and out of the garbage pail.* Moab, UT: Real People.

Perls, F. (1970). Four lectures. In J. Fagan & I. L. Shepherd (Eds.), *Gestalt therapy now* (pp. 14–38). New York, NY: Harper.

Perls, F. (1973). *The Gestalt approach and eye witness to therapy.* Palo Alto, CA: Science & Behavior Books.

Perls, F., Hefferline, R. F., & Goodman, P. (1951). *Gestalt therapy: Excitement and growth in the human personality.* New York, NY: Crown.

Polster, M. (1976). Women in therapy: A Gestalt therapist's view. In C. Hatcher & P. Himelstein (Eds.), *The handbook of Gestalt therapy* (pp. 545–562). New York, NY: Aronson.

Saner, R. (1989). Culture bias of Gestalt therapy: Made-in-U.S.A. *The Gestalt Journal, 12,* 57–72.

Sartre, J. P. (1956). *Being and nothingness.* New York, NY: Philosophical Library.

Slemenson, M. (1998). Gestalt therapy in Argentina: Revolution, evolution, and contributions. *Gestalt Review, 2,* 123–130.

Smith, M. L., Glass, G. V., & Miller, T. I. (1980). *The benefits of psychotherapy.* Baltimore, MD: Johns Hopkins University Press.

Soderbergh, S.(1993). *King of the hill* [Motion picture]. United States: Wildwood.

Stevens, B. (1970). *Don't push the river.* Moab, UT: Real People.

Strumpfel, U. (2004). Research on Gestalt therapy. *International Gestalt Journal, 27,* 9–54.

Van Dusen, W. (1975). The phenomenology of a schizophrenic existence. In J. O. Stevens (Ed.), *Gestalt is* (pp. 95–115). Moab, UT: Real People.

Woldt, A. S., & Toman, S. M. (Eds.). (2005). *Gestalt therapy: History, theory and practice.* Newbury, CA: Sage.

Yontef, G. M. (1988). Assimilating diagnostic and psychoanalytic perspectives into Gestalt therapy. *Gestalt Journal, 11,* 5–32.

Yontef, G. M. (1995). Gestalt therapy. In A. S. Gurman & S. B. Messer (Eds.), *Essential psychotherapies* (pp. 261–303). New York, NY: Guilford.

Yontef, G. M. (1998). Dialogic Gestalt therapy. In L. S. Greenberg, J. C. Watson, & G. Lietaer (Eds.), *Handbook of experiential psychotherapy* (pp. 82–102). New York, NY: Guilford.

Yontef, G. M., & Jacobs, L. (2008). Gestalt therapy. In R. J. Corsini & D. Wedding (Eds.), *Current psychotherapies* (8th ed.). Belmont, CA: Thomson Brooks/Cole.

Zinker, J. (1977). *Creative process in Gestalt therapy.* New York, NY: Brunner/Mazel.

CHAPTER **8**

Behavioral Counseling

BACKGROUND OF THE THEORY

Historical Context and Founder's Biographical Overview

Since about 1900, behavior therapy has been developing as a result of the influence of not primarily one but, rather, several theorists, researchers, and clinicians. Contemporary behaviorists currently view behavior therapy as having evolved in three waves or generations (Hayes, 2004; Spiegler & Guevremont, 2009; Wilson, 2008; see Table 8.1 for an overview).

The first generation of behavior therapy developed over roughly the first half of the twentieth century (Spiegler & Guevremont, 2009). Ivan Pavlov, a Russian physiologist, discovered a learning process that came to be known as classical conditioning. This process fit with the views of John B. Watson, a Johns Hopkins University experimental psychologist. Watson "rejected mentalist concepts such as consciousness, thought, and imagery" (Spiegler & Guevremont, 2009, p. 18) and emphasized instead the objective study of observable behaviors. He came to be known as the father of behaviorism, the theory upon which behavior therapy and behavioral counseling were originally based (Spiegler & Guevremont, 2009). Other clinicians successfully applied the principles of classical conditioning to problems of phobias, bedwetting, and tension-related disorders. In particular, Joseph Wolpe (pronounced WOHLpee; A. Lazarus, personal communication, July 30, 2009) in South Africa developed systematic desensitization for the treatment of fear and anxiety, for which he is sometimes considered the founder of behavior therapy (Spiegler & Guevremont, 2009, p. 23). Meanwhile, Columbia University psychologist Edward Thorndike and Harvard University psychologist B. F. Skinner developed the principles of operant conditioning, the other learning process in traditional behavioral *learning theory*. Clinicians applied these principles to the treatment of targeted problem behaviors and to the development of token economies in psychiatric institutions (Spiegler & Guevremont, 2009).

Prior to 1950, despite developments in behaviorism, psychoanalysis dominated the field of psychotherapy. Only after World War II did clinicians criticize that psychoanalysis took too long to treat the masses of people who had been traumatized by the war and questioned its effectiveness. These conditions provided a fertile ground for the simultaneous, and apparently independent, development of behavior therapy in the United States, South Africa, and Great Britain during the 1950s (Spiegler & Guevremont, 2009). By the 1960s, first generation behaviorists had conducted a great deal of research substantiating the efficacy (from research under ideal controlled conditions), effectiveness (from research in real-world clinical settings), and efficiency of behavior therapy. Beginning in the 1960s, behaviorists developed numerous professional organizations and journals.

TABLE 8.1   Overview of Behavior Therapies

Generation	Emergence	Class	Focus	Assumptions	Causality	Goals re: Distress	Examples	Original Developer
First	(Precursors 1900–1940s) 1950s–1960s	Traditional Behavioral Therapy	Observable behaviors	People's behavior is the product of their environments; their behavior reflects the contingencies/ conditions in their environments.	Linear: Environmental contingencies (e) control overt behavior (ob). e → ob	Reduce distress by changing relevant environmental contingencies.	Based on classical conditioning theory: —Systematic desensitization for phobias —Bell-and-pad for enuresis; Based on operant conditioning theory —Reinforcement and extinction for targeted behaviors —Token economy for hospitalized psychiatric patients	Ivan Pavlov; John B. Watson; Mary Cover Jones; Edmund Jacobson; Joseph Wolpe; Hobart & Willie Mowrer; Edward L. Thorndike; B. F. Skinner; Teodoro Ayllon & Eric Haughton; Teodoro Ayllon & Nathan Azrin
Second	Mid-1960s–1980s	Cognitive-Behavioral Therapy	Observable behaviors + cognitive processes	People's behavior is the product of their cognitions about and actions	Reciprocal: Environmental contingencies (e) and	Reduce distress by changing relevant environmental	Based on social cognitive theory: —Multimodal therapy	Albert Bandura; Arnold Lazarus

Generation	Time	Type	Components	View of behavior	Relationship	Goal	Techniques	Key figures
				on the environment; their behavior reflects their perceptions of and effects on environmental contingencies.	both overt and covert behavior (ocb) affect each other. e ↔ ocb	contingencies and cognitions about contingencies and self.	—Skills training —Self-instruction training —Stress inoculation training	multiple / Donald Meichen-baum
							Based on cognitive theory (related to social learning theory): —Cognitive therapy	Aaron Beck (not a behaviorist)
Third	1990s–present	Mind-fulness Therapy	Observable behaviors + cognitive processes + nonjudg-mental awareness	People's behavior is the product of the extent to which they are nonjudgmentally aware of and identify/disidentify with cognitions and other experiences.	Interactive: non-judgmental awareness (a), environmental contingencies (e), and both overt and covert behavior (ocb) mutually affect each other. a / e ↔ ocb	When possible, reduce distress by changing relevant contingencies and cognitions; when not possible, accept distress as inevitable but not an obstacle to meaningful life.	—Acceptance and Commitment Therapy (ACT) —Dialectical Behavior Therapy for borderline personality disorder (DBT) —Mindfulness-Based Cognitive Therapy (MBCT)	Steven Hayes / Marsha Linehan / Zindel Siegal, John Teasdale, & Mark Williams

By the 1970s, "behavior therapy emerged as a major force in psychology" (Spiegler & Guevremont, 2009, p. 27).

The second generation of behavior therapy is sometimes termed *the cognitive revolution*. Probably the single greatest contribution to its emergence was the work of Stanford University psychologist Albert Bandura during the 1960s. He developed and researched social learning theory that included the principles of classical and operant conditioning as well as the social factors of modeling and imitation and the cognitive factors of thought, image, and expectation in learning (Bandura, 1977, 1986). He came to call his view *social cognitive theory* (Bandura & Davidson, 2003). Meanwhile, psychotherapists from a psychoanalytic rather than behavioral background developed cognitive approaches to psychotherapy, most notably Aaron Beck (see Chapter 9) and Albert Ellis (see Chapter 10). Beck credited Bandura's work as a contribution to the development of cognitive therapy, stating that some aspects of cognitive therapy "endorse" and are "related to" social learning theory (Beck & Weishaar, 2008, p. 271). These aspects include the idea that people acquire and maintain their thoughts through the same learning conditions that they acquire and maintain their observable behaviors. Mental health practitioners who incorporate first generation behavior therapy along with interventions based on social cognitive theory and/or cognitive approaches are called *cognitive-behavioral therapists*. Among the developments in the 1980s that enhanced the applicability and acceptance of behavior therapy was that "cognitive-behavioral therapy emerged as a major force" (Spiegler & Guevremont, 2009, p. 27).

In the 1990s, cognitive-behavioral therapists instigated the third generation of behavior therapies. In addition to first- and second-generation theory and technique, their approaches included an additional perspective reflecting five common themes (Spiegler & Guevremont, 2009): Some *pain is inevitable* in life; rather than resist it (a futile expenditure of energy) one can practice being *mindful* (nonjudgmentally aware) of whatever is occurring, thereby cultivating *acceptance* (especially of unavoidable pain) and, despite the pain, use one's energy to create and pursue a *life worth living according to one's most cherished values*. From this perspective, the therapeutic goal is not first order change—reducing or eliminating pain to live a more satisfying life but, rather, *second order change*—changing one's relationship to pain in order to live a more satisfying life (Spiegler & Guevremont, 2009, pp. 386–390). In short, third generation behavior therapists retain the first and second generation goal of helping their clients reduce or eliminate pain when possible, and they add the third generation goal of helping their clients accept pain and act purposefully despite it whenever necessary. Among the prominent third generation behavioral approaches are Steven Hayes's Acceptance and Commitment Therapy (ACT), Marsha Linehan's Dialectical Behavior Therapy (DBT), and Zindel Siegal, John Teasdale, and Mark Williams's Mindfulness-Based Cognitive Therapy (MBCT; Spiegler & Guevremont, 2009). Since they depart substantially from the approaches of the previous two generations, mindfulness approaches are controversial even within the field of behavior therapy (Spiegler & Guevremont, 2009; Wilson, 2008).

Philosophical Underpinnings

Each generation of behavior therapy represents an evolution in philosophical assumptions. We begin this section by tracing that evolution.

Western philosophical thought from the 1600s through the end of the twentieth century has been dominated by the assumptions of modernistic science (Richards &

Bergin, 1997). Like Freud and his psychoanalytic followers in the early twentieth century, Watson and other early behaviorists were committed to developing psychology as a science. In this pursuit, they subscribed to "naturalism, determinism, universalism, reductionism, atomism, materialism, mechanism, ethical relativism, ethical hedonism, classical realism, positivism, and empiricism" (Richards & Bergin, p. 24). Monte (1999) classified the philosophical underpinnings of what would now be considered first generation behaviorism into four main areas: empiricism, reductionism, determinism, and evolutionary continuity.

Empiricism is a focus on the observable, the measurable, and the testable. Early behaviorists endorsed a more rigorous positivism and empiricism than did the other leading theorists of the time, psychoanalysts. These behaviorists eschewed inferences about covert phenomena, those that could not be directly observed, such as not only the psychoanalytic inference of unconscious processes but also people's emotions and, especially, thoughts. Instead, they endorsed the view that an accurate formulation of the laws of behavior would result from considering only overt phenomena, that is, from testing hypotheses about what observable, measurable conditions made observable, measurable changes in observable, measurable behaviors.

Reductionism is the process of considering behavior in terms of its components. Rather than the holistic view that "the whole is *greater* than the sum of its parts," which implies that taking the whole apart would result in *losing* something essential, the reductionist or aggregate view is that "the whole *is* the sum of its parts," which implies that taking something apart is the way to *get at* what is essential. Thus, from this perspective, personality is the sum total of discrete behaviors, and a problem such as a person feeling awkward in social situations is addressed through components such as skills in how to select, physically approach, and make eye contact with a potential conversation partner and how to start, maintain, and end conversations.

Determinism is the view that all behavior has a direct physical cause and is never unpredictable or random. From an early behavioral perspective, a person's previous and, especially, current environmental conditions—reinforcement contingencies—determine that person's behavior.

Evolutionary continuity refers to the assumption that the behavior of nonhuman animals is fundamentally identical to, though less complex than, the behavior of humans (Watson, 1967). Thus, rat behavior is the same as human behavior in quality though not quantity. Operating from this premise, early behaviorists conducted experimental research on rat, pigeon, monkey, and other nonhuman animal behavior to discover principles they considered applicable to human behavior.

Second generation behavior theorists and therapists softened on most of these assumptions. Regarding empiricism, Bandura's work (1969, 1977, 1986, 1997) showed that people learned not only by direct experience with environmental contingencies but also vicariously—by observing and selectively imitating others' behavior. His work also showed that when objective measures of people's environmental conditions contradicted their reported covert thought processes (their *perceptions and expectations about* those conditions) their covert processes often predicted their behavior better than the objective measures did. Thus, cognitive behaviorists shifted from a strict focus on overt, objective phenomena to an additional focus on covert, subjective phenomena—people's perceptions and cognitions. However, they retained their commitment to empirical investigation of hypotheses about behavior and therapeutic interventions to change it.

Furthermore, Bandura (1997) found that people's reported thoughts about not only environmental conditions but also *themselves as agents in their environments* influenced their behavior. Chief among these thoughts was *perceived self-efficacy,* the belief that one can be successful at a task, which may or may not reflect one's objective chances of being successful. Concepts of self-efficacy and self-regulation conveyed that people not only are affected by, but also affect their environments. Thus, regarding determinism, the first-generation linear stance that people's environments cause their behaviors became a second-generation reciprocal stance that people's environments and their behaviors cause each other.

Regarding evolutionary continuity, the introduction of people's verbalized cognitions into behavioral theory and therapy clearly indicated the limits of generalizing principles of nonvocalizing animals' behavior to vocalizing human animals' behavior. Another distinguishing feature of humans is that they clearly have changed their environments in form and degree far beyond what other animals have. People's capacity for language and environmental modification indicates a qualitatively different level of cognition compared to other animals. Thus, people's cognitions constitute a unique factor to be considered and addressed in understanding and helping them change their behavior.

Third generation behavior therapy includes features that, from a historical behavioral perspective, are unique. Behavior theorists apparently have not yet addressed how the third generation relates philosophically to the first and second. To us, it appears to have the potential to soften the earlier philosophical assumptions even more.

However, contemporary behavior therapists Spiegler and Guevremont (2009, pp. 6–8) identified four themes and three characteristics that they believe define all three generations of behavior therapy, and Wilson (2008, p. 225) identified seven common characteristics; some of these two listings overlap. These themes or characteristics may represent the closest thing available to a philosophy that consistently underlies all three generations.

First, behavior therapists are *scientific,* being precise in defining what behaviors will be targeted for change and what the treatment goals will be, in assessing targeted behaviors throughout therapy, and in specifying treatment procedures and conducting empirical research on the efficacy, effectiveness, and efficiency of those procedures. Second, because people presumably acquire and maintain most of their problem behaviors the same way they acquire and maintain their nonproblem behaviors, behaviorists take a *depathologizing* stance, referring not to illnesses or disorders but to "problems in living" that call for the application of the same principles that are involved in nonproblem behaviors. Specifically and third, behavior therapists believe all behavior is at least affected by, if not completely the result of, *learning,* and they focus on helping clients learn how to reduce unwanted behaviors and increase desired behaviors. Fourth, both therapists and clients are *active*—doing rather than just talking—to achieve agreed upon treatment goals. Fifth, based on the belief that no matter how someone originally developed a behavior, one continues it because of current, not past, conditions (including current thoughts about the past and future), behavior therapy is primarily *present-focused.* Sixth, because each person's specific behaviors, learning history, and current maintaining conditions are unique, treatment is *individually tailored* to each client's unique needs. Seventh, treatment will almost certainly be characterized by strategies that involve *stepwise progression* from less challenging to more challenging tasks and by *treatment packages* consisting of more than one specific behavioral technique. Eighth, especially because of its specificity and focus on the present, treatment is likely to be *brief* compared to several other therapeutic approaches.

PERSONALITY DEVELOPMENT

As with philosophy, behavioral personality theorists have not yet incorporated third-wave approaches into one commonly recognized and embraced perspective. In addition, you can learn about Beck's cognitive therapy, and even a bit about MBCT, in Chapter 9. For both these reasons, the following discussion of personality development will tend to reflect what is unique to behavior therapy: first-generation and the social cognitive aspects of second-generation behavior therapy principles.

Nature of Humans

Function of the Psyche

From a first-generation behavioral perspective, each person at birth is like a *tabula rasa*, a blank slate, with no presumed innate motives, drives, needs, or tendencies except the capacity to learn behavior. Except for a few innate involuntary responses, each person learns all behavior as a result of environmental contingencies. Each person is a passive product of one's environment. Watson expressed this perspective in his claim that, hypothetically, he could employ behavioral learning principles to make any infant pursue any given vocation as an adult.

From a second-generation behavioral perspective, each person at birth has innate biologically based capacities and tendencies, such as the ability to "attend to environmental stimuli, interpret them, encode them, and selectively remember them" (Wilson, 2008, p. 236), and one actively employs these innate capacities when encountering environmental contingencies. In addition, because of innate factors, even very young children sometimes respond differentially to the same environmental contingencies. For example, in a recent study (Alexander, Wilcox, & Woods, 2009), infants as young as three months of age spent more time looking at toys associated with their own sex (boys the toy truck, girls the doll) indicating innate sex-linked toy preferences; presumably, a preferred toy would have greater reinforcement value. Thus, not merely the external environmental contingencies, but also innate psychological functions that play a role in a person's response to environmental contingencies include attention, interpretation, memory, and preference, determine a person's behavior.

Structure of the Psyche

First generation behaviorists viewed personality as a person's *behavioral repertoire*—the sum total of a person's voluntary and involuntary overt behaviors—observable actions. Second generation behaviorists added to this definition covert behaviors—cognitions. Each person is born with several involuntary responses, such as the orienting and sucking reflexes. The person learns all the rest of behavior—voluntary and involuntary, overt and covert.

Each personality includes behaviors that tend to be consistent across environmental conditions that generalize from one environmental situation to another, as well as those that are unique to specific environmental conditions and that involve discrimination between one situation and another. For example, in social situations, Gale was typically quiet—a consistent behavior pattern; also, no one has ever seen Gale dance in public, but occasionally, when she was alone, she danced expressively around the room—a discriminate behavior pattern. Her capacities to be withdrawn and inexpressive as well as active and expressive are both part of her "personality."

Role of the Environment

Aside from several inborn reflexes, a person's behavior consists of the voluntary and involuntary responses one learned as a result of experience in the environment. Learning is defined as *a relatively permanent, observable change in behavior that results from experience or practice.* "Relatively permanent" means the person tends to repeat the response (action or cognition) under the same environmental conditions, or antecedents. "Observable change" means that the person is responding differently in some measurable way than one used to respond; it includes doing either more or less of a particular response than previously. "Results from experience or practice" means that an environmental event that preceded or followed the previous occurrence of the response apparently caused the subsequent occurrence of the behavior. This definition is sometimes characterized as "ABC" (antecedent, behavior, consequence; Spiegler & Guevremont, 2009), reflecting the notion that current behavior, whether action or cognition, is the result of the events that occurred before and after that behavior. Once again, as second generation behaviorists contend, the learning process is not purely mechanistic in that person factors of attention, memory, preference, and so forth do mediate it (Wilson, 2008).

A particular learning process corresponds to each category of behavior: voluntary and involuntary. A person learns voluntary behavior through operant conditioning and involuntary behavior through classical conditioning. The basic principle behind each of these forms of conditioning is that a person tends to repeat behavior that is reinforced and tends not to repeat behavior that is not reinforced. In a circular definition, reinforcement is any environmental contingency related to a response that is followed by an increase in the response (Spiegler & Guevremont, 2009, p. 120).

Operant Conditioning

The basic principle behind operant conditioning is that when a person makes a voluntary response of any kind, if it is followed fairly quickly by some form of reinforcement, the person is likely to make that response again under the same or similar environmental conditions. Phenomena that often serve as positive reinforcers include attention, praise, and money.

Before addressing what maintains or decreases the frequency of a voluntary behavior, we will first address how a voluntary behavior occurs for the very first time. Being voluntary, the behavior presumably is not inborn. Rather, a person emits a voluntary response initially through one of three processes.

Consider a person who is learning a new computer program. In *random or accidental* emission of a novel response, the person involved in one maneuver accidentally clicks something on the computer screen that is followed by some form of reinforcement. In *trial and error,* the person tries one maneuver and then another until one is found that is followed by reinforcement. In *imitation of a model,* the person does something new by following the instructions in the manual or following the example of someone who knows the program. Of these three phenomena, modeling through demonstration and prompting is most often involved in a process specific to operant conditioning called *shaping,* whereby a complex behavior is broken down into simpler components, and the person sequentially acquires and is reinforced for each component until the entire

TABLE 8.2   The Four Processes of Operant Conditioning

		To Have This Effect on the Frequency/Strength of a Voluntary Response	
		Increase	Decrease
Using a consequence that is	Pleasant	Positive reinforcement	Extinction
	Unpleasant	Negative reinforcement	Punishment

Source: Adapted from Holden, J. M., In D. C. Locke, J. E. Myers, & E. L. Herr (Eds.), *The Handbook of Counseling*, pp. 131–150, Sage, Thousand Oaks, CA, 2001.

complex behavior is learned. Anyone who has successfully taught a child to tie her shoes is familiar with this process ("First take this shoelace in this hand like this, and this other shoelace in this other hand like this ...").

From a behavioral perspective, once a voluntary response occurs for the first time, the subsequent presence, absence, strength, and frequency of the response is the result of one of the four processes listed in Table 8.2.

In positive reinforcement, a person in a particular environmental circumstance emits a voluntary response; fairly quickly some reinforcement occurs in the environment that the person notices, values, and considers a consequence of the response; and thereafter the likelihood increases that the person under the same or similar environmental conditions will emit a similar voluntary response. For example, in a classroom a teacher asks a question (specific environmental condition), a child answers the question (voluntary response), and the teacher praises the child (reinforcement), after which the child is more likely to offer answers to the teacher's future questions.

In the case of positive reinforcement, a person emits some observable voluntary response because in the past it has been followed by *something the person finds pleasurable*. In the case of negative reinforcement, the person emits an observable voluntary response because it has been followed by the *avoidance of something the person finds aversive*. For example, as midnight of April 15 approaches in the United States, many citizens converge on their local post offices to get their U.S. tax returns into the mail (voluntary response), not because they will get anything like attention, praise, or a financial bonus (positive reinforcement), but because they will avoid losing money as a result of a late charge penalty (negative reinforcement). They are increasing "mailing" behavior in order to avoid a fine.

One factor in reinforcement is the *schedule of reinforcement. Continuous reinforcement* occurs each time the person emits a particular response. *Intermittent reinforcement* occurs only some of the time the person emits the response. *Regular intermittent reinforcement* occurs either at the end of a particular *interval* of time in which the person emitted the response (such as monthly payment of salary) or in *ratio* to a specific number of times the person emitted the response (such as a salesperson getting a bonus for every 10th sale). *Irregular intermittent reinforcement* occurs at irregular times, a schedule of reinforcement that results in the most frequent and long-lasting response pattern—as seen with gambling, in which the gambler persists in gambling despite winning only some of the time and usually unpredictably.

Another interesting phenomenon regarding reinforcement is illustrated by *superstitions*. Consider Pat who, dressing for a ballgame, puts on a particular pair of new socks, then proceeds to win the game. True to the irregular intermittent reinforcement principles of operant conditioning, Pat insists upon wearing those same socks for each subsequent game that season, even though Pat does not always win. Pat's superstition illustrates not only the endurance of voluntary responses that are intermittently reinforced, but also the fact that there need not be an *actual* causal connection between a response and a reinforcement for the response to be reinforced. Pat herself may agree that she cannot imagine how wearing these socks could possibly have an influence over the outcome of her ballgame, yet she will continue to insist upon wearing those socks for each game because wearing them has been followed, even if irregularly, by victory. True to second generation behavioral theory, her *perception* of a possible causal connection between her sock-wearing response and game outcome is the critical factor in reinforcement.

REINFORCEMENT AND YOU

Take a sheet of paper and divide it vertically down the middle. In the left column, list 20 voluntary behaviors you do. Be sure to list only things you do, not things you do not do or purposely avoid doing. Begin with routine daily behaviors, but be sure to include any behaviors you wish you did not do or would like to stop doing. Then in the right column, list positive or negative reinforcement(s) you have experienced following each behavior, even if only once. See the examples below. If you are unable to identify a reinforcement for any behavior, consult with someone else to try to identify at least one. Here are some examples:

Voluntary behavior	Reinforcement (positive [+] or negative [–])
Brush teeth	Look attractive (+), avoid rejection from others due to bad breath (–), avoid pain of cavities and dentist's drill (–)
Wear "in" clothes	Approval from others (+), avoid criticism and rejection (–)
Eat too much chocolate	Tastes good (+); supposedly releases endorphins, the "natural opiates" in the human body (+)

After completing your list, ask yourself, "What is the role of reinforcement in my life? Did I list any behavior for which I couldn't identify a reinforcer?"

Once a person has emitted a voluntary response, then that response likely will reduce or discontinue if the response either is no longer followed by positive reinforcement (extinction) or is followed by an aversive event (punishment). Certain secondary responses accompany each of these processes.

For example, in extinction, a person will likely display some or all of the reactions associated with grief identified by Elisabeth Kübler-Ross (1997): denial (persist in the behavior temporarily), anger, bargaining (increase the behavior or associated behaviors in an attempt to regain the reinforcement), and acceptance (discontinuation of the behavior). Consider Francis, who talks on the phone while his sister often interrupts him. Employing extinction, Francis ignores his sister's interruptions, that is, withdraws the reinforcement of attention. Francis can expect his sister to persist at first, to show signs of anger, and actually to increase the interruptions before she finally stops interrupting. (However, if he even once responds to an interruption, he probably will have inadvertently, powerfully reinforced interruption through intermittent reinforcement! In extinction, consistency is vital.) Finally, even after his sister discontinues interrupting, at some future time she may suddenly interrupt again, a phenomenon termed *spontaneous recovery*; if Francis continues to ignore her, she will again discontinue interrupting.

Whereas a person experiencing extinction tends to reduce gradually the behavior being extinguished, the person experiencing punishment, as in the case where a behavior is followed by physical pain, tends to discontinue the behavior rapidly. The recipient of punishment may exhibit some of the same behaviors associated with extinction, such as intense anger. In addition, the recipient may display anxiety and may subsequently avoid the punisher. The recipient may imitate punishing behavior in relationships with others, such as the abused child who becomes abusive to others. For these reasons, punishment is usually a behaviorist's strategy of last resort (Spiegler & Guevremont, 2009).

EXTINCTION, PUNISHMENT, AND YOU

Take a sheet of paper and divide it vertically down the middle. In the left column, list 20 voluntary behaviors you have done but no longer do, or could do but do not do. Include both behaviors you are glad you don't do and those you regret you don't do. Then in the right column, list examples of extinction (discontinued pleasurable event following the behavior), and label them "e," and/or punishment (aversive event following the behavior), and label them "p." See the examples below. If you are unable to identify an absent reinforcement or present aversive consequence for any behavior, consult with someone else to try to identify at least one. Here are some examples:

Decreased/discontinued voluntary behavior	Extinction (e) or punishment (p)
Stopped calling Fred	He stopped returning my calls. (e)
Reduced dessert eating from everyday to weekends only	I was gaining weight. (p)
Reduced how often I work out all day	I was losing sleep and feeling crabby from getting up early to work out. (p)

Then ask yourself, "What is the role of extinction and punishment in my life? Did I list any behavior for which I couldn't identify an extinction or a punishment?"

A final disadvantage accompanies both extinction and punishment. Both serve only to decrease a response rather than to increase the likelihood of an alternative, more desirable response.

Extinction and punishment are pervasive in human experience. Due to less distressing or destructive side effects, behavioral therapists prefer extinction to punishment. In addition, whenever possible, prompting (instructing someone in a more desirable response) and then reinforcing that response is considered preferable to extinction or punishment of the undesirable response. For example, which of the following alternatives seems to be the most constructive way to teach a child to wait her turn in conversation: slapping or humiliating her when she interrupts (punishment); ignoring her when she interrupts (extinction); warning her that if she interrupts again, she will be sent to her room until she is prepared to wait for a pause before speaking during conversation (negative reinforcement; she can avoid the confinement by waiting for a pause in conversation); or telling her it's polite to wait for a pause before beginning to speak and then giving an approving nod when she does so (prompting and positive reinforcement)? Behaviorists would generally agree that the foregoing examples are provided in an order from least to most constructive.

Once an operant response is learned, two other processes come into play. A person may *generalize* a response from the original situation in which the response was learned to a new, similar situation. Going back to the computer program example, the person learning the new program might transfer a learned response from an old program to the new one. In *discrimination,* when the person makes a generalized response, she is not reinforced in the new situation, so she ends up continuing the response in the old situation but not the new, thus discriminating between old and new.

From a behavioral perspective, the processes described in the foregoing discussion of operant conditioning can explain the part of personality comprised of voluntary responses. As a person interacts with the environment, the person acquires new voluntary responses and discontinues others. As the person's perception of environmental conditions either continues or changes, so too will the person's voluntary responses that result from those conditions either continue or change.

Classical Conditioning

Each person is born with a host of involuntary responses to innately eliciting environmental conditions. For example, assuming normal salivary capabilities, a newborn infant will salivate the first time milk enters his or her mouth. Classical conditioning is the process by which we learn to emit those involuntary responses to new, rather than only to the innately eliciting environmental conditions.

Ivan Pavlov is credited with the discovery of classical conditioning while studying digestion in dogs. The reader can have a similar experience by following the instructions in the box.

CLASSICAL CONDITIONING

Read the following imagery, then take about 3 minutes to close your eyes and engage in the imagery.

> Imagine you are at home in your kitchen, standing at a counter. On the counter is a freshly cut, juicy half grapefruit and an empty juice glass. Squeeze the grapefruit juice into the glass. Rotate the grapefruit and squeeze again until most of the juice is squeezed out into the glass. Pick up the glass and take some of the grapefruit juice in your mouth, not swallowing but rather holding it in your mouth. Swish it around. When you feel compelled to swallow, do so. Take another mouthful and repeat the holding and, finally, swallowing.

Now close your eyes and, in as much detail as possible, imagine this scenario. When you open your eyes, answer the following questions:

- Did you find that you salivated during the imagery, or even as you read the description of the imagery?
- If so, are you aware you were salivating to mental pictures or words in the complete absence of any actual grapefruit?

- Do you believe you were born salivating to the mental image or written description of drinking grapefruit juice? If you had never experienced anything like a grapefruit, and on your first sight of a grapefruit, before actually tasting or smelling it, had imagined squeezing it and drinking its juice, do you think you would have salivated to that imagery?
- Did you intend to salivate or did it happen involuntarily?
- Try vividly imaging the scene again and not salivating. How successful were you?
- If you were to engage in an experiment, and every day for a week you were to spend 10 minutes imagining a grapefruit, and during that week you were to have no exposure to any citrus fruit, what do you think would happen to your amount of salivation throughout the week?

Classical conditioning begins with an unconditioned (unlearned) stimulus, in this case the grapefruit juice on one's tongue, and an unconditioned (unlearned/innate involuntary) response, in this case salivation. If someone put a drop of grapefruit juice in a newborn's mouth, the baby would salivate (though, of course, it's actually not appropriate to feed newborns anything but breast milk or formula). A third ingredient in the classical conditioning process is a conditioned (learned) stimulus, in this case the sight of a grapefruit. If someone merely showed a grapefruit to a child who had never seen or tasted anything like it, the child would not salivate. But if the child saw or imagined the grapefruit (conditioned stimulus) while the grapefruit juice was on one's tongue (unconditioned stimulus), he would salivate (unconditioned response). And after a few experiences like this, the child would salivate to the sight of the grapefruit alone (conditioned response). Salivation to the sight alone of the grapefruit has been learned/conditioned: Whereas he did not formerly salivate to the sight of a grapefruit, now, as a result of experience, he does. And salivation is an involuntary response to the sight of the grapefruit; it occurs without the child's intention, and it occurs even if the child intends that he not salivate; it is an involuntary learned response.

Some of the same processes that apply to operant conditioning also apply to classical conditioning. In *generalization,* a person responds to a similar conditioned stimulus. For example, if the child was originally conditioned with the sight of a yellow grapefruit, he will also salivate to the sight of a pink grapefruit. In *extinction,* the conditioned response dies out if the person is exposed repeatedly to the conditioned stimulus without the unconditioned stimulus. For example, salivation to the sight or mental image of a grapefruit would reduce and discontinue if one were repeatedly to see or imagine a grapefruit without actually tasting any grapefruit juice during that time. The process of *discrimination* involves repeated exposure to one conditioned stimulus along with the unconditioned stimulus, and repeated exposure to a similar conditioned stimulus without the unconditioned stimulus, resulting in a conditioned response to the one conditioned stimulus but not to the other. In the example, it would involve the person repeatedly tasting grapefruit juice while seeing yellow grapefruit but never while seeing pink grapefruit, resulting in salivation to the sight or image of the former but not the latter.

From a behavioral perspective, the processes described in the foregoing discussion of classical conditioning can explain the part of personality comprised of involuntary responses. As a person interacts with the environment, the person acquires involuntary responses to various conditioned stimuli. As the environmental conditions either continue or change, so too will the person's learned involuntary responses that result from those conditions either continue or change. Probably the involuntary responses most salient to the counseling process are emotional responses, most notably fear and anxiety but also others.

The Relationship of Operant and Classical Conditioning

As stated previously, a person's personality consists of the voluntary behaviors the person learned from operant conditioning and the involuntary behaviors he learned from classical conditioning. However, almost any observable behavior the person emits has both operant and classical conditioning components. Thus, one's personality is actually a complex interconnection of these two processes.

Consider the man who is sitting under a tree daydreaming, and who reports he was thinking about his beloved. A behaviorist would speculate the following. In the actual presence of his beloved (unconditioned stimulus), he feels physical pleasure as the hormone phenylethylamine (Love & Robinson, 1994) is released in his body (unconditioned response). Any reminder of his beloved (conditioned stimulus) results in similar hormone release and pleasurable feelings (conditioned response). So he takes himself to a quiet spot under a tree (voluntary response) where he can purposely indulge in thoughts of her (voluntary response, conditioned stimulus) and feel pleasure (conditioned response, reinforcement). Note that the pleasure he feels is both *a classically conditioned response to the thoughts* and *an operant reinforcement for purposely engaging in the thoughts* and purposely placing himself in a situation where he has a good chance of being able to think about her prolongedly without being interrupted.

Consider the person with a phobia of water that began after the person nearly drowned. Water (conditioned stimulus) has become associated with drowning (unconditioned stimulus; asphyxiation naturally evokes panic response), which elicited fear (unconditioned response). Now, at the sight or even thought of a body of water, the person becomes fearful (conditioned response). Since going near water (voluntary response, conditioned stimulus) results in powerfully aversive feelings of fear (conditioned response, punishment), the person avoids being in proximity to bodies of water. Notice that the fear is both *a conditioned response to the sight or thought of bodies of water* and a *punishment for going within sight of bodies of water*, which is why he reduces the voluntary behavior of putting himself within eyeshot of bodies of water.

Typically, people reportedly experience involuntary responses as unpleasant (fear, anxiety, sadness), pleasurable (excitement, happiness), or neutral (salivation). These feelings are involuntary, classically unconditioned and conditioned responses and also serve as reinforcers and punishers of people's voluntary behavior. From the viewpoint of first and second generation behaviorist, a person's personality is the sum total and the complex interaction of these processes of operant and classical conditioning—of both overt responses (actions, physiological responses) and covert responses (cognitions: verbal thoughts and picture images) as that interaction has developed based on the individual's unique innate characteristics (for example, preferences) and learning history (what conditioning events have occurred, both those instigated by external conditions and those instigated by the person). Again, third generation behaviorists have not yet put forth a unified theory of how mindfulness functions in this personality equation—a topic to which we return toward the end of this chapter.

Impact of the Familial Versus Extrafamilial Environments

Behaviorists acknowledge the important role the family plays in personality development. A child's first conditioning experiences occur in the family environment and can have a relatively lasting effect on the child's behavior. Therefore, parents can have a direct impact on the shaping and reinforcement of both behaviors that are personally and socially constructive and/or destructive for the child. Many studies have indicated that behavioral training of the parents can lead to the improvement of many childhood problems such as conduct disorder (Graziano & Diament, 1992), fire setting (Kolko, 1983), and phobias and fears (D'Amico & Friedman, 1997; Friedman & Campbell, 1992).

However, the behaviorist view is that one's current environment primarily maintains one's current behavior. Therefore, behaviorists emphasize the contingencies in one's present environment as crucial in understanding and influencing one's present behavior.

Model of Mental Health

Unhealthy Functioning

From a behavioral perspective, all learned behavior, both functional and dysfunctional, is acquired through the same two processes of classical and operant conditioning. As we said earlier, a person's dysfunctional behavior is viewed from the behavioral perspective not as pathology but as "problems in living." These problems arise from the failure to learn needed behaviors or from having learned behaviors that, in one's current environment, result in a lack of reinforcement or in punishment.

Healthy Functioning

Noteworthy sources on behaviorism, such as Nezu, Nezu, and Lombardo (2004), Spiegler and Guevremont (2009), and Wilson (2008), have not included a description of a model of optimal human functioning. However, the behavioral notion of optimal functioning one would gain from a survey of behavioral journals would include painlessness and competency to solve problems and obtain reinforcement (Jones, 1988, p. 165). John Gottman (1999) found that marital relationship health was related to the ratio of pleasant to unpleasant interactions, such as compliments, good-natured kidding around, and helpful, cooperative actions versus criticism, indifference, and opposition. If the ratio was at least 5:1, the couple continued in a lasting relationship in which each spouse reportedly felt happy; if it fell below 1:1, divorce was virtually inevitable; and if it was between, the relationship became unhappy for at least one of the spouses and became less stable. An interesting possibility is that this ratio might apply to all relationships—and to the reinforcement versus extinction/punishment ratio for individuals.

In recent years, cognitive behaviorists have alluded to "well-being" with reference to cognitions and behaviors that promote physical health as well as subjective experiences such as "optimism, hope, greater self-esteem and self-confidence ... and a strong sense of overall life satisfaction" (Nezu, Nezu, & D'Zurilla, 2006, p. 3; see also D'Zurilla & Nezu, 2006) through effectively solving life's inevitable problems. Some practitioners have even referred to "central or core messages common across most religions and spiritual philosophies ... messages of love, acceptance, compassion, forgiveness, a commitment to help others, a sense of purpose, surrender to a higher power, and the experience of personal peace" (Nezu & Nezu, 2004, p. 6). Though these descriptors are not universally or even widely endorsed in the behavioral literature as together comprising mental health, when combined with principles of reinforcement/extinction/punishment ratios, they appear to be compatible with a third generation behavioral perspective and, thus, could serve as a model of the direction in which behavior therapists help clients to move.

THE PERSONALITY CHANGE PROCESS

From a behavioral perspective, personality change involves learning: the decrease/disappearance and/or the appearance/increase of specific overt responses—along with related covert responses. Learning occurs when someone either encounters or implements changing environmental contingencies.

Behavioral counseling, therefore, is the implementation of *corrective learning experiences* (Wilson, 2008) aimed directly at specific overt responses and often associated covert responses. Through modification of responses that one has learned and/or acquisition of new responses in areas of previous learning deficits, one's response repertoire (one's personality) changes.

Client's Role

Regarding motivation to seek counseling, people presumably seek counseling to increase pleasurable conditions and decrease aversive conditions in their lives. Thus, a behavioral counselor expects that a client comes into counseling reporting one's own unique variation on the theme of a relative dearth of reinforcement and/or spate of punishment in some aspect(s) of one's life.

Regarding capacity to change, a client's responses are maintained entirely by current conditions—actual environmental contingencies and/or one's interpretations of those contingencies. To the extent that these factors can be changed, the client's behavior will change. Thus the client is theoretically capable of extensive personality change, though the focused attention on only the problematic aspects of one's personality means that client and counselor will target only selected aspects of personality for change.

Regarding the focus and process of therapy, behaviorists differ in their views of the client's role. For example, Wilson (2008) stated explicitly that "the client controls what; the therapist controls how" (p. 238). That is, the client determines exactly *what* outcomes one desires in terms of specific changes, with the counselor assuming a "following" role; and the counselor—the expert in behavior change strategies—determines how they will proceed to achieve that outcome, with the client assuming a following role. However, Spiegler and Guevremont (2009) spoke in more moderate terms of the client and counselor taking "the major responsibility" (p. 52) respective to goals and strategies. Counselor input is needed in establishing goals because clients tend to speak in generalities and need help pinpointing specific targets of change (p. 52). Client input is needed in establishing change strategies because more than one strategy often exists for addressing a particular problem, and even when only one strategy exists, it should be adapted to each unique client; in both cases client preferences play a decisive role (Swift & Callahan, 2009).

Once the team has agreed on treatment goals and a treatment plan, the client's role is to be active in carrying out each subsequent step of the plan, regularly reporting to the counselor one's progress and pitfalls and seeking counselor input on how to overcome the pitfalls. Client resistance, that is, a client not carrying out one or more steps of an agreed upon treatment plan, is understood like any other response or lack of response: in terms of maintaining conditions. For example, a client will continue to make undesirable responses if those responses continue to be reinforced; a client seeking to quit smoking might cheat and smoke a cigarette in a situation in which the clear and immediate pleasurable sensation of smoking outweighs the obscure, long-term pleasure of feeling generally better. Conversely, a client will tend not to make a desirable response heretofore absent from the client's response repertoire for any of a number of possible reasons, such as if that response has not been adequately modeled for the client and/or if the response is too complex for the client to enact all at once. For example, a client learning to say "no" to unreasonable requests rather than say nothing and acquiesce is likely to need to rehearse several skills before real-life implementation, such as speaking in I-language, remaining firm but nice through the "broken record" technique, and reminding oneself of the cognition that a good friendship will not dissolve in the face of occasional refusal of requests. Until the client has developed each of these skills—and some other(s) that the client–counselor team might discover they had overlooked in their original assessment of the problem—the client is likely to resist saying no in real life.

Counselor's Role

The foundation of the behavioral counselor's role is to communicate genuine empathy and positive regard for the client. Behavioral counselors affirm both research and clinical experience indicating that these qualities are necessary for successful collaboration and positive therapeutic outcome. Wilson (2008) used several words to describe the behavioral counselor's demeanor in relationship with the client: "concerned—a problem solver and a coping model ... open ... genuine, and ... disclosing" (p. 238). The counselor employs positive reinforcement; typically this includes paying attention to the client, acknowledging the client's existing strengths (adaptive responses), acknowledging and/ or praising any client changes that constitute progress toward the counseling goals, and being generally pleasant and patient. The skillful counselor is also observant of what each client finds uniquely reinforcing and adapts accordingly; for example, some clients respond well to joking and kidding, whereas others respond well to businesslike seriousness. However, behavioral counselors consider that these relationship factors are not sufficient for positive outcome. They affirm both research and clinical experience that therapeutic techniques play a crucial role.

Thus, in Wilson's (2008) words, the behavioral counselor's role is also to ask, "What is causing [the client] to behave in this way right now, and what can [the client and I] do right now to change that behavior?" (p. 229). In so doing, the counselor focuses less on the client's past and more on the present and the future. Although acknowledging and addressing client emotion, the counselor considers behaviors and cognitions to be the appropriate foci of change. Through an aggregate view of personality, the counselor focuses on specific behaviors and cognitions rather than the whole of the client's personality.

The effective behavioral counselor can listen to client complaints and translate them into goals consisting of measurable changes in specific behavior. This process involves detailed analysis of the target behaviors and the application of classical and/or operant conditioning principles and/or social cognitive principles to the plan for behavioral change. The behavioral counselor is active and directive in guiding the client through new learning experiences.

In addition to using positive reinforcement, when confrontation seems necessary to the achievement of counseling goals, the behavioral counselor addresses client discrepancies with the client and challenges the client to tackle somewhat difficult behaviors or procedures in the service of goal achievement. Here, Gottman's (1999) finding of the 5:1 ratio that characterizes satisfying marriages may be applicable also to the therapeutic relationship. The counselor who maximizes the use of positive reinforcement along with the occasional use of well-timed confrontation increases the likelihood that clients will experience both the counseling process and progress as reinforcing and thus will persevere to a positive outcome.

Stages and Techniques

Assessment

Relationship building and assessment occur simultaneously. Behavioral counselors make extensive use of a variety of assessment methods. From most to least frequently used, these include interview by the counselor, direct self-report inventory completed by the client, self-recording of the frequency of and conditions surrounding a particular behavior, checklist or rating scale of the client's behavior completed by someone other than the client, systematic observation of the client by the counselor in a natural and/or a simulated setting, role playing during counseling, and physiological measurement in the counseling or a naturalistic setting (Spiegler & Guevremont, 2009, p. 78).

Spiegler and Guevremont (2009) identified several ways in which behavioral assessment differs from traditional assessment. One difference is a narrow focus on target behaviors rather than a global assessment of personality, based on the behavioral belief that specific behaviors can be singled out for lasting change. Another difference is identifying the current antecedents and consequences that maintain target behaviors rather than seeking to determine the past origin of the behaviors.

The behavioral counselor's goal in the initial assessment is to devise an individualized treatment plan that specifies observable behavioral goals and the means to achieve them. The counselor also uses assessment throughout the counseling process to ascertain progress toward the goals and to use new or additional information to adjust the treatment plan as needed. Client termination—or recontracting for a new set of goals—is clearly indicated when the client achieves the original treatment plan goals.

Change Strategies

First and second generation behavioral change strategies are numerous. First generation strategies can be categorized as based primarily on either operant or classical conditioning principles. In most cases, behavioral counselors assist clients to acquire new responses in the actual counseling setting. In addition, through assignment of homework, they encourage clients to practice newly acquired responses and to acquire further new responses in the environment outside the counseling setting. Although behaviorists typically work with individuals, they also work with couples (Jacobson, 1998), families, and groups.

Strategies Based Primarily on Operant Conditioning   In the following discussion, we address the best known of the numerous operant change strategies described in the clinical behavioral literature. We first describe strategies to help a client increase desirable, adaptive voluntary behavior, then describe strategies designed to decrease unwanted voluntary behavior.

In *modeling*, someone demonstrates a voluntary behavior that the client reports wanting to do but never having done and the client imitates the model. Models can include other people from the client's life, the counselor, actors in film or on television, or even a videotape of the client rehearsing the behavior oneself. Behavioral counselors use modeling extensively to help people develop social skills and assertiveness (Jakubowski & Lange, 1978; Lange & Jakubowski, 1976). A related use is when a client avoids an adaptive behavior, reportedly because of anticipating a negative consequence; if the client observes a model performing the behavior without negative consequences, the client is more likely to imitate the model's behavior.

In *behavioral rehearsal/role-play,* a client first practices a new voluntary behavior in the counseling setting and then performs it outside of counseling. The counselor often provides prompting (suggestions and directions to help the client refine the behavior) and responds to each improvement with positive reinforcement. If the behavior is too complicated for the client to perform all at once, the counselor and client use shaping to break the behavior down into "smaller response pieces" and then to progress systematically from simpler to more complex or from easier to more difficult pieces, mastering each piece before moving on to the next.

The previous strategy, termed *graded task assignment,* is one of a group of strategies termed *guided discovery* that cognitive counselors (see Chapter 10) have developed employing the principles of operant conditioning. Two additional strategies can be helpful when a client, particularly one exhibiting depression or anxiety, reports low motivation to engage in adaptive behavior. In *activity scheduling,* the counselor and client chart the client's daily activities for the near future. This structure helps the client with depression stay active rather than lapse into inactivity and helps the client with anxiety not avoid activities the client reportedly fears, on the assumption that once the client engages in the activities, the client likely will experience reinforcement. In *mastery and pleasure rating,* the client rates anticipated pleasure prior to engaging in adaptive behavior and actual pleasure after engaging in it. For the client whose preactivity scores are consistently lower than postactivity scores, this exercise helps the client learn to take action despite negative anticipation and to reap the reinforcement.

To decrease or eliminate unwanted voluntary behavior, behaviorists prefer some strategies over others. In *reinforcement of a competing response,* whenever the client begins to engage in the undesired behavior, he stops and engages instead in another behavior that he finds reinforcing and that makes it impossible for him to engage in the undesirable behavior. Cognitive counselors employ diversion as a form of competing response. This strategy is exemplified by the Alcoholics Anonymous (AA) practice that when one feels the urge to drink, one instead calls one's sponsor or attends an AA meeting; one cannot easily drink while talking under these circumstances, and the social interaction provides reinforcement such as attention, sympathy, and/or amusement.

When reinforcement of a competing response is not a viable option for reducing an unwanted behavior, the counselor next explores the possibility of using *extinction.* Only if extinction also is not viable does the counselor consider *punishment.* The client who can self-administer punishment might snap a rubber band on her wrist each time she begins to engage in the undesired behavior. For example, a client with trichotillomania who wants to stop pulling out her hair snaps the rubber band on her wrist each time she finds herself reaching for her hair.

Counselors also use therapeutic punishment with children with developmental disabilities whose self-injurious behaviors threaten their health or their very lives (Spiegler & Guevremont, 2009). Using a mild electric shock comparable in discomfort to having a rubber band snapped on one's wrist, the counselor delivers the shock whenever the child engages in the self-injurious behavior, and the child quickly stops the dangerous behavior.

In most cases, counselors can use less aversive strategies to help clients decrease unwanted behavior. In *time out,* whenever the client engages in an unwanted behavior, she separates herself—or is separated—from any possible source of positive reinforcement for a previously specified brief period of time. In *response cost,* the client loses something valuable each time he enacts an undesired behavior (punishment); conversely, when he engages in activities other than the undesired behavior for a specified period of time, he not only avoids losing the valuable thing (negative reinforcement), but actually regains it (positive reinforcement). An example of response cost is the client who wants to stop fighting with classmates. She gives her school counselor six $5 bills and the name and address of the person she most dislikes. Each time the client reports or is reported having fought, her counselor arranges for the disliked person to receive one of the $5 bills. In addition, if the client engages actively in any of a variety of nonfighting behaviors (such as working cooperatively on a project, playing amicably with others), first for a few days and then for increasing periods of time, at the end of each time period not only does the disliked person not receive one of the $5 bills, but the client herself gets one back.

In structured settings, such as schools and psychiatric hospitals, counselors employ operant conditioning principles in the form of *token economies*. When students or patients behave in appropriate ways, the staff reinforces those behaviors with tokens that can be traded for goods or privileges. When students or patients behave inappropriately, the staff, whenever possible, usesless aversive strategies, such as time out, to decrease the inappropriate behaviors. Due to the potential for staff abuse of power, ethical (professional) and moral (personal) guidelines are vital components of token economy programs (Spiegler & Guevremont, 2009).

Strategies Based Primarily on Classical Conditioning   For client problems involving anxiety, the behaviorist employs a category of interventions involving *exposure and response prevention*. The client comes to counseling distressed and/or debilitated by classically conditioned anxiety. Anxiety also has likely influenced the client's operant responses. In the case of a phobia, the client likely reduced engaging in circumstances in which the anxiety might occur, because being in those circumstances was accompanied by the noxious feeling of anxiety—punishment; people with social phobias usually reduced participation in social situations. In the case of obsessive-compulsive disorder (OCD), the client likely increased certain responses because they enabled the client ultimately to escape from the noxious feeling of anxiety—negative reinforcement; people with OCD typically spend inordinate amounts of time in repetitive behaviors. The operant response of avoidance or repetition has, itself, become a problem.

To remedy the problematic operant behavior, the counselor must help the client reduce the anxiety from which the client is seeking to escape. The counselor achieves that reduction by arranging for the client to expose herself repeatedly or prolongedly to the anxiety-producing situation (conditioned stimulus) while preventing herself from making the anxiety-reducing operant response. Assuming that the unconditioned stimulus (frightening circumstance) that elicited the unconditioned response (anxiety) is consistently absent, according to the principle of extinction, the client's repeated exposure to the conditioned stimulus without the unconditioned stimulus will result in reduction of the conditioned response (anxiety).

One procedure of this type is *systematic desensitization*. Counselor and client first collaborate to develop a stimulus hierarchy: a list of anxiety-eliciting conditioned stimuli, ranked from least anxiety-producing to most anxiety-producing. For example, a person with a water phobia might list hearing the sound of the ocean, seeing the ocean, putting a toe in the ocean, and immersing one's entire body in the ocean. The counselor–client team then puts the list aside while the client learns relaxation, most typically progressive relaxation of the muscle groups of the body by progressively tensing and relaxing them, starting at the head and ending at the toes. When, after practice, the client can quickly become relaxed, the client encounters the least frightening stimulus from the list, either in imagery or in vivo—in real life. The client uses a subjective units of distress (SUDs) scale from 1 (low) to 10 (high) to report his level of anxiety. If the client reports a SUDs of 3 or more, the counselor guides him temporarily to relax; if a SUDs of 1 or 2, the counselor guides him to refocus on the anxiety-eliciting stimulus. With each repetition of this process, the client remains more and more relaxed in the real or imagined presence of the conditioned stimulus, at which point the next stimulus on the hierarchy is encountered. Ultimately, the client can focus on the previously most frightening stimulus and remain relaxed, reporting a SUDs of 1 or 2. Applying the constructs of classical conditioning, the person encountering the conditioned stimulus now elicits the conditioned response of relaxation rather than anxiety. Interestingly, some research indicates that the effectiveness of systematic desensitization rests on the client's growing cognitions of self-efficacy as much as or more than straightforward classical conditioning principles.

A second procedure involving exposure and response prevention that a counselor might use is flooding. The client, instead of gradually encountering increasingly frightening conditioned stimuli, attends a long counseling session during which he continuously encounters the most frightening conditioned stimulus. Again, with prolonged exposure to the conditioned stimulus without the unconditioned stimulus (something that innately elicits the unconditioned response of anxiety), the conditioned response of anxiety extinguishes. Of the two exposure and response prevention procedures, counselors and clients tend to favor systematic desensitization (Spiegler & Guevremont, 2009), a kinder, gentler approach to the extinction of anxiety.

The counselor and client also can employ classical conditioning principles in the treatment of enuresis. People (usually children) with bedwetting typically have no trouble controlling urination while they are awake. The problem seems to be that while deeply asleep, they do not awaken to the rather subtle sensations of a full bladder and urination. Awakening is an involuntary response to an unconditioned stimulus such as a loud noise. If a loud noise, such as an alarm, could somehow occur just as the client experiences the sensation of a full bladder (conditioned stimulus) and begins to wet the bed, then within a few nights, when the client has the sensation of a full bladder (conditioned stimulus), he would awaken (conditioned response). To achieve this, the counselor and client arrange for the client to sleep on a special mattress pad or use a small device attached to pajamas that, at the moment of contact with moisture, sets off an alarm. Once the client is conditioned to awaken to the sensation of a full bladder, he goes to the bathroom, an operant response that had been conditioned prior to the intervention.

Another counseling intervention based on classical conditioning principles is *aversion therapy*. When a client has had a strong positive association to something, the pursuit of which has brought about negative consequences for the client, aversion therapy can help the client develop a negative association to that thing. Examples include addictions to alcohol, cigarettes, food, and illicit substances as well as sexual attraction to things or people that are deemed illegal or inappropriate. In aversion therapy, the counselor and client use an aversive unconditioned stimulus and unconditioned response, such as discomfort from a painful but not harmful electric shock, or nausea induced by the counselor graphically describing something disgusting or by injection of the drug apomorphine. The client experiences the aversive reaction (unconditioned response) while she attends to the conditioned stimulus, for example, seeing, smelling, and smoking a cigarette, or imagining the sexual object. After repeated trials, whenever she encounters the conditioned stimulus in reality or imagery, she experiences the aversive reaction (conditioned response). According to the operant principle of negative reinforcement, the client then avoids the conditioned stimulus so she can escape from the aversive response.

For a number of reasons, counselors and clients use aversion therapy only when the client faces potentially catastrophic negative consequences from the original condition and when other less distressing change interventions are not viable or have failed. The use of aversion therapy in certain cases, such as clients seeking to change their homosexual orientation to heterosexual, has generated a great deal of controversy in the professional mental health literature (Donaldson, 1998); we return to this topic later in this chapter.

Treatment Packages and Manuals   Most behavioral treatment packages include strategies from more than one of the four primary treatment modalities: classical-conditioning-based, operant-conditioning-based, social-cognitive-based, and mindfulness-based. In addition, a major trend in behavioral therapy is the use of *treatment manuals* that detail procedures for a counselor to follow each session in the treatment of specific disorders (Spiegler & Guevremont, 2009, p. 73). Such protocols increase the likelihood that a therapist will pursue the therapeutic strategies that research has shown to be efficacious and/or effective, yet they do not preclude the therapist from individualizing treatment as is usually appropriate.

Termination and Follow-Up   When objective measures indicate that the client has reached the original agreed upon therapeutic goals, the team either terminates counseling or recontracts for additional goals. Termination is rarely abrupt; rather, counseling fades out with one or more follow-up sessions and/or phone contacts at increasingly longer intervals between contacts. If relapse occurs, the team will hold one or more booster sessions followed again by fading follow-up.

Addressing Client Resistance   From the behavioral perspective, client reluctance or unwillingness to use a change strategy offered by the counselor is the result of the same dynamics as any other behavior. For example, the client who wants a romantic relationship but feels anxious and lacks social skills to develop such a relationship will probably resist being thrown into an intense social situation without preparation. The preparation might include the counselor modeling and prompting the client in the nonverbal and verbal skills of social conversation, systematic desensitization of anxiety while imagining making conversation, and graded task assignment accompanied by a behavioral record that enables the client to observe a general trend of success.

Behavioral counselors avoid resistance through a number of strategies. One is agreement with the client on the goals of counseling and explanation of how each change strategy has the potential to bring the client closer to those goals. Another is the maintenance of a balance of more pleasant to fewer aversive contingencies throughout the counseling process.

CONTRIBUTIONS AND LIMITATIONS

Interface With Recent Developments in the Mental Health Field

The Nature–Nurture Question

Behaviorists have come a long way since Watson's claim that people are entirely the products of their environments. Authors of respected sources in behavior therapy, such as Spiegler and Guevremont (2009) and Wilson (2008) have stated explicitly that biological factors predispose people to particular behavior and, specifically, to particular problems in living.

However, even beyond linear arguments that environment determines behavior or that biology sets limits within which environment determines behavior, recent research has illustrated how truly interactive biology and environment are. Bandura (1997) demonstrated how high self-efficacy could impact physiological (genetic) processes and control or improve neurotransmitter secretions, stress levels, and blood pressure. Neuroimaging of the brain has demonstrated that in the successful treatment of some problems, such as OCD, cognitive-behavioral therapy (CBT) and medication both change brain functioning in the same way that corresponds to improvement in the condition; thus, environment and behavior clearly influence biology. Refinement of clinical understanding of these interacting factors continues, as in a recent study in which neuroimaging enabled prediction of which clients with depression would benefit from CBT (Siegel, Carter, & Thase, 2006).

DSM–IV–TR *Diagnosis*

"Most behavior therapists … assign DSM-IV diagnoses" (Spiegler & Guevremont, 2009, p. 82), primarily because work settings and third-party reimbursers require it. Although "philosophically, diagnosis is antithetical to the fundamental premises of behavior therapy and behavioral assessment" (p. 82), if the therapist remains mindful of avoiding the pitfalls of diagnosis, it can serve a constructive role in a comprehensive and "detailed description of a client's unique problem and the antecedents and consequences that are maintaining it" (p. 82). Diagnosis also points a behavioral counselor to treatment protocols and manuals that describe empirically supported treatment approaches. Despite behaviorists' seemingly antidiagnosis stance, the diagnostic community seems very probehaviorist, in that diagnostic criteria—symptoms—are mostly behavioral in nature.

Pharmacotherapy

Regarding pharmacotherapy, again, behaviorists value the empirical literature that endorses the use of psychoactive medication in certain cases. However, "it is noteworthy that behavior therapy fares well in comparison to medication, which is the treatment most frequently employed for psychological disorders" (Spiegler & Guevremont, 2009, p. 473). Behaviorists are likely to use psychoactive medication only as a temporary assist in behavior therapy rather than as a long-term solution.

Managed Care and Brief Therapy

Behavior therapy is, by philosophy, a brief therapy aimed at changing specific, current behaviors. Despite an absence of established guidelines for length of treatment, most behavior therapy is short-term, though "therapy lasting from 25 to 50 sessions is commonplace … in excess of 100 sessions is relatively rare" (Wilson, 2008, p. 243). Norcross and Wogan (1983) reported that among theoretical approaches, behavioral therapists saw their clients less in both frequency and duration. Managed care has come increasingly to favor empirically supported therapies, and one need only peruse the list of such therapies to conclude that behavioral and cognitive-behavioral interventions strongly dominate the list. Therapists of other theoretical orientations have come to cite behavioral and cognitive-behavioral treatments in their documentation to managed care—hopefully, from our perspective, when their theories endorsed technical eclecticism and they could conceptualize the treatment in a way consistent with their guiding theory.

Technical Eclecticism

The term *technical eclecticism* was coined by Arnold Lazarus, originally a behavior therapist who remained true to behavioral theory yet adopted and adapted techniques from other psychotherapeutic approaches to develop his multimodal therapy (Lazarus, 1994, 2008). Lazarus apparently is not alone. According to Spiegler and Guevremont (2009), other behavior therapists, valuing empirical evidence as they do, have increasingly included validated nonbehavioral approaches in their psychotherapeutic repertoires. True to the spirit of theoretical purity and technical eclecticism, the authors challenged behavior therapists "to incorporate non-behavioral treatments without violating the fundamental behavioral approach, which would preserve the integrity of behavior therapy" (p. 501) and expressed hope but uncertainty that this challenge can be met.

Effectiveness of Psychotherapy

Spiegler and Guevremont (2009) asserted that "behavior therapy arguably has the broadest and strongest empirical base among psychotherapies" (p. 473). However, Wilson (2008) countered that

> Behavior therapy consists of a broad range of different strategies and techniques, some of which are differentially effective for different problems. Hence, it is difficult to evaluate some global entity called "behavior therapy." Instead, evaluation must be directed at specific methods applied to particular problems. (p. 251)

Wilson (2008) went on to describe "the most rigorous and complete evaluations of both the psychological and the pharmacological treatment of different clinical disorders" (p. 253) that the National Institute for Clinical Excellence (NICE) in the United Kingdom published in 2004. In this analysis, the empirical support for behavioral treatments typically received the highest of three possible ratings. Wilson (2008) and Spiegler and Guevremont (2009) cited how behavioral and cognitive-behavioral treatments dominate the American Psychological Association's (APA) list of empirically supported treatments.

However, Wilson (2008) pointed out that "overall evaluation of the *relative efficacy of behavior therapy versus other psychotherapies* is so far inconclusive" (p. 230, italics added). As we stated in Chapter 1, the best comparative analysis so far (that of the APA) is flawed in its exclusion from the analysis any approach that didn't involve a treatment manual. It is probably fairest to conclude that behavioral and cognitive-behavioral therapies have the strongest empirical support of any particular approaches but that their effectiveness relative to other therapies is not yet well established.

Diversity Issues

"Over the past 20 years, behavior therapists have become increasingly aware of the need to be responsive to *specific* issues of ethnic and cultural minorities" (Spiegler & Guevremont, 2009, p. 479). Whereas one source on behaviorism included the statement that "behavior therapy … has … been shown to be effective with diverse patient populations, including disadvantaged minority groups" (Wilson, 2008, p. 230), another stated that, with a few exceptions, research on "the efficacy and effectiveness of behavior therapies with culturally diverse clients … to date, has generally not been done" (Spiegler & Guevremont, 2009, p. 482).

Social cognitive theorists have addressed the role of culture in the phenomenon of self-efficacy: "Cultural context shapes how efficacy beliefs are developed, the purposes to which they are put, and the social arrangements through which they are best expressed" (Bandura, 1999, p. 185). Spiegler and Guevremont (2009, pp. 479–482) provided examples of cultural factors that might play into diverse clients' willingness to seek and/or participate in behavior therapy and that behavior therapists should consider in relating to, assessing, and treating diverse clients. They also critiqued the degree to which the behavioral literature so far has included attention and sensitivity to diversity issues, and they seemed to find it not yet commendable but improving. They also pointed out that so far, the proportion of diverse behavior therapists in training has lagged far behind the proportion of diverse members of the population.

Regarding sexual orientation in particular, at one time behavioral technology was at the center of a controversy: Should aversion therapy be used to attempt to alter a client's sexual orientation from homosexual to heterosexual? Within the past decade, every major mental health organization has taken a negative stand regarding practitioners' use of conversion or reparative therapies—those aimed at converting sexual orientation from homosexual to heterosexual or to "repairing" homosexual orientation. The stands these organizations have taken range from firm positions based on ethical and clinical issues, such as the premise widely endorsed among mental health organizations that homosexual orientation is not a mental disorder in need of repair, to more equivocal positions focused on an inadequate research basis for conversion and reparative therapies(APA, 2000, 2008). Conversely, cognitive therapists have produced videos demonstrating how to assist clients struggling with sexual orientation issues (see Chapter 9).

Regarding religion, Skinner (1953) discussed how religious agencies use "religious control" (p. 350) to reinforce, extinguish, and/or punish certain behaviors. For example, people who behave sinfully face the threat of being barred from the eternal pleasure of heaven and/or condemned to the eternal pain of hell, whereas those who behave virtuously face the promise of heaven and/or release from the threat of hell (Skinner, 1953, p. 353). Indeed, whether or not a religion includes an explicit concept of heaven or hell, each one prescribes behavior that presumably leads to more pleasurable outcomes and proscribes behavior that presumably leads to more painful outcomes.

Spiegler and Guevremont (2009, pp. 247–248) provided an example of the use of behavior therapy to "restore normal religiosity" (Ozer & Bandura, 1990). A client suffering from religious-related obsessions and compulsions participated in in vivo and imaginal flooding to significantly reduce his anxiety and increase his satisfying engagement in life. In their discussion, the authors commented on the value of consulting with clergy in such cases.

As early as 1979, behaviorists addressed the integration of spiritual and behavioral approaches to counseling (Elkins, Anchor, & Sandler, 1979; Miller & Martin, 1988). Martin and Booth (1999) outlined practical behavioral methods for enhancing one's spiritual development. Richards and Bergin (1997) showed how the assumptions of modernistic science that underlie traditional behaviorism contradict the assumptions underlying theistic religious (Western) traditions, though some assumptions may be compatible with the objective idealistic (Eastern) religious worldview (see Balodhi & Mishra, 1983; de Silva, 1984; Mikulas, 1981). This latter point addresses the extent to which the incorporation of mindfulness practices, which cognitive-behaviorists have adapted from their origins in Zen Buddhism, do and do not fit theoretically with first and second generation behaviorism.

Limitations

Regarding limitations of the behavioral approach to psychotherapy, former charges that its practitioners are impersonal and mechanistic have mostly been allayed. Furthermore, cognitive therapists have ventured outside the domain of waking actions and thoughts by developing a theoretically based and consistent approach to dreamwork (Hill, 1996; see Chapter 9).

However, behavioral theory does not account for the origin of transpersonal/ spiritual experiences that many people have found valuable, if not compelling, in enhancing the quality of their lives. For example, numerous researchers have documented the profound transformation that people usually manifest in the aftermath of near-death experiences (Holden, Greyson, & James, 2009); behavioral theory does not account for such experiences. This limitation could become clinically relevant, as in the case of an agnostic who undertook meditation for its stress-reducing benefits and apparently encountered psychic, reincarnation, and other spiritual phenomena, such that he became not merely a believer in, but a knower of God (Kaplan, 1996). Even third generation behaviorists have not offered theory to encompass such phenomena. Nevertheless, although behavior theory cannot incorporate the spiritual domain, a spiritual perspective can incorporate much of what is good and useful from behavior therapy.

However, in our view, the greatest limitation of behavior therapy is even more fundamental. One illustration of it is in a comparison of two editions of a prominent behavior therapy text. In their third edition, Spiegler and Guevremont (1998) noted that behaviorists were increasingly incorporating nonbehavioral treatments into their practices and said, "We believe that the challenge ... for behavior therapy is to incorporate nonbehavioral treatments without violating the fundamental behavioral approach, which would preserve the integrity of behavior therapy. Whether this can be done remains to be seen" (p. 501). A decade later in their fifth edition, they did not even address how psychotherapy integration posed a threat to behavior therapy's integrity. Apparently, their plea for theoretical consistency was not reinforced by behavior therapists' practices, so the authors discontinued the plea (extinction). Instead, they said, "there is no single definition of behavior therapy. Although some common points of view are shared by most behavior therapists, there is a wide diversity among those persons who call themselves behavior therapists" (2009, p. 494). They went on to provide a definition that included the features of applying findings from behavioral science, checking on therapeutic effectiveness by monitoring progress, being present focused, and helping clients improve self-control by expanding skills, abilities, and independence (pp. 494–495). These features, taken together, are hardly exclusive to behavior therapy. In addition, they do not represent a comprehensive theory of how people are innately endowed, develop, and change.

In our view, behavior therapy has lost its theoretical base. It has become a mix of techniques—not merely technically eclectic, nor even theoretically eclectic, but essentially atheoretical. This "anything empirically supported goes" mentality leaves a counselor adrift without a theoretical lifeboat when encountering problems for which empirically supported approaches do not exist—of which leading behaviorists acknowledge there are many (Spiegler & Guevremont, 2009; Wilson, 2008).

Contributions

More than any other approach, behavior therapy has contributed to psychotherapy by providing specific treatment procedures for many specific counseling issues. These include anxiety disorders, OCD, post-traumatic stress disorder, unipolar depression, eating and weight disorders, schizophrenia, childhood disorders, and problems in behavioral medicine such as medication compliance and the prevention and treatment of cardiovascular disease (Wilson, 2008). Indeed, under Spiegler and Guevremont's (2009) index entry

"Problems (treated by behavior therapy, representative examples)," over 100 client concerns are listed (p. 607).

Treatment manuals are another contribution of behavior therapy. Such manuals enable a therapist to apply the specific procedures that research has shown to be efficacious and/or effective for specific disorders, and behavior therapists' attention to the subjective dimension of each client enables the counselor to customize and individualize treatment to the client's particular needs and circumstances. Behaviorists' commitment to scientific research has sometimes yielded more than one successful approach to a given client complaint, thereby providing clients with choices that can enhance their commitment to and engagement in the therapy process and thereby increase the likelihood of positive outcome.

SUMMARY

Since its origin around 1950, behavior therapy reached prominence in the 1970s, at which time it became closely affiliated with cognitive therapy. Today, cognitive-behavior therapy is arguably the most influential approach to counseling and psychotherapy. Backed by the most empirical evidence for efficacy, effectiveness, and efficiency, it is the treatment modality preferred by managed care. Behavior therapy continues to develop as its proponents, believing strongly in empirical evidence, incorporate and integrate nonbehavioral strategies that have been shown to be effective.

RECOMMENDED RESOURCES

Books

Nezu, A. M., Nezu, C. M., & Lombardo, E. R. (2004). *Cognitive-behavioral case formulation and treatment design: A problem-solving approach.* New York, NY: Springer. The authors provide specific treatments for 11 of the most common issues for which clients seek counseling.

Spiegler, M. D., & Guevremont, D. C. (2009). *Contemporary behavior therapy* (5th ed.). Belmont, CA: Wadsworth. Clear and comprehensive with a minimum of contradictions.

Audiovisuals

American Psychological Association. (2003). *APA psychotherapy series III: Behavioral health and health counseling* [Motion pictures]. Washington, DC: Author. Discussion and demonstration of behavioral approaches to a variety of health concerns, including cardiac psychology, chronic illness, drug and alcohol abuse, exercise, headaches, pain management, sexual health, sleep and sleep disorders, smoking cessation, and weight loss. (Available at http://www.apa.org/videos/series3.html)

Krumboltz, J. (1998). *Cognitive-behavior therapy* [Motion picture]. In J. Carlson & D. Kjos, *Psychotherapy with the experts*. Boston, MA: Allyn & Bacon. Discussion and demonstration by a pioneer of behavior therapy. (Available through multiple internet sources.)

Lazarus, A. A. (1994). *Multimodal therapy* [Motion picture]. In T. Plott (Ed.), APA psychotherapy videotape series. Washington, DC: American Psychological Association. Discussion and demonstration by another pioneer of behaviorally based therapy. (Available through multiple internet sources.)

Web Sites

http://www.abct.org/dHome/ Association for Behavioral and Cognitive Therapies. Founded in 1966 as the Association for Advancement of Behavior Therapy, in 2005 the organization changed to its current name. It has served as the primary professional organization for behavior therapy (Spiegler & Guevremont, 2009). This site is a rich source of current print and video resources.

http://www.bfskinner.org/BFSkinner/Home.html B. F. Skinner Foundation. This site provides biographical information on B. F. Skinner, important publications, and a self-instruction program designed to teach the principles of behavior analysis.

http://psych.athabascau.ca/html/aupr/ba.shtml This site features articles, tutorials, and demonstrations on a variety of specific topics within behaviorism.

REFERENCES

Alexander, G. M., Wilcox, T., & Woods, R. (2009). Sex difference in infants' visual interest in toys. *Archives of Sexual Behavior, 38,* 427–433.

American Psychiatric Association. (2000). *Therapies focused on attempts to change sexual orientation (reparative or conversion therapies).* Retrieved from http://www.psych.org/Departments/EDU/Library/APAOfficialDocumentsandRelated/PositionStatements/200001a.aspx

American Psychological Association. (2008). *Answers to your questions: For a better understanding of sexual orientation and homosexuality.* Washington, DC: Author. Retrieved from http://www.apa.org/topics/sorientation.html#whatabout

Balodhi, J. P., & Mishra, H. (1983). Pantanjala yoga and behavior therapy. *Behavior Therapist, 6,* 196–197.

Bandura, A. (1969). *Principles of behavior modification.* New York, NY: Holt, Rinehart & Winston.

Bandura, A. (1977). *Social learning theory.* Englewood Cliffs, NJ: Prentice-Hall.

Bandura, A. (1986). *Social foundations of thought and action.* Englewood Cliffs, NJ: Prentice-Hall.

Bandura, A. (1997). *Self efficacy: The exercise of control.* New York, NY: Oxford.

Bandura, A. (1999). Social cognitive theory of personality. In L. A. Pervin & O. P. John (Eds.), *Handbook of personality: Theory and research* (2nd ed., pp. 154–196). New York, NY: Guilford.

Bandura, A. (Writer/Narrator), & Davidson, F. W. (2003). *Bandura's social cognitive theory: An introduction* [Motion picture]. San Luis Obispo, CA: Davidson Films. (Retrieved from http://www.davidsonfilmsstore.com/Bandura.htm)

Beck, A. T., & Weishaar, M. E. (2008). *Cognitive therapy.* In R. J. Corsini & D. Wedding (Eds.), *Current psychotherapies* (8th ed., pp. 263–294). Belmont, CA: Thomson Higher Education.

D'Amico, P. J., & Friedman, A. G. (1997). Parents as behavior change agents in the reduction of children's fears. In L. VandeCreek, S. Knapp, & T. L. Jackson (Eds.), *Innovations in clinical practice: A sourcebook* (Vol. 15, pp. 323–339). Sarasota, FL: Professional Resources Press.

De Silva, P. (1984). Buddhism and behaviour modification. *Behaviour Research and Therapy, 22,* 661–678.

Donaldson, S. M. (1998). Counselor bias in working with gay men and lesbians: A commentary on Barret and Barzan (1996). *Counseling and Values, 42*(2), 88–91.

D'Zurilla, T., & Nezu, A. M. (2006). *Problem-solving therapy: A positive approach to clinical intervention* (3rd ed.). New York, NY: Springer.

Elkins, D., Anchor, K. N., & Sandler, H. M. (1979). Relaxation training and prayer behavior as tension reduction techniques. *Behavioral Engineering, 5,* 81–87.

Friedman, A. G., & Campbell, T. A. (1992). Children's nighttime fears: A behavioral approach to assessment of treatment. In L. VandeCreek, S. Knapp, & T. L. Jackson (Eds.), *Innovations in clinical practice: A sourcebook* (Vol. 2, pp. 139–255). Sarasota, FL: Professional Resource Press.

Gottman, J. M. (1999). *The marriage clinic: A scientifically based marital therapy.* New York, NY: W. W. Norton.

Graziano, A. M., & Diament, D. M. (1992). Parent behavioral training: An examination of the paradigm. *Behavioral Modification, 16,* 3–38.

Hayes, S. C. (2004). Acceptance and commitment therapy, relational frame theory, and the third wave of behavioral and cognitive therapies. *Behavior Therapy, 35,* 639–666.

Hill, C. (1996). *Working with dreams in psychotherapy.* New York, NY: Guilford Press.

Holden, J. M. (2001). Cognitive-behavioral Counseling. In D. C. Locke, J. E. Myers, & I. L. Herr, *Handbook of counseling* (pp. 131–150). Thousand Oaks, CA: Sage.

Holden, J. M., Greyson, B., & James, D. (2009). *The handbook of near-death experiences: Thirty years of investigation.* Santa Barbara, CA: ABC-CLIO.

Jacobson, N. (1998). *Acceptance and change in couple therapy: A therapist's guide to transforming relationships.* New York, NY: W. W. Norton.

Jakubowski, P., & Lange, A. J. (1978). *The assertive option: Your rights and responsibilities.* Champaign, IL: Research Press.

Jones, S. L. (1988). A religious critique of behavior therapy. In W. R. Miller & J. E. Martin (Eds.), *Behavior therapy and religion: Integrating spiritual and behavioral approaches to change* (pp. 139–170). Newbury Park, CA: Sage.

Kaplan, M. (1996). Ambushed by spirituality. *Time.* Retrieved from http://www.time.com/time/magazine/article/0,9171,984754-1,00.html

Kolko, D. J. (1983). Multicomponent parental treatment of firesetting in a six year old boy. *Journal of Behavior Therapy and Experimental Psychiatry, 21,* 349–353.

Kübler-Ross, E. (1997). *On death and dying* (reprint ed.). New York, NY: Simon & Schuster.

Lange, A. J., & Jakubowski, P. (1976). *Responsible assertive behavior: Cognitive/behavioral procedures for trainers.* Champaign, IL: Research Press.

Lazarus, A. A. (2008). Multimodal therapy. In R. J. Corsini & D. Wedding (Eds.), *Current psychotherapies* (pp. 368–401). Belmont, CA: Thomson Brooks/Cole.

Love, P., & Robinson, J. (1994). *Hot monogamy.* New York, NY: Plume.

Martin, J. E., & Booth, J. (1999). Behavioral approaches to enhance spirituality. In W. R. Miller (Ed.), *Integrating spirituality into treatment: Resources for practitioners* (pp. 161–175). Washington, DC: American Psychological Association.

Mikulas, W. L. (1981). Buddhism and behavior modification. *Psychological Record, 31,* 331–342.

Miller, W. R., & Martin, J. E. (Eds.). (1988). *Behavior therapy and religion: Integrating spiritual and behavioral approaches to change.* Newbury Park, CA: Sage.

Monte, C. F. (1999). *Behind the mask: An introduction to the theories of personality* (6th ed.). New York, NY: Harcourt Brace.

Nezu, A. M., Nezu, C. M., & D'Zurilla, T. (2006). *Solving life's problems: A 5-step guide to enhanced well-being.* New York, NY: Springer.

Nezu, A. M., Nezu, C. M., & Lombardo, E. R. (2004). *Cognitive-behavioral case formulation and treatment design: A problem-solving approach.* New York, NY: Springer.

Nezu, C. M., & Nezu, A. M. (2004). *Awakening self-esteem: Spiritual and psychological techniques to enhance your well-being.* Oakland, CA: New Harbinger.

Norcross, J. C., & Wogan, M. (1983). American psychotherapists of diverse persuasions: Characteristics, theories, practices and clients. *Professional Psychology, 14,* 529–539.

Ozer, E. M., & Bandura, A. (1990). Mechanisms governing empowerment effects: A self-efficacy analysis. *Journal of Personality and Social Psychology, 58,* 472–486.

Richards, P. S., & Bergin, A. E. (1997). *A spiritual strategy for counseling and psychotherapy.* Washington, DC: American Psychological Association.

Siegel, G. J., Carter, C. S., & Thase, M. E. (2006). Use of fMRI to predict recovery from unipolar depression with cognitive behavior therapy. *American Journal of Psychiatry, 163,* 735–738.

Skinner, B. F. (1953). *Science and human behavior.* Toronto, Canada: Free Press.

Spiegler, M. D., & Guevremont, D. C. (1998). *Contemporary behavior therapy* (3rd ed.). Pacific Grove, CA: Brooks/Cole.

Spiegler, M. D., & Guevremont, D. C. (2009). *Contemporary behavior therapy* (5th ed.). Belmont, CA: Wadsworth.

Swift, J. K., & Callahan, J. L. (2009). The impact of client treatment preference on outcome: A meta-analysis. *Journal of Clinical Psychology, 65,* 368–381.

Watson, J. B. (1967). *Behavior: An introduction to comparative psychology.* New York, NY: Holt, Rinehart and Winston.

Wilson, G. T. (2008). Behavior therapy. In R. J. Corsini & D. Wedding (Eds.), *Current psychotherapies* (8th ed., pp. 223–262). Belmont, CA: Thomson Higher Education.

CHAPTER 9

Cognitive Counseling

REALITY TESTING

6/25/2009. I've been working the last few days on this chapter on Cognitive Counseling. Last night, in the middle of the night, I awoke abruptly from a vivid image of a big black spider on the white baseboard of my bedroom. From where I lay in bed, I had only to open my eyes to see that length of baseboard. And in the dimness of the room, with my night vision, I saw an uninterrupted length of white. No black spider. The spider had been a reasonable possibility—a credible hypothesis—but it had failed the empirical test of its actual existence. It had been only an image in my mind. Without moving another muscle, without the least elevation of my heart rate, I closed my eyes and went immediately back to sleep.—JMH

BACKGROUND OF THE THEORY

Historical Context

The two decades following World War II were characterized in the United States at large by both the optimism of economic expansion and the anxiety of the Cold War, with its issues of nuclear threat and deterrence. The relative social conservatism of the 1950s, with an emphasis on conformity, gave way to the social liberalism of the 1960s, with an emphasis on dissent. The trend was toward valuing independence of thought and having the intellectual integrity to "tell it like it is" (Landon, 1998).

The domain of clinical psychology also was undergoing change. By 1960 in the United States, behaviorism had begun to displace psychoanalysis, the Rogerian approach was gaining momentum, and the treatment of mental disorders with psychoactive medication was becoming well established. Nevertheless, many clinicians who had become dissatisfied with psychoanalysis also found behavioral approaches too narrow, the Rogerian approach too inefficient, and the medical approach too mechanistic to produce meaningful change.

In this social and professional climate of the early 1960s, Aaron Beck developed cognitive therapy. Through his own research and clinical experience, he detected client psychological dynamics that had gone unidentified by psychoanalysts, behaviorists, and Rogerians. Moving beyond his own psychoanalytic training and the growing trend to treat mental disorders with medication, Beck "called it as he saw it," thus pioneering a unique theory and therapy. He asserted that each of the various mental disorders was characterized by a particular cognitive pattern and that the most effective, efficient, and lasting psychotherapy involved intervention in that cognitive pattern. His autonomous stand in reference to the psychological "establishment," including a principled willingness to dissent and even rebel (Weishaar, 1993), paralleled the social tenor of the times. Despite his breaking free of the constraints of the prevailing psychological perspectives, his was not a rejecting stance but one that retained what was useful about those perspectives and also moved beyond them (Beck & Weishaar, 2008; J. S. Beck, 1995).

Often throughout history, two or more people have virtually simultaneously pursued the same innovations. It is as if the time is ripe for the innovation, and more than one individual picks up on the "readiness" for the development to emerge. Such was the case with the cognitive revolution of the 1970s in psychology, in which Beck was a key figure (Leahy, 1996; Weishaar, 1993). During the same period, Albert Ellis developed Rational Emotive Behavior Therapy also as a cognitively based psychological theory and therapy. However, the two theorists worked independently, unaware for some time of each other's work. Although both approaches are cognitively based, the similarity practically ends there, with the two innovators taking substantially divergent perspectives and approaches (Beck & Weishaar, 2008; Ellis, 2000).

Founder's Biographical Overview

Aaron Temkin Beck was born on July 18, 1921, the youngest child of Harry and Elizabeth Temkin Beck. The Beck parents were Jewish Russians who migrated to the United States as older teenagers in the early 1900s. The first and third of their five children died, to which Elizabeth responded with a year-long depression that mostly abated with Aaron's birth. Beck "smiles at the notion that he was able to cure his mother's depression at such an early age" (Weishaar, 1993, p. 9).

At age 7, Beck had an accident in which he broke his arm. A complication developed when the bone became infected and the infection spread to Beck's blood. He underwent a traumatic surgery, and for two months, he was expected to die. He survived, but he developed anxieties and phobias related to his health, and he missed so much school that he was held back in first grade. He concluded that he was stupid, but, disliking being behind his friends in school, he devised a plan to catch up. He ended up not only succeeding but actually exceeding his peers, an experience that contributed to his reformulated belief that he actually was quite bright and could "dig [himself] out" of a hole (Weishaar, 1993, p. 10).

Beck has attributed a lifelong "sensitivity to others' unexpected mood changes" (Weishaar, 1993, p. 11) to his childhood experiences with an emotionally erratic mother and an emotionally abusive first grade teacher. His interests during his school years included science and nature, Scouts, and editorship of his high school newspaper. In reference to Beck's middle name, a high school friend nicknamed him "Tim," the name that Beck's wife and close associates still call him (Weishaar, 1993, p. 11).

Beck graduated first in his high school class. After beginning the study of liberal arts at Brown University, and despite being discouraged by a dean from pursuing medical school because of a "quota system enforced against Jews" (Weishaar, 1993, p. 12), Beck pursued a premed curriculum and graduated magna cum laude in 1942.

Over the next decade, Beck became a psychiatrist—by circumstance more than purposeful design (Weishaar, 1993)—and a reluctant, but ultimately convinced, recruit to psychoanalysis. Wanting to correct the absence of research demonstrating the effectiveness of psychoanalysis, Beck embarked on studies of his own. However, rather than finding corroboration, he found substantial evidence that psychoanalytic concepts neither accurately predicted nor explained how depressed people actually functioned. Rather, he found that these patients had constructed a distorted view of reality that involved inaccurately pessimistic views of themselves and their capacity to achieve success and happiness. From these roots, Beck went on to create the innovation of cognitive therapy for the treatment of depression, anxiety, and numerous other mental disorders (Leahy, 1996; Weishaar, 1993). Since his groundbreaking book in 1976, *Cognitive Therapy and the Emotional Disorders,* he has gone on to publish prolifically. Most recent is his coauthored 2008 book, *Schizophrenia: Cognitive Theory, Research, and Therapy.*

While a student at Brown University, Beck met fellow student Phyllis Whitman; the two married in 1950. Her career developed from newspaper reporter to Pennsylvania Superior Court judge, and his career development culminated in a psychiatry professorship at the University of Pennsylvania and directorship of the Beck Institute in Pennsylvania. During that time, the Becks had four children, all of whom are now adults with children of their own. Their daughter, Judith, is a major figure in her own right in the field of cognitive therapy (J. S. Beck, 1995).

Throughout Beck's professional development, he achieved mastery over phobias and anxieties that he traced back to childhood traumas (Weishaar, 1993). In particular, he overcame a blood/injury phobia that originally caused him to faint at the sight of movie hospital scenes, as well as a public speaking phobia. Some of his students believe a residue of performance anxiety causes him to come across in filmed psychotherapy demonstrations as much less warm and engaging than he is with patients in real life.

The extent of Beck's mastery over these impediments makes Beck's professional honors even more impressive. In 1982, the prestigious journal *American Psychologist* conducted a survey of clinical and counseling psychologists who identified Aaron Beck as one of the "Ten Most Influential Psychotherapists." Today, he "is the only psychiatrist to have won the highest research awards from both the American Psychiatric and the American Psychological Associations" (Weishaar, 1993, p. 43). With his distinguishing head of white hair, his trademark bow tie, his intellectual autonomy, and his personal humility, Aaron Beck continues to solidify and further the cognitive revolution that currently dominates U.S. psychology and psychotherapy.

Philosophical Underpinnings

Beck and Weishaar (2008) named three conceptual foundations of cognitive therapy, two of which specifically involve philosophy. The first is phenomenology. This perspective dates back to the Greek Stoics who asserted that people can have erroneous isolated cognitive impressions as well as real knowledge in which a cognition is part of a larger, internally consistent system of cognitions and "is secure, firm and unchangeable by reason" (Baltzly, 2008). Beck and Weishaar (2008) also cited the eighteenth century philosopher Immanual Kant as having emphasized the importance of conscious subjective experience. It is noteworthy that both Aristotle and the Stoics advocated achieving happiness by the control and the annihilation, respectively, of irrational passions through the use of reason (see http://www.utm.edu/research/iep/s/stoicism.htm).

The second philosophically related "pillar" of cognitive therapy was "the structural theory and depth psychology of Kant and Freud, particularly Freud's concept of the hierarchical structuring of cognition into primary and secondary processes" (Beck & Weishaar, 2008, p. 267). As you may recall, primary process refers to the mind's unconscious, irrational workings, whereas secondary process refers to its conscious, rational workings. Elsewhere in this book, see Chapter 2 for a more in-depth refresher on these processes. As you read this chapter on cognitive counseling, you will see continuous references to these Stoic and Kantian concepts.

A third component in the foundation of Beck's cognitive therapy has been others' research and theory in cognitive psychology (Beck & Weishaar, 2008). An early contemporary influence was George Kelly (1955), who based his cognitive model of personality on the concept of psychological structures he called "personal constructs." Kelly's model never achieved widespread application in the United States, however, in part because of its incompatibility with prevailing views of the 1950s (Leahy, 1996). Other contributors to a shift in focus toward the cognitive domain were Magda Arnold (1960) and Richard Lazarus (1984), who pointed to the role of cognition in emotion and behavior; Albert Bandura (1977), who demonstrated how, even more than external environmental reinforcement conditions, internal cognitive processes such as expectancy and belief predicted behavior; structuralists like Piaget (1954, 1965, 1970) and Chomsky (1965) who demonstrated that, cross-culturally, people cognitively structure reality in predisposed and evolving ways (Leahy, 1996); Loftus (1980), who showed how cognitive structures, once formed, actually limit further cognitive innovation and change by modifying and directing attention and memory; and researchers who studied the factors to which people attributed their relative successes and failures and how those attributions influenced future success and failure (Leahy, 1996).

Yet another influence is empiricism and its brainchild, the scientific method. This influence has manifested in two ways. One is the use of hypothesis testing in the therapeutic process itself. Client and counselor first identify the cognitive conclusions about life to which the client has come, collaboratively consider them not as conclusions but as hypotheses, and then test the validity of those hypotheses. True to empirical procedure, the client who realizes the evidence does not support a hypothesis is likely to reject that hypothesis and replace it with an alternate one that the evidence better supports. The other influence of empiricism on cognitive therapy has been research on the method itself: both Beck's own research on psychotherapy that spawned cognitive therapy and the extensive research on cognitive therapy that Beck and others have conducted.

PERSONALITY DEVELOPMENT

Nature of Humans

Function of the Psyche

At birth, an infant is endowed with the motive to survive. Later in life, another "evolutionary derived objective" will emerge: to procreate (Beck, 1996, p. 5). To accomplish these aims, the individual must process information, that is, perceive, interpret, and remember experiences; draw conclusions, make predictions, and formulate goals. Information processing is, itself, informed innately by pleasurable feelings and emotions, which are crude indications that survival and procreation are being served, and painful feelings and emotions, which are crude indications that survival and procreation are not being served and which motivate corrective action.

To process information, the infant is endowed with a variety of functions: not only sensation and emotion, but also memory and the potential for increasingly voluntary motor movement. Crucial to information processing is cognition, the ability to form mental images—visual, auditory, tactile, olfactory, and gustatory memories and constructions—and verbal thoughts. The cognitive aspect of information processing in the infant is quite primitive, involving nonverbal images. As the child develops cognitively, information processing becomes increasingly verbal, abstract, and subject to a growing ability to reason, though always retaining its sensory basis. At every stage of development, "the processing of information is crucial for the survival of any organism" (Beck & Weishaar, 2008, p. 263).

From a cognitive counseling perspective, experience does not fall on a mind that, endowed with the above functions, is otherwise a metaphorical blank slate. Cognitive theorists acknowledge the extensive research indicating "different temperaments at birth. Temperamentally, [a person] may tend to be more frightened, active, outgoing, or shy.... [T]emperaments push [people] in certain directions" (Young, n.d.). Thus, even shortly after birth, two infants are likely to perceive the same event differently, and perceptual differences can become only more idiosyncratic as individuals move through their unique life experiences. In addition, related to research on innate temperament is research on innate genetic/neurochemical predisposition to psychopathology, which cognitive thera-pists also acknowledge.

However, despite their affirmation of innate predispositions, cognitive therapists do not see individuals as passive victims of inborn tendencies but as "active participants in their environment, judging and evaluating stimuli, interpreting events and sensations, and judg-ing their own responses" (Beck & Weishaar, 2008, p. 267). People actively create and seek to achieve goals they believe will serve both their vital and their less-than-vital interests.

It is, therefore, only natural that individuals become distressed when they experience a threat to their interests (Beck & Weishaar, 2008). From the infant who cries in hunger to the teen who fears failure on an exam to the adult who grieves the death of a spouse, psychological upset is tied to the perception of a threat to one's well-being—ultimately, one's ability to survive and procreate. The more vital to one's perceived well-being, the more intense the upset. In other words, the perception of threat to one's vital interests results in a more highly charged or energized response than does the perception of threat to less-than-vital interests. A newborn infant is more likely to become more emotionally upset from extreme hunger than from mild hunger. As adults, most people are more likely to become more intensely upset at the loss of a beloved spouse than at the loss of a valued piece of jewelry.

Structure of the Psyche

From a cognitive perspective, personality is the unique and relatively consistent and stable way a person has developed to maximize survival and procreation. The interre-lated structures of personality are *systems, schemas,* and *modes.* Whereas some cognitive therapists use the terms "schema" and "core belief" interchangeably (Riso & McBride, 2007, p. 7), others differentiate between them (Rasmussen, 2005). We follow the latter practice: To explain these structure or functions, we will expand on Rasmussen's analogy of the file folder (p. 23).

Systems and Schemas   Personality begins with five survival-supporting *systems:* cogni-tive, emotional, physiological, motivational, and behavioral. Think of these as five single-drawer file cabinets arranged in a semicircle. Within each file cabinet are *schemas:* file folders that pertain to the core phenomena of that system.

For example, within the *cognitive system* file cabinet are *cognitive schemas:* file fold-ers organized by themes such as one's beliefs about perceived danger, violation, loss, and gain in life. Jeffrey Young (2003a) has elaborated on these general themes and identified 18 specific schemas, each with a brief name representing the maladaptive end of the schema continuum, such as vulnerability to harm or illness (see Table 9.1). In our anal-ogy, these schemas are the file folders in the cognitive system file cabinet.

TABLE 9.1   Young's List of Cognitive Schemas

Schema domain	Early maladaptive schema	Description: The extent to which one perceives oneself to be
Disconnection and rejection	Abandonment/ instability	Prone to abandonment by significant others due to others' instability or proneness to death or to loss of their favor
	Mistrust/abuse	Prone to be exploited or hurt, either through others' purposeful intention or extreme neglect
	Emotional deprivation	Prone to have one's normal emotional needs for others' nurturance, empathy, and/or protection go unmet
	Defectiveness/shame	Essentially worthwhile to, and/or lovable by, oneself and others
	Social isolation/ alienation	Similar to, accepted by, and/or belonging to groups of others or society
Impaired autonomy and performance	Dependence/competence	Competent to manage one's everyday affairs substantially on one's own
	Vulnerability to harm/ illness	Prone to medical, emotional, or external catastrophes
	Enmeshment/ undeveloped self	Needing to receive and/or give excessive emotional closeness with one or more significant others—at the expense of individual and/or social development
	Failure	Prone to inadequacy and failure in areas of achievement such as school, career, or avocations
Impaired limits	Entitlement/grandiosity	Prone to feel superior to other people; entitled to special rights and privileges; or not bound by the rules of reciprocity that guide normal social interaction
	Insufficient self-control/ self-discipline	Unwilling or unable to manage one's emotions in order to achieve goals or responsibly coexist with others
Other-directedness	Subjugation	Prone to feel coerced to suppress one's needs and/or emotions in favor of others'
	Self-sacrifice	Prone to voluntarily deny one's own needs and desires in favor of others'
	Approval- or recognition-seeking	Prone to base one's esteem on others' evaluations rather than one's own

TABLE 9.1   Young's List of Cognitive Schemas (Continued)

Schema domain	Early maladaptive schema	Description: The extent to which one perceives oneself to be
Overvigilence and inhibition	Negativity/pessimism	Prone to negative outcomes in life
	Unrelenting standards	Prone to one's own or others' criticism if one does not meet very high standards of behavior or achievement
	Punitiveness	Entitled or obligated to punish oneself and/or others harshly for their mistakes

Source: Adapted from Young, J. (2003a) *Early maladaptive schemas and schema domains.* Retrieved from http://www.schematherapy.com/id73.htm

Despite the maladaptive terminology, the schema file folder label actually represents a continuum. For example, in the case of vulnerability to harm or illness, the core belief is one of danger: At one extreme is the belief that catastrophe is imminent and that one cannot prevent it or must take extreme measures to prevent it (Young, 2003a), and at the other extreme is that catastrophe rarely if ever occurs because one is usually capable of preventing it or, if it does occur, one can likely manage it. Theoretically, each person, based on innate predisposition and life experiences, has formed a specific *core belief* that could be located somewhere on that continuum. The core belief represents a person's particular range of belief and typical position point on the continuum. So, from a cognitive perspective, everyone has a vulnerability-to-harm-or-illness schema theme file representing a continuum of *potential* belief, and everyone has one's own unique *core belief*—a specific range and typical point on that continuum—that makes up the *actual contents* of the file. For example, within the *vulnerability* cognitive schema file, one person might hold the core belief that catastrophe is often to always imminent (range) and typically believe that it is quite imminent (typical point), whereas another might believe catastrophe is rarely to never imminent (range) and typically believe it is not imminent (typical point). Those core belief file contents include not only the range and typical position on the continuum but also all the word thoughts and mental images associated with that position. The core belief file contents also include the application of the continuum position to numerous life circumstances; in the case of vulnerability, for example, one's core belief may apply not only to germs in one's home, workplace, and other settings, but also to the threat of pandemic. Together, a person's 18 cognitive schema files and their specific core belief contents (continuum range and typical position, word and image associations, and numerous applications) comprise the individual's cognitive system file cabinet: one's system of beliefs about self, the world—the physical and social environment, and the future.

The *emotional system* file cabinet contains file folders organized around core emotions, such as anxiety, anger, sadness, and happiness. Again, each person has a collection of *emotional schema* file folders, each representing a potential continuum of emotional intensity. Each file folder contains the individual's unique, specific *core emotions*: the range and typical intensity with which one experiences that emotion. For example, within the *fear* emotional schema file, one person's core emotion might range from feeling mild to extreme fear with a typical position of quite fearful, whereas another person ranges from completely calm to moderately fearful with a typical position of calm. Together, a person's several emotional schema files and their specific core emotion contents comprise the individual's emotional system file cabinet.

Physiological schemas refer to the core ways that the body's autonomic, motor, and sensory systems are energized. Motivational schemas are the core impulses: to escape or avoid, to attack, to grieve, or to seek and approach. Behavioral schemas are core actions, including shaking, scowling, crying, and smiling. Again, for each schema type, each person has a collection of schema file folders containing the individual's unique, specific *core physiology, motivation,* or *behavior* with range and typical expression.

In addition to the five survival-supporting systems, each infant also is born with the potential to develop a *conscious control system.* You'll probably understand this system best by first understanding how the other five systems interact in modes.

Modes Perhaps you have noticed the parallel construction of the examples in discussion of the five survival-supporting systems: The cognitive perception of danger is accompanied by the emotion of fear, charged physiology of fast heart rate and tense muscles, the motive to escape or avoid, and the behavior of shaking. Together, this combination of core phenomena from schema file folders within each system file cabinet comprises the *anxiety mode*; see Figure 9.1. This is one of several *major modes*, subpersonality structures characterized by intense core phenomena. Examples of other major modes are

- *Anger mode* in which the cognitive perception of having been violated in some way is accompanied by the emotion of anger, charged physiology, the

FIGURE 9.1 Anxiety mode.

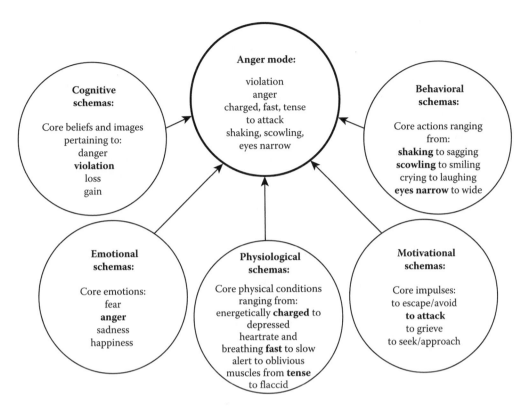

FIGURE 9.2   Anger mode.

motive to attack, and the behaviors of shaking, scowling, and narrowed eyes (see Figure 9.2);

- *Sadness mode* in which the cognitive perception of loss is accompanied by the emotion and physiology of sadness, slowed physiology, the urge to grieve, and, typically, the actual behavior of crying (see Figure 9.3); and
- *Joy mode* in which the perception of gain is accompanied by the emotion and physiology of happiness, charged physiology, the urge to seek and approach, and the behaviors of smiling, laughing, and wide eyes (see Figure 9.4).

Notice that in each case, it is as if schemas from each file drawer are "color coded" such that those files tend to "get pulled" together: maybe the schema files related to anxiety mode are colored yellow (thinking of danger, feeling fearful, shaking, etc.), those related to anger are red (thinking of violation, feeling angry, feeling motivated to attack, etc.), those related to sadness are blue (thinking of loss, feeling sad, crying, etc.), and those related to joy are green (thinking of gain, feeling happy, physiologically charged, etc.). However, modes can be idiosyncratic, such as a person smiling when anxious. In any case, when a major mode is operating, it dominates the person's functioning.

Major modes are one of three types that function during waking life. The *orienting mode* is the network involved in the almost constant process of scanning the environment for threats and opportunities related to one's interests, both vital and otherwise. The cognitive schemas of the orienting mode contain one's core beliefs about threat and opportunity, such as one's perception of potential danger, failure, rejection, or benefit. These beliefs

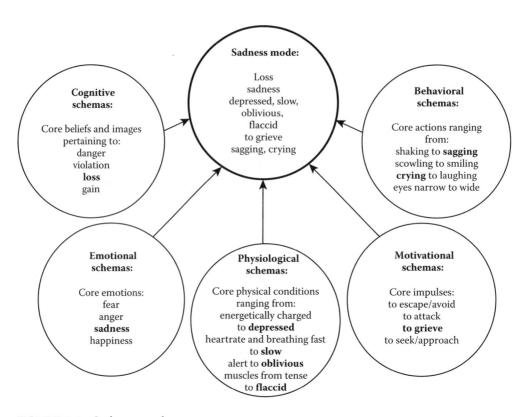

FIGURE 9.3   Sadness mode.

comprise a kind of template that a person constantly "lays over" whatever is currently happening to determine whether current circumstances "match" the template. When one perceives no match between the template and current environmental circumstances, one is likely to be in a *minor mode* (Beck, 1996, p. 10), pursuing less-than-vital interests. Minor modes include working at one's job or in one's garden, conversing with a friend or playing a computer game, and experiencing mild emotional states such as concern, irritation, disappointment, and satisfaction. When a perceived environmental circumstance matches the template of threat or opportunity to one's vital interests, the match activates simultaneously the powerfully energized cognitive, emotional, physiological, motivational, and behavioral components of a major mode such as the anxiety, anger, sadness, or joy mode. Beck also referred to major modes as primal modes, referring to the primitive, universal, survival-related nature of these modes (Beck, 1996; Beck & Weishaar, 2008, p. 264).

To extend the file cabinet analogy, the orienting mode is like a person standing in the center of the semicircle of the five file drawer system, monitoring the physical and social environment for a template match involving danger or opportunity, and pulling the relevant color-coded files of either a minor (worry, irritation, disappointment, or satisfaction) or a major mode (anxiety, anger, sadness, joy). We suspect that even the degree to which the orienting mode is active or on alert varies from person to person; perhaps that degree is influenced by a person's typical point on one's core phenomena continuums, such that if the typical point is at the lower end of intensity, one's orienting mode is also less intense or on alert, and if the typical point is at the higher end of intensity, one's orienting mode is also more intense or on alert.

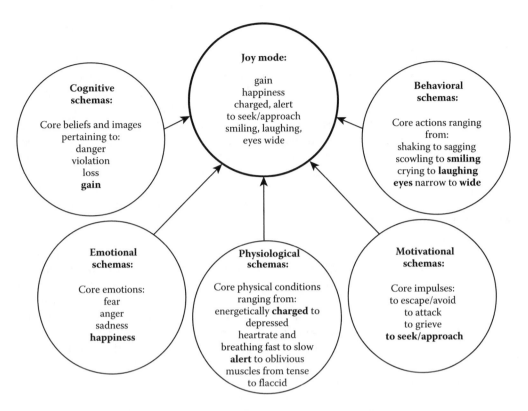

FIGURE 9.4 Joy mode.

To summarize, while awake, a person's orienting mode is always active to some degree, and one is also always in either a minor mode or a major mode. For example, a driver is driving along on an errand one day; he is, in effect, in his minor driving mode. Suddenly, a dog darts out in front of his car. The driver's orienting mode perceives a match between the template of danger and these circumstances. Instantly he thinks, "I must not hit the dog!" (automatic thought), which activates his anxiety mode: Frightened (emotion), his body is energized (physiology), he feels the impulse to avoid hitting the dog (motivation), and he follows that impulse by swerving the car (behavior). He misses the dog, which happily darts out of sight between some parked cars. The driver's orienting schema no longer perceives a match between the template of danger and existing circumstances, and he gradually returns to the minor mode of driving. The potential to develop modes and shift from mode to mode is an innate endowment.

A difference between major/primal and minor modes is that major/primal modes are more intensely charged with energy, and the charge lingers for some time after the template-matching external event has passed. In the above example, the driver will need some time to calm down.

Another crucial difference involves the one remaining structure/function of the psyche, the *conscious control system*. This system "is separate from, and relatively independent of, [modes]. When activated, this control system has the potential ... to de-energize the mode" (Beck, 1996, p. 14) by thinking about and acting on one's cognitive and behavioral systems. The driver who averted disaster can facilitate the calming process by purposely enacting the behavior of relaxing his muscles, taking a few deep breaths, and purposely engaging the cognitions, "Everything is okay. The dog wasn't hurt. Everything is fine."

However, while a primal mode is activated, access to the conscious control system is limited. The automatic thoughts of the cognitive system, in particular, are characterized by narrowed focus, selective attention, and extreme, absolutistic evaluation, and the remaining components of the mode instantaneously shift into gear. The driver thinks only about how he must avoid hitting the dog and only about the features of the environment relevant to that goal. Unlike the cognitive rigidity of the major/primal modes, cognitive flexibility characterizes the minor modes that, in turn, are more easily influenced by the conscious control system (Beck & Weishaar, 2008). In the file drawer analogy, the conscious control system is like a boss who has the ability to oversee the whole process of orientation and mode activation but who has the potential to lose control of the process when a major mode is activated.

Levels of Cognition   Cognitive therapists are so named because they are particularly interested in the cognitive component of modes, believing that component to be the "prime mover" of change. The basic contents of the cognitive system—its core beliefs—are not in place at birth. Rather, an infant is endowed with *protoschemas*, the basic, general structures pertaining to broad, survival-related themes such as danger, violation, loss, and gain. Protoschemas are analogous to a file cabinet's color-coded files that are originally empty of specific labeled files and their contents—though they may, through biological influence, be prone to contain relatively more adaptive or maladaptive contents. With experience, these protoschemas become specific schemas with unique contents. In other words, humans are innately endowed with the basic potential to recognize circumstances relevant to their vital interests, signaling such things as danger, violation, loss, and gain. Specific core beliefs, however, result from some combination of innate predisposition and specific experiences in one's learning history.

Core beliefs are not the only level of cognition in the psyche. Cognitive therapists view cognitions as *hierarchically organized based on their availability to awareness and their stability* (Beck & Weishaar, 2008). The least available to awareness and most stable cognitions are one's core beliefs about self, the world, and the future. People form these beliefs during childhood's preoperational level of cognitive development—when the child is not yet able to reason abstractly (Leahy, 1996). Consequently, core beliefs can be reasonable or can reflect some degree of error in logic.

Consider a person's core belief regarding the abandonment/instability schema—the degree to which one believes that others are available or unavailable as sources of continuous support and connection and that one tends to be either secure or prone to abandonment (Young, 2003a). You might be thinking, "Where do I fall on that continuum?" If so, you are experiencing, right now, how core beliefs are normally completely out of awareness. As fundamental as this single belief is to your basic approach to any relationship with another person, you formed it at such an early age that it became part of the foundation from which you operate rather than a conclusion that you periodically question or reevaluate. Nevertheless, cognitive therapists do not believe that cognitive schemas are deeply buried in the unconscious; though not the cognitions most readily available to consciousness, one can become conscious of core beliefs *if* one seeks to be—which few people do, or know how to do, outside the context of counseling.

Core beliefs remain relatively stable because, once formed, they act like a pair of tinted glasses that one is unaware of wearing. For example, the person who believes people are completely unstable and unreliable sources of support and connection is likely to have an orienting mode that sniffs out any hint of abandonment. Consequently, the person more readily notices abandoning behavior in others, more readily interprets even neutral behavior as abandonment, and thus remembers more of such behaviors. Thus, once a core belief is formed, it further influences the processing of information. In addition, this person probably inadvertently perpetuates abandoning behavior in others. To understand this last point, imagine that the person perceives abandonment in a series of neutral actions on the part of a friend. The person is likely to shift into anxiety mode, including behaviors such as clinginess, accusations of abandonment, and frequent requests for reassurance. Over time, the friend may come to find these behaviors unpleasant and break off the friendship—thus abandoning the person with the abandonment schema and reaffirming the person's core belief.

Moving up the hierarchy, somewhat more available to awareness and less stable are the cognitions that arise out of schemas: *assumptions* (Leahy, 1996) or *intermediate beliefs* (J. S. Beck, 1995) consisting of rules. These rules take the form of if-then propositions and shoulds that apply generally across situations. Someone toward the more secure end of the abandonment–instability continuum might hold the assumption that "If I am reasonably considerate to others, I am not likely to be abandoned" and "I should be reasonably considerate to others." Someone toward the insecure end might believe, "If I take care of others, they will never leave me" so "I should make every effort to take care of others," and "If I focus exclusively on others' needs, I don't have to think about my own needs and how I might be abandoned" so "I should put all my attention on what others need" (Leahy, 1996, p. 198).

Further up the hierarchy, even more available to awareness and less stable are *automatic thoughts,* the cognitions) verbal thoughts and mental images) that arise from the intermediate beliefs in the context of specific situations. The secure person who sees his partner scowl might think, "She must have had a bad day." He is likely to remain in a minor mode and might actually tell her (sympathetically) that she looks like she might have had a rough day. The insecure person might think, "Oh, no! She must be upset with me!" He is likely to shift into a major mode and ask with some emotional desperation, "What's wrong? Did I do something to upset you?"

Finally, most available to awareness and least stable are *voluntary thoughts*. An example of a voluntary thought is, "Let's see. Would I rather have broccoli or carrots for dinner?" or "I need a pair of scissors to open this package."

Summary

An infant is born with the innate disposition to survive and procreate. Throughout life, the individual fulfills that disposition through processing the information that arises from experience, using innate feelings of pleasure and pain as a guide. Each person is equipped to process information using the five systems of cognition, emotion, physiology, motivation, and behavior. Certain innate connections exist between these systems, which comprise modes, such as between the cognition of danger, the emotion of fear–anxiety, the motivation to escape or avoid, and the behavior of fleeing, which comprise the anxiety mode. The personality consists of several modes—the orienting mode that operates continuously in waking life; the minor modes that, for most people, operate most of the time; the major/primal modes that are activated when one perceives threats or opportunities related to one's vital interests of survival and/or procreation—along with the conscious control system that has the ability to deactivate primal modes.

The cognitive system is comprised of verbal thoughts and mental images that exist in a hierarchy: Beyond the most accessible and unstable voluntary thoughts lie the still relatively accessible, unstable, and situation-specific automatic thoughts; which arise from the less accessible and more stable and general intermediate thoughts that take the form of rules; which arise from the least accessible (though still accessible), most stable, and most fundamental beliefs about self, the world, and the future: core beliefs. Newborn infants are endowed with protoschemas that, through experience, become schemas with their specific core belief contents. Most people from their core beliefs during childhood when they are developmentally prone to make errors in reasoning. Some cognitive systems, right down to the core beliefs, are more reasonable and functional—more truly facilitative of surviving and procreating—than others. In addition to the role of innate temperament and predisposition, how some people develop more reasonable, functional cognitions, and yet others develop less reasonable and more dysfunctional cognitions is the subject of the next section.

Role of the Environment

For the cognitive therapist, environment refers to both a person's physical and social surroundings (Beck & Weishaar, 2008, p. 271). A person serves the goals of survival and procreation by processing information about Earth's gravity and the behavior of plants and other animals as well as processing information about one's interactions with other humans.

Cognitive therapists subscribe to social learning theory. That is, they believe that, even more than people's behaviors themselves, people's cognitions (their beliefs, their conclusions, expectations, and predictions that underlie their behaviors) are influenced by modeling, by the presence and form—or absence—of reinforcement and punishment, and by vicarious learning from significant others. Whereas cognitive therapists acknowledge innate predispositions to perceive stimuli in particular ways, they more strongly "[emphasize] the individual's learning history, including the influence of significant life events" (Beck & Weishaar, 2008, p. 249) on the development of personality. Whereas personality results from the interaction between innate disposition and environmental factors, the greater influence is considered to be the environment.

Since children create core beliefs (Young, 2003a), the single greatest influence on the development of one's core beliefs is the aspect of the environment that most frequently and powerfully provides modeling, reinforcement, and punishment during one's early years: That environment typically is one's family. As the child seeks to adapt in the pursuit of survival, the messages one perceives from one's early caretakers, both behavioral and verbal, contribute most to one's core beliefs about self, the world, and the future. So, for example, a child is likely to develop an abandonment/instability schema if, when he or she was young, a parent "died or left the home permanently ... was moody, unpredictable, or an alcoholic ... withdrew or left [one] alone for long periods of time" (Young, 2003b, p. 92), failed to protect one from abuse, or the like.

Additional influences include the extrafamilial domains of the larger social environment—one's culture—and, as previously stated, the physical environment. At the same time that these environmental factors impinge strongly on one's development, the environment is not solely responsible for one's schemas. The individual's innate predispositions play a role in how one perceives environmental contingencies. In addition, with cognitive development comes the increasing ability to engage one's conscious control system to deactivate dysfunctional major/primal schemas and even to access and modify them.

Model of Mental Health

Healthy Functioning

Beck and Weishaar (2008) offered a succinct summary of the cognitive perspective on personality development. Cognitive therapists, they asserted, view "personality as reflecting the individual's cognitive organization and structure, which are both biologically and socially influenced. Within the constraints of one's neuroanatomy and biochemistry, personal learning experiences help determine how one develops and responds" (p. 271).

The less bias in a person's thinking, the healthier the person is. The individual with adaptive core beliefs exhibits a kind of modal flexibility. Under normal life circumstances, she spends most of her time in minor modes with easy access to her conscious control system. When circumstances call for a shift into a major/primal mode, she makes that shift, and when those circumstances end, she shifts back to minor mode functioning. Her core beliefs probably go something like, "I'm pretty competent. Others are usually trustworthy and supportive. The world is usually a safe place where I can usually achieve my goals. The future looks essentially bright."

Unhealthy Functioning

The relationship between healthy and unhealthy adaptation is one of degree—quantity rather than quality. "The phenomena of psychopathology ... are on the same continuum as normal ... reactions, but they are manifested in exaggerated and persistent ways" (Beck & Weishaar, 2008, p. 270). So, for example, assuming an absence of objective threats to personal well-being, a well-adjusted person experiences occasional concern and brief anxiety, whereas the poorly adjusted person experiences chronic, intense anxiety.

Thus, the individual with biased core beliefs exhibits a kind of modal rigidity. Under normal life circumstances, one or more of her major modes is chronically activated. She does not experience just the occasional minor mode of worry or even just the occasional major mode of anxiety but the intense, chronic dysfunctional mode of anxiety disorder; not irritation or anger but rage; not disappointment or sadness but depression; not satisfaction or joy but mania. Almost everyone probably has one or more core beliefs that stray from the ideal range on the schema continuum. However, when someone's core beliefs are located rather far, or very far, from that ideal range, their symptoms meet the criteria for *DSM–IV–TR* (American Psychiatric Association, 2000) Axis I disorders and Axis II personality disorders, respectively.

Various disorders reflect specific *cognitive profiles*. For example, in anxiety-related disorders such as generalized anxiety, panic disorder, phobia, obsession, compulsion, anorexia, and hypochondria, core beliefs reflect themes of exaggerated and relatively persistent danger. In depression, core beliefs about self, the world, and the future contain themes of exaggerated and relatively persistent loss. In hypomania, core beliefs contain themes of exaggerated and relatively persistent gain. Though chronic hostility is not an official *DSM–IV* disorder, Beck (1996) asserted "that it should be included ... to account for individuals' excessive reactions leading to violence and homicide" (p. 13). In these disorders, core beliefs contain themes of an exaggerated and relatively persistent sense of being violated. In personality disorders, such as narcissistic and borderline, core beliefs are at such an extreme end of the continuum range that the person spends virtually all of her time in major/primal modes.

Though each client's schemas will be unique, the cognitive counselor expects to find this profile in some form in a client presenting with the specified disorder. For example, depression, the mode of exaggerated and persistent loss, is accompanied by the profile of the cognitive triad: an exaggerated and persistently negative view of oneself, the world, and the future. The depressed client sees oneself as incapable, abandoned, and valueless; the world as overwhelmingly demanding with huge obstacles to goal achievement and complete absence of satisfaction; and the future as holding no improvement over the present negative conditions. This latter perception is associated with the emotion of hopelessness, which Beck and other researchers (Beck & Weishaar, 2008) have found to be a highly reliable predictor of suicide. Other symptoms include the motivational component of "paralysis of will" (Beck & Weishaar, 2008, p. 272) and the behavioral components of inactivity and eating and/or sleeping too little or too much. These other symptoms and the cognitive component mutually feed back to each other to maintain the depressive mode. For example, believing himself incompetent, he feels unmotivated to set and achieve even a simple goal, spends several hours sleeping; having accomplished nothing, he then is reinforced in the belief that he is incompetent.

Cognitive Distortions The cognitions that comprise psychological disorders' cognitive profiles both reflect and perpetuate a systematic bias in information processing (Beck & Weishaar, 2008, p. 272). This bias takes several characteristic forms, called cognitive distortions, which can be detected beneath the voluntary thought level of the client's cognitive system—in his automatic thoughts, intermediate thoughts, and core beliefs. The forms are:

Arbitrary inference: Jumping to a conclusion in the absence of supporting evidence or even despite evidence to the contrary. For example, a teacher who struggles with a particularly difficult class concludes, "I'm a horrible teacher."

Selective abstraction: Conceptualizing an entire situation based on taking one detail out of context and ignoring other aspects of the context. For example, a husband who, along with his wife, enjoys fairly frequent sex, describes in counseling a recent night when his wife declined to make love. He states, "My sexual needs are not getting met."

Overgeneralization: "Abstracting a general rule from one or a few isolated incidents and applying it too broadly and to unrelated situations" (Beck & Weishaar, 2008, p. 272). For example, a successful store owner is robbed one day and concludes, "People can't be trusted. I'll never get ahead."

Magnification and minimization: Attributing much more or less importance to something than is warranted. Magnification is often manifested in catastrophizing, such as the man who believes, "If my date sees my anxiety on our first date, she'll want nothing more to do with me." Minimization is often manifested in denial, such as the woman who believes her husband's frequent bouts of physical abuse are "not the real him."

Personalization: Attributing the cause of external events entirely to oneself without evidence supporting a causal connection (Beck & Weishaar, 2008). For example, a child's parents divorce, and the child concludes, "It's all my fault."

Dichotomous thinking: Conceptualizing shades-of-gray phenomena in black-or-white categories. For example, a student believes, "If I don't get the best grade in the class, I'm a total failure."

David Burns (1980, 2007) offered different, possibly more user-friendly, terms for some of these cognitive distortions, and he has added a few to Beck's list:

Jumping to conclusions: Burns's term for arbitrary inference.

Mental filter: Burns's term for selective abstraction.

Blame: Listed by Burns with, and as a converse to, personalization: attributing internal responsibility entirely to external events. For example, a student who is failing a class attributes his poor performance entirely to the teacher's "bad teaching."

All-or-nothing thinking: Burns's term for dichotomous thinking.

Disqualifying the positive: Akin to minimization, this distortion specifically involves arbitrarily concluding that positive experiences "don't count" in an evaluation process.

Emotional reasoning: The assumption that emotions reflect reality. For example, in procrastination, one thinks, "I don't feel like doing [a particular task] right now, so it's actually not a good time to do it."

Should statements: Distorted attempts to motivate oneself and others by psychological force.

Labeling and mislabeling: A form of overgeneralization and all-or-nothing thinking in which one labels a total phenomenon based on one experience. This distortion can be directed at oneself, as when a salesman loses one account and thinks of himself as incompetent; at someone else, as when a friend forgets a lunch date and is labeled inconsiderate; or at a thing or activity, as when a computer program uncharacteristically quits and is labeled totally worthless.

As previously stated, Young (2003a) has identified 18 maladaptive schemas that underlie most psychological disorders. Take a moment to refer to Table 9.1, and see if you can generate some distorted intermediate and automatic thoughts that might arise from a few of the dysfunctional schemas, such as: entitlement/grandiosity, the belief that one is superior to other people, entitled to special rights and privileges, or not bound by the rules of reciprocity that guide normal social interaction; self-sacrifice, an excessive focus on voluntarily meeting the needs of others in daily situations, at the expense of one's own gratification; and unrelenting standards/hypercriticalness, the underlying belief that one must strive to meet very high internalized standards of behavior and performance, usually to avoid criticism (Young, 2003a).

The problem with distorted cognitions is that they are associated with unnecessarily distressing emotions and nonadaptive behaviors that often serve as a feedback loop, perpetuating further distorted thinking and associated self-defeating feelings and behaviors. The person who thinks, "I'm boring; if I talk to people, they'll reject me," is likely to feel anxious at a party and avoid social interaction. In this social phobia mode, he experiences cognitive deficits: His ability to access his conscious control system, which has the potential to "turn off idiosyncratic thinking, to concentrate, recall, ... reason ... [engage] reality testing and [refine] global conceptualizations" (Beck & Weishaar, 2008, p. 270), is reduced. Failing to find evidence that disputes the cognition, he is likely to come away from the party believing even more firmly that, indeed, he must be boring.

A final note on the maladaptive personality is that, in the case of dysfunctional modes, the associated intermediate beliefs—rules—reflect themes of *avoidance* or *overcompensation* (Leahy, 1996, pp. 193–194). Consider, for example, the person with social phobia related to a core belief of "defectiveness/shame: The feeling that one is defective, bad, unwanted, inferior, or invalid in important respects" (Young, 2003a). One might avoid experiencing the schema by avoiding social situations in which conversation is necessary ("If I avoid parties, I won't be seen as boring, so I should avoid all parties"). One might overcompensate by becoming a center-of-attention clown ("If I am always clowning around, people won't see how boring I am, so I must be the perpetual clown at parties"). When one is avoiding and/or overcompensating for a schema, one is responding to the schema rather than stopping to examine it. Thus, the schema continues unchallenged.

In summary, distorted cognitions are, by nature, self-perpetuating, and people tend to respond to them with avoidance or overcompensation. For all these reasons, distorted cognitions themselves tend to go unidentified, unexamined, and, therefore, unchanged.

THE PERSONALITY CHANGE PROCESS

From a cognitive perspective, personality change occurs when a person's core beliefs change. In terms of adaptiveness, personality can devolve, as when an adult with no apparent history of psychological problems undergoes extreme stress and develops post-traumatic stress disorder. It also can evolve when a person removes systematic bias—cognitive distortions—from one's core beliefs, leaving one less prone to future dysfunction. Such change is most solidified when the person also learns the process of how to realize if biased information processing is occurring and how to remove that bias. Since biased thinking tends to be self-perpetuating and to go unidentified and unexamined, constructive personality change is less likely to occur spontaneously in the course of normal life and more likely to occur under the special conditions of the therapeutic situation.

In the process of cognitive therapy, the counselor relies on the client's desire to change. The counselor invites the client to collaborate by learning some of the basic principles of cognitive therapy. With that knowledge, the client can then join the counselor in a process of coinvestigation that can result in change. With the counselor's help and in response to guiding questions, the client identifies situations in which he felt extreme or undue emotional reactions and/or behaved in some undesirable, self-defeating way; identifies the cognitions (thoughts and/or images) in his mind at the time of the extreme emotions or unwanted behavior; considers the cognitions not as self-evident conclusions but as testable hypotheses; tests those hypotheses for their reasonableness and usefulness; finding any that are unreasonable and/or not useful, modifies them in the direction of more reasonable and/or useful cognitions; and practices the modified cognitions and, often, the new behaviors that the new cognitions potentiate. As the client learns these skills, he becomes increasingly active and directive during sessions and the counselor less so, until he is reasonably well equipped to discontinue therapy and proceed on his own.

Beck and Weishaar (2008) summarized that "cognitive therapy employs a learning model" (p. 277) that "teaches patients to use conscious control to recognize and override maladaptive responses" (p. 264). "The shift to normal cognitive processing is accomplished by testing the erroneous inferences that result from biased [information] processing. Continual disconfirmation of cognitive errors, working as a feedback system, gradually restores more adaptive functioning" (p. 266).

Leahy (1996) noted that "cognitive therapy is the power of realistic thinking, not the power of positive thinking" (p. 24). Beck concurred and added that, similarly, the concept that client problems are essentially "cognitive" is not meant to imply that their problems are "all in their head" or imaginary. Quite the contrary:

Patients may have serious social, financial, or health problems as well as functional defi-cits. In addition to real problems, however, they have biased views of themselves, their situations, and their resources that limit their range of responses and prevent them from generating [effective] solutions. (Beck & Weishaar, 2008, p. 276)

It is those biased views that cognitive therapy targets to create lasting, constructive change in all aspects of functioning.

Client's Role

Motivation to Change

Clients usually come to counseling complaining of persistent, intensely distressing emo-tions or painful consequences to such emotions and associated behaviors. From the cog-nitive perspective, those distressing emotions and behaviors are components of major/primal modes activated by distorted cognitions. When in pain, people naturally seek corrective action. Due to the self-perpetuating nature of the modes, the person is unable to generate a corrective alternative for himself, so he seeks counseling in an attempt to find less painful, more pleasurable alternative ways of being.

Indeed, the client's pain is the counselor's ally. "[A mechanism] of change common to all successful forms of psychotherapy [is] ... the patient's emotional engagement in the problem situation" (Beck & Weishaar, 2008, p. 280). Without that engagement, as is often the case with mandatory clients such as those referred by the court, counseling is much less likely to be successful.

Capacity for Change

Beck and Weishaar (2008) described the characteristics of the client most likely to benefit from cognitive therapy. Socioeconomically, "cognitive therapy is effective for patients with different levels of income, education, and background" (p. 281). Attitudinally, it works best with clients who can accept the client role and who take responsibility for actively coping with their problems. Emotionally, the ideal client can tolerate the anx-iety of carrying out experiments and can persist to complete the counseling process. Cognitively, clients can best benefit if they "have adequate reality testing (i.e., no hallu-cinations or delusions), good concentration, and sufficient memory functions.... As long as the patient can recognize the relationships among thoughts, feelings, and behaviors and takes some responsibility for self-help, cognitive therapy can be beneficial" (Beck & Weishaar, 2008, p. 281).

Responsibility for Change

The client in cognitive therapy is expected to join the counselor in sharing equal responsi-bility for client change. The client must be active, collaborating with the counselor to set the session agenda, describing situations in which problems occurred, and providing infor-mation about distressing emotions and behaviors and associated cognitions (mental images and/or verbal thoughts) that occurred during those situations. The client actively learns how to mentally convert convictions into hypotheses and test them for validity as well as how to modify invalid hypotheses into more functional cognitions. The client must be will-ing to carry out homework assignments after each session, consisting of activities like keep-ing thought records, conducting behavioral experiments to test the validity of cognitions, and practicing thinking reformulated cognitions and doing new behaviors that they make possible (Beck & Weishaar, 2008). The client also is best served who is willing to give the counselor honest feedback after each session about what was and was not helpful.

Source of Resistance

Cognitive therapists (Beck, 1996; Beck & Weishaar, 2008; J. S. Beck, 1995) tend not to refer to client *resistance* to change, perhaps because of the adversarial connotation of the phrase that seems inconsistent with a collaborative approach, and tend more to speak simply in terms of why a client in cognitive therapy does not change. Before embarking on possible reasons, it is important to note that the feedback a counselor solicits at the end of each session, inquiring into what the client found helpful or not helpful, is designed to help the counselor continuously tailor counseling specifically to the client's needs and thereby avoid resistance. Nevertheless, even with the routine solicitation and use of client feedback, clients sometimes still do not change (Beck & Weishaar, 2008).

Perhaps the most fundamental reason is that the client does not perceive herself to have a problem, or does not perceive her problem to be a real threat to her vital interests. In either case, she will lack the emotional involvement to carry her through the risks and challenges of changing her basic beliefs (Beck & Weishaar, 2008).

Even if she sees her problem as a vital threat, changing her thinking and staying with the therapy process involves effort, some discomfort, and perseverance. Her tolerance for discomfort may be insufficient to the challenge of change (Beck & Weishaar, 2008). Other client factors in the absence of change include dysfunctional beliefs about therapy, such as that it requires no effort on the client's part, or about the therapist, such as that he or she will be controlling.

Some reasons clients do not change have less to do with the client than with the therapist. "The therapist may lack rapport or may have failed to provide a rationale for a procedure; an assignment may be too difficult for the patient ... there may be a lack of consensus on the aims and goals of therapy" (Beck & Weishaar, 2008, p. 284). Therefore, when clients do not change, counselors look to themselves as much as to their clients for causes and solutions.

Counselor's Role

Goals of Counseling

"The goals of cognitive therapy are to correct faulty information processing and to help patients modify assumptions that maintain maladaptive behaviors and emotions" (Beck & Weishaar, 2008, p. 275). The counselor seeks to engage the client's conscious control system to meta-cognize: think about the cognitive system involved in the client's problematic mode; inquire into the reasonableness and usefulness of the automatic thoughts, intermediate thoughts, and, ultimately, the core beliefs, that underlie her distressing, self-defeating emotions and behaviors; and when cognitions fail the test of reasonableness and usefulness, reformulate them into a more reasonable and useful form.

"Cognitive therapy initially addresses symptom relief, but its ultimate goals are to remove systematic biases in thinking and modify the core beliefs that predispose the person to future distress" (Beck & Weishaar, 2008, pp. 275–276). It also aims to arm the client with the skills to address future distress if and when it does occur.

Characteristics of an Effective Counselor

Cognitive therapists affirm the research on the critical role the counseling relationship plays in positive outcome in psychotherapy (Asay & Lambert, 1999). Therefore, the cognitive counselor is, first and foremost, warm, empathic, and genuine (Beck & Weishaar, 2008; Burns, 1992). These attitudes, and their associated skills such as nonverbal attending and verbal reflection, are considered absolutely necessary for constructive client change.

However, they are not sufficient. In addition, to the essential therapeutic qualities, a cognitive counselor must have expertise in the theory and techniques of cognitive therapy. She actively inquires into the unique meaning that each client attributes to his experiences. She is collaborative, working with, not on, the client. She respects the client as the expert on his own experience and "does not regard the patient's self-report as a screen for more deeply concealed ideas" (Beck & Weishaar, 2008, p. 265). She provides a rationale for each procedure she uses, demystifying the counseling process. She has interest and aptitude in investigation, joining the client in discovering his own unique manifestations of the cognitive profiles of psychological disorders and in testing the clients often credible, but not necessarily valid, beliefs.

"The cognitive therapist eschews the word 'irrational' in favor of 'dysfunctional' because problematic beliefs are nonadaptive rather than irrational. They contribute to psychological disorders because they intervene with normal cognitive processing, not because they are irrational" (Beck & Weishaar, 2008, p. 266). Consequently, once a client experiences the emotional arousal associated with a potentially dysfunctional belief, the cognitive therapist does not employ *disputation* strategies but invites the client to stay with the aroused feelings while collaborating in a *coinvestigation* of the validity of the related belief. In this process, she is able to empathize with feelings as well as to use logic and to question skillfully, guiding the client through the reasoning process and helping the client focus on the attenuating effect on his distressed feelings when he discovers invalidity of his beliefs. She opts for coinvestigation on the assumption that a client will more easily accept, and more likely put to use, conclusions he arrives at through his own conscious control system rather than arguments forcefully asserted by an external authority.

The effective cognitive therapist is observant and flexible, able to notice and respond to changing client needs. If the client needs support, she provides it. If the client seems ready to learn, she can competently teach the client the principles of cognitive therapy. As clients express cognitive distortions in their normal course of speech, she can identify them. When clients are first learning how to identify and evaluate cognitive distortions, they often need considerable guidance; the effective cognitive counselor can then take the lead. Toward the end of counseling, clients usually have become quite able to move on their own through the process of identifying, examining, and reformulating distorted cognitions; the counselor is then able to relinquish the lead and, instead, follow. Another aspect of the cognitive counselor's flexibility is the ability to use self-disclosure when it serves the client's counseling goals.

> Flexibility in the use of therapeutic techniques depends on the targeted symptoms. For example, the inertia of depression responds best to behavioral interventions, whereas the suicidal ideation and pessimism of depression respond best to cognitive techniques. A good cognitive therapist does not use techniques arbitrarily or mechanically, but with sound rationale and skill and with an understanding of each individual's needs. (Beck & Weishaar, 2008, p. 277)

The effective cognitive therapist also displays flexibility by being open to client feedback. Receiving and incorporating client feedback affirms the counselor's respect for the client as expert on his own well-being and strengthens the collaboration between counselor and client.

Finally, the effective cognitive therapist has received formal, supervised training in cognitive therapy (Beck & Weishaar, 2008). She takes responsibility for continuing education to fortify and add to her therapeutic skills.

Stages and Techniques

Overall Structure

Cognitive therapy is designed to be short-term. Most clients with *DSM–IV–TR* Axis I disorders achieve their counseling goals within 12 to 16, and up to 25, weeks. Clients with personality disorders may require longer duration. Cognitive counselors usually meet with clients weekly for 45-minute sessions. Some will conduct longer intake sessions, and in the case of moderate to severe client problems, they will see a client twice a week for a few weeks and then move to weekly sessions. After clients have met their therapeutic goals, they typically return once a month for two months for follow-up or booster sessions (Beck & Weishaar, 2008).

A cognitive counselor usually see clients in her office, but in the case of clients with phobias, the counselor will meet with the client in a real-life setting relevant to the phobia, such as, in the case of an elevator phobia, a building with elevators. "Cognitive therapists give their patients phone numbers at which they can be reached in the event of an emergency" (Beck & Weishaar, 2008, p. 287).

> Whenever possible, and with the patient's permission, significant others, such as friends and family members, are included in a therapy session to review the treatment goals and to explore ways in which the significant others might be helpful. This is especially important when family members misunderstand the nature of the illness, are overly solicitous, or are behaving in counterproductive ways. Significant others can be of great assistance in therapy. (Beck & Weishaar, 2008, p. 287)

Throughout counseling, the counselor enacts several roles. As necessary, the counselor serves as nurturer. Some clients benefit from little or none, others from nurturance around the beginning of counseling when they are severely distressed and have not yet begun stable improvement, and yet others, usually clients with personality disorders, may require intense nurturance well into the process of therapy. On a related note, Burns (1992) distinguished between the counselor's relationship establishment and maintenance skills—including nonverbal attending; reflection of feeling, content, and meaning; and gentle, open-ended questioning—and specific change strategies that enable the client to shift modes by intervening in the cognitive system, including Socratic questioning (further explained below), designing behavioral experiments, and assigning relevant homework. He estimated that he spends, on average, 50% of therapeutic time enacting each of these two skill sets. With clients who arrive at therapy functioning relatively well, he might spend 5% of time on relationship and 95% on change; with poorly functioning clients, such as those with personality disorders, he might spend 90% on relationship and 10% on change.

During the change strategies portion of the therapeutic process, cognitive counselors generally progress through a series of roles that begin more directive and end less directive: teacher of cognitive principles, guide for how to apply the principles in the client's unique case, catalyst of corrective experiences in which clients experience change and its benefits, and consultant who responds to requests for points of refinement by increasingly self-reliant clients (Beck & Weishaar, 2008).

Assessment

Regarding assessment, cognitive therapists use both objective and subjective approaches throughout the course of therapy. At the outset of counseling, the counselor inquires deeply into the client's developmental history and the unique meanings the client attributes to experiences (Beck & Weishaar, 2008), determines initial severity of client distress, and joins with the client in specifying problems and related goals. As counseling progresses, the collaborative team assesses client progress toward goals, and the counselor solicits feedback from the client throughout the course of counseling. Clients are asked to complete objective data prior to the first session as well as before and after each session. Prior to the first session, cognitive clients are likely to complete a background questionnaire. One of us (JMH) has adopted Arnold Lazarus's Multimodal Life History Inventory (Lazarus & Lazarus, 1991) for this purpose. Depending on the client's presenting problem, he might complete one or more self-report inventories at the beginning of, and periodically throughout, counseling to assess initial severity of, and progress in overcoming, those specific problems. At Beck's Center for Cognitive Therapy, therapists most frequently use the Scale for Suicide Ideation, the Anxiety Checklist, the Dysfunctional Attitudes Scale, the Beck Depression Inventory (BDI), the Beck Hopelessness Scale, and/or the Beck Anxiety Inventory. Also useful in identifying clients' vulnerable schemas is Young's (2003b) Schema Questionnaire.

To learn about the client's subjective perspectives, the cognitive counselor uses the clinical interview at the beginning of counseling and clinical inquiry—both verbal and through some routine forms—throughout counseling. The counselor uses the initial clinical interview:

> to obtain background and diagnostic data; to evaluate the patient's stress tolerance, capacity for introspection, coping methods, ... to obtain information about the patient's external situation and interpersonal context; and to modify vague complaints by working with the patient to arrive at specific target problems to work on. (Young, Weinberger, & Beck, 2001, p. 283.)

The interview also enables the counselor to learn the client's expectations of the counselor and the counseling process and, when necessary, negotiate and modify those expectations (Beck & Weishaar, 2008).

Verbal forms of clinical inquiry throughout counseling include the counselor opening each session with a question about how homework went. The counselor supplements clients' verbal reports with their completion of routine forms. These include the Daily Record of Dysfunctional Thoughts, in which the client identifies an upsetting event; the specific emotion(s) involved; the strength of those emotions using a scale from 1 (lowest the client ever experienced) to 100 (highest the client ever experienced); the automatic thoughts (verbal thoughts and/or mental images) that seemed to "feed" the distressed emotions; the cognitive distortions evident in those thoughts; more realistic and useful reformulated thoughts; and, upon substitution of the original thought(s) with the reformulated thought(s), the strength of one's emotions, from 0 to 100. Another routine form for feedback purposes is Burns' (1989) Client's Report of Counseling Session. The form includes the Empathy Scale that asks the client to rate 10 items addressing the "health" of the therapeutic relationship, and it provides a place for the client to write anything that bothered them about the last session, what they found helpful from the last session, and what they might want to address in their next session.

> In general, relief from symptoms is indicated by changes in scores on standardized inventories such as the BDI, changes in behavior as indicated through self-monitoring and observation by others, and change in thinking as evident in such measures as the Daily Record

of Dysfunctional Thoughts ... by the outcome of the [weekly] homework assignments ... in the relative ease with which a patient challenges automatic thoughts, the decrease in frequency of maladaptive cognitions and behaviors, the increase in ability to generate solutions to problems, and improved mood. (Beck & Weishaar, 2008, p. 283)

Change Strategies and Techniques

Cognitive therapists always employ verbal and behavioral strategies to help clients develop the skills to identify, evaluate, and reformulate dysfunctional cognitions and to notice the relationship between the relative functionality of their beliefs and level of distressing emotions and behaviors. Though cognitive therapists reflect the general counseling profession's preference for "skills over pills" in combating dysfunction, they are not averse to employing medication under certain circumstances. Those circumstances conform to the general standard of care: when the client is a serious danger to himself (suicidal) or someone else (homicidal), when the client is so distressed that he is unable to benefit from talk–action therapy, or when the client is strongly in favor of medication, even after experiencing in the first counseling session how cognitive techniques can relieve distressing symptoms. The cognitive counselor sees medication as only a short-term solution and believes that long-term improvement and reduced chances of relapse result from change in the client's core beliefs and the client's acquisition of skills to shift to, and maintain, more functional modes.

One of the counselor's goals in the first session is to give the client a taste of how cognitive therapy can relieve distressing symptoms. Enabling the client in the first session to experience how cognitive therapy can bring relief, can instill hope—particularly important if the client is feeling hopeless/suicidal—and help the client feel motivated to carry out the first homework, which usually involves self-monitoring of feelings, behaviors, and thoughts. For example, a client with depression mentioned in his first session that he worried that his difficulty concentrating might indicate a brain tumor.

Counselor: So when you think you might have a brain tumor, you feel worried or anxious. On a scale from 1 (low) to 10 (high), how worried or anxious do you feel when you think about the possibility of having a brain tumor?

Client: I don't know. (Pauses to think) Probably a 7.

Counselor: Okay. About a 7. So you feel pretty worried. And you've been to the doctor, and she doesn't think you have a brain tumor, but you don't seem convinced.

Client: No. I think she's missing it. Because I'm having such a hard time concentrating on things.

Counselor: Well, let's look at other evidence. Now, actually, you've described several symptoms of depression, such as your feeling sad a lot of the time, feeling low energy, not feeling hungry, feeling like sleeping a lot more than usual, and feeling worthless. I notice you haven't mentioned any typical symptoms of a brain tumor like a rather sudden increase in severe, prolonged headaches; loss of the actual ability to move or speak; or loss of actual physical sensation. Is that right that you haven't noticed any symptoms like that?

Client: No, not those kinds of things.

Counselor: Well, actually, difficulty concentrating is a well-known symptom of depression. Because you haven't had any of the more typical symptoms of brain tumor, but you have several symptoms of depression, and difficulty concentrating is one of those, it's fairly certain that your difficulty concentrating is just part of your depression, which we can address here, and is not a brain tumor.

Client: Hmm (appears to be thinking about what the counselor said).

Counselor: You look a bit relieved. When you think about the evidence that your difficulty concentrating is much more likely an aspect of your depression than an indication of a brain tumor, how anxious do you feel on that scale from 1 to 10?

Client: Not as much. Probably about a 2 or 3.

Counselor: Okay. So, when you examined the actual evidence, and revised your original thought accordingly, your worry and anxiety went down from a 7 to a 2 or 3. It's a lot less distressing to feel a 2 or 3 than a 7. This is pretty much the process that we'll be doing, and that you'll be learning how to do on your own, with other troubling feelings you are having, like your sadness and lack of motivation.

After the initial session, later sessions follow a kind of formula (Burns, 1980; Greenberger & Padesky, 1995; Padesky & Greenberger, 1995). The client brings in situations that occurred since the last session in which he felt distressed and/or acted in some self-defeating way. This specificity of concerns sets the agenda for the session. Then, together, counselor and client move through a series of steps. Early in counseling, the counselor guides the client through the steps; later, as the following description will illustrate, the client moves through the process virtually independently.

The client prioritizes the situations. Focusing on the top priority, he describes the upsetting event, identifies what emotion(s) he was experiencing and what actions he took, and specifies how strong the emotion(s) were by rating from 1 to 100. Thinking back, the client takes himself back to the moment in the situation when he first realized he was emotionally upset, and he or the counselor asks what Beck has called "the fundamental cognitive probe for identifying automatic thoughts" (Dattilio & Padesky, 1990, p. 29): "At the moment I first realize I am upset, what is going through my mind in the way of thoughts or images?" He jots down what usually is a list of verbal thoughts and/or mental images, stopping when he has gotten them all down. Out of this list, one thought usually stands out as the "hot thought" (Greenberger & Padesky, 1995)—the one that seems most to feed the distressing feeling. He identifies the hot thought and then examines it for cognitive distortions. Finding some distortions, he examines the evidence for and against the thought. If he finds that the evidence is not very strong, he reformulates the thought into a form that the evidence better supports. Thinking that thought, he again rates the strength of his emotion.

During the early and middle phases of counseling, when the client is learning the process described above, the counselor and client spend a large amount of time with the counselor asking questions (a particular type of questions) and the client responding. This special question-and-answer dialog is called Socratic dialog. The counselor carefully forms questions to facilitate new client learning. Though Socratic dialogue is used at every stage of the process, it is especially important during the phase of "examining the evidence." Socratic questions are not "leading questions" that imply a predetermined answer (Beck & Weishaar, 2008, p. 278); however, the counselor uses certain questions to guide the client toward what the counselor considers probable answers, always holding the possibility in mind that the answer the counselor anticipates may not actually turn out to be the one she gets. In other words, the counselor asks Socratic questions in a truly open manner, prepared to hear the client respond differently than she expects.

With client and counselor truly in agreement on, and both invested in, therapeutic goals, a good therapeutic relationship in place, a relevant hot thought identified, and the counselor's open attitude and skillful posing of questions, the client is highly likely to examine his automatic thoughts—and eventually his intermediate thoughts and core beliefs—nondefensively and, in the process, discover something new and useful.

Following is a Socratic dialogue between counselor and client. The client is the husband in couples counseling during an individual session. He is describing a situation that occurred two days previously in which his wife declined to have sex with him. He responded with angry hostility, and she had not spoken with him since. As he describes the incident and his reactions to it, he becomes increasingly upset and concludes by declaring, "My sexual needs in this marriage are not getting met!"

Counselor: Zero!

Client: That's right: Zero!

Counselor: And how angry are you feeling right now, on a scale from 1 (low) to 10 (high)?

Client: An 8!

Counselor: Okay. So you're pretty angry! You tell yourself that your sexual needs are getting met at a zero level, and you feel really mad! (Counselor pauses) I wonder if you're willing to stop and examine this situation a little more closely.

Client: (Calming down slightly, says begrudgingly) I guess.

Counselor: Okay. Let's take a look at that automatic thought. (Pauses briefly to give the client a little more time to shift into his conscious control system.) Let's review what you and your wife have told me during our conjoint sessions so far. The two of you have sex once or twice a week. Is that right?

Client: Yes.

Counselor: And both of you enjoy sex when you have it?

Client: Yes.

Counselor: You also have some complaints. You would like sex somewhat more often, sometimes within a day or two of the last time, and with more variety and novelty, not just the same routine. Is that right?

Client: Exactly.

Counselor: In fact, your wife has responded to some of your requests for novelty from time to time?

Client: That's right, on occasion.

Counselor: So taking everything into account that we've just reviewed—the frequency of your sexual encounters and the quality of them—both the extent that you enjoy them and the ways you'd like them to change, overall, how satisfied do you feel with your sex life, on a scale from 1 to 10?

Client: Well, usually around a 5 or 6.

Counselor: What's the lowest you've experienced?

Client: Probably a 5.

Counselor: And the highest?

Client: Probably a 7 or 8.

Counselor: So your average satisfaction is a 5 or 6, ranging from 5 to 7 or 8.

(Client nods)

Counselor: So, then, how true is it that your sexual needs are being met at a zero level?

Client:	It's not true. But I'm not really satisfied.
Counselor:	Yes, I understand that you'd like more frequency and novelty. Let's do a cost/benefit analysis of telling yourself zero and generating a lot of anger in yourself. What are the advantages of that?
Client:	I get my point across. I get to let her know how frustrated I feel.
Counselor:	Okay! You can feel pretty confident that she knows how much you're hurting. Anything else?
Client:	I guess when I'm angry, I don't notice my frustration so much. I'd rather feel angry than frustrated.
Counselor:	Okay! The power of anger feels better to you than the powerlessness of frustration. Anything else?
Client:	(Introspects for a moment) No, I guess that's it, mainly.
Counselor:	Okay. How about the costs?
Client:	She hasn't talked to me for 2 days. That's been pretty miserable. That tension all the time.
Counselor:	So you don't like the feeling of tension and isolation between the two of you. Anything else?
Client:	It will probably be more than a week before things calm down enough that she'll want to have sex again.
Counselor:	So you actually end up having sex less often. Anything else?
Client:	I have to apologize and make it up to her. That takes extra effort and is uncomfortable.
Counselor:	So you end up spending a lot of mental and emotional energy repairing things between the two of you. Anything else?
Client:	No, those are the main things.
Counselor:	Okay. So on the plus side, you get your point across that you're hurting and you get to feel powerful rather than powerless–at least for awhile. On the negative side, you end up putting up with the tension and isolation, having sex less often, and spending a lot of mental and emotional energy repairing things between the two of you.
(Client nods)	
Counselor:	So, if you had to distribute 100 points between the two sides, the benefit side and the cost side, like 50/50 or 60/40, what does the proportion feel like to you, of which side weighs out heavier, the benefits or the costs?
Client:	I'd say, 35/65.
Counselor:	So the costs outweigh the benefits. So let's review. When your wife declines to have sex with you, you tell yourself your sexual needs are getting met at a zero level, and you feel really angry and say something hostile. In fact, you feel satisfied at about level 5 or 6, ranging from 5 to 8. And getting angry and saying something hostile ends up costing you about twice as much as it gains you. So what would be a more accurate thought that might save you from that cost?
Client:	I guess to keep a perspective and remind myself that one "no" doesn't make my sexual satisfaction a zero; it's actually a 5 or 6 overall, even with the "no's."
Counselor:	And when you do think "I'm satisfied overall at a level 5 or 6," how angry do you feel, 1 to 10?
Client:	About a 3.

Counselor: So thinking "zero" is less accurate and less useful, and reminding yourself that you're satisfied at a 5 or 6 level is more accurate and more useful and helps you feel less angry: from an 8 on the anger scale to a 3. And when you're less angry, you're less likely to be hostile. And it doesn't change the fact that you still have requests of her that you still want to pursue. So that "5 to 6" thought sounds like a good thought to rehearse mentally.

Client: (noticeably more calm) Yeah, but what am I supposed to do? She's never going to change.

Counselor: Never?

Client: (chuckles, catching himself in his distorted automatic thought) Okay! But you have to admit, the evidence isn't very promising!

Counselor: (smiling) I hear you. And I think you posed a great question: What else could you do that holds more promise in getting you what you want than getting angry and hostile does? Let's look at that. [Counselor proceeds to the topic of effective communication.]

You may have noticed that the Socratic questions employed some purposeful strategies. In the example, the counselor used not only *examining the evidence,* but also *scaling* and *cost/benefit analysis.* She chose scaling, asking him to look at the evidence and rate his sexual satisfaction, as an antidote to his all-or-nothing thinking (zero). Scaling is a form of "thinking in shades of gray" (Burns, 1980). She chose cost/benefit analysis as an antidote to what she perceived as emotional reasoning; when her client said, "Yes, but I'm not really satisfied," it was as if he was saying, "If I feel dissatisfied, it follows that I act on what I'm feeling." The cost/benefit analysis helped the client evaluate the actual advantages and disadvantages of acting on his hostile impulse.

Other cognitive strategies include what Leahy (1996) called "examining criteria" and what Burns called "define terms": The client is asked to define key terms and labels such as "worthless," "success," and "failure," which often results in the client moving from global, overgeneralized concepts to specific, often achievable goals. On a related note is Burns's (1992) "semantic method." He gave the example of the client who believed, "I am a defective human being." After trying a few cognitive strategies unsuccessfully, Burns suggested that the client try the slightly semantically different thought, "I am a human being with defects." The client reported a noticeable shift: Being a defective human being meant he was essentially "wrong," whereas being a human being with defects meant he was essentially okay with identifiable problems he could potentially improve upon.

The "double standard technique" involves the client applying his own beliefs about himself to someone he loves. A client who was sexually abused as a child and believes "I am damaged goods" is invited to imagine that his best friend was similarly abused as a child and to imagine telling his friend "You are damaged goods." Clients usually recoil at such a suggestion. They then can be invited to role-play what they *would* say to the friend who believed that about himself, and then to practice saying the same things to oneself.

Reattribution (Beck & Weishaar, 2008) is an antidote for the cognitive distortions of personalization and blame. In the case of personalization, the client reduces excessive guilt by identifying factors besides himself that contributed to some occurrence. In blame, the client reduces anger at others for their role in some occurrence by taking appropriate responsibility for his own contributions.

In externalization of voices (Leahy, 1996), the client who has successfully challenged a distorted belief is invited to switch roles with the counselor. The counselor tries to convince the client of the distorted beliefs, and the client argues how the beliefs are inaccurate and not useful and argues in favor of more accurate and useful beliefs.

Sometimes, clients' automatic thoughts are realistic, yet their responses seem excessive. For example, the client who became despondent when she heard her mother's cancer diagnosis reported the automatic thought, "My mother might die soon." Under the circumstances that thought was true. In such cases, the cognitive counselor uses the "downward arrow technique": Proceeding from that automatic thought, the counselor asks, "What if that were true? What would that mean to you?" In this case, the client said, "I will be all alone in the world." Taking the arrow one level further, the client said, "I'll be miserably lonely for the rest of my life"—most likely a cognitive distortion and one that explained her despondency.

According to Beck and Weishaar (2008), cognitive therapists also use behavioral strategies:

> to modify automatic thoughts and assumptions, ... also ... to expand patients' response repertoires (skills training), to relax them (progressive relaxation) or to make them active (activity scheduling), to prepare them for avoided situations (behavioral rehearsal), or to expose them to feared stimuli (exposure therapy). Because behavioral techniques are used to foster cognitive change, it is crucial to know the patient's perceptions, thoughts, and conclusions after each behavioral experiment. (p. 286)

Burns (2007) listed more than 50 techniques for inquiring into the functionality of a cognition. Obviously, it is beyond the scope of this introductory chapter to describe them all. The interested reader is referred to the recommended resources at the end of this chapter.

As therapy progresses, a counselor looks for, and invites the client to look for, themes among similar and recurring automatic thoughts that suggest rules and, ultimately, core beliefs by which the client lives. Since particular phrasing seems to really fit, the counselor is open to the client taking time to search for and find the most fitting words and to reword phrases the counselor has offered. Since a client's deepest beliefs are tied modally to his deepest feelings, clients often are deeply moved when a schema is empathically identified. In fact, a client's tears are often an indicator that client and counselor have hit precisely on one of the client's core beliefs (Beck & Weishaar, 2008, pp. 284–285). Of course, the display of emotion in cognitive therapy is not an end in itself; lasting change results from modification of cognitions. That modification also can be deeply touching; consider the client abused in childhood at the very moment when he first truly grasps that he is not damaged goods.

Responding to Resistance

When a cognitive counselor finds a client is not changing, she applies cognitive principles to the situation. If she has erred, she accepts responsibility without engaging in the distortion of personalization, and she takes corrective action. If the problem arises from a cognitive distortion on the part of the client, such as mistaken expectations of the counselor, the counseling process, or the process or consequences of change, she invites the client to identify and examine those expectations as he would any cognition (Beck & Weishaar, 2008).

Judith Beck (1995) noted that cognitive therapy is present-focused. That is, after the in-depth exploration of the client's history at the very outset of counseling, counselor and client focus on how clients are distressed in their *current* lives. However, she clarified that the cognitive therapist shifts attention to the client's past in three situations: "if the client strongly desires it, if the focus on the present produces no change, and/or if the counselor believes that a client's understanding of how he developed his cognitions will significantly facilitate the counseling process" (p. 7). Thus, cognitive therapists believe that a failure to explore past origins of clients' cognitions can sometimes contribute to an absence of change in counseling.

Like all counselors, cognitive counselors feel challenged when working with challenging diagnoses such as personality disorders and with clients who have histories of unsuccessful therapy. For such cases:

> Beck, Rush, [Shaw, and Emery] (1979) provide [the following] guidelines … 1) avoid stereotyping the patient as being the problem rather than having the problem; 2) remain optimistic; 3) identify and deal with your own dysfunctional cognitions; 4) remain focused on the task instead of blaming the patient; and 5) maintain a problem-solving attitude. By following these guidelines, the therapist is able to be more resourceful with difficult patients. The therapist also can serve as a model for the patient, demonstrating that frustration does not automatically lead to anger and despair. (Beck & Weishaar, 2008, p. 287)

CONTRIBUTIONS AND LIMITATIONS

Interface With Recent Developments in the Mental Health Field

The Nature–Nurture Question

Probably more than any mental health practitioners, cognitive therapists explicitly incorporate into their conceptualization of clients' functioning recent research on genetic origins of behavior. They believe that, by virtue of innate temperament and other hereditary and biological influences, each person is predisposed to develop relatively healthy functioning or the cognitive profile of one or more psychological disorders. One possible difference between research and theory is that whereas researchers have found, overall, a slightly greater influence of environment than heredity in personality development, cognitive therapists tend to attribute a relatively greater influence of one's learning history on one's development of personality, including degree of healthy versus unhealthy functioning.

DSM–IV–TR Diagnosis

Along with behavior therapists, cognitive therapists explicitly reference *DSM–IV–TR* diagnoses. However, whereas *DSM–IV–TR* descriptions of mental disorders do not include speculation about psychological processes and dynamics that underlie the various constellations of symptoms, Beck has gone a step further, supplementing cognitive therapists' understanding of mental disorders by offering cognitive profiles for many of the diagnostic categories.

Pharmacotherapy

Probably more explicitly than proponents of other therapeutic approaches, with the possible exception of behavioral, cognitive therapists specify the conditions in which they affirm the use of psychotropic medication. Though cognitive therapists' goal is to arm the client with cognitive techniques instead of medication whenever possible—"skills instead of pills"—they do not eschew the use of medication under certain circumstances. They affirm its value as an aid at the beginning of counseling if clients' symptoms are so intense that they are suffering excessively, and/or are unable to participate in and benefit from the counseling process, and/or have a strong desire for medication based on a belief in its necessity or importance (J. S. Beck, 1995). They also affirm that clients make ongoing use of medication if they have been diagnosed with a psychotic condition such as psychotic depression, schizophrenia, or bipolar disorder. In cases of moderate to severe depression, research indicates that in initial treatment, cognitive therapy can be as effective as medication, and that in the aftermath of treatment, clients who participated in cognitive therapy with or without medication are less prone to relapse than those who used medication alone (Beck & Weishaar, 2008).

Managed Care and Brief Therapy

Cognitive therapy is a darling of managed care. It is inherently a brief approach, making it cost-effective. It has extensive research backing that affirms its effectiveness. Its procedures are described in treatment manuals that increase the consistency of counselors' services, thereby enhancing the quality of client care. Its inclusion of *DSM–IV–TR* diagnosis fits the managed care requirement to diagnose. Its inclusion of objective data and observable, measurable phenomena to assess clients at the outset of counseling, set therapeutic goals, and assess progress toward those goals throughout counseling, fits the managed care requirement for accountability in objective terms. In every way, cognitive therapy fulfills the requirements of managed care.

Diversity Issues

Several examples from the cognitive therapy literature (both print and audiovisual) indicate the attention cognitive therapists have paid to diversity and the applicability of cognitive therapy to diverse populations. Beck and Weishaar (2008) stated early in their overview of cognitive therapy that "some beliefs are tied to one's culture, gender role, religion, or socioeconomic status. Therapy may be directed toward problem solving with an understanding of how these beliefs influence the patient" (p. 265). Later they cited research to substantiate that "cognitive therapy is effective for patients with different levels of income, education, and background" (p. 281).

More explicitly, Padesky and Greenberger's (1995) *Clinician's Guide to "Mind Over Mood"* included the section "Adapting Mind Over Mood to a Client's Culture." In that section, the authors addressed how to use cognitive therapy with clients representing various specific ethnic groups, socioeconomic statuses, religious–spiritual affiliations, gender and sex-role values, and minority sexual orientation.

Another example of explicit attention to diversity is a video/DVD entitled *Psychotherapy with Gay, Lesbian and Bisexual Clients, Part 2: Individual Assessment and Psychotherapy* (Scott & Reyna, 2005). In it, leading cognitive therapists explained the value of cognitive therapy with this diverse population and discussed diagnostic and therapeutic considerations. Then Christine Padesky provided a two-session demonstration of work with a client with internalized homophobia who questions his homosexual orientation. In the first session she showed how she approaches his sexual identity issue, and in the second how she approaches his issues around coming out.

Regarding religion, one of us (JMH) has been intrigued by the similarity between basic cognitive precepts and the very first of the sayings of the Buddha: "We are what we think; all that we are arises with our thoughts; with our thoughts, we make the world" (Byrom, 1976, p. 1). Interestingly, numerous studies have revealed that integrating the practice of mindfulness, which originated in Buddhism, with cognitive therapy greatly enhances the latter's effectiveness in preventing relapse in the treatment of depression (Segal, Williams, & Teasdale, 2002). Segal demonstrated his approach in the DVD *Mindfulness-based Cognitive Therapy for Depression* (American Psychological Association, 2004). Ladner demonstrated the integration of mindfulness practices in psychotherapy more generally in *Mindful Therapy* (American Psychological Association, 2007).

Though the issue of racial/ethnic diversity does not come up in it, another video demonstrates European American leading cognitive therapist Judith Beck working with a severely depressed African American woman (American Psychological Association,

2006). This resource, along with those described above and numerous others, illustrate how theorists–practitioners have actively addressed the application of cognitive therapy to clients representing various types of diversity.

Technical Eclecticism

Though explicit cognitive strategies are clearly cognitive and behavioral in nature, Beck and Weishaar (2008) clarified that any technique consistent with the cognitive theory of emotional disorders is, essentially, fair game. This technical eclecticism includes the use and adaptation of experiential techniques such as the empty chair technique that grew out of Gestalt therapy (J. S. Beck, 1995). In essence, any technique is endorsed that a counselor employs to help a client modify dysfunctional cognitions and acquire self-help skills.

Though none of the best-known resources on cognitive therapy alludes to dream-work, an excellent text, Hill's (2003) *Dream Work in Therapy,* describes in detail a cognitively based approach. In brief, Hill asserted that recurrent and other salient dreams that people recall upon awakening reflect the psyche's attempt to accommodate incongruent experience into existing schemas. By discovering the meaning of dream symbols, which are idiosyncratic to the dreamer, the accommodation process can be facilitated. This process is often an emotional as well as cognitive one, and in the case of recurring dreams, it often marks the end of them.

For example, you may recall from Chapter 2 the dream of an adult female client. This dream was very simple. It began with a baked potato with a lengthwise cut and the white part of the potato "plumped up" through the opening. A single green pea came and landed in the potato. The potato was dry, and the pea was supposed to moisten it, but the pea was completely inadequate to the job.

Using Hill's (2003) approach, the client explored associations to the dream, such as peas being her husband's favorite vegetable, "pea" associating with "penis." At one point, after several associations, the meaning of the dream became absolutely clear to her. Over the past several months, her husband had become increasingly impotent (im-potato-ant?), and she had become increasingly frustrated, sexually. But her frustration was more than sexual. Over the past couple of years, she'd had the increasing sense that she was continuing to grow, to be psychospiritually "fertile," while her husband seemed to be languishing, remaining in a familiar but "small" and, for her, inadequate and unsatisfying lifestyle. Up to the time of this dreamwork, she had had very vague feelings that now became crystal clear to her. Her marriage, which had been extremely satisfying for many years, had gradually over the past couple of years become unsatisfying. This shift in her basic perception of her marriage was only the beginning of an important chapter in this client's counseling, but it was major catalyst in her forward movement.

Effectiveness of Psychotherapy

Much research supports the value of cognitive and cognitive-behavioral therapy, the latter that Beck and Weishaar (2008) defined as "CBT, the atheoretical combination of cognitive and behavioral strategies" (p. 282). Among the American Psychological Association's list of empirically supported approaches to the treatment of mental disorders, the number of cognitive and cognitive-behavioral treatments is second only to that of behavioral treatments (Crits-Christoph, 1998). A structured approach, it is amenable to description in treatment manuals that enable clinicians to follow standardized procedures that increase consistency in the care they provide to clients.

In psychotherapy research, a highly valued indication of a treatment's efficacy is a large effect size, which indicates a strong relationship between a treatment and positive outcome, that a researcher determines through meta-analysis, the analysis of several studies. Butler, Chapman, Forman, and Beck (2006) recently reviewed 16 meta-analyses of cognitive therapy and found:

> large effect sizes for unipolar depression, generalized anxiety disorder, panic disorder with or without agoraphobia, social phobia, and childhood depressive and anxiety disorders, [m]oderate effect sizes … for marital distress, anger, childhood somatic disorders, and chronic pain, [and r]elatively small effect sizes … for adjunctive [cognitive-behavioral therapy] for schizophrenia and for bulimia nervosa. (Beck & Weishaar, 2008, p. 282)

Regarding individual studies, researchers using randomized control trials have found cognitive interventions to be efficacious in the treatment of a wide variety of additional psychological disorders (Beck, 2005). Thus the research support for cognitive therapy is both extensive and quite strong.

Limitations

Until the mid-1990s, Beck's theory was based on a linear model of cognitions, emotions, and behavior. To accommodate recent research, he modified his model (Beck, 1996), adding the holistic concepts of modes and the energetic concepts of charges to his personality theory. The theory has become more accurate, but less elegant. It continues to evolve, and elegance may still be in its future.

Considering the extent to which cognitive therapists are willing to modify the theory in light of research, one of us (JMH) finds it curious that a particular, seemingly salient research finding has not been incorporated. Several researchers have found that "[nondepressed] people are highly vulnerable to illusions including unrealistic optimism, overestimation of themselves, and an exaggerated sense of their capacity to control events. The same research indicates that depressed people's perceptions and judgments are often less biased" (Alloy, 1995, p. 4). These findings suggest that the extent to which one's cognitions fit the evidence, that is, the extent to which they are "realistic," is not as adaptive as the extent to which they help people genuinely survive and thrive. Leahy (1996) asserted that cognitive therapy is not the power of positive thinking but of realistic thinking, and Beck referred to both realistic and useful thinking (Beck & Weishaar, 2008). Research seems to indicate, however, that the most important feature of a belief is not how realistic it is but how useful or helpful it is for the client's survival and well-being.

Contributions

Before cognitive therapy, person-centered therapists honored the client's phenomenological perspective and respected the client's wisdom about his own well-being, but it lacked structure and efficiency. Behavior therapy, on the other hand, brought to psychotherapy specificity and a systematic approach to problem identification and treatment, but many practitioners found it mechanistic. Cognitive therapy has combined the best of both approaches: the humanity and respect of the person-centered approach with the structure and efficiency of the behavioral approach.

The cognitive profiles of mental disorders offer a foundation for the conceptualization of clients. The use of treatment manuals has improved the quality of client care, specifying what works and enabling uniform application of those specifications. Extensive research in cognitive therapy has established its usefulness.

Current Status

Cognitive therapy is a major, if not the major, force in current psychotherapy. The Center for Cognitive Therapy at the University of Pennsylvania, affiliated with the University of Pennsylvania Medical School; the Beck Institute in Bala Cynwyd, Pennsylvania; and 10 other centers in the United States offer training in cognitive therapy. As of 1999, the Accreditation Council of Graduate Medical Education has required psychiatry training programs to train residents in the competent use of cognitive therapy (Beck & Weishaar, 2008).

Several publications, including a newsletter and several professional journals, are devoted to the dissemination of information about ongoing developments in cognitive therapy. Cognitive therapy is well represented among presentations at conferences of mental health professionals. Research is ongoing as mental health practitioners apply cognitive therapy principles to an ever-growing list of client concerns.

SUMMARY

Since the 1960s Beck and others have been developing cognitive therapy, an active, problem-focused approach to psychotherapy in which mental health practitioners target the cognitive aspect of the personality to affect constructive change in all aspects: emotional, behavioral, motivational, and physical. Extensive research has supported the efficacy of cognitive therapy across a wide variety of mental disorders. As practitioners continue developing cognitive techniques and researchers continue their investigations, the cognitive approach to counseling will continue to evolve.

RECOMMENDED RESOURCES

Books and Print

Beck, A. T., & Weishaar, M. E. (2008). Cognitive therapy. In R. J. Corsini & D. Wedding (Eds.), *Current psychotherapies* (8th ed., pp. 263–294). Belmont, CA: Thomson. An excellent overview of the theory and therapy.

Beck, J. S. (1995). *Cognitive therapy: Basics and beyond.* New York, NY: Guilford Press. An extremely clear presentation, replete with clinical examples of specific techniques.

Burns, D. (2007). *Therapist toolkit.* An invaluable resource packet for any counselor venturing into the use of cognitive therapy; well worth the initial investment. Available for purchase at http://www.feelinggood.com/therapist's_toolkit.htm

Dattilio, F. M. (2009). *Cognitive-behavioral therapy with couples and families: A comprehensive guide for clinicians.* New York, NY: Guilford Press. As of the writing of this chapter, this book has not yet been released. However, Dattilio is a recognized expert on the application of CBT to conjoint therapy, and the book is endorsed with a foreword by Aaron Beck.

Frieberg, R. D., & McClure, J. M. (2002). *Clinical practice of cognitive therapy with children and adolescents: The nuts and bolts.* New York, NY: Guilford Press. Outstanding guide for counselors who specialize in work with children.

Greenberger, D., & Padesky, C. A. (1995). *Mind over mood: Change how you feel by changing the way you think.* New York, NY: Guilford Press. An excellent client introduction to cognitive therapy and step-by-step workbook.

Hill, C. E. (2003). *Dream work in therapy: Facilitating exploration, insight, and action.* Washington, DC: American Psychological Association.

Padesky, C. A., & Greenberger, D. (1995). *Clinician's guide to Mind Over Mood.* New York, NY: Guilford Press. Indispensable counselor's accompaniment to the client workbook.

Rasmussen, P. R. (2005). *Personality-guided cognitive-behavioral therapy.* Washington, DC: American Psychological Association. Based on Millon's personality theory and assessment, this book takes counselors to a new level of fulfilling the cognitive edict to adapt the theory to individual differences.

Riso, L. P., du Toit, P. L., Stein, D. J., & Young, J. E. (2007). *Cognitive schemas and core beliefs in psychological problems: A scientist-practitioner guide.* Washington, DC: American Psychological Association. Detailed explanation of how to address client's maladaptive schemas.

Audiovisuals

In addition to the video recordings we've mentioned already, we recommend:

Beck, A. (1986). *Cognitive therapy. Three approaches to psychotherapy III, Part 3* [Motion picture]. Corona Del Mar, CA: Psychological & Educational Films, 3334 East Coast Highway, #252, Corona Del Mar, CA 92625. Dr. Beck works with a depressed client, Richard.

Gladding, S. (Director), & Holden, J. M. (Featured Counselor and Editor). (2002). *Cognitive counseling* [videotape]. Produced by Association for Counselor Education and Supervision and Chi Sigma Iota. Available from Microtraining Associates, 25 Burdette Ave., Framingham, MA 01702. Dr. Holden demonstrates her "10 steps of the cognitive counseling routine" with three clients: a young, a middle-aged, and an older adult. Accompanied by a 20-page student workbook.

Padesky, C. (2008). *Cognitive therapy training on disc*™ *7PAK.* Noted cognitive therapist provides seven exceptionally clear and instructive demonstrations: case conceptualization, Socratic dialog, thought record, underlying assumptions & behavioral experiments, core beliefs, panic disorder, and social anxiety. Available at http://www. store.padesky.com

Web Sites

Jeffrey Young has an excellent Web site at http://www.schematherapy.com/

David Burns's resources are listed at his Web site at http://www.feelinggood.com/

The Beck Institute Web page is at http://www.beckinstitute.org

Another excellent Web site is Robert Leahy's at the American Institute for Cognitive Therapy: http://www.cognitivetherapynyc.com/

REFERENCES

Alloy, L. B. (1995, April). Depressive realism: Sadder but wiser? *The Harvard Mental Health Letter,* 4–5. (74 Fenwood Road, Boston, MA 02115)

American Psychiatric Association. (2000). *Diagnostic and statistical manual of mental disorders* (4th ed., text rev.). Washington, DC: Author.

American Psychological Association. (2004). *Mindfulness-based cognitive therapy for depression.* (Available from American Psychological Association Service Center, 750 First Street NE, Washington, DC 20002-4242; http://www.apa.org/videos/4310714.html)

American Psychological Association. (2006). *Cognitive therapy.* (Available from American Psychological Association Service Center, 750 First Street NE, Washington, DC 20002-4242; http://www.apa.org/videos/4310736.html)

American Psychological Association. (2007). *Mindful therapy.* (Available from American Psychological Association Service Center, 750 First Street NE, Washington, DC 20002-4242; http://www.apa.org/videos/4310795.html)

Arnold, M. (1960). *Emotion and personality* (Vol. 1). New York, NY: Columbia University.

Asay, T. P., & Lambert, M. J. (1999). The empirical case for the common factors in therapy: Quantitative findings. In M. A. Hubble, B. L. Duncan, & S. D. Miller (Eds.), *The heart and soul of change* (pp. 23–55). Washington, DC: American Psychological Association.

Baltzly, D. (2008). Stoicism. In E. N. Zalta (Ed.), *The Stanford encyclopedia of philosophy.* Retrieved from http://plato.stanford.edu/entries/stoicism/

Bandura, A. (1977). *Social learning theory.* Englewood Cliffs, NJ: Prentice-Hall.

Beck, A. (1976). *Cognitive therapy and the emotional disorders.* New York, NY: Meridian.

Beck, A. (1996). Beyond belief: A theory of modes, personality, and psychopathology. In P. Salkovskis (Ed.), *Frontiers of cognitive therapy* (pp. 1–25). New York, NY: Guilford Press.

Beck, A. (2005). The current state of cognitive therapy: A 40-year retrospective. *Archives of General Psychiatry, 62,* 953–959.

Beck, A. T., Rush, A. J., Shaw, B. F., & Emery, G. (1979). *Cognitive therapy of depression.* New York, NY: Guilford Press.

Beck, A. T., & Weishaar, M. E. (2008). Cognitive therapy. In R. J. Corsini & D. Wedding (Eds.), *Current psychotherapies* (8th ed., pp. 263–294). Belmont, CA: Thomson.

Beck, J. S. (1995). *Cognitive therapy: Basics and beyond.* New York, NY: Guilford Press.

Burns, D. (1980). *Feeling good: The new mood therapy.* New York, NY: New American Library.

Burns, D. (1989). *The feeling good handbook: Using the new mood therapy in everyday life.* New York, NY: William Morrow.

Burns, D. (1992, February 28). *Feeling good: Fast and effective therapy for anxiety and depression and the resistant client.* Paper presented at the 24th Annual North Texas Counseling Conference, Denton, TX.

Burns, D. (2007). *Therapist toolkit.* http://www.feelinggood.com/therapist's_toolkit.htm

Butler, A. C., Chapman, J. E., Forman, E. M., & Beck, A. T. (2006). The empirical status of cognitive-behavioral therapy: A review of meta-analyses. *Clinical Psychology Review, 26*, 17–31.

Byrom, T. (1976). *Dhammapada: The sayings of the Buddha.* Boston, MA: Shambhala.

Chomsky, N. (1965). *Aspects of the theory of syntax.* Cambridge, MA: Massachusetts Institute of Technology.

Crits-Christoph, P. (1998). Training in empirically validated treatments: The division 12 APA task force recommendations. In K. S. Dobson & K. D. Craig (Eds.), *Empirically supported therapies: Best practice in professional psychology* (pp. 3–25). Thousand Oaks, CA: Sage.

Dattilio, F. M., & Padesky, C. A. (1990). *Cognitive therapy with couples.* Sarasota, FL: Professional Resource Exchange.

Ellis, A. (2000). Rational emotive behavior therapy. In R. J. Corsini & D. Wedding (Eds.), *Current psychotherapies* (6th ed., pp. 168–204). Itasca, IL: F. E. Peacock.

Greenberger, D., & Padesky, C. A. (1995). *Mind over mood: Change how you feel by changing the way you think.* New York, NY: Guilford Press.

Leahy, R. (1996). *Cognitive therapy: Basic principles and applications.* Northvale, NJ: Jason Aronson.

Kelly, G. (1955). *The psychology of personal constructs.* New York, NY: W. W. Norton.

Landon, P. J. (1998). *Review of the history channel presents the fifties, film & history, H-Net reviews.* Retrieved from http://www.h-net.msu.edu/reviews/showrev.cgi?path=118

Lazarus, A. A., & Lazarus, C. N. (1991). *Multimodal life history inventory* (2nd ed.). Champaign, IL: Research Press.

Lazarus, R. (1984). On the primacy of cognition. *American Psychologist, 39*, 124–129.

Leahy, R. (1996). *Cognitive therapy: Basic principles and applications.* Northvale, NJ: Jason Aronson.

Loftus, E. (1980). *Memory.* Reading, MA: Addison-Wesley.

Padesky, C. A., & Greenberger, D. (1995). *Clinician's guide to Mind Over Mood.* New York, NY: Guilford Press.

Piaget, J. (1954). *The construction of reality in the child.* New York, NY: Basic.

Piaget, J. (1965). *The moral judgment of the child.* New York, NY: Free.

Piaget, J. (1970). *Genetic epistemology.* New York, NY: W. W. Norton.

Rasmussen, P. R. (2005). *Personality-guided cognitive-behavioral therapy.* Washington, DC: American Psychological Association.

Riso, L. P., & McBride, C. (2007). Introduction: A return to a focus on cognitive schemas. In L. P. Riso, P. L. du Toit, D. J. Stein, & J. E. Young (Eds.), *Cognitive schemas and core beliefs in psychological problems: A scientist-practitioner guide* (pp. 3–10). Washington, DC: American Psychological Association.

Scott, R. L., & Reyna, E. (Producers). (2005). *Psychotherapy with gay, lesbian and bisexual clients. Program 2: Individual assessment and psychotherapy* [Motion picture]. Santa Ana, CA: Buendia Productions. http://www.buendiaproductions.com/home.htm

Segal, Z. V., Williams, J. M. G., & Teasdale, J. D. (2002). *Mindfulness based cognitive therapy for depression: A new approach to preventing relapse.* New York, NY: Guilford Press.

Weishaar, M. E. (1993). *Aaron T. Beck.* Thousand Oaks, CA: Sage.

Young, J. (2003a). *Early maladaptive schemas and schema domains.* Retrieved from http://www.schematherapy.com/id73.htm

Young, J. (2003b). *Schema therapy YSQ-L2.* Retrieved from http://www.schematherapy.com/id53.htm

Young, J. (n.d.). *Coping styles.* Retrieved from http://www.schematherapy.com/id62.htm

Young, J. E., Weinberger, A. D., & Beck, A. T. (2001). Cognitive therapy for depression. In D. H. Barlow (Ed.), *Clinical handbook of psychological disorders: A step-by-step treatment manual* (3rd ed.; pp. 264–308). New York, NY: Guilford Press.

CHAPTER 10

Rational Emotive Behavioral Counseling

BACKGROUND OF THE THEORY

Historical Context and Founder's Biographical Overview

Albert Ellis, the father of Rational Emotive Behavior Therapy (REBT), was born in Pittsburgh, Pennsylvania in 1913. When Ellis was 4 years old, his family moved to New York, where he subsequently made his home. Ellis was the oldest of three children and struggled with serious kidney problems that continued throughout his life. In addition to his physical ailments, Ellis learned to survive on his own, as his father was a traveling businessman and Ellis perceived his mother to be emotionally absent. To deal with his physical and family issues, young Ellis developed a philosophy of viewing life that he later turned into REBT. A famous example of his early application of REBT ideas is how a teenage Ellis confronted his reluctance to approach girls. He approached 100 girls in a 30-day period to test his fear that rejection would lead to some personal catastrophe. The experiment proved to be a success: He was rejected and the horrible tragedy that he feared never occurred.

Ellis earned his bachelor's degree from City College of New York in 1934 and, eight years later, decided to pursue a graduate degree in clinical psychology. He earned his PhD in 1947 from Teachers College, Columbia. Heavily influenced by psychoanalysis, for six years Ellis practiced psychoanalytic therapy and wrote in the areas of personality assessment and marriage and family therapy.

In the early 1950s, Ellis became increasingly dissatisfied with the impact of analytic forms of therapy. Having personally undergone analysis for over three years and being seemingly perplexed and uncertain of its long-term impact, he began to experiment with briefer forms of analysis, adding components that were more congruent with his personal philosophy of change. Time after time, he found the passive approach of the analyst to have little effect on the belief systems that seemed to sustain symptom reformation in clients.

> Why, when I seemed to know perfectly well what was troubling a patient, did I have to wait passively, perhaps for a few weeks, perhaps for months, until he, by his own interpretive initiative, showed that he was fully ready to accept my own insight? Why, when patients bitterly struggled to continue to associate freely, and ended up by saying only a few words in an entire session, was it improper of me to help them with several pointed questions or remarks? (Ellis, 1962, p. 7)

In an attempt to find a more efficient solution for his clients, Ellis explored several modes of therapy and philosophy. In 1956, at the American Psychological Association's conference, Ellis introduced the psychological community to his philosophy of change. Labeled Rational Therapy, the method largely resembled his own experiments as a child and adolescent. This form of therapy directly confronted clients' irrational belief systems and taught and encouraged clients to learn how to dispute and conquer their maladaptive ways of thinking.

Since the theory's inception, Ellis revised it several times with modifications and name changes. Unhappy with the interpretation that Rational Therapy meant ignoring emotion, Ellis changed the name to Rational Emotive Therapy. Finally, in 1993, he again modified the name to REBT to honor the theory's "highly cognitive, very emotive, and particularly behavioral" elements (Ellis, 1993, p. 1). Throughout the various name changes of his therapeutic approach, Ellis remained a prolific writer and presenter. His abrasive and energetic presentation style was as unique as his philosophy of therapy. He wrote more than 60 books and 700 scholarly articles on the theory and practice of REBT and continued to refine and expand his approach up to his death in 2007 at the age of 93.

Philosophical Underpinnings

Like every other theorist, Ellis formed REBT on the foundation of his own philosophical leanings. According to Bernard and Joyce (1984), REBT's philosophical underpinnings address questions such as, "how we know what we know (epistemology), the role of logical thought and human reason in the acquisition of knowledge (dialectics), goals for which individuals strive (values), and the criteria and standards for deciding how to relate to others (ethics)" (p. 39).

Epistemology and Dialectics

REBT rests on the assumption that human knowledge is based on selective interpretations of the world. In other words, how a person perceives events and people will largely impact how that person thinks, feels, and acts. This constructivist philosophy has its roots with the first century AD. Roman slave philosopher, Epictetus (1955), who wrote, "humans are disturbed not by things, but by the views they take of things" (p. 19). Consider the following scenario: A professor hands back graded exams to her students and announces, "Everyone did very well on this exam." As she gives each exam to a student, she notices various facial expressions, some positive, some distraught. Below are some of the students' internal interpretations in response to identical stimuli.

Professor: Everyone made above an 80 on this exam. Therefore, everyone did great.
Student #1: I made an 85. That's horrible. I always make A's. Maybe I'm not cut out for graduate school. I guess I didn't study enough.
Student #2: I made an 85. That stinks. The professor did not teach us the material very well. I feel cheated. The test was so unfair.
Student #3: I made an 85. That's so cool. I've never made above a C before on an exam. I am going out to celebrate!

The philosophy underlying REBT also can be considered relativistic, because its adherents assume that no absolute truth or reality exists but that each person's truth or reality is internally defined and experienced. The belief that reality exists only as one perceives it might be comforting, but it also carries the possibly less comforting implication that other realities are just as appropriate as one's own. Therefore, being understanding of others' subjective views and being flexible in one's own is essential within the REBT philosophy.

The role of logic in the acquisition of knowledge is central to REBT. The practice of rationality and logic dictates that individuals consider all pertinent evidence before drawing conclusions. At the very least, a rational thinker would understand that no conclusion can be based on all information; consequently, the thinker who discovers relevant new evidence will likely have to modify or change the belief. However, most people fail to be flexible or logical in their thinking. In fact, people typically make judgments based on very little data. For example, the adolescent girl who believes, "He hates me" when her boyfriend does not call her one evening; the father who thinks his son is not interested in spending time with him because the son has something else planned on one particular date; or the employee who believes the boss is angry at him because she did not say hello to him in the hall are all examples of how people affect themselves emotionally and behaviorally when they draw conclusions based on limited information. Since REBT practitioners hold that rational thinking is the mediator between the world and the individual, their primary therapeutic activity is teaching clients how to identify irrational thinking and how to replace it with rational thinking.

Responsible Hedonism

According to REBT philosophy, enjoying life is a legitimate primary goal, and rational individuals strive to maximize pleasure. People who practice pure hedonism achieve pleasure at any cost, but REBT adherents, who emphasize personal responsibility, advocate responsible hedonism. A responsibly hedonistic person is able to create short- and long-term goals that maximize pleasure potential. Practitioners of this philosophy use "hedonic calculus" to determine the relationship between short-term pleasure and long-term goals (Bernard & Joyce, 1984). A pure hedonist would sacrifice long-term goals for short-term pleasure, whereas a responsible hedonist would forgo short-term pleasure if it meant achieving long-term pleasure goals. Consider the example of marriage. For many people the decision to get married means commitment to a long-term goal that includes a multitude of individually perceived pleasurable components, including consistent companionship, reduced loneliness, increased emotional support, caretaking when ill, a relatively consistent sexual partner, children, and financial support. Faced with the opportunity for a casual sexual encounter, a pure hedonist would participate in the affair with the justification, "Pleasure is the goal. I'm not going to consider how this fling might destroy my marriage. I want to have fun now." A responsible hedonist, using hedonic calculus, would reason that one's moment of pleasure in the affair very likely would greatly jeopardize the long-term pleasures of marriage. Therefore, she would consider participating in the affair to be irrational and would avoid it to maximize future pleasure potential.

Humanism

REBT proponents embrace the humanistic philosophy of appreciating the individuality, creativity, and autonomy of each person. They believe in the innate worth of every individual and believe that dysfunction arises when one criticizes oneself and makes comparisons between self and others. Ellis viewed these comparisons and self-evaluations as thoroughly destructive and irrational. No universal criteria exist regarding right and wrong, pretty and ugly, or good and bad. Therefore, all such criteria are arbitrary, and by criticizing oneself for not living up to some arbitrary standard, a person generates within oneself unnecessary distress. Self-evaluations that arise out of such comparisons are equally harmful. Ellis believed that rational beings are unconditionally self-accepting and have no need or desire to put themselves down. The REBT proponents hold that comparisons and evaluations contradict a person's ability to rationally experience a situation and that they degrade the inherent worth of every human being.

PERSONALITY DEVELOPMENT

Nature of Humans

Function of the Psyche

According to REBT proponents, humans have the innate desire to survive, feel pleasure, and attain self-actualization. Ellis contended that humans are largely influenced by two innate biological tendencies. One is the overwhelming tendency to think and behave irrationally. According to Ellis, people seem to have an inborn need to self-evaluate and self-criticize as well as to accept assumptions about self, others, and the world that they cannot validate empirically. Ellis believed that even the person who has grown up in the most rational of environments will still construct irrational beliefs about self, others, and the world (Ellis, 2000b).

The other innate biological tendency is for humans to think rationally and be proactive in identifying and disputing irrational beliefs in order to live a more rational, self-actualizing life. Ellis contended that, because of this biological capacity, each person has power over, and responsibility for, one's own change process. As one chooses to dispute irrationality and be more logical and flexible, one is actively self-actualizing. Although a person may naturally slip into irrationality, Ellis believed it is equally natural for each person to live a rational life. In essence, every person chooses to succumb to the innate tendency to be emotionally disturbed and can choose at any time to follow the equally innate tendency to become undisturbed again.

Structure of the Psyche

Ellis parsimoniously summarized the basic structure of the personality according to REBT in his ABC model (see Figure 10.1). The model is traditional in that it includes

A (Activating Event)
My father yelled at me and grounded me for the weekend.

B (Belief About A)	**Disputation**
"He is unfair. He should be more caring."	(1) What evidence supports these beliefs?
"I am always a victim."	(2) Are these beliefs helping or hurting me?
"He must understand me. Because he doesn't, my life is ruined."	(3) Is it really as awful as I believe?

C (Consequences)	**New Effect**
Unhealthy negative emotions	Healthy emotions
Rage	Frustration
Shame	Regret
Betrayal	Disappointment
Self-defeating behaviors	Self-actualizing behaviors
Denies responsibility for actions	Accepts responsibility for own actions
Refuses to build relationship with dad	Communicates directly with father
Sneaks behind dad's back	

FIGURE 10.1   ABC model of intervention.

specific internal structures of the psyche like those Freud hypothesized. However, unlike Freud's three parts of the personality, Ellis's structural model is comprised of a universal processing system. In this system, A stands for the *activating* event or activating experience, which may be external, such as one's beloved spouse filing for divorce, or internal, such as a sharp pain in the abdomen. The C stands for the emotional and/or behavioral *consequence*. After hearing of the divorce plans, one might feel depressed or angry and might not go to work for awhile. After noticing the sharp pain, one might feel anxious and contact one's physician.

Most people reading the scenarios above would assume that A, such as the divorce, caused C, the feelings of depression and anger and the behavioral withdrawal. However, from the REBT perspective, A does not cause C; instead, B (one's *beliefs* about A) causes C. In other words, one's emotions and actions are not the consequences of internal or external activating events; they are the consequences of one's beliefs about those activating events. In the divorce scenario, the beliefs about divorce that led to depressed and angry feelings and behavioral withdrawal were probably something like, "My spouse is the only one I could ever love. Without my spouse, I'll never be happy. My spouse has 'done me wrong' by initiating divorce and should have been more loyal." According to REBT, the beliefs about the activating event, not the activating event itself, cause the emotional and behavioral consequences.

Some readers might conclude that the person in the above scenario is rational: that divorce would always cause the kinds of feelings and behavior that the individual in the scenario experienced. However, such feelings and thoughts are not inevitable; the ABC model demonstrates that how one thinks about a stimulus is the greatest predictor of how one will react to the stimulus. In addition, because individuals construct their beliefs on the basis of their experiences and perceptions, no belief is universal in response to the same stimulus. Consider the different beliefs that different people generated to the same activating event of divorce, along with the corresponding emotional/behavioral consequences, listed in Table 10.1.

If A *caused* C, the same C would always follow a given A. But this is not the case; different Cs follow the same A. As the ABC model clearly demonstrates, the different Cs are the result of different Bs. It is beliefs, not activating events, that cause emotional and behavioral consequences in the aftermath of activating events. As you will soon see, REBT practitioners utilize this dynamic ABC model to assess and promote change in clients' irrational beliefs into more rational beliefs that produce more satisfying consequences.

TABLE 10.1   Alternate Beliefs About, and Related Emotional and Behavioral Consequences to, the Same Activating Event

A	B	C
Divorce	"That is unfortunate, but not the end of the world. She is free to make her own choices, and I can move on with life."	Brief mourning Resume dating
Divorce	"That is horrible! I must be a complete loser. No one will ever love me again! I am all alone, unlovable, and I can't live without her."	Intense depression Hopelessness Extensive withdrawal Suicide
Divorce	"Who cares? I can find someone else. I never really loved her anyway and am definitely better off without her; think of all the money I'll save! I can't wait to start dating again!"	Apathy Excitement Relief Resume dating

Role of the Environment

Although Ellis affirmed a biological basis for irrational and rational living, he also believed a person's environment has an impact on personality development. Specifically, Ellis (1979) listed the following possible environmental influences that we have updated to include modern examples: instruction from parents, teachers, other relatives, and coaches; media, such as radio, music, television, books, magazines, and the internet; environmental rewards such as wages, honors, or anything else that fits a societal definition of success; environmental consequences such as legal sanctions, social sanctions, and anything that does not fit a societal definition of success; organized groups such as churches, athletic teams, gangs, socioeconomic status, political affiliation, and occupation; peer groups and romantic affiliations. All of these—and this list is not exhaustive—influence an individual's thoughts, emotions, and behaviors. In terms of dysfunction, Ellis asserted that many beliefs involving absolutistic musts and shoulds emanate directly from environmental injunctions, such as "You must make all A's to be a good son," "You should marry before age 25 or you are unlovable," "You must do what you are told or you are bad," or "Life should be fair."

Overall, Ellis hypothesized an interdependent relationship between biology and environment. "REBT holds that people's environment . . . reaffirms but does not always create strong tendencies to think irrationally and to be disturbed. . . . People naturally and easily add rigid commands to socially inhibited standards" (2000b, p. 179). Demonstrating a stance consistent with REBT philosophy, Ellis declined to identify either influence as absolutistically causative. Instead, he affirmed the influence of both heredity and environment, along with the individual's responsibility for perceiving, interpreting, and believing in a uniquely personal way.

Model of Mental Health

Healthy Functioning

In REBT philosophy, the rationality of one's belief system is directly related to one's level of mental health. A rational individual is "pragmatic, logical and reality based" (Dryden & DiGiuseppe, 1990, p. 3). Rational people are flexible in their approaches and conclusions, are willing to make mistakes and learn from them, and base interpretations and conclusions on realistic data. When faced with situations they find difficult, rational people interpret the events as hurtful or disappointing but not catastrophic. For example, a rational person who is confronted with a disagreement with a friend will form beliefs about this activating event that are characterized by a *rational evaluation of badness* ("I do not like fighting with Justin, but it is not the end of the world"); a sense of *tolerance* (being open to other points of view, understanding that disagreements are a part of every relationship, and actively pursuing other aspects of life while attending to the disagreement); and a sense of *acceptance* ("I am human, so I can make mistakes. I might be wrong about this, and that is fine. I can live with being wrong. If this relationship ends because of this disagreement, I can move on, too.").

Expressing a philosophical kinship with the existential writers of his time, Ellis (1962) considered the work of Braaten (1961) to be a fitting summary of rational health. Following are the main themes Ellis (1962, p. 124) cited, along with added commentary on how they fit within a rational life, including movement toward self-actualization.

1. **You are free; define yourself.** A rational person accepts both the privilege and responsibility of free will. With the knowledge that one is free comes an understanding that "I alone" am accountable for personal feelings, thoughts, and behaviors.
2. **Live in dialog with your fellow human beings.** REBT proponents maintain that under normal circumstances, a person has many opportunities to acquire feedback about reality from one's environment. The person who isolates oneself breeds belief stagnation and raises the risk of reindoctrinating oneself with irrational beliefs. By openly dialoging with others, free of negative comparisons and self-evaluations, a person is most likely to promote self-acceptance and self-actualization. A rational person is open to receiving input from others and weighing it while keeping in mind the next theme.
3. **Your own experiencing is the highest authority.** Taken in isolation, this theme might seem inherently selfish and possibly contradictory to the preceding theme. However, this theme directly addresses the dynamic of each person being responsible for self and not blaming others and/or putting too much credence in other people's views and opinions of one's life. Overall, intertwined with the other themes, this theme is the heart of self-actualization: unconditional self-acceptance of strengths and weaknesses.
4. **Be fully present in the immediacy of the moment.** According to REBT practitioners, a person cannot be rational and live in the past or the future. Both worrying and moping about what happened 10 years ago, and being consumed with anxiety about what might happen tomorrow, are ineffective and do not maximize a person's potential for long-term happiness. The person who confronts current self-defeating thinking and who collects information from the present is on the road to change that leads ultimately to more effective, satisfying living.
5. **There is no truth except action.** As we discussed in the biographical overview, Ellis became disillusioned with psychoanalysis because of its emphasis on insight over action. Ellis believed that in order to change, a person needs to actually do something different. Merely understanding why a behavior or belief developed will not necessarily lead to change. A person enacts the hallmarks of a rational life by actively disputing irrational beliefs and participating consistently in new, more rational forms of thinking, feeling, and behaving.
6. **You must learn to accept certain limits in life.** Ellis maintained that rational individuals recognize personal strengths and weaknesses, and although it is appropriate, even courageous, to try continuously to improve, one must recognize that no one is perfect. Perfection is an impossible goal; therefore, a person is irrational to believe that one can or should be able to attain perfection. A key element to rationality and, thus, self-actualization is for a person to accept one's own fallibility as a condition of life and not as a catastrophe.

Unhealthy Functioning

Unlike many practitioners of schools of therapy who focus on why and how maladjustment develops, REBT practitioners are more concerned with how individuals maintain psychological disturbance. As we noted previously, Ellis believed all people have a biological predisposition to act and think irrationally. Their biology coupled with their experiences provide a vulnerability to disturbance that is then solidified when they reindoctrinate themselves with irrational beliefs in the present. Basically put, all people are vulnerable to "crooked thinking," and the only way they can remediate the problem is by working passionately to "think straight."

Although REBT proponents espouse psychological interactionism, wherein a person's thoughts, feelings, and behaviors are seen as interdependent and overlapping, they consider the core of maladjustment to be one's belief system. They hold that humans tend to think absolutistically about activating events. These absolute conclusions tend to take the form of three basic musts, shoulds, and oughts (Dryden & DiGiuseppe, 1990), which we outline below.

1. **Musts about self:** These beliefs are declaratives about one's worth and expected success. Examples include, "I must be liked by others, and if someone does not like me, then I am horrible," or "I can't stand it when I am not picked first for the team. I am a failure if I am not the best." As a result of self-directed musts, a person typically experiences emotional consequences of guilt, shame, and feelings of inferiority, and the behavioral consequences of underachievement.
2. **Musts about others:** A person directs these beliefs at others and makes demands on others' behavior. "You must treat me with respect, because when you don't, I fall apart," and "You mustn't get angry with me, because if you do, it means you do not love me and I can not handle that," are common examples. Emotional consequences of anger, resentment, and jealousy, and behavioral consequences of passive-aggressive behavior and acts of violence are common results of these musts.
3. **Musts about the world:** With these beliefs, a person makes demands about how life should be at all times and under all conditions. Examples include, "Life must be fair, and if it is not, then I am a victim," and "Life should be happy, and if I'm not completely happy, then I am miserable." The emotional consequences of helplessness and hopelessness and the behavioral consequences of procrastination and suicide are all possible outcomes of these beliefs.

By using such beliefs, a person constructs a "musturbatory" belief system or ideology. The REBT practitioners consider such a system to be, at its core, irrational, because it increases the probability that the beliefs will interfere with the person's goal achievement and satisfaction in and with life (Ellis, 1977a).

Individuals who adhere to an irrational philosophy based on the core musturbatory beliefs typically derive specific types of thinking based on the three core musts. These thoughts, contrasted with rational thoughts, reflect the qualities of extremeness and rigidity. Typical forms of irrational musturbatory derivative thoughts include:

1. **Awfulizing:** The person perceives the situation as 100% bad. "I missed my bus and that is horrible. My whole week is ruined!"
2. **I-Can't-Stand-It-itis:** With this type of thoughts, a person generates a low tolerance for frustration and an expectation that a catastrophe will occur if one continues to encounter the current level of perceived stress. "I can't stand my job. It's too mundane and stupid. I will explode if I have to work there one more day."
3. **Damnation:** With these types of thoughts, a person produces intense criticism of self, other(s), or the environment. An example of damnation of self is, "I am such a complete loser. No wonder I can't get dates. I'm worthless." An example of damnation of others is, "She is a bitch to treat me in this disrespectful way." Inherent in damnation are expectations about how things *should* be; hence, Ellis sometimes referred to these kinds of thoughts as "shoulding" on self, others, and/ or the world.

TABLE 10.2   Principles that Differentiate Appropriate and Inappropriate Negative Emotions

Inappropriate Negative Emotions	Appropriate Negative Emotions
Experienced as emotional pain	Experienced as a warning, an alert
Motivate self-sabotaging behaviors	Motivate self-actualizing behaviors
Paralyze; inhibit goal achievement	Energize; facilitate goal achievement

4. **Always and Never Thinking:** In this irrational thought style, a person uses a small amount of evidence to make sweeping conclusions about self, others, or the environment. "My mom won't take me to the movies. She never does anything for me."

Ellis believed that once people have disturbed themselves with irrational beliefs and thoughts, they tend to reindoctrinate themselves—reconfirm to themselves the validity of those beliefs and thoughts. This self-perpetuation of the irrational belief cycle renders it resistant to change. A practice through which people render themselves particularly resistant to change is secondary disturbance. In secondary disturbance, people overlay a second disturbance on top of a primary one. Common examples of secondary disturbances include becoming anxious about being anxious (see APA, 2000, section on Panic Disorder with Agoraphobia), feeling hopeless about depression, and worrying about insomnia. Another example involves condemnation, which generally follows the formula, "It's your fault I'm so [insert any emotional consequence] that I can't [insert any behavioral consequence];" for example, "It's your fault I'm so depressed that I can't get up and go to work." These secondary disturbances not only make the symptoms of the primary problem worse but also make the primary problem more difficult to treat because the secondary disturbance acts as a barrier between rational disputation and the primary problem. In each example the secondary disturbance prevents treatment of the primary disturbance, increases the level of irrationality, and thus increases the amount of psychological disturbance the person has generated.

Before leaving the topic of mental health and unhealth, we want to clarify that not all negative emotions are unhealthy and not all positive emotions are healthy. Everything depends on the extremeness and rigidity of one's beliefs and, consequently, one's emotions and behavior. It is one thing to feel sad about a loss; it's another to become enraged or become paralyzed with depression. It is one thing to feel delighted about a gain; it is another to become recklessly elated. Crawford and Ellis (1989) discussed how rigid beliefs about activating events yield self-defeating consequences, whereas flexible beliefs about activating events yield self-actualizing consequences. Table 10.2 contains principles that differentiate appropriate and inappropriate *negative* emotions. Through this aspect of the theory, REBT parallels existential theory by differentiating inappropriate from appropriate negative emotions based on their impact on the individual.

Table 10.3 outlines Ellis's view of common irrational and rational beliefs and serves to summarize the REBT perspective on unhealthy and healthy functioning.

THE PERSONALITY CHANGE PROCESS

People change their feelings and actions by changing their beliefs and thinking. Since of the innate human tendency toward rationality, people have the capacity to change their beliefs and thinking on their own in the normal course of life. However, because of the innate human tendency toward irrationality, combined with exposure to, and incorporation of,

TABLE 10.3   The 10 Major Irrational and Rational Beliefs of REBT

Ten Major Irrational Beliefs	Ten Major Rational Beliefs
1. I must have love or approval from all people I find significant.	1. Although it is desirable for me to be approved of and loved, I do not need it to survive. It is most desirable to concentrate on self-acceptance and on loving instead of being loved.
2. I must be thoroughly competent, adequate, and achieving.	2. It is more advisable to accept myself as an imperfect creature with human limitations and fallibilities.
3. When people act obnoxiously and unfairly, I should blame and damn them and see them as bad, wicked, or rotten individuals.	3. People often behave unfairly, stupidly, and inconsiderately and it would be better if they were helped to change their ways rather than to be severely damned and punished. It is not legitimate to rate their total worth on the basis of their individual acts.
4. Things are awful, terrible, and catastrophic when I get seriously frustrated, treated unfairly, or rejected.	4. Although it is undesirable to fail to get what I want, it is seldom awful nor is it intolerable.
5. Emotional misery comes from external pressures, and I have little ability to control or change my feelings.	5. Since I mainly create my own emotional upsets, I can change them by thinking more rationally.
6. If something seems dangerous or fearsome, I must preoccupy myself with and make myself anxious about it.	6. Worrying will not magically make things disappear. I will do my best to deal with potentially distressful events and when this proves impossible, I will accept the inevitable.
7. It is easier to avoid facing many life difficulties and self-responsibilities rather than to undertake more rewarding forms of self-discipline.	7. In the long run, the easy and undisciplined way is less rewarding than is the longer range approach to pleasure and enjoyment.
8. My past remains all-important, and because something once strongly influenced my life, it has to keep determining my feelings and behavior today.	8. Continual rethinking of my old assumptions and reworking of my past habits can help minimize most of the pernicious influences from my childhood and adolescence.
9. People and things should turn out better than they do, and I must view things as horrible and awful if I do not find good solutions to life's grim realities.	9. Whether I like it or not, reality exists, and I'd better accept its existence before I set about trying to change it.
10. I can achieve maximum happiness by inertia and inaction or by passively and uncommittedly "enjoying myself."	10. I will tend to be happiest if I get involved in long-term, challenging work that requires me to take risks and forces me to act against my own inertia.

Source: From Ellis, A., & Harper, R. A. (1997) *A New guide to rational living.* North Hollywood, CA: Melvin Powers.

irrational beliefs and thinking in their social environments, people tend to create and reindoctrinate themselves with irrationality. Thus, people are most likely to change in the special situation of psychotherapy that is structured to facilitate maximum actualization of their innate rational tendencies.

Client's Role

REBT is an active and directive form of therapy. A client who will benefit is the client who is interactive and cooperative. The client needs to be motivated to learn about the REBT philosophy, to be open to exploring one's belief system as the point of change, and to possess enough cognitive sophistication to grasp the process. Clients who enter therapy expecting to explore past experiences and have their feelings extensively validated will be disappointed within the REBT framework. Dryden (1990, p. 14) outlined the following steps the client must be willing to take when working in collaboration with an REBT therapist.

1. Acknowledge the problem.
2. Identify and overcome any secondary disturbances about this problem.
3. Identify the irrational belief that underpins the primary problem.
4. Understand why the irrational belief is irrational (illogical, inconsistent with reality, and will give them poor results in life).
5. Realize why the rational alternative to this irrational belief is logical, is consistent with reality, and will give them better results in life.
6. Challenge the irrational belief to strengthen the conviction in the rational alternative.
7. Learn to use a variety of cognitive, emotional, imaginal, and behavioral assignments to strengthen the conviction in the rational belief and weaken the conviction in the irrational belief.
8. Identify and overcome obstacles to therapeutic change using the above structure, while simultaneously accepting the tendency to personally construct such obstacles.
9. Keep working against the tendency to think and act irrationally.

Counselor's Role

Although the client–counselor relationship is important in REBT, it differs from the relationship endorsed in many of the other theories we discuss in this textbook. Unlike Rogers, Ellis disagreed with the notion that a warm relationship provides the necessary and sufficient conditions for change. In fact, Ellis believed that devoting energy to developing warmth between counselor and client could actually interfere with and distract from the therapeutic goals. Furthermore, it could feed into a client's irrational belief that "I must be loved by everyone I find important." However, Ellis stressed that it is essential for a counselor to accept a client unconditionally if the client is to change. Therefore, effective REBT counselors learn how to actively dispute and reject the client's irrational emotions and behaviors, along with the antecedent irrational beliefs and thoughts, while unconditionally accepting the client as a striving, yet fallible, human being (Dryden & DiGiuseppe, 1990; Ellis, 1962; Ellis & Dryden, 1997; Weinrach, 1995). Novice therapists might find this "despise the behavior but embrace the person" dynamic difficult to grasp. The example below demonstrates the process.

Client: I don't know. It's just that I feel so stupid, like everybody is judging me.

Counselor: Based on that statement, you are saying that you feel stupid because everyone is judging you?

Client: Yeah, I guess.

Counselor: I don't think "everyone" has anything to do with it. I think you believe that you are stupid and are using other people to take the blame for your feelings. Let's take "everyone" out of the picture. Let's stick with you. Say "I am stupid " and then prove to me why you are "stupid."

Client: Well, I don't know.

Counselor: Sure you do. The self-evaluation that concluded that you were stupid comes from within you, so let's hear it. Convince me.

Client: Well, I'm not doing a very good job here. I feel confused.

Counselor: Is it such a catastrophe to feel confused? Is it so horrible? Confusion is part of the human condition. It seems that the only failure here today was in your ability to convince me, part of the "everyone," that you are stupid. What's your take on that failure?

Client: (laughing) It's not so bad.

In this example the counselor attacks the irrational label of stupid by pushing the client to personalize and define the term. The counselor normalizes the feelings of the client while demonstrating that the belief is not only internally based but also lacks empirical support. In the end, the counselor disputes the conclusion that the client is stupid and conceptualizes the original irrational belief as a mistake (failure).

Ellis (1997a) maintained that effective REBT therapists are active and directive; are skilled teachers, communicators, and problem solvers; have a good sense of humor that they use appropriately in session; are not afraid to take appropriate therapeutic risks such as confronting clients; are energetic and forceful; and accept themselves as imperfect and have the courage to work on their imperfections. REBT practitioners focus primarily on the present, actively exploring to identify clients' irrational beliefs, disputing those beliefs, and instructing clients in the art of REBT. Therefore, counselors do not take lengthy histories and put little weight on childhood and unconscious factors when considering present client dysfunction. Although REBT counselors are present-oriented and typically move quickly, they may find therapeutic benefit in moving more slowly in the case of certain client styles and presenting problems, for example, trauma such as rape or incest (Dryden, 1990; Ellis, 2000b; Zachary, 1980).

Practitioners of REBT need to be aware of how their own absolutistic beliefs may interfere with client work. Ellis (1983, pp. 4–7) outlined several common irrational beliefs that therapists need to modify to work effectively with clients.

1. I have to be successful with all of my clients all of the time.
2. I have to be respected and loved by all of my clients.
3. I must be a great counselor and be more competent than any other counselor I know.
4. As I am working so hard, my clients must also work hard and listen to what I say.
5. Since I am human, I must be able to have a good time in the session and use these sessions to get something useful for myself such as emotional satisfaction or learning how to solve my own problems.

As behavioral consequences of any of these beliefs, a counselor may inappropriately push the client to change. For example, a counselor who believes that his worth is linked to client change may push the client to change before she is ready or may develop feelings of resentment toward the client when she is not moving at the counselor's pace: "That client is just stuck. She's resistant to therapy." Conversely, a therapist who believes the client must like him at all times may not confront the client enough for fear that the client may dislike him. It is vital for REBT practitioners to explore their own belief systems and actively dispute irrational beliefs that may interfere with therapy. Two examples of ways for a counselor to monitor one's own beliefs and, thus, improve one's practice of counseling are to seek supervision and to pursue one's own counseling.

Stages and Techniques

Although Ellis never specified a stage progression of REBT, several authors have outlined steps or stages of the therapeutic process (Dryden, 1990; Dryden & DiGiuseppe, 1990). In this section, we discuss the main stages—beginning, middle, and ending—along with the techniques associated with each stage.

Beginning

In the beginning stage, the counselor builds rapport with the client and teaches the client the basics of REBT. Although Ellis believed that a warm relationship was not a necessary or sufficient condition for change, he did believe that the counselor and client need a good working relationship to make progress. Dryden (1990) asserted that a counselor contributes to the establishment of a good working relationship by setting the parameters of counseling (fees, length of sessions, frequency of sessions), collaborating with the client on goals, encouraging discussion of issues, demonstrating unconditional acceptance, and establishing therapeutic credibility by adopting a problem-solving approach. As the therapeutic alliance solidifies, the client will be more open to the counselor's confrontations and disputations.

The REBT practitioner takes an active–directive approach from the start of therapy. Assuming that the client knows nothing about the therapeutic process and specifics of REBT, the therapist instructs the client in the art of irrational belief disputation. During sessions, the counselor asks the client to identify situations, which the counselor labels "A" along with the client's feelings and actions in those situations, which the counselor labels emotional and behavioral "C," and helps the client identify the beliefs, "B," that led to the client's C. In some situations, the client will report having felt and acted rationally, and counselor and client can identify the client's rational beliefs that potentiated the client's rational response. In others, such as the target problem(s) the client came to counseling to address, the client will report having felt and possibly acted irrationally. In this case, counselor and client would identify the client's irrational beliefs and the counselor would dispute (D) them so the client could experience how such disputation results in the effects (E) of more rational thinking and, consequently, more self-enhancing feelings and actions. By repeating this process with several client examples, the client begins to internalize the ABC model and the therapeutic process. The counselor encourages the client to maximize learning by completing homework assignments that counselors can find in a variety of REBT-oriented workbooks (Dryden & Gordon, 1990; Ellis, 1988). The therapist's goals for the end of the beginning stage are for the therapeutic alliance to be formed and for the client to have a working knowledge of the basics of REBT.

Middle

In the middle stage, counselor and client use the ABC model to identify and dispute core irrational beliefs. Whereas disputing target problem irrational beliefs will remediate that problem, identifying and disputing core irrational beliefs will also result in more widespread changes in other aspects of life. For example, a person who was having problems at work because of the irrational belief, "I must always be liked by my coworkers" can identify a core irrational belief, such as, "I must be liked by everyone, or I am a complete loser." Disputing the target problem irrational belief and, later, the core irrational belief, can have an impact on the target problem site, work, and also on the client's other relationships, such as with one's intimate partner and children.

During this stage, the therapist often employs a wide range of techniques to help the client engage in a rational existence and integrate new rational beliefs. Ellis and other REBT practitioners have categorized these techniques into cognitive, emotive, and behavioral groupings.

Cognitive Techniques   As the name implies, cognitive techniques involve the client employing reason to produce more rational situational responses and a more rational philosophy overall. Some of these techniques include:

1. **Rational self-statements:** The counselor encourages the client to create a list of rational statements that dispute common irrational beliefs. "It is normal to make mistakes. It means I am human." "I would like to make my husband happy, but if I sometimes don't, it is not the end of the world." "Smart people do not have to say smart things all of the time." Having this list can help clients in their disputation work.

2. **Becoming an REBT teacher:** Others' irrational beliefs are usually much easier to identify than one's own. By encouraging clients to actively teach the principles of REBT to others, counselors help clients gains additional practice in the REBT process. The personal impact of learning through teaching is an important aspect of REBT homework and of REBT-oriented group work (Ellis, 1997b; Ellis & Dryden, 1997).

3. **Semantic precision:** An important aspect of disputing irrational beliefs is paying attention to and correcting irrational language (Dryden, 1990). For example, a client can change, "I can't possibly speak to that professor" to "I am choosing not to speak to that professor because I am afraid;" or "It would be devastating if my girlfriend did not call me this evening" to "It would be disappointing, but bearable, if my girlfriend did not call me this evening." Inherent in this precision is the recognition that thinking and speaking in terms of anticipated catastrophe or other extremes is irrational and that distinguishing between needs and preferences—and thinking and speaking in terms of the latter rather than the former—is rational.

Emotive Techniques   Again, as the name implies, with these techniques, counselor or client purposely evoke emotion as a means to facilitate disputation of irrational beliefs.

1. **Imagery:** The use of imagery can take many forms in REBT. One method is to fix an image of an unpleasant activating event (A) and mentally switch from an irrational belief about A to a rational thought belief about A and feel the difference in the sensation of the emotional consequence (C). The goal is for the client to experience the change in emotion by changing the thought. In another method, the therapist uses imagery to dispute A by following that thought to its catastrophic consequence. For example:

Client: If Melissa breaks up with me, my life will be over.

Counselor: Let's take a trip through time and get snapshots of your life assuming that Melissa breaks up with you right now. What will you look like in 2 hours?

Client: I would be a wreck, crying and alone in my room.

Counselor: That sounds pretty sad. Let's take a look 2 weeks from now. What will you be doing?

Client: I don't know. Probably still sad.

Counselor: But you will still be here, right?

Client: Yeah.

Counselor: Good. What about 6 months from now?

Client: Wow, that's a long time. I guess I would be working, and dating someone else.

Counselor: You are a fast mover! What about 10 years from now?

Client: I'll be out of college. I'll have my degree and hopefully a job. Who knows, I might even be married.

Counselor: So, getting back to Melissa. You will be sad if she breaks up with you, but it is NOT the end of the world. Right?

Through imagery, the client is able to work past the catastrophe that is tied to the irrational belief about the break up.

2. **Humor:** The judicious use of humor can be an excellent way for a counselor to demonstrate the irrationality of a client's beliefs. When extended to its illogical end, the inherent nature of an irrational belief is that it is unbelievable, and sometimes even funny. One way Ellis used humor is through constructing humorous songs that both client and therapist can sing. The very creative therapist and/or client can tailor such songs to the client's personal irrational beliefs. A couple constructed the following song during their time in therapy:

I Hate Me, You Hate You
(Sung to the tune of "I Love You," the *Barney & Friends* song)

I hate me, You hate you
Now there is no one to be mean to
I am so bad, You could not love me
We're the worst example of matrimony

I hate me, You hate you
Now there's nothing left to do
But sit in the house and cry our life away
No one would miss us anyway

3. **Shame-attacking exercises:** A counselor uses these experiments to help clients feel less intimidated and impacted by how others feel about them. Counselors can encourage clients to break minor social mores, such as skipping down the street, singing to oneself, or asking silly questions, while making note of how others respond. One of two things will happen: Either people will not notice or will respond neutrally or positively, or they will respond negatively. In the

first scenario, clients will learn that they put too much pressure on themselves worrying that others will notice them making mistakes. In the second scenario, clients will learn that even when people actually think they are weird, clients can think differently. As one client put it, "You cannot imagine how liberating it was to act completely goofy. This one guy thought I was nuts. He said, 'Cut it out, you freak.' The old me would have been humiliated, but I just walked away and continued my day. I was fine!" Shame-attacking exercises can be fun and freeing for clients who obsessively worry about others' negative reactions to them, but it is crucial that the activities be legal and that they not risk possible physical injury to the client or others.

Behavioral Techniques   Once again, as the name implies, with this category of techniques, counselors employ client actions to dispute irrational, and promote rational, thoughts and beliefs. The REBT practitioners realize that, to be effective in attacking irrational beliefs, clients need to practice consistently both inside and outside of the therapy session. Thus, counselors routinely assign activity-oriented homework based on in vivo desensitization and flooding models (For more details, see Chapter 8). With these techniques, counselors intend to help clients tolerate discomfort or encourage them to avoid procrastination (Grieger & Boyd, 1980). For example, in the case of a client who is afraid that his wife will reject him if he requests affection from her, the counselor might assign him to ask her 10 times a day for various levels of affection, such as holding hands, hugging, and kissing, and to record the outcome of each request. At the next session, counselor and client will discuss the results of this experiment, and the client very likely will realize that he gets more affection when he is assertive and that although he will be turned down some of the time, his wife's refusal is situational—not a wholesale rejection of him—and, thus, is not catastrophic.

Ending

The last part of the REBT counseling process is called the ending stage. This stage is marked by a client's resolution of presenting problems and, more importantly, demonstrated ability to utilize the REBT disputation process as a method for current and future problem solving. Along with termination of the therapeutic relationship, counselors can expect clients to express irrational beliefs about their ability to maintain their progress without counseling. For example, a client might say or imply, "I must have therapy to cope. Without therapy I will go back to the way things were." Ellis (1996, pp. 96–100) encouraged clients to maintain their therapeutic gains by doing the following:

1. Reinforce therapeutic learning by reviewing what worked in counseling.
2. Continuously risk and try new behaviors. You can use successes to add to a success mentality and mistakes to reaffirm that you can survive poor decisions.
3. When you do not get what you want, use rational thinking continuously to generate appropriate negative feelings, such as sadness, disappointment, and/or frustration, and note the difference between those thoughts and feelings and irrational thoughts and their associated inappropriate negative feelings, such as panic, depression, shame, and/or extreme guilt.
4. Encourage self-motivation and dispute procrastination.
5. Practice using REBT, and teach it to friends. Practicing reinstills rational living, and the more members of your social system know about REBT, the more support you are likely to receive.

6. Find pleasure in life. Developing new interests provides intrinsic and extrinsic rewards that give you something to strive to attain.

CONTRIBUTIONS AND LIMITATIONS

Interface With Recent Developments in the Mental Health Field

The Nature–Nurture Question

When Ellis first developed REBT, he posited that, for the most part, children learned disturbance from their environments. After working with clients for many years, Ellis changed his view to incorporate the growing evidence of the role that heredity plays in psychological dysfunction. He came to believe that a person's capacity to be rational and irrational is not determined by any one source but instead is the outcome of intertwining biological and environmental variables. In REBT theory, neither nature nor nurture holds ultimate sway over an individual's thought processes. Although Ellis believed that everyone has irrational thoughts and is born vulnerable to irrationality, all humans have an innate tendency toward both irrationality and rationality, one's environment encourages both, and each person has the capacity to reinstill rational or irrational belief systems in oneself.

DSM–IV–TR *Diagnosis*

In this age of managed care, REBT practitioners use diagnosis as necessary. Ellis believed that, regardless of diagnosis, REBT can be helpful to the client through uncovering and disputing the irrational beliefs that contribute to the reporting of catastrophic symptomatology. However, Ellis (1998) noted that REBT is more effective with single-issue clients than with more seriously disturbed clients, as is the case with other psychotherapeutic approaches. Outcome studies have demonstrated a correlation between clusters of certain irrational beliefs from Ellis's original list and certain specific diagnostic mental disorders (Woods, 1992).

Pharmacotherapy

Consistent with most theories of therapy, REBT practitioners support using medication as an adjunct to counseling in cases in which empirical studies have validated a pharmacological treatment. Ellis (2000b) commented that REBT is appropriate for clients with numerous profiles including "overt psychotics ... when they are under medication" (p. 191). For REBT practitioners, a client's beliefs about medication would be as instructive and important as the chemical outcome. For example, a client who believes that medication is a magic bullet or an instant cure would probably forgo therapy and thus remain irrational. The REBT proponents encourage disputation of all absolutistic beliefs, even those regarding treatment.

Managed Care and Brief Therapy

Consistent with its directive, high-energy style, REBT seems well suited for brief therapy. As noted previously, Ellis developed REBT out of his dissatisfaction with the slow and arduous process of analysis. Even when Ellis was experimenting with more active forms of psychoanalysis, he reported cutting analysis time from 100 sessions to around 35 sessions, often with better results (Ellis, 1962).

Research analyzing treatment length yielded the finding that the average number of sessions in the course of REBT treatment was 16.5 (DiGiuseppe, 1991). Meanwhile, Ellis wrote extensively about applying REBT to even shorter time frames: from 1 session to as many as 20 structured sessions (Ellis, 1992, 1996). Ellis (2000b) outlined several approaches that can accelerate the REBT therapeutic process. For example, during the time between sessions, clients can listen repeatedly to the audiotapes of previous sessions. Clients can experience new insights, learning, and reindoctrination of disputed irrational beliefs outside the weekly session and, thus, can reduce the overall time they spend in therapy. Additionally, they can use homework and worksheets specifically designed for REBT between sessions. Such written activities also can help the client rely less on the therapist for disputation and more on individual skills the client can continue to use after having completed counseling.

Technical Eclecticism

Although REBT shares many similarities with person-centered, Adlerian, existential, Gestalt, cognitive, behavioral, and other theories of change, REBT is a unique theory with a distinctive approach to treatment. Thus, REBT practitioners, like all practitioners well versed in counseling theory, would not endorse theoretical eclecticism. Regarding technical eclecticism, REBT proponents would engage only in a technique or process that was specifically designed to illuminate and dispute a client's irrational beliefs. Indeed, REBT practitioners can utilize a broad range of techniques from various schools of thought that help with these processes. In this regard, REBT proponents support and encourage technical eclecticism.

Diversity Issues

As we discussed in Chapter 1, U.S. culture is quickly moving in the direction of increasing diversity. The basic tenets of REBT support people's flexibility in their thinking and attitudes about self and others. In considering cultural diversity, Ellis (1998) encouraged counselors not to assume that clients share the same worldview as the counselor. It is equally important for counselors to realize that cultural beliefs can be irrational, rigid, and absolutistic or rational, flexible, and preferential. Clients who believe that all people must respect their culture are likely to feel angry, frustrated, and victimized when a counselor (or anyone else) does not appreciate their diversity. Internally, if clients believe they must absolutely adhere to their cultural rules at all times, they will constantly evaluate themselves and denigrate themselves for the slightest infraction of those rules. REBT practitioners urge all clients, regardless of culture, to replace the demandingness of musts and shoulds with the flexibility of preferential beliefs. It should be noted that in enacting this very practice, counselors could be violating the values of some conservative cultures that, themselves, emphasize rigid adherence to cultural norms.

Beyond the general applications of REBT to various cultures, authors have pointed to specific examples utilizing REBT in a multicultural setting. Ellis (2002) detailed the use of REBT with clients from various Asian cultures. Lega and Ellis (2001) adapted the Attributes and Beliefs Inventory for Spanish speaking clients and studied its effectiveness on clients from Colombia, Spain, El Salvador, and the United States. Sapp, McNeely, and Torres (2007) used REBT to counsel African Americans who were dealing with end of life issues and found the approach effective.

Regarding gender diversity, congruent with its underlying humanistic philosophy, REBT can help both men and women lead rational lives and move beyond rigid, stereotypical gender roles. Ellis firmly believed in the right of all individuals to live the type of lives they desire and opposed having one set of standards for men and another for women. REBT proponents recognize that women in the past have experienced gender roles that stressed dependence and inferiority and currently experience gender roles containing musts and shoulds regarding independence and power. Ellis and other REBT proponents have been extremely active in designing programs for women to explore and dispute irrational beliefs related to gender roles. They have built these programs around various components such as consciousness raising through group counseling; bibliotherapy emphasizing other women's struggles and successes; assertiveness training; encouraging and developing female friendships and mentorships; developing positive self-messages such as, "I am making a valuable contribution as a full-time mom;" disputing culturally based irrational relationship demands such as, "I need a man to survive" or "I should be married by the time I am 28;" and self-pleasuring assignments, including the belief, "I have a right to have fun" (Bernard, 1991; Wolfe & Russianoff, 1997).

Ellis's view of sexual orientation rested on the belief that humans are born bisexual, with the ability to enjoy sexual relationships with any partner. Individuals exhibit irrationality in believing, "I must have sex only with women" or "I must have sex only with men." Ellis's 1965 book, *Homosexuality: Its Causes and Cure*, although laced with terminology linking homosexuality to dysfunction as was customary at that time, stressed that homosexuality was not inherently problematic or abnormal. However, Ellis did believe that homosexuality could be viewed as irrational because the social costs of the supposed choice of homosexual orientation are high. Faced with constant opposition, a homosexual's freedom is reduced, so choosing to continue such behavior when it is obviously harmful would be, by definition, irrational. Mylott (1994) outlined 12 irrational beliefs that "drive gay man and women crazy" (p. 61). True to Ellis's conceptualization, many of the irrational beliefs are not gay specific and could easily apply to heterosexual men and women, such as "I need to have sex with another person" (p. 62) and "I need to be loved" (p. 63). However, a few pertain exclusively to a homosexual lifestyle: "People shouldn't be homophobic" (p. 66); "I can only accept my homosexuality if I know for certain that it is genetically determined, or that God made me gay. Otherwise, I cannot accept myself" (p. 67).

The issue of spirituality is an excellent example of REBT's flexibility and growth over time. In early formulations of his theory, Ellis saw religious beliefs as irrational and contributory to emotional disturbance (Ellis, 1960, 1971, 1973). He contended that spiritual beliefs in higher powers, ultimate dictums of right and wrong, and eternal damnation or punishment usually lead people to surrender self-direction or to engage in constant self-evaluation in the form of assessment of sin, which leads to self-criticism, guilt, and shame. As Ellis (1980) concluded, "devout faith in supra human entities and powers always leads to poor emotional health and long range unhappiness" (p. 327).

Over time, numerous REBT practitioners and researchers have studied the integration of REBT philosophy with spiritual and religious ideas and philosophies (DiGiuseppe, Robin, & Dryden, 1992; Johnson, 1993; Johnson, Ridely, & Nielsen, 2000; Nielsen, Johnson, & Ridley, 2000). Although most of these authors have focused on organized forms of religion, some have found basic philosophical similarities between REBT and many religious–spiritual philosophies (Ellis, 2000b; Johnson, 1994; Johnson et al., 2000; Nielsen, 1994; Nielsen et al., 2000). Some of this common ground includes:

- The view that all people are worthy of forgiveness and that imperfection is a part of the human condition.
- The use of education as a change agent.
- The perspective that all people have free will and thus largely create their own health or disturbance and are responsible for behaving and thinking differently ("God helps those who helps themselves").
- The encouragement of high frustration tolerance; spiritual proponents often discuss this capacity in the context of faith.

Ellis reviewed these discussions and research and, consistent with his philosophy of flexibility, integrated the new ideas into REBT. He was most persuaded by the studies that demonstrated that people who viewed their chosen God as supportive, loving, and caring were more likely to lead healthier lives than those who viewed their God as vengeful or angry (Gorsuch, 1988; Hood, Spilka, Hunsberger, & Gorsuch, 1996; Kirkpatrick, 1997). Upon considering these writings, Ellis moderated his earlier view and acknowledged that some absolutistic spiritual beliefs could be healthy, but he continued to believe firmly that most devout, dogmatic, rigid beliefs still contribute to irrational thinking. "My view now is that religious and nonreligious beliefs in themselves do not help people to be emotionally 'healthy' or 'unhealthy.' Instead their emotional health is significantly affected by the kind of religious and nonreligious beliefs they hold" (2000a, p. 30).

If you are interested in evidence of REBT proponents that have integrated spirituality into their theoretical perspectives, we encourage you to read Weinrach et al.'s (2006) article in which seven experts on REBT reflected on the events of September 11, 2001 in which terrorists destroyed the two World Trade Center buildings in New York City. Each author wrote from a personal–theoretical perspective and commented specifically on the role of one's own religious–spiritual views and how those views impacted one's conceptualization of the events. The confluence of personal, spiritual, and professional values with such a profound event provides an excellent example of the authors' struggles to balance all three and yet emphasizes the value of doing so and arriving at a well-integrated theory—indeed, a well-integrated philosophy of life.

Effectiveness of Psychotherapy

In 1977, Ellis (1977b) wrote an exhaustive review of studies in which results supported the therapeutic effectiveness of REBT. He not only summarized outcome studies but he outlined the key philosophical underpinnings of the theory and included over 950 citations that supported the various elements of the approach. DiGiuseppe and Miller (1977) also conducted a review of empirical outcome studies and reported substantial support of the efficacy of REBT with a wide range of problems and populations. Since these two overviews, hundreds of other researchers have published articles citing the effectiveness of REBT when compared with other forms of therapy or with no therapy (see Engels, Garnefski, & Diekstra, 1993; Lyons & Woods, 1991; Silverman, McCarthy, & McGovern, 1992). More recently David, Szentagotai, Lupu, and Cosman (2008) conducted a randomized clinical trial comparing REBT, cognitive therapy, and pharmacotherapy in treating major depression and found REBT to be significantly more effective at the 6-month follow-up measurement.

REBT theorists would have both assenting and dissenting views of Asay and Lambert's (1999) findings regarding factors that contribute to positive therapeutic outcome. For example, they would concur that extratherapeutic factors such as chronicity of the problem, client's motivation, and social support have an impact on outcome, but most REBT clinicians would assert that the client does have a modicum of control over these factors—if not direct control, then at least their interpretation of, and attitudes toward, these factors. REBT counselors as a whole would disagree with the need for a therapeutic relationship characterized by counselor warmth. The REBT would replace "warmth" with the counselor characteristics of "unconditional acceptance" and willingness to attack the client's irrational behaviors. Some critics might see the disputation process as attacking, yet REBT practitioners emphasize the "attack" is on the client's beliefs, not on the client.

Contributions

Ellis's contribution to the field rests primarily in three areas: his ability to translate Adler's ideas into a more present-oriented and focused approach, his ABC model, and his forceful personality. First, he has readily credited Adler with being the pioneer of cognitive forms of therapy and with contending that people generate their own disturbance via personally created beliefs about events. Ellis integrated Adler's core ideas and stripped away the childhood, family, and life task concepts, thus producing a theory based strictly on waging active war on present irrational beliefs. This here-and-now, no-nonsense approach makes even the common sense psychology of Adler seem complicated. REBT's simplified cognitive approach represented a divergence from conceptually dense intrapsychic theories, such as self-psychology, psychoanalysis, and Adlerian, and proved more pragmatic than what Ellis would probably consider some of the "touchy-feely" theories of his time, such as person-centered or Gestalt.

The ABC model that Ellis developed for specific application in REBT represents another distinguishing characteristic. The ABC structure provided an innovative way to demonstrate not only the change process but also the basic workings of the personality. Counselors use the ABC model as a tool for in-session demonstration and education as well as for client homework and ongoing learning outside of sessions.

Although some commentators might debate whether a theorist's personality could be a contribution to the field, Ellis's instructional and therapeutic manner has had an impact on the world of therapy. His abrasive, humorous, and confrontational style represented a stark contrast to past and contemporary theorists and practitioners. His personal style not only corresponded to the directive ideas found in his theory but it also demonstrated to a world of therapists that not all effective mental health professionals are warm and cuddly. Counseling students often respond strongly to Ellis's handling of clients in video demonstrations. One therapist (Johnson, 1980) responded to Ellis's therapeutic style by publishing a journal article titled, "Must the Rational Emotive Therapist Be Like Albert Ellis?" (His answer to the title question, in a nutshell: No!) Whatever one's viewpoint, Ellis's personality has been a primary contribution to his theory and thus to the field.

CURRENT STATUS

Considering the recent loss of REBT's creator, what is its current status? It is an interesting question that REBT experts answered and later reiterated. In 1995, nine members of the Institute for Rational-Emotive Therapy's International Training Standards and Review Committee published an article in the *Journal of Mental Health Counseling* titled, "Rational Emotive Behavior Therapy after Ellis: Predictions for the Future." Eleven years later, they republished the article in the *Journal of Rational-Emotive and Cognitive-Behavior Therapy* (Weinrach et al., 2007). Interestingly, the opinions about the future of REBT fell between the pessimism of Dryden, who predicted a collapse, and the optimism of Ellis (!), who stated that "fifty years after my death ... REBT will be alive and kicking!" (p. 204). Most of the experts felt that REBT would continue to have success in the areas of preventive education, dealing with low frustration tolerance, and other counseling issues. Now that Ellis is gone, therapists who practice REBT are challenged to carry the theory beyond his influence and drive. One year into this journey, the structure still exists. Researchers and clinicians can publish articles relevant to REBT in the *Journal of Rational-Emotive and Cognitive-Behavior Therapy*. Individuals interested in training or continuing education can enroll in the many seminars organized through the Albert Ellis Institute (formerly the Institute for Rational-Emotive Therapy).

SUMMARY

Albert Ellis created REBT as an active/directive/educational theory in which a therapist could address and dispute a client's irrational belief system. REBT includes an ABC model of personality, whereby a person's beliefs about events lead directly to emotional and behavioral consequences. Beliefs can be irrational or rational. Irrational beliefs are characterized by rigidity, self-evaluation, and absolutistic demands. These beliefs lead to magnified, self-defeating emotional and behavioral consequences, whereas rational beliefs, characterized by flexibility, lead to moderate, self-enhancing consequences or no consequences. Although everyone's biology and environment influence them to think both rationally and irrationally, most people lean toward the irrational.

Working within these basic therapeutic premises, REBT counselors do not rely on a warm relationship or uncovering of past experiences as change agents but, instead, focus on actively uncovering and disputing clients' irrational beliefs in the here and now. To facilitate effective disputation, REBT therapists use a variety of cognitive, emotional, and behavioral techniques. In therapy, clients and counselors work together to dispute irrationality, and clients learn the REBT process and integrate the methods so they can continue to use the techniques long after they have terminated formal therapy.

RECOMMENDED RESOURCES

Books

Dryden, W. (Ed.). (1990). *The essential Albert Ellis: Seminal writings on psychotherapy.* New York, NY: Springer. This edited work is very thorough and contains many of Ellis's most important written contributions. The text's two main sections, Theory and Practice, provide the reader with a broad scope of information that is easy to access and use.

Ellis, A. (1962). *Reason and emotion in psychotherapy.* Secaucus, NJ: Lyle Stuart. This classic text is comprehensive and gives the reader an excellent theoretical and historical flavor of REBT.

Audiovisuals

Interested viewers will be impressed by most of the tapes available from the Albert Ellis Institute. The videos include taped sessions with real clients presenting with a wide variety of issues. Below are three that we have found students seem to like the best. Except for the first, the remaining tapes can be ordered directly from the Institute by calling 212-535-0822.

Baxley, N. (Producer), & Ferraro, E. (Director). (1982). *Rational emotive therapy* (video recording). Champaign, IL: Research Press. Though dated, this video still provides an excellent overview of REBT as Ellis and others demonstrate it at Ellis's institute in New York City.

DiGiuseppe, R. *Coping with anger.* New York, NY: Albert Ellis Institute.

Wolfe, J. *Woman coping with depression and anger.* New York, NY: Albert Ellis Institute.

Web Sites

The best choice is the official Web site for the Albert Ellis Institute (http://www.rebtinstitute. org/). This site contains valuable information about REBT and the application of the theory. Readers have access to catalogues and informational resources. It is also the site to enroll in a wide array of training opportunities.

REFERENCES

American Psychiatric Association. (2000). *Diagnostic and statistical manual of mental disorders* (4th ed., text rev.). Washington, DC: Author.

Asay, T. P., & Lambert, M. J. (1999). The empirical case for the common factors in therapy: Quantitative findings. In M. A. Hubble, B. L. Duncan, & S. D. Miller (Eds.), *The heart and soul of change* (pp. 23–55). Washington, DC: American Psychological Association.

Bernard, M. (1991). *Staying rational in an irrational world.* New York, NY: Lyle Stuart.

Bernard, M. E., & Joyce, M. R. (1984). *Rational emotive therapy with children and adolescents.* New York, NY: Wiley.

Braaten, L. J. (1961). The main theories of "existentialism" from the viewpoint of a psychotherapist. *Mental Hygiene, 45,* 10–17.

Crawford, T., & Ellis, A. (1989). A dictionary of rational-emotive feelings and behaviors. *Journal of Rational-Emotive and Cognitive Behavior Therapy, 7,* 3–27.

David, D., Szentagotai, A., Lupu, V., & Cosman, D. (2008). Rational emotive behavior therapy, cognitive therapy, and medication in the treatment of major depression: A randomized clinical trial, posttreatment outcomes and six month follow-up. *Journal of Clinical Psychology, 64,* 728–746.

DiGiuseppe, R. (1991). A rational-emotive model of assessment. In M. E. Bernard (Ed.), *Using rational-emotive therapy effectively: A practitioner's guide* (pp. 151–172). New York, NY: Plenum.

DiGiuseppe, R., & Miller, N. J. (1977). A review of outcome studies on rational-emotive therapy. In A. Ellis & R. Grieger (Eds.), *Handbook of rational-emotive therapy* (pp. 72–95). New York, NY: Springer.

DiGiuseppe, R., Robin, M. W., & Dryden, W. (1992). On the compatibility of rational emotive therapy and Judeo-Christian philosophy: A focus on clinical strategies. *Journal of Cognitive Psychotherapy: An International Quarterly, 4,* 355–368.

Dryden, W. (1990). *Rational emotive counselling in action.* London, UK: Sage.

Dryden, W., & DiGiuseppe, R. (1990). *A primer on rational emotive therapy.* Champaign, IL: Research Press.

Dryden, W., & Gordon, J. (1990). *How to be a happier you: Solving your emotional problems by rational thinking.* London, UK: Sheldon Press.

Ellis, A. (1960). There is no place for the concept of sin in psychotherapy. *Journal of Counseling Psychology, 7,* 188–192.

Ellis, A. (1962). *Reason and emotion in psychotherapy.* Secaucus, NJ: Lyle Stuart.

Ellis, A. (1965). *Homosexuality: Its causes and cure.* New York, NY: Lyle Stuart.

Ellis, A. (1971). *The case against religion: A psychotherapist's view.* New York, NY: Institute for Rational Living.

Ellis, A. (1973). *Humanistic psychotherapy: A rational-emotive approach.* New York, NY: Institute for Rational Living.

Ellis, A. (1977a). The basic clinical theory of rational-emotive therapy. In A. Ellis & R. Grieger (Eds.), *Handbook of rational-emotive therapy* (pp. 3–34). New York, NY: Springer.

Ellis, A. (1977b). Research data supporting the clinical and personality hypotheses of RET and other cognitive-behavior therapies. In A. Ellis & R. Grieger (Eds.), *Handbook of rational-emotive therapy* (pp. 35–71). New York, NY: Springer.

Ellis, A. (1979). Toward a new theory of personality. In A. Ellis & J. M. Whitely (Eds.), *Theoretical and empirical foundations of rational-emotive therapy* (pp. 33–60). Monterey, CA: Brooks/Cole.

Ellis, A. (1980). Psychotherapy and atheistic values: A response to A. E. Bergin's psychotherapy and religious values. *Journal of Consulting and Clinical Psychology, 48,* 635–639.

Ellis, A. (1983). How to deal with your most difficult client: You. *Journal of Rational Emotive Therapy, 1,* 3–8.

Ellis, A. (1988). *How to stubbornly refuse to make yourself miserable about anything— yes, anything!* Secaucus, NJ: Lyle Stuart.

Ellis, A. (1992). Brief therapy: The rational-emotive method. In S. H. Budman, M. F. Hoyt, & S. Friedman (Eds.), *The first session in brief therapy* (pp. 36–58). New York, NY: Guilford.

Ellis, A. (1993). RET becomes REBT. *IRETletter, 1,* 4.

Ellis, A. (1996). *Better, deeper, and more enduring brief therapy: The rational emotive behavior therapy approach.* New York, NY: Brunner/Mazel.

Ellis, A. (1997a). REBT and its application to group therapy. In J. Yankura & W. Dryden (Eds.), *Special applications of REBT: A therapist's casebook* (pp. 131–161). New York, NY: Springer.

Ellis, A. (1997b). The evolution of Albert Ellis and rational emotive therapy (REBT). In J. K. Zeig (Ed.), *The evolution of psychotherapy* (pp. 69–78). New York, NY: Brunner/Mazel.

Ellis, A. (1998). *How to control your anxiety before it controls you.* Secaucus, NJ: Carol.

Ellis, A. (2000a). Can rational emotive behavior therapy (REBT) be effectively used with people who have devout beliefs in God and religion? *Professional Psychology: Research and Practice, 31,* 29–33.

Ellis, A. (2000b). Rational emotive behavior therapy. In R. J. Corsini & D. Wedding (Eds.), *Current psychotherapies* (6th ed., pp. 168–204). Itasca, IL: F. E. Peacock.

Ellis, A. (2002). *Overcoming resistance.* New York, NY: Springer.

Ellis, A., & Dryden, W. (1997). *The practice of rational emotive therapy.* New York, NY: Springer.

Ellis, A., & Harper, R. A. (1997). *A guide to new rational living.* North Hollywood, CA: Melvin Powers.

Engels, G. I., Garnefski, N., & Diekstra, R. F. W. (1993). Efficacy of rational-emotive therapy: A quantitative analysis. *Journal of Consulting and Clinical Psychology, 61,* 1083–1090.

Epictetus. (1955). *The enchiridion* (T. W. Higginson, Trans.). Indianapolis, IN: Bobs-Merrill.

Gorsuch, R. L. (1988). Psychology of religion. *Annual Review of Psychology, 39,* 201–221.

Grieger, R., & Boyd, J. (1980). *Rational-emotive therapy: A skills-based approach.* New York, NY: Van Nostrand Reinhold.

Hood, R. W., Spilka, B., Hunsberger, B., & Gorsuch, R. (1996). *The psychology of religion* (2nd ed.). New York, NY: Guilford.

Johnson, N. (1980). Must the rational emotive therapist be like Albert Ellis? *The Personnel and Guidance Journal, 59,* 49–51.

Johnson, W. B. (1993). Christian rational emotive therapy: A treatment protocol. *Journal of Psychology and Christianity, 12,* 254–261.

Johnson, W. B. (1994). Albert Ellis and the religionists: A history of the dialogue. *Journal of Psychology and Christianity, 13,* 301–311.

Johnson, W. B., Ridley, C. R., & Nielsen, S. (2000). Religiously sensitive rational emotive behavior therapy: Elegant solutions and ethical risks. *Professional Psychology: Research and Practice, 31,* 14–20.

Kirkpatrick, L. A. (1997). A longitudinal study of changes in religious belief and behavior as a function of individual differences in adult attachment style. *Journal for the Scientific Study of Religion, 36,* 207–217.

Lega, L. I., & Ellis, A. (2001). Rational emotive behavior therapy (REBT) in the new millennium: A cross-cultural approach. *Journal of Rational-Emotive and Cognitive—Behavioral Therapy, 19,* 201–222.

Lyons, L. C., & Woods, P. J. (1991). The efficacy of rational-emotive therapy: A quantitative review of outcome research. *Clinical Psychology Review, 11,* 357–369.

Mylott, K. (1994). Twelve irrational ideas that drive gay men and women crazy. *Journal of Rational Emotive and Cognitive Behavioral Therapy, 12,* 61–71.

Nielsen, S. L. (1994). Rational-emotive therapy and religion: Don't throw the therapeutic baby out with the holy water! *Journal of Psychology and Christianity, 13,* 312–322.

Nielsen, S. L., Johnson, W. B., & Ridley, C. R. (2000). Religiously sensitive rational emotive behavior therapy: Theory, techniques, and brief excerpts from a case. *Professional Psychology: Research and Practice, 31,* 21–28.

Sapp, M., McNeely, R. L., & Torres, J. B. (2007). Dying a 'good' death, the desire to die, and rational-emotive behavior therapy: Focus on aged African Americans and Hispanics/Latinos. In L. A. See (Ed.), *Human behavior in the social environment from an African-American perspective* (2nd ed., pp. 695–713). New York, NY: Haworth.

Silverman, M. S., McCarthy, M., & McGovern, T. (1992). A review of outcome studies of rational-emotive therapy from 1982–1989. *Journal of Rational-Emotive and Cognitive-Behavior Therapy, 10,* 111–186.

Weinrach, S. G. (1995). Rational emotive behavior therapy: A tough-minded therapy for a tender-minded profession. *Journal of Counseling and Development, 73,* 296–300.

Weinrach, S., DiGiuseppe, R., Wolfe, J., Ellis, A., Bernard, M., Dryden, W., ... Vernon, A. (2007). Rational emotive behavior therapy after Ellis: Predictions for the future. *Journal of Rational-Emotive and Cognitive Behavior Therapy, 24,* 199–213.

Weinrach, S., Dryden, W., DiMattia, D. J., Doyle, K. A., MacLaren, C., O'Kelly, M., & Malkison, R. (2006). Post-September 11th perspectives on religion, spirituality, and philosophy in the personal and professional lives of selected REBT cognoscenti. *Journal of Rational-Emotive and Cognitive-Behavioral Therapy, 24,* 257–288.

Wolfe, J., & Russianoff, P. (1997). Overcoming self negation in women. *Journal of Rational-Emotive and Cognitive Behavior Therapy, 15,* 81–92.

Woods, P. J. (1992). A study of belief and non-belief items from the Jones irrational beliefs test with implications for the theory of RET. *Journal of Rational-Emotive and Cognitive- Behavior Therapy, 10,* 41–52.

Zachary, I. (1980). RET with women: Some special issues. In R. Grieger & J. Boyd (Eds.), *Rational emotive therapy: A skills based approach* (pp. 249–264). New York, NY: Van Nostrand.

CHAPTER 11

Reality Therapy and Choice Theory

BACKGROUND OF THE THEORY

Historical Context

In the years when William Glasser first began formulating his views about the human change process, the psychological community at large was beginning to make an important shift. Starting primarily with Adler and Jung in the 1940s, mental health professionals were noting that human experience seemed to involve more than psychoanalysis had explained. By the 1950s, many practitioners and researchers were forming ideas that honored people's ability to choose and control their thoughts, feelings, and actions, thus freeing themselves from the chains of determinism. As the psychological Zeitgeist moved toward existentialism, psychotherapy increasingly reflected a focus away from a client's internal drives and toward a client's perception of the world; from a deterministic view of the past toward free will in the present; and from the counselor as anonymous analyst toward the counselor as involved participant in a relationship that was, itself, a factor in healing. It was in the context of this psychocultural revolution, when innovators were developing such theories as person-centered, existential, and Gestalt, that the genesis of reality therapy began.

Founder's Biographical Overview

William Glasser was born in 1925 in Cleveland, Ohio. His father was a small business owner who, as a young boy, had come to the United States with his Russian Jewish family to escape religious persecution. Glasser's mother emphasized education and encouraged young Glasser to read. During those early years, Glasser developed his views about relationships, personality, and control. "If the Olympics had an event in controlling, my mother could have gone for the gold medal. My father was totally choice theory. Never in the more than sixty years that I knew him did I ever see him try to control another person" (Glasser, 1998b, p. 90). Through his parents, Glasser experienced a continuum of behaviors that he eventually reflected in his theoretical constructs: his mother's investment in controlling others and his father's intention not to control others but, rather, to specialize in self-control.

Glasser followed his older brother and sister to college and followed his father's advice that a major in engineering would be "practical" (Wubbolding, 2000a). Glasser worked as a chemical engineer for about a year, but he wanted to pursue a career in psychology. During one of his graduate psychology courses, the instructor encouraged Glasser to pursue psychiatry. Glasser doubted that he would qualify for medical school due to his poor undergraduate grades, but he decided to complete some foundational work and apply. Case Western Reserve accepted him, and he excelled in his studies.

During his internship, Glasser chose to spend two years at the Veterans Administration Center in Los Angeles and then moved to University of California – Los Angeles (UCLA's) outpatient division for his third year. Throughout his medical education, Freudian theory dominated the thinking of the time, but this theory never really fit for Glasser. During his time at UCLA, G. Harrington supervised him. The two became very close and shared views that were at variance with pychoanalysis. In an interview, Glasser (Wubbolding, 2000a) recalled the moment when he chose to practice psychiatry in a different way. A client, who had been coming to the clinic for four years, met with Glasser and proceeded to discuss her problems with her grandfather, a topic she had discussed repeatedly with four other psychiatrists over the four-year span. Glasser responded:

> I can tell you that if you want to see me, I don't have any interest in your grandfather. There is nothing I can do about what went on with him, nothing you can do about what went on with him. He's dead. Rest in peace. But if that's what you want, then you'll have to say that you want a new psychiatrist because I think you have some problems, but you have been avoiding them for a number of years by talking about your grandfather, and I want to talk about what is going on in your life right now. I have no interest in what was wrong yesterday. (Wubbolding, 2000a, p. 49)

When Glasser reported the confrontation to Harrington, Harrington was supportive and remarked, with a handshake, "Join the club" (Wubbolding, 2000a, p. 49).

While still in his third year of internship, Glasser began work at the Ventura School for Girls, a residential facility for delinquent girls in Ventura, California. Glasser noted that the school was really run like a prison, where the authorities routinely punished the girls harshly and did little to create a sense of community. Glasser sensed that because the authorities viewed the girls as losers, the girls came to believe they were losers. Glasser adapted the program to give each girl responsibilities, taught that each person was responsible for her own behavior, treated each girl with kindness and respect, and verbally praised the residents (Berges, 1976). With the implementation of Glasser's program, the school's effectiveness improved markedly.

From these two seminal experiences, Glasser's reality therapy began to take shape. In 1965, he wrote *Reality Therapy*, and several other books followed, including those he wrote with his wife, Naomi, who was his personal and professional partner from the time of their marriage during his college years to her death in 1992. Glasser continuously lectured, taught, conducted private practice, and consulted with school systems during his early years of developing the approach. In 1977, Glasser used a work by William Powers (1973), *Behavior: The Control of Perception*, as a theoretical backdrop for his therapeutic approach. The basic theoretical tenet was that people's choices are attempts to control their perception that they are meeting their needs in the world.

As reality therapy has evolved, so has its name. With the integration of Powers's ideas, Glasser began to call his approach control theory. In the late 1990s, Glasser modified the theory, largely to avoid the negative connotation of the word *control*. Glasser wanted his theory to reflect the ideas of self-control and the power of choice. Therefore, he changed the name to choice theory. Today, choice theory provides the basis for the counseling model known as reality therapy.

Probably the best-known reality therapist besides Glasser himself is Robert Wubbolding. Because Wubbolding has contributed substantially to both the practice and research aspects of the professional reality therapy literature, we cited him extensively throughout this chapter.

Philosophical Underpinnings

In several of Glasser's works, he maintained that he developed choice theory primarily from his own experiences with patients. Unlike many of his predecessors who developed counseling theories, Glasser has not identified underlying ideas that may have contributed to his viewpoint. However, he has noted that many of his ideas are similar to, and concur with concepts in, several other theories of counseling. Therefore, in the following discussion, we focus on those similarities and points of divergence.

Reality therapy and Adlerian therapy seem to share many points of agreement. Adler viewed behavior as purposeful, and reality therapists concur with this teleological perspective. Adler posited that all humans strive for superiority and that this process could be healthy, striving for the betterment of humanity through cooperation with others, or unhealthy, striving for one's own superiority at the expense of others. This concept of motivation is similar to reality therapy's concept of responsible and irresponsible ways to fulfill one's needs. Glasser's recent focus on the central importance of the love and belonging need echoes Adler's emphasis on the need to belong as the primary goal of one's striving throughout life. Both theorists share the phenomenological stance of understanding the subjective worldview of the client. The points of divergence that most clearly differentiate these two theories include respective views on the importance of attending to and having insight into past experience: Adlerians consider these components vital to constructive change, whereas reality therapists consider them a diversion from constructive change.

Person-centered theory also shares similar philosophical beliefs with choice theory. Both include a belief in the purposefulness of all behavior. Each theory also includes the contention that the client–counselor relationship, based on empathy, unconditional positive regard, and genuineness, is necessary for the client to change. However, whereas person-centered therapists believe that the relationship conditions are sufficient for change, reality therapists believe that more is needed. On the other hand, both theories emphasize different aspects of the psyche, although Glasser's concept of one's quality world and inner picture album is not too far removed from Rogers's organismic valuing system. Perhaps the largest philosophical difference is in the role of the counselor. In general, reality therapists are more active, directive, technique, and education-oriented than their person-centered counterparts.

Existential therapy and reality therapy also share many of the same philosophical constructs. Practitioners of both theories emphasize the personal responsibility of the individual and the need for a constructive client–counselor relationship. The most interesting commonality rests within the similarity between reality therapy's needs and existential therapy's givens of existence. Existential theorists maintain that every human must attend to the givens of meaninglessness, death, freedom, and isolation. Similarly, reality therapists contend that all people must attend to five basic needs. Although the needs and givens differ in some ways, they appear to overlap substantially.

PERSONALITY DEVELOPMENT

Nature of Humans

Function of the Psyche

According to choice theory, all humans are born with five basic needs: survival, love and belonging, power, fun, and freedom. Every human is genetically endowed with the motivation to seek fulfillment of these needs in order to avoid the pain that results when they are not fulfilled. However, the strength of each need varies among individuals. Additionally, although each need is distinct, several can interact and overlap in the same situation. For example, eating a good meal while on a date can serve the needs for survival, belonging, and fun.

Beginning at birth, a person has the potential to translate the needs into specific *wants*—the people, objects, or circumstances that the person desires because they meet one or more of his needs—and to revise those wants throughout life. Also beginning at birth, to get the wants that meet the needs, a person has the potential to generate *total behavior*: thinking, doing, feeling, and physiology. In this context, thinking refers to the cognitive processes of voluntary and involuntary thought. Doing refers to observable actions. Feeling refers to emotions, and in choice therapy feelings are discussed not in the passive terminology of getting angry, becoming depressed, or feeling relieved, but in the active—and distinctive—verbiage of *angering, depressing,* or *relieving.* Finally, physiology includes biological processes such as heart rate and perspiration. From a choice theory perspective, a person's every behavior—thinking, doing, feeling, and physiology—constitutes that person's current best effort to meet one or more basic needs.

Every human also is born with the potential to fulfill one's needs with total behavior that is either *responsible* or *irresponsible* and *effective* or *ineffective*. In responsible behavior, one fulfills one's own needs without preventing others from fulfilling theirs. Irresponsible behavior involves fulfilling one's own needs in a way that prevents others from fulfilling theirs.

The various needs sometimes come into conflict as each person attempts to find a balanced fulfillment of the needs. To clarify understanding of these concepts, each need is defined below along with examples of wants that arise from the needs and of total behaviors (both responsible and irresponsible) that people generate to satisfy their needs.

The *survival* need is the one need that is not purely psychological. The human biological imperative is to survive and to procreate to ensure future survival. Behaviors that increase an individual's chance for survival, such as eating healthfully, exercising, and paying the electric bill, and those that increase the chance of survival of the human species, such as sexual behavior, fall into the category of survival needs. An example of responsible fulfillment of the survival need is the child who, having forgotten her lunch money, borrows from a friend and, the next day, pays it back. Irresponsible fulfillment would involve something like stealing another child's lunch money. An example of the survival need coming into conflict with another need is eating a half pint of rich ice cream: This action may fulfill the fun need but, for many people, runs counter to the survival need. A responsible way to resolve this conflict is to exercise regularly and eat the ice cream only occasionally.

Human beings are social creatures who have a need for *love* and *belonging*. The desire to congregate, to have friends, and to engage in sexual intimacy are all manifestations of this basic need. Infants seek nurturing and approval from their caretakers. Beginning in childhood, people seek the comfort of friendship. In adolescence, peer groups become even more important, not only as a means to belong but as an extension of and a laboratory for a developing sense of personal identity. Also in adolescence, a new kind of belonging emerges: intimate relating. The need for this blend of love and sex is very powerful; people feel both plagued by the desire for it and fulfilled by the satisfaction of it throughout life. Wubbolding (2000a) noted that in a society in which survival needs are largely met, the need for love and belonging will be in the forefront of client concerns. Glasser (2000) went a step further and stated that forming relationships with others and meeting the need for love and belonging is the barometer of healthy and unhealthy behavior. As Glasser (2000) remarked, "To satisfy every other need, we must have relationships with other people. This means that satisfying the need for love and belonging is the key to satisfying the other four needs" (p. 23).

People satisfy the need for *power* through a sense of accomplishment and competence. This need also can be understood as a desire for a felt sense of personal worth to others. As one client remarked, "It means so much to be needed in my marriage, to know I am valuable to him." "How do you know you are needed?" the counselor asked. "Because he listens to my opinions and ideas," the client stated firmly. Responsible fulfillment of this need includes getting good grades in school or a raise at work. Gaining power at the expense of others, through such actions as bullying, unethical business practices, or gossip, constitutes irresponsible fulfillment of this need. Infants realize power the moment their crying leads to instantaneous comfort from their caretakers. As any parent would attest, temper tantrums are a powerful tool. During adolescence, the struggle for independence from parental bonds is a prime training ground and battleground for developing the ability to meet power needs. The adolescent carries into adulthood the pictures (mental images of successful strategies) of how to attain power, whether those strategies involved irresponsible or responsible behavior.

The need for *fun* is defined as the quest for enjoyment. Wubbolding (2000a) affirmed that the need should not be construed as shallow silliness but, instead, as a feeling of invigorating playfulness and deep intimacy. According to Glasser (1998b), "fun is the genetic reward for learning" (p. 41). Through the meeting of the fun need, people not only learn about self and others but also build more satisfying relationships with others. Infants and children spend most of their time pursuing fun by playing. Through play, infants learn to define themselves, and through play with others, children learn valuable lessons about how to connect interpersonally and thus fulfill the belonging need. Adolescents pursue fun in both childlike and newer adult ways. Through this pursuit, the teenager learns about more complex relationships. Play also continues into adult life or should, anyway! Having fun in relationships creates intimacy and forges a "pleasure bond" between the people that help maintain the relationship. This process is nowhere more important than in couple relationships.

The need for *freedom* is expressed in the human desire for autonomy: to be able to make a choice, relatively unrestricted, from among several options. Like other needs, it may be identified most clearly through the pain one experiences when the need is thwarted: No one relishes the idea of working under a tyrannical boss or being imprisoned. In both cases, the opportunity to fulfill one's remaining needs is restricted; for example, one has no chance to go to a friend's house for a party when one is in jail. Or one can meet a particular need only at the expense of another need; for example, with a boss who forbids socializing during work, one's love and belonging need is met only at the expense of one's survival need: job insecurity. It is important to note a core belief in choice theory: that every human at every moment *is* free to choose. The *need* for freedom is reflected in the innate human desire to expand one's options and to seek circumstances whereby one can fulfill each need without thwarting the fulfillment of the others.

The need for freedom can be seen in the infant's desire to explore the environment unrestricted, the adolescent's desire to choose his own friends, the adult's desire to pursue the career that she finds satisfying. According to Glasser (1998a), responsible behavior that meets the freedom need often involves creativity, a defining human characteristic. Someone unjustly imprisoned can either irresponsibly and uncreatively withdraw into despair or responsibly and creatively take every legal action to establish his innocence and secure his release, in the meantime using creativity to maximize the responsible satisfaction of his other needs. Someone with a tyrannical boss can respond irresponsibly and uncreatively with hostility or can responsibly and creatively seek both to influence the boss to become more humane and also to find alternative ways to responsibly meet her other needs. In choice theory, at the heart of responsible fulfillment of the freedom need—indeed, all the needs—is a central tenet: One can influence but not control others; one can control only oneself.

Structure of the Psyche

In choice theory, the central structure is the brain: the controlling system for the organism. Glasser (1990) conceptualized the function of the psyche, or the need fulfillment process, through the metaphorical structure of an automobile. In this example, the basic needs represent the car's engine, while the individual's unique wants steer the vehicle. The wheels of the car are connected to the elements of total behavior. The front wheels are represented by thinking and doing, whereas the rear wheels are feelings and physiology. The car model represents the philosophical belief that behavior, total behavior, is purposeful. All four components work together to one end: fulfilling the needs as directed by the navigation of the person's inner picture album.

In Glasser's (1990) theory, humans are like front-wheel drive vehicles, an analogy that ascribes importance to the thinking and doing aspects of total behavior. Glasser maintained that people have much more control over thinking and action than feeling and physiology. It is easier to adjust one's thinking about a situation, for example, to stop dwelling on the difficulty of a situation and start thinking about possible solutions, or to run faster or slower than it is to make oneself instantly feel differently or make oneself spontaneously sweat or digest one's food more quickly. People have the innate potential to control their thoughts and actions directly, but to control their feelings and physiology only indirectly through changing their thoughts and actions. For example, to sweat less, stop running or, in the case of anxious sweating, think calming thoughts. This assumption has important implications for change. Namely, if one wants to have the highest probability of successful change, one needs to target those areas of total behavior that one can control: thinking and doing; then the car (all four aspects of the whole person) will move in a new direction.

People are born with the potential to develop several psychic structures. Among these is the *quality world*, also known as the *inner picture album*. Out of all a person has ever perceived, the quality world consists of the perceptions of all the phenomena that have fulfilled—and, the person believes, can continue to fulfill—one or more basic needs. According to Glasser (1998a), the pictures in this mental album represent three main categories: "the people we most want to be with; the things we most want to own or experience; and the ideas or systems of belief that govern much of our behavior" (p. 45). Although most people are only dimly aware of the basic genetic needs and the many ways they seek to fulfill them, each person has an internal feeling of what works—what fulfills needs—and what does not. People single out mental pictures of satisfying phenomena to store them in the picture album for future reference. This dynamic explains the wide variety of people's likes and dislikes and, even more importantly, the vastly wide array of choices different people make to fulfill the basic needs.

As each person grows and develops, the innate tendency is to continually assess the mental pictures in the quality world and, when encountering more satisfying pictures, replacing the old, less satisfying with the new, more satisfying. Although people may keep pictures that are ineffective due to a lack of more need fulfilling pictures, most people routinely update the inner picture album. Consider the person who plays soccer to fulfill the needs for fun, survival (physical fitness), and belonging. As she gets older or suffers an injury, playing soccer may cease to be a realistic option. She then can replace the picture of soccer with another or a combination of other activities that work to fulfill these needs. For example, she might have fun watching soccer on television, achieve a sense of belonging by coaching a team, and stay fit by adopting a less strenuous exercise regimen. If she chooses to keep the picture in the album, she will feel frustrated in her need fulfillment, and she may begin to choose symptoms as an ineffective means to fulfill her needs. This process will be further explained in the section below on unhealthy functioning.

Role of the Environment

As you can probably guess from the preceding discussion on development, reality therapists view every person's internal processes as the primary decision-making agent. Each person, regardless of environmental influences, has the choice as to what one perceives and uses in daily life to fulfill the basic needs. Wubbolding (2007) asserted, "Behavior originates from inside of them and is not thrust upon them by their external world: society, culture, personal history, or other external events" (p. 253). Although this assertion may be interpreted to mean that the external world does not matter, reality therapists would say that such an interpretation is too narrow. Instead, reality therapists honor a client's environmental circumstance while empowering the client to recognize the choices inherent in any circumstances (Wubbolding & Brickell, 2008). Following is more detail about the role of environment in personality development.

Familial Environment

In their writings, talks, and demonstrations, many reality therapists have avoided discussing familial impact because their approach to change is always to focus on present relationships. Dwelling on how one constructed pictures of need satisfaction in the past is not as important or useful as exploring new ways of fulfilling needs in the present and future. With that caveat, reality therapists hold that family factors provide the growing child with initial need-fulfilling opportunities. A person can be aware of only those need-fulfilling people, things, and ideas one has experienced. Thus, the family contributes substantially to the quality of a child's picture album—the people, things, and ideas the child has experienced as need-fulfilling and from which the child can choose to fulfill needs in the future. The family does not determine behavior, but the experiences a child has in the family tend to play a significant role in impacting the child's picture album.

Extrafamilial Factors

Just as a person's family provides opportunities for need fulfillment, the environment outside the home (church, school, neighborhood, culture, and geographic location) all influence the person by providing unique environmental opportunities and limitations for need satisfaction. For example, I (KAF) grew up in a South Texas town that was close to the beach. My geographic surroundings provided a means for me to place "going to the beach" in my internal picture album as a way to fulfill my need for fun. My son, Dylan, has lived in the South all of his life and has never seen snow. This environmental factor limits his ability to choose "playing in the snow" as an effective way to fulfill his need for fun.

As mentioned earlier, environment is obviously more than just geography. Using the examples mentioned above, one's school officials decide on the means and topics of instruction—how and what one is taught; one's church encourages certain values and promotes a collective belief in the difference between "good" and "evil"; one's neighborhood can provide examples of social living; and one's culture provides a foundation for everything from community rituals to language and what foods are appropriate to eat. With all of the possible environmental opportunities every individual encounters, it is important to note that, from a reality therapy perspective, it is not the environment itself, but what experiences in the environment the person found to be need fulfilling, that influence the choices a person will make in the future and the person's total behavior. Again, a person can choose in the future only those people, things, and ideas the person experienced in the past to be need-fulfilling. This concept provides the basis for a counselor to suggest alternatives to a client that the client has not previously experienced and, therefore, cannot know the need fulfilling potential of the new alternatives.

Model of Mental Health

Healthy Functioning

From the perspective of choice theory, healthy functioning is characterized by responsible behavior: the ability to meet one's own needs without preventing others from meeting theirs. It follows, then that healthy people are able to build relationships with others and are able to develop and maintain vital connections to fulfill needs. As stated previously, Glasser (1998a) identified the love and belonging need as the key to meeting the other needs. One is not likely to sustain relationships with others if one is meeting one's own needs at their expense. In addition, choice theory includes the tenet that a good balance of the other needs is necessary for healthy adjustment. Although the need for love and belonging is primary, one must attend to all the needs to achieve a sense of well-being.

Wubbolding (2000a) outlined a stage model of achieving the basic needs in a balanced manner. He called the model "effective life direction" (p. 70), and its stages are outlined as follows:

1. *I Want to Change and I Want to Grow* (p. 71): This stage requires that a person desire a change in current lifestyle. This statement of change is necessary before any concrete change in behavior can occur. Healthy individuals are not immune from choosing unwisely and hurting self and others, but these individuals make the commitment and are open to making more effective choices.
2. *Effective Behaviors* (p. 71): After verbalizing or thinking about a commitment to change, healthy individuals take action. Their commitment to more effective living does not exist within self-understanding alone; it must be put into action. Behaviors Wubbolding (1988) discussed that indicate a choice for a healthier lifestyle include:
   a. Assertive and Altruistic Behaviors: Healthy people are goal-oriented and take responsibility in setting and achieving long- and short-term goals. Choosing actions that help the individual connect in positive ways with others is a hallmark characteristic of these behaviors. Such actions might include

participating in charitable activities, conducting oneself in an ethical manner at work, and contributing to one's family and intimate relationship.

b. Positive Thinking Behaviors: In the total behavior model, cognitions are vital, constituting one of the two wheels of the front-wheel drive system. Healthy individuals use positive inner statements to help steer their lives. For example, thinking thoughts such as, "I can control only myself and not others," "I am responsible for my actions," "I am free to make my own choices," and "I can and will choose positively and effectively" are all thoughts that help facilitate effective living.

c. Effective Feeling and Physiological Behaviors: Healthy people also use the back wheels of the total behavior system for effective living. They cultivate feelings that facilitate need fulfillment, and those feelings manifest in the rest of their total behavior. For example, being patient, trusting, and hopeful tend to generate specific behaviors characterizing each emotion. Healthy individuals also enact behaviors that enhance physiology. Such behaviors might include eating a balanced diet and getting regular exercise and an appropriate amount of sleep.

3. *Positive Addictions*: According to Wubbolding (2000a), very few people are able to achieve and maintain this third stage. To develop a positive addiction, a person must engage daily in a behavior that produces a natural high and requires little concrete concentration so the mind is free from the minutiae of day-to-day existence. The behavior must not take up so much time that it creates obstacles in the person's relationships, yet the behavior is not merely a trend but is an activity to which the person is dedicated. In his book, *Positive Addiction*, Glasser (1988) proposed jogging as an example that fits the criteria for a positive addiction. Many runners jog daily and report the "runner's high" that accompanies a good run. Many jog early in the morning so as not to interfere with work or family, and they report that their brains go into a kind of autopilot mode as they run. Finally, to achieve the high, one must jog for many months so the exercise becomes ingrained into the physical and mental regimen of the runner's life. Another example of a positive addiction is meditation. Running and meditation are obviously not the only positive addictions. We encourage you to think of examples and realize that any behavior that enhances effective living is a positive step.

Unhealthy Functioning

As early as 1965, Glasser's view was that people exhibiting maladjustment are not crazy and should not be considered mentally ill. Glasser contended that people are responsible for their own behavior and that the range of behaviors that mental health professionals call abnormal are just more examples of the ways people choose to behave when they feel thwarted in their attempts to responsibly satisfy one or more of their five basic needs.

Beginning in 1998 with the book *Choice Theory*, but more clearly explained in *Reality Therapy in Action* (2000), Glasser precisely defined the root of almost all human maladjustment: "the lack of satisfying present relationships" (p. xvii). Glasser posited that maladjustment is a disconnection between the person and others. According to Glasser (2000), "what is called mental illness is a description of the ways in which huge numbers of people … choose to deal with the pain of their loneliness or disconnection" (p. 1). In other words, maladjustment involves choosing one form of pain to avoid an even greater form of pain.

But why would clients choose to be miserable at all? And wouldn't anyone suffering from depression or an anxiety disorder be highly offended at the notion that they are somehow responsible for their pain? Glasser (1985) cited three main reasons why people create and endure misery.

1. Choosing intense symptoms such as depression and anxiety helps keep angering under control. Because angering may lead to relatively more painful consequences, such as being arrested or injured, one chooses instead to depress, which tends to bring about less painful consequences.
2. By choosing intense symptoms, one brings other people into one's service. As a client stated, "If I am not depressed, you will not see me in therapy." When a person chooses to depress, other people begin to comfort and take care of that person. The person is enduring the pain of loss of power, freedom, and fun that accompanies intense symptoms in order to avoid the even greater pain of loneliness. Glasser would contend that a person who was not coddled when choosing to depress would quickly give the behavior up because it would not fulfill any need for love and belonging.
3. Choosing intense symptoms enables people to avoid doing what they are afraid of doing. An adolescent who sees himself as inept may choose to depress so he can avoid relationships or academic challenges at school. He chooses the pain of depression to avoid the even greater pain of embarrassment, rejection, or humiliation.

In all three cases, by choosing the symptom, the individual thwarts any possibility for truly satisfying relationships and overall effective and responsible total behavior. Despite great discomfort, the person will likely report feeling paralyzed or trapped in the symptom and, from a choice theory perspective, will choose to persist in the symptom because it is the best way the person knows to meet his needs, even if only partially and self-defeatingly.

Reality therapists' framing of symptoms not as the nouns "depression" and "anxiety" but as the verbs "depressing" and "anxiety-ing" constitutes a semantic shift consistent with the theory's emphasis on self-responsibility. In reality therapy, clients are not depressed without a choice in the matter but are, instead, choosing to depress. This terminology is not meant to blame or criticize the client. The new terminology is designed to demonstrate to the client that the control to change lies within and that the choice of any behavior is an attempt to satisfy a need or needs using the best strategy in the client's awareness. By believing that the responsibility for change rests within the client, reality therapists lay the foundation for counseling.

THE PERSONALITY CHANGE PROCESS

To a reality therapist, change consists of a person taking responsibility to choose different total behavior that more effectively and responsibly meets one's needs. For the behavior change process to be most effective, one must begin to realize the multitude of options in any given situation. Glasser (1992) noted that people change when they realize that present behavior is not getting them what they want and that other behavior has a greater probability of success. Once one takes an active and responsible role in the choice process, one can assess the effectiveness of any new choices. From a reality therapy perspective, it is this process—choice and assessment—that is at the heart of the change process. Although this process can and does occur outside of counseling, the more restricted the pictures in a person's internal picture album, the more likely the person will require the organized resources of counseling to supplant less effective pictures with more effective ones.

Client's Role

The client in reality therapy must be willing to focus on and change total behavior. Some clients enter into therapy wanting and expecting to explore past relationships and family dynamics. Reality therapists do not spend time focusing on these phenomena, because they perceive such time to be wasted. Clients must be willing to accept the here-and-now focus and be open to being educated about choice theory. Glasser (2000) remarked that he expects his clients to be motivated and encourages them to read *Choice Theory* as homework.

In reviewing the case study books on reality therapy, *Control Theory in the Practice of Reality Therapy* (N. Glasser, 1989) and *Reality Therapy in Action* (W. Glasser, 2000), we found a pattern among the case study clients. In the beginning of therapy, as the relationship was forming, most clients seemed offended at the notion of choosing symptoms. For example, in W. Glasser's (2000) casebook, the client Jerry, made statements such as, "I don't choose [obsessive-compulsive behaviors]. What are you talking about? I'm sick" (p. 18). Lucy retorted, "What do you mean I choose to be depressed? What are you talking about? I don't want to feel this way" (p. 31). As Glasser developed the therapeutic relationship, provided education in reality therapy principles, and employed the techniques of the approach, each of these clients respond to Glasser's challenges and began to take responsibility for making more effective choices. Clients in reality therapy must be open to building a relationship with the therapist and have the strength to maintain the relationship and persist in the process even when they experience the counselor challenging them.

Counselor's Role

The role of the counselor and the relationship between counselor and client are closely tied to the primary goal of counseling. Glasser (2000) asserted that "the continuing goal of reality therapy is to create a choice theory relationship between client and counselor" (p. 23). By experiencing a satisfying relationship, clients can learn a lot about how to improve the troubled relationship(s) for which they sought counseling. Thus, in many ways, the client–counselor relationship becomes the cure agent for the client: a laboratory for learning how to forge relationships based on the tenets of choice theory.

The client–counselor relationship is so important in reality therapy that Glasser asserted if the counselor fails to connect with the client, the client will not change. Therefore, the first stage in the counseling process is known as "making friends." This friendship is based on respect, boundaries, and choices; it contains many facets; and the counselor establishing it does so most effectively by following several dos and don'ts. Wubbolding (1988) and Wubbolding and Brickell (1998) listed some of the characteristics of good therapists:

- Continuously Practicing the AB's (Always Be): Wubbolding (1988) summarized the first collection of effective counselor characteristics by using an easy-to-remember ABCDEFG approach. The AB stands for *always be*, while the other letters remind the therapist to be *courteous* to the client, even in the face of anger; *determined* that the client can change and that change comes through making different choices; *enthusiastic* toward the client; *firm* regarding the plans and commitments that the client has made in therapy; and *genuine* with the client, thus treating each client with openness and honesty.

- Focusing on the Present: Glasser has contended that the road to change lies within the client making new choices in the here and now. Reality therapists use the client–counselor relationship as it is occurring in the present and spend little time discussing past issues or circumstances.
- Using Humor: Fun is one of the basic needs, and laughter is not only an excellent way to fill the fun need, but it also leads to greater psychological intimacy between therapist and client. Counselors should model the use of responsible humor as a relationship-enhancing agent.
- Using Empathic Confrontation: The primary task of the counselor is to influence the client to make more effective choices. The foundation of influence is the ability to connect with and understand every client. As an outcome of this understanding, the counselor will effectively confront the client and encourage total behavior in the direction of more responsible need satisfaction. Thus the effective counselor is able and willing to connect with and confront clients.

In addition to the above characteristics, Wubbolding (1988) included several behaviors an effective counselor avoids:

- Don't Accept Excuses: Many therapists from other schools of thought are interested in the reasons behind client behaviors. From a reality therapy perspective, asking or even wondering why a client behaved in a particular manner invites the client to excuse her behavior rather than take responsibility for it: "I am depressed because my wife is angry at me," "I am anxious because I did not study for my test and I am afraid I will fail and have to repeat the class." It can also invite the counselor to make excuses for the client, thus failing to encourage the client to take responsibility for, and make more effective, choices: "He is depressed because he has a chemical imbalance," "She is an addict because she grew up in a troubled family." Reality therapists posit that all behavior is a choice that represents the client's best attempt to satisfy needs at the present time. Figuring out the why's of behavior is more than useless; it counterproductively draws both client and counselor away from the essence of healing: making more responsible choices.
- Don't Argue or Criticize: Counselors often feel frustrated to see clients make ineffective choices over and over again. However, counselors who fully understand choice theory respect clients' freedom to make any choice and understand that those choices represent clients' best attempts to meet their needs. Arguing with clients or criticizing them represents an unhealthy need fulfilling behavior—probably for power—on the part of the counselor. Concentrating on the AB's and the advice in the next paragraph will help the counselor refocus.
- Don't Give Up Quickly: Clients will not give up ineffective total behaviors quickly, because that behavior has, probably for a long time, been their most effective way to meet their needs. Change is difficult because it involves clients trying new behaviors—behaviors they have never before experienced as need-fulfilling—in order to create new pictures of satisfying people, things, and ideas that help them

feel motivated to more consistently reorient their behavior. If the counselor's over-arching goal is to form a choice theory relationship with the client that supports this sometimes painstaking and halting process, then the client–counselor relationship will have highs and lows like any other relationship. The task of the counselor is to maintain an empathic and challenging attitude toward the client and never give up on the client's ability to choose more responsible and effective behavior.

Stages and Techniques

To describe the process in which a counselor both challenges and encourages a client to make new and better choices, Wubbolding (1988, 1991, 2000a) outlined the "WDEP" steps of reality therapy. He did not intend counselors to use this system as a lockstep approach but, rather, as a web of skills and techniques, all aimed at helping the client choose more effective, healthy, responsible behavior. Our goal here is to introduce, rather than fully explain, each of the WDEP steps. For a complete explanation, we encourage you to consult Wubbolding (1988, 2000a).

W (Wants)

In this first step of the cycle, the counselor assesses the client's wants, needs, and perceptions with regard to self, others (spouse, children, boss, the counselor, etc.), and the environment. The counselor helps the client more clearly identify the core components of the quality world/inner picture album. This exploration is not as nebulous as it sounds. Asking a series of questions such as, "What do you want?" "What are you not getting from your relationship(s) that you would like to get?" "What options are available to you now that you have found need-satisfying in the past?" and "What is preventing you from getting what you want?" all provide the counselor and client with a better picture of the client's quality world. Reality therapists often use a client's answers to these more standard questions by formulating follow-up questions that elicit further information. As Wubbolding (2000a) noted, "As with any list or series of questions, making them unique to the client constitutes the art of Reality Therapy" (p. 99). Consider the following case excerpt as an example of how elegant questioning can elicit quality world information.

Client: I am just so unhappy in my relationship with my wife.
Counselor: What do you want in your marriage?
Client: What all people want, to be happy and loved.
Counselor: How would you know you were being loved? (This question clarifies the client's specific picture of "love in a relationship.")
Client: I guess we would spend more time together. The more we are apart the more depressed I get.

This response provides information about the picture in the client's quality world: being with and spending time with his wife. This information provides the foundation for new choices. It gives the counselor a view of the client's purpose in choosing to depress: It might spark attention from his wife. The answer also provides a possible solution to his problem: Choose behaviors that increase the probability of spending time with his wife.

D (Direction and Doing)

In this step, the counselor inquires into the client's current life direction. Counselors can best assess current direction through the client's observable behavior. Using the automobile analogy of total behavior, counselors during this step seek to illuminate how the four wheels are guiding the client's direction. Counselors can ask clients, "What are you doing?" Wubbolding (2000b) provided an interesting analysis of the significance of each word in this important question.

- "What" directs the client to be specific. It moves the client away from excuses and vague answers that *why* questions could evoke. Reality therapists are interested in helping the client pinpoint specific aspects of total behavior to retain or modify.
- "Are" is a verb that signifies present tense. The here and now is the domain of change, according to reality therapists, and the most effective questions and explorations reflect this focus. What a client *was* doing is relatively unimportant unless the past behavior is having a direct impact on the present.
- "You" puts the focus on the client and not on others. The philosophical root of personal responsibility is found in this word. It demonstrates that the client will not find change by hoping others will act differently. One can control only one's own behavior; therefore, the new direction must begin with self.
- "Doing" puts the focus on behavior, which clients are likely to interpret only as action, but which opens the door to educating clients about the concept of total behavior. Through counseling, clients learn that they have more control over their total behavior, especially cognitions and actions, than they previously realized, and, as stated earlier, the true assessment of change can be found only in doing something different in one or more of the four domains of total behavior. As clients make better choices—particularly thinking and acting in new ways—their emotional and physical lives will also improve, thus yielding an improvement in total behavior.

E (Evaluation)

In the previous two steps, the counselor and client have discovered what the client wants and what the client is currently doing. The E step puts these two pieces of information together when the counselor asks, "Is what you are doing getting you what you want?" or, more open-endedly, "How well is what you're doing getting what you want?" If the answer is "yes" or "pretty well," then the client is not experiencing a problem, and the counselor does not pursue the matter as a therapeutic goal. If the answer is "no" or "not very well," then the client can either make the same choices and get the same response or the client can choose differently and then reassess to determine the relative success of the new choice. Continuing with the case excerpt, counselor and client might enact the E step as follows:

Counselor: It seems as though you want to spend more time with your wife and that you are currently choosing to depress. Behaviorally this choice is demonstrated through sleeping most of the day, not going to work, and complaining about how bad you feel. Is this behavior getting you what you want in your relationship?

Client: Hell no! It did in the beginning, when she was worried about me. Now it seems to repel or exhaust her.

Counselor: By "it" you mean your behavior.

Client: Yeah.

Counselor: If this set of behaviors is not working, wouldn't you be more likely to get what you want by choosing some others?

At the Evaluation stage, the counselor's main task is to facilitate the client's assessment of the effectiveness of any chosen behavior. The counselor should remember and convey to the client that current ineffective behavior does not make the client a bad person but represents the best choice the client could make at the given time. Counseling is about learning that new choices are possible and learning a process to evaluate future choices.

P (Plan)

Reality therapists hold that a client's understanding of one's effective and ineffective behaviors is not enough to create new behaviors. Change requires action, and a client is most likely to adopt a consistent pattern of effective behavior by making and following a plan. Plans are physical that is, written down representations of client decisions to behave in new, more effective ways. In reality therapy, to be more effective, behaviors must meet the criteria of responsibility: need fulfillment that does not infringe on the rights or well-being of others. Once the client's chosen behaviors pass this litmus test, counselor and client can script the plan. Reality therapists can assess client plans using the SAMI2C3 system (Wubbolding, 2004). According to this system, plans need to be:

- Simple: The plan needs to be straightforward and easy for all parties to understand.
- Attainable: The plan needs to be within the client's grasp. Some clients, infused with energy over the decision to change, will make plans that exceed reality. For example, a student who decides, after failing three out of four grading periods, that he will get all A's and end up with a passing average for the year, may have a positive plan, but not a very realistic one.
- Measurable with regard to outcome and timeline: The specifics of the plan need to be as detailed and concrete as possible. For example: "I will tell my husband 'I love you' every night" is more measurable than, "I will show my husband love throughout our marriage."
- Immediate: The execution of the plan needs to be as soon as possible, preferably the day of or day after the counseling session. The quick turnaround enables the client to avoid procrastination and to evaluate the new behavior promptly.
- Involves counselor: By including the counselor, the client provides for oneself both support and objective feedback. The client should have primary input on the level of counselor involvement in the plan.
- Controlled by the client: The client takes responsibility for forming and executing the plan. This idea honors the reality therapy focus on each person being personally accountable for one's decisions.
- Commitment: As we've stated, for change to occur, the client must decide to do something different and then choose to enact this decision behaviorally. The counselor does not accept excuses for not committing to the plan and does not accept "I will try." A client demonstrates commitment to change through "I will" statements coupled with follow through.
- Consistent: True change involves the client making the new behavior a regular part of one's life. Symptoms that the client reports are ineffective behavior patterns the client uses consistently in an attempt to meet the basic needs. Clients must enact healthy behaviors equally consistently to have the desired result of more effective, responsible living.

Once the client carries out the plan on a consistent basis, client and counselor can address other issues by cycling back through the WDEP process. More than a linear process, therapy is likely to address many issues that the client is processing at various levels in the WDEP system. Likewise, the counselor will move among the components of the process, encouraging the client to let go of behavior that is not need-fulfilling and to choose new total behavior that helps the client get what the client wants.

CONTRIBUTIONS AND LIMITATIONS

Contributions

Reality therapy has made a significant contribution to the field of education. In *Schools Without Failure* (1968) and *The Quality School*, Glasser (1998b) outlined the application of choice theory to an educational setting. Since his first work at the Ventura School for Girls, Glasser and other reality therapists have trained teachers, parents, and school counselors to work effectively with children using the principles of reality therapy. In a quality school, all participants are trained in choice theory. Currently, over 260 schools have begun the quality school process (Wubbolding, 2000a). The action-oriented, short-term focus is appealing to the hectic schedule of the school counselor, and the focus on instilling responsibility is appealing to teachers, principals, and parents.

Glasser's formulation of the basic genetic needs and the quality world are unique to reality therapy, as is Wubbolding's WDEP system. Each of these concepts helps add depth and definition to the theory and also provide constructs for future research. The WDEP model provides students and practitioners with a structure to explore the principles and process of reality therapy. The fluid model is easy to understand, theoretically consistent, and flexible enough for advanced practitioners to expand. The model is also fairly easy for clients to comprehend and integrate into their own lives.

Limitations

One potential weakness of the theory is that upon a superficial reading, the therapy seems very easy to execute. Before writing this text, while teaching Counseling Theories using another text, I (KAF) would routinely ask my graduate students, "As you end your first Counseling Theories course, what are some of your general impressions of the theories covered in the text?" Students often indicated that both person-centered and reality therapy seemed very elementary in terms of procedures, with many students indicating that reality therapy seemed like "just asking a bunch of questions." Keep in mind that these results are by no means empirically validated and that beginning graduate students comprised the sample. However, research on reality therapy has substantiated this limitation (Murphy, 1997; Wubbolding, 2000a). The critique is that many practitioners are conducting reality therapy without a full understanding of what reality therapy really involves. This weakness has more to do with how people are educated about the theory and less with the theory itself, but partial responsibility lies with the authors who write about reality therapy. Authors of several seminal works wrote in self-help format with little attention to key clinical detail. Hopefully, books that eloquently explore clinical issues, such as Wubbolding's (2000a) *Reality Therapy for the 21st Century*, will help dispel this misconception.

Interface with Recent Developments in the Mental Health Field

The Nature–Nurture Question

Reality therapists posit that every person is genetically endowed with the five basic needs, and each person's environment, to one degree or another, offers ways to meet those needs. Apart from these basics, reality therapists contend that each person determines one's own life through one's own perceptions and choices. In other words, a person is responsible for the unique choices she makes to fulfill her genetically based needs within the ranges of options she perceives in her environment. Simply put, genes and environment impact but do not dictate behavior: *Choice* dictates behavior.

This perspective seems to ignore recent research findings that several phenomena addressed in counseling have a known or a strongly suspected genetic influence. Indeed, choice theory has been criticized for not giving at least a nod to the possibility that, for a person whose brain is deficient in certain neurochemicals, the ability to make certain admittedly more healthy choices may be extremely challenging, at best. However, reality therapists are in agreement with mental health practitioners who acknowledge genetic influence in psychological distress and who nevertheless conclude that "biology is *not* necessarily destiny" (Baker & Clark, 1990, p. 599). Such practitioners assert that in the case of known genetic influence, environmental accommodations often can maximize or minimize the genetic influence. Reality therapists endorse the idea of just such an environmental accommodation.

DSM–IV–TR *Diagnosis*

From a theoretical standpoint, reality therapists view diagnostic labeling as inappropriate or unnecessary within the therapeutic environment. Diagnoses are clusters of symptoms, and symptoms, from a reality therapy perspective, represent ineffective choices a client has made in the process of fulfilling one's needs. Providing a diagnostic classification for a person's choices often gives the client and the therapist relief from the responsibility for change. As one client stated, "If I just knew I had ADHD, then I would feel better. I would know it was not my fault." Although reality therapy is not designed to blame and criticize clients for their difficulties, the theory does stress responsibility as the basic ingredient of change. Glasser (2000) summarized this view from a practical and theoretical position: "Clients should not be labeled with a diagnosis except when necessary for insurance purposes. From our standpoint, diagnoses are descriptions of the behaviors people choose to deal with the pain and frustration that is endemic to unsatisfying present relationships" (p. 24).

Pharmacotherapy

Glasser has consistently and adamantly opposed the use of medication for mental problems. He (2000) reported never having to use medication with any of his clients. Reality therapists posit that clients choose all four components of their total behavior as their best attempt to meet their five basic needs. Because all behavior is chosen, a biochemical rationale for behavior and its associated medical remedy take the responsibility away from the client. Glasser asserted that all parties (pharmaceutical company, insurance company, client, and mental health professional) enjoy a relief from responsibility when they participate in the practice of prescribing medication to deal with problems.

Glasser (2000) proposed that money is a prime reason why the psychiatric and pharmaceutical companies propagate the medical cure for mental distress. He observed that, "since our society will never run out of disconnected people and as long as we believe in mental illness, the industry will never stop producing new drugs to treat it" (p. 229). Glasser contended that prescribing medicine not only is ineffective, but also serves purposes either that are not associated with client care or that run counter to the basic principles of change that reality therapists have outlined. Clearly, from the perspective of mental health professionals who believe that pharmacotherapy sometimes actually saves lives and frequently contributes to the quality of life for people debilitated by genetically faulted neurochemistry, Glasser's position is radical though theoretically consistent. Glasser's strict opinion is somewhat peripheral to the theory, in that it would be possible to hold a more liberal view on the use of medication and maintain the basic tenets of reality therapy.

Managed Care and Brief Therapy

Regarding brief therapy and managed care, reality therapy poses some interesting advantages and disadvantages. Insurance companies routinely require a DSM–IV diagnosis and approve of medication as an adjunct to therapy. Both of these approaches run contrary to the pure version of reality therapy. However, as Glasser's previously cited quote indicates, at least he is pragmatically flexible on the issue of diagnosis. A practical reality therapist most likely uses diagnosis as a tool to help the client get what both client and counselor want—reimbursement for therapy expenses—while they proceed with reality therapy.

Reality therapy seems to be well suited for two preferences or requirements of managed care: a time-limited framework and change strategies that counselors can characterize as cognitive-behavioral. Glasser (2000) stated that some clients change in one session, whereas most show change in 10 to 12 sessions. These figures correspond roughly to those cited in Chapter 1 of this text regarding research on psychotherapy at large (Asay & Lambert, 1999). Wubbolding (2000a) asserted that although reality therapy can be time limited, it is by no means a quick cure. He cited Sleek (1994) who concluded that, for clients engaged in a cognitive-behavioral approach, 16 weeks is the minimum time they need to see results. Glasser emphasized that the reality therapy system does not determine the length of therapy as much as the ability to form a choice theory relationship between counselor and client coupled with the client's own motivation to change. Without these two elements, therapy not only will take longer but also will most likely fail.

Regarding counselors' ability to characterize reality therapy change strategies as cognitive-behavioral, of course reality therapy and cognitive-behavioral therapy differ philosophically in some fundamental ways. However, in that reality therapists facilitate change by focusing, metaphorically, on the front wheels of the car (thoughts and actions) and, as we discuss in the next section that they can exercise technical eclecticism including techniques that cognitive-behavioral therapists first developed, reality therapists' change strategies can be characterized as cognitive-behavioral.

Technical Eclecticism

Reality therapy is, by design, a flexible system of psychotherapy in which counselors can easily incorporate any techniques from other theories that help clients choose more effective behavior in the present. To accomplish this feat, counselors must have a firm understanding of the principles of choice theory or run the risk of employing techniques that contradict the goals of the therapy. Reality therapists avoid techniques aimed at insight into unconscious processes, dream work, focusing on the past, or any other technique in which the aim is more on awareness and insight than on immediate commitment to behavioral change. Therefore, choice theorists would certainly discourage theoretical eclecticism among reality therapy practitioners, whereas they would encourage a practitioner informed in choice theory to practice theoretically consistent technical eclecticism.

Diversity Issues

Probably more than any other theoretical proponents we described in this text, reality therapists have made an effort to adapt choice theory to a wide array of culture and to study these applications of the theory. Wubbolding (2000a) provided an excellent overview of the multicultural applications of reality therapy to a variety of populations: Japanese, Chinese, Koreans, Singaporeans, Puerto Ricans, Native Americans, African Americans, and Irish. In addition, reality therapists have worked with Jewish and Arabian students (Renna, 1998) as well as Eastern Russians (Bogolepov, 1998).

Reality therapists believe that choice theory is flexible and can and should be modified to incorporate the client's cultural worldview. Because one's quality world is formed within the context of one's culture, the counselor who considers the client without respect to culture would fail to understand the world of the client. Without this clear understanding, a counselor would not be able to form a choice theory relationship, and therapy would fail. Wubbolding (2000a) encouraged reality therapists to obtain knowledge about the client's culture and to adapt the WDEP system to fit the needs of the client. Wubbolding asserted that the WDEP system is flexible. A good example of its possible cultural adaptation involves modifying its typically liberal use of direct questioning. People from many Eastern cultures view direct questioning as intrusive and rude. Reality therapists can honor this perspective by asking more indirect forms of the traditional direct question. For example, Wubbolding (2000a, pp. 185–186) suggested that instead of asking, "What do you want?" the therapist could ask, "What are you looking for?" And instead of asking, "How hard do you want to work at solving the problem?" ask, "What would happen to your life if you decided to do things differently?" Because such clients are likely to find the results of these subtle semantic shifts more acceptable, therapy is likely to be more effective.

Unlike the impressive attention to cultural issues, authors in the reality therapy literature have made little reference to gender or sexual orientation issues. Because gender represents a genetic given that both restricts and expands possible behavioral choices, the absence of attention to such issues represents a deficit in the theory's literature. Additionally, the choice and genetic aspects of sexual orientation beg to be addressed by choice theorists. Glasser (2000) discussed a case in which a man wanted to become a woman, but the case description failed to include a full exploration of sexual orientation issues. The absence of a thorough treatment of both gender and sexual orientation represents a deficit that, hopefully, future authors will address in the choice theory–reality therapy literature.

Within the context of reality therapy, a counselor best views spirituality through each client's pictures in his quality world. In fact, the number of different spiritual denominations can be interpreted as evidence that no single correct spiritual direction exists but that each person can choose the spiritual path that best fulfills that person's needs. Often through spirituality, people acquire pictures and values regarding the nature of an afterlife and how to conduct oneself in life. In light of these internal factors, people choose ways to fulfill needs that are in accordance with the spiritual belief system they have chosen. Many of the tenets of reality therapy are similar to various spiritual principles. For example, responsibility, defined as the fulfilling of needs in a way that does not hinder or hurt others, is quite similar to the Golden Rule—to do to others only what one would want done to oneself—that many spiritual scholars consider to be universal among spiritual systems.

Linnenberg (1997) and Mickel and Liddle-Hamilton (1996) further detailed how to incorporate spiritual components into the reality therapy perspective. Like any behavior, spiritual behavior can be responsible or irresponsible. For example, attending religious services can be a responsible way to fulfill the belonging need. Conversely, believing that one need not change because one's deity has caused one's circumstances or because one's deity will bring about any needed change are irresponsible cognitions. Litwack (2007b) made a case for reality therapists to consider spirituality to be one of the basic needs, stating that

> This is a need to connect with something beyond the self. This need becomes especially important in later life, but the groundwork for its satisfaction is laid all through life. We can fulfill it through spiritual experiences or connection to God or other spiritual entities. We can fulfill our need for spirituality through the experience of connection with nature. We can fulfill it by creating higher, more universal meaning in our lives. We can also fulfill it by devoting ourselves to the welfare of people, either by directly helping people or by working for social change. (p. 30)

Reality therapists do well to treat the spiritual domain as a vital component in many clients' quality worlds and also to assess the extent to which clients' total behavior related to spirituality promotes or impedes clients' responsible fulfillment of their needs.

Effectiveness of Psychotherapy

Regarding the relationship between the reality therapy perspective and the conclusions from research on the effectiveness of psychotherapy (Asay & Lambert, 1999), we have inferred several conclusions. Reality therapy appears to be in alignment with the research findings that the therapeutic relationship, specific therapeutic interventions, the client's expectation for improvement, and certain extratherapeutic factors, such as the client's motivation to improve, play a determining role in a positive psychotherapeutic outcome. However, reality therapists would probably weigh these factors somewhat differently than research has suggested. Reality therapists would probably give more weight to the therapeutic relationship, the client's motivation, and the counselor's specific interventions, along with less weight to certain extratherapeutic factors, such as the severity and chronicity of the client's problem, the client's capacity to relate to other people, ego strength and psychological mindedness, and the quality of the client's social support system. Some reality therapists might consider these latter factors as irrelevant, perceiving that the therapist has the potential to influence them and/or that they are under the client's choice control. Indeed, from a reality therapy perspective, many of these factors smack of being excuses that clients use to avoid responsibility for choices over which they actually have control.

Litwack (2007a), in a response to the criticism that reality therapy lacked empirical support, collected and cited over 60 dissertations on the efficacy of reality therapy that researchers had produced between the years 1970 and 2007. Although this compilation does not necessarily substantiate the effectiveness of the approach, it does demonstrate that a substantial number of investigators are actively and continuously researching the theory.

Researchers have examined the validity of reality therapy concepts, such as the basic needs (Deci, 1995; Harvey & Retter, 1995), as well as the effectiveness of reality therapy with a variety of populations, such as students (Comiskey, 1993; Dryden, 1994; Edens & Smryl, 1994), reality therapy trainees (Cullinane, 1995), clients with addictions (Honeyman, 1990), and perpetrators of domestic violence (Rachor, 1995). Radtke, Sapp, and Farrell (1997) analyzed the outcomes of more than 20 studies on reality therapy and concluded the therapy produced a medium effect, indicating fairly good effectiveness.

Murphy (1997) and Wubbolding (2000a) criticized reality therapy research and encouraged future research to focus on the following:

- Use theoretically pure forms of reality therapy that Glasser (1998a) and Wubbolding (2000a) have provided. In many existing studies, researchers used mutated forms of the therapy, a practice that confounds results about the theory's effectiveness and hampers replication studies.
- Use practitioners who are trained and certified in reality therapy. Many researchers so far have failed to assess the level of expertise of the counseling or training providers. Because the development of a choice theory relationship is crucial to success in therapy, inexperienced or untrained therapists could adversely impact results.
- Design studies to be longitudinal in nature. To date, many researchers conducted their studies over brief time periods, a condition that could have negatively affected the results.

CURRENT STATUS

William Glasser is semiretired but continues to speak worldwide about choice theory and reality therapy and to direct the William Glasser Institute in California. After the death of his first wife, Naomi, Glasser remarried, and his current wife, Carleen, is very active in the application of reality therapy in the schools. Robert Wubbolding has continued to advance reality therapy, holds executive positions at Glasser's Institute, and directs his own Center for Reality Therapy in Ohio (The William Glasser Institute, 2008).

Counselors can pursue training and certification in reality therapy through the William Glasser Institute. They can also enhance their knowledge and skills by consulting *The International Journal of Reality Therapy* devoted to ongoing development of research and practice. Whatever the name of the underlying theory, reality therapy continues to impact the psychological and educational community, especially in the school counseling arena.

SUMMARY

Reality therapy is a present-oriented psychotherapeutic approach through which practitioners focus on ways clients can make more effective choices in their lives. People behave to fulfill the basic genetic needs of fun, freedom, power, love and belonging, and survival, in the most effective ways they know at any given time. Therapists help clients identify what they want, assess how effectively current total behavior is helping them get what they want, and, if current strategies are not very effective, both support and challenge clients to adopt new behaviors that are both responsible and more effective. This process requires clients' commitment to do something different and to continuously evaluate behavior in terms of its effectiveness in meeting clients' needs and fulfilling their wants. The change process is also predicated on counselors' ability to form choice theory relationships with clients—therapeutic relationships based on empathy, respect, a here-and-now focus, and honest confrontation to adopt new and more effective and responsible ways of forming relationships and fulfilling needs. Although the theory has undergone several revisions since its conception in the 1960s, the clarifications have refined the basic underlying structure of the theory.

RECOMMENDED RESOURCES

Books

Glasser, W. (1998). *Choice theory: A new psychology of personal freedom*. New York, NY: Harper Collins. This book provides the reader, practitioner, or client with all the basic information about choice theory. In the book, Glasser explained each theoretical concept using understandable language and many examples. Reality therapists often assign this book as homework for clients.

Glasser, W. (2000). *Reality therapy in action*. New York, NY: Harper Collins. This is Glasser's most recent conceptualization of the theory in which he has made several adjustments. He used case studies to demonstrate application of choice theory. Although this format is illuminating, we encourage you to have some background in reality therapy before reading this book. Otherwise, you might come away from the book with the false impression that treating serious issues can be fairly simple.

Wubbolding, R. E. (2000). *Reality therapy for the 21st century*. Philadelphia, PA: Brunner-Routledge. We consider this book by far the most comprehensive work available on reality therapy. In it, Wubbolding provided an overview of basic theoretical concepts, several in-depth chapters on the specifics of treatment application, a whole chapter on multicultural issues, and an informative interview with Glasser. The writing style and content are appropriate for a clinical audience that is likely to find Wubbolding's liberal use of case examples helpful.

Audiovisuals

Wubbolding, R. (2001). *Reality therapy in family counseling* [Motion picture]. North Amherst, MA: Microtraining Associates and Chatsworth, CA: The William Glasser Institute.

Wubbolding, R. (2007). *Reality therapy* [Motion picture]. Washington, DC: American Psychological Association and University Park, IL: Governors State University.

Web Sites

http://www.wglasser.com This Web site of the William Glasser Institute is an excellent source of information about the newest ideas and applications of reality therapy. Visitors can also get information on how to get certified in reality therapy through the institute's 18-month program.

http://www.realitytherapywub.com This Web site of Bob Wubbolding's Center for Reality Therapy contains up-to-date information about current use and special applications of the WDEP system.

REFERENCES

Asay, T. P., & Lambert, M. J. (1999). The empirical base for the common factors in therapy: Quantitative findings. In M. A. Hubble, B. L. Duncan, & S. D. Miller (Eds.), *The heart and soul of change* (pp. 23–55). Washington, DC: American Psychological Association.

Baker, L. A., & Clark, R. (1990). Introduction to special feature. Genetic origins of behavior: Implications for counselors. *Journal of Counseling and Development, 68,* 597–600.

Berges, M. (1976). A realistic approach. In A. Bassin, T. E. Bratter, & R. L. Rachin (Eds.), *The reality therapy reader: A survey of the work of William Glasser.* New York, NY: Harper & Row.

Bogolepov, S. (1998). From Russia with love. *International Journal of Reality Therapy, 17,* 30.

Comiskey, P. (1993). Using reality therapy group training with at-risk high school freshmen. *Journal of Reality Therapy, 12,* 59–64.

Cullinane, D. K. (1995). The influence of Glasser's control theory and reality therapy on educators. *Dissertation Abstracts, 56*(09A), 3546.

Deci, E. (1995). *Why we do what we do.* New York, NY: Penguin.

Dryden, J. (1994). The quality school consortium: Insights into defining, measuring, and managing for quality schools. *Journal of Reality Therapy, 16,* 47–57.

Edens, R., & Smyrl, T. (1994). Reducing classroom behaviors in physical education: A pilot study. *Journal of Reality Therapy, 13,* 40–44.

Glasser, N. (Ed.). (1989). *Control theory in the practice of reality therapy: Case studies.* New York, NY: Harper & Row.

Glasser, W. (1965). *Reality therapy: A new approach to psychiatry.* New York, NY: Harper & Row.

Glasser, W. (1968). *Schools without failure.* New York, NY: Harper Collins.

Glasser, W. (1985). *Control theory: A new explanation of how we control our lives.* New York, NY: Harper Collins.

Glasser, W. (1988). *Positive addiction.* New York, NY: Harper & Row.

Glasser, W. (1990). *The basic concepts of reality therapy.* Canoga Park, CA: Institute of Reality Therapy.

Glasser, W. (1992). Reality therapy. *New York State Journal for Counseling and Development, 7,* 5–13.

Glasser, W. (1998a). *Choice theory: A new psychology of personal freedom.* New York, NY: Harper Collins.

Glasser, W. (1998b). *The quality school.* New York, NY: Harper Collins.

Glasser, W. (2000). *Reality therapy in action.* New York, NY: Harper Collins.

Harvey, V. S., & Retter, K. (1995). The development of the basic needs survey. *Journal of Reality Therapy, 15,* 76–80.

Honeyman, A. (1990). Perceptual changes in addicts as a consequence of reality therapy based on group treatment. *Journal of Reality Therapy, 9,* 54–58.

Linnenberg, D. (1997). Religion, spirituality and the counseling process. *International Journal of Reality Therapy, 17,* 55–59.

Litwack, L. (2007a). Basic needs: A retrospective. *International Journal of Reality Therapy, 26,* 28–30.

Litwack, L. (2007b). Dissertations on reality therapy and choice theory: 1970–2007. *International Journal of Reality Therapy, 27,* 14–16.

Mickel, E., & Liddle-Hamilton, B. (1996). Black family therapy: Spirituality, social constructivism and choice theory. *Journal of Reality Therapy, 16,* 95–100.

Murphy, L. (1997). Efficacy of reality therapy in schools: A review of research from 1980–1995. *Journal of Reality Therapy, 16,* 12–20.

Powers, W. (1973). *Behavior: The control of perception.* New York, NY: Aldine Press.

Rachor, R. (1995). An evaluation of the first step PASSAGES domestic violence program. *Journal of Reality Therapy, 14,* 29–36.

Radtke, L., Sapp, M., & Farrell, W. (1997). Reality therapy: A meta-analysis. *International Journal of Reality Therapy, 17,* 4–9.

Renna, R. (1998). Israel: Conflict and the quality world. *International Journal of Reality Therapy, 18,* 4–7.

Sleek, S. (1994). Merits of long, short term therapy debated. *Monitor, 25,* 41–42.

The William Glasser Institute. (2008). *Who we are.* Retrieved from http://www.wglasser.com/index.php?option=com_content&task=view&id=29&Itemid=59

Wubbolding, R. E. (1988). *Using reality therapy.* New York, NY: Harper & Row.

Wubbolding, R. E. (1991). *Understanding reality therapy.* New York, NY: Harper Collins.

Wubbolding, R. E. (2000a). *Reality therapy for the 21st century.* Philadelphia, PA: Brunner-Routledge.

Wubbolding, R. E. (2000b). *Reality therapy training manual* (11th ed.). Cincinnati, OH: Center for Reality Therapy.

Wubbolding, R. E. (2004). *Reality therapy training manual* (13th ed.). Cincinnati, OH: Center for Reality Therapy.

Wubbolding, R. E. (2007). Glasser quality school. *Group dynamics: Theory, research and practice. 11,* 253–261.

Wubbolding, R. E., & Brickell, J. (1998). Qualities of the reality therapist. *International Journal of Reality Therapy, 17,* 47–49.

Wubbolding, R. E., & Brickell, J. (2008). Frequently asked questions and not so brief answers: Part II. *International Journal of Reality Therapy, 27,* 46–49.

Constructivist Approaches*

For those of us alive to the excitement of ideas, some of the proposals of constructive metatheory are music to make us dance. (Mahoney, 1991, p. 113)

BACKGROUND OF THE THEORY

Historical Context and Philosophical Underpinnings

Much like existentialism (see Chapter 5), constructivism has historically been more of a philosophy than a counseling theory. Since its historical context and its philosophical underpinnings are so closely connected, we discuss them interconnectedly in this introductory section.

During the nineteenth and much of the twentieth century, a search for objective truth through reductionism and strict empiricism—relying exclusively on direct observation and experimentation to acquire knowledge—dominated Western thought. This perspective peaked in the early twentieth century with the emergence of logical positivism. Not long after, some thinkers pointed out the irony that when they applied logical positivist assumptions to the perspective itself, it negated itself (Mahoney, 2005). Thus did philosophers and scientists begin to identify the limits of, and move beyond, the prevailing perspective of narrow empiricism and the search for objective truth (Mahoney, 1991; Sexton, 1997; Tarnas, 1991; Wilber, 2000). In large measure, it was this disbelief in the validity of an exclusively objectivist philosophy that gave rise to twentieth century constructivism.

However, the philosophical roots of constructivism date back many centuries. Two contemporary but geographically separate sixth century BC philosophers, Lao Tzu, Chinese philosopher and founder of Taoism, and Greek philosopher Heraclitus, believed that change occurs constantly, reflecting a dynamic interplay between opposites such as dark and light, chaos and order, stability and change. The fifth century BC East Indian founder of Buddhism also addressed the impermanent nature of life and emphasized how humans use their minds and thinking to create and maintain their experiences of reality.

Jumping ahead to the early eighteenth century, the Italian philosopher Giambattista Vico, credited as a founder of constructivism (Mahoney, 1991), described a process by which people create personal meaning. When they encounter something previously

---

* Parts of this chapter are adapted from "Integral Constructivism and Dynamic Systems in Psychotherapy Processes," by M. Mahoney and A. Marquis, 2002, *Psychoanalytic Inquiry, 22*(5). Copyright 2002 by Copyright Clearance Center, Inc. With permission from Taylor & Francis.

unknown, they make sense of it by transposing known psychological structures onto it. In other words, by relating new experiences to what one already knows, one continually builds (constructs) one's worldview. Thus, human knowing involves an imaginative construction of order in experience. It is a process that takes place in social contexts including culture and relationships.

Beyond Vico, scholars also frequently have cited eighteenth and nineteenth century philosophers Immanuel Kant, Martin Heidegger, Friedrich Nietzsche, and Hans Vaihinger as influences on constructivist thought. Each of these philosophers focused on the central idea that there is no single, absolute truth and placed each human being at the center of the creation of a personally held truth about self, others, and the world.

Kant (as cited in Mahoney, 1991) emphasized the power of categories and patterns in people's thinking to organize, interpret, and filter what they perceive. Although these patterns place limits on what people know, Kant did not view people as prisoners of their minds. He believed in both freedom and an autonomous will, and he related these to an ethic of action. He believed that people participate in the construction of a universal lawfulness and that integrity and good will are essential to that process.

In *The Philosophy of "As If,"* Vaihinger (1965) argued that the primary purpose of mind and mental processes is not to portray or mirror objective reality but to create "functional fictions" that help people make meaning of their experiences as they navigate through life circumstances. Vaihinger's principle of functional fictions would later form a cornerstone of Alfred Adler's theory of individual psychology.

These philosophers' perspectives found support in some noteworthy twentieth century psychology research. Frederic Bartlett (1932), in his classic work on reconstructive processes in memory, found that people often fail to observe aspects of experience that don't conform to their preexisting ideas and that, in recalling those experiences, people fill gaps in observation with material from their preexisting ideas. Thus, people often don't remember what actually happened but instead construct their own renditions of what happened.

At about the same time, Jean Piaget began his series of influential studies on children's cognitive development. He found that as people develop throughout childhood and adolescence, they show characteristic changes in the ways they construct their perceptions and knowledge: They become capable of understanding self and world in new ways such that an adult's understanding and a child's are qualitatively different. Drawing on the dynamic view of learning that Johann Herbart (1776–1841) had put forth, Piaget described knowing as a person's quest for a dynamic balance between what is familiar and what is novel. People accomplish this balancing act by coordinating the processes of assimilation and accommodation. They create mental structures, such as categories. Whenever possible, they assimilate (integrate) new experiences into those structures—even when they sometimes have to disregard certain aspects of the experiences to "make them fit" into the structures. When necessary—when new experiences just cannot fit into existing structures—people accommodate (modify) the structures so those structures can include and make sense of the new experience. Piaget emphasized that people organize their worlds by organizing themselves, and this theme of self-organization pervades constructivist views of human experience.

An example of each phenomenon, assimilation and accommodation, comes from one of our (JH's) childhoods. Jan's father liked to tell the story of the day when Jan was about five years old and the family, driving through the countryside, drove past a bull and cow in the act of mating. Her dad saw from the corner of his eye that the scene had gotten Jan's attention. He braced himself for questions he anticipated would be very awkward to answer. He reported that after some lengthy silence, the exchange went like this:

Jan: Dad?
Dad: Yes?
Jan: Do cows sometimes walk on their back legs?
Dad: Yes.
Jan: Oh.

And that was it. With relief, he realized he would not need to elaborate on a lot of new information that Jan would have had to accommodate involving the nature of sexual relations between animals ... and possibly humans. Instead, Jan simply added "cows"—not even yet differentiating between male and female cattle—into her existing list of "four-legged animals that sometimes walk on two back legs." Notice all the information that Jan had to disregard—and, in fact, never even thought to question—in order to fit what she'd seen into existing psychological structures.

On the other hand, Jan remembers vividly the moment she learned about sexual intercourse in humans. It was third grade, and she and Debbie T. had gotten the teacher's permission to go to the bathroom at the same time. In the restroom, Debbie commented that she was tired because her parents had kept her awake the night before making noise while having sex in the next room.

Jan: Having sex?
Debbie: Yes. (Realizing Jan didn't understand, she added) You know: When a man puts his penis in a woman's vagina.

No, Jan didn't know. And she remembers for the next few days looking at adults and thinking, "They do *that*?" with a mixture of surprise, wonder, and dismay. To accommodate this novel information, she modified or expanded her psychological structure about "things that adults do."

These examples illustrate how, as ways to integrate new experiences into one's cognitive structures, the process of assimilation can be an emotionally easier, if sometimes less accurate, process, whereas accommodation is often a more accurate, if more emotionally intense, process. Piaget and constructivists focus on the fact that all people all the time are involved in having experiences that range from mildly novel (such as discovering that a coworker engages in a particular hobby), to profoundly novel (such as experiencing the death of a beloved person or experiencing the horrors of combat), and are in the process of assimilating those experiences into their existing cognitive structures when they can and accommodating those structures to include the experiences when they must.

In his 1952 treatise *The Sensory Order,* philosopher and Nobel laureate Friedrich A. von Hayek offered a powerful theoretical presentation of constructivism. He showed that "much that we believe to know about the external world is, in fact, knowledge about ourselves" (pp. 6–7). In other words, what someone proclaims to "know" reflects as much or more about the person's process or way of organizing experience as it does about the object of knowledge. In the examples from Jan's childhood, the stories reveal more about what Jan knew about sex and how she processed new information about it than about the sexual behavior of cattle and humans.

In the field of psychotherapy, another major event in the emergence of constructivism was George Kelly's 1955 publication *The Psychology of Personal Constructs*. Kelly's theory of "constructive alternativism," better known as "personal construct theory," emphasized both pattern and possibility in the self-organization of personality. In his original theory of personality, constructs are psychological structures through which a person forms and tests one's sense of reality. Constructs (organizing processes) are dichotomous (either/or) in structure and exhibit dynamic (ever-changing) aspects (that is, qualities such as their relative permeability/impermeability and tightness/looseness). Kelly translated his theory into a novel approach to psychotherapy in which the therapist's role is to skillfully challenge the client's ways of construing self, others, the world, and the ways those three phenomena might be related, so that the client can discover new alternatives. Kelly's work has stimulated substantial research on personality and psychotherapy.

Psychotherapist Milton Erickson (1980; Haley, 1973) added to constructivist psychotherapy the dimension of focusing on client strengths. The best example of this contribution is his concept of utilization, in which the counselor makes use of the client's assets as a way for the client to overcome difficulties. Until Erickson, practitioners had focused on exploring client problems. Thus, utilization represented a major shift in the mental health paradigm.

Although scholars can trace the legacy of constructivism far back into written and oral history, the term does not yet appear in most dictionaries of psychology or counseling. However, over the past quarter century, in the literature of academic fields ranging from biology and brain science to cognitive behavioral, psychoanalytic, humanistic, and integral psychotherapies, authors are more often using the terms *constructive* and *constructivist* to describe developing perspectives.

Founder's Biographical Overview

During the late twentieth century, mental health practitioners became increasingly interested in constructivism. Unlike the case with many theories in this book, no one person is the single founder of constructivist psychotherapy. In fact, congruent with the philosophical approach, constructivist practitioners differ in their clinical foci and their translation of constructivist theory into practice. For example, a prominent constructivist, Robert Neimeyer, has focused specifically on grieving as a meaning-making process (Neimeyer, n.d.). Another, Bill O'Hanlon, has written 29 books on his solution-oriented approach, with similarities to solution-focused therapy; several of his books are available at his Web site (O'Hanlon, n.d.). To provide a sampling of constructivist approaches, we have chosen three that honor the philosophical core yet look different in practice: solution-focused therapy, narrative therapy, and Mahoney's constructive psychotherapy. In the following section, we briefly introduce the professionals most prominently associated with each approach and describe its emergence.

Solution-Focused Therapy

Beginning in the early 1980s, husband-and-wife team Steve de Shazer and Insoo Kim Berg and their clinical team at the Brief Family Therapy Center in Milwaukee, Wisconsin developed solution-focused therapy. Over the next two decades, they published works in which they described their approach (de Shazer, 1985; DeJong & Berg,

2008). De Shazer died in September 2005 at the age of 65 and Berg in January 2007 at the age of 72.

The approach rests on the assumption that people create and maintain their realities through social interaction. Thus, practitioners carefully design the social situation of the psychotherapeutic encounter to join with the client in creating the client's therapeutic goal by focusing not on problems but on solutions; in identifying and amplifying what is happening on those occasions in which a problem is not occurring—exceptions; in tapping client resources to move toward solutions; and in focusing on both small and big moves the client makes toward solutions and promoting further movement toward them.

Narrative Therapy

The most prominent early contributors to the development of narrative therapy were Michael White and his colleague David Epston in New Zealand. With their 1990 book *Narrative Means to Therapeutic Ends*, they brought the approach to widespread awareness in the United States, and both they and colleagues continued to be prolific with publications over the next two decades. White died in April 2008 at the age of 59. Epston, codirector of the Family Therapy Centre in Auckland, New Zealand, continues to practice, speak, and conduct trainings.

Narrative therapists believe in the postmodern idea that people can interpret any event in a number of ways. They believe that within people's sociocultural contexts, they selectively perceive their experiences and create stories of their lives—narratives—that either inspire them or oppress them as they proceed in life. When people's stories become problem saturated (oppressive) they often seek counseling. Narrative counselors collaboratively dialog with clients to identify such aspects as the client's hopes, dreams, and assets and to use these aspects in a reauthoring of the client's story into an inspiring form that helps people live in ways they prefer.

Mahoney's Constructivist Psychotherapy

Michael Mahoney (2000) described his theoretical orientations first as behaviorist (see Chapter 8), then cognitive (see Chapter 9), and then constructivist. With publications including his 1974 book *Cognition and Behavior Modification,* he made a pioneering contribution to the cognitive revolution in psychology and psychotherapy. With other books including his 1991 *Human Change Processes,* he made pioneering contributions to the constructivist revolution. Mahoney died in May 2006 at the age of 60.

Unlike radical constructivists who believe so strongly in the ultimately subjective nature of knowing that they deny the existence of an objective real world, Mahoney was a critical constructivist who acknowledged the "existence and influence of an unknowable but inescapable real world ... the individual is conceived as a 'co-creator' or 'co-constructor' of personal realities, with the prefix *co*-emphasizing an interactive interdependence with [one's] social and physical environments" (Mahoney, 1991, p. 111).

Unlike theorists who believe human behavior changes through simple, linear, predictable processes, Mahoney's (1991) research demonstrated that, instead, people change through complex, nonlinear processes in which the specifics are unpredictable. Consequently, he believed psychotherapists need concepts from traditional philosophy as well as chaos theory (Gleick, 1987), dynamic systems theories (Thelen & Smith, 1994), and other studies of complexity (Kauffman, 1993) to work most effectively with clients. Admonishing counselors to be mindful of the philosophical roots of psychotherapy and, at the same time, to remain in close empathic contact with clients' pain, he said, "We are so caught up in the demands of day-to-day practice that we have lost sight of where we came from and what our work is primarily about. Life is complex, and suffering is more than an abstraction" (Mahoney, 2005, pp. 337–338).

One final important point concerns the *theory* status of the three approaches we discuss in this chapter. In telling "The Theoretical Story of Narrative Therapy," Wendy Drewery and John Winslade (1997) acknowledged a theoretical basis to what narrative therapists do. However, in their discussion, they addressed some aspects of our Personality Development section explicitly, addressed some implicitly, and did not address others. By contrast, solution-focused therapist Michael F. Hoyt (2008) cited two recent solution-focused authors to make the point that proponents from founder Steve de Shazer through current practitioners firmly hold the position that solution-focused therapy is "not a Theory of how people develop, how people change, or how therapy should be conducted" (Simon & Nelson, 2007, p. 7; cited in Hoyt, 2008, p. 282). Thus, authors describing this approach also have addressed only some aspects of our Personality Development outline, and mostly implicitly rather than explicitly. By even further contrast, because Mahoney (1991, 2003) integrated into his approach knowledge from a vast array of physical, biological, psychological, social, and spiritual fields, he considered it a metatheory and asserted that "constructive metatheory may be a particularly promising candidate for the continuing exploration of 'integrations' and convergence among the major psychological theories" (1991, p. 113). These points about each approach's status as a theory may be helpful to you as you embark on the next section of this chapter.

PERSONALITY DEVELOPMENT

In our review of constructivist literature, we found two authors who explicitly addressed the topic of personality development. One was Sandra Rigazio-DiGilio (1997) who drew from constructivist learning theory rooted in Piagetian ideas. She postulated that people create worldviews throughout life by using four main systems: (1) images and perceptions; (2) concrete action and thought; (3) abstract and reflective reasoning; and (4) recursive interaction—mutual influence—between self and environment. The structure of the psyche represents each individual's own way of making sense of the world using each of the four domains in different ways throughout development.

Mahoney (2003) also addressed the topic in terms of themes and core-ordering processes (COPs). He considered the basic themes of constructivism to be (1) people as active agents; (2) people organizing/bringing order to their experiences; (3) self/identity as both an ever-changing product of the organizing/ordering process and a factor in how people organize/order their experiences; (4) social/symbolic relatedness (social relationships) as continual, pervasive, and often nonconscious influences on how people organize/order their experiences; and (5) dynamic dialectical life span development—how people, through a back-and-forth influence between oneself and one's physical and social environments, change throughout life in the ways they organize/order their experiences. In addition to and interacting with those five themes are the four COPs, "deeply abstract [and overlapping] processes that are central to our psychological experiencing" (2003, p. 49): (1) worldview: each person constructing a sense of reality; (2) value: each person constructing emotional judgments about experiences; (3) self: each person constructing a sense of personal identity; and (4) power: each person constructing a sense of agency, which is the ability to exercise some degree of freedom and choice.

Nature of Humans

Function of the Psyche

Most constructivists appear to believe that each person is born with a *capacity for experience with its sensory, emotional, and cognitive aspects.* The aspects of experience typically develop into more complex forms over time. For example, newborn eyesight (sensory) is blurry beyond about 15 inches but typically improves to some degree over time, and cognitive experience probably first takes the form of sensory images, for example, an infant's visual memory of a caretaker's face and auditory memory of the sound of a caretaker's voice—and later takes the form of word thoughts—such as the labeling of a caretaker as mother.

Most constructivist authors seem to imply that inseparable from experience is an innate *valuing process*—to like experiences that increase a felt sense of satisfaction and dislike those that increase a felt sense of suffering. Presumably, in an infant this process is immediate and predominantly sensory and emotional, becoming increasingly cognitive with development but without ever losing its sensory and emotional aspect. Both an infant and an adult with the stomach flu are likely to feel repulsed by food that usually is the person's favorite; this temporary devaluation is an immediate sensory/emotional response in both, but in the adult it is likely to include concepts such as illness and nausea.

By making explicit reference to pain and suffering (de Shazer, 1991, p. 12; Epston, 1999, pp. 141–142; Mahoney, 2005, pp. 337–338), most constructivist authors seem also to imply that inseparable from each person's valuing process is a *motive to reduce suffering and increase satisfaction.* Newborn infants appear to be endowed with the innate behavior of crying in response to the suffering of biological need, which crying usually serves as a valuable signal to caretaking adults to take action that meets the infant's need and reduces his suffering. Throughout life, people take action to reduce suffering and increase satisfaction; pause for a few moments to try to think of an example of anyone who has ever done anything that they did not find *ultimately* to be the most satisfying course of action. Test cases include difficult decisions in which people struggle to determine which course of action will ultimately be most satisfying, and sacrifice in which people choose certain forms of suffering in order to attain an ultimately greater sense of satisfaction.

Constructivists appear to agree that both at birth and throughout life, when a person has a new experience, it is not yet organized into one's psyche; that is, it does not yet have a place in one's psychological system. According to constructivists, each person's innate and nonconscious response is *to organize each new experience into a system of meaning making* related to suffering and satisfaction. Early in life, this ability involves primarily sensory and emotional processes. For example, in a very young infant, the sight of nurturing caretakers may come to mean what, if he had language (which he doesn't yet), he might describe as "good, pleasure, happy, yes." Although the ability to bring order to experiences never loses its sensory and emotional foundation, it increasingly includes some degree of cognitive processes—first concrete (again, sensory images), then increasingly abstract (language and reasoning).

Constructivists have more explicitly agreed that innate to the function of creating meaning is *conceptualizing in terms of opposites* (Freedman & Combs, 2008, p. 239; Mahoney, 2003). For example, someone might conceptualize an acquaintance as relatively tall or short, kind or cruel, humorous or serious—and each quality has meaning only with reference to its opposite.

Among constructivists, Mahoney (2003) appears to have gone the furthest in discussing innate psychological functions in people. He drew on self psychology concepts (Kohut, 1971) in asserting that each person has an innate *need for selfobjects*. Selfobjects are external objects, usually people, that an individual subjectively experiences as providing one or more intrapsychic functions, such as validating one's subjective experiences, especially emotional ones; soothing one's physical and emotional distress; and esteeming one's abilities and felt-sense of "I" (Bacal, 1990; Kohut, 1971). Due to the fundamentally emotional nature of people's meaning systems, this need is profound in early life and typically, but not always, reduces by adulthood but never disappears (Mahoney & Marquis, 2002).

It is important to note that we found differences among constructivist therapy authors on the topic of emotion. Narrative therapy authors (Freedman & Combs, 2008; Monk, Winslade, Crocket, & Epston, 1997) were relatively silent on the subject. Solution-focused authors (Hoyt, 2008; Miller & de Shazer, 1998, 2000), through their statement that emotion was neither avoided nor sought in the therapeutic process, explicitly downplayed its primacy in the change process (Hoyt, p. 277) and seemed to imply a less central role in the development process, as well. Mahoney (2003) drew on neuroscientists' recent research findings that emotions are fundamental both to how people perceive and to their ability to use higher order reasoning to make complex decisions. For example, a person in whom the emotion center in the brain has been damaged can explain the pros and cons of a complex decision but cannot experience one pro or con as being more emotionally preferable than another; consequently, they cannot make a choice (Damasio, 1995, 1999; LeDoux, 1996).

Constructivists either state (Mahoney, 2003) or seem to imply that every person combines the previously described innate functions in the service of a master function: *to create and continually revise a personal construct of "the good life"*—a system of meaning in which the person perceives and anticipates reduced suffering and enhanced satisfaction. Narrative therapists have spoken of clients' "preferred perceptions, attitudes, and actions" for "stories ... that help people have a sense of choice, agency, purpose and accomplishment" and that "they prefer, that are more just, and that make their worlds more satisfying" (Freedman & Combs, 2008, p. 236). Solution-focused authors have referred to clients seeking "to achieve what they consider reasonable satisfaction" (Hoyt, 2008, p. 263), clients' pursuit of their "wishes and hopes" (p. 264), and clients' "desired" (p. 265) and "preferred" (p. 266) outcomes. In accordance with development, a very young infant's *good life* will be much simpler than an adult's. Ultimately, the process of pursuing one's good life is more complex than just minimizing pain and maximizing pleasure. Rather, constructivists acknowledge that people inevitably experience pain in life; that they sometimes can transform their perception of pain, as in the person who can self-hypnotize anesthesia; and that they can create meanings in which whatever pain they cannot escape or they choose to experience, they experience in a psychological context of enhanced satisfaction, as in the case of religious martyrs who voluntarily underwent torture and death, perceiving their suffering to be in the service of the ultimate and eternal well-being of their immortal souls.

Constructivists more explicitly agree that people are endowed with two more innate potentials—*to choose* and *to create and pursue goals*—which they use in their ongoing creation and pursuit of a good life. At least Mahoney (2003) indicated that as people develop, they become increasingly capable of choosing and of creating goals. Their choices and goals both reflect the meaning system they have created, pointing to what they consider to be satisfaction-increasing and suffering-reducing, and contribute to the further evolution of their meaning system. Throughout life, people are to some degree continuously active in the pursuit of future goals and projects.

Every constructivist author made either explicit or implicit reference to an innate human motive to *create a sense of power and control* to pursue the good life. Each person seeks to feel powerful rather than powerless and in control rather than out of control to enhance satisfaction and reduce suffering. Even under the most extreme circumstances—those of monumental loss, monumental gain, and profound trauma, when a person is confronted with experiences so novel that one cannot either assimilate or accommodate them into one's existing system of meaning and that system enacts its innate potential to *become disorganized*—a person's innate tendency will be to regain power. That is, one will seek to reorganize a new system of meaning in which one can resume the sense that one is an agent with the power to successfully pursue the good life.

Alone among constructivists, Mahoney (2003) made reference to a major innate factor in the meaning-making process: the *influence of a person's genetic and other biological endowment.* For example, at birth, if not before, genetic endowment can powerfully influence temperament. Based on different temperaments, one infant encountering a loud noise in the environment remains relaxed, whereas another becomes distressed. Such basic reactions clearly influence the satisfaction/suffering meaning different infants would make of the same experience. Likewise, the innumerable genetically and organically based abilities (such as sight) and disabilities (such as blindness, from whatever cause) with which people are born and/or that they develop throughout life, play a crucial role in meaning making. They influence what people will experience; how people will interpret their experiences in terms of satisfaction/suffering; and, eventually, what ever-evolving perspective on the good life people will create.

Structure of the Psyche

Each life experience is, to some degree, novel; thus, people are constantly in the process of constructing and reconstructing their systems of meaning to assimilate and accommodate experiences. For this reason, the constructivist view of "structure" is actually more like a snapshot in time of that ongoing function. Like a time-lapse photo of an airborne horse in the process of galloping, the horse's condition of flying through the air is best understood not in isolation but in terms of the cyclical flying-and-falling process of galloping. Thus, it might be said that although constructivists use the words *structure* and *construct* in their noun forms (a structure, a construct), they really mean those nouns to represent verbs—continuous functions (a person structures, a person constructs; Mahoney, 2003).

Mahoney's (2003) four COPs can be understood to comprise the basic structures of the psyche, structures to which other constructivists have explicitly referred (Freedman & Combs, 2008; Hoyt, 2008). Note that the term *core ordering processes* indicates ongoing activities—even if nonconscious—rather than static things. The fact that they tend to be relatively stable can give the false impression that they are fixed.

Operating primarily outside of awareness, COPs are the organizational processes through which people perceive stabilities, continuities, and constancies. Each COP involves dimensions of opposites. The first COP, *reality,* refers to one's worldview. Reality dimensions include what the person considers real/unreal, possible/impossible, and meaningful/meaningless. The second COP, *value,* refers to judgments that, through development, come to have a cognitive component but are always fundamentally emotional. Value dimensions include what the person considers good/bad, right/wrong, to be approached/to be avoided, and worthy/worthless. The third COP, *self,* refers to a sense of personal identity. Self dimensions include what the person considers body/world, me/not me, and us/them. The fourth COP, *power,* refers to one's sense of agency. Power dimensions include active/passive, hopeful/hopeless, in control/out of control, and engaged/withdrawn. Rather than separate systems, the COPs are always interacting with and mutually influencing each other (Mahoney, 2003).

Role of the Environment

From a constructivist perspective, physical/social environmental occurrences are not objective events with predictable effects on people. Rather, each person perceives each environmental occurrence through one's COPs (sense of reality, values, self, and power) that are always in the process of developing and changing, so a person's response to an occurrence can be predicted only to a degree and never absolutely (Mahoney, 1991; Rigazio-DiGilio, 1997).

In addition, people do not, in a linear, cause-effect way, merely respond to their perceptions of occurrences in the physical/social environment. Rather, they are in a circular, "dialectic relationship" with the environment (Mahoney, 1991; Rigazio-DiGilio, 1997). That is, people continually both respond to and act on their environments. Dialectic means two way, back and forth, and dialog-ic. Thus, people not only change in response to their environments but also change the environments to which they, in turn, change—in a perpetually mutually interactive and mutually influencing process.

On a related note, in the social environment, each person brings one's subjective perceptions and unique set of actions to the process of relating to others. Thus constructivists often use the term *intersubjective*—the interplay of two or more people's subjective systems of meaning—to describe the web of human interaction (Mahoney, 2003).

Since a person's feeling/thinking/acting response to any environmental occurrence reflects that person's current construction of reality, self, values, and power, no one can predict with certainty what that response will be or, in the case of a social interaction, with its intersubjectivity, how the interaction will necessarily unfold. Take for example the following event in a household:

> At dinnertime, a parent puts out a meal of roast beef and vegetables for the family. What will be the outcome of this event? In part because each member of the family will interpret this event according to one's unique COPs, the specific outcome is impossible to predict. The vegetarian son may feel insulted or devalued by the parent serving roast beef, or he may see the vegetables as a sign that the parent cares about and values his choice not to eat meat. If he feels insulted or devalued, will he hide his feelings, become sullen and withdrawn, or storm out of the room? If he feels valued and cared for but would like more variety than the vegetables the parent served, will he hide that preference, ask permission to also make a salad for himself (and perhaps anyone else in the family who might like one), state that he wants to make a salad and get up to do so, or simply get up and make a salad without comment? Whatever his response, how will the parent respond to it? Who knows for certain? Because the outcomes rely so much on the complex interpretation and choices of the individuals involved, hypotheses about them are somewhat futile. If the outcomes are so varied over the simple example of a family dinner, consider the enormous difficulty surrounding interpreting the *causal* environmental factors of depression!

Unlike some theorists who search for environmental antecedents to, or causes of, a counseling client's presenting problem, constructivists are less interested in learning about the environment as a means of explanation than they are with how the person's behavior reflects how one makes meaning of one's environment and perceives one's ongoing relationship with it.

Familial Environment

With these caveats in mind, at least one constructivist, Mahoney (1991, 2003) has addressed the role of early experience in the family on the development of a child's COPs. As noted in his second basic theme, he believed that constructivists view emotions as powerful self-organizing processes in human adaptation. Emotions are critical influences on where people direct their attention; how they perceive, value, and organize memory of what they experience; the sense of self they develop; and the extent to which they feel capable and motivated to engage in life.

People usually have the most intense emotions in (intersubjective) relationships with others, particularly those whom Kohut and intersubjective theorists referred to as selfobjects (Kohut, 1971, 1977; Schore, 1994; Stolorow & Atwood, 1992). Again, selfobjects can be thought of as external objects (usually people) that an individual subjectively experiences as providing one or more intrapsychic functions, such as validating, soothing, and esteeming (Bacal, 1990; Kohut, 1971). As a child usually develops one's initial COPs primarily in the self–selfobject relationships of one's family of origin during one's infancy and early childhood, and those initial COPs are the primary basis on which the child will make meaning of all future experiences, those relationships in the early familial environment play a crucial role in a child's development.

Thus, emotions are at the core of selfobject functions, and the extent to which a child's caregivers provide selfobject functions will powerfully influence the child's basic COPs. In general, the more caregivers accept children's emotional experiences and help children assign meaning to and make sense of them, the more likely children are to develop healthy COPs (Mahoney, 1991; Mahoney & Marquis, 2002). We will discuss the characteristics of healthy COPs in more detail in the Model of Mental Health section below.

Extrafamilial Factors

From Mahoney's (2003) constructivist perspective, not only caretakers and other family members but also many other people throughout a person's development and life serve selfobject functions. Although as people mature healthfully they come increasingly to serve those functions for themselves, they never entirely outgrow the need for selfobject functions from others. The extent to which they experience those needs being met continues to influence their COPs throughout life. The implication is clear regarding the role of counselors in clients' lives: Counselors who provide clients with selfobject functions are the ones most likely to influence clients in a constructive way.

Even entire systems in a person's society can serve or fail to serve selfobject functions. An example of the latter is depicted in the movie *Changeling* (Eastwood, 2009). In the 1920s United States, perfectly sane women who defied police injustice were committed to mental institutions where medical personnel physically and emotionally abused them. Although many people suffer predominantly or entirely as a result of the meaning system they have created—in the absence of external sources of abuse—some people's suffering legitimately arises from their social and cultural environments and is better addressed through social action than through change in their constructions of reality, values, self, and agency. Suffering that arises primarily from the self rather than the environment calls for changing the self; that which arises primarily from the environment rather than self calls for changing the world.

Model of Mental Health

To summarize Mahoney's (2003) five constructivist themes, operating fundamentally on emotion-based valuing processes, each person draws on inner factors, such as genetics; outer factors, such as relationships and culture with their language and symbols; and personal choice to continually and nonconsciously organize experiences to create a system of meaning comprised of dimensions of opposites. Central to this system is a sense of self, and the system includes a view of the good life that the person to some degree strives, through some degree of agency, to achieve by creating and pursuing goals.

So far, little we have said implied that one person's system of meaning or view of the good life is healthier than another's. Was Adolf Hitler's view better than, worse than, or equally as good as Mahatma Gandhi's? Indeed, constructivist psychotherapy authors have tended to be much more explicit about *not* operating from preconceived ideas in addressing this question. For example, Hoyt (2008) said solution-focused therapists "avoid traditional diagnostic categories and preconceived notions of what may be healthy/unhealthy or functional/dysfunctional for a particular couple, individual, or family" (p. 260) and that they "[accept] the client's version of what is—and is not—a problem. Primacy is given to clients' experiences, goals, ideas, values, motivations, and worldviews, which are respectfully accepted as valid and real" (p. 261). Narrative therapists Freedman and Combs (2008) also asserted, "We do not subscribe to normative ideas of what constitute ... healthy ...." (p. 235) and that "we are interested in people's own evaluations of what is problematic and what is preferred" (p. 232). However, these latter authors also were explicit that this relativistic stance does have limits: "We want ... stories to support meanings and actions that do not harm or impair other people" (p. 232), and "We are opposed to (among other things) abuse, coercion, and cruelty" (p. 232). Hoyt (2008) also stated, that solution-focused therapists "do respond appropriately to situations of obvious abuse" (p. 277). Although Mahoney apparently did not state these limits explicitly, one of us who worked closely with him (Marquis) is certain he would have agreed unequivocally with regard to them.

Interestingly, despite the solution-focused admonition regarding avoidance of traditional diagnostic categories, Hoyt (2008) did say that proponents of this approach, like those of other approaches, would have low expectations for improvement with clients who are "too psychiatrically impaired" (p. 284). He also referred to "sociopathy and/or domestic violence" (p. 284) as possible cause for special treatment, such as the client participating in individual counseling until the therapist determines the client is safe for couple counseling. However, solution-focused therapists' rejection of established diagnostic procedures makes it unclear how a therapist would determine sociopathy or what constitutes too extreme psychiatric impairment.

So, in summary, what system of meaning and model of the good life is relatively healthier? Combining explicit and implicit messages from various constructivist authors, we identified this list that we believe to be representative but not necessarily exhaustive:

- A system of meaning that is *well defined yet flexible,* as opposed to less well defined at one extreme or rigidly defined at the other.
- A system of meaning that is predominantly *saturated with solutions and hope,* as opposed to saturated with problems and either anxious hypervigilance at one

extreme or depressive hopelessness at the other—or vacillation between these extremes.

- A system of meaning that supports *active engagement in life and balanced pursuit of life goals,* as opposed to hyperactive overinvestment in life goals at one extreme or passive withdrawal from life goals at the other.
- A system of meaning that yields *a sense of balance and wholeness* as opposed to a sense of imbalance and/or of alienation or segregation of parts from the whole—aspects of self from a more whole sense of self, or self from relationship to a greater whole.
- A system of meaning that *supports both one's own and others' freedom and well-being,* as opposed to one that infringes on the freedom or well-being of others.

THE PERSONALITY CHANGE PROCESS

In general, constructivists see development as the process by which individuals continually accumulate and organize personal knowledge about self, others, and the world and, in so doing, create their own "personal realities" (Mahoney, 2008). Social constructionists like Gergen (1985) view a person's statements about the world as "artifacts of communal interchange," not as reflections of the objective world. These theorists focus on how social processes—in particular, language, discourse, artifacts such as the *Diagnostic and Statistical Manual of Mental Disorders* (American Psychological Association, 2000), and the mutual meaning making between counselor and client—shape people's conceptualizations. Thus, people are always changing, usually nonconsciously, through dialog in relationships. Counseling consists of a more intentional change process of shared meaning making in which a helping professional hears, understands, and participates in a client's reconstruction of one's personal reality—one's story.

According to DeJong and Berg (2008) and White and Epston (1990), the first principle of change in counseling is that clients can tell counselors who the clients are and where they want to go developmentally. Whether clients dialog generally about their life stories or specifically about an issue, constructivists believe *clients have the wisdom and competency to determine the focus of change.*

The second principle of change in counseling emphasizes *the role of client strengths* versus presenting problems. Traditional therapists tend to be problem focused by spending considerable time talking about the precursors to and presumed causes of the issue before considering possible solutions. Proponents of the three theories we discuss in this chapter believe that just as clients have the power to change, they also already possess strengths, and if client and counselor can uncover or maximize those strengths, change will follow.

Mahoney (1991, 2003) described another basic principle of change: that *personal transformations*—significant and enduring personal changes, whether they occur in or out of counseling—*are often preceded by brief or prolonged episodes of whole system disorganization.* Such disorganization may be an essential precursor to the emergence of a reorganized system of meaning that is more adaptive. From this perspective, disorder and disorganization are not the enemies of developmental emergence (personal evolution); they may, in fact, be necessary prerequisites for the holistic change necessary for a new, more adequate level of functioning to emerge.

Another of Mahoney's (2003) principles of change is that when the system manages to wrestle new order out of disorder, the *emerging system tends to be both more complex and more capable*. Although even the new system will inevitably contain its own vulnerabilities, constructivists' views of people's potential for constructive change is more hopeful than the views of theorists and therapists from pathology-based models of human dysfunction (Mahoney & Marquis, 2002).

In life and in psychotherapy, *change is not linear* (Mahoney, 1991). Between the multiple forces at work in the client's life and in the relationship between client and counselor and the natural tendency of living organisms to oscillate between activity and inactivity and between expansion/risk and contraction/security, *the particulars of the change process cannot be predicted with certainty*. However, some patterns are more likely than others, and we will discuss some of these patterns below.

Client's Role

Therapists from all three constructivist perspectives agree that from clients' perspectives, their motivation to seek counseling and to change is to reduce pain and suffering in their lives. From constructivist counselors' perspective, the source of people's pain and suffering sometimes is their social environments that somehow obstruct their pursuit of the good life. Much more often, it is their own meaning systems that have unintentionally become problem saturated and, thereby, infused with feelings such as hopelessness that limit possibilities.

Being inherently and fundamentally conservative, once people establish COPs that helped them achieve the good life in the past, they resist changing. The very processes that at one time maximized a sense of meaning become "ruts of being." Like other constructivists, Mahoney (2003) often (though not always) depathologized the reasons people sought counseling: "Periods of disorganization and fluctuations in our experiencing are a natural and necessary part of development. Such episodes may not be pleasant, but they often reflect promise and possibility in our process of being" (p. 11).

Regarding clients' capacity to change, developmental constructivists consider the resilience and resourcefulness of the human system is much greater than is generally appreciated (Mahoney, 1991, 2003). In other words, without ignoring the profound negative influence that genetics or neglectful or abusive early childhoods may exert, people can exert considerable influence over the course of their development throughout the life span. At the same time, their potential for transformation surely is not limitless. According to Mahoney, traditional analysts, behaviorists, and humanists have all grasped part of this issue, but not its complexity:

> People do express their genetic inheritance, but they do it in highly contextual and individualized ways. Early experiences make big differences in developmental trajectories, yet many people transcend them. Environments do select patterns, yet we select and change our environments. Human potential may not be limitless, but it is much greater than most psychological models have yet appreciated. (2003, p. 170)

Similarly, narrative and solution-focused therapists agree that clients often have constructed systems of meaning—stories—composed of perspectives and plots that exclude other possibilities. For these therapists, each client's future is a blank page on which the client has the power—the authority—to create and live a story more in line with the client's good life. As such, their capacity to change is great.

With authorship capacity comes the primary responsibility for constructing new narratives. Clients in constructivist counseling focus on what they can make better in the present and future; if that focus is not their natural initial inclination in counseling—as it often is not, tending as they often do to focus on what has been problematic in the past—they must be open to the therapist guiding them toward solutions in the future. In this process, clients are active participants in goal setting and follow-through. Constructivist counselors see clients as collaborators in the change process who assume neither a passive nor a complete leadership role. Instead, the role of clients can best be described as in identifying and pursuing goals or projects that are meaningful to them.

Regarding client resistance, constructivist therapists are united in the view that when clients do not change in ways counselors expect, counselors do not cast clients as villains and they assume some responsibility in the situation. What some therapists label resistance is not just a client's "stubborn refusal" or "failure" to change. Narrative therapists acknowledge that therapy sometimes becomes difficult, and when it does they themselves must be the ones to resist: resist blaming the client as a way of putting the responsibility for the difficulty on the client and enhancing the counselor's sense of diminished power in the difficulty, and resist using words or meanings like "client resistance" in conversations even with other professionals. "Instead, we might examine the restraints that are operating in the conversation between us [counselor and client] or in the cultural world around us, and we might invite our clients to take part in this examination" (Winslade, Crockett, & Monk, 1997, p. 57). Similarly, solution-focused therapists have declared "the death of resistance" (de Shazer, 1984), reconceptualizing it as inadvertent therapist failure to foster cooperation in light of the kind of relationship the client was ready to enter (Hoyt, 2008, p. 264). Mahoney (2003) also thought more in terms of protective devices that clients understandably use if they do not feel empathic attunement from their counselors around experiences such as a sense that their COPs are changing too quickly or that they might be hurt by the therapist as they were by someone in their past. Therefore, "resistance" is not merely an intrapsychic function of the client but, rather, is a product of the intersubjective field between client and counselor—with the counselor's actions always playing a role (Mahoney & Marquis, 2002; Stolorow, Brandchaft, & Atwood, 1987).

Counselor's Role

Constructivist counselors approach therapy with some assumptions: That clients are creative, capable, changing, and wanting further change in the direction of what they perceive as their more enhancing wishes and hopes; and also that clients are suffering from a system of meaning, with its assumptions and selective attentions, whereby they have come to perceive that they do not have access to what they need to move in preferred directions (Hoyt, 2008, p. 263). Constructivist therapists assume that although they strive to understand clients' worldviews as much as possible, they never can understand perfectly—nor do they need to understand entirely—those worldviews or, especially, clients' views of their problems, in order to help clients move in preferred directions. They assume that little to nothing is fixed about clients or their preferred directions and that both are likely to change and evolve as counseling progresses. Constructivist therapists see counseling as a collaborative enterprise between experts: the client(s), who are experts on what, for them, is the good life and on what does and does not help them move toward it; and counselors, who are experts in facilitating clients' discovery of their abilities to realize more of their good life.

Among skills common to constructivists are the ability to do their part in the therapeutic process of:

- Cocreating an atmosphere of safety and openness: to listen with genuine interest and empathy to clients' stories and to use reflective responses and questions to check the accuracy of their understanding of those stories. ("So you want to feel more confident in conversing with strangers.")
- Setting the stage for possible change: to listen and question in particular ways that help clients expose and evaluate perspectives and practices the client has taken for granted and that draw out, identify, and amplify clients' preferred directions, their strengths, and exceptions to problems—times when the problem was not present. ("Wow! So you somehow found the courage to attend a party at which you knew practically no one. How did you do that?")
- Promoting change: to encourage or invite clients to try experiments and undertake projects they and/or the clients have designed that clients perceive as offering the possibility of movement in clients' preferred directions and that are characterized by such qualities as accomplishment, agency, choice, hope, and purpose. ("You want to make a point to keep listening to upbeat music on the way to a party as a way to enter the party feeling more generally upbeat yourself.")
- Promoting client self-determination: to invite clients to question and assess the extent to which anything from as small as a specific counselor question to as big as an experiment or project, an entire session, or an entire course of therapy are helping the client move in preferred directions; to assess whether, how much, and what form of counseling the client chooses to pursue further; and to make choices based on that assessment. ([At end of session] "Having identified what was helpful to you in our session today and what you want to do this week, what would you like to do regarding another session?")

One theme constructivists typically address is the dynamics of power in relationships—between people in various roles such as man–woman, boss–employee, spouse–spouse, and even the immediate relationship of client–counselor—dynamics that often are implicit in people's stories and experiences. Constructivists seek to make these dynamics explicit so people, being more aware, have more choice. One expression of the view that client–counselor power is not just one way (counselor more powerful, client less powerful) is a view that, among constructivists, Mahoney (2003) voiced most explicitly: Not only clients, but also counselors, are affected and changed through the intersubjective process of counseling.

Another theme in the constructivist counselor's role is self-reflection to enhance therapeutic effectiveness. Mahoney (2003) recommended that constructivist psychotherapists prepare for each session in quiet reflection. Solution-focused therapists typically take a break near the end of each session to reflect and plan how to close the session in the most helpful way for clients (Hoyt, 2008, pp. 270–271). Narrative therapists reflect on ways clients might develop alternative stories even further than they did in session, or on stands clients have taken in relationship to problems, and often send clients letters and documents that express these reflections to "keep a story alive and growing" (Freedman & Combs, 2008, p. 233).

Constructivists also typically eschew counselors using techniques on clients (de Shazer, 1985; Mahoney, 2003). One of us [AM] remembers his first clinical supervisor, John Garcia, saying, "Techniques are what you'll use until the therapist arrives." By this, Dr. Garcia meant that developing counselors rely strongly on techniques until they become truly effective agents of change: able to form safe, trusting, empathic, intimate relationships and to use their own conscious development to create an unconditional healing presence. Though constructivist counselors often do enact certain practices in their interactions with clients, they do so only secondarily to their intentions to meet the person of the client and facilitate the client living in ways the client finds preferred and more satisfying.

Constructivists from the various approaches also differ in their roles. For example, narrative and solution-focused therapists as quickly as possible redirect clients away from a focus on problems and toward a focus on solutions, whereas a focus on client problems is sometimes an explicit level of focus in Mahoney's (2003) approach. Similarly, Mahoney (2003) recommended that counselors "trust that your clients can endure their pain and be strengthened by the process" (pp. 262–263), whereas narrative and solution-focused therapists tend to make only passing reference to client pain—and primarily to its role in people's motivation to enter counseling. Also, whereas Mahoney (2003) recommended that constructivist psychotherapists "teach compassion, forgiveness, and self-care" (pp. 262–263), neither narrative nor solution-focused therapists have voiced such a recommendation.

In line with these differences are varying views on the role of emotion in the therapeutic process. Mahoney (2003) recommended counselors to "encourage (but do not force) emotional expression" and to "allow and invite yourself to feel emotional in the process of counseling" (pp. 262–263). Beyond reference to the emotional resonance of empathy, narrative therapists have tended to be silent on the topic of the role of emotion in the therapeutic process, whereas solution-focused therapists have asserted, "emotion is not avoided, but it is also not sought or elicited as a therapeutic 'royal road' or as an end in itself" (Hoyt, 2008, p. 277); rather, they cooperate with clients by using clients' own feeling and/or behavioral words that relate to solutions.

A final contrast involves constructivists' perspectives on how easy it is for therapists to use constructivist approaches. One solution-focused therapist described that approach as "user friendly" (Hoyt, 2008, p. 259). By contrast, Mahoney (2005) referred to the "illusions of simplicity" (p. 347) in many approaches to psychotherapy (2005, p. 347). He wrote of constructivism that:

> No other family of modern theories asks its adherents to maintain such a degree of self-examining openness, to so painstakingly tolerate and harvest (rather than eliminate) ambiguity, or to so thoroughly question both the answers and the questions by which they inquire. It is not easy to be a constructivist. (2003, p. 207)

Stages and Techniques

The further we move from abstract philosophy toward concrete procedures, the more the three approaches diverge. Thus, in this section, we leave off attempts to draw out similarities and differences between the approaches and merely highlight, in turn, the procedures of each approach.

Solution-Focused Therapy

Hoyt (2008) asserted that although solution-focused therapists employ the practices or tools of client support, client encouragement, and teaching clients specific skills, "the hallmark" of this approach is that counselors "use … questions to invite clients to organize and focus their attention, energy, and understanding in one way—toward a richly detailed description of a solution picture" (p. 265). Therapists ask questions and explore and elaborate on selected client responses "to direct clients toward the realization of their desired outcomes" (p. 265).

Typically in solution-focused therapy, one counselor works with one or more clients for 50- to 60-minute sessions. During each session, the therapist typically takes a break at some point. Client(s) determine the number and temporal spacing of the sessions; Hoyt (2008) reported 1–10 sessions is a typical course of therapy, though some courses may be longer (p. 263). Clients also may return intermittently as they experience the need (Hoyt, 2008).

1. *Initial contact*: When a client first calls to set up an appointment, the counselor typically invites the caller to "bring to the session whomever is involved" in the problematic situation (Hoyt, 2008, p. 263). To begin facilitating a shift in client perspective toward what is already happening that is positive, and to begin promoting cooperation, the counselor is likely to give the client a pre-session task: to observe in the relationship the client describes as problematic, something the client would like to continue to happen—and come to the first session prepared to describe it to the counselor. For example, a client might report in the first session that, for once, her employee responded to her request by agreeably fulfilling it rather than arguing.

2. *First session*: "To build rapport, make space for [clients'] views and theories, and establish a team (therapist-[client] alliance) framework" (Hoyt, 2008, p. 266), solution-focused therapists ask clients to describe what situation brought them to counseling, what they would like to happen regarding that situation, and what role they see the counselor serving in that process. De Shazer and Berg (1997) specified that "at some point in the first interview, the therapist will ask the 'Miracle Question'" (p. 123): "If a miracle occurred overnight and the problem(s) that brought you here were solved, how would you know? What would be different?" Another therapist tool of the first and subsequent sessions is scaling—rating on a 1 to 10 scale things like client hope, motivation, and/or progress toward goals, with 10 always being the positive (hopeful, motivated, goal-achieved) end (Hoyt, 2008, p. 269).

   An important process is for the counselor to join the client in a relationship for which the client is ready. The counselor accomplishes this process in two steps. The first is to assess the client's level of engagement and commitment to change. At any given time, a client might be a *visitor,* with whom the counselor cannot identify a clear complaint or goal; a *complainant,* in which case the client has a clear complaint but is not ready to take action or wants another person or situation rather than oneself to change; or a *customer,* who has a complaint, a clear goal, and readiness to take action toward achieving the goal (Shoham, Rohrbaugh, & Patterson,

1995). The second step is to respond accordingly, a process that is clearest in the last few minutes of the session, which we describe next.

Typically after 40 minutes or so, the counselor takes a break, saying explicitly that this is a time for everyone to reflect on what was or wasn't helpful about the session, where the client(s) will go from here in terms of the directions they've discussed during the session, and whether and when the client(s) will return for a future session. After the break, the counselor typically *compliments* the client(s) on things such as their positive motivation, constructive intentions, and/or actions. For clients who are visitors, the counselor offers politeness, sympathy, and compliments ("I'm impressed that you made the effort to come to counseling even though what your spouse described as a problem for her, you haven't experienced as a problem for you."); for the complainant, accepting the client's perspective, giving compliments ("You clearly care about your children and want them to experience a peaceful home environment."), and possibly suggesting observational tasks such as noticing exceptions ("You might watch to see if you can notice a time when your wife is more patient and even-tempered with your children."); and for the customer, more explicit solution-oriented tasks.

3. *Subsequent sessions*: Solution-focused counselors use many of the same tools from the first session in subsequent sessions. We have already mentioned questions that help clients express their pain, identify exceptions to problems, and scale their hope, motivation, and progress toward goals. Solution-focused therapists also use "agency (efficacy) questions ... to call attention to clients' ... abilities to make a difference in the desired directions" (Hoyt, 2008, p. 268; How did you accomplish that?); "coping (endurance) questions ... to acknowledge ... [pain] ... and also highlight the clients' contributions to their resiliency" (p. 269; How did you manage to persevere in the face of all those obstacles?); and questions to "bring forth and highlight competencies, positive qualities, strengths, and successes" (p. 269; What does achieving that goal say about you as a person?).

As clients move toward increasing customership, counseling becomes increasingly goal focused. Goals are crucial in the solution-focused process. Only with a goal that represents a different approach than the one the client has been taking, will the client realize a more satisfying life. In general, good goals are positive, present-and process-oriented, specific, and understood and controlled by the client. De Shazer (1991) also said it involves a small step, is important to the client, is achievable, is "perceived by the clients as involving their 'hard work'; [is] described as the 'start of something' and not as the 'end of something'" (p. 112), and involves the observable and measurable presence of new behaviors rather than the "absence or cessation of existing behavior(s)" (p. 112). Consider these two goals:

Goal #1:   I want to have a happier marriage. My marriage will be happier if my wife would be nicer to me.

Goal #2:   I want a happier marriage. I am going to improve my part in the relationship by doing one helpful thing per day. I am going to talk with my wife and come up with a list of 10 things that she would find helpful, and I am going to choose one of those per day to complete.

Can you see the difference? Goal #1 is vague and largely outside the client's control. It also lacks specificity and contains no information on the process of being happy other than an expectation of another person's behavior. The nature of this goal would indicate that the client is a complainant—not ready to take action to make improvements. Conversely, Goal #2 focuses on the solution, provides for specific steps of action that the client controls, and includes a means for assessing progress toward its achievement. Will the client feel happier after one week? No one knows, but the opportunity for greater happiness improves with the formation of a good goal. Regardless of the outcome, at the following session, the client and counselor would review the client's activities around the goal and continue what worked, build on any successes, and disregard the rest (de Shazer, 1985).

The example below represents the evolution of that goal and the interventions that resulted in its enactment.

Counselor: What went well this week with your plan?
Client: Well, I talked with my wife. She seemed hesitant to talk about the list. At the end I only had about 7 things, which fell short of my 10.
Counselor: You were able to achieve over two thirds of your goal; that's pretty good. What did you do with the 7 items?
Client: I did 2 of them.
Counselor: So you were able to follow through on your plan despite not getting the cooperation you were hoping for!
Client: Yes, and I even did more than I planned, so that was a pleasant surprise.
Counselor: What else did you experience as positive?
Client: Just talking to her in that way felt a lot better. I think I listened to her and didn't get frustrated. And of course, it was great that I followed through. That was different.
Counselor: Okay, so you felt that your ability to listen and follow through on your goal had a positive impact on you and the relationship.
Client: Absolutely.
Counselor: In fact, on a scale from 1 (low) to 10 (high), how satisfied do you feel with what you were able to achieve?
Client: About a seven.
Counselor: Okay! Let's build on that for next week. How would you like to proceed in term of this goal or another?
Client: I want to get to a 9 or 10 on this goal. I am going to have another conversation with my wife and listen to her view on the relationship. I am also going to continue to commit to doing at least one thing a day to help.

In this phase, solution-focused counselors encourage clients as they make small or big steps in the direction of their goals. Counselors can use scaling questions to help themselves and their clients assess client progress, and when clients regress, the two collaborators refocus on the client's positive aspects that could improve the situation. For example, if the client notes after the first week that the strategy of listening to his wife and following through improved his feelings about the relationship, but in a subsequent session he starts to become discouraged, the counselor could revisit the strategy of listening to his wife and following though to rededicate the client to the change process.

4. *Stabilization of change and decision to continue or terminate counseling*: As clients change, solution-focused counselors maintain focus on progress toward the goal and positive aspects of the client that are contributing to goal attainment. Throughout the counseling process, solution-focused counselors remain vigilant about "problem talk" and redirect to solution talk. In the above example, if the client began to focus on how the wife is uncooperative and, therefore, the client cannot be happy, the counselor would refocus the client on the solution: the goal. Solution-focused therapists believe that by focusing on even very small changes, they facilitate other small and large changes, and successes build. Upon achieving the original goal, the client decides to pursue another goal or to terminate counseling.

Narrative Therapy

Regarding the overall structure of therapy, narrative therapists have not tended to focus on details such as the length of each meeting. However, they have indicated that they "negotiate … each meeting as [they] go along, one session at a time" (Freedman & Combs, 2008, p. 232). They also relate that therapy might last from a few sessions to several years (p. 233).

In narrative therapy, the dialog between client and counselor in the form of the client's story is the central focus. Since the dialog in each therapy session is unique and arises from the interaction between counselor and client, the counseling process does not consist of definitive stages or involve specific techniques per se. In fact, narrative therapists would probably consider the concept of universal stages of client progress to be an affront to client freedom and an impediment to natural story development. However, narrative therapists do emphasize a pattern of story progression: from stories that are problem saturated to those in which authors "[live] out, moment-to-moment, choice-by-choice, life stories that they prefer, that are more just, and that make their worlds more satisfying" (Freedman & Combs, 2008, p. 236). For introductory purposes we have outlined the general elements of the narrative therapy process, but keep in mind that in practice, narrative counseling is not a lock-step approach, and these steps would comprise aspects of a whole integrated process.

1. Telling the story: As *clients tell their stories*, narrative counselors "listen with focused attention, patience, and curiosity while building a relationship of mutual respect and trust" (Freedman & Combs, p. 237). They interrupt periodically to reflect what they are hearing and ask how well the meanings they are making from the client narrative matches what the client intends to convey (p. 237). Through deep and accurate understanding of client stories, counselors can employ what Omer (1997) referred to as narrative empathy: finding emotional and cognitive patterns within clients' stories.

2. Exploring elements of the story: In another important aspect of narrative counseling, counselors help clients *identify various elements of the story,* such as roles, settings, patterns, character perspectives, and final conclusion. Later, counselor and client will use one or more of these elements as possible avenues for change.

   In addition to these explicit story elements is another important category: *meanings that are underlying or implicit.* Every story includes "realities," practices, "purposes, values, hopes, commitments, and the like that are 'absent but implicit' in people's narratives" (Freedman & Combs, 2008, p. 239). Freedman and Combs (2008) provided an example of a couple in which the wife initially defined the problem as "betrayal." "When we hear problematic stories, we particularly listen for implications about what might be treasured" (p. 240). By asking whether trust—the implicit value in the issue of betrayal—was something the wife treasured (she replied yes, with tears), and asking her to identify any ways her husband *had* contributed to her sense of trust (which she could), husband and wife turned the spotlight onto how to promote the growth and flourishing of "trust and commitment" in their relationship. "Listening for the absent but implicit helped us find stories and meanings we might never have found if we had continued to focus on betrayal" (p. 240).

3. Exploring alternatives: As counselor and client dialog about the story, they both (but usually the counselor initially) explore alternatives implicit in the story.

One important alternative is the option to *externalize the problem*, that is, recast the problem as an external character that "costs" the client in some way. Rather than remaining a characteristic of the client, the problem becomes a separate, external (to the client) character in the story to whom the client gives a name. For example, a client who feels anxious about dating identifies "Anxiety" as an antagonist in the client's story that freezes the client's limbs and prevents him from going out on dates and tries to keep him from adding to his life the rewards that dating can bring. Much like in a good work of fiction, by setting up the problem as an external—and villainous—character, the main character—the client(s)—can become a hero who somehow opposes the villain and very possibly gains victory. Externalizing the problem enables the client to separate oneself—the person—from one's difficulty—the problem. In so doing, the client can discontinue the role of victim, with its associated feelings of powerlessness and discouragement, and assume—cast oneself in—the role of hero, with its associated feelings of power and courage.

Another way of exploring alternatives is through *identifying exceptions* to the main plot that hold potential for change. Counselors "try from the first to invite people to explore, describe, and experience new [more preferable] directions in life that are already unfolding" (Freedman & Combs, 2008, p. 233). For example, are there moments in the story when Anxiety does not freeze the client? If so, what did the client do to escape Anxiety's grip? What was special about that situation? Answers to these questions may provide clues to possible new story lines. It is here that the counselor focuses on the inherent strength of the client. Having already externalized the problem, client and counselor are actively looking for ways to beat the villain. Many of these strategies already exist in the "shadows" of the client's story; by turning the spotlight on them, counselor and client increase their potential to play a more "starring role" in the client's story. Each alternative that counselor and client uncover has the potential to infuse the client's story with hope and to promote the client's recognition of one's own power to construct one's life story according to one's highest values and greatest hopes and dreams.

4. Writing new stories: As client and counselor come to understand the client's story, reveal its explicit and implicit elements, and perceive alternatives within and beyond it, the client is likely to feel increasingly empowered to write and rewrite story lines. Although client and counselor achieve this reauthorship through therapeutic dialog, the client also achieves it through practice in life outside of therapy and even by literally writing one's life stories in the form of letters and journals (see Box 12.1).

BOX 12.1 SAMPLE LETTERS

In these sample letters from a 14-year-old client, notice how his shift in perspective from the first to the second letter manifests in changed language and ending.

The Story of My Relationship With My Father (first version)

Dear Dad,

In the beginning, I came into the world with much promise. I have seen pictures of you holding me as a newborn, your face full of awe and wonderment. I imagine that as a baby I received much love and encouragement from you. As I grew, I felt the bond between us grow. I recall you coaching me in baseball and being a fan as I learned new things. Then I turned 13 and something happened. I noticed you pulling away, and I feel a great distance between us. I am struggling with changes in my own life and need you to be there like you were when I was a baby ... or a Little League baseball player. I have gotten angry and sad and nothing has worked. I am now 14 and feel alone. Anxiety, ANGER, and Fear are monsters that live with me constantly. I hang out with them a lot, and you don't seem to notice. As time goes on, I expect that I will continue to live with them. If I go to college, they will become my roommates, and I won't think to call you anymore. The distance will be permanent ... they will have replaced you. I need to do something.

Love, Brian

Letter to Dad (version two)

Dear Dad,

In the beginning, I came into the world with much promise. I have seen pictures of you holding me as a newborn, your face full of awe and wonderment. I imagine that as a baby I received much love and encouragement from you. As I grew, I felt the bond between us grow. I recall you coaching me in baseball and being a fan as I learned new things. Then I turned 13 and something happened. I notice you pulling away, and I feel a great distance between us. I am struggling with changes in my own life and need you to be there like you were when I was a baby ... or a Little League baseball player. I have gotten angry and sad and nothing has worked. I am now 14 and feel alone. Anxiety, ANGER, and Fear are monsters that live with me. I hang out with them a lot, and you don't seem to notice. There are times when I don't hang out with them. I have gotten better at sending them away. When they are gone, I feel hopeful and sad. It is in those times that I seek you out and I find you more willing to talk with me. I enjoy our times in the car. I could ride the bus to school but choose to ride with you because it gives us some time to be together. I am going to be more active in finding stuff for us to do. Anxiety and FEAR tell me I shouldn't do that, but I think it's a good idea. If I can find one thing that we enjoy together, I see our relationship getting better. The more I try, the less those feelings want to hang around me. I realize now that I don't have to rely on you to try. I can always do that ... in any relationship. If I can keep choosing to try, I see our relationship improving over the years. I will feel less isolated and disconnected, and that feels good.

Love, Brian

In addition to clients, counselors also participate in reauthorship exercises.

> We take notes in therapy that document new stories as they develop ... often refer back to these notes and read them aloud [to clients]. When [clients] take [new] stands [in relationship to problems] or achieve new things, or reach turning points, we might create a document or certificate together that formalizes this newly distinguished event in their story ... videotape for ... personal use.... We sometimes write letters between therapy meetings ... reflect on unique outcomes and ask questions that we did not ask in the therapy conversation ... [in the hope of] thicken[ing] and extend[ing] the [new story lines] that had begun to emerge.... We invite couples to share these documents with other people in their lives. (Freedman & Combs, 2008, p. 245)

Unlike solution-focused therapists, for whom goals are a critical aspect of therapy, narrative therapists are "more interested in opening up possibilities" (Freedman & Combs, 2008, p. 236). They are:

> wary of "goal setting" ... single, specific trajectories ... can all too easily close down possibilities.... Instead of goals, we tend to speak of "projects" or "directions in life." ... Problems can be thought of as plots, and projects as counterplots. (p. 236)

The point narrative counselors emphasize is that no story is set in stone. Clients are the creators of their stories and, therefore, have the power at any time to examine, edit, and change their stories in the directions they desire from the present point forward.

Mahoney's Constructive Psychotherapy

On the subject of techniques in psychotherapy, Mahoney asserted that "the art of human helping will not be found in specific words or meticulously repeated rituals, unless those words and rituals reflect something deeper than their own surface structure" (Mahoney, 2003, p. 168). That "something deeper" is counselors' compassionate understanding of clients—their developmental levels, worldviews, and wishes; and caring for them—seeking to uncover and remove obstacles to their well-being. Like Carl Rogers and Fritz Perls before him, Mahoney (2003) was adamant that counselors most fundamentally access their compassion and caring for clients and only secondarily, as an outgrowth of that primary process, employ specific techniques. As such, the most effective counselors use their compassion and caring to choose and tailor interventions to be appropriate to the client's level of development, worldview, and wishes, including the client's desired goals and pace of change.

Nonetheless, in his book *Constructive Psychotherapy*, Mahoney (2003) included six chapters on techniques ranging from basic centering and problem solving to pattern- and process-level work and two additional chapters on techniques he created such as "stream of consciousness" and "mirror time." Moreover, the book includes 14 appendices, most of which are instructions for counselors to practice and use specific exercises, from breathing, relaxation, and meditation to mirror time, self-comforting, and spiritual exercises. The range of techniques reflects Mahoney's ongoing appreciation for the perspectives through which he evolved and/or that he integrated in his own professional development: behavioral, cognitive, analytic, humanistic, and constructivist. In this chapter, we will discuss only those interventions that are more unique to Mahoney's constructivism.

Mahoney believed that both comfort and challenge are essential to optimal therapy. Constructive psychotherapists most fundamentally cultivate their own capacity for compassion, "the heart of constructive psychotherapy" (Mahoney, 2003, p. 17). They seek to establish a genuine bond of affection with clients and foster clients' feeling of safety by maintaining empathic attunement to clients' ongoing experiences—through reflective listening and gentle inquiry. After clients feel safe, constructive psychotherapists also typically challenge them with deeper inquiry and invitations to participate in experiments. Constructivists view clients as agents, not objects. Thus, constructive psychotherapists do the process of therapy *with* clients, not *to* them.

Mahoney believed that a fundamental aspect of healthy development is a person's ability to identify, describe, and integrate into one's system of meaning one's emotional experiences, especially when the person finds those experiences to contradict or disrupt their existing system of meaning (Mahoney, 1991, 2003; Mahoney & Marquis, 2002). Thus, a central role of the constructive psychotherapist is to attend to clients' emotional blocks and/or difficulties in verbalizing their emotions, both in the client's life as they describe it in therapy and as those blocks and/or difficulties arise in the therapeutic relationship. Regarding the latter, counselors begin by being vigilant about when disruptions in the therapeutic bond, or client assumptions about counselor disinterest or dislike, seem to occur. By inquiring into the client's experience, clarifying both client and counselor feelings and meanings, negotiating adjustments in mutual interactions, and reestablishing an unperturbed bond, the client learns how to identify and constructively process distressing feelings in relationship.

Assessment Most instructors of assessment and appraisal courses typically spend most course time on instruments that yield quantifiable measures or categorical labels. For a variety of reasons, Mahoney did not favor using such instruments; for example, they do not reveal clients' personal meanings or that which is most near and dear to their hearts, and the categories and labels they generate might create additional obstacles for both clients and counselors to overcome in clients' processes of change. Constructive psychotherapists focus instead on learning how the client herself classifies or categorizes herself. Does she believe she can change? How does she view her personality and her core self? What does she believe are her strengths, weaknesses, and available options? "The client's theory of change is often at least as important as the theory believed by the therapist" (Mahoney, 2003, p. 41).

Constructivist psychotherapists continually seek to understand what it is like to be the specific client(s) with whom they're working, especially with regard to the five basic themes and four COPS previously described. To aid counselors in this process, Mahoney (2003) created an idiographic assessment instrument: the Personal Experience Report (PER). In addition to providing clients with the opportunity to provide background information, current concerns, client strengths, and how they cope, it includes numerous queries into clients' emotional, spiritual, and recreational lives. In Mahoney's practice, he would meet initially with a client and, if they concluded mutually that they were a good therapeutic fit, he would ask them to complete the PER at home. He would then review it with the client in a relational assessment process in which he often discovered a "knowing" of the client that was "much more subtle and profound than our logical, linguistic, and mathematical consciousness can imagine" (2003, p. 54). He found that this knowing of his clients and how he could best be of service to them was powerfully informed by his own internal reactions to them during all his interactions with them. Thus, he concluded that "the processes of knowing another person and knowing one's self are intimately related" (Mahoney, 2003, p. 54).

Change Strategies Mahoney asserted, "I emphasize homework—experiments in living—as crucial to personal development" (p. 44). Thus, constructive psychotherapists' primary practice is to collaborate with clients in developing experiments—novel experiences that challenge clients' old, less satisfying patterns of acting/thinking/feeling and open new, more satisfying ways of being. The process of developing experiments often calls for a spirit of adventure and creativity from the constructive practitioner (Mahoney & Marquis, 2002). As Mahoney stressed, "that creativity and spirit cannot be formalized in a particular procedure. . . . [Likewise,] *constructive practice recognizes that the power to change lies in processes* rather than specific procedures" (2003, p. 58, italics in original). For example, the *process* of learning to relax can be acquired from numerous different *techniques*: from meditation, yoga, and self-massage to progressive muscle relaxation, autogenic training, and guided imagery. Every competent therapist navigates the process of, on the one hand, learning a technique from sources such as training manuals and supervision and, on the other, determining whether, when, and how to use it in light of the uniqueness of a particular client (Marquis, 2009).

Moreover, Mahoney stressed that any specific technique will be far more effective if both the client and the therapist are *prepared* for them and in an appropriate state of consciousness. Thus, it is critical that therapists prepare for powerful, experiential interventions, such as empty-chair work, guided imagery, or early recollections, with some form of centering method, which might involve a few deep cleansing breaths, a few moments of silent contemplation, and the setting of positive intentions (Mahoney, 2003). Equally important is the counselor's explaining to the client the rationale for an experiment so the client can give informed consent to participate in the intervention. It also is essential for counselors to allow plenty of time after the intervention to process the experience with the client and reflect upon the meanings the client and counselor generated around the experience.

Problem, Pattern, and Process Mahoney found it useful to think of interventions as addressing three interwoven levels: problem, pattern, and process. The domain of *problem-focused work* is the most familiar to clients and most counselors, and many clients come to therapy wanting to focus on solving specific problems. Problem-solving work usually involves predominantly behavioral and cognitive interventions, from recording the frequency of the problem to exposure methods.

However, specific problems very rarely exist in isolation; they are usually part of a pattern, which implies the recurrence of related problems, even if those relationships are not immediately evident to the client or counselor. Mahoney (2003) thought of *pattern work* as involving a "dance" between experiencing (immediate, emotional work) and explaining (reflective, cognitive work; 2003). Some of the techniques Mahoney used to address pattern-level work included personal journaling, bibliotherapy, unsent letters, life review exercises, and narrative reconstructions.

Despite the value of both problem- and pattern-level work, Mahoney believed that the level of focus that held the most promising potential for enduring, significant change was that of process, which he considered:

> among the most difficult challenges for therapists as well as clients . . . some of the most powerful and important work that can be done . . . work [that] goes on at levels of experiencing that are above, below, or between words and languaging. Process work is always work in the immediate, living moment, and it is difficult to wrap such work in neat verbal packages. (Mahoney, 2003, p. 46)

Some of the interventions Mahoney used with clients who chose to work with their process include embodiment exercises, from those involving range of motion (yoga, stretching), resistance (strength training), and rhythm (music, dance) to touch (petting pets, referral for massage) and voice (singing, laughing); fantasy and dreamwork; stream of consciousness; mirror time; and varieties of meditative practices. In all of these cases, counselors invite clients to "look inward" with as little judgment as possible and to attempt to simply observe the many activities—from physical and emotional to mental and spiritual—that constitute their moment-to-moment experience. As the reader may notice:

> Process-level work shares parallels with "depth," experiential, and transpersonal approaches to psychotherapy. It is not a simple and superficial tinkering, but rather a complex excursion into core ordering processes.... Process work can be risky, because it can be so deep. Intimations of basic ordering processes can reflect and induce changes. Process work can be powerful, because it taps into the very engines of experiencing. For some clients, intellectualizing and living in their heads, so to speak, is their best bet at adaptation.... Just as one should never push for strong emotions, one should never push for process-level work.... If the therapist initiates process-level work, it should be done with gentleness and only after assurances of a client's capacities to maintain or regain a sense of center. (Mahoney, 2003, pp. 47–48)

Another important point is that "growing pains," ranging from mild discomfort to intense suffering, are more central to development than most people like to admit. From the perspective of Mahoney's constructivism, strategic interventions that seek to quickly suppress the pain of systemic disorganization often carry a significant risk: "Tension reduction or the resolution of conflict does not necessarily lead to growth ... and it may in fact retard development by diminishing both the energy and the challenges required for such development" (Mahoney & Mahoney, 2001, p. 660). Thus, at times, constructivists will "hold" clients' pain so that they can more fully understand their situation rather than quickly try to solve the problem. It is also worth noting that perturbations in the therapeutic bond are rich sources of opportunities for development, but only when they are negotiated in ways that honor and encourage the client's emotional experience and competence (Fosha, 2000; Safran & Muran, 2000; Stolorow et al., 1987). This process may require repeated experiences of "optimal frustration" (see Chapter 3) followed by a deepening of the relationship. It calls for extensive skill on the therapist's part.

Following are descriptions and contraindications for two practices Mahoney (2003) developed.

Stream of Consciousness Mahoney's stream of consciousness technique is geared toward helping clients explore, experience, and communicate their internal worlds *as they are living them*. As such, it shares many similarities with some meditative practices and Freud's free association. Regarding the latter, there are two important differences. First, Mahoney respected clients' needs for privacy by informing them that they do *not* need to report everything they are aware of (in my [AM] experience, this instruction usually lowers clients' resistance and thus, paradoxically, results in their actually sharing *more* of their internal worlds). The second difference involves the locus of authority regarding the interpretation of the client's experience. Whereas traditional Freudian analysts tend to give more validity to their own interpretations than to their clients' interpretations, constructivists do not. In fact, when clients asked Mahoney what he thought of their experiences in "streaming" sessions, he was less likely to respond from his own perspective than to ask such questions as "What did it remind you of?" "What feelings seemed most prevalent or important?" "How are you feeling now as we discuss this?" "What is your intuition about the experience?" "What do you hope or fear it means?" (2003, p. 142). Since constructivists are trying to help their clients create their own meanings, rather than "get in line with" some universal truth or meaning, Mahoney deemed clients' specific interpretations less important than their engagement in the processes of becoming more self-aware and creating meanings that serve their well-being. The only time Mahoney offered interpretations to clients that differed from their own was when clients' interpretations were repeatedly negative or pathologizing of their experience (2003). Following is a description Mahoney provided of this technique:

> Streaming is an exercise intended to help me get a better sense of what it is like to be you. First I will ask you to relax and to set positive intentions for learning more about yourself. I will ask you to close your eyes and to pay attention to what is going on inside you from moment to moment. You may find that there are many things going on at the same time and that they keep changing. Some may be thoughts, some sensations. There may be images and memories and mixtures. If we think of your inner life as a stream, this exercise is intended to help me understand what your stream is like today in these few minutes. I would like you to dip a bucket into your stream every once in a while and toss me some words as examples of what you caught in the bucket. Don't worry about making sense of how it sounds. If something feels too private to share, then keep it secret. Let's start with a brief streaming trip—perhaps 5 or 10 minutes—and then we will pause and take a break. We can always do more if you want. Just be gentle with yourself and let yourself explore this as a little experiment in looking inside. Do you have any questions before we start? (2003, pp. 143–144)

Mirror Time   As Mahoney often remarked, "The self is a central mystery in consciousness ... a self is itself always under construction. Indeed, one of the paradoxes of the self is its changing stability. The self is not a fixed entity" (2003, p. 152). He also remarked that the only person one has to be with all of the time is oneself. It follows, then that much of one's quality of life is a function of the relationship one has with one's self. Mahoney believed that the theme of self-relationship (which is more than self-image, self-esteem, self-concept, and so forth) should be central in counseling, and that, with many clients, helping them develop self-compassion is among the most valuable things that counselors can do. Of all of Mahoney's ways of assessing and assisting clients' self-relational skills, mirror time was among his favorites. A slightly modified version of the instructions Mahoney would use to introduce this technique follows:

> The purpose of this exercise is to learn to take a good look at yourself and into yourself. It involves spending about 10 minutes in front of a mirror without "doing anything" usual (such as combing your hair, brushing your teeth, or other cosmetic activities). Before you begin, set clear, positive intentions for the exercise. The goal is not to "face" some cold, harsh truth. The goal is for you to look into your own eyes and connect with yourself in a compassionate way.
>
> Begin by taking a few relaxing release breaths [these are described in an appendix of *Constructive Psychotherapy*]. Then look at your face. Look into your own eyes. [After about a minute] Now, close your eyes and take another release breath. Be aware of your body. What are you feeling? Where are you feeling it? Take another release breath. Take your time and be gentle with yourself.
>
> Open your eyes and again look at yourself. Your attention may be drawn to many parts of your face and head. Remember to bring your gaze gently back to your eyes. Alternate

between looking in the mirror and closing your eyes. When your eyes are closed, invite yourself to relax and feel centered. When your eyes are open, simply invite yourself to witness and feel.

You may feel happy or sad. You may feel a mixture of feelings. You may alternate between noticing features of your face and sensing your insides. Looking into your own eyes can be a portal for connecting the outside you and the inside you.

If you feel comfortable doing so, experiment with talking out loud while looking in the mirror [This is where Mahoney would often "coach" or guide clients. Since it is common for clients to assume different voices and phenomenological "positions" during mirror time, he would often guide them in dialogues between polarities such as good me/bad me, critic/wimp, strong self/weak self, and so forth. It is common for clients to become highly self-critical of themselves during this exercise. In such cases, Mahoney would encourage a dialog between their harsh critic and the part of them that is being criticized—similar to Leslie Greenberg's demonstration in the video mentioned at the end of this chapter.]

[When the counselor deems that it is appropriate]: Bring this exercise to a close with a release breath and an explicit thought or statement of appreciation. Express gratitude to yourself for taking the time and energy to honor who you are and to refine how you see and feel yourself. Remember to be gentle and compassionate with yourself. (Adapted from M. Mahoney, Appendix H of *Constructive Psychotherapy: A Practical Guide*, 2003. With permission to reproduce kindly granted from Guilford Press, New York, NY.)

Spiritual Skills   Whereas exercises such as stream of consciousness and mirror time usually begin with a "self-focus," they may lead beyond the self into what may aptly be described as spiritual or transpersonal (Mahoney, 2003; Wilber, 2000). Referring to the point made by the existential therapist Frankl that the healthy eye does not see itself, but itself "does the seeing," Mahoney believed that "eye-to-eye" and "I-to-I" practices can help people cultivate paths that both lead into and then transcend self-focus. Some of the spiritual skills that involve various meditative practices are described in Chapter 14 of this book. Other spiritual skills involve cultivating a sense of connectedness, timelessness, meaningfulness, gratitude, peace, and hope. Consistent with the work of Segal, Williams, and Teasdale (2002), Mahoney stressed that a counselor's effectiveness in teaching any spiritual skill dramatically improves after she herself has practiced and cultivated the skill. Mahoney wrote

> It is also important to emphasize that spiritual skills are neither easy nor assured paths to happiness. Despite popular marketing ploys, personal happiness is not the primary goal of most spiritual traditions.... The paths of spiritual enlightenment do not avoid or deny that pain. To paraphrase Thomas Merton, one does not become a monk in order to suffer more or less than other human beings, but in order to suffer more efficiently. (2003, pp. 165–166)

Contraindications   Very importantly, Mahoney cautioned against using powerful process techniques such as stream of consciousness and mirror time in the following situations: with clients who are struggling to maintain, recover, or develop an integrated, personal sense of self; with clients who are feeling highly unstable, emotionally vulnerable, or suicidal; with clients who have recently experienced a trauma; with clients who are reluctant to engage in experiential, process-level work; with clients who are not skilled in centering or regaining their sense of psychological balance; in early sessions prior to the establishment of a therapeutic alliance; or late in a given session or late in the course of therapy, when there may not be sufficient time afterward to adequately process the experience (Mahoney, 1991, 2003).

CONTRIBUTIONS AND LIMITATIONS

Interface With Recent Developments in the Mental Health Field

The Nature–Nurture Question

Constructivists see the role of nature and nurture as mutually interacting influences on a person's personality but see the person not as a product of those influences but as an agent able to make choices, perceptions, stories, and constructions about those influences. Prawat and Floden (1994) commented on the role of those factors by asserting that constructivists "[recognize] the need to shift back and forth between environmental and organismic reference points, assigning top priority to neither" (p. 45). Rather, they give top priority to the individual's interpretation and integration of the given influences.

An analogy is a child molding clay. Regardless of restrictions or influences such as the clay's size, color, or texture, every child who molds clay will produce something different. Even if someone exerts influence over the process in a biological (supplies purple clay) and environmental sense (suggests making a tree), each child will interpret and respond to the influences in a very idiosyncratic way. The child can make a tree despite the purple clay (objective reality would say trees are not purple), and the shape of the tree will be the child's own interpretation of what a tree looks like, which may be very different from some consensus concept of how trees look. In this way, people interact with both nature and nurture to construct a reality that reflects their uniqueness. Constructivists acknowledge biological and environmental influences but do not see them as absolute determinants.

DSM–IV–TR *Diagnosis*

It should be no surprise that constructivists do not rely heavily on a purportedly objective criteria system such as the *DSM*. Manualized diagnosis and labeling of client experiences directly opposes constructivists' underlying philosophy. They see symptoms as merely a part of the complexity of clients' experiences and as relatively insignificant when isolated from the whole person. From a constructivist perspective, how the client weaves symptoms—particularly the *meanings* the symptoms have for her—into her story is much more important and instructive than the symptoms themselves. Constructivist therapists also stress the strengths of the client as a means of creating change, rather than diagnosing and focusing on a symptom as the locus of change. The more time counselors spend focusing on problems, the more clients are likely to become "deficit focused." By emphasizing strengths in counseling, clients can begin to construct realities that highlight assets and possibilities rather than weaknesses and limits.

Rather than pathologizing client symptoms, constructivists tend to frame them as challenges that provide clients with opportunities to prevail. For example, Mahoney (2003) considered a "disordered person" not necessarily as someone with an "objective" mental illness but, rather, as one whose life circumstances currently exceed one's developed integrative skills. He offered the concept of "phase transitions" and other temporary conditions of disorder in the normal dynamics of development that deserve to be acknowledged for their potential to lead to greater development rather than considered disorders or mental illness.

Pharmacotherapy

Like proponents of most of the theories in this book, constructivists do not view medication as a necessary component in the resolution of many clients' psychological issues. Since these proponents do not think in terms of psychological dysfunction as mental illness but, instead, in terms of systems of meaning that have somehow become problem-saturated, they do not consider the biological solution of medication as a panacea.

However, could psychoactive medication be an important element in the client's solution to issues? With some people, in some situations, yes. For example, narrative therapists have stated explicitly that "we are not opposed to the responsible, thoughtful use of medication," (Freedman & Combs, 2008, p. 233) because "we support people in exploring whatever kind of approach they think might be helpful" (p. 246), and they describe consulting with a psychiatrist when working with such a client. Of primary importance within a constructivist approach would be the client's opinion of medication and the unique role it could play in the client's pursuit of a more satisfying life. The client decides if and how medication is used. An excellent resource regarding this issue is Ingersoll and Rak (2006).

Managed Care and Brief Therapy

Constructivist forms of therapy fit nicely into brief counseling models. In fact, solution-focused therapy is considered a prime example of a brief counseling approach. DeJong and Hopwood (1996) conducted a study of 275 clients in solution-focused therapy, and only 17% of the population attended more than four sessions. Rothwell (2005) similarly reported that the average client attended three sessions. It is no surprise that this approach is commonly referred to as solution-focused brief therapy. Talmon (1990) highlighted the importance of using every minute of contact with clients to facilitate change and orient the client to the strength-based approach of constructivism. Narrative counseling length can vary depending on the needs of the client and the flow of the dialog. There is no predetermined time, even for session length, in which the flexibility of nonstandard session times, such as more than 50 minutes, enables client and counselor to collaborate creatively on the session length the client needs and the counselor can accommodate.

Technical Eclecticism

As alluded to earlier,

> *constructive psychotherapy is not defined by techniques*, but by an overall conceptualization of human experience, knowing, and development. A constructive practitioner can therefore draw on the full spectrum of therapeutic and teaching techniques. More importantly, he or she need not be constrained by that spectrum. (Mahoney, 2003, p. 58)

Toward the end of his career, most of the clients that Mahoney (2003) counseled were, themselves, therapists. To demonstrate the way Mahoney practiced technical eclecticism within a metatheoretical (constructive) purity, consider the following:

> Some of my therapist clients are looking for solutions to problems, and I can sometimes draw on skills I learned as a behavior therapist, and, later, a cognitive therapist. Many of my therapist clients are painfully aware of patterns in their pain. Just like me, they revisit personal "issues" that remain stubbornly demanding of their attention and energies. Here I find myself drawing more on existential-humanistic and wisdom [spiritual] traditions. (Mahoney, 2005, p. 348, bracketed material added for clarification)

Constructivists are free to appropriate techniques that arose from other schools of thought and that reflect constructivist philosophy. Several authors also have described how other theorists have woven constructivism into their theories (Angus & McLeod, 2004; Carlson, Watts, & Maniacci, 2006; Mahoney & Marquis, 2002; O'Connell, 2005; Stolorow et al., 1987; Watts, 2003).

Diversity

"I believe that diversity lies at the heart of development" (Mahoney, 2008, p. 26). Constructivists are philosophically well positioned to honor cultural differences in client diversity because they give an individual's perspective and interpretations the most power and weight in the counseling relationship. Since constructivists assume a position in relationship with the client of "not knowing" and are poised to learn the client's worldview about what is real and desirable, they are perhaps best positioned among therapists to honor client diversity of every kind.

The influence and use of language are central components in constructivist approaches, so it would be important for clients to be able to express their views in their native language. Wentworth and Wentworth (1997) saw the constructivist as a cultural anthropologist of sorts, facilitating clients' awareness of their cultural identity and opening it up for exploration and possible change.

As with culture, constructivists are attuned to issues of gender and how clients have integrated varying perspectives on gender into their worldviews. In essence, men and women construct solutions and narratives that are significantly influenced by gender roles. Henehan (2003) illustrated the power of the narrative in honoring and transforming gender expectations and roles. Moreover, Mahoney's criticism of the pervasive "rationalist supremacy" that so dominates most current research methods and empirically supported treatment lists was paralleled by his appreciation for other modes of knowing—especially those that are more embodied, emotional, connected, and intuitive—adjectives traditionally associated with femininity rather than masculinity. Indeed, Mahoney was the only male invited to author a chapter in the renown *Knowledge, Difference, and Power: Essays Inspired by Women's Ways of Knowing* (Goldberger, Tarule, Clinchy, & Belenky, 1996).

Regarding sexual orientation, we found only one explicit reference in the narrative therapy literature: to "the power of heterosexist masculinity and its denigration of homosexuality" (Harker, 1997). Presumably, constructivist therapists, with their nonpathological, phenomenological stance, would consider the meaning systems of people of all sexual orientations according to the same principles, that is, how problem saturated those systems are, the extent to which the problems people describe are self- and/or socially generated, the role of power dynamics in personal relationships and social contexts, and how people can engage their agency to create preferred systems of meaning and related stories.

Constructivists consider spirituality to be a construction of the individual that can take many forms in a person's life. Counselors gain a full appreciation of the landscape of the client only by including consideration of her spirituality, whether it plays a small or large role in the client's meaning system—both conditions a constructivist considers in the context of the client's good life. More aptly put, it is *how* clients conceive of and embody their own spirituality that is important. Spirituality need not be theistic or tied to an established religion. Nonetheless, most constructivists recognize the potentially helpful role that a person's spirituality can play in her change processes. Moreover,

> Atheists and mystics alike make leaps of faith. Faith is the essence of hope, of continued engagement in the mystery.... Life is itself a sacred mystery whose relentless elusiveness is central to its sanctity. Psychotherapy is a form of spiritual service. Practicing psychotherapy can be a form of spiritual practice. (Mahoney, 2003, p. 207)

The Effectiveness of Psychotherapy

Just as the philosophy of constructivism eschews the narrow empiricism that purports to ascertain "objective" truth, constructive counselors tend to place little stock in experimental and other highly controlled quantitative studies, at least those that do not reflect real-world practice or the complexities and uniqueness of human beings, such as Empirically Supported Treatment and Evidence-Based Practice protocols (Marquis & Douthit, 2002). To be fair, constructivist approaches are fairly new compared to most other theories in this book, so perhaps in time their research base will increase.

Without further explanation, Hoyt (2008) asserted that solution-focused therapy is "often effective" (p. 259). A few studies have demonstrated the effectiveness of solution-focused therapy (Conoley et al., 2003; Georgiades, 2008; Gingrich & Eisengart, 2000; Seidel & Hedley, 2008; Wettersten, Lichtenberg, & Mallinckrodt, 2005). Solution-focused therapy holds research promise. Its approach is the most suited of the constructivist therapies to be manualized; its structure of counseling would most likely appeal to managed care companies; and it fits the Asay and Lambert (1999) model in terms of the weight of various factors in contributing to positive therapeutic outcome.

Freedman and Combs (2008) summarized research on narrative therapy:

> Researchers ... interested in narrative approaches tend to do qualitative rather than quantitative studies.... The published qualitative studies we could find ... are all supportive of narrative therapy as an effective treatment modality in which clients improve and therapists do what they say they do. (p. 246)

In addition to the six studies Freedman and Combs cited, we found two others that supported the effectiveness of narrative therapy (Coulehan, Friedlander, & Heatherington, 1998; Malgady & Constantino, 2003).

Limitations

As a relatively new family of theories, two of the three approaches discussed in this chapter suffer from the growing pains associated with any new venture. Nonetheless, these theories have enjoyed quite a bit of success and attention over the past few years, and as research increases, these approaches will expand and improve in clarity. As growth has occurred, splits and rifts have diffused some of the focus of a central constructivist approach. Students and practitioners new to constructivism struggle with the similarities and distinctions between its different expressions.

As we teach beginning graduate students about theory and practice, we have noticed more interest in solution-focused approaches, which are much simpler than Mahoney's process-focused, integrative approach. This trend has caused us some concern, especially regarding the emphasis (in solution-focused counseling) on questions as a primary counseling technique. In social relationships, the main way to get information is to ask questions, but therapist educators usually teach therapists-in-training a different form of relating and understanding. As a result, we tend to de-emphasize questions until students have developed reflective skills. Students who are initially drawn to solution-focused therapy are often enticed by the permission and safety of being able to ask lots of questions and are especially prone to early advice giving. Although we understand these practices are not necessarily the essence of the approach, it is sometimes difficult for beginning students to understand such nuances.

Another potential weakness that I (AM) have observed in master's level students—in the four years that I have used *Constructive Psychotherapy* as one of the texts in a

Theory and Practice of Counseling course—is that many students respond along the lines of "Well, that's obvious" (even though the majority of students have reported it's their favorite of the four books in that course). On the one hand, I understand that much of what Mahoney wrote about does seem almost irrefutable, but beneath the apparent simplicity of his messages (in ink on each page) lay deep complexities with many subtle intricacies that he and many more advanced thinkers and practitioners recognize and continue to wrestle with. This commentary is not to suggest that Mahoney's (2003) is not an excellent text for such a course; rather, it is a goad to deeply contemplate his work, for most readers will mine more wisdom each time they read and reread his work.

Contributions

As an approach, solution-focused therapy contains many practices that therapists from other theoretical orientations can adopt and still remain theoretically consistent. Both it and narrative therapy have contributed particularly positive- and strength-focused orientations to the psychotherapeutic endeavor.

Similarly innovative, Mahoney's constructivist psychotherapy "suggest[s] a view of the person that is 'integral' in the sense of embracing many of the apparent dualities that have traditionally dominated psychology and philosophy" (Mahoney & Marquis, 2002, p. 800).

> So how is constructive therapy different from any other kind? I don't think of constructive therapy as a separate school, and it certainly will not be manualized or defined by techniques. In a sense, constructivism is a philosophy of knowing that affords a broad spectrum of expressions and sub-theories. Indeed, this integrative and transtheoretical capacity of constructivism appeals to me, as well as the fact that it is inherently an organic philosophy (i.e., one that is both capable of and dedicated to growing in response to the challenges it faces). (Mahoney, 2008, p. 25)

With the possible exception of integral counseling, Mahoney's developmental constructivism is perhaps the most comprehensive, "big picture" integrative view in all of counseling and psychotherapy—honoring and integrating not only body, mind, and spirit but also counseling perspectives ranging from behavioral and cognitive to humanistic and transpersonal; as well as other disciplines, from evolutionary biology, computer science, brain and cognitive sciences to history, literature, and philosophy—and all within a compassionate relationship that rests at the heart of the entire venture to help clients. Significant figures from approaches as diverse as behavioral, cognitive, psychodynamic, humanistic-existential, experiential, transpersonal, and integral (i.e., Bandura, Beck, Stolorow, Bugental, Greenberg, Vaughan, Wilber, respectively, to name just a few) all find Mahoney's work immensely important, both philosophically, theoretically, and pragmatically. In my (AM) opinion, no other therapeutic writer has managed to consistently hold the dialectical tensions between scientific, theoretical, and technical rigor, on the one hand, and the (he)art of human helping that resides in compassion, care, empathic concern, as well as philosophical issues (i.e., are psychotherapists doctors of mental health?, clergy to the soul?; are our clients victims of mental disorders or are they suffering from issues better addressed by moral philosophy?) that are far from mere abstractions. Despite his intellectual and scholarly contributions, Mahoney's writings reflect a warm and sensitive human spirit, whose message was both simple and inspiring: human change processes are complex "and the secret is to ever be in quest." (2003, p. 190).

Current Status

Of the three constructivist approaches we described in this chapter, it is our subjective impression that, currently, solution-focused is most widely known and practiced, followed by narrative, then by Mahoney's constructivist psychotherapy. Two international journals are devoted to constructivism. *The Journal of Constructivist Psychology*, formerly the *Journal of Personal Construct Psychology* is published by Taylor & Francis. It is currently edited by Robert A. Neimeyer and Greg J. Neimeyer. *Constructivism in the Human Sciences* was edited by Mahoney; at the time of this writing, it is unclear if the journal will continue after Volume 12, an en memoriam double issue devoted to Mahoney's lifework.

SUMMARY

The family of theories known as constructivism span a considerable spectrum yet also share some core themes. Perhaps the most important is the postmodern insight that there is not one absolute, objective truth, reality, or goal for the good life, but, rather, that all people play significant (but not absolute) roles in the construction of our personal realities. It follows, therefore, that constructive counseling is the opposite of an authoritarian, expert-driven approach. Yes, there are some general principles of human nature and people's change processes (see, for example, appendices L and N in Mahoney, 2003), but there is also no such thing as a single, fixed approach or a set of techniques that will be helpful to everyone. Thus, if one thinks of some counseling approaches as metaphorically teaching information and/or selling maps about the terrain of life (often advocating one destination as the "best," i.e., that theory's version of health), constructive counseling is much more a matter of intimately joining clients in their journey. Along that therapeutic journey, constructive counselors may at times lead, but more often they are at their client's side or following; constructive counselors honor each client's pace of change by letting them rest when they need to, but also balance that need with developmentally appropriate challenges: "But the power for movement and the responsibility for choices of direction always return to the client" (Mahoney, 2003, p. 209).

RECOMMENDED RESOURCES

Books

DeJong, P., & Berg, I. K. (2008). *Interviewing for solutions* (3rd ed.). Pacific Grove, CA: Brooks/Cole. This book provides a comprehensive yet easy to understand outline of the solution-focused approach. The case examples help illuminate the approach.

Mahoney, M. J. (2003). *Constructive psychotherapy: Theory and practice*. New York, NY: Guilford Press.

White, M., & Epston, D. (1990). *Narrative means to therapeutic ends*. New York, NY: W. W. Norton. This book provides a nice introduction to the narrative approach from two of its leading originators. The style and language of the text is a good reflection of the theory.

Audiovisuals

Accelerated Experiential Dynamic Psychotherapy with Diana Fosha, PhD (part of the Systems of Psychotherapy APA Psychotherapy Video Series). Washington, DC: American Psychological Association. Fosha is another noted constructivist who demonstrates what Mahoney calls process-level work, primarily through the use of moment-to-moment tracking of the client's affective experience in the session. The DVD consists of a pre-session interview, a therapy session, and a post-session discussion.

Carlson, J., & Kjos, D. (2000). *Narrative therapy with Stephen Madigan.* Boston, MA: Allyn & Bacon. This video from the *Psychotherapy with the Experts* series provides a counseling example along with case discussion.

Emotion-Focused Therapy for Depression with Leslie S. Greenberg, PhD (part of the *Specific Treatments for Specific Populations* APA Psychotherapy Video Series). Washington DC: American Psychological Association. Greenberg is a noted constructivist who demonstrates what Mahoney calls process-level work, primarily through the use of empty chair interventions. The DVD consists of a pre-session interview, two therapy sessions with the same client, and discussion of those sessions.

Love, P. (n.d.). *Hot monogamy* [video]. Produced by International Association of Marriage and Family Counseling (http://www.cmtipress.com/videos.htm). Although the first part of this video is not about solution-focused therapy, Dr. Love's demo session with a couple is an excellent example of the solution-focused approach. Students can watch the session and actually list, and witness the effectiveness of, various solution-focused practices.

The Web site listed below for the Solution-Focused Brief Therapy Association contains an online bookstore where you can buy many DVDs and videos pertaining to solution-focused therapy.

Web Sites

Solution-Focused Brief Therapy Association (http://www.sfbta.org): This is the new site for the Brief Therapy Center. After the death of Insoo Kim Berg, the information contained on the previous site was moved to this new location. The SFBTA site is a well-organized site with easily accessible information, links, and products such as books and videos that site visitors may order.

Narrative therapy (http://www.narrativeapproaches.com): This Web site contains information related to narrative therapy including workshops, research links, and overviews of the theory. The site is informative, but we found the graphics and page setup a little distracting.

Developmental constructivism (http://sites.google.com/site/constructingworlds/): This Web site contains information related to the Mahoney-Founded Society for Constructivism in the Human Sciences, including an overview of the theory, links to its journal, and links to conferences, listservs, newsletters, and references.

REFERENCES

American Psychiatric Association. (2000). *Diagnostic and statistical manual of mental disorders* (4th ed., text rev.). Washington, DC: Author.

Angus, L. E., & McLeod, J. (Eds.). (2004). *The handbook of narrative and psychotherapy: Practice, theory and research*. Thousand Oaks, CA: Sage.

Asay, T. P., & Lambert, M. J. (1999). The empirical case for the common factors in therapy: Quantitative findings. In M. A. Hubble, B. L. Duncan, & S. D. Miller (Eds.), *The heart and soul of change* (pp. 23–55). Washington, DC: American Psychological Association.

Bacal, H. (1990). Heinz Kohut. In H. A. Bacal & K. M. Newman (Eds.), *Theories of object relations: Bridges to self psychology* (pp. 240–252). New York, NY: Columbia University Press.

Bartlett, F. C. (1932). *Remembering*. Cambridge, England: Cambridge University Press.

Carlson, J., Watts, R. E., & Maniacci, M. (2006). *Adlerian therapy: Theory and practice*. Washington, DC: American Psychological Association.

Conoley, C. W., Graham, J. M., Neu, T., Craig, M. C., O'Pry, A., Cardin, S. A., ... Parker, R. I. (2003). Solution-focused family therapy with aggressive and oppositional acting children: An N=1 empirical study. *Family Process, 42*, 361–374.

Coulehan, R., Friedlander, M. L., & Heatherington, L. (1998). Transforming narratives: A change event in constructivist family therapy. *Family Process, 37*, 17–33.

Damasio, A. R. (1995). *Descartes' error: Emotion, reason, and the human brain*. New York, NY: Harper.

Damasio, A. R. (1999). *The feeling of what happens: Body and emotion in the making of consciousness*. San Diego, CA: Harcourt.

DeJong, P., & Berg, I. K. (2008). *Interviewing for solutions* (3rd ed.). Pacific Grove, CA: Brooks/Cole.

DeJong, P., & Hopwood, L. E. (1996). Outcome research on treatment conducted at the Brief Family Therapy Center, 1992–1993. In S. D. Miller, M. A. Hubble, & B. L. Duncan (Eds.), *Handbook of solution-focused brief therapy* (pp. 272–298). San Francisco, CA: Jossey-Bass.

De Shazer, S. (1984). The death of resistance. *Family Process, 23*, 79–93.

De Shazer, S. (1985). *Keys to solutions in brief therapy*. New York, NY: W. W. Norton.

De Shazer, S. (1991). *Putting difference to work*. New York, NY: W. W. Norton.

De Shazer, S., & Berg, I. K. (1997). "What works?": Remarks on research aspects of solution-focused brief therapy. *Journal of Family Therapy, 19*, 121–124.

Drewery, W., & Winslade, J. (1997). The theoretical story of narrative therapy. In G. Monk, J. Winslade, K. Crocket, & D. Epston (Eds.), *Narrative therapy in practice: The archaeology of hope* (pp. 32–52). San Francisco, CA: Jossey-Bass.

Eastwood, C. (2009) *Changeling* [Motion picture]. United States: Imagine Entertainment.

Epston, D. (1999). Co-research: The making of an alternative knowledge. In *Narrative therapy and community work: A conference collection* (pp. 137–157). Adelaide, Australia: Dulwich Centre.

Erickson, M. H. (1980). *The collected papers of Milton H. Erickson on Hypnosis* (Vols. 1–4). (E. L. Rossi, Ed.). New York, NY: Irvington.

Fosha, D. (2000). *The transforming power of affect*. New York, NY: Basic Books.

Freedman, J., & Combs, G. (2008). Narrative couple therapy. In A. S. Gurman (Ed.), *Clinical handbook of couple therapy* (4th ed., pp. 229–258). New York, NY: Guilford Press.

Georgiades, S. D. (2008). A solution focused intervention with a youth in a domestic violence situation: Longitudinal evidence. *Contemporary Family Therapy: An International Journal, 30*, 141–151.

Gergen, K. (1985). The social constructionist movement in modern psychology. *American Psychologist, 40*, 266–275.

Gingrich, W. J., & Eisengart, S. (2000). Solution-focused brief therapy: A review of the outcome research. *Family Process, 39,* 477–497.

Gleick, J. (1987). *Chaos.* New York, NY: Viking Press.

Goldberger, N. R., Tarule, J. M., Clinchy, B., & Belenky, M. F. (1996). *Knowledge, difference, and power: Essays inspired by women's ways of knowing.* New York, NY: Basic Books.

Haley, J. (1973). *Uncommon therapy: The psychiatric techniques of Milton H. Erickson.* New York, NY: W. W. Norton.

Harker, T. (1997). Therapy with male sexual abuse survivors: Contesting oppressive life stories. In G. Monk, J. Winslade, K. Crocket, & D. Epston (Eds.), *Narrative therapy in practice: The archaeology of hope* (pp. 193–214). San Francisco, CA: Jossey-Bass.

Hayek, F. (1952), *The sensory order.* Chicago, IL: University of Chicago Press.

Henehan, M. P. (2003). *Integrating spirit and psyche: Using women's narratives in psychotherapy.* Binghamton, NY: Haworth Pastoral Press.

Hoyt, M. F. (2008). Solution-focused couple therapy. In A. S. Gurman (Ed.), *Clinical handbook of couple therapy* (4th ed., pp. 259–295). New York, NY: Guilford Press.

Ingersoll, R. E., & Rak, C. F. (2006). *Psychopharmacology for helping professionals: An integral exploration.* Belmont, CA: Thompson Brooks/Cole.

Kauffman, S. A. (1993). *The origins of order.* Oxford, UK: Oxford University Press.

Kelly, G. A. (1955). *The psychology of personal constructs.* New York, NY: W. W. Norton.

Kohut, H. (1971). *The analysis of the self.* New York, NY: International Universities Press.

Kohut, H. (1977). *The restoration of the self.* New York, NY: International Universities Press.

LeDoux, J. E. (1996). *The emotional brain: The mysterious underpinnings of emotional life.* New York, NY: Simon & Schuster.

Mahoney, M. (1974). *Cognition and behavior modification.* Cambridge, MA: Ballinger.

Mahoney, M. (1991). *Human change process: The scientific foundations of psychotherapy.* New York, NY: Basic Books.

Mahoney, M. (2000). Behaviorism, cognitivism, and constructivism: Reflections on persons and patterns in my intellectual development. In M. R. Goldfried (Ed.), *How therapists change: Personal and professional reflections* (pp. 183–200). Washington, DC: American Psychological Association.

Mahoney, M. J. (2003). *Constructive psychotherapy: A practical guide.* New York, NY: Guilford Press.

Mahoney, M. (2005). Suffering, philosophy, and psychotherapy. *Journal of Psychotherapy Integration, 15*(3), 337–352.

Mahoney, M. (2008). Autobiography: Behaviorism, cognitivism and constructivism: Reflections on persons and patterns in my intellectual development. *Constructivism in the Human Sciences, 12*(1&2), 11–28.

Mahoney, M. J., & Mahoney, S. (2001). Living with essential tensions: Dialectics and future development. In K. J. Schneider, J. F. T. Bugental, & J. F. Pierson (Eds.) *The handbook of humanistic psychology: Leading edges in theory, research, and practice* (pp. 659–665). Thousand Oaks, CA: Sage.

Mahoney, M., & Marquis, A. (2002). Integral constructivism and dynamic systems in psychotherapy processes. *Psychoanalytic Inquiry, 22,* 794–813.

Malgady, R. G., & Constantino, G. (2003). Narrative therapy for Hispanic children and adolescents. In A. E. Kazdin & J. R. Weisz (Eds.), *Evidence based psychotherapies for children and adolescents* (pp. 425–435). New York, NY: Guilford Press.

Marquis, A. (2009). An integral taxonomy of therapeutic interventions. *Journal of Integral Theory and Practice, 4*(2), 13–42.

Marquis, A., & Douthit, K. Z. (2002). The hegemony of 'empirically supported treatment': Validating or violating? *Constructivism in the Human Sciences, 11,* 108–141.

Miller, G., & de Shazer, S. (1998). Have you heard the latest about …?: Solution-focused therapy as a rumor. *Family Process, 37,* 363–378.

Miller, G., & de Shazer, S. (2000). Emotions in solution-focused therapy: A re-examination. *Family Process, 39,* 5–23.

Monk, G., Winslade, J., Crocket, K., & Epston, D. (Eds.). (1997). *Narrative therapy in practice: The archaeology of hope.* San Francisco, CA: Jossey-Bass.

Neimeyer, R. A. (n.d.). *About me.* Retrieved from http://web.mac.com/neimeyer/iWeb/ Home/About%20Me.html

O'Connell, B. (2005). *Solution-focused therapy* (2nd ed.). London, UK: Sage.

O'Hanlon, B. (n.d.). *Bill O'Hanlon's book store.* Retrieved from http://astore.amazon. com/billohanlon?node=2&page=2

Omer, H. (1997). Narrative empathy. *Psychotherapy, 34,* 19–27.

Prawat, R., & Floden, R. (1994). Philosophical perspectives on constructivist views of learning. *Educational Psychology, 29,* 37–48.

Rigazio-DiGilio, S. A. (1997). From microscopes to holographs: Client development within a constructivist paradigm. In T. Sexton & B. Griffin (Eds.), *Constructivist thinking in counseling practice, research and training* (pp. 74–100). New York, NY: Teachers College.

Rothwell, N. (2005). How brief is solution-focused therapy? A comparative study. *Clinical Psychology and Psychotherapy, 12,* 402–405.

Safran, J. D., & Muran, J. C. (2000). *Negotiating the therapeutic alliance.* New York, NY: Guilford Press.

Schore, A. N. (1994). *Affect regulation and the origin of the self.* Hillsdale, NJ: Lawrence Erlbaum Associates.

Segal, Z. V., Williams, J. M. G., & Teasdale, J. D. (2002). *Mindfulness-based cognitive therapy for depression: A new approach to preventing relapse.* New York, NY: Guilford Press.

Seidel, A., & Hedley, D. (2008). The use of solution-focused brief therapy with older adults in Mexico: A preliminary study. *American Journal of Family Therapy, 36,* 242–252.

Sexton, T. (1997). Constructivist thinking within the history of ideas: The challenge of a new paradigm. In T. Sexton & B. Griffin (Eds.), *Constructivist thinking in counseling practice, research and training* (pp. 3–18). New York, NY: Teachers College.

Shoham, V., Rohrbaugh, M., & Patterson, J. (1995). Problem- and solution-focused couple therapies: The MRI and Milwaukee models. In N. S. Jacobson & A. S. Gurman (Eds.), *Clinical handbook of couple therapy* (2nd ed., pp. 142–163). New York, NY: Guilford Press.

Simon, J. K., & Nelson, T. S. (2007). *Solution-focused brief therapy practice with long-term users of mental health services: "I am more than my label."* New York, NY: Haworth Press.

Stolorow, R. D., & Atwood, G. E. (1992). *Contexts of being.* Hillsdale, NJ: The Analytic Press.

Stolorow, R. D., Brandchaft, B., & Atwood, G. E. (1987). *Psychoanalytic treatment.* Hillsdale, NJ: The Analytic Press.

Talmon, M. (1990). *Single session therapy.* San Francisco, CA: Jossey-Bass.

Tarnas, R. (1991). *The passion of the Western mind: Understanding the ideas that have shaped our world view.* New York, NY: Ballantine Books.

Thelen, E., & Smith, L. B. (1994). *A dynamic systems approach to the development of cognition and action.* Cambridge, MA: MIT Press.

Vaihinger, H. (1965). *The philosophy of "as if"* (C.K. Ogden, Trans.). London: Routledge and Kegan Paul.

Watts, R. E. (2003). *Adlerian, cognitive and constructivist therapies: An integrative dialogue.* New York, NY: Springer.

Wentworth, W. M., & Wentworth, C. M. (1997). The social construction of culture and its implications for the therapeutic mind-self. In T. Sexton & B. Griffin (Eds.), *Constructivist thinking in counseling practice, research and training* (pp. 41–57). New York, NY: Teachers College.

Wettersten, K. B., Lichtenberg, J. W., & Mallinckrodt, B. (2005). Associations between working alliance and outcome in solution-focused brief therapy and brief interpersonal therapy. *Psychotherapy Research, 15,* 35–43.

White, M., & Epston, D. (1990). *Narrative means to therapeutic ends.* New York, NY: W. W. Norton.

Winslade, J., Crocket, K., & Monk, G. (1997). The therapeutic relationship. In G. Monk, J. Winslade, K. Crocket, & D. Epston (Eds.), *Narrative therapy in practice: The archaeology of hope* (pp. 53–81). San Francisco, CA: Jossey-Bass.

Wilber, K. (2000). *The collected works of Ken Wilber, Sex, ecology, spirituality* (Vol. 6). Boston, MA: Shambhala.

CHAPTER 13

Systems Approaches

BACKGROUND OF THE THEORY

Historical Context

Until the 1930s, mental health counselors functioned from an accepted paradigm: conceptualizing and treating dysfunctions they presumed to reside within individuals. All of the preceding theories discussed in this book were founded on this individual-based paradigm, and although most proponents of those theories treated families, they retained a focus on how to ameliorate the symptoms of usually one individual within the family—an "identified patient" or client.

The historical road to the mental health field including a very different paradigm—the systemic paradigm—has been a bumpy one (Nichols & Everett, 1986). Interestingly, the systemic orientation in mental health grew primarily out of the public's need and demand for more socially holistic approaches to child guidance, marriage counseling, and the treatment of schizophrenia than the prevailing theories of the time provided. Particularly in the United States, the tide of support from the public met with opposition from the psychoanalytic community's commitment to the idea that psychological dynamics were the exclusive domain of an individual's inner workings. Until the years following World War II, the ideologically and politically powerful psychoanalytic community largely choked out forms of therapy that involved conjoint sessions, in which two or more clients attend together, and that involved a conceptualization of client concerns that included the social context (Nichols & Everett, 1986).

Unlike systemically oriented clinicians in the United States, those in Europe encountered little opposition when, in the early 1900s, they began treating marital concerns by working conjointly with the marital dyad. In the 1920s, Abraham and Hannah Stone emigrated from Europe to New York where they began one of the earlier marriage therapy practices in the United States. In the 1930s, U.S. therapists such as Paul Papanoe and Emily Mudd began treating couples together and conceptualizing problems within the marriage as being of a mutual rather than individual nature (Broderick & Schraeder, 1991). In 1945, marriage counselors identified themselves as a distinct group affiliated with a unique philosophy and approach to therapy when they established the American Association of Marriage Counselors, which later became the American Association for Marriage and Family Therapy (AAMFT).

Then, in the 1950s, came the most important historical event in the family therapy movement. In Palo Alto, California, a group known as the Mental Research Institute (MRI) conducted therapy and research with hospitalized patients with schizophrenia and their families. What they discovered profoundly changed the way many people viewed the source of dysfunction and the process of therapy to alleviate it. Gregory Bateson, Don

Jackson, Jay Haley, and John Weakland (1956) presented the double-bind hypothesis that involved a consistent and contradictory pattern of communication from parent to schizophrenic child. According to this hypothesis, the parent would place the child in a double bind by giving the child an either/or choice and then responding negatively no matter what choice the child made. For example, the parent would communicate that the child should be more loving and affectionate; if the child did not exhibit more affection, the parent would express disapproval, yet if the child did, the parent would ignore or demean the child. In essence, this no-win situation was "crazy-making."

The importance of these findings was that they demonstrated the systemic nature of symptoms—that not all pathology was rooted in the individual but, rather, could be caused by patterns of communication and behavior within the family, and that pathology could be reduced or eliminated by addressing those interpersonal communication and behavior patterns rather than by addressing the intrapsychic dynamics of the individual. Bodin (1981) stated that these findings and the research that emerged as a result constituted the "definitive landmark in the revolutionary shift from individual to systems focus in concepts of pathogenesis" (p. 281).

Although research since that time has not supported the double-bind hypothesis, it has revealed a different systemic dynamic. People with schizophrenia typically have periods of relative stability, in which their symptoms are chronic but less severe, punctuated with periods of relapse, in which their symptoms become more severe. Research has revealed that persons with schizophrenia who stabilize in an extrafamilial setting, such as the psychiatric hospital, run a much greater risk of relapse if they return to a family with at least one member who is high in "expressed emotion," showing "signs of hostility or emotional overinvolvement or speak[ing] critically of the patient when interviewed or answering a questionnaire" (Relapse and Expressed Emotion, 1999, p. 6). Researchers have found similar patterns in patients with mood and eating disorders (Butzlaff & Hooley, 1998). Thus, although most mental health professionals no longer accept the specifics of the original double-bind hypothesis, they continue to affirm a systemic conceptualization of dysfunction.

Early family systems theorists drew upon several threads of emerging scientific knowledge to synthesize their new findings. From Norbert Weiner's (1948) cybernetics, they drew the concept that through continuous feedback loops, a system maintains and corrects itself. From anthropologists such as Talcott Parsons and Robert Bales (1955), they drew the concept of psychological and functional boundaries within a family. And they drew from the biologist Ludwig von Bertalanffy (1950, 1968) his formulation of general systems theory that seemed to tie together several concepts, including feedback and boundaries. Out of the work of these pioneers emerged a new way of thinking about the human change process.

Founders' Biographical Overviews

Whereas most of the other theories in this textbook arose primarily from the thinking of one person, systems theory arose from the thinking of several people. In fact, the term *systems theory* is an umbrella term that includes numerous unique theories that address mental health issues from a shared foundational perspective.

Throughout the reading of this chapter, you will notice references to Table 13.1. This table outlines the theories subsumed under the systems perspective, each with its own points of emphasis, founder of the theory, and view of maladjustment and change. Since each of these systems-oriented approaches is a theory in its own right, it seems superficial to try to explain each in one chapter. Instead, this chapter is designed to provide an

TABLE 13.1 Comparison Chart of Major Family Therapies

Name of Founder	Murray Bowen	James Framo	Ivan Boszormenyi-Nagy
Name of Therapy	Family Multigenerational Therapy	Object-Relations/Family of Origin Therapy	Contextual Family Therapy
View of family	The family is an emotional unit—a network of interlocking relationships, best understood when viewed from a multigenerational framework.	The family is an intricate system with its own unique bonding, rules, homeostatic mechanisms, secret alliances, communication network, myths, regressive features, and dynamic influences from previous generations.	The family understanding is based on the principle of "reciprocity," having received and having to reciprocate. Each spouse brings the heritage and loyalties of previous generations into the context of the new family.
The healthy family	Intellect characterized by emotional detachment is the hallmark of the healthy family. Members have learned to establish their own identities, to differentiate themselves from the family of origin.	In the healthy family: parents are well differentiated, generational boundaries are clear, the loyalty of the spouses is greater to the family of procreation than the family of origin, spouses view the marital subsystem as primary, and autonomy for all family members is encouraged.	Spouses who experienced a high degree of relational equitability in the families of origin bring to the marriage a ledger of indebtedness and entitlements that is balanced. Thus they are able to focus on the mutual welfare interests of the entire family.
Dysfunction	Members of the marital dyad have poor differentiation of self and are emotionally "stuck-together" to their families of origin. Styles of origin are repeated in marital relationships and are passed on to children.	Intrapsychic conflicts derived from the family of origin are replicated with spouse and/or children. Efforts at the interpersonal resolution of the inner conflict are at the heart of the kinds of distress found in troubled couples and families.	Dysfunction occurs when the adult child is not able to transfer loyalty from the family of origin to the new marital relationship; loyalty owed to previous/ subsequent generations conflict with loyalty owed to spouse, siblings, friends, and peers.
Role of therapist	The therapist is a "coach"—an active expert who educates family members (primarily the marital dyad) but remains disengaged from the family system: detached, objective, and neutral.	The therapist is active and very structured, moving from empathy to confrontation. The therapist usually works with a cotherapist who is of the other gender. The therapist works primarily with the marital dyad only and has a strong "educative" function.	The therapist is an active, encouraging guide. Using "multidirectional partiality" he/she is an advocate for all persons involved in therapy, moving from gentle exploration to a more confrontive style while holding participants responsible for their own movement.

(Continued)

TABLE 13.1   Comparison Chart of Major Family Therapies (Continued)

Name of Founder	Murray Bowen	James Framo	Ivan Boszormnenyi-Nagy
Name of Therapy	Family Multigenerational Therapy	Object-Relations/Family of Origin Therapy	Contextual Family Therapy
Goal of therapy	The basic overarching goal is to assist family members—primarily the marital dyad—toward a better level of differentiation of self. Growth in differentiation will facilitate reduction of anxiety and relief from symptoms.	The two major goals for each member of the marital dyad are: (1) to discover what issues/agendas from the family of origin impact the current family, and (2) to have a corrective experience with parents and siblings from the family of origin.	The goal is to enable participants to move toward relational integrity, relational commitments, and balances of fairness, and to enable family members to gain trust in one another's increasingly trustworthy input.
Primary techniques	Genograms, therapist detachment as a primary technique, defining the roles/relationships in the family system, teaching the "I" position, defusing emotion and avoiding blame, examining/reestablishing contact with the family of origin.	Male–female cotherapy team; standard techniques of *Couples Therapy*; *Couples Group Therapy*; *Family of Origin Sessions*—bringing in the family of origin with individual members of the marital dyad to deal directly with unresolved attachment issues.	Three-generational assessment, conjoint family therapy as the norm, multidirectional partiality, self-disclosure, guiding, confrontation, instruction in building trusting and equitable relationships, suggestions, directives, loyalty framing, exoneration, some use of cotherapy.

Name of Founder	Virginia Satir	Mental Research Institute	Jay Haley
Name of Therapy	Process/Communications Approach	Brief Family Therapy	Strategic Family Therapy
View of family	Families are balanced, rule-governed systems that, through the basic components of communication and self-esteem, provide a context for growth and development.	The family is an interacting communications network in which every member from the newborn to the elderly grandparent influences the nature of the entire system and is, in turn, influenced by it.	The family is a system that involves power relations and has rules by which it operates. The power struggle is not a question of who controls whom but rather of who controls the definition of the relationship and by what maneuvers.

The healthy family	In the healthy family, members are in touch with their own feelings, communicate in a congruent manner, accept others as different from themselves, and view those differences as a chance to learn and explore rather than as a threat.	The healthy family is able to maintain its basic integrity even during periods of stress. Changes are accommodated as needed. Communication is handled in a clear and logical manner.	Functional families develop suitable up-front methods of dealing with conflict/control struggles. In addition, they have clear rules and a balance of stability and flexibility.
Dysfunction	Dysfunctional families consist of persons whose freedom to grow and develop has been blocked. Dysfunctional behavior results from the interplay of low self-esteem, incongruent communication, poor system functioning, and dysfunctional family rules (both overt and covert).	Incongruent communication—contradictions between verbal and nonverbal communication—is at the heart of dysfunction. Family problems develop by the mishandling of normal life difficulties; attempted solutions often maintain or exacerbate family difficulties.	Symptoms are understood as an attempt to control a relationship. The maneuver to control is understood as dysfunctional if one or both participants deny the issue of control and/or exhibit symptomatic behavior in the process of doing so.
Role of therapist	The therapist is a facilitator, a resource person, an observer, a detective, and a teacher/model of congruent communication and warmth and empathy. The therapist is highly active, personally involved in the system yet able to confront when necessary.	The therapist is actively in charge of the case and all aspects of the case, including who is seen for treatment. The therapist is a data collector, case planner, treatment hypothesis tester, and communications teacher/model. The therapist is actively in charge of therapy.	The therapist takes an active, directive, and authoritative "take-charge" approach to the power struggle that is therapy. The therapist assumes the role of family change maker; he/she assumes temporary leadership of the family.
Goal of therapy	Three overarching goals: each family member will (1) grow in understanding of self and in the ability to communicate congruently, (2) increase respect for the uniqueness of each family member, and (3) view individual uniqueness as an opportunity for growth.	The basic goal of therapy is symptom abatement: to bring about change in behavior and/or view the problem that reduces the client's/family's pain sufficiently that the client/family no longer desires treatment. The focus is entirely on action and problem solving.	Change in the system is the basic goal of therapy. Therapy is focused on altering behavior patterns maintaining the presenting problem.

(Continued)

TABLE 13.1   Comparison Chart of Major Family Therapies (Continued)

	Virginia Satir	Mental Research Institute	Jay Haley
Name of Founder			
Name of Therapy	Process/Communications Approach	Brief Family Therapy	Strategic Family Therapy
Primary techniques	Family life chronology, conjoint family therapy (marital dyad seen first), family reconstruction, psychodrama, guided fantasy, family sculpting, therapist as communications model/teacher.	A variety of managerial techniques to maintain control over the therapy process, focus on the marital dyad or one person from the system, extensive data collection, reframing; the "one-down" position, homework, paradoxical injunctions (therapeutic double-bind).	Focuses on behavior and communication patterns; one therapist, with one or more therapists behind a one-way mirror; straightforward advice, directives, and so on, with compliant families; paradoxical interventions with noncompliant families.

	Salvador Minuchin	Carl Whitaker	
Name of Founder			—
Name of Therapy	Structural Family Therapy	Symbolic/Experiential Family Therapy	
View of family	A family is more than the individual biopsychodynamics of its members. Family members relate according to certain arrangements that govern their transactions. These arrangements form a whole: the structure of the family.	The family is an integrated whole, and each member derives the freedom to individuate and separate from the family through a sense of belonging to the whole. The power of the family—for good or for ill—is the key to individual growth and development.	
The healthy family	The well-functioning family has an underlying organizational structure that allows for fluid and flexible responses to changing conditions through the family life cycle. Thus the family provides both for mutual support and for autonomy of its individual members.	Health is a process of perceptual becoming. The healthy family: has a sense of wholeness, maintains generational boundaries along with role flexibility, is creative and playful, encourages expression of autonomy, and grows in spite of adversity and resultant stress.	

Dysfunction	Symptoms arise when family structures are inflexible, whether enmeshed or disengaged, and the family does not make appropriate structural adjustments; the family responds in an inflexible manner to changing conditions in the family life cycle.	Dysfunctional families are characterized by interactional rigidity and emotional deadness. The specific symptom is often related to the preestablished roles and triangles of family members. Symptoms serve to maintain the status quo.
Role of therapist	The therapist's role is paradoxical: supportive while challenging, attacking while encouraging, being *for* the family yet *against* the dysfunctional system. The therapist is an active, authoritative agent of change: an actor, director, and producer in family change.	The therapist focuses on *being* fully with the client/family; to use him/herself to help family members fully express/communicate what they are experiencing. The therapist is very active but usually not very directive—a coach or a surrogate grandparent; cotherapy is normative.
Goal of therapy	The basic goal is the restructuring of the family's system of transactional rules, such that interactions become more flexible, with expanded availability of alternative ways for family members to relate to one another.	The goal is growth and creativity rather than reduction of symptoms because individual growth and creative freedom will reduce the need for the symptom; growth occurs when family members are able to experience the present moment and communicate that experience with other family members.
Primary techniques	Structural/family mapping: "joining" techniques: maintenance, tracking, accommodation, mimesis; "disequilibriating" techniques: reframing, use of metaphors, enactment, boundary marking, blocking, punctuation, unbalancing.	The therapist as a person as a primary technique; conjoint family therapy and the use of a cotherapist is the norm; reframing; modeling, therapeutic absurdity; affective confrontation; fantasy; paradoxical intentions; "as if" situations.

introductory overview of systems thinking. The current standard of practice in mental health calls for a counselor to approach an understanding of each client by using multiple perspectives, including intrapersonal/individual, interpersonal/systemic, and biological. For this reason, we encourage you to build on the knowledge you gain in this chapter by enrolling in at least one course devoted to couple and/or family counseling.

Philosophical Underpinnings

To understand and apply systems theory, mental health practitioners have to shift their perspective from an individual to a system focus. They probably can make that shift more easily by understanding the origin of the systems perspective: the work of scientists who explained the nature of biological and cybernetic systems. Readers who are interested in seminal work on general systems theory should consult Ludwig von Bertalanffy (1968). Family therapists drew upon his work, among others, adapting and applying his general systems theory to family systems. Salvador Minuchin (1985) provided a comprehensive yet understandable outline of the basic principles of systems theory. Two of the principles specifically address core philosophical assumptions and are detailed below.

Any System is an Organized Whole, and Elements Within the System Are Necessarily Interdependent

(Minuchin, 1985, p. 289). This one statement is the philosophical core of systems theory. In other holistic theories, the individual is the system in which one's dimensions of feeling, thinking, and acting are inseparably interrelated and are understandable only in the context of the interaction of all dimensions: the whole person. By contrast, in systems theory, the social group is the system in which individual members are inseparably interrelated and are understandable only in the context of the interaction of all members: the whole social group. In other words, when considering the social group of the family from a systems perspective, someone can fully understand individual members of the family only in the context of the entire family. In other words, one can understand individual members outside their social contexts, but one loses a great deal of understanding without information about those contexts.

By way of illustration, Satir (1972) used the analogy of a mobile (a hanging art piece consisting of various components hanging by threads in suspended balance). Moving any one component results inevitably in the movement of all other components. If an observer focused only on component B, trying to understand its movement outside of its relationship to component A, the observer's understanding would be incomplete. Likewise, in the family, a change in the functioning of one person is considered a reflection of a change in the family system to which that person belongs.

Systems theorists maintain that by understanding *the interactive, interdependent relationships* of the members of a family system, a counselor can more fully understand and address the systemic factors in the family's functioning as a whole and each family member's relative functioning and satisfaction. For example, in the case of schizophrenia described above, the goal of therapy becomes a family goal: how the family can maintain a relatively consistently supportive family atmosphere—neither hostile nor overinvolved—and how they can respond most effectively if the supportive family atmosphere is disrupted. The focus is not merely shifted from the schizophrenic to the emotionally expressive family member(s); it is shifted to the role that *each* family member plays in influencing each other and the overall functioning that characterizes the family atmosphere.

Patterns in a System are Circular Rather than Linear

(Minuchin, 1985, p. 290). According to traditional therapies, one person's dysfunctional symptoms can be traced back to a cause within that person. In the case of schizophrenia, for example, linear causality yields the conclusion that the schizophrenic's biological disorder causes her relapses. Systemic thinkers do not merely shift the focus of responsibility from the "identified patient" to someone else in the patient's system: For example, it also would be linear thinking to conclude that the emotionally expressive family member(s) are responsible for the schizophrenic's relapses.

Circular causality involves the concept that mutual interaction means *mutual influence.* One of the challenges in talking about circular influence is that one must start somewhere in the circle, and starting in one place can mistakenly imply linear causality. To transcend any tendency toward linear thinking, notice what you experience as you read the following two sentences that pertain to the family containing a member with schizophrenia.

- The stress of living with the symptoms of a person with schizophrenia contributes to emotional expressiveness on the part of other family member(s); at the same time, the stress of other family member(s)' emotional expressiveness exacerbates the symptoms of a person with schizophrenia.
- The stress of other family member(s)' emotional expressiveness exacerbates the symptoms of a person with schizophrenia; at the same time, the stress of living with the symptoms of a person with schizophrenia contributes to emotional expressiveness on the part of other family member(s).

Notice that both sentence sequences make sense. No one factor is *the* cause of a schizophrenic's relapse. Both factors *cause* each other and result in relapse. Relapse is a development of family members' mutual influence on each other. However, rarely is the family interaction pattern this simple. For example, another family member may provoke emotional expressiveness by such behaviors as teasing the "emotionally expressive" member who, in turn, expresses hostility toward the schizophrenic member. By focusing on the entire family interaction pattern, the counselor can reframe the problem as one in which every family member plays a role in, and thus shares responsibility for, the quality of the family atmosphere.

Another more ubiquitous example illustrates the concepts of interdependency and circular causality. A pervasive systemic dynamic among couples is one variously named the pursuer/avoider, pursuer/distancer, or critic/stonewaller. This dynamic can be observed most clearly when a couple argues.

Consider the case of Justin and Kelly, whose arguments usually end without resolution of the issue of disagreement. In traditional counseling, the goal would depend in part on who came for counseling.

If Justin came, the following linear pattern might emerge (the arrow, →, means *causes*): During arguments, Justin immediately becomes defensive and then increasingly withdraws, both emotionally and physically → the issue of disagreement remains unresolved. The counseling goal might be to help Justin understand intrapsychic reasons for his defensiveness and withdrawal, be accountable for his responses, and work on ways to be less defensive and remain engaged in problem solving with Kelly.

If Kelly came for counseling the linear pattern might be: During arguments, Kelly diffuses focus from the issue at hand by bringing up numerous other issues and by blaming Justin and criticizing his personality → the issue of disagreement remains unresolved. In Kelly's counseling, the focus may be on the reasons for and/or purpose of Kelly's diffusive and critical, blaming attitude and style. Kelly and her counselor might address how she can communicate in a way that more productively leads to problem solving of the original issue.

In both of these counseling sessions, the therapist focuses on individual responsibility and largely ignores what the other person is doing or not doing to contribute to the problem. In fact, the problem is not diagnosed as an interpersonal problem but as an intrapersonal one.

Since systems theorists believe in the mutual influence of the members of the system, they assume causation to be circular. Using the principle of circular causality, a systemic counselor would understand Justin and Kelly's arguments as follows: Kelly brings up an issue of dissatisfaction → Justin responds defensively by minimizing her complaint, arguing his innocence of any fault, or countercriticizing Kelly → Kelly intensifies her complaint by bringing up additional dissatisfactions → Justin begins to withdraw by folding his arms and looking away → Kelly turns the focus to a criticism of Justin's personality—by describing him in derogatory terms, describing how he "always" and "never" does certain things, and so on → Justin retreats in stony silence to his lounge chair → Kelly stomps out of the room → when the issue resurfaces, Kelly brings it up again in a critical, blaming way → Justin is quick to respond defensively → and so on.

The temptation of linear thinking is to conclude that if Kelly just wouldn't complain or would just be consistently gentler, Justin would not be so defensive and withdrawing. However, it's equally possible that if Justin didn't immediately respond defensively, Kelly would not escalate into diffusion, criticism, and blame. In fact, research (Gottman, 1994) has shown both conclusions to be accurate: Both the pursuer's criticism and blame and the distancer's defensiveness and stonewalling, especially when they go unchecked by repair mechanisms such as listening to the other's point of view and affirming the validity of the other's perspective, contribute to a pattern of communication associated with relationship distress and a high likelihood of relationship dissolution. In addition, the longest and happiest relationships were characterized by the wife complaining (but not criticizing) *early and often* in the relationship (Gottman & Krokoff, 1989)!

The philosophical principle in systems theory of circular causality provides a foundation for assessment and change. "Change must be directed toward the cycle, although the point of entry and the manner of interrupting the cycle are matters of choice" (Minuchin, 1985, p. 290).

THE THEORY: DEVELOPMENT AND CHARACTERISTICS OF FAMILY SYSTEMS

Nature of Family Systems

Family systems are ubiquitous

Most children are born into or, soon after birth, enter a family system, their *family of origin*. Most humans also participate in the creation of at least one family system, their *family of creation*, which may or may not produce children of its own. Family systems take many forms across cultures: monogamous (two spouses) or polygamous (more than two spouses); nuclear (the core of which is one set of parents and possibly their children living together) or extended (the core of which is three or more generations living together). In the following discussion, we address characteristics of systems that are universal across the various forms of families, and, for ease of explanation, we sometimes make particular use of the form of family system most strongly associated with prevailing U.S. culture, the heterosexual, monogamous, nuclear family.

Function of Family Systems

We organized this section around two motivational functions of systems: *goal-directedness* and *the maintenance of dynamic equilibrium*. In the process of discussing these two motivational functions, we also discuss several operational functions of systems. Also, it is customary in systemic thinking to make little or no reference to intrapsychic processes, such as awareness. However, as you read the following information, you will be thinking (an intrapsychic process) and one of the things you may be thinking is, "In all my years of membership in family systems, I never really noticed what these authors are describing here." The systems literature does occasionally make reference to the fact that members of a system function within the system largely nonconscious of the operating principles in which they are participating—principles that they themselves are, in fact, enacting. For that reason, we will frequently remind you of the largely nonconscious nature of systemic functioning.

Goal-Directedness Every system, including the family system, has a goal or purpose. Regarding the human family in particular, consider the fact that some form of family is found in every culture (Brown, 1991). Therefore, it stands to reason that the family, a universal social institution, serves some universal purpose. Although some systems theorists object to the concept of purposefulness, considering it a culturally based assumption (Becvar & Becvar, 2008), others consider purposefulness—more specifically, *goal-directedness*—to be inherent in systems, particularly cybernetic systems (Heylighen & Joslyn, 2001; Weiner, 1948). As we have found the concept of teleology not to detract from, but rather to enhance, our understanding of systems theory as it applies to families, we will proceed on the assumption that the family system exists for the purpose of facilitating the greatest overall survival, health, and development of its members. Indeed, the same theorists who decried the concept of purposefulness offered a definition of family as "individuals operating ... *in support of* the mutual welfare of all and the individual development of each" (Becvar & Becvar, 2008, p. 97; italics added). The phrase "in support of" implies a purposeful goal of the system.

However, we argue with the phrase "mutual welfare of all and ... individual development of each." Although these are the *ideal* aims of the family system, several phenomena show that such aims are not *definitive* of families. Among the most salient examples are geriatricide and infanticide: the practice in some cultures of killing elderly parents and newborn children perceived as a liability rather than an asset to the overall family's welfare. Even in the current United States, infanticide occurs; some people believe geriatricide does, as well. Clearly, the victim's welfare—and very life—is sacrificed for the overall welfare of the family; thus, welfare is hardly mutual or supportive of the individual development of each member. More commonly, family systems theorists have postulated that some families bolster their existence by *scapegoating* one family member, beating them down psychologically or even physically. Clearly, the scapegoat's welfare and development are sacrificed, rather than supported, in the service of maintaining the soundness of the family system. Even more salient is the case of an *abusive* family in which a spouse (in a heterosexual couple, almost always the wife) and, often, the children subject themselves to psychological and physical violence out of the perception that these circumstances constitute their best chance at their greatest welfare overall.

In all these cases, the family is still a family—their definition remains in tact—although the ideal, the *mutual* welfare of all and *maximal* development of each, is far from achieved. On a hopeful note, family therapy has demonstrated that, for example, regarding the practice of scapegoating, a family can develop ways to maintain its soundness through alternative strategies. When a family functions in such a way that the ideal (mutual welfare and maximal development of each member) is realized, the family might be said to be maintaining its integrity in *both* senses of the word.

Thus, one motivational function of a system is teleology, purposefulness, goal-directedness intentionality. The purpose of the family system is, by our definition, to support the welfare of its members and, ideally, to promote the maximal development of each family member. The fact that you may not have actually thought about the purpose of the family brings up the mostly nonconscious nature of the family purpose. An additional example of the goal-directedness of families comes from John Gottman and Julie Gottman's (2008) work with couples. They noted that, through skillful questioning by a counselor, each member of a couple will uncover a "dream"—a subjective, desired goal that the member perceives the marriage will help to achieve. Chronic conflict can be reframed—understood in a more positive light—and thus better managed in light of both members' conscious awareness of each one's dream. For the purpose of understanding systemic thinking, suffice it to say that the family system is purposeful.

Maintenance of Dynamic Equilibrium   John and Mary meet. The purpose of their interactions at first may or may not be a "family purpose." On the one hand, one or both of them may be seeking to pair-bond and may perceive the other as a potential partner; on the other hand, one or both of them may be seeking something else, such as friendship or sex. In either case, as they interact, two fundamental operational functions come into play, which are the mechanisms of the creation and maintenance of a social system: *morphogenesis and morphostasis. Morphogenesis is the tendency arising out of interaction for a system to create and recreate its own structure* (morph = structure, genesis = creation). In other words, *systems self-organize and reorganize into their own characteristic patterns of interaction*. More specifically, John and Mary's goal-directed interactions form into patterns of interaction that uniquely characterize their relationship; as they continue to interact, they continue to create and recreate such patterns. It is this mostly nonconscious self-organization into unique patterns, rather than any particular pattern itself, that is universal among family systems.

For example, Gottman (1979) has found that equally lasting, happy marriages can be, in our terms, high, medium, or low volume. High-volume couples have frequent, passionate debates and arguments; medium-volume couples have occasional discussions characterized by open communication of thoughts and feelings; and low-volume couples spend relatively less time together and spend much of their together time in silence or with minimal interaction. By way of another example, I (JMH) recall an overnight stay at my cousin's house when I realized how her family's way of frequently cutting up and teasing each other contrasted with my family's way of being relatively quiet and serious. The fact that her family's interaction pattern was a realization to me underscores the nonconscious nature of such patterns: It had never occurred to me that a family could function any differently than my own did. All of these examples illustrate the self-organization of systemic interactions into *some* form of patterns through which it fulfills its purpose, though the specific pattern in one system may vary greatly compared to the pattern in another.

If systems operated only on the basis of morphogenesis, they would be constantly recreating themselves, constantly changing, and thus would lack a sense of continuity. Another fundamental operational function provides for a system's continuity: morphostasis. *Morphostasis is the system's fundamental tendency to keep its structure the same, stable* (morph = structure, stasis = no movement). Actually, the above examples also illustrated morphostasis: Once a couple morphogenetically creates their interactional volume level, that level tends to remain a stable, unique pattern of interaction; once a family establishes its level of seriousness, it tends to maintain that level.

Like all systems, family systems establish and maintain characteristic levels of interaction around myriad aspects of the systemic relationship: not only the levels of "volume" and "seriousness" but also levels of such things as openness/privacy, dominance/submission, generosity/selfishness. Virtually any aspect of systemic functioning revolves around a level of functioning that characterizes that systemic relationship. It is as if the members of the system calibrate, that is, establish particular set points, for each aspect of systemic functioning.

To maintain functioning within an acceptable range around a particular set point, family members establish mostly nonconscious family rules, such as, "Thou shalt remain within a certain range of seriousness." Then family members mostly nonconsciously monitor deviation from the set point or rule. When members detect deviation, they perceive a perturbation of the system's dynamic equilibrium—*dynamic* referring to the fact that the system is always "in motion" as people continuously act and interact, and *equilibrium* referring to the maintenance of balance around a set point. When family members detect disequilibrium, they mostly nonconsciously employ corrective strategies to decrease disequilibrium. Technically, we could speak of the family seeking either to restore equilibrium or to decrease disequilibrium. For reasons that will become clear in a moment, we are purposely speaking in the latter terms.

For example, in a high-volume couple, if interactions drift away from emotional intensity, one member of the couple will provoke a debate that the other member is likely to join willingly; in a low-volume couple, if interactions drift toward emotional intensity, both members are likely to nonconsciously cooperate in a way to create a more comfortable distance. The joking family that drifts toward seriousness instigates jokes; the serious family that drifts toward levity instigates calming strategies. Now that I (JMH) understand systemic thinking, I find it not at all surprising that one trigger of my childhood asthma was laughing long and hard; nothing aborts levity like an asthma attack. What a creative way to maintain a serious family atmosphere! Notice that anyone, child or adult, can be involved in the maintenance of a family rule.

Perturbations—those changes that provoke or threaten to provoke disequilibrium— can take a few different forms. They may arise from *inside* or *outside* the system; they may be *passive*, such as the "drifts" just discussed, or *active*, such as some acute event; and they may actually have *already occurred* or merely *threatened to occur*. Examples of active perturbations include a member of the system being added (birth or adoption of a child, grandparent or other person comes to live with the family) or taken away (death, marriage, imprisonment, off to college); a member becoming unable to perform a certain role (due to illness, additional employment, or additional responsibilities at school or work) or for the first time, becoming able to perform a certain role (due to reduced employment or outside responsibilities or to developmental progress such as the ability to do household chores or to drive a car); a member stepping outside a given role (a child begins swearing, a heterosexual spouse at work develops a best friend of the other sex). Notice that some of the examples involved perturbations that arose from outside the family (more responsibilities at work) and others from inside (developmental progress of a child). Examples of *threats* of a challenge to the system's equilibrium include when a teenage child starts *talking about* getting a driver's license or a job, a couple *learns* they are expecting a child, or a spouse *begins researching* a new, potentially time- or finance-consuming hobby.

The *corrective strategies* family members employ when they detect disequilibrium can have one of two effects: they can decrease the disequilibrium or increase it. For example, if a parent notices a child has begun to swear, and swearing violates a family rule that "thou shalt not swear," the parent (and probably the child, as well) will experience a sense of systemic disequilibrium. If the parent uses the corrective strategy of frowning at the child, and the child stops swearing, disequilibrium has been decreased. If the parent frowns and the child continues, swears more, makes a hostile remark to the parent—all of which children sometimes do in response to parental corrective strategies and all of which constitute further family rule violation—disequilibrium has been increased. Information about the effect of a corrective strategy on the system's disequilibrium is termed *feedback*. Information that a corrective strategy has *decreased disequilibrium* is termed *negative feedback*, and information that a corrective action has *increased disequilibrium* is termed *positive feedback*. See why we worded it this way? It's harder to think of *negative* feedback as information that *equilibrium has been restored*; it's easier to remember it in terms of *disequilibrium being decreased*. In addition, our wording conveys the "feel" that family (and all systemic) interaction is "all about" monitoring and managing *dis*equilibrium.

We want to clarify a few key points about corrective strategies and negative and positive feedback. First, any single corrective strategy can result in either negative or positive feedback. We already illustrated this principle in the case of the swearing child. Consider also the heterosexual wife who develops a new best friend at work—a friend of the other sex, violating the family rule that "thou shalt not have sexually intimate or even very emotionally intimate relationships with members of the other sex," and thus disequilibrating the couple system. The husband might employ any number of corrective strategies. He could protest the friendship; if the wife agrees and acts accordingly by cooling the outside friendship, disequilibrium is reduced, and the husband's protest yielded negative feedback. However, if she responds to his protest by disagreeing, they argue, and they refuse to speak to one another, disequilibrium was increased, and his protest yielded positive feedback. He might employ a different corrective mechanism: lavishing attention on her. If she responds positively and they become emotionally closer, disequilibrium has decreased: negative feedback. If she recoils from his smothering attentiveness and retreats increasingly to the friendship, disequilibrium in the couple relationship has increased: positive feedback. It may be surprising to learn that even the husband's *saying and doing nothing different* can constitute a corrective strategy. If he says nothing and the wife's friendship remains simply a platonic one and the marital relationship continues undisturbed, his nonresponse constituted negative feedback, whereas if the friendship evolves such that the marital relationship deteriorates, his nonresponse constituted positive feedback.

As the examples illustrate, the words "negative" and "positive" do not clearly correlate with "unpleasant" and "pleasant." The parent's unpleasant frown and the husband's pleasant attention have the potential to function as either negative or positive feedback. A related point is that, as the above examples also illustrate, whether a particular response will *actually* function as negative or positive feedback *cannot always be predicted*, but it *can almost always be observed*, a point to which we will return.

Another point regarding feedback is that "negative" and "positive" do not mean "good" or "bad." Both types of feedback are constructive to the extent that they succeed in restoring dynamic equilibrium. The family systems literature represents negative feedback as always constructive, and positive feedback as sometimes destructive but sometimes constructive, the latter when it results in the restoration of dynamic equilibrium by establishing a new set point that is more functional for the evolving system (Goldenberg & Goldenberg, 2008). Whereas these principles may accurately reflect mechanical cybernetic systems, we believe it makes sense in the case of human systems to consider the possibility that both negative and positive feedback can also be destructive: Negative feedback (deceleration or decrease in deviation from the set point) is not good if the rigid system actually needs to respond to current perturbation by morphogenetically reorganizing itself around a new set point, which it can discover only by creatively deviating from the current set point. Positive feedback (accelerating or increasing deviation from the set point) is not good if the chaotic system actually needs to revert to functioning around an established set point enough to morphostatically stabilize itself.

The overuse of negative feedback is illustrated by the parents who become increasingly controlling in response to an older teen's increasing bids for independence; they may succeed temporarily in restoring equilibrium, but the teen is highly likely at some point to rebel big time. The parents are like the heating system in a home that turns on more and more frequently in response to the slightest deviation from the set point; that system is likely to burn out and be unable to regulate the temperature at all. The overuse of positive feedback involves a family responding to perturbation with increasingly intense deviation from the "old way," as in the case of an argument that spins out of control, resulting in destruction to property or people. The arguers are like a lady I (JMH) knew who, at the slightest temperature discomfort, reset her thermostat several degrees—up and down, and then even more extremely up and down—resulting in chaotic temperature fluctuations rather than the slight adjustments she actually needed. Thus, both negative and positive feedback, which serve respectively to decrease or increase deviation from a given set point, have the potential to constructively restore dynamic equilibrium or destructively upset dynamic equilibrium even further—either by squelching its dynamism or disrupting its equilibrium. The ways a family manifests positive and negative feedback and the extent to which those manifestations result in restoration or further disruption of dynamic equilibrium are the foci of the family therapist.

A final point regarding feedback is that, to define the concepts of negative and positive feedback, we resorted to linear causality (did you notice?): Cause (perturbation and deviation from set point): effect (response). Although our examples did avoid determinism by illustrating that a parent or jealous husband might respond in any of a number of ways, we still invoked linear causality by specifying a starting point. In fact, in systemic thinking, even the cause is seen potentially as an effect. For example, a child starting to swear can be a response to the perturbation of not enough connectedness in the parent–child relationship (a bid for attention) or of too much connectedness (a bid for independence). Similarly, a wife developing a best friendship at work with a member of the other sex can be a response to not enough closeness in the marital relationship (a bid for attention and more intimacy with husband) or to too much closeness (a bid for distance from husband). Systemically speaking, every response is a response to a response, and the function of any one response—its effect on the system—can be understood only in the context of the systemic relationship.

Two final operational functions should round out your understanding of the function of systems: the two types of change. Related to morphostasis, first-order change involves the family *adapting* their *current* mode of operation; related to morphogenesis, second-order change involves a family *adopting* a *new* mode of operation. When a young child begins swearing, first-order change is illustrated by the parents who devise a new penalty relevant to the child's current interests: A child who recently developed an interest in video games is prohibited from playing those games for a specified period of time.

This kind of change may or may not succeed in restoring equilibrium. By contrast, when an adult child begins swearing, second-order change is exemplified by the parents deciding that swearing is to be tolerated, even if they still do not like that kind of language. The young child's parents who do not consistently enforce the rule against swearing facilitate second-order change; the adult child's parents who intensify enforcement of the rule exemplify first-order change. Again, both types of change are potentially helpful and/or harmful to a system, depending on such factors as the context of the situation, such as the child's age, and whether a family makes excessive use of either type of change in response to perturbations. A system so morphostatically rigid that it cannot adapt is in danger of collapsing in on itself, a kind of "implosion," whereas a system so morphogenetically changeable is in danger of falling apart, a kind of "explosion."

In summary, from a systemic perspective, *the members of a system are always monitoring and regulating the dynamic equilibrium of their system*. To apply the concepts addressed in this section, consider that all family systems, in the course of the *family life cycle*, experience some common challenges or perturbations. Work through the box on this page to explore your own family system's approach to the maintenance of dynamic equilibrium through morphostasis/morphogenesis, feedback, and change. Remember: Very different strategies can be effective in the face of perturbation.

Consider the events listed below that occur in a typical family during its life cycle. Make note of how your family responded to the change. You may use your *family of origin* (the one, or one of the ones, in which you were raised) or your *family of creation* (the one, or one of the ones, you have created). If you have experienced two or more families, work through the events using at least two of the family systems. What changes did you note after the event? What new patterns emerged?

- Marriage
- Birth of a first child
- First child goes to school
- Birth of second child
- Child goes to high school, starts dating, gets driver's license
- Death of parent/grandparent
- The 18-year-old child leaves home to establish separate residence or attend college
- Child gets married

What other challenges, perturbations, or disequilibrating circumstances did your family(s) face, for example, serious or chronic illness, unemployment, or unwanted pregnancy? What strategies did your family employ to cope with the perturbation? How effective was the strategy in maintaining the family system's equilibrium?

Structure of Family Systems

Family system theorists postulate that every system contains *subsystems*, those smaller than and contained within it, and that virtually every system exists within *supersystems*, those larger than it. These various contexts comprise multiple layers (see Figure 13.1). Since it would be overwhelming to consider all systemic contexts involved in a therapeutic

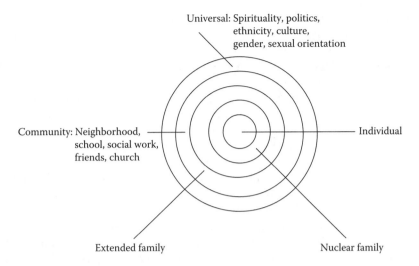

Universal: Spirituality, politics, ethnicity, culture, gender, sexual orientation

Community: Neighborhood, school, social work, friends, church

Individual

Extended family

Nuclear family

FIGURE 13.1   Systemic levels.

situation, family therapists have bracketed the following as the systems of focus: the family system, the family subsystems; and, to some degree, the extended family, community, and cultural systems.

Beginning with the family itself, family systems theorists honor the family's own definition of itself. Consider the Jackson family:

> Mr. and Mrs. Jackson have two children, Iesha, 12, and Ben, 8, and they live in downtown New Orleans, Louisiana. Mr. Jackson's mother, Grandma, also lives in the house. Both Mr. and Mrs. Jackson work full time outside the home, so Grandma fulfills most of the parenting duties. Grandma, Mr. Jackson, and Iesha all play the piano. Mrs. Jackson is a former ping-pong champion, and Ben, in particular, likes playing ping-pong with her and learning competitive tips. The members of this family system are Mr. Jackson, Mrs. Jackson, Iesha, Ben, and Grandma.

A system's subsystems are structures that distribute and carry out all functions within the larger system. Subsystems in a family include the spousal subsystem, which is monogamous or polygamous, depending on the cultural context, and may include the parental subsystem, meaning all those who caretake the children; the sibling subsystem, which in some cultures may mean brothers and sisters, whereas in others, brothers, sisters, and cousins; gender subsystems; and other subsystems. In the Jackson family, the most salient subsystems are:

Spousal: Mr. and Mrs. Jackson
Parental: Mr. and Mrs. Jackson and Grandma
Sibling: Iesha and Ben
Gender: (Male) Mr. Jackson and Ben; (Female) Mrs. Jackson, Grandma, and Iesha
Avocation: Piano: Grandma, Mr. Jackson, and Iesha; Ping-pong: Mrs. Jackson and Ben

At all levels of supersystem, system, and subsystem, systemic structures are differentiated by *boundaries*. Boundaries are comprised of the mostly nonconscious, unwritten *rules* about who belongs and does not belong to a system (or supersystem or subsystem); what the members of a system do and do not do; and how members of the system relate to nonmembers (members of other systems). A system's boundaries and rules establish and maintain the uniqueness of it and its members. Boundaries and rules also provide guidance about how the system processes internal information, carries out system tasks, and integrates information from other systems.

I (KAF) had an explicit discussion about a family rule with my then-six-year-old son Dylan (he's now 13). He came home from school and wanted to know what the "F-word" meant. I said, "We don't talk that way in our family. You don't need to know what the F-word means. If someone is talking like that around you, just walk away." In that single, brief interchange, I communicated a family rule: "We don't use the F-word or curse in this family"; a firm boundary between outside information and the family: "Don't use that word; You don't even need to know what it means"; and a rule or method for handling such information should it come up again: "Ignore people who talk like that."

Boundaries and rules are structures that play a role in every interaction within the system. Examine the following interaction within the Jackson system and identify the boundaries and rules around the issue of grades. Note the boundaries/rules that differentiate the subsystems pertinent to this issue.

Iesha: Here's my report card. I didn't do so hot this quarter, but my math teacher stinks.

Grandma: Well, your other grades are pretty good, mostly A's and a few B's, but you are right, a C in math in not acceptable. When your parents come home we will discuss it.

(Parents come home)

Mr. Jackson: Well, Iesha this is really disappointing.

Iesha: But, dad, the teacher is such an idiot.

Mrs. Jackson: No excuses! Your grade has nothing to do with your teacher. We don't make excuses, Iesha.

Grandma: You know, if we saw you studying more, then we wouldn't be so upset. You don't do your homework until late, and you're on the phone for half the evening. That has to stop.

Mr. Jackson: I agree. You will do your homework first thing when you get home. I or your mom will check it when we get home. Phone time will be from 7:00–7:30, if you have your homework done, no exceptions.

Mrs. Jackson: If you bring your grades up, we will consider expanding your privileges.

By examining the dialog, the parental subsystem (Mr. Jackson, Mrs. Jackson, and Grandma) is identifiable. In this case the parental subsystem is in charge of assessing the child's grades and providing consequences for any deviation from the norm. A member of the child subsystem is represented, Iesha. There are clear boundaries between the subsystems as evidenced by the parents' holding the power of assessment and consequence. In other words, there is no mistake who is in charge and who is in trouble in this scenario. The rule being discussed is the value or expectation of academic performance. Inferring from the discussion, the boundary/rule is something like, "Only grades of A or B are acceptable for members of the sibling subsystem." Iesha's breaking of that rule constituted a perturbation that was experienced as disturbance of the family's equilibrium, to which the parental subsystem responded with a corrective strategy. Iesha also seemed to break a family rule by blaming her teacher for her unacceptable grade. The parental subsystem sought to regain equilibrium by enforcing the rule, which is issuing consequences for the rule violation.

Iesha complained briefly, then sullenly accepted the stipulations laid down by the parental subsystem. Thus, this situation exemplified negative feedback, in that further deviation from the norm pertaining to grades is decelerated. If positive feedback had occurred, it could have taken any of several forms. For example, the parental subsystem could have altered the rule right away, on the basis that, "Because junior high work is more challenging, one 'C' is acceptable as long as the other grades are 'A's' and 'B's.' " Another positive feedback scenario might have been Iesha persisting in her protest: "He really *is* a jerk; I've tried going early and staying late to get help from him, and he's always impatient and mean." After Mr. Jackson talks with the teacher and finds him rather uncooperative, he puts a call in to the principal. In the meantime, he consults with the parental subsystem and concludes that, under the circumstances, they will lift the phone restrictions they had imposed.

The flexibility or rigidity of the rules and boundaries are important to the structure of the system. Systems thinkers refer to the degree of *openness or closedness* of the boundaries/rules to describe the extent to which a system lets external information in or internal information out. Akin to the concept of dynamic balance between morphostasis and morphogenesis is the delicate balance between openness and closedness. Neither is healthy all the time. In this state of balance between openness and closedness, "the system is allowing in information and permitting change as appropriate, while screening out information and avoiding changes that would threaten the survival of the system" (Becvar & Becvar, 2008, p. 84). In order to adapt and change, the system must have boundaries and rules that are flexible and allow for new information. Without new knowledge, the system could not survive. Likewise, systems must have boundaries and rules stable enough to provide a consistent identity for the family. Imagine how chaotic it would be if expectations, values, and rules were constantly changing.

The last ubiquitous systemic structure we will discuss is the *triangle*. In systems thinking, a two-person system, like a two-legged stool, is relatively unstable; as with the addition of a third leg to the stool, a dyadic system is stabilized by the inclusion of a third person. In times of relative equilibrium, the third person can serve to provide a sense of togetherness for the twosome. For example, consider the two possible triangles in Figure 13.2.

Each of the third persons, mother-in-law and secretary, can serve to strengthen the couple's sense of togetherness. When either the husband talks with the wife's mother, or the wife talks with the husband's mother, each of the spouses' membership in the marital system is affirmed. When either husband or wife talks with their respective secretaries about

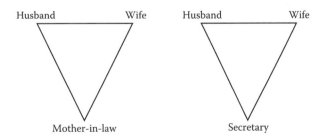

FIGURE 13.2   Examples of Systemic triangles.

such things as upcoming events the couple will be attending, the spouses' "coupleness" is affirmed.

In times of relative disequilibrium, the third person can serve to decrease the intensity experienced within the twosome. Intensity is usually defined as conflict within the twosome that escalates to the point at which the system is threatened. For example, if a spouse feels neglected or pressured by the partner, he or she may call a friend in whom to confide and from whom to receive consolation and support. Having been supported, the intensity of the conflict between spouse and partner would likely be reduced. If the reduction in conflict helps the couple resolve the issue, the triangulation has been constructive. If it promotes a bypassing of the issue, leaving the issue unresolved, it has been destructive.

Guerin, Fogarty, Fay, Kautto, and Kautto (1996) described four common family triangles, as shown in Figure 13.3. In each of these triangles, conflict within the twosome intensifies the triangulation. For example, in the first triangle the husband and wife are having marital problems and fight frequently. The child begins failing in school. As the parents join in solving the child crisis, the conflict between them abates. In the same scenario, the parents may pull the child in by being critical of the child's work at home or school. The "shared enemy" of the child gives the subsystem an avenue for ventilation so the marriage does not disintegrate. It is in this way that the identified patient, in this case the child, may not be the *source* of the problem; rather, the child is (usually nonconsciously) expressing for the family the unresolved conflict between the parents.

Again, triangulation is an equilibrating force that is not inherently good or bad. If it results in too much conflict reduction, the incentive to resolve the issue is temporarily lost, and the issue goes unresolved, only to recur in the future. If it results in some conflict reduction—enough for the dyad to resolve the issue, usually through a form of second-order change—the triangulation has been constructive. The latter illustrates the intended role of the therapist: to be constructively triangulated into the family system.

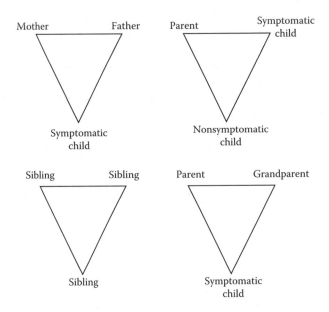

FIGURE 13.3 Four common family triangles.

Role of the Environment

Familial

The family is the system of focus for family therapy, so its influence and importance is primary.

> In all cultures, the family imprints its members with selfhood. Human experience of identity has two elements: a sense of belonging and sense of being separate. The laboratory in which these ingredients are mixed and dispensed is the family, the matrix of identity. (Minuchin, 1974, p. 47)

Regardless of the variability of systems models, all systems theorists believe that the foundation of behavior, healthy or unhealthy, is closely associated with the interactions among members of the family system. The information contained in this chapter details the influence of the family system on its members.

Extrafamilial

Extrafamilial factors include everyone and everything outside the family system: neighbors, friends, teachers and classmates, bosses and coworkers, members of one's church, nature, and culture. Through contact with each of these factors, family members gain information that they bring into the family system and that may serve to contribute to or perturb the family equilibrium. Iesha's grades were an example of perturbing information. Another example: Consider the family system in which the boundary/rule regarding sexual activity among the unmarried has been abstinence only. If a child learns at school about safe sex and brings that information into the family system, the family's equilibrium may be perturbed. To regain equilibrium, the parental system may take corrective action by providing counterinformation. They may be sure to attend their religious institution at the next opportunity to interact with like-minded others and to hear a sermon on the sin of premarital sex and the value of abstinence before marriage. If the child "returns to the fold" regarding this issue, the family-generated information has served as negative feedback; equilibrium has been restored. If the child revolts, the information has served as positive feedback and the equilibrium of the family continues to be challenged.

Interaction of Nature and Environment on System Development

Healthy Functioning

Answering the question "What is a healthy family?" proves to be a daunting task. Each specific theory under the umbrella of systems thinking includes its own answer (see Table 13.1).

Consider the following examples of how three separate families respond to perturbations and strive to reestablish equilibrium. Look for examples of the various concepts introduced so far in this chapter.

> The Browns are a very close family. All family members live within 50 miles of each other, and most work in the family business. Jill, upon graduation from high school, decides to attend a university 5,000 miles away. One week before she leaves for college, her father becomes very depressed and refuses to go to work. Her mother and older siblings become very angry with Jill and repeatedly tell her, "You are killing your father." Jill decides to stay home and attend a community college nearby. Within a week, her father is feeling much better, though the family has taken on an atmosphere of uneasiness.

The Garzas also are a close family. Mr. Garza loses his job and feels as if he is letting his family down. Feeling ashamed and guilty, he becomes irritable, losing his temper more often. The other members are sensitive to his feelings. They realize that he needs support and a way to know that he is contributing to the family, but they are unsure how best to respond. Although he cannot provide financially like he used to, the family discovers that in addition to other things he used to do, such as yard work, Mr. Garza can cook for the family, easing the burden on his full-time-employed wife, and that he can help the children with their schoolwork such that their teachers report they are doing noticeably better at school, both academically and socially. Understanding that, due to the economy and the nature of Mr. Garza's work, it may be some time before he finds work again, the family also has agreed on strategies to conserve money while Mr. Garza continues to seek work. In the meantime, Mr. Garza and his family appreciate his contributions. The stress within the family subsides.

The Smith's also are a close family until their fourth child is born with Down's syndrome and requires fairly intense and continuous care. Mrs. Smith responds by focusing her attention almost exclusively on the youngest child. When Mr. Smith expresses dissatisfaction, they argue, and Mrs. Smith becomes depressed. Mr. Smith gradually spends more and more time at work. Meanwhile, the other three children develop various health and school-related problems. Eventually, Mr. Smith has an extramarital affair, remaining half-heartedly in the role of husband and father; more and more frequently, he contemplates divorce.

While reading the three vignettes, you may have an internal reaction that one family is healthier than the others. One employs excessive morphostasis, one balances morphostasis and morphogenesis, and one exercises excessive morphogenesis. It is worth repeating that, from a systems perspective, various strategies to maintain equilibrium are neither good nor bad, though some are more functional than others, that is, some actually serve to maintain the system, whereas others threaten the system. For example, in the case of the Smiths, Mr. Smith may have undertaken the affair to meet his emotional and sexual needs without placing further stress on the marriage/family system—an attempt to maintain the system—yet it ended up threatening the system as he increasingly contemplated divorce. However, the strategy might have worked: In Sonya Friedman's (1994) book *Secret Loves: Women with Two Lives*, she described women she interviewed who had sustained long-term affairs—some as long as 20 years and still going—that reportedly enabled them to *maintain* their marriages and families by compensating for what they felt was lacking in their marriages and perceived their spouses unable to provide. From a family systems perspective, even a phenomenon as charged as an extramarital affair is evaluated in light of its effect on the system: Although affairs often threaten the system, they apparently, at times, can serve to stabilize it. Fortunately, most strategies families use to maintain their system's existence are less morally controversial. The seminal works of Prigogine (1973) and Maruyama (1963) described how systems can respond to disequilibriating forces by exploring new alternatives, creating new patterns, and thus reaching a new sense of balance and stability that is appropriate to the new circumstance.

Walsh (2002) provided an excellent collection of literature intended to define and describe "normal family processes." Fenell and Weinhold (2003) succeeded in transcending the variations in families and theories by outlining the following general characteristics of healthy families.

Clear Subsystem Boundaries and Clear Family Roles   A colleague of mine (KAF) is fond of saying, "In families, you need to be able to tell the difference between the kids and the parents." His advice points up the importance of establishing clear subsystem boundaries and member roles. Most systemic theorists believe that well-differentiated subsystems are keys to healthy functioning because they make the roles and rules easier for system members to define and fulfill; thus the system is less chaotic, that is, equilibrium is more easily maintained. A number of approaches advocate defined hierarchies: a prioritizing of subsystems based on power (Framo, 1992; Minuchin, 1974). In particular, a well-defined parental subsystem is vital; for example, by and large, parents care for children, not vice versa.

Another important challenge many families face is distinguishing the parental subsystem from the spousal subsystem. In healthy families, the members of the spousal subsystem spend time with each other and apart from the rest of the family system in order to nurture the spousal relationship as separate and distinct from their roles in the parental subsystem. "The [spousal subsystem] is especially important to the family: Any dysfunction in the spousal subsystem is bound to reverberate throughout the family [and spill over into the parental subsystem], resulting in the scapegoating of children or co-opting them into alliances with one parent against the other" (Goldenberg & Goldenberg, 2008, p. 405).

Clear Family Rules with Consistent and Fair Enforcement   Healthy families also have rules that all members of the system know and understand; when infractions occur, consequences are fair and consistent. The idea is that if the members know what to expect, they have a higher probability of maintaining equilibrium and are less likely to erupt in rebellion if a consequence is warranted and enforced. A client in a group counseling session shared the story of how his teenage daughter missed curfew; as a consequence, she was not allowed to attend a party the following night. He stated, "When she came home, I laid down the law [well-defined parental and child subsystem]. I told her that because she missed curfew, she would be staying in the next night. It's on her, as far as I'm concerned. She knew she had done wrong, so she just went to her room to sulk." His story provides a good example of how rules are handled in a manner that is known to all, with minimal surprises in expectations or outcomes.

Respect for Individual Autonomy Coexisting with Respect for Family Connection   Healthy families also respect the individuality of their members while encouraging membership in the system. The concept of *differentiation* can be helpful in understanding this characteristic of a healthy family. Kerr and Bower (1988) defined differentiation as "the ability to be in emotional contact with others yet still autonomous in one's emotional functioning" (p. 145). Healthy systems encourage members to form distinct identities and voice beliefs and knowledge gained through interaction with other systems without being threatened by members' distinct ways of thinking and functioning. Different points of view are honored within healthy systems and can actually form the basis of the cohesion experienced by the members. The operating belief in this type of system might be, "I can speak my mind and not fear losing my place in the family or expect intense coercion from other members." At the same time, "I listen to others' points of view and, if differences exist between our perspectives, I express my position and do not coerce them." A useful strategy in such cases is to "agree to disagree."

Clear and Direct Communication   The last aspect of a healthy family is clear and direct communication patterns. A number of systemic thinkers (Alexander & Parsons, 1982; Beavers & Hampson, 1990; Minuchin, 1974; Olsen & Gorall, 2002; Satir, 1983) have concurred that effective communication includes good listening skills, the sending of direct messages, using "I" language (e.g., "I would like for you to hug me" instead of, "You never want to be around me"), a willingness to share personal feelings about the relationship and oneself, the ability to stay on the topic at hand, and the willingness to be open to alternatives.

Unhealthy Functioning

Clearly defining what constitutes an unhealthy family is as challenging as defining what constitutes a healthy one. Table 13.1 offers descriptions of how different family therapies address the characteristics of a dysfunctional system. For the sake of consistency, we used Fenell and Weinhold's (2003) elements of family dysfunction.

Subsystem Boundaries are Either Too Rigid or Too Diffuse   In dysfunctional systems, the boundaries that differentiate one subsystem from another can be conceptualized along the following continuum:

Diffuse ------- (------- Healthy -------) ------- Rigid

When the boundary is too diffuse, one cannot tell one subsystem from the other, and members have difficulty identifying the various subsystems in their own family. Families with diffuse boundaries may have adults and children who alternate between acting like adults and acting like children. The impact of diffuse boundaries on the family is confusion and chaos. The family belief or motto is, "We have no beliefs or mottos." Conversely, when boundaries are too rigid, the system becomes paralyzed and incapable of change. Families with rigid boundaries fear the disequilibriating effect of outside information and, as a result, become very insular in their interactions. The family mottos are "We fear change," and "This is the way it has always been done."

Rules and Enforcement are Either Too Rigid or Very Inconsistent   When subsystems are poorly or rigidly organized, one can expect that the rules governing these systems will follow suit. In diffuse systems, the only consistent rule is that there are no rules. Rules are arbitrary, open for constant revision, and inconsistently enforced. Any attempt to challenge the chaotic balance is met with fierce resistance. Consider a true story from therapy in which one parent recounted a feeble attempt to set a rule and establish a new pattern in a diffuse system.

> Mrs. Jones heard on a talk show that families should eat together every evening. She thought about her own family: Dad worked crazy hours, often eating out and then going to bed upon getting home; daughter was 16, had just earned her driver's license, and often stayed out with friends, even on school nights; son was 13 and played on three different soccer teams—when did he eat, anyway? Mrs. Jones announced that starting tomorrow, "We will eat together as a family." The family's reply? Dad said, "Okay" and then did not come home until 11:45. Daughter left a post-it note on the refrigerator saying, "Went on a date with Ricky. C-ya!" Mom herself got caught up at work on a project and forgot to come home. Son showed up at appointed time but left when no one else arrived.

Rigid subsystems follow rigid rules in which the appropriate behavior is often narrowly defined and deviations are countered with extreme prejudice. The rules in the system are designed to keep all members within a narrow homeostatic range; even the smallest perturbance leads to extreme reactions by the system—often over what most people would consider small issues. Consider the following case, and see if you can detect the rule and the extreme reaction.

George knew his parents liked to keep the house clean, so before he went to play, he made sure his room was spotless. He hung up his clothes and put all of his toys away. One day George was playing at a friend's house when his mother called on the telephone, saying, "You need to come home right away." George told his friend goodbye and walked home. When he arrived, he found his mother in his bathroom. She said, "You left the cap off of the toothpaste again! You need to learn to keep your room clean, and when you don't, you embarrass the whole family. Now clean this mess up, and you can stay in your room for the rest of the day."

Rigid rules tend to be static and fail to change over time. As time passes, contexts change. If the system is unable to adapt to the changes by modifying old rules or adopting new ones, disequilibrium occurs increasingly frequently, and the system must become increasingly rigid to withstand it.

Roles and Expectations of Members are Either Too Rigid or Not Clearly Defined   Dysfunctional roles operate with the same effect as dysfunctional rules. Diffuse roles fail to help the individual members forge personal or family identities. Members feel very confused, often not knowing what they are supposed to be doing in the family. The following case excerpt demonstrates the chaos of a diffuse boundary between parent and child subsystems and the corresponding role confusion.

I don't know what to do. 6 months ago, my husband and I divorced, and my 12-year-old son and 15-year-old daughter have been punishing me ever since! I am a nervous wreck, so I started smoking again. I wasn't sure if I should, so I asked my son. He said that I should not start smoking, but I started last week. When he caught me, he ripped the cigarette out of my hand and threw it on the ground. I just cried. My daughter is now failing biology, so I grounded her, but she won't listen. I am going to stick to my guns though. I'm her mother! In addition to all this mess, I am dating someone but keeping it a secret from the kids. They would die if they found out. I don't think they would let me if I told them.

Individual Identity Is Not Encouraged or Even Recognized   Minuchin (1974) discussed the difference between enmeshed and disengaged families; correspondingly, Bowen (1978) spoke in terms of a lack of differentiation within families. Both were addressing the dysfunctional system's approach to individuality and autonomy. In *enmeshed families* or systems with low differentiation, autonomy is a threat to the system. All members must think the same thoughts, feel the same feelings, and behave in similar ways. It is as if all the members of the system share the same brain; whoever possesses the lead brain dictates the identity of the system. Decision making is a very trying process in which the typical response is, "I don't care. I'll do whatever you want to do." Guilt, the message that one did something wrong, and shame, the message that one is inherently faulty, are two frequently used enforcement strategies.

Disengaged families have little sense of system identity, so the individual identity is virtually all the person has to work with. The system's balance revolves around an "I'll do my thing, you do yours" mentality. Members are emotionally distant from one another and fail to provide support when needed. Since the affection and support is not found within the family and is even resisted, members typically find it within another systemic level such as school, work, church, or friends.

Communication Is Unclear, Indirect, Abusive, and/or Coercive   In systems characterized by diffuse structures and inconsistency, communication is vague, confusing, and often limited. Simply put, it is common for these systems to fail to communicate, and when they do, the signal is often very weak or full of static. In rigid systems the message is clear—LOUD AND CLEAR—delivered in an authoritarian or abusive manner. Consider the father who tells his college-bound daughter, "You don't need to stay out past 11 o'clock when you are at school. There is nothing going on after 11. If you want to stay out past 11, then you will just be hanging around with low-lifes and whores. If you are going to be doing that, then you can just come back home and live with us." He is using threats and derogatory terms to enforce a rigid family belief that fails to recognize the changing context of his daughter's life.

Theories vary widely in their concepts of what is healthy and what is not in families. How particular theorists answer the question of what is healthy guides their interventions. In the next section, we build on this foundation and address the elements of change.

THE SYSTEM CHANGE PROCESS

From a systems perspective, for a therapist to facilitate constructive change, the family must be able to see the problem as a systemic issue and not an individual one. For many families, this means that the first step toward change is to redefine the problem. Once the systems focus has been established, the emphasis becomes quite different from other nonsystems approaches in which the focus is on restoring order or returning the client to a previous state of healthy functioning. Instead, systems therapists believe that systems enter therapy when negative or positive feedback has proven ineffective in restoring dynamic equilibrium. The system must change how it addresses change; the existing strategies, intended as they are to restore equilibrium, are not doing so.

Although Table 13.1 highlights the variety of methods and approaches different family therapists employ, a few common threads of systems thinking weave through those various approaches. Goldenberg and Goldenberg (2008, p. 417) highlighted those common threads:

1. People are products of their social connections, and attempts to help them must take family relationships into account.
2. Symptomatic behavior in an individual arises from a context of relationships, and interventions to help that person are most effective when they address and alter the faulty interactive patterns from which the symptomatic behavior arises.
3. Individual symptoms are maintained externally in current family system transactions.
4. Conjoint sessions in which the family is the therapeutic unit and the focus is on family interaction are more effective in producing change than attempts to uncover intrapsychic problems in individuals by therapy via individual sessions.
5. Assessing family subsystems, including the permeability of boundaries within the family and of those between the family and the outside world, offer important clues regarding family organization and susceptibility to change.
6. The goal of family therapy is to change maladaptive or dysfunctional family interactive patterns—those that maintain dysfunctional symptoms.

By putting these ideas into practice, a family counselor emphasizes the mutual causality of symptoms and, along the same lines, the mutual nature of change. Consider the following situation that counselors frequently see:

Mr. and Mrs. Smith bring their 8-year-old son and only child, Damien, into therapy. Both parents claim Damien is a hell-raiser; he is failing in three subjects, and he bullies other children. Mom and Dad fight over how to handle Damien. Dad gets frustrated and stays at work until Damien goes to bed. Mom coddles Damien and resents Dad.

How would a systems thinker conceptualize this problem? Obviously there are many directions to go and avenues to pursue, but, generally speaking, a systems therapist would view Damien's school problems as a family issue, not solely a Damien problem. A possible hypothesis of the circular causality within this system is represented in Figure 13.4. From a systems perspective, each response is connected to the other, and no method of communication—verbal or nonverbal—exists in isolation.

Within the systems perspective, *change* means *altering the method of solving a problem*. As previously stated, change can be of the first or second order (Becvar & Becvar, 2008). A first-order change involves *clarifying and following the system's existing rules*, whereas second-order change involves *creating and implementing new rules*. In the case of Damien, if the existing family rule is that each parent independently does what (s)he believes will promote their child's achievement, Mr. Smith may decide to spend regular study time with Damien; although Mrs. Smith continues to exercise her right to buy Damien special treats such as the PlayStation, she is less likely to do so if she no longer perceives Damien to be abandoned by his father.

First-order change may seem simplistic, and often it is the overuse of first-order change that, from a systems perspective, constitutes the problem. However, first-order change often is an effective strategy, and some families too quickly implement second-order change, thereby promoting more chaos than order in the family's functioning. In the latter case, less second-order change and more first-order change is needed.

If first-order change does not restore equilibrium, the Smiths and their counselor might seek second-order change in a variety of ways. For example, Dad and Mom may agree that it is better for them to collaborate on the problem than fight. Dad may come home and take a walk with Mom to discuss the day and any problems/challenges that face the family. The family may decide that Damien is responsible for his school work and his behavior at school and that he is also responsible for any consequences that arise from his choices. Mom and Dad may provide support through helping Damien study or hiring him a tutor. They may agree to make special treats, such as a PlayStation, contingent on Damien's reasonable success in school, as reflected in his grades and other aspects of his school record. These second-order changes represent vast revisions in the philosophical approach to the problem when compared to the former methods. As Becvar and Becvar (2008) noted, "By changing the rules, we change our perception, or the way we view the problem, and new behavioral alternatives become possible in the process" (p. 107).

FIGURE 13.4 Circular causality.

Most often, by the time most families get to counseling, they have tried numerous first-order changes and, in some cases, second-order changes without succeeding in restoring equilibrium in the family. Less often, a family presents as chaotic due to repeatedly seeking second-order change, in which case first-order strategies (the establishment of reasonable rules and their consistent, fair enforcement) is more likely to restore (or create) equilibrium. As Watzlawick, Weakland, and Fisch (1974) commented, "a system which may run through all its possible internal changes (no matter how many there are) without effecting a systematic change ... is said to be caught in a Game Without End. It cannot generate from within itself the conditions for its own change" (p. 22). It is exactly in these moments of systemic paralysis that counseling is indicated.

Client's Role

Members of a system usually enter therapy with the expressed desire for the therapist to fix the identified client. Families routinely view the problem as individually based and rarely have a strong desire to explore the mutual causality of the symptoms. In the most basic of forms, the system is asking the therapist to return the identified client to the way he or she was before the symptoms spiraled out of control. Part of the client's role in systemically based therapy is the willingness to view the problem as systemically, rather than individually, based.

Resistance is a predictable and normal part of the therapeutic process that arises from the system's natural homeostatic function: The therapist perturbs by suggesting new perspectives and behaviors; the system resists. Ineffective as are the family's existing change strategies, they are likely to find the change strategies the counselor suggests to be new, alien, and unknown—potentially *further* threatening to the family's equilibrium. The role of the family member is to express the resistance so the therapist can be aware of it and seek ways to help the family get past it.

Counselor's Role

From a systems perspective, the moment the family enters counseling is the moment the counselor becomes a part of the system. The counselor presents new information into the system and acts as a disturbance to the balance of the system. The nature and method of the disturbance depends on the personality of the counselor and the specific theory of operation (see Table 13.1). However, regardless of theoretical orientation, systems therapists tend to see themselves less as change agents and more as dispensers of new information that perturbs the system to action. As Becvar and Becvar (2008) noted,

> By virtue of our presences, we help define a new context and thus a new family within which the members behave differently.... [W]e must provide new information, which the system may choose to incorporate into a self-corrective process that at the same time facilitates self-maintenance. (p. 114)

In my (KAF) attempts to think of a metaphor for the role of the systems therapist, I consulted a colleague. He likened the role of a systems practitioner to that of an agitator in a washing machine. The agitator is the pole-like mechanism in the middle of the machine drum that rotates the clothes and churns them in the water and soap solution. The really good ones are shaped with screw-like ridges that not only push the clothes from side to side, but also move them up and down. A systems therapist is like an agitator, the system is the clothing, and the therapy is the machine. The therapist's job is to move the system in various directions and agitate/perturb them enough to facilitate change. Perhaps at the end of the "cycle" of therapy, the system is a little "cleaner" than when it started.

Stages and Techniques

Stages

Each of the different models of family therapy offers a different model of the stages of therapy. For overview purposes, we refer to the general stage model that Nichols and Schwartz (2008) proposed. The stages in this model include the initial contact, the first interview, the early phase of treatment, the middle phase, and termination.

The Initial Contact   The goal of the first contact, usually over the telephone, is to set up an appointment with the entire system. The therapist needs to get only a brief overview of the reason for therapy, so as to avoid any in-depth discussion that might begin to create an alliance with the caller that excludes other members of the system. After hearing the presenting problem, the focus shifts to structural concerns such as time and place of appointment and who should attend.

Although some systems-oriented therapists will work with individual clients when necessary, they believe strongly in the value of working with the entire system whenever possible. In the initial contact, they often feel challenged to persuade the caller, who typically views the issue as an individual problem, to bring the entire family for the session. Nichols and Schwartz (2008) maintained that resistance is normal and that an understanding yet firm approach on the part of the therapist generally works through most resistance. The therapist conveys understanding of the caller's perspective and simultaneously asserts that a meeting with everyone for informational purposes is a vital first step. Although there are many ways to wrangle entire systems into therapy, the following conversation should provide an example of the delicate balance of empathy and insistence.

Caller:	Yes, I need to make an appointment to bring my son into therapy.
Therapist:	Okay, can you tell me a little about the reason for seeking counseling?
Caller:	Sure: The school counselor told me to call. He's failing math and he's just not trying. I mean …
Therapist:	How has the family responded to his grades?
Caller:	Oh, we are very angry. Especially his father! I mean, Billy, that's my son, just doesn't try.
Therapist:	I think I have enough information for now and will certainly have time to learn all about the issue when you come in. For the first session, I would like for the whole family to come.
Caller:	Oh, I don't think that's possible. His father is very busy and his sister has basketball practice.
Therapist:	I understand that everyone is very busy, but to get the best information possible and to formulate the best way to help you, I really need to talk with everyone, especially during this first session. Let's discuss what time slots would be most convenient for everyone, especially considering your husband's and daughter's demanding schedules.

In the dialogue, the counselor gathers quite a bit of information about the family. The counselor can note that the mom is calling to make the appointment, that Billy is the identified client who has seemingly broken a family rule regarding grades and "trying," that the father is "busy" and "angry," and the sister is "busy" as well. The therapist gently but firmly insists that meeting with the family is the ideal way for treatment to proceed at this point. Nichols and Schwartz advised that because families might be reluctant to come to therapy, a reminder call the day before the first session might cut down on "accidental" no-shows.

The First Interview   The goal of the first interview in systems-based counseling is essentially the same as in many of the individual-based theories discussed in this text: rapport building. The difference is that instead of connecting with an individual client, the counselor is forming a relationship with the system. The counselor orients the family to the therapy experience and, with Mom's consent, briefly discusses what they discussed during the phone conversation. Counselors make sure to give each member a proportionate amount of time to discuss their view of the problem and also to spend some time discussing the family's strengths. While the family is detailing various views of the problem, the therapist is gathering information about the family dynamics by paying attention to who speaks and in what order, who sits next to whom, how differences in opinion are tolerated, who is the identified client, how the family has tried to handle this problem before, and any other systemic dynamics. Each dynamic the counselor observes provides an additional piece to the puzzle that is this particular family's unique system. Counselors may use graphic representations of generational patterns, such as family maps or genograms, to gain a perspective on family dynamics. Let us continue to follow the case of Billy's family during the first session.

The counselor greets the family in the waiting room. The counselor notes that Dad and Brianna, the daughter, are sitting side-by-side on the couch, and that Billy and Mom are squeezed into a loveseat across the room. Dad looks frustrated, Mom looks worried, Brianna looks disgusted, and Billy looks defeated. The counselor collects the paperwork the family has completed while waiting and invites the family into the counseling room. Dad and Brianna choose the loveseat, while Billy sits in an oversized chair. Mom moves a chair from across the room to sit next to Billy.

Therapist:	Welcome. I spoke to you (Mom) on the phone and you stated there was some concern about Billy's recent grade in math. That is about all I know about this situation, so I would like to give each of you an opportunity to discuss what you see as the important issues in your family at this time. Who would like to start? [The therapist lets the family know what she knows from the first contact so everyone knows where to begin. The initial invitation to discuss "important issues in your family" is a subtle message that emphasizes the system rather than the presenting, individually-based problem. Although it is doubtful the family will shift this soon, building a gradual transition to a systems perspective is often more effective than a quick jump.]
Brianna:	I'll start. Billy just needs to try a bit more. All he does is hang out with his creepy friends and play video games. Me, I study four or five hours a day and still manage to play varsity basketball.
Therapist:	It seems as though you are very disciplined as well as talented. How did you learn self-discipline? [The therapist avoids focusing on the presenting

problem and instead connects with a resistant family member by focusing on her strengths. Her statement and next answer begin to illuminate some key family rules about self-discipline.]

Brianna: I guess I just do it, you know. Mom is real good at helping me when I need help, but you have to ask.

Dad: Well, I think this is a load of crap. He's lazy and needs to pull himself up and work. I tell him that, but he just ignores me.

Therapist: It sounds like you have a pretty good idea of what you want to have happen, but your current strategies are not helping you get there. [Once again, instead of focusing on the specific issue, the therapist personalizes each person's unique role.]

The dialogue continues and at the end of the session, the therapist is able to construct a genogram based on information gathered (see Figure 13.5).

Through examination of the genogram, counselor and family can learn about patterns within the system. Triangles can also become apparent. For example, the following patterns emerge from Billy's family genogram.

- The three lines connecting Mom and Billy denote an enmeshed, or overinvolved relationship. This pattern is multigenerational, as evidenced by the same pattern between Mom and maternal grandmother.
- The two lines connecting Dad and Brianna denote a close relationship. This pattern is also replicated in Dad's family of origin between paternal grandfather and Dad's sister, Sylvia.
- The dotted line between Dad and Billy represents a distant or diffuse relationship. Dad reported a similar type of relationship with his father.

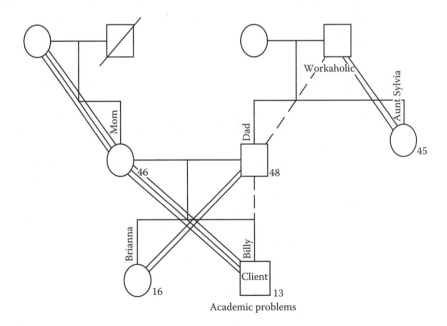

FIGURE 13.5   Billy's family genogram.

An abundance of useful information can surface from a well-constructed genogram. A counselor can add other demographic information and additional generations to further illuminate family patterns. For a more in-depth discourse on genograms consult Gerson, McGoldrick, and Petry's (2008) book *Genograms: Assessment and Intervention*.

The Early Phase of Treatment   The early phase of treatment is marked by a shift in focus characterized by a move away from rapport building and toward a stance of perturbing the system so change can occur. Remember, the system usually enters counseling because its dynamic equilibrium has been disrupted and its self-correcting method of feedback is not reestablishing equilibrium. The system might be experiencing a negative feedback loop that is restricting the possibility of constructive reorganization or a positive feed-back loop that is stuck in only amplifying the deviation. The good news is that the system will act out its pattern in real time during the sessions, which is one reason why it is important to have the entire system in the room. One of the easiest ways to challenge the system is to concentrate on the system's conceptualization of the problem.

Tasks in this phase of treatment include the emphasis on circular or mutual causality of the family's problem and influencing the family to work for change within the session and at home. Homework assignments that target changes in patterns are most effective. Billy's family has now entered the early phase of treatment, and their struggles are described below.

After working and connecting with the family, the counselor generated the following hypothesis about the system: When the system is perturbed, the members use the following strategies to restore balance: Dad uses anger and shame and then withdraws; Mom uses nurturing and, to some extent, "babying"; Brianna uses aloofness and often follows Dad's lead, and Billy hits his "shut down" switch. When the usual strategies fail to work, the system intensifies its strategies, creating a positive feedback loop that has served only to amplify the disequilibrating forces: The family is caught in a cycle. The therapist knows that because of mutual causality, it does not matter where the intervention occurs within the cycle, as long as the cyclical nature of the interactional dynamics is addressed. The following dialog provides one example of a systemic challenge.

Therapist:	It seems to me that this family is a little stuck. All families get stuck, but I am wondering about your perspective about *how you* are stuck.
Dad:	Well, he just won't listen to me, and he is so damn lazy.
Mom:	Oh, honey, you are being too hard on him. [The therapist hypothesizes that the tension between Dad and Billy leads to a triangulation of Mom to cool off the conflict.]
Therapist:	It seems like the two of you are going in two different directions. Dad, you try the hostility thing, and Mom, you try to smooth it over. When they do that, what do you think of all that, Billy?
Billy:	They usually start fighting, and I walk away.
Therapist:	Dad, when you yell, Mom jumps in to break it up, and Billy walks away. The problem never gets resolved. Because each of you plays a role in the stuckness, each of you will need to do something different to get a different result. [The therapist is noting the mutual causality of the problem and challenges each member to change.]

The Middle Phase of Treatment   Once the therapist has succeeded in formulating a hypothesis regarding the patterns within the family system and has begun work on perturbing the system to facilitate change, the middle phase is largely devoted to encouraging interactions among members and testing out new ways of being. Once the family gets used to the process, the therapist can move to the periphery of the system and be less directive and challenging. The therapist becomes a system process observer, pointing out interactions that experiment with new ways of relating and alerting the family to interactions that reflect a return to old patterns. Homework is especially important in this phase so that family members can experience new learning directly and generalized it to the "real world."

Therapist:	Well, it has been six weeks since we started therapy. Billy, how are things going?
Billy:	Okay, I guess. My grades in math are getting better.
Therapist:	What is different?
Billy:	Well, since we've been coming here, my family listens a little more to me.
Therapist:	You seem very observant. Can you describe the changes you have seen in each member of everyone in your family? [Here the therapist turns the table on the family. The person whom they initially labeled as "the problem," the therapist is now treating as a valuable source of information about the family. The risk of the family shutting the process down or reacting in a negative way is minimized because the focus is on positive change.]
Billy:	Hmmm.... Well, Mom is not hovering as much. You know, coming by my room every 5 minutes checking to see if I'm all right. I think that homework where she kept a log of her "fly bys" really helped her. I actually go ask her stuff more often now because I have more room to breathe. [Note the new pattern that has developed.] Brianna has been around more and seems happier. She's really smart and has taken a lot of the classes I am in right now. She is less bossy and more helpful. Dad has really changed! Instead of yelling at me, he spends a half hour with me every night just going over stuff. That's been pretty cool. I try to get my homework done so we can just hang out some of the time instead of spending it all on math.
Therapist:	Wow, very nice! That is a lot of change in four weeks. It sounds as if you have made changes, too. Without your willingness to be open to doing something different, this whole new pattern could not have developed.

Termination   Termination occurs when the family decides that change is not necessary or that the problem has been resolved. In a sense, termination begins with the first contact, so therapists must be mindful and honor the process of ending the therapy. Termination issues can be discussed as family functioning is assessed. Questions such as, "What are you doing differently?" "How have things changed?" "How will you know if you are sliding back into the old pattern?" are important to the process of termination. Highlighting the changes the family has made and the skills they are using to make them provides the family with resources upon which they can draw when future problems occur.

Techniques

Although we have discussed some systems therapy techniques, systems theorists have created a vast number of innovative techniques that focus on illuminating and modifying interactional patterns within the system. We discuss a few of these below to give you a taste of what systems therapists use, and we encourage you to consult specific books for a more comprehensive explanation of systems therapy techniques (see Sherman & Fredman, 1986; Watts, 1999).

Reframing Reframing is a verbal technique designed to enable system members to shift their perspective on a problem and, thereby, generate new ways of responding to it. In a sense, it means looking at the issue at hand from a different viewpoint, often putting a more positive spin on the issue. For example, the father of two sons, ages five and eight, complains that his sons do not listen to authority. The therapist notices that the sons do have conflicts but work hard to figure problems out for themselves. The therapist reframes disobedience as "independent thinkers who like to solve problems on their own" and explores with the father the parenting skills that encouraged such healthy behavior in his sons. The outcome: Instead of getting into a power struggle within the family, the therapist helped the system see the problem in terms of assets.

Sculpting Sculpting is an experiential technique that illuminates each member's perspective on the dynamics of the system. The therapist invites each member in turn to be the "sculptor," physically arranging the members of the family in the room and perhaps giving them a line or motto to say. The result is a symbolic structure representing the sculptor's perspective on the family's interaction patterns. Consider the case example of a 10-year-old boy named Sam, sculpting his family.

Sam:	I would put my brother, Ben, right here in the middle of the room.
Therapist:	How would he look? Arrange his body in some gesture that demonstrates his role in the family.
Sam:	I don't understand.
Therapist:	Okay, how would you describe Ben?
Sam:	Oh, I guess he's all right, but he thinks he is real great and knows a lot more than me.
Therapist:	I see. So if I walked in the room and saw your sculpture, how would Ben be posed so I would look at him and say, "Oh, that guy thinks he's pretty smart"?
Sam:	I get it. I'm going to have Ben smirking and raising his finger and saying over and over, "I'm number 1!"
Therapist:	I think you've got a handle on this.
Sam:	My Mom would be standing with her arm around Ben looking proud.
Therapist:	Does she have something to say?
Sam:	How about, "Ben is number 1!" My Dad, hmmmm, well, he is so worried all the time. I think I'll have him walking around in circles saying, "Where is all the money?" I guess that's it.
Therapist:	Not yet, Sam. Where are you in this sculpture?
Sam:	Oh, I forgot me. I am in the corner. I think I would look sad. Maybe I would wave every once in a while to get people to look at me, but no one notices.
Therapist:	Okay, everyone, take your places and when Sam says, "Go," everyone act out their roles.

Just reading the preceding dialog, you might have a sense of the vivid and powerful family dynamics at play in sculpting. After family members enact the sculpture, the counselor leads them in discussing their feelings and thoughts about the role they played and any new insights they have about the sculptor's perspective, how their family works, and/or new ideas about how they might like to be different in the family.

Prescriptions Prescriptions are instructions the counselor gives the family that are designed to disequilibriate the system and promote an alternative to the current pattern. In a sense, the therapist is creating a positive feedback loop to amplify any deviation from the current pattern. Following are a few of the many types of systems therapy prescriptions.

Paradoxical. With this type of prescription, the therapist may instruct the system to create and/or maintain the symptom for a specific period of time. For example, if the problem is anger, the assignment might be fighting as actively or more actively than usual—only at a prescribed time and duration, such as 7:00–7:30 p.m. on Wednesdays. The effect of this type of prescription often results in an increase in awareness about the futility of the dysfunctional pattern and, even more importantly, that the system controls the pattern.

Counter Systemic. This prescription provides a direct contradiction to the system's ordinary pattern. For example, a mother who complains about the irresponsibility of the children—but who also cleans up after them—is told that she has been fired from maid duty for the rest of the week. During the next session, the therapist processes changes that occurred in the system. Did the Mom find it hard to stay off the job (this highlights Mom's role in the pattern)? How did the other members try to get Mom back on the job? How did other members respond over time to the vacant job and the responsibilities left open by the vacancy?

Restructuring. This prescription injects new skills or new patterns into the system. For example, the counselor may prescribe parenting classes for the parents with the plan that the classes will provide new information to the parental subsystem that may perturb the system and lead to constructive change. The therapist may prescribe responsibilities in the family that may elicit cooperation among disengaged members (cleaning the yard together) or an individual sense of responsibility among enmeshed members (each person is responsible for waking oneself for school or work).

CONTRIBUTIONS AND LIMITATIONS

Interface With Recent Developments in the Mental Health Field

The Nature–Nurture Question

Regarding the nature–nurture question, systems theorists postulate that a person's identity and personality are formed through the dynamic interplay of one's genetic makeup, environment, and one's perception of both. One's genes and environment provide the individual with numerous opportunities and limits, and if one fails to perceive the given opportunities or limits, then they hardly matter. Family systems theorists hold that people are proactive beings, neither predetermined by genes nor completely determined by the environment. Instead, a system perspective focuses on the interaction among the variety of influences within the system.

Systems theorists tend to be quick to point out a finding of research on the genetic basis of psychological dysfunction: that of everyone with a particular genetic makeup often associated with a psychological disorder, not everyone develops the disorder. Systems theorists look to the system of which an individual is a part and consider how the system might be contributing to whether and how the individual is manifesting a disorder for which they are known or suspected to have a genetic basis.

DSM–IV–TR *Diagnosis*

Regarding diagnosis, the traditional diagnostic process of the *DSM* is rooted in labeling individually-based pathology. Rendering a diagnosis for an individual within a system using a classification that does not take the system into account is, therefore, categorically inconsistent with systems thinking. Furthermore, the diagnostic "symptom as bad" connotation does not mesh well with the system perspective that views symptoms only as a piece of the greater systemic balance. Becvar and Becvar (2008) posed the question of whether diagnosis is even an ethical behavior for a systems practitioner. We gathered a few quotes on diagnosis from prominent systems thinkers who have generated their own systems-based perspectives:

> Part of the difficulty in beginning therapy properly has been the confusion between diagnosis for institutional reasons and diagnosis for therapy reasons. For an institution and for medical insurance reasons, it was necessary to see a person alone and classify him or her as a diagnostic type according to some scheme, such as the DSM. That procedure was irrelevant to therapy and could even handicap the therapist. (Haley, 1987, p. 11)
>
> An individual diagnosis is a static label, which emphasizes the individual's most salient psychological characteristics and implies that these are resistant to changes in the social context. In family therapy, individuals and families are seen as relating and changing in accordance with their social context. The advantage of an evolving diagnosis related to context is that it provides openings for therapeutic intervention. (Minuchin, 1974, p. 131)
>
> There are three problems with making concrete diagnoses. First, is that our language is not structured to describe process. The result is that a diagnosis may have iatrogenic effects on the life of the family by reifying the problems. The second is that diagnostic terms are expended metaphor, an attempt to make one kind of reality conform to another type of reality. The third problem is that each family has a private culture and language system to which the therapist has only partial access. The diagnostic process may be crippling to the family and/or mystifying. (Whitaker & Keith, 1981, p. 197)

Obviously, traditional diagnosis does not fit well within the systems approach. However, systems practitioners do make use of what they call interactional or relational diagnosis (Kaslow, 1996). Each systems theorist will emphasize different aspects of the system, but most will look for the general characteristics of the healthy family and will also assess how the family responds to the therapeutic encounter, especially toward the entrance of the therapist into the system. Minuchin (1974) pointed out that interactional diagnosis comprises every information-gathering technique necessary for the therapist to get an accurate read on the context of the family's functioning. The foci can include communication patterns, subsystems, boundaries, nonverbal cues, the family's reaction to questioning and probing (a systemic perturbance), and multigenerational patterns. The last important point concerning interactional diagnosis is that it is always changing. As the family changes, usually experiencing morphogenesis, new boundaries and rules form, and a new dynamic equilibrium is established. Systems counselors understand that interactional diagnosis involves ongoing assessment of the system. Fortunately for systems practitioners, the *DSM* committees have agreed to consider interactional diagnosis for the next edition of the *DSM*.

Pharmacotherapy

Regarding the prescription of medication, systems purists may consider medication as treating the symptom instead of dealing with the family dynamics that create the dysfunction. However, to ignore the research on the benefits of medication for a number of disorders exposes the client to unneeded suffering and opens the counselor's door to malpractice suits. Ethical systems clinicians are encouraged to form cooperative relationships with psychiatrists when a family enters counseling with a preexisting psychiatric relationship and to refer families to psychiatrists who understand and respect the systems perspective (Brock & Barnard, 2008). Just as a diagnosis and medication can be a distraction from what systems counselors consider to be the relevant therapeutic focus, a turf battle between therapist and psychiatrist can be equally distracting from and disruptive to treatment. Therapists can work with clients taking medication as long as all parties understand that the medication is not a cure-all for the problems within the system.

Managed Care and Brief Therapy

Overall, systems approaches are time-limited, problem solving forms of therapy that lend themselves to brief treatment. One could conclude from the literature that the systems approach was a brief-oriented modality from the inception of the theory. When systemic thinkers were trying to gain a foothold in the professional therapeutic community, the battle was with the lengthy treatment regimen of psychoanalysis, so shortening the span of treatment was one way to differentiate the systems perspective. Whereas some approaches outlined in Table 13.1, such as strategic, structural, or MRI's brief therapy, are more time-limited than others, most systems therapists treat the system by perturbing the system, exploring new alternatives to dealing with the challenge, and then letting the family terminate therapy and work on the changes themselves. The literature contains many examples of brief family systems applications (Berg & de Shazer, 1993; Epstein, Bishop, Keitner, & Miller, 1990; O'Hanlon & O'Hanlon, 2002).

Technical Eclecticism

The systems perspective serves as the unifying force that connects all theories outlined in Table 13.1. Once proficient in one of those approaches, a therapist could conceivably draw from the techniques of other approaches and still maintain theoretical consistency due to the shared assumptions of systems thinking. Because of the unifying theme of systems thinking, practitioners of the various approaches might very well have a better chance at developing an integrative approach than would the many and diverse individual-based theorists. In fact, a number of theorists and practitioners have already advocated for an integrative approach that encompasses and unites all the systems approaches (Lebow, 1984; Nichols and Everett, 1986; Pinsof, 1995). It will be interesting to observe the growth of systems theory over the next few decades to see if theorists realize their dream of integration.

Diversity Issues

Systems theorists have devoted a substantial literature to exploring cultural factors in couple and family therapy. Excellent books by Ho, Rasheed, and Rasheed (2003) and McGoldrick, Giordano, and Garcia-Preto (2005) give readers an overview of specific cultural outlooks and how to integrate various cultural perspectives into a systems framework. Systems practitioners appreciate that cultural influences are complex forces that must be examined from the family's context to fully appreciate their role in the dynamics of the system. McGoldrick, Giordano, and Garcia-Preto (2005) encouraged therapists to adopt the role of a "culture broker, helping family members to recognize their own ethnic values and to resolve the conflicts that evolve out of different perceptions and experiences" (p. 31). Pakes and Roy-Chowdhury (2007) emphasized that culture is embedded into the systemic balance and encouraged counselors to actively explore interconnected and disconnected elements of the interaction between counselor and systemic cultures.

Gender issues have been a concern historically for systems theorists and practitioners. At the inception of systems thinking, the family system reflected a model nuclear family: husband, wife, and child. Since the early days of family therapy, the 1950s and 1960s when model families were of the "Leave It to Beaver" and "Father Knows Best" variety, times have changed. From a gender perspective, many of the foundational ideas of systems thinking pathologized the roles of women and failed to acknowledge modern family configurations. Early writers in systems thinking linked mother behaviors to dysfunction, putting forth concepts like "the schizophrenogenic mother" (Fromm-Reichmann, 1948) and stereotyping mothers as overprotective and fathers as distant.

Sexual orientation is an issue that has received much attention within the systems framework over the past decade. Systems theorists have addressed the complex impact that sexual orientation, like any other aspect of a system, has on the system. They have approached the topic not in terms of sexual orientation as good or bad but in terms of the impact of acceptance or rejection of sexual orientation on the system. Authors have explored such diverse topics as system responses to transgender issues (Lev, 2004; Zamboni, 2006), gay and lesbian relationships (Adams, Jaques, & May, 2004; Duffey, 2006), and the ethics involved in working with these issues and related treatments such as conversion therapy to attempt to change a person's homosexual orientation to heterosexual (Janson & Steigerwald, 2002; Steigerwald & Janson, 2003). Notably, systems theorists have recently launched the *Journal for GLBT Family Studies* to focus specifically on issues related to this population.

Although many people would note that gender bias predominantly hurts women, systems theorists have made a concerted effort to demonstrate that gender bias injures all members of the system, both males and females. Lewis (1992) provided excellent guidance to system therapists by encouraging them to practice gender-sensitive therapy. Some of the guidelines include:

- Treating male and female clients equally.
- Avoiding gender stereotypes in diagnosis and treatment.
- Being aware of one's own gender beliefs and biases.
- Monitoring the use and misuse of power within the therapeutic relationship.
- Understanding the system's definition of gender roles.

If you are interested in further reading on gender issues in family therapy, Luepnitz (1992) conducted a feminist critique of the major family system theories.

Regarding spirituality, one content analysis of the major marriage and family journals revealed only 13 articles related to spirituality and/or religion (Stander, Piercy, MacKinnon, & Helmeke, 1994). This finding led the researchers to conclude that the profession of family therapy viewed spirituality as being outside the scope of therapeutic practice. However, in the past 10 years, the amount of literature exploring the role of spirituality in the context of systems practice has increased dramatically (Frame, 2000; Hodge, 2000; Turner, Fox, & Kiser, 2007; Walsh, 2008; Weld & Eriksen, 2006). The overall conclusion from the theoretical and practical literature is that spirituality plays a potentially significant role in the family system that presents for therapy. Therapists who dismiss or ignore the role of spirituality run the risk of operating with less than complete information regarding that system.

The Effectiveness of Psychotherapy

Despite the relative newness of the systems perspective, a large amount of outcome research exists on it. Although very few studies exist that compare different forms of family therapy, outcome research supports the efficacy of family therapy when compared to no treatment or individual-focused forms of therapy (Baucom, Shoham, Mueser, Daiuto, & Stickle, 1998; Dunn & Schwebel, 1995; Pinsof, Wynne, & Hambright, 1996; Shadish, Ragsdale, Glaser, & Montgomery, 1995).

Friedlander, Wildman, Heatherington, and Skowron (1994) provided an excellent overview of the literature on family therapy research and concluded that although much is known about the process and efficacy of family approaches, much also is not known. They encouraged future researchers to focus on the family members' cognitive, emotional, and behavioral experience in therapy, how change occurs in more experiential forms of family therapy, and the role of cultural issues in therapy.

Regarding Asay and Lambert's (1999) findings on the effectiveness of therapy, systems theory would concur with the important elements noted in that research. The importance of the therapeutic relationship is a key aspect of all the systems theories, with most theorists viewing the counselor as entering temporarily into the family system. Techniques play an important role. Perhaps more than most of the theorists we discuss in this book, systems theorists appreciate the impact of extratherapeutic influences on the change process, particularly contextual factors such as the cultural and social systems in which a family is embedded.

Limitations

The most glaring weakness of systems thinking is derived from its philosophical grounding in mutual causality. As an outcome of the theory's emphasis that behavior is not linearly caused and that interactions among members of a system produce systemic behavior, researchers and practitioners in the field of family violence have historically criticized systems theorists as participating in victim blaming. As one of those family violence researchers and clinicians, I (KAF) am concerned about many systems thinkers who continue to conduct family therapy with violent families despite well-established therapeutic contraindications and despite the potential risks to the family members.

The literature suggests that the dynamics of domestic violence do not follow the mutual or circular causality model and, instead, are much more linear in nature. The batterer co-opts the power in the system, and this dynamic of control becomes the pattern that the batterer dictates (Jackson & Oates, 1998; Jacobson & Gottman, 1998; Jones, 1994). Avis (1992) asserted that:

> as long as we train therapists in systemic theories without balancing that training with an understanding of the non-neutrality of power dynamics, we will continue producing family therapists who collude in the maintenance of male power and are dangerous to the women and children with whom they work. (p. 231)

Since family violence is a concern that has reached epidemic proportions in the United States (United States Department of Justice, 1998), family therapists will routinely confront issues of spousal physical and sexual abuse and child neglect and physical and sexual abuse. Until systems thinkers consider some of the issues inherent in situations of family violence, the treatment may not only be ineffective with these populations but may also lead to more violence. For a more in-depth understanding of the treatment of domestic violence, consult such sources as Fall and Howard (2004), Pence and Paymar (1993), and Wilson (1997).

In our view, another weakness of the systemically oriented professional organizations is their retention of the term *marriage* in their titles. Until such time as gay marriage might become universal, that retention not only reflects heterosexism (failing to recognize homosexuals as legitimate consumers of relationship therapy) but also therapeutically disenfranchises dating or cohabiting couples who manifest the full range of systemic issues, including physical and sexual abuse. It is our personal, and probably improbable, dream that AAMFT change its name to AART: the American Association for Relationship Therapy.

Contributions

Most notably, systems thinking represents a paradigm shift in the way mental health professionals view the human change process. Systems thinking spawned numerous independent theories based on the common philosophical assumptions of the systems approach. The shift in conceptualization from an identified client to a family based perspective on pathology and growth has produced a lasting impact on the treatment of families and couples and has led to the establishment of a distinct profession centered around the systems perspective. The next section details the gains made in this area over the past 60 years.

CURRENT STATUS

The practice of family therapy has come a long way since the first clinics opened in Europe and later in the United States. The American Association for Marriage and Family Therapy oversees the credentialing of family therapists and has established training guidelines that include attention to theory (systems and developmental concepts), practice, research, and ethics (AAMFT, 1994). Many marriage and family training programs require 60 hours of graduate coursework at the master's level, with additional coursework required for a doctorate. The AAMFT's Commission on Accreditation for Marriage and Family Education (COAMFTE) accredits master's and doctoral degree programs, and, to date, 37 states have accredited institutions. In addition to university degrees, numerous training institutes, such as the Philadelphia Guidance Center, the Minuchin Center for the Family, and the Menninger Foundation, all provide advanced training in family therapy. Most states offer the Licensed Marriage and Family Therapist (LMFT) credential that recognizes the practice of family therapy as a field with distinct training requirements.

To guide the practice of family therapists, numerous journals address continuing education needs. Some of the more popular include *American Journal of Family Therapy, Family Process, International Journal of Family Therapy, Journal of Marital and Family Therapy, The Family Journal,* and *Journal of Marriage and the Family.* Professional organizations at the national, regional, and state levels routinely hold conferences devoted to the discussion of the latest research and practice trends in couple and family therapy. The AAMFT and the International Association of Marriage and Family Counselors (IAMFC) have written ethical codes specific to the practice of marriage and family therapy (AAMFT, 2001; IAMFC, 2005).

DO YOU HAVE TO HOLD AN LMFT LICENSE TO PRACTICE FAMILY OR COUPLE'S THERAPY?

The answer to this question is more a question of competency than what license one holds. A person with an LMFT has met the curriculum, exam, and supervision requirements and is deemed competent to treat couples and families. However, many graduate programs in counseling, psychology, social work, and psychiatry do not meet the AAMFT requirements, and yet their graduates can be competent to treat couples and families. The primary concern is whether your license allows you to practice with this population. In most areas, it is extremely rare to be excluded from treating a population based on license type, so the real question becomes, "Are you competent to treat this population?" A safe and ethical way to answer the question is to consider the triad of competency. The triad consists of three basic questions: (a) Do you have graduate coursework training in this area? (b) Do you have supervised experience with this population? and (c) Do you regularly seek out continuing education in this area? If these three criteria are met, one could conclude basic competency to treat the population.

SUMMARY

Systems theory represents a shift in thinking about human growth and dysfunction from the individual to the larger systems in which the individual is embedded. Systems thinking rests on a set of assumptions about the mutual causality of behavior and the interdependence of members of any given system. The systems approach is actually an umbrella term that connects many diverse approaches to this type of therapy. Family and couple therapy has blossomed into a distinct professional identity represented by professional organizations, training centers, and licensure requirements.

RECOMMENDED RESOURCES

Books

Due to the vast amount of material devoted to general systems theory and each theory under its umbrella, we decided to do something a little different with this chapter's recommended print resources. Resources are included for most of the systemic approaches.

General Systems

Becvar, D. S., & Becvar, R. J. (2008). *Family therapy: A systemic integration* (7th ed.). Boston, MA: Allyn & Bacon. This text is great for an introduction to systems thinking, and it also goes into depth on several applications and descriptions. It serves as a very nice resource book.

Bertalanffy, L. von (1968). *General systems theory*. New York, NY: Braziller. This seminal work on general systems theory provides an in-depth description of the theory applied to various types of systems. The reader can really get a sense of the roots of family therapy when reading this book.

REFERENCES

Adams, J. L., Jaques, J. D., & May, K. M. (2004). Counseling gay and lesbian couples: Theoretical considerations. *The Family Journal, 12*, 40–42.

Alexander, J. F., & Parsons, B. V. (1982). *Functional family therapy*. Pacific Grove, CA: Brooks/Cole.

American Association for Marriage and Family Therapy. (1994). *Membership requirements and applications*. Washington, DC: Author.

American Association for Marriage and Family Therapy. (2001). *Code of ethics*. Washington, DC: Author.

Asay, T. P., & Lambert, M. J. (1999). The empirical case for the common factors in therapy: Quantitative findings. In M. A. Hubble, B. L. Duncan, & S. D. Miller (Eds.), *The heart and soul of change* (pp. 23–55). Washington, DC: American Psychological Association.

Avis, J. M. (1992). Where are all the family therapists? Abuse and violence within families and family therapy's response. *Journal of Marital and Family Therapy, 18*, 225–232.

Bateson, G., Jackson, D. D., Haley, J., & Weakland, J. (1956). Towards a theory of schizophrenia. *Behavioral Sciences, 1*, 251–264.

Baucom, D., Shoham, V., Mueser, K. T., Daiuto, A. D., & Stickle, T. R. (1998). Empirically supported couple and family interventions for marital distress and adult mental health problems. *Journal of Consulting and Clinical Psychology, 64*, 333–342.

Beavers, W. B., & Hampson, R. B. (1990). *Successful families: Assessment and intervention*. New York, NY: W. W. Norton.

Becvar, D. S., & Becvar, R. J. (2008). *Family therapy: A systemic integration* (7th ed.). Boston, MA: Allyn & Bacon.

Berg, I. K., & de Shazer, S. (1993). Making numbers talk: Language in therapy. In S. Friedman (Ed.), *The new language of change* (pp. 5–24). New York, NY: Guilford Press.

Bertalanffy, L. von. (1950). An outline of general systems theory. *British Journal for the Philosophy of Science, 1*, 139–164.

Bertalanffy, L. von. (1968). *General systems theory*. New York, NY: Braziller.

Bodin, A. M. (1981). The interactional view: Family therapy approaches of the mental research institute. In A. S. Gurman & D. P. Kniskern (Eds.), *Handbook of family therapy* (pp. 267–309). New York, NY: Brunner/Mazel.

Bowen, M. (1978). *Family therapy in clinical practice*. New York, NY: Jason Aronson.

Brock, G. W., & Barnard, C. P. (2008). *Procedures in marriage and family therapy* (4th ed.). Boston, MA: Allyn & Bacon.

Broderick, C. B., & Schraeder, S. S. (1991). The history of professional marriage and family therapy. In A. S. Gurman & D. P. Kniskern (Eds.), *Handbook of family therapy* (Vol. 2, pp. 5–38). New York, NY: Brunner/Mazel.

Brown, D. (1991). *Human universals*. Philadelphia, PA: Temple University Press.

Butzlaff, R. L., & Hooley, J. M. (1998). Expressed emotion and psychiatric relapse. *Archives of General Psychiatry, 55*, 547–552.

Duffey, T. (2006). When a spouse comes out: As told from a straight spouse's point of view. *The Family Journal, 14*, 88–91.

Dunn, R. L., & Schwebel, A. I. (1995). Meta-analytic review of marital therapy outcome research. *Journal of Family Psychology, 9,* 58–68.

Epstein, N. B., Bishop, D. S., Keitner, G. I., & Miller, I. W. (1990). A systems therapy: Problem centered systems therapy of the family. In R. A. Wells & V. J. Gianetti (Eds.), *Handbook of brief psychotherapies* (pp. 405–436). New York, NY: Plenum.

Fall, K. A., & Howard, S. (2004). *Alternatives to domestic violence* (Rev. ed.). Philadelphia, PA: Accelerated Development.

Fenell, D. L., & Weinhold, B. K. (2003). *Counseling families* (3rd ed.). Denver, CO: Love.

Frame, M. W. (2000). The spiritual genogram in family therapy. *Journal for Marital and Family Therapy, 26,* 211–216.

Framo, J. (1992). *Family-of-origin therapy: An intergenerational approach.* New York, NY: Brunner/Mazel.

Friedlander, M. L., Wildman, J., Heatherington, L., & Skowron, E. A. (1994). What we do and don't know about the process of family therapy. *Journal of Family Psychology, 8,* 390–416.

Friedman, S. (1994). *Secret loves: Women with two lives.* New York, NY: Crown.

Fromm-Reichmann, F. (1948). Notes on the development of treatment of schizophrenics by psychoanalytic psychotherapy. *Psychiatry, 11,* 253–273.

Gerson, R., McGoldrick, M., & Petry, S. (2008). *Genograms: Assessment and intervention.* New York, NY: W. W. Norton.

Goldenberg, I., & Goldenberg, H. (2008). Family therapy. In R. J. Corsini & D. Wedding (Eds.), *Current psychotherapies* (8th ed., pp. 402–436). Itasca, IL: F. E. Peacock.

Gottman, J. (1979). *Marital interaction: Experimental investigations.* New York, NY: Academic Press.

Gottman, J. (1994). *What predicts divorce?* Hillsdale, NJ: Erlbaum.

Gottman, J. M., & Gottman, J. S. (2008). Gottman method couple therapy. In A. S. Gurman (Ed.), *Clinical handbook of couple therapy* (4th ed., pp. 138–164). New York, NY: Guilford Press.

Gottman, J., & Krokoff, I. (1989). Marital interaction and satisfaction: A longitudinal view. *Journal of Consulting and Clinical Psychology, 57,* 47–52.

Guerin, P. J., Fogarty, T. F., Fay, L. F., Kautto, J., & Kautto, J. G. (1996). *Working with relationship triangles.* New York, NY: Guilford Press.

Haley, J. (1987). *Problem-solving therapy* (2nd ed.). San Francisco, CA: Jossey-Bass.

Heylighen, F., & Joslyn, C. (2001). Cybernetics and second order cybernetics. In R. A. Meyers (Ed.), *Encyclopedia of physical science & technology* (Vol. 4, 3rd ed., pp. 155–170). New York, NY: Academic Press.

Ho, M. K., Rasheed, J. M., & Rasheed, M. N. (2003). *Family therapy with ethnic minorities* (2nd ed.). Thousand Oaks, CA: Sage.

Hodge, D. (2000). Spiritual ecomaps: A new diagrammatic tool for assessing marital and family spirituality. *Journal of Marital and Family Therapy, 26,* 217–228.

International Association of Marriage and Family Counselors (2005). *Ethical codes and standards.* Alexandria, VA: Author.

Jackson, N. A., & Oates, G. C. (Eds.). (1998). *Violence in intimate relationships.* Woburn, MA: Butterworth-Heinemann.

Jacobson, N., & Gottman, J. (1998). *When men batter women.* New York, NY: Simon & Schuster.

Janson, G., & Steigerwald, F. (2002). Family counseling and ethical challenges with gay, lesbian, bisexual and transgendered (GLBT) clients: More questions than answers. *The Family Journal, 10,* 415–418.

Jones, A. (1994). *Next time, she'll be dead.* Boston, MA: Beacon.

Kaslow, F. (Ed.). (1996). *Handbook of relational diagnosis and dysfunctional family patterns.* New York, NY: Wiley.

Kerr, M. E., & Bower, M. (1988). *Family evaluation.* New York, NY: W. W. Norton.

Lebow, J. L. (1984). On the value of integrating approaches to family therapy. *Journal of Marital and Family Therapy, 19,* 127–138.

Lev, A. I. (2004). *Transgender emergence: Therapeutic guidelines for working with gender variant people and their families.* Binghamton, NY: Haworth.

Lewis, J. A. (1992). Gender sensitivity and family empowerment. *Topics in Family Psychology, 1,* 1–7.

Luepnitz, D. A. (1992). *The family interpreted: Psychoanalysis, feminism and family therapy.* New York, NY: Basic Books.

Maruyama, M. (1963). The second cybernetics: Deviation-amplifying mutual causal processes. *American Scientist, 51,* 164–179.

McGoldrick, M., Giordano, J., & Garcia-Preto, N. (2005). Overview: Ethnicity and family therapy. In M. McGoldrick, J. Giordano, & N. Garcia-Preto (Eds.), *Ethnicity and family therapy* (pp. 1–43). New York, NY: Guilford Press.

Minuchin, P. (1985). Families and individual development: Provocations from the field of family therapy. *Child Development, 56,* 289–302.

Minuchin, S. (1974). *Families and family therapy.* Cambridge, MA: Harvard University Press.

Nichols, M. P., & Schwartz, R. C. (2008). *Family therapy: Concepts and methods* (8th ed.). Boston, MA: Allyn & Bacon.

Nichols, W. C., & Everett, C. A. (1986). *Systemic family therapy: An integrative approach.* New York, NY: Guilford Press.

O'Hanlon, S., & O'Hanlon, B. (2002). Solution oriented therapy with families. In J. Carlson & D. Kjos (Eds.), *Theories and strategies of family therapy* (pp. 190–215). Boston, MA: Allyn & Bacon.

Olsen, D. H., & Gorall, D. M. (2002). Circumplex model of marital and family systems. In F. Walsh (Ed.), *Normal family processes* (3rd ed., pp. 459–486). New York, NY: Guilford Press.

Pakes, K., & Roy-Chowdhury, S. (2007). Culturally sensitive therapy? Examining the practice of cross-cultural family therapy. *Journal of Family Therapy, 29,* 267–283.

Parsons, T., & Bales, R. F. (1955). *Family, socialization, and interaction processes.* New York, NY: Free Press.

Pence, E., & Paymar, M. (1993). *Education groups for men who batter: The Duluth model.* New York, NY: Springer.

Pinsof, W. M. (1995). *Integrative problem-centered therapy.* New York, NY: Basic Books.

Pinsof, W. M., Wynne, L. C., & Hambright, A. B. (1996). The outcomes of couple and family therapy: Findings, conclusions, and recommendations. *Psychotherapy, 33,* 321–331.

Prigogine, I. (1973). Can thermodynamics explain biological order? *Impact of Science on Society, 23,* 159–179.

Relapse and Expressed Emotion. (1999, February). *Harvard Mental Health Letter,* *15*(8), 6.

Satir, V. (1972). *Peoplemaking.* Palo Alto, CA: Science and Behavior.

Satir, V. (1983). *Conjoint family therapy* (3rd ed.). Palo Alto, CA: Science and Behavior Books.

Shadish, W. R., Ragsdale, K., Glaser, R. R., & Montgomery, L. M. (1995). The efficacy and effectiveness of marital and family therapy: A perspective from meta-analysis. *Journal of Marital and Family Therapy, 21,* 345–360.

Sherman, R., & Fredman, N. (1986). *Handbook of structured techniques in marriage and family therapy.* New York, NY: Brunner/Mazel.

Stander, V., Piercy, F. P., MacKinnon, D., & Helmeke, K. (1994). Spirituality, religion and family therapy: Competing or complementary worlds? *American Journal of Family Therapy, 22,* 27–41.

Steigerwald, F., & Janson, G. (2003). Conversion therapy: Ethical considerations in family counseling. *The Family Journal, 11,* 55–59.

Turner, T. E., Fox, N. J., & Kiser, J. D. (2007). Uniting spirituality and sexual counseling: Semitic traditions. *The Family Journal, 15,* 294–297.

United States Department of Justice. (1998). *Crime statistics.* Washington, DC: Author.

Walsh, F. (2002). *Normal family processes* (3rd ed.). New York, NY: Guilford Press.

Walsh, F. (2008). *Spiritual resources in family therapy* (2nd ed.). New York, NY: Guilford Press.

Watts, R. E. (1999). *Techniques in marriage and family counseling.* Alexandria, VA: American Counseling Association.

Watzlawick, P., Weakland, J. H., & Fisch, R. (1974). *Change: Principles of problem formation and problem resolution.* New York, NY: W. W. Norton.

Weiner, N. (1948). Cybernetics. *Scientific American, 179,* 14–18.

Weld, C., & Eriksen, K. (2006). The challenge of religious conflicts in couples counseling. *The Family Journal, 14,* 383–391.

Whitaker, C., & Keith, D. V. (1981). Symbolic-experiential family therapy. In A. S. Gurman & D. P. Kniskern (Eds.), *Handbook of family therapy* (pp. 187–225). New York, NY: Brunner/Mazel.

Wilson, K. J. (1997). *When violence begins at home.* Alameda, CA: Hunter House.

Zamboni, B. D. (2006). Therapeutic considerations in working with the family, friends, and partners of transgendered individuals. *The Family Journal, 14,* 174–179.

Integral Counseling: The Prepersonal, Personal, and Transpersonal in Self, Culture, and Nature

Integral: The word means to integrate, to bring together, to join, to link, to embrace. Not in the sense of uniformity, and not in the sense of ironing out all the wonderful differences, colors, zigs and zags of a rainbow-hued humanity, but in the sense of unity-in-diversity, shared commonalities along with our wonderful differences.

—Wilber, 2000c, p. 2

BACKGROUND OF THE THEORY

Historical Context

For much of his career, Ken Wilber developed his ideas in association with the field of transpersonal psychology, although he has not called himself a transpersonal thinker, per se, for more than 20 years. Yet one of the outstanding features of his theory, which he has termed *integral*, is its explicit inclusion of a transpersonal dimension of psychological and spiritual experience. The following section will begin with an explanation of the term *transpersonal*, provide a brief overview of the history of the field of transpersonal psychology, and conclude with a discussion of the relationship between transpersonal psychology and integral psychology and counseling.

Throughout history and across cultures, many people have reported transpersonal experiences, and some of these people have manifested what appear to be transpersonal levels of development. The term *transpersonal* means "beyond the personal," that is, beyond the sense of oneself as merely a separate entity who functions in the space/time world of earthly existence; in other words, beyond what Alan Watts (1966) referred to as the isolated, skin-encapsulated ego.

Expanding a definition Stanislav Grof (1998) offered, a *transpersonal experience* can be defined as a spontaneous, transient experience involving perception or action that *transcends* the ego's usual limits of space and/or time yet, paradoxically, that the ego, with consensus reality in tact, perceives as authentic or potentially authentic (Holden, 1999). Intuitive, paranormal, and mystical experiences are included among transpersonal experiences.

Intuitive experiences can be understood as those moments of direct, immediate, holistic knowing that involve more than merely one's sensory input and one's reasoning. Judith Orloff, MD (1996), provided an example. One day she received an answering machine message from a woman, Robin, who stated briefly that she wanted to make an appointment. Knowing no more than this, Judith proceeded to have a strong, distinctively negative feeling about Robin—to the point that she hesitated to return Robin's call and schedule an appointment. A few hours later, Judith received a call from her local district attorney's office.

> He told me that he'd been assigned to a suit filed against Robin. "Robin is under a court order to receive psychotherapy and treatment for drug addiction and alcoholism," he explained. "You should also know the district attorney is processing a complaint against her by two of her former psychotherapists, both women. Is seems she became obsessed with them. They're charging her with harassment."
>
> Mr. Young went on to describe how Robin would show up at the therapists' offices unscheduled and call them at all hours of the day and night. A restraining order was finally issued by the Superior Court. Now, learning from Robin that she was planning to start treatment with me, Mr. Young advised that I not take her on, suggesting that she would do better with a male therapist.
>
> I agreed and thanked him. (pp. 118–119)

Paranormal experiences involve the everyday, earthly world and also include phenomena that appear to defy the known physical laws of that world. One category of paranormal experiences is extrasensory perception (ESP), knowledge that a person has gained without the mediation of the physical senses and that can take any of a number of forms. In *precognition*, one inexplicably knows the future, such as when a person, in a wakeful "flash" or a dream, foresees a car accident involving a loved one and, before he can contact the loved one to warn them, the accident occurs. In *telepathy*, one inexplicably shares the thoughts, feelings, or physical experience of someone out of physical contact, such as the father who, driving down the road one day, clutches his chest in excruciating pain and thinks of his son on active duty in the Middle East. The pain passes, but he goes to a nearby hospital emergency room where they admit him for 24-hour observation. Finding nothing wrong, they send him home. The next day, military personnel come to his home to inform him that his son died of a chest wound during a military operation two days before. In *clairvoyance*, one is able to envision things out of visual range, as in the case of the successful Central Intelligence Agency (CIA) training in remote viewing whereby researchers would give a trainee latitude and longitude coordinates and the trainee was able to visualize in accurate detail what was located at that site (Targ & Katra, 1999).

In *mystical experiences*, one encounters a perceived reality beyond the everyday world in which one's sense of self expands to include such phenomena as all of humanity, the world, deity, or the entire universe. Near-death experiences are fairly well-known phenomena that often include mystical features. One such feature is a reunion with deceased loved ones and communing with a deific being of light. Another is experiencing a life review in which one reexperiences one's own thoughts and feelings while also experiencing the thoughts and feelings of others with whom one interacted: The person experiences being both oneself and the other. With one's identity thus expanded, one fully experiences how it felt to be on the receiving end of one's actions throughout one's lifetime.

Transpersonal development involves transformation into a new, relatively stable mode of functioning beyond a merely healthy self. One concept of the farther stages of transpersonal development is "enlightenment," presumably involving levels of wisdom and compassion that transcend what is achievable by a separate self whose purpose is individual or collective physical survival. According to integral theory, a transpersonal experience is a temporary *state* of consciousness, whereas transpersonal development involves the integration of such states into a relatively enduring *trait* of consciousness.

Thus, transpersonal refers to the expression of the transcendent in, through, and as the person. It is a basic assumption of transpersonal psychology that if one looks within one's being deeply enough, one paradoxically finds that which is far greater than and beyond the person: the transpersonal.

Wilber (2000b), in summarizing the work of numerous scholars, presented a strong argument that, historically, Western psychologists have attended almost exclusively to the domain of personal development—the ego and self—whereas Eastern psychologists have attended almost exclusively to the domain of transpersonal development. Nevertheless, Wilber (2000b) credited several Western pioneers with having contributed to a vision of human development that integrates both domains. Foremost was Prussian psychologist Gustav Fechner (1801–1887), often credited as the originator of experimental psychology but who clearly believed that the material world is an expression of spiritual consciousness. Also important was the American James Mark Baldwin (1861–1934), upon whose conceptual foundation current developmental psychology is substantially built and whose concept of development included a hyperlogical domain that, in contemporary terms, is clearly transpersonal. Wilber also affirmed the East Indian philosopher sage Sri Aurobindo (1872–1950), the American psychologist Abraham Maslow (1908–1970), and the contemplatives from every major religion for their invaluable contributions to an evolutionary and transpersonal view of human development.

One hallmark in the development of the transpersonal perspective was William James's 1901 classic book, *The Varieties of Religious Experience*. In it, the eminent American psychologist referred to religion as an individual's apprehension of himself or herself in the presence of the spiritual (p. 42) and as "the belief that there is an unseen order, and that our supreme good lies in harmoniously adjusting ourselves thereto" (p. 58). He described numerous experiences that, today, would fall into the category of the transpersonal. He argued that psychologists should approach the understanding of such phenomena not by reducing them to more basic, materialistic psychological dynamics but rather by nonreductionistically acknowledging them in their own right as valid subjective human experiences and inquiring into their meaning and function.

James's transpersonal experience-affirming attitude was echoed by Carl Jung. Over the first half of the twentieth century, Swiss psychiatrist Jung developed a psychological and psychotherapeutic theory called analytic psychology. He both agreed substantially with Freud and also hypothesized psychological structures and processes beyond those that Freud addressed in his published works.

Regarding the unconscious, for example, Jung hypothesized in each person's psyche not only a personal unconscious but also a collective, or universal, unconscious. The collective unconscious is the repository of the sum total of human experience, and it consists of archetypes, or preexisting forms (Singer, 1972, p. 118). For example, it is now known in the field of linguistics that children all over the world learn language in a specific, predictable sequence. They appear to be innately endowed with psychological "deep structures" that provide the form and pattern to acquire the "surface structures" of their specific language (Chomsky, 1969). Decades before linguists had discovered this phenomenon, Jung hypothesized such deep structures—archetypes—as underlying not only language acquisition but all aspects of human functioning. Examples of preexisting psychological forms that are universal to all humans across time, space, and culture include the Hero's Journey, the Inner Child, the Mother, the Goddess, the Victim, and the Wise Old Man (Douglas, 2000). Thus, a person's unique unconscious and conscious patterns arise from the collective unconscious that is every person's birthright. Jung agreed with Freud's hypothesis of the Oedipus complex, but he saw it as only one archetype among many in the collective unconscious. Other archetypes, Jung believed, included those pertaining to spirituality that were equally valid and powerful in their own right and that one could not, as Freud believed, best understand them by reducing them to the mere sublimation of more primitive, basic motivations.

Jung also embraced the nonrational quality of the unconscious as sometimes regressively irrational, as Freud had described, but also as sometimes progressively transrational—fostering development through processes that did not involve, and that one could not understand completely by exclusively using, linear reasoning. An example was Jung's hypothesis of synchronicity, "meaningful coincidences that cannot be explained through linear causality" (Grof, 1998, p. 91). In a well-known clinical example, Jung (1969) was in session one day with a patient who had dreamt that she had been given a golden scarab, a representation of a beetle. During dream analysis, Jung brought up the point that, since ancient times, the scarab has been symbolically associated with transpersonal phenomena. As had been the case with this patient, she was resistant to the idea of the transpersonal domain, in general, and a transpersonal aspect of her own psyche, in particular. Their dream work was interrupted by a distracting clicking at Jung's window. When he went to the window, he found a rare specimen of beetle, one he had never seen before. He brought it to the patient, who was profoundly affected by this highly unlikely but extremely meaningful coincidence.

Wilber (2000b, pp. 248–249) noted that because of a misinterpretation of Jung, some people have been confused in their thinking about the relationship between the prepersonal stages of development—the first few years of life prior to the emergence of a clear sense of self, and the transpersonal stages—those occurring, if at all, after the emergence, consolidation, and elaboration of the self. Wilber called this confusion *the pre-trans fallacy*, which has both reductive and elevative forms. In the reductive form, someone misinterprets phenomena of the transpersonal realm as prepersonal. For example, a mental health professional diagnoses as schizophrenic an otherwise extremely well-functioning individual who had an experience during meditation of communing with a deity; Freud was guilty of this kind of error. In the elevative form, someone misinterprets phenomena of the prepersonal realm as transpersonal. For example, a mental health professional sees only lofty spiritual implications in a client's chronic, debilitating hallucinations; Jung was guilty of this type of error. If you'd like a better understanding of Jung, we encourage you to read Joseph Campbell's (1972) *The Portable Jung* and June Singer's (1972) *Boundaries of the Soul: The Practice of Jung's Psychology.*

Despite the dominance of psychoanalysis and behaviorism in the field of psychology for almost its first 100 years of existence, eminent figures such as James and Jung, along with other lesser-known figures, carried the thread of the transpersonal through the twentieth century. One such lesser-known figure was Italian psychiatrist Roberto Assagioli (1965, 1991), who called his humanistically and transpersonally oriented approach *psychosynthesis*. His psychological perspective included concepts of a higher self, a higher unconscious or superconscious, and spiritual awakening. However, only in the late 1960s did modern-day transpersonal psychology begin to grow out of the humanistic psychology movement.

In the early 1960s, Abraham Maslow and Anthony Sutich, noteworthy figures in both the humanistic and transpersonal movements (Walsh, 1993b), first joined other like-minded professionals in establishing humanistic psychology, the "third force" after psychoanalysis and behaviorism. These professionals aimed to study and nurture an understanding of some of the more healthful and meaningful, as opposed to pathological and reductionistic, aspects of human nature, such as the human capacity and tendency to fully actualize one's inherent potential.

Eventually, Maslow and Sutich joined others like Assagioli in realizing that the concept of self-actualization seemed inadequate to capture the full essence of humans' developmental potential. They struggled to find a term that captured the transcendent essence of this emerging "fourth force" in psychology. Then Stanislav Grof, an experimental and clinical psychologist who studied higher states of consciousness with individuals under the influence of LSD, proposed to Maslow the term *transpersonal* that apparently William James had first used in a 1905–1906 syllabus (Perry, 1936, pp. 444–445). Maslow believed the term captured the transcendent quality he and his cohorts sought: "beyond individuality, beyond the development of the individual person into something which is more inclusive" (cited in Schwartz, 1995, p. 345). In 1967, Maslow presented the paper "The Farther Reaches of Human Nature," in which he proposed his ideas regarding a

> "higher" Fourth Psychology, transpersonal, transhuman, centered in the cosmos, rather than in human needs and interest, going beyond humanness, identity, self-actualization and the like....Without the transcendent and the transpersonal, we get sick, violent, and nihilistic, or else hopeless and apathetic. (Maslow, 1968, pp. iii–iv)

In the past three decades, numerous key figures and cultural developments have bolstered the field of transpersonal psychology. Among the key figures was Ken Wilber whose prolific writings included numerous articles in the *Journal of Transpersonal Psychology* and other transpersonally oriented publications. However, for a number of reasons, including atheoretical and contradictory theoretical perspectives associated with the transpersonal movement, Wilber has disassociated himself from that movement, notwithstanding his affirmation of the fundamentally transpersonal orientation of his theory.

Founder's Biographical Overview

The man who, for many years, has been acknowledged by colleagues as the leading theoretician of consciousness and transpersonal psychology, Ken Wilber, was born in Oklahoma City to two devoted parents. Largely due to his father's career as an Air Force officer, Wilber's family moved frequently. Thus, at an early age, long before he knew of Buddhism, Wilber realized the Buddhist insight of impermanence. Eager to be liked, and sorrowed by frequently having to say goodbye to friends, the young Wilber "learned to get involved with people very quickly and intimately, but also to hold everything lightly. It was a genuine Buddhist education: to be open, and yet to know that everything comes and goes" (Wilber, cited in Schwartz, 1995, p. 347). Although Wilber reported feeling overprotected, smothered, and a bit overwhelmed by his mother, he deeply appreciated the support and intellectual freedom his parents gave him.

Since childhood, Wilber has been passionate about science. He wrote, "I fashioned a self that was built on logic, structured by physics, and moved by chemistry.... My mental youth was an idyll of precision and accuracy, a fortress of the clear and evident" (cited in Schwartz, 1995, p. 348). With bachelor's and master's degrees in chemistry, Wilber was working toward his PhD in that same subject when he began to realize that science was not "wrong" but profoundly narrow and limited in its scope—and silent with regard to the meaning of life. As always, he was spending far more time in his self-education than in his formal schooling. Mentally devouring numerous disciplines within philosophy, religion, and psychology, he was trying to reconcile what appeared to be contradictory views of such diverse geniuses as Einstein, Freud, and the Buddha. "I felt they were all saying something true," wrote Wilber, "but that *none* of them had it entirely figured out.... It slowly dawned on me that these people weren't all addressing the same *level* of consciousness" (cited in Schwartz, 1995, p. 351). Thus, the question was no longer "Whose view is correct?" but "How do these differing insights fit together in such a way that they don't contradict one another?" What Wilber (1977) called his "Grail search" culminated in his leaving chemistry studies and writing *The Spectrum of Consciousness* (1977), which the 23-year-old wrote in longhand for 12 hours each day over a three-month period (Schwartz, 1995).

Since then, Wilber has written 25 books (including more than 350 foreign editions of his books), making him the most widely translated academic writer in America. Professors from Harvard and numerous other universities have used his books as texts, and renowned thinkers in fields as diverse as business and philosophy have bestowed critical acclaim on his published works.

Wilber's own development is of utmost importance to him. He has extensively practiced transcendental meditation (TM), Zen, and Tibetan Buddhism as well as participated in psychoanalytic and Gestalt therapies. Thus, although he is not himself a clinician, he has firsthand and in-depth familiarity with the terrain of human change processes. He also has devoted himself consistently to a "full-spectrum" approach by attending to each of the broad domains of physical, emotional, mental, and spiritual work. Physically, he lifts weights regularly and labored manually as a dishwasher throughout his early years as a writer. Emotionally, he has undergone extensive psychotherapy and continues to explore this domain via his personal relationships. Mentally, he reads, studies, and writes voraciously. Spiritually, he has developed what many people from diverse spiritual traditions recognize as a rare and precious realization of many of the most sublime and exalted religious truths.

Currently living in Denver, Colorado, Wilber reportedly spends his time mostly writing, reading, or meditating. Although he declined most offers to teach, speak, or be interviewed for the first two decades of his career, he recently decided that devoting some of his time to personally educating people about his work would be valuable indeed. Nonetheless, he prefers to live a nonpublic and contemplative life surrounded by a circle of brilliant, loving friends (Schwartz, 1995).

> The main work I do in the world is writing. I average six to ten hours a day, seven days a week, 365 days a year. On intense writing days, I go up to fifteen to eighteen hours. When I first started meditating, I sat for three to four hours a day. Once a week, I'd take a whole day and sit ten or twelve hours. I still sit every day for at least two hours. These are my two main practices: meditating and writing. They are very solitary, and what I do is very cognitive. My strong point is my mind, no question. That's the talent I was given. (Schwartz, 1995, p. 362)

Wilber's intellect has been hailed as truly extraordinary in its penetrating, synthesizing, and discerning capacities. His knowledge of psychology, philosophy, sociology, comparative religion, mysticism, anthropology, and even "hard" sciences such as biochemistry and physics is virtually encyclopedic, but, most importantly, he has personal experience with the states and levels of consciousness about which he writes (Schwartz, 1995; Wilber, 2000b, Vol. 8). Wilber has commented that without his meditative practice, his work, which involves reading literally hundreds of books each year and writing, on average, a book each year, would be "severely limited" (Walsh & Vaughan, 1994, p. 19).

Although people would not be accurate in viewing him as only an intellectual, his affinity for the mental and spiritual realms, as opposed to the bodily and emotional realms, is clear. Likewise, although his passion is greater for transpersonal than preper- sonal and personal stages of development, he has nonetheless consistently emphasized the dire need for everyone, including himself, to recognize and embrace a full-spectrum view of consciousness and humanity's place therein.

Philosophical Underpinnings

> Our normal waking consciousness, rational consciousness as we call it, is but one special type of consciousness, whilst all about it, parted from it by the filmiest of screens, there lie potential forms of consciousness entirely different.
>
> —James, 1993, p. 94

We believe that integral counseling represents the most inclusive, comprehensive point of view of any system presented in this book. Since all the other systems address the ego or self almost exclusively and make little or no reference to the transpersonal domain, integral counseling provides a unique perspective on the nature of one's ultimate identity and on what constitutes "reality." Upon reading this material, you may feel anything from powerful disconcertion to a deep, familiar resonance.

Integral psychology is not a subset of psychology but, rather, an integration of many disciplines including psychology, philosophy, spiritual traditions, anthropology, cognitive sciences, consciousness studies, and neuroscience. It is the product of an integrative quest spanning the entire spectrum of human possibilities as manifested in both the individual and the collective, from both interior/subjective and exterior/objective perspectives. Integral psychology honors both ancient wisdom and modern knowledge, both East and West.

Perennial Philosophy

Although a postmetaphysical version of it is incorporated, the philosophical foundation of integral counseling resides largely in what scholars generally term the *perennial phi- losophy* (Huxley, 1946; Schumacher, 1977; Smith, 1976, 1992), the "common core of the world's great spiritual traditions" (Wilber, 2000b, p. 5). "Perennial" refers to the remarkable consistency with which this philosophical perspective has emerged through- out human history, across both time and culture, suggesting its universality.

Among the essential claims of the perennial philosophy is that the phenomenal, mate- rial, "gross" world—what people typically agree is real—is not actually primary but is a secondary manifestation of a nonmaterial Ground of Being that authors have termed in various ways, such as the spiritual ground, spirit, or consciousness. Thus, this Ground of Being, rather than its manifestation as matter, is primary and irreducible; the Ground of Being is what is really real. Perhaps even more important, humans not only can know *about* this realm but also can experience and know it *directly*; such mystical experiences involve the knower *communing with*, and then *identifying as*, the Ground or Spirit itself (Huxley, 1946, 1993). Ultimately, a person who identifies with this domain neither denies the existence, at one level, of one's separate self-sense nor inflates that self-sense with self-importance, -omniscience, -omnipotence, or -superiority over other humans; one merely affirms experientially the *ultimate* nature of *each* human. From the perspective of the perennial philosophy, realization of one's own identity as God, Atman, the Self, Buddha, Nature, or whatever name one may use "is the *summum bonum*: the highest goal and greatest good of human existence" (Walsh, 1999, p. 8). It is important to bear in mind that the perennial philosophers have not claimed these ideas as dogmatic assertions that everyone should blindly believe. Rather, every major religion has its mystical tradition consisting of a set of contemplative or esoteric practices, such as meditation and/or prayer; if a person ardently undertakes them, these practices will enable one to use one's own consciousness as a personal laboratory within which one can test these spiritual claims for oneself.

Another of the core concepts of the perennial philosophy, and a central one for integral psychology, is the *great chain of being*. The great chain is a model of the *kosmos*, a word the ancient Greeks used to refer comprehensively to the patterned nature of the entire physical and spiritual universe rather than simply to only the physical universe or "cosmos." Proponents of this model consider the kosmos to be comprised of different but continuous "levels of existence—levels of being and of knowing—ranging from matter to body to mind to soul to spirit" (Wilber, 2000b, p. 5). In other words, these levels emerge in an invariant order, from the most gross, fundamental, nonconscious, and limited, characterized by a relative reality of ever-changing conditions, to the most subtle, significant, conscious, and inclusive, characterized by realization of an absolute, eternal reality.

More accurate than the metaphor of a chain or ladder is that of a series of nested, concentric spheres with each successive sphere both including and exceeding the preceding sphere: a *great nest of being* (see Figure 14.1). Thus, out of matter emerges life, out

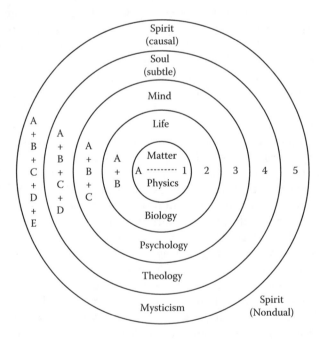

FIGURE 14.1 *The Great Nest of Being.* Spirit is both the highest level (causal) and the nondual Ground of all levels. (From Wilber, K., *Integral psychology: Consciousness, spirit, psychology, therapy,* Shambhala, Boston, MA, 2000b. P.6. Reprinted with permission.)

of life emerges mind, and so forth. Each successive stage includes the qualities of the previous stage: Life includes matter; mind includes life. At the same time, each stage adds its own unique and emergent qualities to the previous stage: Whereas matter cannot reproduce itself, usually is not mobile, and is unaware of its environment, life has these capabilities; whereas a living organism without a developed cortex cannot reflect on its own life and activity, the adult, human mind can (Wilber, 2000a, Vol. 6).

The great nest of being constitutes a particular kind of hierarchy. Each sphere is a *holon:* a complete *whole* at one level and, simultaneously, a *part* of the next level. Thus, the sequence of spheres is a *holarchy*, a hierarchy composed of holons. Holarchies exist everywhere in nature: Atoms are wholes that are parts of molecules, which are wholes that are parts of cells, which are wholes that are parts of organs, and so forth. Wilber (2000a, Vol. 7) posited that "all developmental and evolutionary sequences that we are aware of proceed in large measure by hierarchization, or by orders of increasing holism" (p. 454).

Currently, many scholars disfavor the concept of hierarchy, largely because they equate normal, "actualization" hierarchies found everywhere in nature and complex systems with what Wilber (2000a, Vol. 6) has called pathological or domination hierarchies, in which "one holon assumes agentic dominance to the detriment of all. This holon doesn't assume it is *both* a whole and a part[;] it assumes it is the whole, period" (p. 31). It may help readers to know that the term *hierarchy* was introduced originally by the Christian contemplative Saint Dionysius and referred to "governing one's life by spiritual principles"; *hiero* means sacred or holy, and *arch* means rule or governance (Wilber, 2000a, Vol. 7, p. 453). Inherent in this original meaning is the constant reminder that one's current developmental level is both a whole and a part of a larger whole that is the spiritual Ground of everything. More spirit/reality/consciousness is incorporated or *enfolded* into the structure of each successive level, which is simultaneously a greater revelation or *unfolding* of spirit/reality/consciousness.

Four Quadrant Model

Early in Wilber's professional development, he recognized that various influential people in human history, such as Freud, Piaget, Marx, Newton, and the Buddha, each appeared to offer a valid but partial truth regarding humanity and the universe (Wilber, 1999b, Vol. 1). In grappling with the question of how the diverse and seemingly contradictory views of these people might fit together in complementarity rather than in opposition, Wilber (2000a, Vol. 6) incorporated the perennial philosophy into an encompassing *four quadrant model*. Considering various perspectives such as those offered by Western psychology, the natural sciences, spiritual traditions, economic structures, technological modes, linguistics, and cultural worldviews, he discovered that each perspective fit into a model in which two axes intersect, differentiating individual phenomena from collective phenomena and, in each case, differentiating the interior, experienced aspect of those phenomena from the exterior, observed aspect (see Figure 14.2).

The individual domain includes phenomena pertaining to an individual person/holon, whereas the collective domain refers to phenomena shared by two or more persons/holons. The interior domain consists of that which is subjective, which is unequivocally experienced but cannot be objectively observed and measured. By contrast, the exterior domain consists of that which can be observed and measured relatively independently of subjective experience. All four quadrants are inextricably related to each other but cannot be reduced to each other.

Take, for example, being in love. The experiential (individual-interior) quadrant includes the unmistakable subjective feeling of having fallen in love. The behavioral

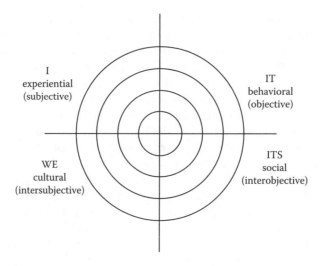

FIGURE 14.2   The Great Nest with the Four Quadrants. (From Wilber, K., *Integral psychology: Consciousness, spirit, psychology, therapy*, Shambhala, Boston, MA, 2000b, p. 67. Reprinted with permission; update of one term.)

(individual-exterior) quadrant includes the objective fact that, when in love, one's bloodstream shows increased levels of phenylethylamine and other endogenous chemicals. Notice that, inextricably linked as the feelings and the chemicals are, the subjective experience of being in love could never reveal knowledge of the endogenous chemicals, nor does knowledge of the chemicals inform the subjective experience; the two phenomena are inseparably related to, but irreducible to, each other.

Moving to the collective quadrants, the cultural (collective-interior) quadrant contains the shared ideas of what falling in love means to the people of a given culture. Consider, for example, most people in Western cultures perceive falling in love to be a basis for the decision to marry, whereas many people in Eastern cultures perceived falling in love to be irrelevant to a decision that one should make based on social and economic rather than emotional considerations. Indeed, it has been said that members of traditional Western cultures love, then marry, whereas members of traditional Eastern cultures marry, then love. The social (collective-exterior) quadrant includes such societal aspects of phenomena as the technological, political, and economic systems in which the phenomena occur. For example, a couple in love may be together when their society is at peace but separated when their society becomes involved in war (society's political system); and couples separated by war in the most advanced early twentieth century society typically communicated by letter, whereas those in the most advanced early twenty-first century typically communicate by e-mail (society's technological system).

In essence, a complete understanding of any phenomenon requires all four quadrants: the *experiential, behavioral, cultural,* and *social perspectives.* The following summary provides a more complete overview of the model. In your reading of it, we suggest that you worry not about getting all the details but rather about getting the overall point of the model: That the way to understand any phenomenon most completely is to consider all four very different perspectives that cannot be reduced to one another without distorting the significance of each view and losing some understanding of a valid aspect of the phenomenon.

Upper Left, Interior-Individual (UL; Experiential)   The subjective, phenomenological dimension of individual consciousness: one's experience "from the inside." This quadrant
includes sensations, perceptions, feelings, and thoughts that a person may, to some
degree or other, be able to describe subjectively in "I" language: "I feel...; I remember...;
I want...." Prominent theorists who focused on this quadrant include Freud, Jung, Piaget,
Aurobindo, Plotinus, and the Buddha. It is on this quadrant that proponents of the perennial philosophy concentrated. Clinically, the counselor understanding the client from
this perspective focuses on her subjective experience: her sensations, feelings, thoughts,
values, intentions, and so on that she reports to her counselor with some degree of completeness and accuracy.

Upper Right, Exterior-Individual (UR; Behavioral)   The relatively objective, scientific perspective of individual structure and/or behavior that oneself or other(s) view "from the outside." This quadrant includes individual structures and processes that other(s) describe
objectively in "it" language: "My/his/your pulse (it) is...; her/your facial expression (it)
appears...; my/his/your attendance (it) has been...." Prominent theorists and proponents
who have primarily taken the perspective of this quadrant include Skinner, Watson,
Locke, empiricists, behaviorists, and natural scientists such as physicists and biologists.
Clinically, the counselor understanding the client from this perspective appraises objective
aspects of her such as her sensory, physical, and mental functioning; medical conditions
and any medications she is taking; her diet, including drug and alcohol use; patterns of
exercise, sleep, and rest; and diagnoses for which her symptoms meet specified criteria.

Lower Left, Interior-Collective (LL; Cultural)   The intersubjective dimension of collective consciousness: the group's experience "from the inside." This quadrant includes the shared
subjective experiences of the members of a culture: the worldviews, linguistic seman-
tics, symbolic meanings, and communal values they hold in common. Members of a
culture may, to some degree or other, be able to describe these phenomena subjectively in
"we" language: "We believe...; we do...; we don't...." Prominent thinkers who theorized
predominantly from this perspective include Kuhn, Dilthey, Gebser, Kohut, Stolorow,
Atwood, and Habermas. Clinically, a counselor understanding a client from this perspective inquires sympathetically into *client meanings related not to individual experience
but to the groups of which the client is a member.* For example, each client will have a
unique idea about the meaning of success that is related to the views of the communities
to which the client belonged and belongs—such as familial, ethnic, socioeconomic, political, religious, sexual affiliation, and friendship communities.

Lower Right, Exterior-Collective (LR; Social)   The interobjective, scientific perspective of collective structure and/or behavior as viewed "from the outside." This quadrant includes
relatively objective aspects of a society, such as its economic, political, religious, and
technological systems, including education, health care, transportation, and communication systems. A person objectively describes these phenomena in what Wilber called "its"
language, though people don't actually use that term: "This economy...; my computer...;
racism...; my religion...." Prominent theorists and proponents who have primarily taken
the perspective of this quadrant include Comte, Marx, Lenski, and systems theorists/
scholars of complexity. Clinically, a counselor understanding a client from this perspective considers the influence of systems of which the client is a part on the issues the client is
addressing in counseling. These can include a wide variety of phenomena, such as noticing
repetitive patterns of interaction in couple, family, or group counseling; acknowledging

the possible role of lead in the deteriorating cognitive ability of a client from a low socio-economic household; and considering the role of a weak economy on a client's challenge to find a job.

The important overall point is that each quadrant provides a *different* perspective on a given phenomenon, each of which is *valid* for that quadrant. Implications of this model are far more complex and far-reaching than is appropriate to explore in this chapter. Suffice it to summarize that each holon within a given holarchy exists not only in relationship with the holons within and beyond it, but also interdependently with holons in the other three quadrants. In a comprehensive integral vision, individual human development is understood as it relates to all four quadrants. No holon exists in isolation. Rather, each holon is always in relational exchange, both within its own quadrant and with other quadrants. Each person and phenomenon has a subjective, an objective, an intersubjective, and an interobjective aspect. Even the simple process of feeling hungry and planning what to eat (experiential) involves certain brain structures and neurochemistry (behavioral); occurs in a context indicating when, what, and how to eat (cultural); and utilizes some technological means to produce and ingest the meal (social; Wilber, 2000a, Vol. 6).

Complete a four-quadrant assessment of the following two phenomena relevant to contemporary psychotherapy:

  1. A client with clinical depression
  2. A highly empathic counselor

PERSONALITY DEVELOPMENT

Wilber's writings explicitly address many, but not all, of the topics addressed for each theory described in this text. Where his own work does not provide an explicit answer, we have drawn on the writings of psychotherapists who have explicitly identified themselves as integral, including Jan Holden, Elliott Ingersoll, Robert Kegan, Michael Mahoney, Andre Marquis, Frances Vaughan, and Roger Walsh, and those transpersonal therapists whose techniques are theoretically compatible with integral counseling, such as Seymour Boorstein.

Nature of Humans

Function of the Psyche

> By their own theories of human nature, psychologists have the power of elevating or degrading that same nature. Debasing assumptions debase human beings; generous assumptions exalt them.

> **—Allport, cited in Walsh and Vaughan, 1994, p. 18**

No theorist of counseling holds a more optimistic and elevating view of human nature than Ken Wilber, for he has conceptualized humans as spiritual in nature, despite the fact that most people are unaware of their ultimate identity as spirit, the source, and

Ground underlying all manifestation. In fact, Wilber has contended that human nature is inseparably interconnected with the entire kosmos and that humans' core is essentially spiritual, loving, and positively directed. Likewise, Adi Da, perhaps the most integral of spiritual teachers and an influential figure in Wilber's developmental model, declared that spiritual transformation is a potential for "every human being. It is only more consciously activated or served in extraordinary or more perfectly awakened individuals. But it is present in everyone.... [T]he human individual is natively or structurally disposed ... to grow beyond his [sic] present limits" (Da, 1980, pp. 50–51).

From an integral perspective, each person's underlying motivation is *to realize one's ultimate/spiritual nature*: a condition of original perfection, unity, and happiness. This realization does not involve a pleasurable or pain-free existence but, rather, involves a deep and profound peace and a radical freedom from the binding power of exclusive identification with any one thing. Wilber (1999b, Vol. 2) called this yearning for and struggle toward realization of one's true nature "the Atman project": "All things are driven, urged, pushed and pulled to manifest this realization" (p. 60).

Rather than a discovery, realization of one's true nature is actually a *remembering*: "the Buddhist *smriti* and *sati-patthana*, the Hindu *smara*, the Sufi *zikr*, Plato's *recollection*, Christ's *anamnesis*: all of those terms are precisely translated as remembrance" (Wilber, 1999b, Vol. 2, p. 268). Thus, it may be inferred that by assuming human form and developing psychological structures such as the ego, one tends to severely limit awareness and experience of the spiritual light of one's true nature. Although for many people that light shines at first as a very faint beacon, it is the light toward which all life movement is aimed. Each phase of development constitutes an increasing realization of that light, which is experienced as a recognition or remembering of what always has been, and realizing union with that beacon constitutes spiritual awakening—enlightenment: "Time past and time future / What might have been and what has been / Point to one end, which is always present" (Eliot, 1943, p. 14).

The process of realization is one of *development*, which involves several functions. First, throughout life, people experience the yearning for realization as the felt motivation of *needs*. If development proceeds well, fulfillment of needs at one level provides the foundation for fulfillment at the next level. The following discussion distills multiple, nuanced needs into four major categories.

The newborn and very young infant is dominated by *physical needs*. Through the course of normal development, the infant's emerging capacity for interpersonal relationship is accompanied by the emergence of *emotional needs*. Throughout childhood, mental faculties develop accompanied by the emergence of *mental needs*, such as for knowledge, for "making sense of things," and for other forms of mental stimulation. Finally, *spiritual needs* emerge, to become increasingly aware of each person's "relationship with a Source and Ground that gives sanction, meaning, and deliverance to our separate selves" (Wilber, 2000b, p. 118). Thus, from an integral perspective, each level of need fulfillment, of development, is an increasingly exquisite expression of, and progression toward fulfilling, the ultimate human desire for spiritual realization.

At each level, people experience the inability to meet the emerging need as painful, disruptive, even potentially lethal. Being motivated to avoid this pain, disruption, and death, they develop increasingly complex psychological structures—relatively stable patterns in consciousness. As each new need emerges, they typically at first feel unequipped to satisfy it and overwhelmed with its onslaught. Ideally people gradually *metabolize experiences*—incorporate them through organization and mastery—thus creating the capacity to meet the new need in a systematic way. With each newly emerging need, this process involves integrating qualitatively different structures or functions with the previously existing one[s]. Thus, the process of development is a recapitulation of the cycle of *identification* with and consolidation of one level of functioning; then, as new needs emerge, *disidentification*, that is, transcendence of exclusive identification with that level; which enables *realization* of a broader mode of functioning than the previous level had allowed; then *integration*, the inclusion of the previous level[s] with the new one, resulting in a qualitatively different and broader level of being and functioning.

This process is not entirely smooth, however. Leaving the familiarity and security of the old structure and entering the unfamiliarity and uncertainty of the new is, in itself, an experience of pain, disruption, even death—a letting go of a familiar yet relatively limited way of life in order to be born into a new, more whole way. Consequently, as a function of the same underlying motives (to seek happiness and to avoid pain, disruption, and death) people both seek and resist development.

An analogy of the developmental process is upgrading one's living quarters. The realization can be painful and unsettling that one's formerly secure haven has recently become inadequate. At first one might try to rearrange the furniture in an effort to make the existing quarters satisfactory, a process Wilber called *translation*: change within one's *existing* level of development (horizontal growth). As a person acknowledges the inadequacy of translation to meet emergent needs, one must confront the pain, disruption, and death involved in *transformation*: change to a *subsequent* level of development (vertical growth). One must find the resources for upgraded housing, must undertake the stressful process of searching for adequate housing, and must accomplish the disruptive process of moving, resettling, and reorienting. The best possible new housing will have the useful features of the old but also more features that better meet one's emerging needs. Yet, to leave the security and familiarity of the old house can feel like a kind of death. If the move is successfully resolved, one looks back on the old home with nostalgia—appreciating what it provided at one time—while simultaneously looking on the new home with excitement and with well-founded trepidation, for, as anyone knows who has ever moved, the new home brings with it both new satisfactions and new challenges all its own.

A key structure in the process of development is the self, or self-system, the seat of a host of functions. Some of these have already been described, such as identification, gaining identity by associating with a level of functioning; organization, providing a sense of cohesion to experiences; and metabolism, psychological digestion that transforms one's discrete experiences, or one's *states*, into enduring modes of functioning and levels of development, or one's *traits*. Also involved are *will*, exercising choice and initiating action; *defense*, nondevelopmental strategies that mitigate against pain, disruption, and death; and *navigation*, wending one's way through the developmental labyrinth. It is through such self-functions that a person is capable of choosing how to respond to givens such as heredity and environment, mostly within the limits of one's current developmental capabilities. Yet one can exceed even those limits at times through *creativity*. Whereas creativity as a human capacity is addressed in other systems of psychology, it is understood in those systems to be a kind of wild card inherent in human nature, having no clear source. From an integral perspective, creativity involves temporary access to that which is beyond one's prevailing developmental level, a reach into the *all that is* that seems beyond one's purview but actually is the Ground of all, the essence of one's own nature that, therefore, is always potentially available.

To summarize thus far, each human is innately endowed not only with a motivation to meet physical, emotional, and mental needs but also with an impulse, however faint, to meet spiritual needs that ultimately involve transcendence of the separate self-sense and identification with spirit, the source of everything. Ultimately, this transcendental, transformational disposition does not involve a detached avoidance or abandonment of the material world but rather an involvement in the world along with a transcendence of it into its source. To transcend and transform is both to include and to go beyond one's previous developmental level.

Wilber (1999b, Vol. 2) wrote also about the human potential to fail to develop:

> prior to ... spiritual awakening, all things seek Spirit in a way that actually prevents the realization.... We seek for Spirit in the world of time; but Spirit is timeless.... We seek for Spirit in this or that object ... but Spirit is not an object.... In other words, we are seeking for Spirit in ways that prevent its realization, and force us to settle for substitute gratifications. (p. 60)

Thus, people are often more absorbed in such substitute gratifications as money, food, sex, power, or fame, all of which can bring temporary and imperfect peace and none of which, therefore, can quench the thirst for ultimate freedom. "All our desires, wants, intentions, and wishes are ultimately 'substitute gratifications' for unity consciousness—but only half satisfying, and therefore half frustrating" (Wilber, 1999b, Vol. 1, p. 569).

Thus it is that humans are prone to be misguided, seduced by half-satisfactions that "feel like" development, "feel like" they meet people's deepest needs. By seeking happiness in the phenomenal realm of ever-changing conditions that can never provide lasting happiness, by seeking peace in the inertia of routine and the placation of the familiar, people actually maintain the peaceless status quo of half-satisfaction. When combined with the fact that developmental progress involves directly facing the very phenomena of pain and disruption from which one seeks to escape, the difficulty of development becomes clear. This, then, is the condition of tension in which humans face the purpose of life: spiritual development (Holden, 1993; Marquis, 2002; Walsh, 1999). Again, it is worth stressing that achievement of the "farther reaches of human nature" does not mean a life of exclusive ecstasy and bliss but, rather, an ongoing, underlying sense of peace and well-being that, in essence, gives the individual an ultimate resource with which to meet the vicissitudes of life.

Structure of the Psyche

Integral theory addresses both *conscious* and *unconscious* aspects of the human psyche. The conscious aspects include the totality of which one is aware, and the unconscious aspects include those potentials that have yet to become conscious as well as phenomena from past experience that one has defensively relegated out of awareness (Wilber, 2000b, p. 101). Integral theory and this section explicitly address several important psychological structures: developmental levels and lines, states of consciousness, personality types, subpersonalities, the self, and five different types of unconsciousness.

Levels In Wilber's view, the great nest of being manifests in humans as levels or stages of development. Perhaps the easiest way to understand a stage of development is to think of it as a unique way to make meaning of one's experiences resulting in a unique sense of identity. The word "levels" connotes that each stage of development is qualitatively distinct, that the stages occur in a sequence, and that each sequential stage is more complex than the previous one because it includes both the feature of and features that go beyond the previous stage. Wilber has also referred to stages as "structures" to underscore the integrated, holistic, relatively stable nature of each stage, and as "waves" to emphasize the fluidity with which the stages flow into one another.

Another important point is that, although we will focus in the following discussion on the development of the self, "the basic structure or basic waves themselves are devoid of a sense of self.... [T]he basic structures are simply the waves of being and knowing that are available to the [proximal] self as it develops toward its highest potentials" (Wilber, 2000b, p. 35).

Since healthy development involves integrating previous stages into one's current developmental stage, individuals have access to not only their current stage but also their previous ones, and thus may function, perceive, and exist from several different levels or perspectives, even within the same day. Nonetheless, most people will *tend* spontaneously to act from the most developed meaning-making system or perspective that they have mastered. Integral theorists call this preferred perspective—or "central tendency" from which individuals make meaning—their developmental "center of gravity" (Cook-Greuter & Soulen, 2007, p. 183), a phrase that Cook-Greuter (1999) originally found in William James's (1901) *Varieties of Religious Experience*. Another important point is that integral theorists and practitioners focus primarily on a person's full developmental potential and only secondarily on the extent to which the person has realized that potential—the person's current developmental level.

PREPARATORY ACTIVITY: DESCRIBING A RAINBOW

How many colors are in a rainbow? Most people would say a rainbow contains an infinite number, covering the full spectrum of visible color. Yet, if you were to meet someone who was familiar with colors but had never seen a rainbow, how would you describe it? Take a moment to write down your answer.

Probably your answer included something like, "an infinite blending of one color into another, from red to orange to yellow to green to blue to purple." Though arbitrary, the identification of three primary and three secondary colors from among the infinite number present in the rainbow provides a structure for at least a preliminary understanding of what constitutes a rainbow. Likewise, Wilber (1999b, Vol. 4) noted the arbitrariness of separating the continuous process of development into any particular number of stages, yet affirmed the conceptual value of doing so. Consequently, he conceptualized the levels of human development as 10 holarchical spheres clustered into three realms: *prepersonal, personal*, and *transpersonal*. The prepersonal realm, corresponding roughly to the great nest spheres of matter and life, and the personal realm, corresponding roughly to the great nest sphere of mind, are corroborated by Western academic psychology (Freud, 1971; Kohut, 1977, 1984; Mahler, Pine, & Bergman, 1975; Piaget, 1977). Empirical evidence for the transpersonal realm, which corresponds to the Great Nest spheres of soul and spirit, rests primarily in the developmental mappings of the contemplative traditions, both Eastern and Western (Aurobindo, 1970; O'Brien, 1984). With transformation into each progressive level of development, the individual potentially retains the resources afforded by the previous level and acquires additional capacities to draw upon in the process of living.

Another term Wilber (1999a) used synonymously with *level* is *fulcrum*. Imagine a fulcrum progressing along a 10-point line. At any given time, one's self identifies primarily with one of the 10 basic structures of development yet accesses adjacent levels and, to a progressively lesser degree, more distant levels. As such, one's sense of self often teeters, identified primarily with the predominant level of functioning—one's developmental center of gravity—sometimes dipping slightly backward into previous levels, but increasingly reaching slightly forward, until transformation renders a qualitative forward shift: the fulcrum advances to the next, broader/deeper/more complex level of meaning-making, identity/sense of self, and functioning. Referring to the word "fulcrum," Wilber used the designation "F-" to refer to each of the 10 levels of identity development: F-1 through F-10.

Each human typically spends the first 7 years of life proceeding through three fulcrums or basic structures of development that, together, comprise the *prepersonal* realm. During this time, the person's stable, coherent, individuated self-sense is, as yet, only in the process of emerging. Psychological functioning in this realm is *prerational*. At birth, the infant enters the *sensoriphysical level* (F-1) in a state of psychological undifferentiation from her environment. During her first 18 months of life, she takes her first tentative steps toward individuation by developing an identity as a *physical self*, a body separate from the environment. Then, in the *phantasmic/emotional level* (F-2), the toddler develops a sense of her *emotional self*, realizing she feels different emotions than other people do and, therefore, developing a sense of identity separate from other people. Between the second and third years of life, at the *representational mind level* (F-3), the *mental self* emerges: What the child previously knew only directly and immediately through her senses, she now is capable of representing through mental images she can keep in mind even when the source of the image is not directly and immediately present. Piaget (1977) classified this third level as the preoperational period in which the capacity for symbols and language provides the child access to an entirely new world of objects and ideas in both the past and the future.

Since levels four through six involve the stabilization and elaboration of a coherent, individuated self, they comprise the *personal realm*. Psychological functioning in this realm is relatively *rational*. The seven-year-old typically enters the *rule/role mind level* (F-4), a stage that corresponds to Piaget's (1977) concrete operations. The child at this stage develops the capacity to take the perspective (role) of others and assumes an identity as a *role self*, learning the rules associated with various social roles. The dawn of adolescence is accompanied by the *formal-reflexive level* (F-5), corresponding to Piaget's (1977) formal operations: The young teenager becomes capable of thinking about thinking. This development enables the person for the first time to introspect, marking the emergence of a *conscientious self*: one no longer merely learns the rules and roles of life but can question such things as their source, purpose, and appropriateness. Many people continue into and through adulthood at this fifth level of functioning that tends to involve dichotomous, either/or thinking. However, around age 21, the potential develops for the young adult to emerge into the *vision-logic level* (F-6). This level involves a transcendence of dichotomous thinking and an emergence into integral-aperspectival thinking: The individual can simultaneously hold multiple, apparently contradictory perspectives in her attention and, through synthesis and integration, can conceptualize networks of interactions among the various perspectives. At this level, existential concerns characterize the self that Wilber called the *centaur*, borrowing the term Erikson used "to denote a mature mind-and-body integration, where 'human mind' and 'animal body' are harmoniously one" (Wilber, 2000b, p. 44).

Whereas the first four or five levels tend to emerge without a person's intentional effort, progressive emergence of the higher order structures tends to require a person to more and more purposefully pursue contemplative practice. Since the last four levels involve increasing disidentification from a sense of self as isolated, separate, and individual, these structures are termed *transpersonal*, including as well as transcending the personal. Psychological functioning in this realm is often deemed *transrational* in that it seems to involve direct and immediate apprehension without using the physical senses or thinking. You should be forewarned that you may have difficulty fully grasping the following description of any transpersonal realm that you have not experienced yourself.

In the *para-mental, or psychic, level* (F-7), psychic or other paranormal experiences, which, as described above, include references to the natural, "gross" world, often—but not always—occur as one's identity expands to include all of cosmic nature; thus, one experiences *nature mysticism*. One's identity emerges as a *universal self* that transcends the individual self's sense of space and time. This oneness with the universe is not to be confused with the undifferentiated state of a newborn infant who has not yet developed a clear sense of self. Rather, the universal self includes a sense of oneself as an individual, and the sense of self also expands to include all natural phenomena.

Experiences of the *meta-mental, subtle, level* (F-8) involve the transcendence of gross referents; that is, the contents of these inner experiences transcend the everyday physical world and typically involve archetypal forms and patterns, interior luminosities and sounds, and subtle currents of bliss. One's identity expands in a union of one's soul with deity; thus, one experiences *deity mysticism*. For example, some near-death experiences include a state of union with a being of light that a Christian experiencer is likely to interpret as Jesus or God. *If* one metabolizes the experience, one will report that throughout much of waking life, one experiences a trait of union: an ongoing feeling of inseparable connection with God that is subtle but unmistakable. Again, the person retains a separate self-sense while that self-sense also has expanded to include union with deity.

In experiences of the *over-mental, or causal, level* (F-9), one realizes the formless Ground from which all phenomena, of both exterior and interior worlds, arise. These are experiences of pure consciousness, devoid of all content, in which attention—the root-essence of mind—abides without effort, strategic manipulation, or self-consciousness. In this witness-consciousness (Avabhasa, 1985), one does not merely know about, but directly experiences/realizes, the unmanifest source, Ground, support, and *cause* of all of the previous levels. When a person metabolizes such experiences, one's identity abides as the unmanifest source of all arising phenomena.

By contrast, in the *supra-mental, or nondual, level* (F-10), the experiencer transcends even the distinction between the formless Ground and the phenomena that arise from the Ground. This level actually is not a discrete level apart from other levels but, rather, is the reality, suchness, or condition of *all* levels. In other words, in this ultimate state of unity consciousness, one realizes spirit and its manifestations, consciousness and its display, emptiness and form, nirvana and samsara—the ultimate reality or truth and the conditional realm of suffering in which most people are engrossed—to be "not-two." When one metabolizes such experiences, the self retains and integrates all its previous forms into the stable realization and experience of its true nature as the All.

Wilber's developmental model, which he has termed the *spectrum of development*, is summarized in Table 14.1.

Lines In addition to navigating through the levels of development, the self also consists of various *lines* or "streams" of development. A line of development can be thought of

TABLE 14.1   Ken Wilber's Spectrum of Human Development

Realm	Great Nest Sphere	Psychological Functioning	Fulcrum	Developmental Fulcrum/Level	Approximate Age in Years	Identity
Prepersonal	Matter/life	Prerational	F-1	Sensoriphysical	0–1.5	Physical self
			F-2	Phantasmic/emotional	1.5–3	Emotional self
			F-3	Representational mind	3–7	Mental self
Personal	Mind	Rational	F-4	Rule/role mind	7–12	Role self
			F-5	Formal-reflexive	12–21 (potential)	Conscientious self
			F-6	Vision-logic	21 (potential)	Centaur
Transpersonal	Soul	Transrational	F-7	Para-mental	(potential)	Universal self (nature mysticism)
			F-8	Meta-mental	(potential)	Includes union with deity
	Spirit		F-9	Over-mental	(potential)	Witness-consciousness/unmanifest source
			F-10	Supra-mental	(potential)	Unity consciousness

Source: From Wilber, K., Integral psychology: Consciousness, spirit, psychology, therapy, Shambhala, Boston, MA, 2000b. With permission.

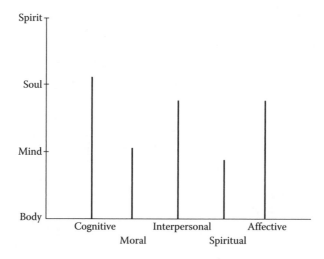

FIGURE 14.3 The Integral Psychograph. (From Wilber, K., *Integral psychology: Consciousness, spirit, psychology, therapy*, Shambhala, Boston, MA, 2000b, p. 30. Reprinted with permission.)

as an aspect of the individual's overall development, and as Wilber (2006) has noted, "a 'level of development' is always a 'level in a particular line'" (p. 61). Each line or stream proceeds sequentially, yet quasi-independently, through the 10 waves or levels. Empirical research indicates that at least two dozen of these relatively independent lines exist, including cognitive, self, values, moral, worldview, aesthetic, spiritual, needs, kinesthetic, emotional, and interpersonal.

Each line manifests in a relatively identifiable way at each wave or level; however, the lines can and do develop at different rates. Consequently, a person may be more developed in some lines and less developed in others (see Figure 14.3). Thus, although *specific* developmental lines and levels unfold sequentially, *"overall development ... is far from a sequential, ladder-like, clunk-and-grind series of steps, but rather involves a fluid flowing of many waves and streams in the great River of Life"* (Wilber, 2000a, Vol. 6, p. xvii).

REFLECTION

Using only the lines identified in Figure 14.3, sketch your own integral psychograph, knowing that it will be your best guess or approximation. Then sketch the psychographs of two other individuals you know well. How do these lines help to illuminate a person's individuality? How might lines of development help one to understand how a spiritual authority (such as a minister, priest, or guru who is genuinely developed in many ways) might engage in behavior such as sexual or other exploitation of one or more followers?

States Wilber (2000b) noted that although the self at any given time predominantly reflects the structure of one's developmental center of gravity, it is not confined only to experiences associated with those structures. Rather, in addition to predominant functioning at one's current center of gravity, the self can temporarily regress to earlier levels of functioning or temporarily progress to subsequent levels of functioning through a range of states of consciousness that are *potentially* available. Thus, virtually anyone can have a temporary transpersonal experience or state.

Wilber (2000b, p. 13) identified two general categories of temporary states of consciousness. *Natural* or ordinary states include waking functioning at one's current developmental level; dreaming, the nightly, mostly unconscious excursion into the subtle domain; and deep sleep, the nightly unconscious excursion into the causal domain. *Altered* or nonordinary states include those regressive or progressive experiences that people tend to experience under a variety of conditions or circumstances such as fasting, fever, drugs, EEG biofeedback, contemplation, prayer or meditation, or profound stressors such as intense exercise or being near death, but that also can occur spontaneously without an identifiable precondition.

People in the transpersonal field have tended to focus more on temporary altered *states* rather than the metabolism of those states into relatively stable, enduring transpersonal *traits*/levels/waves of development. However, Wilber (1999b, Vol. 4; 2000a, Vol. 7) has contended that although anyone at any level of development can have a temporary experience of any transpersonal state; whether that state will be metabolized into an enduring trait depends on certain factors. These factors include the frequency and duration of the temporary states, the "distance" between one's current fulcrum or level of development and the level from which the experience or state arose, the degree of awareness that the person brings to the process of metabolism, and the amount of intentional practice one devotes to integrating the new awareness into one's daily life.

Consider, for example, a young child who had a para-mental experience, such as precognition of a disastrous event involving a loved one. Since para-mental-level understanding is, as yet, developmentally unavailable to her, she is unlikely to conclude that she temporarily gained access to a transpersonal source of information. Rather, she is likely to interpret the experience with concrete, self-centered thinking and conclude that she caused the event, that is, thought it into existence—a conclusion with which she is likely to feel distressed. Another example is an adult in the fifth formal/reflexive level of functioning who has a meta-mental experience, such as a near-death experience that involves communion with an all-knowing, all-loving Being of Light. He might dismiss the experience or deny its reality because it is incongruent with his current worldview. In these cases, distress and denial will likely impede the integration of the experience. The individual is, so to speak, developmentally unprepared to metabolize the experience into a quasipermanent realization/mode of functioning/stage of development. The more isolated and short-lived the temporary state or experience and the more advanced the wave from which it arose, the less likely the self will consolidate it into a new level or wave of functioning. The greater the frequency, duration, and awareness brought to the temporary state or experience—as results most reliably from a regimen of contemplative practice—and the more "adjacent" to one's current level is the level from which the state or experience arose, the more likely it is that the self will consolidate the experiences into the next level of development: increasingly stable functioning at a more inclusive level of being and knowing. In short, integral theorists remain mindful of how a person's current center of gravity will influence how they will tend to interpret their experience. Table 14.2 displays probable, even if highly stylized, examples of how differently the same mystical experience would be interpreted as a function of a person's developmental center of gravity.

TABLE 14.2   Different Interpretations of a Highly Similar Spiritual Experience

Developmental Stage	How a Christian is Likely to Interpret a Subtle/Meta-Mental Experience of Seeing and Communing With Jesus
Phantasmic-emotional (magic; ego-centric)	Jesus is *my* personal savior and He will miraculously transform the world to meet my whims and desires.
Representational-mind (mythic; ethnocentric)	Jesus is the bringer of the One Eternal Truth. Everyone who believes in the literal interpretation of the Bible will be saved; everyone who does not will burn eternally in hell.
Early formal-reflexive (rational; transition from ethno- to world-centric)	Jesus is fully Divine, yet he is also a more humanized and believably human being; he represents universal love that facilitates people finding their salvation through him or through other religious and/or spiritual paths.
Late formal-reflexive (pluralistic; world-centric)	Jesus is my specific culturally influenced symbol of a kind of God-union that everyone has the potential to experience.
Vision-logic (integral; universe-centric)	Jesus is the historical figure who represents Christ-consciousness—present to varying degrees in different people—and described in various terms by adherents to various religious, spiritual, and secular traditions.

Source: Adapted from Marquis, A. (2008) *The integral intake: A guide to comprehensive idiographic assessment in integral psychology*, p.133, New York, NY: Routledge.

Types and Subpersonalities   At any level of any line, a person might be characterized by any number of *types* of orientations, such as those assessed by the Myers-Briggs Type Indicator, the five-factor model of personality, the Enneagram, or other typological systems. Wilber (1999c) has even hypothesized gender to be a kind of "type." It is important to recognize that whereas levels can be thought of vertically and are universal structures through which all individuals may pass, types are horizontal phenomena that are highly individual and nonuniversal. Thus, types add to the fluid and nonlinear appearance of overall self-development.

The self also contains *subpersonalities*, which Wilber (2000b) defined as "functional self-presentations that navigate particular psychosocial situations" (p. 101). In other words, a subpersonality is a particular thought/feeling/action/physiology mode that kicks in to cope with certain types of situations. A common example is the harsh critic who, when confronted with her own and/or others' fallibility, responds with judgmental thoughts; with angry, superior feelings; with critical words and punitive actions; and with tense physiology.

Wilber (2000b) and others (Rowan, 1990) suggested that the average person has about a dozen subpersonalities. A person can form one or more subpersonalities at any level of development and often does form at least one at each level. Consequently, various counseling theorists have identified some relatively common subpersonalities as personality parts: psychoanalysis's id, ego, and superego; transactional analysis's child, parent, and adult ego states; Gestalt's top dog and underdog; focusing's critic. Subpersonalities revolve around particular archetypal forms and can include social roles such as the father role or wife role. Wilber noted that people can even form subpersonalities associated with transpersonal levels of development. The crucial issue for healthy functioning is the extent to which the self can dis-identify from a subpersonality so that the self can take charge of it—having choice as to when and how one engages the subpersonality—rather than being taken over by it.

Self In this section, adapted from Marquis (2008, pp. 155–163), we address in greater depth a central structure in integral psychology: *the self*. Wilber has conceptualized human development prior to the transpersonal stages from a predominantly psychodynamic perspective. Thus, structures such as the ego and self are central to integral psychology and counseling. Importantly, *the self is not so much a thing or noun as it is an action or verb*—the dynamic and usually tacit *process* that holds together the sundry developmental lines, subpersonalities, and so forth, constructing something of a cohesive whole that recursively serves as each person's psychological universe. As previously mentioned, the self is also the locus of a host of important operations and capacities, such as organization, identification, defenses, metabolism (psychological digestion of one's experiences), will, and navigation (one's journey through the developmental labyrinth). The goal of this section is not to fully explain all of the detailed depths of an integral view of the self-system; rather, the goal is to pique your interest enough so that you will seek out other primary integral therapy resources that address the self-system more fully (Ingersoll & Cook-Greuter, 2007; Marquis, 2008; Wilber, 2000b).

To begin, integral theory distinguishes between the self-sense (UL view; the self as a person experiences it phenomenologically from inside) and the self or self-system (UR view; the self as structurally analyzed and conceptualized from outside). As in all cases, integral therapists are mindful of the imperative need to allow first-person views to inform third-person descriptions and explanations. Wilber (2000b) described the *overall self as* consisting of several aspects. The ground of the self is "pure Consciousness ... Spirit that transcends all ... the transcendental Self, antecedent Self" (p. 34), what Wilber termed the ultimate *witness*. The witness manifests in each individual as a *proximate self*, a person's immediate *felt-sense of* oneself, and a *distal self*, everything one *knows about* oneself. As an example: I (Marquis) counseled a client years ago who was court-ordered to attend therapy because of his violent tendencies. When I initially asked him to tell me about himself, the first words he spoke were "I'm a violent man"—as if that was the *whole* of who he was (proximate self). Although it took a few months, he came to respond to that same query with "*Part* of who I am is aggressive or violent, but those are really just adjectives that describe the real me, which is more difficult to explain." In this case, what he was previously subject to, identified with, and embedded in—violence—became an *object* of his awareness (part of his distal self) with which he (the *subject/* proximate self) no longer exclusively identified.

Wilber described the relationship between what is subject and what is object to oneself as a process in which "a *mode* of self becomes merely a *component* of a higher-order self" (1980, p. 81, italics in original). He further described the above process in a number of different ways. In addition to the notions that *what was subject becomes object* and *what was the whole becomes a part*, he also wrote that "what is *identification* becomes *detachment* ... what is *context* becomes *content*" (1980, p. 81, italics in original). The overall self does not undergo development; rather, one aspect of it navigates the sequence of developmental levels. By contrast, the proximate self does proceed through that developmental sequence that we previously described in the Levels section.

Self-System Pathology The 1-2-3 Process. At each successive stage of self-development, an individual ideally experiences that what was first-person "I" becomes first-person "me" or "mine" (Wilber, 2006). What was one's subjective sense of self with which the self was totally identified ("I am x") becomes an objective aspect of one's self from which the self can disidentify yet that the self still owns ("X is part of me...").

For example, consider a client who is having difficulty with her anger. Various meditative techniques—especially what Wilber (2000a, 2000d) referred to as the "witness exercise"—can foster clients' experiential sense of the antecedent self as a state of consciousness involving a perspective of nonattachment that "can give the client a feeling of I or self that is free from problems. In this sense the state can provide temporary respite from the suffering that comes from attachment" (Ingersoll & Cook-Greuter, 2007, p. 197). So, the therapist invites the client to dis-identify from her anger by saying to herself "I have anger, but I am not my anger. I am that which is aware of my anger. If I can observe my anger arise and fade away, I must be the observer, not that which I observe. I am the witness. I have anger, but I am not my anger." When that exercise proceeds well, the client does indeed realize that she is not exclusively her anger, but, equally importantly, she recognizes that the anger that she experiences is *hers*—it has emerged from within, and as a part of, her own body–mind. That is part of the importance of the phrase "I have anger" rather than "I am aware of anger." In the latter case, the client could be aware of another's anger (second-person) or of dissociated anger overcoming him (as a third-person "it" or "other": "I don't know what happened... I was overcome by the anger"); in either case, the client would be viewing the anger as "other" to herself and, thus, would not own and integrate it.

By contrast, in unhealthy self-development, first-person "I" becomes other than I: second-person "you" or third-person "it" (Wilber, 2006). Rather than assuming responsibility and ownership for aspects of one's self, the person somehow disowns those aspects: dissociates from or projects them onto others or the world at large. Although differentiation and dis-identification are essential to healthy development, also essential is that whatever one dis-identified with, one still owns as an object of oneself. Integral theorists refer to the disowning of first-person aspects of self as second- or third- person phenomena as the "1-2-3 phenomenon" (Wilber, 2006, p. 136).

An example of how a person projects one's disowned experiences—such as feelings, thoughts, and motives—onto others or dissociates from them so that they are perceived as third-person "its" is the case of the client with violent tendencies. During one of our sessions, he seemed to be in the process of becoming angry, as evidenced by a tense face, gritting his teeth, and clenching the arms of his chair so tightly that his knuckles were literally white. When I commented that he appeared angry, he burst out, "Me! I'm not angry, but *you* seem infuriated with me." My supervision group observed the session: Both my introspection and their observation indicated that I was not and had not appeared angry. Moreover, that same client, especially in the beginning of our work together, often spoke not of "I became angry" but as "being overcome with anger [it] or violent thoughts [its]"—as if they were third person it/its: not part of him but, rather, separate from and alien to his sense of self.

To summarize, it is usually unhealthy for someone to convert a first-person dynamic (such as "I am angry") into second-person ("I'm not angry, *you* are!") or third-person ("the anger, *it* just took control of me"). Regarding the "1-2-3" process, what is often therapeutic is the reversal of that dynamic, what Wilber referred to as "the 3-2-1 process of (re)owning the self before transcending it" or more simply as the "3-2-1 process" (2006, p. 136), which we will discuss further under the Techniques section.

To reiterate: healthy self-development transforms "I" into "me" or "mine"; pathological self-development transforms "I" into "you" or "it." *Dis-identification* is an essential component of the process; along with ownership, it can lead to growth and liberation, whereas along with dis-ownership, it usually leads to symptoms and an intensification of problems.

Self-System Pathology: Repression   All forgetting is not repression. At one end of the continuum of forgetting is simple, meaningless inattention to phenomena; at the other end is meaningful, forceful, yet unconscious submersion of psychological material into forgetfulness. Likewise, all forgetting is not problematic; only repressed material seeks expression in the form of disguised, symbolic symptoms. Integral theorists consider repression a pathology of the self-system because a person unknowingly relegates into nonawareness those experiences in the environment or aspects of oneself that one finds actually or potentially threatening to the self.

Five Different Types of Unconsciousness   Many counseling theorists have deduced from clinical experience that people have some kind of unconscious psychological structure-function. An integral conceptualization of unconscious psychodynamics reveals not just one unconscious *structure* but five qualitatively distinct types of unconscious *processes*. Wilber's (1980; 1999c) conceptualization includes not only the dynamic and structural features other theorists like Freud, Jung, Rogers, and Perls have described, but also developmental and evolutionary aspects. For example, although adults who have learned various rules, roles, and responsibilities may repress guilt for some action or failure to act, it makes no sense to speak of a two-year-old as having repressed guilt. Thus, what is in "the" unconscious is a function of development (Wilber, 1999c). Following are five different *types* (not levels) of unconsciousness.

At birth and throughout life, each person's psyche consists of the *ground-unconscious*. It contains all of the most fundamental and as-yet formless deep structures from which all the person's future psychological structures will arise. In the ground-unconscious, these developmental potentials are undifferentiated and enfolded, though humanity has programmed them, so to speak, to emerge, unfold, and take form in a particular sequence. A person has not repressed these potentials because they have not yet emerged into awareness; they are originally unconscious (Wilber, 1999c, p. 247).

The *archaic-unconscious* involves the most primitive forms to emerge from the ground-unconscious (Wilber, 1999c, p. 249), such as nutritional sustenance drives, emotional-sexual energies, and mental-phantasmic images. Like the ground-unconscious, this type of unconscious is not the result of personal experience but is innate in humans by virtue of their phylogenetic heritage (Freud, 1963; Jung, 1969; Wilber, 1999c). As such, it also is not repressed but is simply unconscious from the beginning of a person's life. Mostly emergent at birth, and being psychologically primitive, the archaic-unconscious is mostly preverbal, a quality it retains throughout life (Wilber, 1999c, pp. 249–250).

The *submergent-unconscious* is what most therapists probably consider "the unconscious;" it consists of material that had previously emerged from the ground- and/or archaic-unconscious into a person's consciousness, only to be submerged once again out of awareness. It can include any and all types of material: individual or collective; prepersonal, personal, or transpersonal. The reasons that specific content is in the submergent-unconscious span the continuum of forgetfulness, from simple inattention to actual repression. Like Jung (1969), integral theorists refer to the personal dimension of the submergent-unconscious as the "shadow" that spans a spectrum: from the preverbal, barely differentiated primal material of a person's archaic unconscious, to a person's relatively developed verbal scripts and injunctions about how self, others, and life are and should be (Wilber, 1999c, p. 251).

The *embedded-unconscious* refers to those psychological structure-functions that are fundamental to people's perception and organization of experience yet are out of their awareness. Piaget's (1977) and Beck, Rush, Shaw, and Emery's (1979) notions of *schemas* and Adler's (cited in Ansbacher & Ansbacher, 1956) *schema of apperception* are examples of embedded psychological structures that influence, connect, and organize a person's perceptions and experiences without the person being conscious of the structures or their operations. In addition to these structure-functions, the embedded-unconscious includes the aspect of the self that enacts repression—that, outside of one's conscious awareness, feels threatened by some phenomenon and relegates memory of it to the submergent-unconscious (Wilber, 1999c, p. 254).

Regardless of a person's developmental stage in life, one's conscious self does not, in its natural course of operation, directly observe the very structure-functions that comprise the self, that is, in which one's self is embedded. However, with effort, most people can become somewhat more aware of these structures and processes. An analogy is that a person who is wearing tinted sunglasses will have her perception of the environment colored by the lenses she is looking through, yet she won't see the colored lenses while looking *through* them, but only if she removes them from her face and looks *at* them.

The *emergent-unconscious* refers to those deep structures that a person has not yet identified with or realized out of their potentiality. Thus, the contents of the emergent unconscious change as a person develops—as the person realizes—and thereby becomes increasingly conscious of more and more of one's potential. For example, for a person whose center of gravity hovers around the representational mind, every basic structure of consciousness beyond the representational mind (F-3) is part of that person's emergent-unconscious, in this case the rule/role mind, formal-reflexive, vision-logic, and the suprapersonal (you may find it helpful to consult Table 14.1). Along these lines, Freud wrote that every mental process

> first exists in an unconscious state or phase, and only develops out of this into a conscious phase, much as a photograph is first a negative and then becomes a picture through the printing of the positive. But not every negative is made into a positive, and it is just as little necessary that every unconscious mental process should convert itself into a conscious one. (1935, p. 260)

In summary, the primary structures of the human psyche are the *levels* and *lines* of development, various *states* of consciousness, personality *types*, the *self* and its *subpersonalities,* and different forms of *unconsciousness.* The universality of these structures accounts for commonality among humans; the combinations and permutations of these numerous factors, as each person creatively expresses them in the context of one's own culture and society, accounts for the uniqueness of each human.

To close this section, we want to make the point that integral theorists do not speak of an individual being *at* a particular stage or level of development but, more likely, something like *currently manifesting* a particular stage or level. This wording acknowledges that the entire spectrum of development is present within each person as a potential for the person to realize. It also acknowledges that stages are not actually concrete, reified structures but are *probability waves* or *psychological spaces* that a person adopts and from which the probability is quite high that the person will manifest—and the person and/or others will observe—specific patterns of thinking, feeling, and acting that characterize a given level of development (Marquis & Wilber, 2008). Likewise, Wilber (2000b) repeatedly asserted that the psychological structures that humans have manifested "can better be understood as formative habits of evolution,

'Kosmic memories', ... and not pregiven modes into which the world is poured" (p. 145). Thus, it seems more fitting to describe a person as "currently manifesting" a probability of expressing the characteristics humans have created and come to know as a given level or stage of development.

Role of the Environment

From an integral perspective, the existence of every holon at every level depends on *inter-relationship* with its environment. In particular, an individual and one's environment are constantly engaged in an ongoing system of relational exchange involving the needs associated with one's level of development and the environmental provision of the food that meets those needs. Indeed, Wilber (2000b, p. 118) has characterized the environment as consisting of a *holarchy of "food"* that corresponds to the needs at each level of the holarchy of individual development. Physical food includes nutrition and physically safe surroundings. Emotional food includes emotional connection and nurturing and, when developmentally appropriate, sexual intimacy. Mental food includes the psychological stimulation of thinking and communicating about ideas. Spiritual food includes opportunities "to be in relationship with a Source and Ground that gives sanction, meaning, and deliverance to our separate selves" (p. 118). You may have noticed that Wilber did not specify social needs, although need fulfillment often occurs through relationship with other people. This seeming exclusion is because individual holons are *always* members of social holons; therefore, social interaction is inherent in the system of relational exchange throughout life.

The environment can provide the various forms of food or can fail to provide them or even provide seemingly toxic experiences. In particular, Wilber (2000b, p. 101) mentioned three environmental conditions that can be detrimental to developmental progress, although he did not elaborate on them. "Developmental miscarriages" probably refers to conditions of *chronic deprivation* that preclude normal development, for example, starvation, lack of contact comfort, or any other absence of food at any level. *Repeated trauma* probably refers to actual assaults on the developing organism, that is, multiple exposures to conditions for which one is not developmentally prepared to cope, for example, ongoing childhood sexual abuse. *Recurrent stress* probably refers to conditions with which one is developmentally prepared to cope except for the severity and chronicity of the conditions that gradually wear away at one's coping resources, for example, trying to find work in a chronically depressed economy. As the examples show, these conditions can exist in either or both the familial and/or extrafamilial environments, both of which are represented by the bottom two quadrants of integral theory's four quadrant model.

Familial

In accordance with psychodynamic principles, Wilber has identified the familial environment as a crucial factor in early development. In his view, object relations and self psychology, as well as other modern schools of psychoanalysis, have provided the best explanations of the first four levels of development, both of which include the fundamental contention that the quality of early child–caregiver relationships greatly influences the quality of the child's sense of self.

One's family can continue to exert influence on a person throughout that person's life. Yet, as an individual progresses through the spectrum of development, influence shifts increasingly from familial to extrafamilial, particularly to one's cultural group.

Extrafamilial

An individual's inextricable embeddedness in, and interrelationship with, one's culture and society plays a crucial role in development. The collective provides the background without which a self-sense—the felt sense of being an "I"—would not even emerge (Wilber, 2000a, Vol. 7). A given culture itself can be understood as having its own developmental structure around which it is centered and that reflects its collective level of development within the great nest of being. This collective center of gravity exerts powerful pressures on individual development.

> The center of gravity of a given culture tends to act as a 'magnet of development': if you are below that average, the magnet pulls you up; if you try to go beyond it, it pulls you down.... [T]hus, with any postformal and post-postconventional developments, not only are you on your own, you are sometimes actively discouraged. (Wilber, 2000a, Vol. 7, pp. 730–731)

In particular, a culture that does not include belief in the realities of development beyond the separate, individual self will certainly not foster such development.

> Cultures seem to function ... as collective conspiracies to constrict consciousness.... [S]ociety may encourage development up to societal norms but hinder development beyond them ... [which] explain[s] the fate of all too many saints and sages who throughout human history have ended up poisoned, crucified, or burned. The net result is that our latent capacities and geniuses may be covertly suppressed rather than encouraged and expressed. (Walsh & Vaughan, 1993, pp. 110–111)

Another developmentally restrictive aspect of Western culture, in particular, is what anthropologists such as Laughlin, McManus, and Shearer (1993) termed its *monophasic* quality: valuing and deriving a worldview from a single state of consciousness, the normal waking state. In contrast, most cultures are *polyphasic* in that their values and worldviews reflect an appreciation of multiple states of consciousness, including waking, dreaming, and numerous mystical or contemplative states. Since *state-specificity*, insights and understandings derived from a given state of consciousness are likely to be incomprehensible to those who have not experienced that state (Tart, 1983; Walsh, 1989). This phenomenon may explain why contemplative or mystical experiences and disciplines have been so widely misunderstood in the West.

Thus, one's culture, and how it is expressed in one's social environment of family, friends, coworkers, and so forth, play a powerful role in one's development. Maslow (1968) encouraged people to create optimal environments to facilitate personal and spiritual growth. These "euspychian environments" involve sharing the company of those who value personal and transpersonal development, who are practicing their cultivation, and who provide conditions of safety that allow each other the opportunity to reduce defenses and emerge into new ways of being. More specifically, Wilber (2000b) has repeatedly emphasized the necessity for a person to have an ongoing relationship with a spiritual teacher to facilitate transpersonal development.

Interaction of Human Nature and Environment

From an integral perspective, a comprehensive view of development includes reference to all developmental levels as they manifest in all four mutually influencing quadrants: interior and exterior, individual and collective. Nevertheless, for an introductory chapter such as this one, we will focus primarily on the experiential quadrant, as that has been the traditional purview of counseling. In addition, although the environment provides both opportunities and limits, the individual can choose what meaning she makes of circumstances she cannot control and can use her creativity to generate new opportunities and exceed external limits. However, her choices and creativity are probabilistically related not only to cultural (LL) and social (LR) constraints, but also to her level of psychological development (UL): She is most likely to choose from the resources available to her at her current center of gravity, and to this extent her free will is limited, though, again, in only a probabilistic rather than an ultimate way, because all humans, at all times, at the deepest level of being, have access to—in fact, *are*—all that is. Indeed, the history of human development is highlighted by the creative acts of people who exceeded the limits of both exterior, and even seemingly interior, conditions. The point to keep in mind in the following upper-left-quadrant-focused discussion is that human development is actually a highly complex, all-quadrant affair.

Healthy Functioning

Integral counselors consider optimal human functioning to be far more than the absence of symptoms of mental disorder. A substantial amount of research accumulated in the last 40 years strongly suggests that average adults have by no means realized their developmental potentials (Alexander, Druker, & Langer, 1990; Assagioli, 1991; Maslow, 1968, 1971; Snyder & Shane, 2005; Wade, 1996; Wilber, 2000b, Vol. 4; Wilber, Engler, & Brown, 1986). As Maslow (1968) asserted, "what we call 'normal' in psychology is really a psychopathology of the average, so undramatic and so widely spread that we don't even notice it" (p. 16). Even in the absence of diagnosable mental disorders, people may suffer from a host of what Maslow (1971) termed "metapathologies": "failure[s] to recognize and satisfy our transpersonal nature and needs," wrote Walsh and Vaughan (1993), "[that] may underlie much of the individual, cultural, and global suffering that surrounds us" (p. 137).

An integral view of optimal functioning involves at least four notions. First, *the farther one has traversed the developmental journey*, the more resources one has to bring to the process of living. With each subsequent level of development, one retains the abilities of the previous levels and adds to them. This process does *not* mean that someone at a higher stage of development is *better* than someone at a lower stage, any more than an oak tree is better than an acorn: Given its stage of development, the acorn is just as perfect as the oak. The acorn, however, is more vulnerable to environmental dangers, such as fires or hungry squirrels, than is the oak tree. Similarly, even though each individual is a radiant expression of the spiritual, people who experience themselves as only their bodies and minds have fewer resources with which to meet the vicissitudes of life than do those who have awakened to their identities beyond the separate self-sense. In a sense, the more developed one is, the freer one is of previous limitations.

Second, healthy functioning is associated with the *completeness of identification with one's level* of development, whatever that level is. Healthy developmental progress involves the individual disidentifying with one level, identifying with the next level, and integrating the preceding level within the new level. Pathology involves either/both a failure to disidentify from, or entirely from, the previous level, resulting in developmental arrest or fixation, respectively, and/or failure to integrate the previous level, resulting in repression, fragmentation, and alienation (Wilber, 1999b, Vol. 4). This aspect of health involves the notion of how "stabilized" a person is at any given stage (Ingersoll & Cook-Greuter, 2007; Marquis, 2008), a notion we'll discuss further below.

Third, given that the self includes numerous *lines* that can develop rather independently of each other, an integral notion of health involves a relative *balance among the lines*. For example, an individual with high cognitive and moral development but low interpersonal development is likely to feel isolated and lonely, whereas one with high cognitive and interpersonal development and low moral development may be manipulative and exploitive. Thus, the more similarly developed one's various lines of development are, the less distressed one is likely to feel and the less distressing to others one is likely to be.

Finally, integral health includes a *balance among the quadrants* within one's level of development. For example, regardless of one's level, excessive emphasis on the "I" (experiential quadrant) leads to egocentrism; inordinate concern for "we" (cultural quadrant) results in conformity; and too much focus on "it" (behavioral and social quadrants) produces dissociation from interior individual and collective experiences and processes. Thus, the integral view of optimal functioning includes one's place among the 10 levels of development, one's completeness of identification with one's current prevailing level, balance among one's lines of development, and balance among the four quadrants.

Healthy people are happy people. Happiness does not imply a hedonistic or pain-free life. In fact, healthy people do not avoid pain; rather, they fully experience and explore it (Puhakka, 1994; Walsh, 1995). When one understands pain and suffering, one knows that their source is one's attachment to specific conditions. In the words of T. S. Eliot (1943), "Desire itself is movement not in itself desirable" (p. 20). Unhappiness is essentially a discrepancy between what one desires and what one has. "Happiness lies not in feeding and fueling our attachments but in reducing them and relinquishing them. Nowhere is this summarized more succinctly than in the Buddha's Third Noble Truth: 'Freedom from attachment brings freedom from suffering' " (Walsh, 1999, p. 41). This message was also expressed by the Christian mystic, Meister Eckhart: "the greatest and best virtue with which man [*sic*] can most completely and closely conform himself to God … [is] a pure detachment from all things" (cited in Walsh, 1999, p. 41). Thus, healthy people address their physical, emotional, mental, and spiritual needs while giving relatively less energy and attention to the fulfillment of specific desirable conditions and giving relatively more energy and attention to the realization of peace and happiness in the midst of whatever conditions arise or pass away.

In many ways, healthier people appear to be more developed beings (Vaughan, 1985; Walsh, 1999). Such people are more loving, compassionate, and serving than most; they appear less motivated by fear and greed and more concerned with living in harmony with all beings; they experience more inner peace, gratitude, reverence for life; and they appreciate both unity and diversity. Such people are humorous, generous, forgiving, wise, accepting, and more open and, therefore, more vulnerable. Finally, health demands wholeness, which requires integration of not only the "shadow"—relegated to the submergent-unconscious—but also the integration of the physical body, emotionality, mental ego, existential self, and spiritual self. So, whereas "mental and existential identifications represent essential stages of human growth, healthy maturation and wholeness require growing beyond them" (Vaughan, 1985, pp. 30–31).

Unhealthy Functioning

Conversely, an integral view of suboptimal functioning includes a relatively lower prevailing level of development, incomplete identification with one's current prevailing level, imbalance among one's lines of development, and/or imbalance among the four quadrants.

More specifically, Wilber (1999a, Vol. 4) has posited that each stage of development, if unsuccessfully navigated, will produce its own psychogenic pathology. For each of the 10 stages respectively, these pathologies are psychoses, borderline/narcissistic personality disorders, neuroses, script pathologies, identity neuroses, existential pathologies, psychic disorders, subtle disorders, and causal disorders; the nondual stage is pathology free.

Within the prepersonal realm, *psychoses* represent "a failure to differentiate and integrate the physiosphere" (Wilber, 1995, p. 211). Reflecting "the most profound and primitive lack of psychological organization" (Marquis, 2002, p. 19), they include such conditions as schizophrenia and psychotic depression. In *borderline/narcissistic personality disorders*, having differentiated from others physically but not emotionally, people

> feel overwhelmed or engulfed by their emotional environment (borderline disorders), treat their environment as an extension of their own feelings (inflated narcissism), or derive their sense of self-worth from their perceptions of how others feel about them (fragile narcissism) ... [and] employ primitive defenses such as splitting and denial. (Marquis, 2002, p. 20)

Neuroses involve "the more mature defenses such as repression or displacement" such that "the mental self [dissociates] from the emotional self or [remains] fixated upon certain bodily or emotional impulses"; as a result, "that which was repressed returns in the form of 'disguised symptoms' forcing themselves into consciousness (Wilber, 1995; Wilber et al., 1986)" (Marquis, 2002, pp. 21–22).

Within the personal realm, *script pathologies* refer to a broad array of manifestations that have as their source role confusion (Erikson, 1963); rule confusion, distortion of the rules of logic in one's thinking (Beck & Weishaar, 1989); and/or duplicitous transactions. In the latter, overt messages mask hidden agendas or covert messages (Berne, 1961), such as the boss who asks her late-arriving secretary, "What time is it?" a message overtly seeking information but covertly expressing hostile criticism. *Identity neuroses* refer to a broad array of manifestations that have as their source the distresses and vulnerabilities of the emerging introspective self (Marquis, 2002). These include obsession over possible losses and the struggle to resist social pressures in order to emerge as one's own person. *Existential pathologies* have as their source questions about the ultimate meaning of life in general and one's own life in particular and can manifest in a broad array of concerns including the givens of life—death, meaninglessness, freedom, and isolation (Yalom, 1980)—and issues of personal autonomy, authenticity, and self-actualization.

Proceeding to the transpersonal realm, we want to alert you again to the fact that transpersonal pathologies may seem alien, not making sense if you have not had experiences from the level we are discussing. Indeed, many writers have argued that the transpersonal realm cannot make sense in the same manner as most everyday discourse, precisely because it is transpersonal: beyond the senses—trans-sensational, and beyond reason—trans-rational.

Psychic disorders fall into three main groups.

> First are the spontaneous awakenings of unsought spiritual energies and capacities, such as kundalini, which 'can be psychological dynamite'. Next are the spiritual crises that, during severe stress, invade the lower levels of development ... psychotic-like episodes [that can be differentiated from actual psychosis].... Third are the many problems of those beginning a contemplative life, such as psychic inflation—attributing the

transpersonal energies to the individual self/ego, structural imbalances—resulting from improper employment of spiritual disciplines, and the 'dark night of the soul'—having tasted unity with the Spiritual and then to have it fade, one enters a profound state of despair [that can be differentiated from personal-realm depression]. (Wilber et al., 1986, cited in Marquis, 2002, p. 37)

Subtle disorders take many forms, two of the most common of which we will describe here. One is a kind of fragmentation in which one *observes* rather than *is* archetypal awareness (Wilber et al., 1986, p. 123). Another is mistaking the phenomena of subtle level experiences—archetypal forms, interior luminosities and sounds, and currents of bliss—as enlightenment itself.

The *causal* disorders involve either a failure to differentiate or a failure to integrate. Either the person fails to

differentiate from, or die to, "the subtlest level of the separate self-sense," or, having differentiated itself from all objects of awareness—to the extent that no objects arise to consciousness—one fails to *integrate* the causal unmanifest with the manifest realm of forms. (Marquis, 2002, p. 44)

For each pathology, Wilber (1999b, Vol. 4) proposed treatment modalities consisting of widely practiced psychotherapeutic approaches, alternative therapies, and practices from the world's contemplative traditions. His spectrum of treatment brings order and harmony to the cacophony of psychological theories and treatment options available to mental health professionals. It is to the psychotherapy process that we now turn.

THE PERSONALITY CHANGE PROCESS

The Self Is Integral; So Must Be Counseling

According to Wilber (1999b, Vol. 4), people change in two basic ways: translation and transformation. *Translation* involves change *within* one's level of development, maintaining the same deep structure of functioning but changing surface structures (horizontal growth). *Transformation* involves change *of* one's level of development, a fundamental shift in the deep structure of one's functioning in the direction of greater complexity (vertical development). As previously stated, translation is analogous to rearranging one's furniture, whereas transformation is analogous to moving to upgraded living quarters (Wilber, 1999b, Vol. 3).

Translation and transformation recur in the process of human development; to this extent, change is a naturally occurring, indeed, an unavoidable phenomenon that people manifest in response to emerging needs: physical, emotional, mental, and spiritual. At the same time, because of people's tendency to avoid pain and disruption, and because of chronic deprivation, repeated trauma, and recurrent stress in the environment, virtually everyone, at one time or another, has become stuck in the process of developmental change. Wilber (2000b) asserted that

the curative catalyst ... is bringing *awareness* or *consciousness* to bear on an area of experience that is (or has been) denied, distorted, falsified, or ignored. Once that area enters (or reenters) consciousness, then it can rejoin the ongoing flow of evolutionary unfolding, instead of remaining behind, stuck, ... sending up painful symptoms.... Encountering (or reencountering) these disturbed or ignored facets [of experience] allows them to be differentiated (transcended) and integrated (included) in the ongoing waves of ever-expanding consciousness. (p. 99, italics added)

Like the process of becoming stuck, the process of becoming unstuck can and does occur naturally. However, a person can achieve the latter process more elegantly in the special circumstance of counseling, an environment specifically aimed at the development of consciousness. The exceptional caring and expertise that characterizes the best counseling environments can facilitate the unearthing and overcoming of impediments to development.

Client's Role

From the client's perspective, he seeks counseling because he wants relief from pain. From the integral counselor's perspective, the client's pain is a manifestation of his being stuck in the process of development; it is a kind of feedback from the proximal self that one is not progressing as one's deepest nature intends. Thus, from the counselor's perspective, the client's felt motivation is to alleviate pain, and his deeper motivation is to continue the process of development.

Although clients may seek counseling for any of the nine pathologies corresponding to the first nine fulcrums of development that Wilber has posited, most clients seek counseling to alleviate suffering that arises from "a few levels: mostly fulcrum-3 (which involves uncovering and integrating repressed feelings and shadow elements), fulcrum-4 (which involves belongingness needs and cognitive reprogramming of harsh scripts), and fulcrums 5 and 6 (which involve self-esteem and self-actualization)" (Wilber, 1999b, Vol. 4, pp. 17–18).

Integral therapists acknowledge that, at the same time clients seek relief, they also resist change. The process of transformative change, in particular, involves the disruption and death of exclusive identification with the previous fulcrum, mode of functioning, or self. "The self, at every level, will attempt to defend itself against pain, disruption, and ultimately death" (Wilber, 2000b, p. 94). As Adi Da put it, the separate self is "at war with its own Help" (cited in Murthy, 1990, p. 31). Wilber (2000b, Vol. 1, p. 563) has posited that people at different levels of development tend to rely on different forms of defense and resistance. For example, whereas a client at F-3 representational-mind tends to resist and disown bodily impulses such as sex and aggression, someone at F-6 vision-logic has accepted and integrated those impulses but tends to resist experiencing the immediate here and now. Likewise, at the transpersonal levels, individuals tend not to resist the present moment but to resist fully surrendering to unity consciousness. At any level, "people will sometimes opt for the known pain of the old adaptive pattern rather than endure the pain of transcendence, disintegration, and reintegration" (Holden, 1993, p. 15).

Since counseling involves the threat of development, a client must be willing to endure the temporary discomfort of transformation to alleviate the chronic discomfort he sought counseling to relieve. Evolutionarily, each person has developed what Mahoney (2003) called "core ordering processes" (p. 48)—emotionality, personal identity, one's sense of reality, and power/control—as special protection against changing; such resistance reflects fundamental self-protective processes that function to maintain the coherence of the living system. From an integral perspective, the problem is that a person is, ultimately, more than simply a living system. Thus, what is most adaptive for the biological organism (life sphere within the great nest of being) may not serve one's deepest nature (soul and spirit spheres).

An effective counselor can facilitate a client's willingness to change and the process of change itself. However, the primary responsibility for change rests with the client. This notion is corroborated by substantial research (Asay & Lambert, 1999; Bohart & Tallman, 1999; Lambert & Bergin, 1994; Mahoney 1991, 2003) suggesting that client variables, such as motivation, presenting concern, and the assumption of responsibility, are more predictive of counseling success than are counselor variables such as theoretical orientation and techniques employed. In addition, integral therapists believe that to each successive fulcrum of development, a person must bring increasing intentionality that is expressed in action. In particular, for one to proceed through the transpersonal fulcrums, one must engage in a program of spiritual practice. Regarding both counseling and spiritual practice, Walsh (1999) wrote that what a person must bring to the processes are

> an open mind and a willingness to experiment.... It takes courage to examine yourself and your life carefully. It takes effort, ... commitment.... Fortunately, the more you practice, the more these essential qualities grow" (p. 15).

In the end, integral theorists' view of the human capacity to change is quite exalted: Each human being has enfolded within her being the entire great nest, from dirt to divinity, from matter to spirit. Thus, like transpersonalists in general, integral therapists believe in each person's "wealth of inner resources and an innate capacity for self-healing" (Vaughan, 1993, p. 160).

Counselor's Role

The counselor's role in integral counseling could be stated most basically as helping clients be happier and suffer less (Walsh, 1999) by promoting their translative and transformative change. Since most clients will seek translation rather than transformation (Wilber, 1999b, Vol. 4), most counselors will pursue what Wilber has termed the *prime directive*: helping clients stabilize and maximize their functioning at their current prevailing level of development. Thus, analogously speaking, the goal is not necessarily to live in the building's penthouse but to live as happily as possible on one's own floor, with some access to the entire building.

To prepare for both translative and transformative work, integral counselors fulfill certain prerequisites. One prerequisite is the ability to conceptualize her clients, herself, and life in terms of integral theory. Another is the counselor's pursuit of her own development. A final prerequisite is the counselor's mastery of the psychotherapeutic techniques associated with the developmental levels of clients with whom she works.

Regarding the first prerequisite of integral conceptualization, studying this chapter is an excellent beginning. Reading primary sources on integral counseling such as Wilber (2000b), Marquis (2008), Forman (2010), and Ingersoll (2010) also is necessary, as is supplementary reading of sources that address transpersonal counseling and spirituality in counseling. Seeking out continuing education through conferences, workshops, and university coursework is also essential. A counselor can also advance integration of integral concepts by revisioning one's own life and experience in terms of integral theory. A specific manifestation of this perspective is that the counselor grasps the counseling process as a sacred journey that involves "[joining] another person in an extraordinarily intimate way ... trying to become a helpful part of [a client's] very evolution" (Kegan, 1982, p. 278). As such, integral counselors *care* for clients such that they are moved by their experiences with clients—a quality potentially as helpful to clients as the counselor's professional knowledge. Another manifestation of the counselor's integral perspective is an appreciation of the mutual influence of the counselor's personal and professional life (Mahoney, 2003). This appreciation leads naturally to the second prerequisite.

Regarding the second prerequisite, pursuit of one's own development, Walsh and Vaughan (1993, p. 154) quoted the Buddha: "To straighten the crooked, You must first do a harder thing—Straighten yourself." Similarly, it is a transpersonal counseling axiom that one can elegantly facilitate others' achievement of only those developmental levels that one has achieved in oneself. To say it another way, one must have "been there and done that" in order to help others "be there and do that" (or something similar to that).

> The depth of [counseling] is necessarily limited by the [developmental] stage of the thera-pist.... [T]he further the therapist has evolved through the stages of Self-awareness at various levels of consciousness, the more effective he or she is likely to be as a healer. (Vaughan, 1985, pp. 184–185)

For transpersonally oriented therapists, including integral therapists, "undergoing their own in-depth, transpersonally oriented psychotherapy and long-term practice of transpersonal disciplines such as yoga or meditation are invaluable ... part of a lifetime practice" (Walsh & Vaughan, 1993, p. 154). Integral theorists believe that a counselor's presence, being, unconditional positive regard, empathy, and compassion are largely a function of the counselor's own spiritual work (Boorstein, 1997; Epstein, 1995; Ram Dass, 1973). In general, "to whatever degree my personal [spiritual] practice keeps *me* loving, keeps *me* compassionate and empathic, to that degree therapy proceeds most effectively" (Boorstein, 1997, p. xvi). In particular, to work with clients in the transper-sonal domain, one must undertake some form of spiritual practice to facilitate a direct and greater understanding of what were, at first, merely cognitive assertions (Vaughan, 1985, 1995; Wittine, 1993).

The third prerequisite, mastery of the psychotherapeutic techniques associated with the developmental levels of clients with whom one works, calls for the counselor to become technically eclectic. As will be discussed below, Wilber's spectrum of development and pathology is associated also with a spectrum of treatment. An integral counselor first decides which developmental levels of client concerns one will address and then devel-ops the skills of the psychotherapeutic approaches that most appropriately address client concerns that arise at those levels. For those clients who are struggling with issues that derive from developmental levels with which the counselor does not work, one identifies qualified practitioners to whom one refers clients with concerns involving those levels. For example, a counselor might be competent to work with clients whose concerns fall primarily into the personal domain but refer clients whose concerns fall primarily within the prepersonal or transpersonal domains. An implication of integrally based technical eclecticism is that an integral counselor will have mastered the psychotherapeutic skills common to all psychotherapeutic approaches, such as basic counseling skills to establish and maintain a therapeutic relationship, session management skills, professional ethics skills, and so forth. Always at the foundation of integral counseling, even more primary than an understanding of the client in terms of quadrants and level of development, is the counselor's valuing of the client as another human being, another manifestation of spirit.

Stages and Techniques

> Just as life is complex, so too, is counseling. (Mahoney, 2003)

Relationship

The integral counseling process begins with the therapeutic relationship. From an integral perspective, any relationship constitutes a small culture of its own, represented by the lower left quadrant. When that culture is healthy, when it is pervaded by intentions of well-being and by mutual vulnerability and influence, it provides for the client "a 'secure base'—a safe, accessible, and compassionate human bond—the therapeutic relationship becomes a context in and from which the client can explore, experiment, and express" (Mahoney, 2003). The therapeutic relationship is thus the primary vehicle of change—the culture in which clients grow (Kegan, 1982).

At its best, the therapeutic relationship provides a client with the security to transform, to disintegrate so that aspects of one's self may be reintegrated at a higher level. Winnicott described this type of relationship as "an environment in which one can safely and easily be in bits and pieces without the feeling of falling apart" (cited in Epstein, 1995, p. 206). When therapy is proceeding well, both counselors and clients can tolerate the discomfort—sometimes terror—of disintegration by seeing it in its place in the developmental process. "More than anything else," wrote Wittine (1993), "our clients need to be seen and felt as the Self they truly are, which is no different from the true Self we are" (p. 169). Thus, beyond the positive regard of person-centered therapy is the positive regard of integral counseling in which the client is regarded at her core as an embodiment of the ultimate goodness, beauty, and truth of Spirit itself.

Assessment

A critical aspect of integral counseling is an accurate and comprehensive assessment of a client's four quadrant profile, level of development, lines of development, states of consciousness, type of personality, and self-system. Only with this information can the client and counselor establish collaboratively the most appropriate counseling goals and processes.

Integral counselors can use the Integral Intake to assess a client's four quadrant profile (Marquis, 2008). A client completes this self-report, short answer instrument prior to the first counseling session or between the first and second sessions. To assemble a conceptual snapshot of the client's experiential quadrant, the counselor notes client responses to items addressing self-image, self-esteem, concerns, and what the client deems meaningful and valuable. To ascertain the client's behavioral quadrant, the counselor reviews client responses regarding more objective phenomena such as medical disorders, medications, diet, alcohol and/or drug use, aerobic and/or strength exercise, and patterns of sleep/rest. To understand the client's cultural quadrant, the counselor examines the client's reported cultural experience: ethnicity, family dynamics, and vocational relationships; political, environmental, and religious or spiritual beliefs; and any experiences of discrimination and/or oppression. Finally, to construct an understanding of the client's social quadrant, the counselor ascertains client responses regarding the more objective aspects of the client's environment, such as socioeconomic status, work environment, conditions of one's neighborhood, layout or state of household, and other environmental stressors and conditions. The Integral Intake also provides a counselor insight into developmental-, state-, and type-related issues of the client that will be relevant to the counselor's conceptualization and treatment planning.

Traditional psychotherapists have tended to favor one quadrant to the relative neglect of others: Psychodynamic and cognitively oriented therapists have focused primarily or exclusively on a client's subjective experiences and psychological dynamics (upper left quadrant), behaviorists on clients' observable behaviors (upper right quadrant), family therapists on clients' social systems (lower right quadrant), and multicultural counselors on clients' cultural contexts (lower left). A unique feature of the integral approach is that counselors can use the Integral Intake to give substantial, structured attention to all aspects of the client's life (all four quadrants) from the outset of counseling. The counselor can use this holistic assessment to formulate an integral profile, including prioritized counseling foci and goals, to present to the client as a way to initiate collaborative goal setting.

Another aspect of assessment is for a counselor to ascertain a client's developmental level. From an integral perspective, people at different stages of development face different struggles, the resolution of which calls for different counseling approaches and practices. The spectrum of development, pathology, and corresponding treatment modalities and, in some cases, contraindications, are summarized in Table 14.2. Wilber (1999b, Vol. 4) stressed that

> the nine general levels of therapy that I outlined are meant to be suggestive only; they are broad guidelines.... There is, needless to say, a great deal of overlap between these therapies. For example, I list "script pathology" and "cognitive therapy" as being especially relevant to fulcrum-4.... Cognitive therapy has excelled in rooting out these maladaptive scripts and replacing them with more accurate, benign, and therefore healthy ideas and self-concepts. But to say cognitive therapy focuses on this wave of consciousness development is *not* to say it has no benefit at other waves, for clearly it does. The idea, rather, is that the farther away we get from this wave, the less relevant (but never completely useless) cognitive therapy becomes. (p. 16)

Regarding *how* to assess a client's level of development and primary psychogenic pathology, very few integral therapists use paper-and-pencil tests. When they do, two available standardized instruments assess ego development, the single best reflection of a person's developmental fulcrum or center of gravity: the Washington University Sentence Completion Test (WUSCT; Hy & Loevinger, 1996) and the Sentence Completion Test integral (SCTi; Cook-Greuter, 1999).

Most integral therapists assess a client's developmental center of gravity informally via observation and inference. In the process, they pay attention to such phenomena as:

- The person's use of language, which reflects thought processes: To what degree is the client's thinking concrete versus abstract? How open is the client to examining the evidence for his thoughts and opinions and revising them on the basis of that evidence
- Signs of developmental arrests or fixations, such as intense needs that appear regressive or age-inappropriate
- The degree of differentiation and complexity in the client's meaning-making activities
- How the client relates to the counselor, that is, reciprocally or merely as an extension of himself; countertransference reactions the counselor observes in oneself that seem related to the client's dynamics rather than the counselor's
- The client's most commonly used defense mechanisms (Marquis, 2008).

So, for example, patterns of highly unstable relationships and the use of primitive defense mechanisms suggest borderline (F-2) disorders; repression of sexual and aggressive impulses resulting in "disguised symptoms" suggest neurotic (F-3) disorders; issues pertaining to role confusion, distorted thinking, "duplicitous transactions" in which hidden agendas or covert messages are masked by different overt messages or overly harsh and rigid internal scripts suggest role or script (F-4) disorders. Some integral counselors find the current edition of the *Diagnostic and Statistical Manual of Mental Disorders* to be a helpful adjunct and use it with awareness of its limitations from an integral perspective, which we discuss near the end of this chapter.

Finally, counselors should explore various *lines* of client development. Again, some integral counselors use assessment instruments such as Kegan's subject–object interview, Hy and Loevinger's (1996) WUSCT or Cook-Greuter's (1999) SCTi, and/or Rest's (1979) and Gilligan's (1982) assessments of moral development; most assess these dimensions more informally through observation and inference. Using results from line-of-development assessment, the counselor formulates an "integral psychograph" (see Figure 14.3) that illustrates to what level a client has developed various lines.

Treatment Plan

Reflecting upon the client's four-quadrant profile, level of development, and integral psychograph, the counselor then tailors integral therapeutic approaches most appropriate to this particular client. At the heart of these approaches are *integral transformative practices* (ITPs): practices that honor and nurture the entire human being, from the body, emotions, and mind, all the way to soul and spirit, as *each* unfolds in self (I), culture (we), and nature (it and its). Thus, regardless of a client's level of development, a counselor attempts to devise a treatment plan that is as "all-quadrant, all-level" as possible for that client (Wilber, 2000c, p. 136). The basic premise is that one is most likely to transform if one exercises and cultivates as many aspects of one's being as possible. Conceptual processes such as adopting an integral philosophy are not sufficient; it is through the actual and consistent engagement of ITPs that one transforms. Wilber recommended that one

> start with the self: the waves of existence ... can be exercised by a spectrum of practices: physical exercises (weightlifting, diet, jogging, yoga), emotional exercises (qi gong, [evocative aspects of] counseling, psychotherapy), mental exercises (affirmation, visualization), and spiritual exercises (meditation, contemplative prayer).
>
> But these waves of existence need to be exercised—not just in self ([a narcissistic affliction Wilber termed] boomeritis!)—but in culture and nature as well. Exercising the waves in culture might mean getting involved with community service, working with the hospice movement, participating in local government, working with inner-city rehabilitation, providing services for homeless people. It can also mean using *relationships in general* (marriage, friendship, parenting) to further your own growth and the growth of others.
>
> Exercising the waves of existence in nature means that nature is viewed, not as an inert and instrumental backdrop to our actions, but as participating in our own evolution. Getting actively involved in respect for nature, in any number of ways (recycling, environmental protection, nature celebration) not only honors nature; it promotes our own capacity to care.
>
> In short, integral transformative practice attempts to exercise all of the basic waves of human beings—physical, emotional, mental, and spiritual—in self, culture, and nature.... [T]his is the most powerful way to trigger transformation to the next wave—not to mention simply becoming as healthy as one can be at one's present wave, what ever it might be (no small accomplishment!). (Wilber, 2000c, pp. 138–139; bracketed material added)

TABLE 14.3 The Spectrum of Human Development, Psychogenic Pathology, Defenses, and Treatment*

General Realm	Level/Fulcrum	Class of Psychogenic Pathology	Common Defenses	Optimal Treatment
Prepersonal (body)	Sensoriphysical	Psychoses	Hallucination, delusional projection, wish fulfillment	**Pharmacotherapy with psychotherapy as adjunct** (Behavioral and Cognitive-Behavioral approaches)
	Phantasmic/emotional	Borderline and narcissistic disorders	Splitting, (projective identification), selfobject fusion	**Structure-building approaches:** object relations, self psychology, (Dialectical Behavior Therapy)
	Representational mind	Neuroses	Repression, (projection), reaction formation	**Uncovering approaches:** Psychodynamic: Jungian, ego psychology; Gestalt; Focusing; (experiential/person-centered)
Personal (mind)	Rule/role mind	Script pathologies	Displacement, duplicitous transaction, covert intention, (repression)	**Script analysis** (collaborative empiricism, cognitive therapy, REBT, Adlerian, Reality Therapy, etc.)
	Formal-reflexive	Identity neuroses	Sublimation, anticipation, suppression	**Introspection, philosophizing, Socratic dialogue** (experiential)
	Vision-logic	Existential pathologies	Inauthenticity, deadening, aborted self-actualization, bad faith	**Existential psychotherapy** (experiential approaches)
Suprapersonal (spirit)	Para-mental	Psychic disorders	Pranic disorder, yogic illness	**Path of yogis** (sometimes temporary suspension of contemplative work)
	Meta-mental (Illumined mind)	Subtle disorders	Failed integration, archetypal fragmentation	Intensification of contemplative practice, increased contact with spiritual teacher
	Over-mental (Intuitive mind) / Super-mental	Causal disorders	Failed differentiation, Arhat's disease	Collaboration between student and spiritual teacher

Source: Adapted from Wilber, K. (199b) *The collected works of Ken Wilber,* Vol. 4. Boston, MA: Shambhala Publications. Reprinted with arrangement from Shambhala Publications, Inc. (www.shambhala.com)

* Items in parentheses are from Marquis (2008), based upon empirical research in the professional literature.

In addition, essential to such a lofty endeavor is some sort of communal support, whether that be a formal institution or a group of family and friends who encourage and inspire such practice (Murphy, 1993; Wilber, 2000c).

Regarding specific treatment plans, Wilber (2000a, Vol. 7) offered these examples:

- A client with borderline pathology, impulsive ego, preconventional morality, and splitting defense mechanism might be offered structure building therapy, bibliotherapy, weight training, nutritional supplements, pharmacological agents (as required), verbalization and narrative training, and short sessions of a concentration-type meditation (no awareness-training meditation, which tends to dismantle psychological/self-structure, which the borderline does not yet adequately possess).
- A client with anxiety neurosis, phobic elements, conventional morality, repression and displacement defense mechanisms, belongingness needs, and persona self-sense might be offered uncovering psychotherapy, bioenergetics, script analysis, jogging or biking (or some other individual sport), desensitization, dream analysis/therapy, and vipassana meditation.
- A client with existential depression, postconventional morality, suppression and sublimation defense mechanisms, self-actualization needs, and a centauric self-sense might be offered existential analysis, dream therapy, a team sport (e.g., volleyball, basketball), bibliotherapy, t'ai chi chuan (or prana circulating therapy), community service, and kundalini yoga.
- A client who has been practicing Zen mediation for several years, but suffers life-goal apathy and depression, deadening of affect, postconventional morality, postformal cognition, self-transcendence needs, and psychic self-sense might be offered uncovering therapy, combination weight training and jogging, tantric deity-yoga (visualization meditation), tonglen (compassion training), and community service (p. 643).

Notice Wilber's wording, "might be offered," which indicates how an integral counselor devises a preliminary treatment plan and then collaborates with a client on modifying it, both initially and throughout counseling, to optimize the likelihood it will help clients reach their therapeutic goals.

Wilber (2000a, Vol. 7) acknowledged the untested nature of integral therapy (Wilber, 2000a, Vol. 7, p. 642). Research is currently in progress to assess how it is actually practiced by expert integral counselors, as well as its effectiveness (Marquis, 2010).

Techniques

Integral counselors use interventions that emerged from the various approaches that constitute the entire spectrum of psychotherapy, from analysis of transference and empty chair work to exposure and response prevention to cognitive restructuring. Since integral counselors have hundreds of interventions from which to draw in facilitating their clients' healing, growth, and well-being, Marquis (2009) created a classifying system with which to lend order and coherence to it: an *Integral Taxonomy of Therapeutic Interventions* (ITTI). Marquis chose the word "therapeutic" instead of "counseling" or "*psycho*therapeutic" to include societal-systemic techniques along with the intra- and interpersonally oriented techniques that have tended historically to characterize counseling and psychotherapy. Marquis's ITTI classifies more than 200 therapeutic interventions within the all-quadrant, all-level model of integral counseling. Figure 14.4 provides a "mini-ITTI."

Upper Left (UL): Interior-Individual	Upper Right (UR): Exterior-Individual
Body	*Body*
• Gendlin's focusing and attunement to immediate "felt-sense"	• Self-management programs; self-monitoring and recording
• Self-comforting and basic centering exercises	• Pharmacotherapy
Mind	*Mind*
• Awareness/consciousness raising	• Cognitive restructuring*
• Dialogues with parts of self	• Reality therapy's WDEP system
Spirit	*Spirit*
• Meditation/contemplative prayer	• EEG biofeedback and brain–mind machines that help induce theta and delta states of consciousness
• Cultivating mindfulness, love, compassion, forgiveness, etc.	• Yoga
Lower Left (LL): Interior-Collective	**Lower Right (LR): Exterior-Collective**
Body	*Body*
• Attending to and mending ruptures in the therapeutic bond	• Basic session management skills and structure of sessions
• Finding stability in relationships	• Involving the client's social support system in at least one session
Mind	*Mind*
• Establishing the therapeutic relationship	• Social skills training
• Role playing	• Genogram analysis
Spirit	*Spirit*
• Compassionate understanding as the heart of counseling	• Serving others and engaging in social activism/to promote social justice
• "Selfless service": compassion; social interest; social liberation	• Relating responsibly to the environment

*Though cognitive restructuring may at first appear to target intrapsychic processes, Marquis (2009) explained his categorization of this technique in the upper right quadrant because of Beck's (Hollon & Beck, 2004, p. 448) emphasis on clients learning to objectify their thoughts and to assess and modify them as objective phenomena.

FIGURE 14.4   A mini-integral taxonomy of therapeutic interventions.

Due to space considerations, we will discuss only selected techniques that are unique to transpersonal and integral counseling. The integral counselor uses these techniques when, and only when, they are appropriate to a client's concerns, goals, and spiritual worldview.

In general, transpersonal practices were developed within the world's wisdom, or spiritual, traditions. "Spiritual practice" usually refers to the manifesting or rehearsal of desired qualities or ways of being, which eventually become natural and spontaneous, whereas "spiritual techniques" are the specific methods or exercises employed in such practice (Walsh, 1999). In general, counselors should recommend only those techniques that they have personally experienced or practiced. Also important to bear in mind is that enjoying solitude in nature, participating in art, meditating, or any other activities that are potentially spiritual practices "can serve either the ego or the soul, depending on the intention with which they are pursued" (Vaughan, 1995, p. 253).

Bibliotherapy   Boorstein (1997) reported that recommending spiritual reading material is often helpful to clients, even for those who are severely disturbed. He posited that not only are they empowered by their perception that he views them as able to do spiritual work, but that his recommending to them spiritual literature that is personally meaningful to him bolsters their self-esteem and ego strength through identification with him. Boorstein (1997) noted that *A Course in Miracles* (Foundation for Inner Peace, 1975), also known as *The Course*, was written in the tradition of Christian mysticism and stresses genuine forgiveness as a powerful means of eradicating barriers that separate people both from each other and from their own spiritual nature. Other books to recommend to clients include Tolle's (2004) *The Power of Now*, Vaughan's (1985) *The Inward Arc*, Hixon's (1978) *Coming Home*, and Walsh's (1999) *Essential Spirituality*.

Great Questions   The intense pondering of profound questions can be powerful in promoting both insight and the disintegration of rigid, limiting, and illusory preconceptions regarding the nature of self and reality. A few of these questions are "Who am I?" "How shall I live?" "Who or what is always already the case before 'I' do anything at all?" and "Am 'I' the one who is 'living' (animating/manifesting) me (the body-mind) now?" (Avabhasa, 1985). Another is the meaning and purpose of suffering in life (Walsh, 1995).

Prayer–Contemplation   Since people from the Judeo-Christian tradition are sometimes put off by the word meditation, a counselor can instead suggest contemplative prayer as a way to elicit a sincere, authentic, contemplative response from Christian clients. In fact, Christian contemplatives such as Father Thomas Merton (1969), Father Thomas Keating (1986), and Brother David Steindl-Rast (1983, 1984) frequently used the words "prayer," "contemplation," and "meditation" interchangeably. They also agreed that petitionary prayer, in which one asks for some desired condition for oneself, is the lowest form of prayer, whereas contemplation, or communing with God's presence or experiencing union with Godhead, is the highest form. Moreover, Steindl-Rast (1984) compellingly argued—from a Christian perspective—that the cultivation of gratefulness is the heart of true prayer (1984).

In essence, contemplation and meditation are the same, although the aim of contemplation is usually said to be communing with the presence of God and, ultimately, union with God, which is possible only when one has quieted and emptied one's mind such that one is capable of resting in silence. Merton's (1969) Christian views sometimes seem indistinguishable from a Buddhist perspective: "We find god in our own being" (p. 134); "God Who is at once infinitely above us and Who yet dwells in the depths of our being" (p. 135); "Then will I truly know Him, since I am in Him and He is truly in me" (p. 139). Keating (1986) and Steindl-Rast (1983, 1984) offered superb descriptions of contemplative practices within the Christian tradition.

Meditation

> We must close our eyes and invoke a new manner of seeing, a wakefulness that is the birthright of us all, though few put it to use.

—Plotinus, in O'Brien, 1984

"The training of attention" is probably as good a definition of meditation as any. Meditative practices fall into one of two categories.

Concentrative meditation increases the mind's ability to focus, analogous to the intense power of a laser compared to the diffused and relative weakness of scattered light. This ability to maintain a concentrated focus on a single object is a prerequisite to the second category of awareness types of meditation. Although description of all the different types of concentrative practices would fill volumes, they all have in common the goal of single-pointed focus, regardless of the object of one's attention. Such single-pointed absorption is experienced as inherently joyous: the "oceanic feeling" of union and bliss.

Meditating on a mantra is a common form of concentrative practice. A mantra is a spiritually meaningful word or phrase that is repeated, either softly or silently, as the object of one's attention. *Metta* (lovingkindness) meditation or prayer involves silently repeating one's hope that all beings feel happy, peaceful, and free from suffering. While visualizing the person(s) to whom these wishes are intended, one silently repeats something along the lines of "May you be at peace; may you be happy; may your heart remain open and sensitive to the light and love of your true nature." This is particularly effective with people who are angry or critical of themselves or others (Boorstein, 1997).

In Tibetan Buddhism, one can find meditations designed to promote almost any virtuous quality. One example is *Tonglen*, an extremely powerful meditation of compassion. Tonglen is Tibetan for "giving and receiving" and essentially involves the taking in of others' pain and suffering and the giving to them of one's love, happiness, and healing energy. Briefly, the practice is to invoke as much compassion within oneself as possible and then to visualize another's pain, suffering, and distress in the form of dark, grimy, tar-like smoke. On the in-breath, the practitioner visualizes breathing in this great mass of suffering to the core of one's being, where it is purified and dissolved. On the out-breath, one visualizes the giving of a radiant, pure, white light of love, joy, and happiness to the one who is suffering. Some people are put off by the intensity of this practice. For them, less extreme versions of Tonglen are available (see Chapter 12 of Sogyal Rinpoche's [1993] *The Tibetan Book of Living and Dying*). "No other practice I know," wrote Rinpoche (1993), "is as effective in destroying the self-grasping, self-cherishing, self-absorption of the ego, which is the root of all our suffering and the root of all hard-heartedness" (p. 193).

Awareness/insight meditation in its classic form is called *vipassana*. After having developed the ability to maintain a concentrated focus, one applies "bare attention" or "choiceless, nonjudgmental awareness" to all that arises in and passes out of one's present field of attention. One practices simply being as aware as possible of everything experienced, from one's breath to sensations, emotions, thoughts, and eventually the felt sense of "I," taking care to notice the difference between what arises and one's appraisals, evaluations, and judgments of what arises. The aim is not to search for anything in particular, not to hold on to or cling to any images or feeling, nor to avoid or deny anything that arises. With arduous practice, one realizes that literally everything that arises also passes, and that one's suffering is due to one's desire to cling to pleasurable, satisfying experiences that will inevitably be lost, while trying to avoid unpleasant experiences. When one truly realizes that everything is constantly in flux, one relaxes one's attachments and the illusion of control and is thus able to be more fully present in each moment. One develops a greatly deepened capacity to tolerate and accept unpleasant conditions. In this disposition, one can see that one is not as much of an active, conscious entity but rather is a *process* of identifying, automatically and unconsciously, with patterns of reactivity. "It is *the* fundamental tenet of Buddhist psychology," maintained Epstein (1995), "that this kind of attention is, in itself, healing" (p. 110).

Many vipassana practitioners claim that this type of meditation, more than dreams, is the "royal road to the unconscious" (Vaughan, 1985; Walsh, 1999; Washburn, 1988; Wilber, 1999b, Vol. 3), because its potential to uncover repressed psychological material is enormous. Counselors should recommend this practice only to those clients who have an already-established, strong ego, because, unlike the goal of concentrative meditations (to facilitate the experiences of peace and bliss), one goal of vipassana is the dissolution of ego boundaries and defenses. For an excellent overview of a wide variety of meditative practices, from the Jesus prayer of Christianity to the zazen of Zen Buddhism, we refer you to Goleman (1972a, 1972b), Epstein's (1990) "The Psychodynamics of Meditation," and Chapter 10 of Wilber's (1997a) *The Eye of Spirit*.

3-2-1 Process. In its most skeletal form, the 3-2-1 process involves the client's converting third-person "its" into second-person "others" or "you's" with which he can then have a dialog. When the technique is successful, the client "owns" or assumes first-person responsibility for previously defended-against material; he no longer represses, dissociates from, or projects it. In the case of the angry client (recall and/or consult the self subsection of the Structure of Psyche section), she takes the third-person anger that "overcomes" her, converts that into another (second-) person who is angry (whether that is the therapist or anyone else), and then, through empty chair or voice dialog work, has a dialog with and as the second-person "other" who is angry, then realizes and experiences the anger as her own. For more details on the 3-2-1 process, consult Wilber (2006).

Yoga. The word *yoga* derives from the word "yoke" and thus involves a set of disciplines designed to consciously yoke or unite the practitioner with her deepest spiritual nature. Yoga is not simply a postural endeavor but a family of practices and technologies of transformation more than four thousand years old that includes ethics, meditation, breathing, postures, movement, intellectual study, devotion, service, sex, lifestyle, and work (Feuerstein, 1997). Interested readers are referred to Feuerstein (1996).

Silence. Frequently, the most powerful therapeutic moments are those of silence, not awkward, dead, or paralyzing silence, but healing silence pregnant with meaning and possibility. "This healing silence, which is an untouched natural resource for the practice of psychotherapy" (Epstein, 1995, p. 187) is possible only when the counselor can be with a client without an agenda, simply being present to the intersubjective field arising between counselor and client. This capacity is greatly augmented by the counselor's meditative or contemplative practice.

Visualization. Visualization can be a powerful aid in the healing process. Although different religions suggest visualizing different forms, such as Jesus, Shiva, or Chenrezig, they all attest to the efficacy of this method. In addition to visualizing deities, Assagioli (1991) recommended visualizing the unfolding of a beautiful rose with the potential of the bud symbolizing one's potential to realize one's hidden, true nature and beauty. For a detailed description of a 12-step transpersonal visualization technique called the Power Within, see Chapin (1989).

Service, Forgiveness, and Devotion. In daily life, authentic spirituality demands some form of service, a service motivated not by a sense of duty or obligation but by the felt need to help others. "If we are awake to our true nature and aware of self and soul, service seems to be a natural expression of who we are" (Vaughan, 1995, p. 287). As the poet Tajore wrote:

> I slept and dreamt that life was all joy.
> I awoke and saw that life was but service.
> I served and understood that service was joy.

—Volunteer Newsletter, 2005

Forgiveness has long been emphasized in Christianity for its transformative power. *A Course in Miracles* even stated that "forgiveness is the key to happiness" (Foundation for Inner Peace, 1975, Vol. 2, p. 210) and that the inability or unwillingness to forgive is an unwillingness to let go of the past (Boorstein, 1997). However, a person must typically have a well-developed self/ego in order to fully forgive another. As with many spiritual practices, forgiveness has prepersonal, personal, and transpersonal dimensions. Thus, recommending that a less-developed client fully forgive someone who has, for example, raped or assaulted them—when what is more healthy and developmentally appropriate is for the client to be in touch with and express justified anger—can be iatrogenic. For an excellent discussion of forgiveness in counseling, from an integral perspective, see Lewis (2005).

Devotion is not a simple issue. Although it has always been emphasized in Christianity and has long been an integral element of Hinduism and Tibetan Buddhism, in modern America, the ideal of the autonomous individual and the emphasis on the equality of each person is greatly at odds with such practice. Even though it is certainly not the appropriate practice for everyone, "when it is done right, Guru Yoga [the practice of devotion to a Spiritual Teacher] is the most powerful yoga there is" (Wilber, 1999c, p. 224); it is a practice reminiscent of Jesus's disciples' devotion to him. Moreover, for individuals working with transpersonal issues, an authentic spiritual teacher, or master, is probably more important than a transpersonal counselor, although working with both would be ideal. For an overview of contemporary spiritual teachers, see Rawlinson (1997) and Berzin (2000).

Addressing Resistance

Therapeutically responding to a client's resistance is a large part of the art, and heart, of integral counseling. Balancing the dialectical tension of a client's desires and fears of developing into the unknown, counselors must walk a razor's edge between support and challenge. This is a fancy way of saying *counselors work with, not against, clients' resistance* (Mahoney, 1991, 2003; Wilber, 1999b, Vol. 1). How does a counselor do this?

First, the counselor adopts the perspective that the client's resistance to change is not an opponent to be conquered but an ally to be honored: Resistance is the self's protection against pain, disintegration, and death. The problem is that in protecting against *all* forms of pain, disintegration, and death, the self can block those forms that are part of the developmental process. Consequently, "the therapist doesn't try to get rid of the resistances, by-pass them, or ignore them. Instead, he [*sic*] helps the individual see how, and secondarily, why he is resisting" (Wilber, 1999b, Vol. 1, p. 564). Thus the counselor is, again, implementing a primary process goal of integral counseling: to bring awareness or consciousness to experience. The integral counselor does not pursue this process initially by facilitating the client's direct contact with and acceptance of that which he is resisting. Rather, the counselor skillfully employs what Wilber termed *special conditions* for the purpose of frustrating the client's resistance. The client is most likely to become aware of resistance when that resistance is frustrated. Only when a client becomes aware that he is actively, even if unconsciously, resisting will he be free to choose to continue, to increase, or to decrease his resistance.

Consistent with his full-spectrum model, Wilber (1999b, Vol. 1) posited a specific technique, or "special condition," to work with the unique type of resistance clients are likely to manifest at each level of development. For example, for an F-3 client with a neurosis who is repressing and resisting his sexual and aggressive impulses, the special condition is the technique of *free association*, in which the client is asked to freely tell the counselor everything that enters his mind. If resistant, the client will have difficulty freely relating his fantasies and associations. At the moment when the client stops associating freely, rather than confronting the client with what the counselor thinks the client is resisting, the counselor simply points out that the client hit a snag of some sort, and, together, they explore the client's experience in the moment, which likely will facilitate the client's awareness of how and why he was resisting. Thus, free association is a special condition that reveals F-3 clients' resistances.

By contrast, consider a centauric (F-6) client. Since she has developed beyond the neurotic level, she has integrated the bodily and emotional aspects of her being with her cognitive/role self and thus is not resistant to the same impulses to which the neurotic client is resistant. Rather, the centauric client is dealing more with issues such as meaning and authenticity, and as such, she is resistant *not* to memories of the past or fantasies of the future but to being immediately and authentically present. The special condition at this level is the client's concentration on

> the immediate present in all its forms and the bodymind which discloses it.... The therapist will watch—not for blocks *in* thought—but for any flight from present awareness *into* thought.... In ego-level therapy a person will be encouraged to explore his past; in centaur-level therapy, he will be prevented from it. (Wilber, 1999b, Vol. 1, p. 565, italics added)

Such special conditions are also available for each of the transpersonal levels of development. The spiritual practice of such conditions discloses that "although the only thing a person fundamentally wants is unity consciousness, the only thing he is ever doing is resisting it" (Wilber, 1999b, Vol. 1, p. 569).

CONTRIBUTIONS AND LIMITATIONS

Interface With Recent Developments in the Mental Health Field

Wilber has always demonstrated a great openness to new evidence and therefore to revising his theory. Since 1973, his work has evolved through five distinct phases, each demanding either revision or additional concepts.

The Nature–Nurture Question

Wilber has written little about how genetics specifically influence one's capacity to realize one's developmental potentials. However, by acknowledging heredity as a component in the upper-right quadrant, he has probably addressed it more explicitly than most counseling theorists. His four-quadrant model also provides an elaboration on the theme of genetic propensities that is virtually absent in other theories. The upper left quadrant addresses how genetic propensities *feel* to the individual. The lower left quadrant addresses the meaning that such propensities are given by the individual's culture, for example, whether shyness, which research has shown to be genetically influenced, is perceived as sensitivity or as cowardice. The lower right quadrant addresses the environmental factors that interact with heredity and greatly influence the extent to which a genetic propensity will actually be expressed—factors such as diet, drugs, physical traumas, exposure to toxins, and the ways the individual and others have adapted the environment to fit the individual's tendencies. Returning again to the upper left quadrant, one is believed to have some degree of ability to be conscious of (to witness) one's genetic tendencies and, thus, to assume at least some degree of agency over those tendencies.

Wilber's view of the relative importance of genetics in the grand scheme of things is reflected in his notion of "tetra-evolution": that the evolution both of the individual and of humanity at large is not predetermined but, rather, is a function of all four quadrants as they manifest and interact with each other (Wilber, 2000b). Referring to the Human

Genome Project, the $3 billion undertaking to systematically map the entire sequence of human DNA, Wilber (1997a) wrote that

> this spectacular project promises to revolutionize our ideas of human growth, development, disease, and medical treatment, and its completion will surely mark one of the great advances in human knowledge. Not as well known, but arguably more important, is what might be called the Human Consciousness Project, the endeavor, now well under way, *to map the entire spectrum of the various states of human consciousness.* (p. 30)

DSM–IV–TR *Diagnosis*

Similar to psychodynamic assessment, integral assessment focuses more on *levels* of development than *specific disorders within a given level.* However, in keeping with their goal of expanding the orthodox perspective by working within it, Wilber and other integral theorists have suggested including *DSM–IV–TR* diagnoses, when appropriate, with the integral psychograph (Ingersoll, 2002; Marquis, 2008). Although attempting to be comprehensive, the *DSM–IV–TR* disorders are all right-quadrant perspectives: Axes I, II, III, and V are exterior descriptions of the individual, the upper right quadrant; and Axis IV is an exterior description of the individual's system, the lower right quadrant. References to the left, interior quadrants appear in the text of *DSM–IV–TR*, but only sporadically (see Douthit & Marquis, 2006). Until the *DSM* gives the interior quadrants what, from an integral perspective, is the attention they are due, it behooves the integral counselor who uses *DSM–IV–TR* diagnosis to rectify the diagnostic neglect of the subjective quadrants by devoting particular attention to them (see Ingersoll & Rak, 2006).

Pharmacotherapy

From Wilber's perspective, pharmaceutical treatment should be limited *primarily* to those clients with the more severe disorders such as schizophrenia, bipolar disorders, autistic disorder, and severe depressions. This is *not* to say that pharmaceutical treatment is never appropriate for other psychiatric problems, because Wilber (2000a, Vol. 7, p. 642) also included pharmaceuticals within the physical realm, the most fundamental of all levels. When something is wrong with one's body, whether it is physical pain, illness, or fatigue, the body is that much harder to transcend. However, the prominence of pharmaceutical use is a reflection of U.S. culture, in which people still focus primarily on the behavioral quadrant. In response to depression, administering a pill is primarily a behavioral (UR) endeavor, as opposed to inquiring into the meaning that the client's depression has for him, a primarily experiential (UL) endeavor. For an excellent discussion of this topic, the reader is referred to Ingersoll and Rak's (2006) *Psychopharmacology for Helping Professionals: An Integral Exploration.*

Managed Care and Brief Therapy

Integral counseling has only recently emerged, and authors have written very little about brief integral counseling. From an integral perspective, brief therapy most likely addresses translative change, whereas long-term therapy is most likely necessary for transformative change. Most clients seek translative change, and most are addressing issues related to fulcrums F-3 through F-6; in many such cases, approaches that managed care endorses are, from an integral perspective, quite appropriate. However, authentic transformation (vertical development) usually demands very hard work and requires patience, diligence, and devoted practice that typically spans years, if not one's lifetime (Mahoney, 2003). When a client is pursuing transformative change, especially involving the transpersonal domain, brief therapy is not applicable, and thus managed care is not likely to be a viable option.

Technical Eclecticism

Also clear to the reader by now is the extent to which technical eclecticism is inherent in integral psychology. In fact, the integral approach offers the practitioner a rationale for utilizing the broadest range of possible techniques within a theoretically pure/consistent context. Rather than assuming a traditional theoretical position—a single-school perspective—and imposing it on every client, integral counselors identify and employ the approach that addresses the level of development from which the client's struggles primarily derive, the quadratic issues most implicated in the client's problems, and/or the client's specific personality type and pertinent states of consciousness.

Along with this wide embrace of a variety of techniques comes an equally weighty responsibility: for the integral counselor to be competent in the techniques one uses. Ethically speaking, competence is based not only on study but also on supervised practice. Therefore, it is possible that an integral counselor might practice only within a specific developmental range of techniques, those in which one is competent, while maintaining the broad integral perspective.

Diversity Issues

Regarding culture, the cultural quadrant reveals that a person absolutely cannot be adequately understood without also considering the cultural context within which she has lived and lives. Thus, cultural issues are central to integral counseling. In addition, Wilber's incorporation and integration of traditions as diverse as Tibetan Buddhism, the !Kung African Spirituality, and Vedantic Hinduism encourage integral counselors to be relatively free of Western ethnocentrism. Likewise, his exposition of the perennial philosophy has revealed that rather than one culture having the doorway to salvation, each major religion has, at its contemplative core, a unique and valid pathway to truth, God, or spirit. The reader is referred to "In a Modern Light: Integral Anthropology and the Evolution of Cultures" in Wilber (2000a, Vol. 7).

Regarding gender, in several of his works, Wilber has considered issues such as whether men and women have different, even if complementary, types of morality and spirituality. Discussing more than a dozen different forms of feminism, particularly that of Carol Gilligan and Peggy Wright, Wilber (2000a, Vol. 7) summarized his view: Men and women *transform* (develop) through the same gender-neutral basic stages of development, "but men tend to *translate* with an emphasis on *agency*, women with an emphasis on *communion*" (p. 588). Neither is better than the other, and, in fact, both genders exist, as do all holons, as agency-in-communion.

As always, Wilber's criticism is not that the various feminist perspectives are wrong but that they tend to be limited and exclusionary, usually focusing on only one of the quadrants and often only on one level within that quadrant. Wilber (2000a, Vol. 7) called for a more integral approach. The interested reader is referred to "Integral Feminism: Sex and Gender on the Moral and Spiritual Path" in Wilber (2000a, Vol. 7).

Regarding spirituality, it should be clear by now that no other theorist of counseling has placed spirituality in such a central role as has Wilber. Wilber (1999d) has dealt with the perplexing issue of defining spirituality by identifying the five more common definitions found in the broad spiritual literature: (a) Spirituality pertains to the highest level of each of the developmental lines; (b) spirituality is the sum total of the individual's development in all the developmental lines; (c) spirituality is itself a separate developmental line; (d) spirituality is an attitude, such as openness or love that one can have at any developmental level; and (e) spirituality involves peak experiences rather than developmental levels. He concluded that each of these definitions has value and that no one definition yet incorporates the useful aspects of each of the five definitions.

Wilber also has postulated both translative/legitimate/exoteric and transformative/ authentic/esoteric aspects of spirituality. Examples of *translative spirituality* include elaboration of one's exoteric system, such as reading more or attending workshops related to one's belief system, or conversion from one belief system to another within the same developmental wave. According to Wilber (1997b) and Feuerstein (1997), translative spirituality is the more commonly observed function of religion: to fortify the self. Through an *exoteric* system of beliefs and rituals, people are helped to understand and perhaps minimize the inherent suffering of the separate self; thus, translative spirituality fosters feelings of security, comfort, consolation, protection, and fortification. Translative spirituality is *legitimate* because it provides a certain sense of legitimacy to one's beliefs about the world and one's place therein.

An example of *transformative spirituality* involves someone who, after sustained contemplative practice, expands from the vision-logic wave of development into the paramental wave, and perhaps beyond. According to Wilber (1997b), transformative spirituality constitutes a less commonly observed function of religion: *to deconstruct the self*. Rather than consoling, fortifying, or legitimizing the self, it involves *esoteric* practices to dismantle, transmute, transform, and liberate the self, ultimately from its illusion of separateness through a series of deaths and rebirths of the self into ever more inclusive developmental waves, all of which constitutes the process of *authentic* spirituality. Authentic spirituality inquires into legitimate spirituality and concludes that the latter tends to entrench a person in the current wave of development and thus prolong, even if more comfortably, the illusion of separateness that is, ironically, the actual source of suffering. In his glib way, Wilber (2000a, Vol. 8) summarized that, in transformative spirituality, "the self is not made content. The self is made toast" (p. 305).

From the integral psychology perspective, both translative and transformative functions of spirituality are vitally important. Equally important is distinguishing the two because of their different goals and processes. Readers interested in addressing spiritual issues in counseling are referred to Marquis, Holden, and Warren (2001) and Scotton, Chinen, and Battista (1996).

Effectiveness of Psychotherapy

Since of its newness, integral counseling itself has not been the subject of much research. However, because integral counselors employ established therapeutic approaches for the majority of clients who are seeking change in the personal domain, and because they concur with research on factors in the effectiveness of psychotherapy, their work in the personal domain reflects many of the best practices indicated by psychotherapy outcome research. In addition, recent research suggests that expert counselors and psychologists evaluate the Integral Intake as the most comprehensive, efficient, and helpful published theory-based idiographic assessment instrument (Marquis, 2008; Marquis & Holden, 2008).

Integral counselors also employ strategies that address the transpersonal domain. Some of these strategies have been researched and found effective. For example, since 1970, beginning with Wallace's groundbreaking publication of "The Physiological Effects of Transcendental Meditation" in *Science,* researchers have conducted more than 1000 studies of meditation and its effects. The consensus is that meditation accelerates psychological development without altering the sequence of developmental stages (Alexander, Druker, et al., 1990; Haruki, Ishii, & Suzuki, 1996; Haruki & Kaku, 2000; Richards & Commons, 1990; Walsh, 1993a).

TM is one type of mantra meditation that researchers have studied extensively with prison inmates, children, young adults, and the elderly. The results have consistently shown numerous benefits, ranging from purely physiological to emotional, cognitive, and spiritual (Alexander, Davies et al., 1990; Brown & Engler, 1986a, 1986b). For example, physically, stress, cholesterol, muscle tension, and blood pressure levels drop (Benson, 1975; Murphy & Donovan, 1989); psychologically, anxiety, post-traumatic stress, phobias, insomnia, and mild depression decrease; intelligence, creativity, and academic achievement are enhanced; and self-control, empathy, peace, and joy increase (Walsh, 1993a, 1999). In one study, researchers found that with regard to Loevinger's scale of ego development, only 1% of a sample of college students appeared to have reached one of the two highest levels, whereas 38% of a similarly matched sample of TM meditators reached those levels (Alexander, Davies et al., 1990). Numerous studies corroborate this notion; the interested reader may consult the Research Appendix in Alexander, Druker, and Langer (1990) and Shapiro and Walsh (1984).

Several studies have measured brain wave activity through the use of the electroencephalograph (EEG), demonstrating with objective, quantitative data that meditation positively affects one's brain. Not only do meditators' brain waves slow down, but also various cortical regions show increased synchronization and coherence (Walsh, 1993a, p. 63). Moreover, Goleman et al. (2003) demonstrated that, with expert meditators, different types of meditation practices yield highly distinct and recognizable positron emission tomography (PET) scans, not to mention some truly remarkable findings such as the ability to completely "turn off" reflexes: A gun loaded with blanks was fired at random times behind yet near the heads of meditating monks as their brains were being monitored with EEG and PET scan machines, and no response to the gun shot was recorded by the machines.

Research has thus revealed a great deal about meditative practices, but not much is known regarding what ones are most effective for specific types of people at varying stages of life. The question remains: What type of ITPs best facilitate transformations in what line of development for what type of people? Also as of yet, no researchers have assessed the validity of Wilber's spectrum of treatment modalities hypothesis. However, a research study is underway that will provide an initial investigation of that hypothesis (more about this study under the Limitations section that follows).

Limitations

The most common criticism of Wilber's work is that it has emerged from a nonclinician and therefore that some of his elegant theory is less than elegant at the practical level. A common target of such is criticism is his spectrum of treatment modalities: A few therapists have claimed that although it makes a tremendous amount of sense, it is too rigid. However, this criticism may stem from a misunderstanding. As we earlier quoted Wilber, he never meant the spectrum of treatment modalities to be a rigid prescription dictating that only one approach was appropriate for a given individual. Moreover, most integral theorists are cognizant of the complexities of human development and pathology and thus recognize that Wilber's proposed spectrum of development and pathology is not a neat and simple one-to-one relationship; an individual's center of gravity can be far more developed than some of the pathological remnants that continue to plague him or her. Most integral therapists are aware of the profound complexity of each human's development and seek to avoid rigidity through such strategies as remembering that the self is not a noun but a process and that the logic of the integral model rarely manifests so neatly in a given person's developmental process (Marquis, 2008).

Another weakness of the integral approach is a lack of research. Since integral psychology and psychotherapy are so new, as long as research is undertaken with the urgency Wilber and other integral theorists have expressed (Forman, Marquis, Ingersoll, Zeitler, & Lewis, 2008; Marquis, 2008), this weakness currently may be forgiven. Indeed, research assessing the utility of a newly developed integral intake instrument has recently been completed (Marquis, 2002; Marquis & Holden, 2008). As previously mentioned, a research study utilizing an intensive "Integral Methodological Pluralism" (Douthit & Marquis, 2006) design to investigate five expert integral therapists as they counsel a client for approximately 50 sessions is currently underway (Marquis, 2010). Among the goals of this research are to inquire into:

- How, specifically, expert integral therapists use the information that clients provide via the Integral Intake to begin formulating case conceptualizations and to create integrative treatment plans.
- How expert integral therapists continue to make their clinical decisions regarding what change processes and interventions to use, and when, with their patient throughout treatment.
- What the effects of these treatment decisions are, that is, how effective are the chosen change processes and interventions with each client.
- How to refine the matching of available treatments according to clients' quadratic dimensions while also providing some empirical illustrations.
- How to refine the matching of available treatments according to a client's developmental center of gravity while also providing some empirical illustrations.

This research project (Marquis, 2010) will hopefully provide the data to create a formalized, data-driven set of clinical guidelines regarding when and how to choose and implement change processes and specific interventions—a *Treatment Manual of Integral Psychotherapy*; the manual will consist of *general principles* of integral psychotherapy, in contrast to a highly prescriptive set of specific procedures.

Contributions

Wilber's contributions to psychotherapy are numerous, and psychotherapy is just one of many disciplines he has addressed. Wilber's three most unique and significant contributions to psychotherapy are the "all quadrant, all level perspective"; his spectrum of development, pathology, treatment, resistance, and special conditions for the resistance; and his emphasis on the necessity of counselors' and clients' commitment to ITPs. Many counselors have found his spectrum of development to be immensely helpful in their understanding of the full spectrum of clients. Understanding developmental hierarchies allows the integral counselor to more fully join, understand, and communicate with clients as they are.

Wilber was also the first to discern and recognize many dynamics that seem increasingly obvious: the need to conceptually separate *lines* and *levels* of development; the difficulties involved with defining a spiritual line of development; that geniuses such as Freud and the Buddha—the former claiming the goal of mental health was a strong ego, the latter claiming the goal was transcendence of the ego, the source of suffering—were not contradicting each other but, rather, were addressing different levels of the great nest of being. His all-quadrant, all-level model, with its honoring of and demand for both objective and subjective approaches to knowledge at both the individual and collective levels, is the most likely candidate to lend credibility in the eyes of orthodox thinkers to unorthodox notions such as transpersonal levels of development.

CURRENT STATUS

In 2000, Wilber founded the Integral Institute, an "all-quadrant, all-level" organization with branches in business, ecology, psychology, politics, medicine, art, law and criminal justice, education, religion, and the university student outreach. He hopes that his theoretical model, which honors the importance of relatively objective, conventional disciplines and approaches and integrates them with the interior, subjective domains of existence at all levels, including transpersonal levels, will foster the building of bridges to the conventional world that the transpersonal field has been unable to achieve. The Integral Institute has been providing week-long seminars in Integral Psychotherapy and work is also underway on *The Handbook of Integral Psychotherapy* (Marquis & Ingersoll, 2011).

Perhaps even more importantly, integral counseling and psychotherapy are no longer the birthchild of just Ken Wilber. Numerous scholar practitioners are currently contributing to the confirmation, criticism, refinement, and fleshing out of clinical practicalities regarding Wilber's theoretical work; among them are Elliott Ingersoll, Andre Marquis, Jan Holden, Tim Black, Durwin Foster, David Zeitler, Bert Parlee, Willow Pearson, and Susanne Cook-Greuter. Now that practicing counselors and psychotherapists have contributed to the theoretical and practical aspects of integral counseling, most of them recognize that the most imperative need for this approach is more empirical research, an undertaking to which many of them are now devoting themselves.

SUMMARY

This chapter is only an introduction to the richness of integral counseling, yet, hopefully, readers who resonate with integral counseling and find it a candidate for their guiding theory are inspired to pursue further study, both intellectual and experiential.

In the words of Walsh and Vaughan (1994), Ken Wilber

has forged a systematic, broad-ranging, multidisciplinary, integrative, visionary yet scholarly worldview based in psychology, grounded in philosophy, spanning sociology and anthropology, and reaching to religion and mysticism.... The scope of his synthesis is perhaps unparalleled. (p. 18)

Ultimately, Wilber's integral philosophy, with its quadrants, lines, and levels like all other theories, is just a map. Its purpose will have been fulfilled if it encourages and helps both counselors and clients live more integral lives. Never before in human history has so much wisdom, ancient and modern, Eastern and Western, been available to humanity. An integral life puts that wisdom to use. Such a life is not intended to be rigid or ascetic. Rather, an integral life embodies health, joy, love, humor, wisdom, and compassion. In Wilber's words:

I don't suggest the mere study of maps. What I actually recommend is finding and engaging a practice that speaks to your potentials and shows you the actual territory.... [T]he practice could be anything—art, community service, raising sane kids, writing novels, sports—so long as it also pulls you out of yourself and into a larger being. The point is that each of us has to take the actual journey, in our own way, in our own time, at our own pace. (Schwartz, 1995, p. 374)

RECOMMENDED RESOURCES

The first 22 years of Wilber's writings are now available in his eight-volume *Collected Works* (1999b; 2000a). We suggest that the interested reader begin with *Integral Psychology* (2000b), then proceed to *A theory of Everything* (2000c). Other key integral works are Marquis's (2008) *The Integral Intake: A Guide to Comprehensive Idiographic Assessment in Integral Psychotherapy,* which actually is not just about assessment but is largely about the entire process of integral counseling; Ingersoll's (2010); Forman's (2010); and the special issue of the journal *Counseling and Values,* 53(3), which was devoted exclusively to integral counseling.

Leonard and Murphy (1995) provided detailed descriptions of how to tailor ITPs so that they become an integral part of one's daily life. If you are interested in joining one of the approximately 40 ITP groups that have begun across the country, you can contact Murphy and Leonard at http://www.itp-life.com

Out of the vast transpersonal literature, we most highly recommend Scotton, Chinen, and Battista (1996), Walsh and Vaughan (1993), and Schwartz (1995). Walsh (1999) is an excellent introduction to central spiritual practices and techniques. Also, Vaughan (1985), who concluded each chapter with an experiential exercise, may prove helpful to counselors. A wealth of videotaped interviews of persons prominent in transpersonal psychology is available in the Thinking Allowed television series: http://www.thinkingallowed.com

REFERENCES

Alexander, C., Davies, J., Dixon, C., Dillbeck, M., Druker, S., Oetzel, R., … Orme-Johnson, D. (1990). Growth of higher stages of consciousness: Maharishi's Vedic psychology of human development. In C. Alexander & E. Langer (Eds.), *Higher stages of human development* (pp. 286–341). New York, NY: Oxford University.

Alexander, C., Druker, S., & Langer, E. (1990). Introduction: Major issues in the exploration of adult growth. In C. Alexander & E. Langer (Eds.), *Higher stages of human development* (pp. 3–32). New York, NY: Oxford University.

Ansbacher, H. L., & Ansbacher, R. R. (Eds.). (1956). *The individual psychology of Alfred Adler: A systematic presentation in selections from his writings.* New York, NY: Harper & Row.

Asay, T. P., & Lambert, M. J. (1999). The empirical case for the common factors in therapy: Quantitative findings. In M. A. Hubble, B. L. Duncan, & S. D. Miller (Eds.), *The heart and soul of change* (pp. 23–55). Washington, DC: American Psychological Association.

Assagioli, R. (1965). *Psychosynthesis.* New York, NY: Penguin.

Assagioli, R. (1991). *Transpersonal development: Dimensions beyond psychosynthesis.* San Francisco, CA: Aquarian.

Aurobindo, S. (1970). *The life divine* (Vols. 1 & 2). Pondicherry, India: All India Press, Sri Aurobindo Ashram.

Avabhasa, D. (1985). *The dawn horse testament*. Clearlake, CA: Dawn Horse.

Beck, A. T., Rush, A. J., Shaw, B. F., & Emery, G. (1979). *Cognitive therapy of depression*. New York, NY: Guilford Press.

Beck, A. T., & Weishaar, M. (1989). Cognitive therapy. In A. Freeman, K. M. Simon, L. E. Beutler, & H. Arkowitz (Eds.), *Comprehensive handbook of cognitive therapy* (pp. 21–36). New York, NY: Plenum.

Benson, H. (1975). *The relaxation response*. New York, NY: Avon.

Berne, E. (1961). *Transactional analysis in psychotherapy*. New York, NY: Grove.

Berzin, A. (2000). *Relating to a spiritual teacher: Building a healthy relationship*. Ithaca, NY: Snow Lion.

Bohart, A. C., & Tallman, K. (1999). *How clients make therapy work: The process of active self-healing*. Washington, DC: American Psychological Association.

Boorstein, S. (1997). *Clinical studies in transpersonal psychotherapy*. Albany, NY: State University of New York Press.

Brown, D., & Engler, J. (1986a). The stages of mindfulness meditation: A validation study. Part I: Study and results. In K. Wilber, J. Engler, & D. P. Brown (Eds.), *Transformations of consciousness: Conventional and contemplative perspectives on development* (pp. 161–191). Boston, MA: Shambhala.

Brown, D., & Engler, J. (1986b). The stages of mindfulness meditation: A validation study. Part II: Discussion. In K. Wilber, J. Engler, & D. P. Brown (Eds.), *Transformations of consciousness: Conventional and contemplative perspectives on development* (pp. 193–217). Boston, MA: Shambhala.

Campbell, J. (Ed.). (1972). *The portable Jung*. New York, NY: Viking.

Chapin, T. (1989). The power within: A humanistic-transpersonal imagery technique. *Journal of Humanistic Psychology, 29*(4), 444–456.

Chomsky, N. (1969). *Deep structure, surface structure, and semantic interpretation*. Bloomington, IN: Indiana University Linguistics Club.

Cook-Greuter, S. (1999). *Postautonomous ego development: A study of its nature and measurement. Dissertation Abstracts International,* 60(06B), UMI No. 9933122.

Cook-Greuter, S., & Soulen, J. (2007). The developmental perspective in integral counseling. *Counseling and Values, 51,* 180–192.

Da, F. J. (1980). *Scientific proof of the existence of God will soon be announced by the White House!* Middletown, CA: Dawn Horse.

Douglas, C. (2000). Analytical psychotherapy. In R. J. Corsini & D. Wedding (Eds.), *Current psychotherapies* (pp. 99–132). Itasca, IL: F. E. Peacock.

Douthit, K. Z., & Marquis, A. (2006). Empiricism in psychiatry's post-psychoanalytic era: Contemplating DSM's "atheoretical" nosology. *Constructivism in the Human Sciences, 11*(1), 32–59.

Eliot, T. S. (1943). *The four quartets*. New York, NY: Harcourt Brace Jovanovich.

Epstein, M. (1990). Psychodynamics of meditation: Pitfalls on the spiritual path. *Journal of Transpersonal Psychology, 22*(1), 17–34.

Epstein, M. (1995). *Thoughts without a thinker: Psychotherapy from a Buddhist perspective*. New York, NY: Basic Books.

Erikson, E. (1963). *Childhood and society* (2nd ed.). New York, NY: W. W. Norton.

Feuerstein, G. (1996). *The philosophy of classical yoga*. Rochester, NY: Inner Traditions International.

Feuerstein, G. (1997). To light a candle in a dark age. *What Is Enlightenment? 12,* 34–43.

Forman, M. (2010). *A guide to integral psychotherapy: Complexity, integration, and spirituality in practice*. Albany, NY: State University of New York Press.

Forman, M., Marquis, A., Ingersoll, E., Zeitler, D., & Lewis, J. (2008, August). *Integral psychotherapy panel*. Paper presented at the meeting Integral Theory in Action: Serving Self, Other, and Kosmos, Pleasant Hill, CA.

Foundation for Inner Peace. (1975). *A course in miracles* (Vols. 1–3). Tiburon, CA: Author.

Freud, S. (1935). *A general introduction to psychoanalysis*. New York, NY: Liveright.

Freud, S. (1971). *A general introduction to psychoanalysis*. New York, NY: Pocket.

Gilligan, C. (1982). *In a different voice: Psychological theory and women's development*. Cambridge, MA: Harvard University Press.

Goleman, D. (1972a). The Buddha on meditation and states of consciousness. Part I: The teachings. *Journal of Transpersonal Psychology, 4*(1), 1–44.

Goleman, D. (1972b). The Buddha on meditation and states of consciousness. Part II: A typology of meditation techniques. *Journal of Transpersonal Psychology, 4*(2), 151–210.

Goleman, D. (Ed.). (2003). *Destructive emotions: How can we overcome them?* New York, NY: Bantam.

Grof, S. (1998). *The cosmic game: Explorations of the frontiers of human consciousness*. Albany, NY: State University of New York Press.

Haruki, Y., Ishii, Y., & Suzuki, M. (Eds.). (1996). *Comparative and psychological study on meditation*. Delft, The Netherlands: Eburon.

Haruki, Y., & Kaku, K. T. (Eds.). (2000). *Meditation as health promotion: A lifestyle modification approach*. Delft, The Netherlands: Eburon.

Hixon, L. (1978). *Coming home: The experience of enlightenment in sacred traditions*. Burdett, NY: Larson.

Holden, J. (1993). Transpersonal counseling. *Texas Counseling Association Journal, 22*(1), 7–23.

Holden, J. M. (1999). *Introduction to the transpersonal perspective in counseling*. Paper presented at the 48th Annual World Conference of the American Counseling Association, San Diego, CA.

Hollon, S. D. & Beck, A. T. (2004). Cognitive and cognitive behavioral therapies. In M. J. Lambert (Ed.) *Bergin and Garfield's handbook of psychotherapy and behavior change*, fifth edition. New York, NY: John Wiley & Sons.

Huxley, A. (1946). *The perennial philosophy*. New York, NY: Harper & Brothers.

Huxley, A. (1993). The perennial philosophy. In R. Walsh & F. Vaughan (Eds.), *Paths beyond ego: The transpersonal vision* (pp. 212–213). Los Angeles, CA: Jeremy P. Tarcher.

Hy, L. X., & Loevinger, J. (1996). *Measuring ego development*. (2nd ed.). Philadelphia, PA: Lawrence Erlbaum Associates.

Ingersoll, R. E. (2002). An integral approach for teaching and practicing diagnosis. *Journal of Transpersonal Psychology, 34*, 115–127.

Ingersoll, R. E. (2010). *Integral psychotherapy: Inside out, outside in*. Albany, NY: State University of New York Press. Manuscript submitted for publication.

Ingersoll, R. E., & Cook-Greuter, S. (2007). The self-system in integral counseling. *Counseling and Values, 51*(3), 193–208.

Ingersoll, R. E., & Rak, C. F. (2006). *Psychopharmacology for helping professionals: An integral exploration*. Belmont, CA: Thomson Brooks/Cole.

James, W. (1901). *The varieties of religious experience*. New York, NY: Holt, Rinehart & Winston.

James, W. (1993). The varieties of consciousness: Observations on nitrous oxide. In R. Walsh & F. Vaughan (Eds.), *Paths beyond ego: The transpersonal vision* (pp. 94–95). Los Angeles, CA: Jeremy P. Tarcher.

Jung, C. G. (1969). Synchronicity: An acausal connecting principle. In G. Adler, M. Fordham, W. McGuire, & H. Read (Eds.), and R. F. C. Hull (Trans.), *The collected works of C. G. Jung* (Vol. 8, pp. 419–519). Princeton, NJ: Princeton University Press.

Keating, T. (1986). *Open mind, open heart: The contemplative dimension of the gospel.* Amity, NY: Amity House.

Kegan, R. (1982). *The evolving self: Problem and process in human development.* Cambridge, MA: Harvard University Press.

Kohut, H. (1977). *The restoration of the self.* New York, NY: International Universities.

Kohut, H. (1984). *How does analysis cure?* Chicago, IL: University of Chicago Press.

Lambert, M. J., & Bergin, A. E. (1994). The effectiveness of psychotherapy. In A. E. Bergin & S. L. Garfield (Eds.), *Handbook of psychotherapy and behavior change* (4th ed., pp. 143–190). New York, NY: Wiley.

Laughlin, C., McManus, J., & Shearer, J. (1993). Transpersonal anthropology. In R. Walsh & F. Vaughan (Eds.). *Paths beyond ego: The transpersonal vision* (pp. 190–194). Los Angeles, CA: Jeremy P. Tarcher.

Leonard, G., & Murphy, M. (1995). *The life we are given: A long-term program for realizing the potential of body, mind, heart, and soul.* New York, NY: G. P. Putnam's Sons.

Lewis, J. L. (2005). Forgiveness and psychotherapy: The prepersonal, personal, and transpersonal. *Journal of Transpersonal Psychology, 37*(2), 124–142.

Mahler, M., Pine, F., & Bergman, A. (1975). *The psychological birth of the human infant.* New York, NY: Basic Books.

Mahoney, M. (1991). *Human change processes: The scientific foundations of psychotherapy.* New York, NY: Basic Books.

Mahoney, M. (2003). *Constructive psychotherapy: A practical guide.* New York, NY: Guilford.

Marquis, A. (2002). *Mental health professionals' comparative evaluations of the integral intake, life-style introductory interview, and the multimodal life history inventory.* Doctoral dissertation, University of North Texas, Denton, TX. (UMI No. 3065703)

Marquis, A. (2008). *The integral intake: A guide to comprehensive idiographic assessment in integral psychology.* New York, NY: Routledge.

Marquis, A. (2009). An integral taxonomy of therapeutic interventions. *Journal of Integral Theory and Practice.*

Marquis, A. (2010). *Integral psychotherapists' treatment-matching decisions: An exploratory study.* Manuscript in preparation.

Marquis, A., & Holden, J. M. (2008). Mental health professionals' evaluations of the integral intake, a metatheory-based, idiographic intake instrument. *Journal of Mental Health Counseling, 30,* 67–94.

Marquis, A., Holden, J. M., & Warren, E. S. (2001). An integral psychology response to Helminiak's (2001) Treating spiritual issues in secular psychotherapy. *Counseling and Values, 45*(3), 218–236.

Marquis, A., & Ingersoll, E. (2011). *The handbook of integral psychotherapy.* Albany, NY: State University of New York Press. Manuscript in preparation.

Marquis, A., & Wilber, K. (2008). Unification beyond eclecticism and integration: Integral psychotherapy. *Journal of Psychotherapy Integration, 18*(3), 350–358.

Maslow, A. H. (1968). *Toward a psychology of being* (rev. ed.). New York, NY: Van Nostrand Reinhold.

Maslow, A. H. (1971). *The farther reaches of human nature.* New York, NY: Viking Press.

Merton, T. (1969). *Contemplative prayer.* New York, NY: Herder & Herder.

Murphy, M. (1993). Integral practices: Body, heart, and mind. In R. Walsh & F. Vaughan (Eds.), *Paths beyond ego: The transpersonal vision* (pp. 171–173). Los Angeles, CA: Jeremy P. Tarcher.

Murphy, M., & Donovan, S. (1989). *The physical and psychological effects of meditation.* San Rafael, CA: Esalen Institute.

Murthy, T. S. (1990). *The life and teaching of Sri Ramana Maharshi.* Clearlake, CA: Dawn Horse Press.

O'Brien, E. (1984). *The essential Plotinus.* Indianapolis, IN: Hackett.

Orloff, J. (1996). *Second sight.* New York, NY: Warner.

Perry, R. B. (1936). *The thought and character of William James.* New York, NY: Harper & Row.

Piaget, J. (1977). *The essential Piaget.* H. E. Gruber & J. J. Voneche (Eds.). New York, NY: Basic Books.

Puhakka, K. (1994). The cultivation of wisdom: An interview with Roger Walsh. *Humanistic Psychologist, 22,* 275–295.

Ram Dass. (1973). *Love, serve, remember* (audiotape). Santa Cruz, CA: Hanuman Foundation.

Rawlinson, A. (1997). *The book of enlightened masters: Western teachers in Eastern traditions.* Chicago, IL: Open Court.

Rest, J. (1979). *Development in judging moral issues.* Minneapolis, MN: University of Minnesota Press.

Richards, F., & Commons, M. (1990). Postformal cognitive-developmental theory and research: A review of its current status. In C. Alexander & E. Langer (Eds.), *Higher stages of human development* (pp. 139–161). New York, NY: Oxford University.

Rinpoche, S. (1993). *The Tibetan book of living and dying.* San Francisco, CA: Harper.

Rowan, J. (1990). *Subpersonalities: The people inside us.* New York, NY: Routledge.

Schumacher, E. F. (1977). *A guide for the perplexed.* New York, NY: Harper & Row.

Schwartz, T. (1995). *What really matters: Searching for wisdom in America.* New York, NY: Bantam.

Scotton, B. W., Chinen, A. B., & Battista, J. R. (Eds.). (1996). *Textbook of transpersonal psychiatry and psychology.* New York, NY: Basic Books.

Shapiro, D., & Walsh, R. (Eds.). (1984). *Meditation: Classic and contemporary perspectives.* New York, NY: Aldine.

Singer, J. (1972). *Boundaries of the soul: The practice of Jung's psychology.* New York, NY: Doubleday.

Smith, H. (1976). *Forgotten truth: The primordial tradition.* New York, NY: Harper & Row.

Smith, H. (1992). *Forgotten truth: The common vision of the world's religions.* San Francisco, CA: HarperCollins.

Snyder, C. R., & Shane, S. J. (Eds.). (2005). *Handbook of positive psychology.* New York, NY: Oxford University Press.

Steindl-Rast, D. (1983). *A listening heart: The art of contemplative living.* New York, NY: Crossroad.

Steindl-Rast, D. (1984). *Gratefulness, the heart of prayer: An approach to life in fullness.* New York, NY: Paulist.

Targ, R., & Katra, J. (1999). *Miracles of mind: Exploring nonlocal consciousness and spiritual healing.* New York, NY: New World Library.

Tart, C. (1983). *States of consciousness.* El Cerrito, CA: Psychological Processes.

Tolle, E. (2004). *The power of now: A guide to spiritual enlightenment*. Novato, CA: New World Library.

Vaughan, F. (1985). *The inward arc: Healing and wholeness in psychotherapy and spirituality*. Boston, MA: Shambhala.

Vaughan, F. (1993). Healing and wholeness in psychotherapy. In R. Walsh & F. Vaughan (Eds.), *Paths beyond ego: The transpersonal vision*. Los Angeles, CA: Jeremy P. Tarcher.

Vaughan, F. (1995). *Shadows of the sacred: Seeing through spiritual illusions*. Wheaton, IL: Quest.

Volunteer Newsletter. (2005, Winter). *I slept ... Volunteer Reporter Quarterly*. Retrieved from http://www.uihealthcare.com/depts/volunteerprogram/newsletter/winter2005.pdf

Wade, J. (1996). *Changes of mind: A holonomic theory of the evolution of consciousness*. Albany, NY: State University of New York Press.

Wallace, R. (1970). Physiological effects of transcendental meditation. *Science, 167,* 1751–1754.

Walsh, R. (1989). Can Western philosophers understand Asian philosophies? *Crosscurrents, XXXIX,* 281–299.

Walsh, R. (1993a). Meditation research: The state of the art. In R. Walsh & F. Vaughan (Eds.), *Paths beyond ego: The transpersonal vision* (pp. 60–66). Los Angeles, CA: Jeremy P. Tarcher.

Walsh, R. (1993b). The transpersonal movement: A history and state of the art. *Journal of Transpersonal Psychology, 25,* 123–139.

Walsh, R. (1995). The problem of suffering: Existential and transpersonal perspectives. *Humanistic Psychologist, 23,* 345–357.

Walsh, R. (1999). *Essential spirituality: The seven central practices to awaken heart and mind*. New York, NY: Wiley.

Walsh, R., & Vaughan, F. (1993). Introduction. In R. Walsh & F. Vaughan (Eds.), *Paths beyond ego: The transpersonal vision*. Los Angeles, CA: Jeremy P. Tarcher.

Walsh, R., & Vaughan, F. (1994). The worldview of Ken Wilber. *Journal of Humanistic Psychology, 34*(2), 6–21.

Washburn, M. (1988). *The ego and the dynamic ground: A transpersonal theory of human development*. Albany, NY: State University of New York.

Watts, A. (1966). *The book: On the taboo against knowing who you are*. New York: Vintage.

Wilber, K. (1977). *Spectrum of consciousness*. Wheaton, IL: Theosophical.

Wilber, K. (1980). *The atman project: A transpersonal view of human development*. Wheaton, IL: Quest Books.

Wilber, K. (1995). *Sex, ecology, spirituality: The spirit of evolution*. Boston, MA: Shambhala.

Wilber, K. (1997a). *The eye of spirit: An integral vision for a world gone slightly mad*. Boston, MA: Shambhala.

Wilber, K. (1997b). A spirituality that transforms. *What Is Enlightenment?, 12,* 22–32.

Wilber, K. (1999a). An approach to integral psychology. *Journal of Transpersonal Psychology, 31*(2), 109–136.

Wilber, K. (1999b). *The collected works of Ken Wilber* (Vols. 1–4). Boston, MA: Shambhala.

Wilber, K. (1999c). *One taste: The journals of Ken Wilber*. Boston, MA: Shambhala.

Wilber, K. (1999d). Spirituality and developmental lines: Are there stages? *Journal of Transpersonal Psychology, 31*(1), 1–10.

Wilber, K. (2000a). *The collected works of Ken Wilber* (Vols. 5–8). Boston, MA: Shambhala.

Wilber, K. (2000b). *Integral psychology: Consciousness, spirit, psychology, therapy.* Boston, MA: Shambhala.

Wilber, K. (2000c). *A theory of everything.* Boston, MA: Shambhala.

Wilber, K. (2006). *Integral spirituality: A startling new role for religion in the modern and postmodern world.* Boston, MA: Integral Books.

Wilber, K., Engler, J., & Brown, D. P. (1986). *Transformations of consciousness: Conventional and contemplative perspectives on development.* Boston, MA: Shambhala.

Wittine, B. (1993). Assumptions of transpersonal psychology. In R. Walsh & F. Vaughan (Eds.), *Paths beyond ego: The transpersonal vision.* Los Angeles, CA: Jeremy P. Tarcher.

Yalom, I. (1980). *Existential psychotherapy.* New York, NY: Basic Books.